VILLAGE LIFE in TUDOR and STUART TIMES

A study of Radcliffe-on-Trent

Edited by

Pamela Priestland and Beryl Cobbing

Cover picture: Anne Ballard from a rubbing of her brass in St Mary's church Radcliffe-on-Trent printed as a positive image. (See pages 125-6.)

ISBN 1 872356 08 7

Published by ASHBRACKEN 14 Cropwell Road Radcliffe-on-Trent Nottingham

Printed by Derry and Sons Limited Nottingham

CONTENTS

INTRODUCTION

This book on Tudor and Stuart Radcliffe completes a study of the village of Radcliffe-on-Trent in Nottinghamshire begun in 1972 under the auspices of the University of Nottingham and the WEA. Covering chronologically the earliest period, it has been produced last. The researchers have therefore had the advantage of already being familiar with the village and its people from later studies, but inevitably the new findings have thrown light on what has already been published.

On the face of it, any attempt to study the early history of Radcliffe (and Lamcote) seems an unpromising project. No village family has left personal papers, and parish records for the period are scanty - even church registers do not begin until Charles I's reign. Much can be gleaned from wills, however, and regional sources such as archdeaconry and civil court records provide occasional insights into the concerns of the community. Moreover, documents in national sources, notably Chancery cases and Inquisitions Post Mortem, have proved particularly enlightening. What was anticipated as a slim volume has therefore emerged as a bulky work.

Any division of material into either chronological or topic-based sections is inevitably artificial. History reflects life which is too complicated to be neatly packaged. Nevertheless, a combination structure has been attempted, so that those only interested in a particular period or a particular subject should find it possible to follow-through their chosen theme.

The main contributors to this study are:

Marjorie Bacon

Marion Caunt

Beryl Cobbing

Jenny Collins

Sue Drury

Joan Epton

Tony Ford

Mary Hall

Jean Lowe

Marjorie Parry

Pamela Priestland

Valuable additional support has come from Denis Berry, Chris Clarke, Gwyneth Farmer, Sue Forrest, Jean Harris, Alice Mossman, Margaret Oxby and Audrey Wise. Technical assistance, photographs and illustrations have been supplemented by Graham Beaumont, Tom Carter, John Cobbing, Ray Jackson, Jean Lowe, Maggie Martin, Neal Priestland, Katherine Southby and Eric Toft. We are also grateful to numerous others who have supplied material and allowed access to their premises.

In addition we would like to thank the staff of the various institutions who have helped us in our research: the University of Nottingham Manuscripts Department, Nottinghamshire Archives Office, and Nottingham Local Studies Library; Leicestershire Archives Office; the Borthwick Institute, York; the Public Record Office, Lambeth Palace Library, the British Museum Manuscripts Library, and the Guildhall Library in London.

The group is grateful to the University of Nottingham's Department of Adult Education and to the WEA for their donations towards the cost of publication.

Beryl Cobbing
Pamcla Priestland

March 1996

Sketch map of Nottinghamshire showing main places mentioned in the text

THE HISTORICAL BACKGROUND

I From Early Times to the Domesday Survey

Radcliffe-on-Trent is a village lying south of the River Trent on the main road between Nottingham, the county town six miles to the west, and Bingham, a market town some three miles to the east. Situated on the margin of the red Mercia mudstone (Keuper marl) and the alluvium, it is slightly elevated above the flood plain, its meadows bordering the river and its arable sloping upwards to the higher ground on the south. To the east dramatic cliffs give the village its name. By Tudor times the settlement clustered around the church and along the main road, its civil boundaries including the hamlet of Lamcote.

Long before Tudor times, however, there were settlements in both Radcliffe-on-Trent and Lamcote. Written evidence does not appear until after the Norman Conquest, but archaeological finds suggest that the site might at least have been traversed, if not settled, from early times. Late Neolithic or early Bronze Age tools have been collected from the fields at Malkin Hill just to the north of the parish, and the site speculatively identified as a barrow (pre-historic burial mound) or beacon. In May 1961 a barbed and tanged flint arrowhead, perhaps from the early Bronze Age, was found in the Clumber Drive area of Radcliffe. By this period the Trent was already an important artery for trade and travel. Three log boats and a spoked wheel, dating from some time between the early Iron Age and the Roman period, have been found at nearby Holme Pierrepont in gravel beds abandoned when the river changed its course. It is hard to believe that the activities along the river did not impinge on the bank at Radcliffe from time to time.

The Roman occupation left a more clearly discernible mark on the area through the remains of a number of villas scattered throughout Nottinghamshire. More important for Radcliffe was the fort built at Margidunum (near East Bridgford), the largest of the posting stations built along the Fosse Way within the present boundaries of the county. The military presence was no doubt feared but it provided security for traders and travellers whether by road or water. This security came to an end with the break up of the Roman Empire from the 4th century, leaving the country at the mercy of plundering tribes. There is some evidence that even the stronghold at Margidunum was attacked.

Dating events in this obscure period is difficult but it seems certain that the Trent valley was occupied by the Anglians sometime in the latter half of the 5th or early in the 6th century, and it is perhaps from this time onwards that the site at Radcliffe became a permanent settlement. The gradual displacement of Roman rule by Anglo-Saxon, then Danish, settlers is partly reflected in place-name evidence. The names of Radcliffe, Lamcote and Saxondale are all derived from the Anglian. Close at hand, too, was a large Anglian settlement at Cotgrave where a cemetery containing 87 burials from the second half of the 6th century has been excavated. In addition, cremation cemeteries have been found at Holme Pierrepont.

It is not until 867 that Nottingham itself appears in written records (as Snottengaham in the Anglo-Saxon Chronicle), the year in which the invading Danes first wintered in the town. If there were any settlers by this time at Radcliffe, they could hardly have escaped the upheaval and terror following the invasion. The subsequent creation of a loose federation of Five Boroughs, including Nottingham, (whether immediately after the Danish occupation or during the later Anglian reconquest of the East Midlands) left a durable legacy. The boundaries of Nottinghamshire and the administrative units of the wapentakes (hundreds) were established, with Radcliffe included in Bingham wapentake.[1]

The Norman Conquest and Domesday Book

The first specific information about Radcliffe and Lamcote occurs after the Norman Conquest when a vast transference of land from English and Anglo-Scandinavian lords to Norman tenants-in-chief took place. King William had to fight hard for his new domain and it was some years before he could feel secure. Rebellion flared up, especially in the north, and the strategic importance of Nottingham, controlling the north-south route and the great waterway of the Trent, was obvious. For this reason William rewarded the most loyal and powerful of his followers with estates which ringed the town and which were subject to relatively light taxation. William Peverel, his illegitimate son, was given a large Honour (a term describing lands made up of more than 60 manors) and custody of the newly built castle at Nottingham. Roger de Busli based in the castle of Tickhill in Yorkshire, which gave its name to another Honour, provided a bulwark against further trouble to the north. These two men, and others only slightly less powerful such as Walter de Aincourt (Deyncourt) and Ralph Buron, acquired property in, among many other places, Radcliffe and Lamcote. As a result of their overlordship Nottinghamshire remained loyal to the king and escaped the devastation of the 'scorched earth policy' with which he punished the north.

With his position secured and after 'much thought and very deep discussion with his Council', at Gloucester on Christmas Day 1085 William ordered his commissioners to discover the extent and value of the lands he and his tenants-in-chief had acquired, and the amount of tax which had been raised from them before the Conquest. Though never fully completed, the result was the great Domesday Book of 1086. It is in this that the records of Radcliffe-on-Trent begin and its inclusion implies that there had been a settlement for some time, though not necessarily a village in the modern sense of the word. As the king was only interested in land which brought him a direct profit, however, the entries cannot be regarded as a full description of the 'township'. The findings are summarised below.

The basic unit used in the Radcliffe section of the Domesday Book was the manor. This term referred to the single administrative unit of a landed estate and could include the hall or residence of the landholder. Here dues to the king were collected and other forms of tribute paid to the lord by his tenants - labour services, food and rent. The size of manors and the number of tenants varied greatly.

One of the two manors described in Radcliffe was conveyed to the king's son, William Peverel, and so became part of the Honour of Peverel, an association which was to continue for nearly 800 years. The Domesday Book describes his manor in these terms:

Fredegis had 1 1/2 carucate of land taxable. Land for 3 ploughs.
Now Fredegis and Wulfgeat have 2 ploughs under William [Peverel] and 15 villagers and 6 smallholders who have 4 ploughs.
Meadow 18 acres; the site of half a fishery and the third part of 1 fishery.
Value before 1066, 60s; now 32s.

Domesday Book language was largely concerned with tax assessment. For example, 'carucate' was a fiscal term (but it could also refer to the amount ploughed by an eight-ox team in a year, perhaps 120 acres - a measurement which varied from place to place). The reference to 'ploughs' may represent an estimate of arable capacity, or be a new term of fiscal assessment. The 'villagers' were the villeins or the free peasantry who held the basic peasant holding subject to certain burdens. None of the manors in Radcliffe and Lamcote had sokemen (freemen), although they made up over 32% of all tenants throughout Nottinghamshire. The 'smallholders', also known as bordars, formed the smallest group within the county and were within the lower rank of peasantry. With a cottage and small adjacent enclosure they eked out a meagre living on the lands of the lord and on those of the more prosperous villeins. Some of them supplemented their livelihood by becoming craftsmen such as blacksmiths, carpenters and wheelwrights and by providing a reserve of labour at harvest and other critical times.

The presence of fisheries is hardly surprising in a riverside community; the River Trent was particularly noted for its salmon in the medieval period. The omission of assets one might have expected - a watermill, a hand mill or a church - does not mean that they did not exist but merely that, if they did, the lord of the manor did not profit from them. Finally, this manor was not unusual in recording a decline in value since Edward the Confessor's time: over 58% of cases recorded in Nottinghamshire did so. Reorganisation is likely to be the cause of such loss, although devastation is another possibility. Nor should it be forgotten that as these records were made for tax purposes, the valuation by landholders might tend to be on the low side.

The other Radcliffe manor went to William de Aincourt (Deyncourt), Lord of Blankeney in Lincolnshire. This manor was linked with the 'knight's fee' of Granby which was the principal Deyncourt manor in Nottinghamshire. Part of the military service required of the Deyncourts in return for holding this knight's fee would be passed down to the lesser manor in Radcliffe, although as time went by it was probably commuted into money payment. The Norman commissioners listed this manor as follows:

Swein had 1 1/2 carucate of land taxable.
Land for 3 ploughs. In lordship 2 ploughs.
14 villagers and 3 smallholders who have 2 ploughs.
Meadow 19 acres.
Value before 1066 and now 40s.

Swein may well have been a wealthy landowner, for his name crops up frequently in the Domesday Book, owning property which extended as far north as Finningley in Nottinghamshire. 'Lordship', or demesne, was that part of the manor over which the lord had proprietary rights or which he retained for his personal use.

In Lamcote three manors are recorded. One went to Roger Bully (or de Busli) within the Honour of Tickhill:

Fran and Odincar had 7 1/2 bovate of land and the third part
of 1 bovate taxable. Land for 1 plough. Roger has 1 1/2 ploughs
and 1 villager.
Meadow, 2 acres.
Value before 1066 and now 15s.

A 'bovate' or oxgang was one eighth of a fiscal carucate, but also a variable measure related to the amount of land an ox could plough in a year. Depending on soil quality, this could range from 10 to 25 acres.

A second Lamcote manor went to Ralph Buron:

Ulfketel had 5 bovate of land taxable. Osmund, Ralph's man,
has 1 plough and
1 villager.
Meadow, 6 acres.
Value before 1066 and now 10s.

The 'king's thegns' or thanes, those pre-Conquest lords who still retained their lands in 1086, held Lamcote's third manor. Such holdings were subsequently known as 'Tayneland':

Ulfkell had 5 bovate of land and the third part of 1 bovate
taxable. Haldane holds from the King. He has 1 plough in
lordship.
Meadow, 6 acres.
Value before 1066, 10s; now 5s.

It appears that Haldane replaced Ulfkell who may have been killed during the northern rebellions or whose loyalty may have been suspect.

Those (such as Fredegis, Swein, Odincar or Ulfkell) who had been replaced by Norman tenants-in-chief would probably have continued on a lower social level as sub-tenants on the land they had formerly owned, though the actual terms of the tenure may have changed very little. From the point of view of the ordinary peasant working beneath them, there may have been little immediate difference between one regime and the other.[2]

II Medieval Manors and Tenants

The medieval village

From the Domesday survey it is clear that even by the end of Anglo-Saxon times Radcliffe had a structured society based on landholding, headed by manorial lords. Defended by both river and red cliffs (hence Radcliffe) and with good arable and pasture land, particularly for sheep (hence Lam[b]cote), the medieval village developed around a simple street pattern. The remains are still evident today in the circuit of Narrow Lane (now Water Lane), and Main Street. It is likely that housing developed around this route, although no remnants earlier than the 16th or 17th centuries can now be identified. Much would have been too ephemeral to survive, but three or four sites can claim manor house connections. Reference to a miller in a document of 1271 indicates that the village had at least one mill. A church, on the present site, and possibly a tithe barn would have been amongst the main buildings.

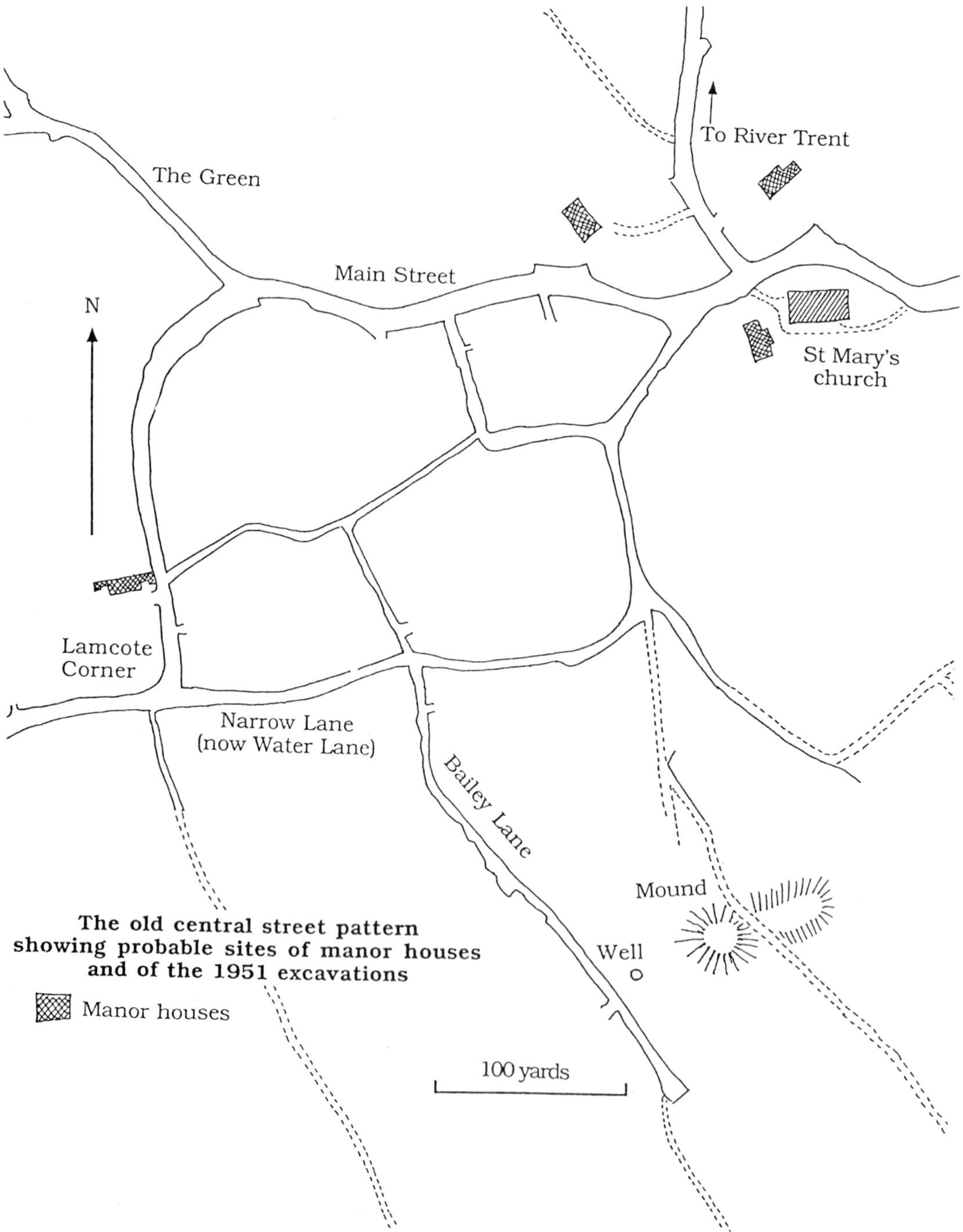

The old central street pattern showing probable sites of manor houses and of the 1951 excavations

Still less visible are the remains of a so-called motte and bailey (perhaps the site of one of the original manor houses) 90 feet in diameter, some 150 yards south-west of the church. This was excavated in 1951. A ditch was also found on the north side measuring 36 feet wide and 8 feet deep. Several smaller 'tumps' were discovered to the west of the main circular mound, identified as the remains of medieval huts belonging to tenants of one of the lords of the manor. (A long rectangular eminence - 241 feet x 77 feet x 3 feet - approximately 15 yards east of the mound, produced no archaeologically satisfactory results.) A well, about 8 feet deep, still existed in 1951 and yielded clean unpolluted water. The site did not give the impression of having been heavily defended against human attack, but was well-drained against flood by its ditch. Surrounding the motte, and acting as a sewer, was a stream, perhaps linked to the Syke Drain, the once-open meandering stream which came down from Saxondale, flowed along the main street, and eventually reached the Trent. Artefacts found on the site were meagre, but green pottery dating from c. 1200 was discovered in a test trench in the mound, and a further hole revealed a medieval tile fragment, a little more 13th century green pottery, and a boar's tusk.[3]

Medieval landholding

Whoever occupied this site had a place on the feudal pyramid, with its permissions and obligations, which ultimately reached up to the crown - in legal terms the owner of all land. Occasionally, a visit in person from the monarch would reinforce this authority and emphasise the gulf between highest and lowest. One such occasion was on 3rd April 1303 when Edward I, his courtiers and supporters, came through Radcliffe on the way to Lenton Abbey, before the start of his seventh Scottish campaign. The prestigious local subjects who may have received the king were the descendants - metaphorical or actual - of the tenants-in-chief of William the Conqueror's time. In the intervening years, however, many of the lands and allegiances of tenants-in-chief had been acquired by sub-tenants, so that a theoretically simple system became ever more complicated. Tenants at all levels became more interested in their estates than in their obligations to the crown, and land transactions led to a sprawling network of interests difficult to disentangle and by no means confined to neat topographical boundaries.

An incomplete picture of the leasing and sub-leasing of the manors of Radcliffe and Lamcote is to be found in deeds of land transfer in the Calendars of State Papers, and in the work of antiquarian writers such as Robert Thoroton (1623-1678). A magistrate and medical doctor, Thoroton rode about the Nottinghamshire countryside collecting material for his great book on the history of the county. Among the most informative of the gentry he visited was Thomas Rosell of Radcliffe who brought out his family deeds and, no doubt with some pride, displayed his collection of manorial records, perhaps embellishing their deficiencies with family tradition and local lore. The story which emerges from these sources is confusing. It is especially difficult to see who might have been resident locally at any stage and what rights of jurisdiction were being exercised. Not until the middle of the 16th century does the situation become clearer, by which time the main manors had been acquired by one resident family - the ancestors of Thomas Rosell himself.[4]

The manor of Peverel

What is certain is that after the Norman conquest William Peverel's heirs continued at the head of their Honour for two or three generations, but they backed the wrong side in the conflicts between Stephen and Matilda and their possessions were taken over by Henry II, Matilda's son, in 1155. Part of Radcliffe continued to be a manor within the Honour which kept the name of Peverel, but it was the Grey family with whom it was next associated.

Their involvement began in the 12th century, when Lord Grey of Codnor, who held six knight's fees of the Honour of Peverel in Nottinghamshire and Derbyshire, is recorded as lord of this manor. It is highly unlikely that such a great man ever visited the place, but a sub-tenant - Ralph, son of William Godenoure - may have done so. He was accounted in 1177 to have owed two marks for half a knight's fee in Radcliffe, leasing his land from the Greys. The Greys continued to own the manor as chief tenants of the Honour of Peverel throughout the Middle Ages, despite the fact that Sir Richard de Grey was on the losing side in the struggle between Henry III and his barons. After the Battle of Lewes in 1264 he was captured by the crown's forces, forfeiting all his possessions including the manor in Radcliffe, which was shortly afterwards passed to another member of the family, Sir John de Grey.

Specific information about this manor comes from an Inquisition held in 1271. (Such enquiries took place on the death of anyone holding land directly from the king.) John de Grey, who died in that year, was said to hold the manor of Radcliffe 'by barony pertaining to Tonenton [i.e.Toton] which is held of the King in chief' (within the Honour of Peverel). This seems to indicate that the manor was administratively linked with Toton. John's heir was Henry, who was not quite 14 years of age, and a full description was given of the land and its values:

> *... They say also that the easements of the homes with a certain croft that contains in itself 6 acres and with the fruit and herbage of the garden are worth yearly 20s. Also they say that there are 4 oxgangs of land in demesne which contain in themselves 92 acres of land which are worth yearly 30s.8d, price of each acre 4d. Also there are 3 acres of meadow which are worth yearly 9s.4d, price of the acre 3s.1¼d. Also there are there freeholders who render yearly 15s.5d. Also there are there 4½ oxgangs of land in villeinage for which and for their works they render yearly 67s.6d. Also there is there a cottage which is worth 4s yearly. Also of chevage yearly from 1 man 3d [i.e. payment to lord for permission to live away from manor]. Also they say that there is a mill which is worth yearly 15s.*

The freeholders referred to, though owing fealty to the lord of the manor, were able to sell or pass on their lands as they wished, unlike those who held in villeinage. This document is of particular interest as it contains the earliest known reference to a mill, and it specifically equates four oxgangs with 92 acres - i.e. 23 acres to an oxgang. This could therefore be regarded as the local standard.

About the time this description of the manor was written, Henry III's queen Eleanor, mother of Edward I, acquired a brief interest in Radcliffe during her widowhood when she was granted 12⅞ knight's fees from the Honour of Peverel including 1⅛ from the land held by Henry de Grey in Toton and Radcliffe. The Grey interest in Radcliffe was to continue until the early 16th century.[5]

The Deyncourt manor

The Deyncourt family, who had acquired a second Radcliffe manor after the Norman conquest, survived until the 15th century when their male line failed. Their inheritance then passed to the Lovels through marriage. Long before this, however, they sub-let their Radcliffe manor whilst retaining the overlordship. For example, as early as 1284 Edmund Deyncourt let his manor, comprising half the 'township', to William de Radeclyve and by 1428 the latter's descendants had been replaced by a Richard Slory (Slurry).

According to Thoroton, the 'posterity' of Hugh Basily 'or some of his family' acquired lands within the manor, presumably holding them from the de Radeclyve and then the Slory families still within the Deyncourt barony. The Basilys 'became, by degrees, possessed of most of this [Deyncourt] fee, and had their most constant residence here'. Certainly, Thomas Basily acquired a good deal of property in Radcliffe in the 1280s: the Lady Hawisia Deyncourt gave him 'divers of her Villeins'; from Walter de Gousell (Gousil, Goushill, Gonsell) he acquired the 'Homages, Rents and Services of certain Tenants'; and from Richard, son of William de Birtun [Burton], came 'certain Villeins, Lands and Houses'. In addition, he obtained 'Lands of divers other persons'.

Thoroton acquired this information from Thomas Rosell in the 17th century, and there is no reason to doubt the story, for the Rosells had Basily links. It was through the marriage of a 14th century Thomas Rosell of Cotgrave to the daughter and heir of Robert Basily that the Rosells came to inherit these lands about 1396, and they probably moved into the village as a result, for hereafter they are known as 'of Radcliffe'. Torre, a late 17th century authority, suggests that the Basilys and Rosells held the manorial title in this medieval period, but the evidence does not support this. In any case, the Deyncourt overlordship and the feudal chain of landholding clearly continued for between 1392-6, on the death of Sir William

Deyncourt, his widow Alice received one knight's fee in Radcliffe valued at five marks a year as part of her dower.[6]

The Lamcote manors

Few Lamcote manorial records have survived after the Domesday era, so any coherent summary is difficult to make. It is known, however, that the manor granted to Roger de Busli reverted to the crown as he died without heirs towards the end of William II's reign. The overall Honour to which this manor belonged retained the title of Tickhill and became part of the Duchy of Lancaster. Thoroton supposed that Roger de Busli's Lamcote holding subsequently went to the Lords of Holme Pierrepont, 'in which Parish all, or a great Part of the Hamlet is'. He based this on information from Thomas Rosell who said that in King John's time the holder of Holme Pierrepont, Michael de Malnoers, handed over several small parcels of Lamcote land to Eustachius the Clerk of Ludham (Lowdham) who may have been Sheriff of Nottinghamshire and Derbyshire.

This same Eustachius of Lowdham and his family accumulated property in the second Lamcote manor which had originally gone to Ralph Buron. The manor had subsequently come under the control of Geoffrey Torkard (Torcard), and it was from the latter's son, Thomas, that Eustachius leased a quantity of land. He also obtained four bovates in Lamcote from Galfr (Geoffrey) de Welleborf, although the latter reserved 11s yearly rent. In addition, a Sir Walter de Lowdham, perhaps a relative of this Eustachius, acquired from John, the son of Robert Torkard of Hucknall, all the service due for a knight's fee in Lamcote and Hucknall. (The prestigious Strelleys, too, owned property in Lamcote for they passed on land worth 11s in rent to John Lowdham, while in 1319 Margaret Strelley granted a freehold to an unknown recipient.) Throughout the 13th and early 14th centuries, therefore, the de Lowdhams built up their hold on property within Lamcote, but they were probably resident elsewhere, as their name indicates. Their absence is confirmed in 1313/14 when Sir John de Lowdham and his wife Alice let their manor to Robert Rasen and his wife Annora to farm for their respective lives for 16 marks sterling a year. Nevertheless, whoever occupied or sub-let the manor, the overlordship for much of this period seems to have remained with the Torkards, for between 1272 and 1307 an Inquisition confirmed that John Torkard and William Pite still held the knight's fees of Lamcote and Hucknall. The de Lowdham connection with this manor ended in 1317/18 when Sir John exchanged it for property belonging to Thomas Basily in Newton and Shelford. Ultimately, however, as with the Deyncourt manor, it was the Rosell family, heirs of the Basilys through marriage, who benefited. (After Thomas Rosell married his Basily heiress, he ratified to his widowed mother-in-law, Audina, a life interest in estates in a number of places including Lamcote.)

The third Lamcote manor is described by Thoroton as 'Tayneland', a reminder that in 1086 it had been held by a pre-Conquest thane. Before 1464 it was held by Agnes Marmion who initially passed it to Sir Thomas Stathom and William Babington esquire. Her heir, however, was her cousin Agnes who was 26 years old at the time of the enquiry into her property. This second Agnes, was the wife of Thomas Pilkington, and through her the manor came into the hands of the Pilkingtons until Elizabethan times.[7]

Examples of other landholders

The great barons dominate the history of the Middle Ages because most surviving records deal with them and their families. Their considerable power was almost certainly wielded at a distance, however, and lesser landholders or sub-tenants may have had more actual contact with the village. Fleeting references to these occur in deeds and Inquisitions Post Mortem. (They appear in the latter either as the deceased subject of the enquiry, or amongst those on the 'jury' hearing the evidence.) Some further information is found in a rental, and legal records.

The Hoveringham name is one linked to medieval Radcliffe, notably through three deeds which Thomas Rosell produced in the 17th century for Dr Thoroton. They concerned Hugh de Hoveringham and still bore impressive seals, which Thoroton described as 'very large, with his [Hugh's] Image on Horseback, and a fair Circumscription of his Name'. In the first of these deeds Osebert, son of Hubert de

Radeclive, paid 30s of silver for a lease of all the land which Hugh de Hoveringham and his father Robert before him had held in 'Radeclive'. In addition, there was a rent of 3s a year to pay, which also covered the pasture of 'Hassegange' (i.e. Hesgang, now across the river). Stephen de Radeclive (Redcliffe) was one of the witnesses, which dates the document to the mid-13th century. It was this Stephen or his son who, according to tradition, gave the pasture to the 'town'. This benevolence was matched by Hugh de Hoveringham's own. In a second deed he granted a toft, or plot of land, with appurtenances to Eustachius de Lowdham, the cleric who was already amassing property in two of the Lamcote manors. The latter also acquired the right to put 60 sheep 'and their sequel of one year' on the common pasture in Radcliffe and on Hesgang and 'Nesse'. The third of Hugh de Hoveringham's deeds reflects the spiritual values of the age when men felt passionately about going on pilgrimage or crusade to the Holy Land, and about the welfare of their souls and those of their family after death. He gave one bovate of land in Radcliffe

> *to God and St Mary, and the House of the Hospital of St John the Baptist, at Jerusalem, and the Brethren there serving God... for his Soul, and the Souls of his Wives, and of his Ancestors and Successors, and for the Journey of his Pilgrimage which he promised to make to St Andrew.*

So began Radcliffe's link with this rather exotic military order through which tenants on its lands had to pay suit at the Court of St John of Jerusalem, at first held in Shelford and then (probably from the late16th century) in Cotgrave.[8]

An example of an Inquisition held sometime between 1279 and 1307 is that concerning the lands and tenements of William de Birton a tenant of William Marshall. (The Birtons and the Marshalls held property in both the manors in Radcliffe.) At the time of his death William de Birton held '9 oxgangs of land demesne and each is worth yearly 12s; and 3 oxgangs of land which only render to him 16d yearly; and he paid to William Marshall for the said 12 oxgangs of land 18s yearly and did foreign service as much as belongs to a fourth part of a knight's fee'. The Birton (Burton) connection would have repercussions for Radcliffe some three centuries later. In due course a marriage between the Birton and Wode families brought property in Grey's manor to the latter, after which the Wode (Wood) name became attached to it. In the 16th century Woodhall manor would come to the Cranmers and then to the Radcliffe Rosells.[9]

The William Marshall from whom William de Birton held his lands belonged to another prestigious local family, confusingly connected with both Radcliffe-on-Trent and Ratcliffe-on-Soar. The Marshalls, along with the Mortons, Gousells, Frends and others, often appeared as jurymen on Inquisitions, or when other matters required investigation. Not only would they would have been amongst the most substantial tenants, but their local knowledge would have been useful in the investigation. Members of these families often performed the same duties for generations. One William Marshall, for example, was involved in three Inquisitions on property in Shelford, Gamston, Bridgford and Oxton. In particular he was amongst those giving evidence in September 1292 at an important enquiry held in Nottingham into the building of weirs on the river Trent - whether they interfered with the passage of ships and were detrimental to trade in Nottingham and whether they damaged the king's fisheries. William de Morton was on the jury in 1294 investigating rents held in Screveton by John de Gousell, then an outlaw. In 1309 Amicellus Perunel and Amicellus Frend of Radcliffe were amongst those enquiring into the possessions of Sir Gilbert de Gaunt at Shelford. Another Frend - William - was one of the jury enquiring into the exchange of lands between Thomas le Clerk and Hugh de Gousell in 1316 in connection with Radcliffe church. Others on that jury were Richard Rempstone of both Lamcote and Radcliffe, William Attetownshend (his name suggesting where in Radcliffe he or his ancestors lived), Robert Sayland (Sayllard), Hugh Hayde, Richard Honlin, John de Botheby and plain William son of Robert. This case dragged on for some years and William Frend helped in the later investigations with Leonard Basseley (Basily) of Lamcote in 1342/3. One of the Frend family served on three other juries in Shelford, Hamelate (Lamcote?) and Bassingfield in the first half of the 14th century. The status attached to such duties suggests that the Frend family had overcome any problem created a century earlier by another William who had killed a miller.[10]

An Inquisition held at Bingham on Henry de Notyngham's holdings in 1327 demonstrates the way sub-tenancies had become the norm. Despite his name he probably lived in Radcliffe, holding substantial property in the village as the tenant of two greater landlords. One was Sir Richard de Grey, who held the Radcliffe manor within the great Honour of Peverel. From Grey, Henry held eight acres of Radcliffe land for which he paid in kind with 1 lb of cumin each Christmas Day. (This spice, imported from the Levant, was a necessary luxury to make meat palatable during the winter when fresh meat was scarce. Cumin and peppercorn rents were therefore more than token payments at this period.) The annual value of this land was given as 4d an acre. Henry held most of his lands, however, from the heirs of Richard de Byngham by knight's service. These comprised 149 acres of arable worth annually 4d an acre, a 'certain several pasture' worth 12d a year which implies that it was enclosed, and three acres of parkland for which he paid 3s a year at 12d the acre. He also held the 'capital messuage worth yearly nothing beyond reprise' (i.e. a manor house or house of some substance worth only an annual charge). Although Henry himself was a sub-tenant, he could sub-let to others, and consequently collected rents from freemen on his lands at the feasts of St Martin (November 11th) and Pentecost (Whitsun), perhaps receiving them in his manor house. They amounted to 39s.8d yearly (just under £2.)[11]

A medieval rental

The de Birton and de Notyngham Inquisitions and the first of the Hoveringham deeds referred to above include some references to rent. Any systematic survival of such information is rare, and only one medieval rental has been found which includes Radcliffe. This is the rental for 1367-68 of the possessions of Robert Hayton of Hayton (Clarborough) in Nottinghamshire. It shows that by this period neat geographical units were a myth, having been broken down by networks of landholders and sub-tenants. Robert Hayton's holdings were scattered through Clarborough, Hayton, Stokeham, South Leverton, Carlton, Colston Bassett, Stapleford, Misterton, Wellow, Retford, Lound, Walkeringham and Radcliffe-on-Trent. He had only four tenants in Radcliffe: Cecilia de Eland, almost certainly a widow, who paid the considerable rent of 14 marks annually (£9.6s.8d); Fabro de Ratclyf probably paying 8s; Thomas, son of Leonis, paying 3d; and Robert Basily also paying 3d. When this local piecemeal example is applied on a large scale, the complexities of the landholding system become apparent.[12]

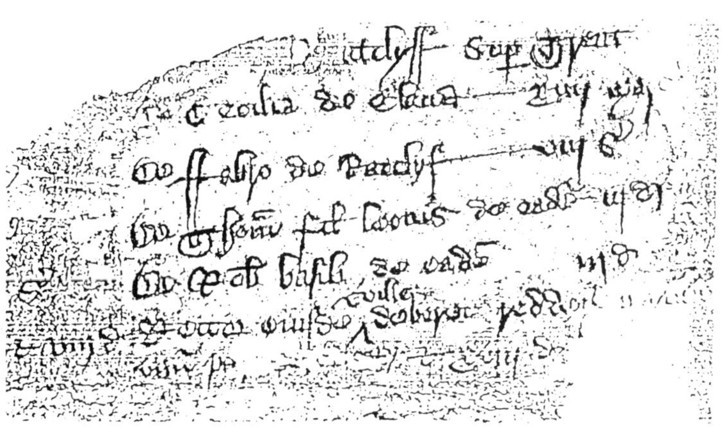

Extract from a rental of 1367-8 showing four tenants on Radcliffe lands belonging to Robert Hayton of Clarborough. (PRO Sc11/536)

Landholders in civil and criminal cases

Information about the landholding élite occasionally comes from legal cases which have survived in national records. For example, two financial disputes involving large sums were recorded in the 1320s. In 1323 the parson, Hugh de Gousell, was owed 40 marks (£26.13s.4d) by Richard Grey, son of the current manorial lord. Similarly, Thomas, son of William le Clerc, acknowledged in April 1327 that he owed William, the son of William Marshall, 25 marks (£16.13s.4d). In both cases the plaintiff was to lcvy what was owed from the goods and chattels of the defendant should he fail to pay.

Occasionally, too, members of this élite were on the wrong end of the criminal justice system. The early 14th century records are again the most revealing. Thomas de Radcliffe, the son of Thomas the clerk, was accused of the rape of Alice de Rughford (Rufford) at Carlton and of carrying her off to Radcliffe. His goods, lands and chattels were seized, but he pleaded 'benefit of clergy' which allowed him the privilege of being dealt with by an ecclesiastical court, in which sentences were less severe than in a temporal court. He was handed over by the justices to the Archbishop of York, so it seems that the younger Thomas was in holy orders, or at least able to read, to justify his treatment. He does not seem to have been brought to trial, but purged his innocence before the archbishop. After this, in August 1330, he was able to reclaim his confiscated possessions from the Sheriff of Nottingham.

In February 1333, Thomas Basily, a member of one of Radcliffe's most prestigious families, was also trying to regain his lands, goods and chattels which had been confiscated by the crown, this time in connection with a robbery. He was accused of harbouring Nicholas de Spalding and other thieves at Radcliffe after the robbery of Robert Race of Saxondale. Nicholas was an 'approver' (a criminal turned informer). To achieve a pardon he would be required to fight and win five battles under the customs laid down for trial by battle. Nicholas presumably lost, for he was hanged. Thomas Basily, however, purged his innocence before the Archbishop of York, and the Sheriff of Nottingham was ordered to restore his confiscated possessions. As the latter subsequently declared that he could not restore them since they had never been in his custody, it is not clear whether Thomas ever recovered his losses.

Two cases coincided with political disaffection and the disruption of the Hundred Years' War. During the reign of Edward II, Walter de Radeclive sided with the king's uncle, Thomas of Lancaster. The latter brought about the execution of Edward's favourite, Piers Gaveston, but was himself executed in 1322. Walter was one of a number of Lancaster's supporters who escaped execution for treason and received a letter of pardon from the king. In the 1330s, Simon and William Sayllard (a name which occasionally appears amongst the Radcliffe élite) were involved in the death of William de Bekyngham. Perhaps in an effort to evade justice, they took the opportunity of the outbreak of hostilities with France to go 'beyond seas' with Edward III's army. In March 1339, with others in a similar position, they were granted a qualified pardon by the king. If anyone took proceedings against them, they were still to stand trial, find surety for their good behaviour, and then return to the king's service whenever called upon to serve for a year at his wages.

Some cases hint at tensions which cannot now be explained. John, the son of Thomas Tydd of Radcliffe, gained a pardon in March 1367 for the death of John de Adbolton the elder and for any consequent outlawry. (By 1393/4 John Tydd, now of Lamcote, was sufficiently prestigious to be on the jury for an Inquisition.) The circumstances of the violence are not explained, nor is the motive of Isobel, the wife of Walter Withors, at whose request John Tydd's pardon was granted.[13]

Obligations to the crown

These cases are a reminder that the crown could wield ultimate authority in legal matters, just as it could in the landholding system. Despite the fragmentation of the latter, old feudal obligations still held good. In particular, a knight's fee - the obligation to provide military support for the crown in return for land - remained a part of landholding terminology until well after medieval times. For example, in 1242/3 Oliver Deyncourt held locally 17½ knight's fees and a fourth part of another, out of which Robert Deyncourt held one fee in Radcliffe. By this date, however, the military obligation was often commuted to a financial payment known as scutage. This became difficult to collect and was last levied in 1327. The provision of armed men in times of need was then often based on the annual value of land, rather than ancient obligation. In January 1345, because of the threat of invasion from France and Scotland, Edward III recruited a mounted archer from those with lands worth 100 shillings yearly, a 'hobbler' (a lightly armed horseman with 'haqueton', visor, burnished 'palet', iron gauntlets and lance) from £10 landholders, a man-at-arms from those with land worth £25, and a further man for each additional £25. (While the local landholder was taxed in this way, the local craftsman could benefit by the enforced increase of trade. In May 1474, prior to an invasion of France, Edward IV's commissioners were ordered to make payments in Nottinghamshire, amongst other counties, to makers of sheaf arrows, bows and bowstaves, arrowheads, and bow strings for the army).

The knight's fee was also the basis for the payment of certain feudal aids to which the crown was automatically entitled. For example, in 1302/3 Edward I collected an aid on the marriage of his daughter at the rate of 40s per knight's fee, previously assessed at the rate of 2 marks (26s.8d). In Radcliffe, Henry Grey (1 fee) and Thomas de Radeclive (1/2 fee) were both obliged to pay. Another occasion for a feudal aid occurred in 1346 when Edward III chose to knight his eldest son. William Eland and Thomas de Radeclive's son, another Thomas, holding some Radcliffe lands, were expected to pay on this occasion. Such dues were unpopular, however, and were mentioned as a specific cause of grievance in the parliament of 1348.[14]

The crown could also make grants of land to tenants in return for some specialised form of personal service. Two cases of tenure by 'sergeantcy' have been linked to Radcliffe: William Hasard in 1299 and the widow Joan Bassett in 1353. The latter's special services included 'mewing a goshawk in summer'. (These cases are not explored further here as it seems more likely that they are associated with Ratcliffe-on-Soar rather than Radcliffe-on-Trent.)[15]

A royal right which provoked much resentment was that of purveyance. By this the crown could buy goods and provisions at prices below market rates. At times corrupt officials compounded the problem. Numerous examples occur from Edward III's reign of vast quantities of Nottinghamshire crops and stock being purchased for the wars against France. When purveyance occurred for a less pressing cause, resentment could lead to violence. In 1348 Thomas le Lord of Radcliffe and his son Richard, with two others, objected to the purveyance of hay, oats and other necessaries for the queen's horses. The purveyor, Richard Hegham, suffered such an assault at Nottingham 'that his life was despaired of'. He was awarded 40 marks (£26.13s.4d) out of the le Lord lands and goods, and initially received £20 worth in goods. When, however, he came to collect the rest from half of Thomas's sown lands, the latter and others mowed the crops by force, carried them and other goods away, and assaulted the purveyor's men and servants 'whereby he lost their service for a great time'. The whole legal process was slow as there was a gap of two and a half years between Hegham's first complaint and the second.[16]

The subsidy of 1332

Those who worked in Thomas le Lord's fields would be amongst the villagers of lesser status whose names and activities remain virtually unknown. From 1348 their numbers may well have been reduced as a result of the Black Death. Just prior to that time it has been estimated that the general population was at the maximum which could be sustained by the methods of medieval farming. In 1332 Edward III's proposed invasion of Scotland meant that the crown needed to raise money from outside its own resources. Consequently, parliament granted permission for a subsidy to be collected on the basis of taxing country dwellers on one fifteenth of the current valuation of certain personal property. The local collectors went from house to house on the appointed day (usually at Michaelmas) valuing the relevant movable goods. As the names of those who were taxed have survived from this subsidy, some impression of the real residents of the community, rather than the grander and usually absentee landholders, can be gained from a time when the village would probably be at its most populous until the Tudor period.

The returns (even allowing for caveats about evasion, underestimates, the absence from the list of those too poor to be taxed, let alone faulty arithmetic!) provide some surprises. Radcliffe was among the four wealthiest 'townships' in the Bingham wapentake. It had the largest number of taxed inhabitants (40), and its total assessment was for £3.19s. Bingham (with 26 names) and Cotgrave (with 33) were each assessed at £4.10s, and Shelford (with 30) at £4.1s.3d. The apparent disparity in the figures can be explained by the presence of one or two exceptionally affluent individuals in Bingham and Shelford who owned a quarter of the assessed wealth. There was a 'middle' group in these two villages (between one third and a half) who paid between 3s and about 5s. Radcliffe and Cotgrave present a more egalitarian picture. In both places those assessed between these rates were the well off, and no doubt represented the resident village élite. There were 13 in Radcliffe who paid at the highest rates - between 3s and 4s.6d. Their combined assessment, however, amounted to well over half the total. In Cotgrave almost half were in this position (including John Rosell assessed there at 4s). The main difference between the two villages was that in Radcliffe there was also a large number assessed at under 2s (25 as against seven in Cotgrave). Cotgrave, however, may have had a larger proportion of its population who were too poor to be listed. The returns suggest that because the great landholders were perhaps resident elsewhere no great fortunes were to be found in Radcliffe, and that the community's wealth in goods was more evenly spread than in other local villages such as Bingham and Shelford. (The returns for the subsidy of 1334 do not contain names, but show some increased values for all four villages, with the greatest rise in Bingham and Radcliffe: i.e. Shelford £4.5s.3d - a rise of 4s, Radcliffe £4.5s.8d - a rise of 6s.8d, Cotgrave £4.15s - a rise of 5s, and Bingham £4.16s.8d - a rise of 6s.8d.)

Although the names on the 1332 list do not reflect the greatest barons or sub-tenants, who lived or had their main holdings elsewhere, the three wealthiest, assessed at 4s.6d each, were certainly men of substance: Thomas de Radclyf, Hugh de Gousell, and Richard de Nottingham. Some dozen of the 40 names indicated a place of Nottinghamshire origin (such as Richard de Annesley, John de Hoveringham, William de Shelford as well as the above), and two were identified by parentage (Thomas son of Leonis, and Henry son of Robert, expressed in the Latin form 'Henrico filio Roberti'). The name of Henry le Plasterer, assessed at 20d, was the only one indicating a trade. Four surnames occurred more than once: Prest and Goderode twice each, and Howelyn and Peronnall three times. Only four women - probably widows - held sufficient property in their own right to be included in the assessment: Scolastica Peronnall (11d), Alicia de Gunthorp (14d), Margeria Prest (18d), and Margeria Basily, from a particularly prestigious family, (3s). Occasionally names can be linked to other activities. William Frend, assessed at 14d, and Robert Sallart (Sayllard) at 2s.6d had sufficient status to appear on Inquisition juries, while Hugh de Gousell was the priest. Only two surnames - Howelyn and Theryuve (Thrave, Thuryff etc) - are found beyond the medieval period.[17]

The agricultural system

Information about tenants at the lower levels of the feudal or manorial system has rarely survived. Occasionally, legal or national records identify those who suffered at the hands of their social superiors. For example, the name of Alexander de Hopwell, a 13th century miller, is preserved because, as already noted, he was unfortunate enough to be killed by William Frend. The latter, of an earlier generation to the William of the subsidy, was granted a pardon in March 1253 for his actions. Another humble 13th century victim of violence was Hugh Godchep. In March 1266 a jury was summoned to decide whether or not Robert, the son of Walter of Lamcote, had killed him in self defence. Similarly, the name of a local smith, Robert Stele, is known because John, the son of Bartholomew de Radcliffe, was responsible for his death in the summer of 1401. (John was subsequently pardoned.) Not until the 15th century is there regular use of the term 'yeoman' (a freeholder or farmer of middling status.) John Ballard and John Smalley, both of Radcliffe, are so described in the reigns of Henry VI and Edward IV respectively. For the rest, the middle and lower ranks remain largely anonymous. The miller, the smith and the yeoman farmers whose names have survived symbolise generations dependent on the annual round of the agricultural system.[18]

Most of these lesser folk would owe allegiance to one of the manorial lords or sub-tenants. Initially, the feudal system was built on labour services for the lord in exchange for rights in the open fields, but wages gradually became the norm, particularly after the Black Death of 1348 when manpower was in short supply and peasants were in a better bargaining position. Although some came to hold their land in socage (a form of freehold with nominal rents and services), most would pay full rents for their land and cottages, and were subject to the jurisdiction of manorial courts which dealt with breaches of the agricultural routine, tenurial matters and sometimes minor misdemeanours. Such customary tenants generally came to hold their possessions by copyhold i.e. by written titles copied from the records of admission on the court rolls. Their right to graze animals, cultivate crops, or collect wood might be indicated in these 'titles'.

Whoever 'owned' the land, it was farmed collectively in large open fields. Whether Radcliffe had the traditional three-field system in medieval times - two in use for crops and one left fallow in rotation - is uncertain, but by the Tudor period a four-field pattern was established. Land was normally measured in oxgangs - the variable area which an ox could plough, depending on soil quality. (As already noted, one Radcliffe document for 1271 equates an oxgang with 23 acres.) The fields in agricultural use were divided into strips on which peasants worked either for wages from their lord, or for themselves, but the whole field would be sown with one crop. A number of parallel strips, each separated from its neighbour by a double furrow, made up a furlong. Numerous furlongs of different shapes and sizes filled the large open fields. The up-and-down ploughing of the long narrow strips threw soil towards the centre, so causing the ridges which often became permanent after arable land was converted to sheep pasture. The 1951 excavation (see p. 13) drew attention to the ridge-and-furrow pattern of the surrounding land (now under

Medieval ridge and furrow alongside the A 52 in January 1995

houses). Much of this medieval legacy has now been eradicated by roads and buildings, but it still survives in many parts of the Midlands. Traces can be seen on the outskirts of Radcliffe near the golf course, beside the RSPCA exit from the village, and particularly in a field alongside the Cotgrave railway line on the A 52.

Despite the open-field system, there is some indication that enclosure of land by individuals was taking place on a small-scale by the early 14th century. The Inquisition on Henry de Notyngham's estate held in 1327 (p. 17) shows that he had 3 acres of parkland in the village, which would probably be used for two or three deer, perhaps for instant venison. Henry also held an enclosed pasture worth 12d a year. The process would continue in the Tudor period, reaching its climax in the 18th century.[19]

Specific evidence of the crops or stock managed in medieval Radcliffe and Lamcote is difficult to find, but records of purveyance (the crown's purchasing rights) indicate for what the county in general was noted. For example, in 1337 at the start of the Hundred Years' War, Edward III's agents were instructed to buy a total of 30,000 sacks of wool - 1,200 of them from Nottinghamshire and Derbyshire. The quality of local wool is indicated in the prices paid: 8 1/2 marks for Nottinghamshire wool compared to the best at 12 marks from Herefordshire, and the poorest in Northumberland, Westmorland and Cumberland at 5 marks per sack.

The name of onc Radcliffe wool supplier of this period has survived in the king's instructions to customs collectors at Hull. William le Kok (or Cocus), having lent money to the King, was one of a number of merchants who were to have their export dues on wool to Antwerp reduced from 40 to 20 shillings a sack. In May 1338, William's concession amounted to £176.8s.2d by this arrangement 'provided that he or his attorney shall take oath each time that he takes out wool, that the wool is his own and that he will not pass the wool of others as his own...'. The order was renewed in 1339, but by July 1343, he had received only £16.16s.2d of his concession, the king issuing a writ in his favour for the remaining £159.12s.

In 1351 as the wars against France continued, Edward III's purveyors were ordered to collect 300 quarters of wheat, 100 quarters of rye, 100 quarters of peas and beans, 500 quarters of barley, 200 beef carcasses and 400 bacon pigs from Nottinghamshire for despatch to Calais, Gascony and Brittany. Local people, through the parish constable, would have had to make their contributions to these demands. Any surplus produce would normally be disposed of in the markets at Nottingham, six miles to the west, or at Bingham some three miles to the east. Access to trade further afield was provided by the Fosse Way and by the river.[20]

The river

For landlords and tenants alike, the River Trent was of supreme importance. The Celts had named it 'Tristanton' or 'Trespasser', for over the centuries it had swung sharply in its course, eroding banks and forming Radcliffe's cliffs. In medieval times it wandered past the village to the north of its present course, allowing access on foot to land (the Hesgang pasture) which by Elizabethan times could only be reached by ford or boat. With no bridges between Newark and Nottingham, ferries were the main means of crossing for the villagers along its banks.

There is no evidence that Radcliffe possessed a wharf in early times, but some benefits must have accrued from the fact that the river was such a busy transport route. Many goods were carried by barge, and when the river was low even sailing boats would have had to be hauled. Here were opportunities for the villagers to find some by-employment when called on to help, and they could also supply the thirsty bargemen with ale. There was a limit to profits, however. A government order of 1382 directed that no tolls were to be taken which would delay 'the vessels navigating that river (which is the King's and of right a common thoroughfare for all)', so pushing up the cost of victuals.

Fisheries, already noted in the Domesday survey, provided a good source of food. Anglo-Saxon fish weirs consisted of wooden fish traps placed across the current between an island and one bank. Remains of this type have been found at Colwick. During the Middle Ages rules were laid down about close seasons for fishing, and commissions of enquiry set up to investigate breaches of the regulations. In 1380 it was reported that 'in the water of Trent... where salmon are taken, divers breaches... are committed and are not punished to enforce the said statute which prescribes a close time for salmon' from 8th September until 11th November (the Nativity of the Virgin until Martinmas) 'and for small salmon by nets and other engines at mill pools from the middle of April until midsummer'. Conservators were empowered to punish first offenders by burning their nets and equipment. Subsequent offences could lead to imprisonment for a quarter of a year.

Because of the river's potential for wealth, the government was alert to the harm that could be done by local landowners who built weirs and dams, obstructing the passage of boats and interfering with fishing, to the detriment of the king's revenues as well as the livelihood of riverside villages. There were frequent commissions of enquiry into such abuses. In 1292, for example, William Marshall of Radcliffe was one of the investigators of several weirs built between Torksey and Nottingham. They were said to disadvantage Nottingham as they hindered the passage of ships, although on this occasion the king's fishery was deemed not to have suffered. In 1316 the construction of a fish weir across the river from Radcliffe at Colwick by William de Colwyck allegedly narrowed the channel of the Trent and diverted its course to his watermill. This not only prevented ships passing to Nottingham Castle, but adversely affected the king's profits from his Nottingham fishery. At the investigation it was stated that the river 'from mid-stream of the said river, from the river Humber to the castle of Nottingham, ought to be of the breadth of one perch at least (16½ feet) and of old time whereof the memory of man exists not, was accustomed to be'. The importance of the river to the medieval economy is clear. A dispute in Elizabethan times would affect Radcliffe people more specifically.[21]

III The Medieval Church

Feudal obligations and even the agricultural routine which affected all, directly or indirectly, emphasised social divisions. Theoretically, ecclesiastical authority, with its spiritual teaching expressed through the parish church, helped to unite all levels of society through common beliefs. While there is no specific record of a church in Radcliffe in William the Conqueror's survey of 1086, there is evidence of its existence by the 13th century, when references to the priests begin to appear in the records. The early building, dedicated to the Virgin Mary, was probably the same as that referred to by Robert Thoroton in 1677, with its traditional chancel window at the east end, and north and south aisles presumably on either side of a central nave. The lay-out and orientation of the building would therefore be similar to that of today, but on a smaller scale. Thoroton does not mention the steeple which was to cause such problems in the 18th century. Lamcote, administered in practical matters with Radcliffe, belonged to Holme Pierrepont parish for ecclesiastical purposes.[22]

The Christian doctrine which the early priests upheld was largely accepted throughout Europe. A hierarchical clergy (celibate only in major orders), headed by the Pope in Rome, conducted services in Latin and administered the seven sacraments - baptism, confirmation, eucharist, penance, extreme unction, holy orders and matrimony. Of these, the eucharist celebrated at mass was to become the most controversial. From 1215 the doctrine of transubstantiation was affirmed: that the inner reality of the bread and wine at the ceremony became the body and blood of Christ. Tithes were paid by the whole community to support both the local clergy and the main part of the church. (The patron of the living traditionally paid for the upkeep of the chancel.) The separate status of the priest from the laity was emphasised by the vestments he wore. He was God's representative to the people rather than the other way round. Much of this was to be challenged in northern Europe by the 16th century.

Early benefactors and clergy

Documents offer only brief glimpses into early religious practices in Radcliffe, but it is clear that the great medieval landholders - such as the Deyncourts, the Gousells or the Hoveringhams - felt the need to be religious benefactors for the sake of their spiritual welfare. The 2nd Baron Deyncourt had founded Thurgarton Priory, some 7 miles from Radcliffe, in the early 12th century, and a descendant, Stephen, gave the priory two bovates (or oxgangs) of Radcliffe land. The links between Radcliffe and Thurgarton were therefore established very early on. Thurgarton, however, was not the only religious institution to benefit from local landholders. As has been seen, Hugh (III) of Hoveringham gave a bovate of Radcliffe land to the Hospital of St John of Jerusalem for the souls of himself, his wives, ancestors and successors, and because he had not fulfilled a promise to go on a pilgrimage. Evidence from 16th century documents shows that Newstead Abbey, Shelford Priory, Dale Abbey in Derbyshire and the local Bingham chantry were also the recipients of lands and rights in Radcliffe or Lamcote. Such religious gifts, their origins now obscure, complicated land holding and the obligations of local tenants for centuries to come.[23]

The great landholders did not forget the local church. For much of the 13th century the Deyncourt and Gousell families were patrons of the living. According to Thoroton, Robert Deyncourt and his wife Hawisia, 'For their Souls health', gave to God and St Mary of Radcliffe a toft 'towards the sustentation of a Priest for ever, to celebrate the Mass of St Mary.' This 'toft' - a small building, or the site where one had stood - was perhaps the first rectory house. Gerard 'the Clerk' was a witness to the agreement, and a man of this name was one of Radcliffe's earliest known priests. (In 1208/9 he was given a bovate (oxgang) of land by Walter de Gousell - with the consent of his wife, Matilda.)

Apart from Gerard the Clerk, the best known name associated with the church in this early period is Stephen de Redcliffe. (Unfortunately, these two names were common to more than one man, so it is not always possible to distinguish between them.) Prior to 1226, however, it is Master Stephen de Redcliffe who is recorded as priest. He was often a witness to charters in the early 13th century, and was probably a canon lawyer. He had three known sons - Stephen, Walter and Thomas of Radcliffe, the latter becoming parson of Flintham. In 1226 Stephen senior was about to change his role in Radcliffe for on August 16th of that year Robert Deyncourt and Walter de Gousell presented Gerard of Radcliffe, clerk, to the living. (He was presumably not the same man who had been the recipient of the earlier de Gousell gift.) Nevertheless, Stephen did not relinquish all his connections with the parish, for he reserved his rights as vicar. This meant that he could still collect the lesser tithes (fruit, eggs etc) while the new priest retained the greater tithes (corn, hay, timber etc). To compensate Gerard for his loss of full income, Stephen agreed to pay him one gold piece annually. (This payment from vicar to rector was still in operation when the status of the living changed in 1379.)

It is probably this Stephen de Redcliffe who, according to Thoroton, gave a pasture to the 'town', subsequently identified as the Hesgang. (See p. 16.) At some point, too, Radcliffe acquired a chantry chapel. In the mid-16th century this was specifically described as having been founded for a priest to say mass there for ever for the soul of Stephen de Redcliffe. (Others subsequently left money to the chantry for their own or their relatives' souls.) Contemporary proof cannot now be produced to confirm the exact nature of either of these benefactions, but Stephen's memory was perpetuated by a distinguished monument - now destroyed - in Radcliffe church. His oak effigy originally lay against the south wall under an arch. It was reputedly burnt on a celebratory bonfire in Napoleonic times, but a tablet to his memory is in a similar position in the present building. This gives the date of his death as 1245 (when W[illiam] de Shenendon was rector), and records his benefaction as being to the church.24

Plaque to Stephen de Redcliffe in St Mary's church

From 1290 to 1340 the powerful Gousell family held the Radcliffe living through two rectors, both named Hugh. Shortly after the first Hugh became priest the living was valued. This was because in 1291 Pope Nicholas IV granted to Edward I six years' tenths from the clergy for a crusade, which was in fact never undertaken. In 1292-3 papal collectors made a survey of every benefice in England to assess the tenth. (The findings were used for assessment purposes until 1534.) Radcliffe's valuation was for 30 marks (£20). Holme Pierrepont and Shelford were both assessed at 24 marks, and Bingham at 80 marks.

In 1295, the church's dedication to the Virgin Mary was, on the order of the Archbishop of York, to be celebrated annually on August 20th (close to the feast day of the Assumption of Mary into heaven on August 15th). Such holy days provided welcome breaks in the medieval routine, and were largely lost at the Reformation. This date, however, meant that a second holy day tended to come in the middle of harvest time, and by September 1303 the parishioners were sufficiently irritated at having to stop mid-week harvesting that they were allowed to change their celebration to the Sunday immediately after the feast of Our Lady's Assumption.25

The era of the two Hugh de Gousells confirms the existence of a parsonage house. In a land transaction of 1317 its scope was extended when a licence was granted to Hugh de Gousell to acquire a messuage (a farmhouse) and a plot of land 137 feet in length and 10 feet in breadth close to his existing house - 'to hold and to have to him and his successors, parsons of the said church, for the enlarging of his house for ever'. The licence was necessary so as not to flout the Statute of Mortmain which had been introduced in 1279 to prevent people making over their land to the church and then receiving it back as tenants, so escaping military service to the king or manorial lord.

An earlier transaction, some time before the end of Edward I's reign in 1307, however, had been of dubious legality. In 1324, the authorities named Hugh de Gousell as one of the participants in a convoluted property chain which was clearly against the Mortmain statute. Land and messuages held by Henry de Grey of Codnor from the Honour of Peverel had been granted for life to Adam de Wetenhale, who had then granted them to Hugh de Gousell with a life interest. They would eventually be returned to the Greys via Henry's son, Richard. Henry's initial 'trespass' was pardoned after a fine of 10 marks. Somewhere along the line Hugh de Gousell found himself 40 marks out of pocket at the hands of Richard de Grey, and judgement was given in his favour to levy payment out of the latter's goods and chattels if the debt was not paid. The two Hugh de Gousells were perhaps typical of the wealthy clergy, as much concerned with estates as with religion.

Other rectors appear as little more than names in the records - John de Kyneton (appointed in 1340), Robert de Alyngton, William Dalby, John Caldewell and Robert de Hanley. The latter, installed in 1377, was the last Radcliffe rector for over six-hundred years.[26]

From rectory to vicarage

The change in the status of the Radcliffe living came in 1379. Already in the previous December Sir Henry Lescrope, who had obtained the advowson of the church along with some small amounts of land and rent, was granted a licence to pass them to Thurgarton Priory. The full appropriation of the Radcliffe rectory by the prior and convent of Thurgarton was formally approved by the Archbishop of York on 30th April 1379. As compensation to the archbishop, who was losing revenue as a result, the priory was to pay 20 shillings annually to him and his successors and 10 shillings to the dean and chapter of York out of the fruits of the rectory. These would include the great tithes, specified as wool and lambs in this case and, as is made clear in later documents, garbs (sheaves of corn) and hay, as well as the glebe land (unspecified) not allocated to the vicar.

The Radcliffe priest from this time (until the Reformation) was to be chosen by the prior and convent of Thurgarton out of their canons. He was to be supported by eight acres of arable land scattered in the open fields and by two acres of meadow. He was also to have all the lesser tithes (minor produce which was often difficult to collect), oblations (donations for pious use), mortuaries (gifts to the priest on the death of parishioners, traditionally of the second best animal), and other payments for the maintenance of the altar. Out of his profits, the vicar was routinely to provide the bread and wine for divine celebration, lights in the choir, pay procurations (entertainment for the Bishop or other visitors), synodals and Peter's Pence (taxes to the diocese and Pope respectively). Any other burdens, ordinary and extraordinary, connected with the church were to be borne by Thurgarton. The first vicar was John de Thurgarton, a canon of the priory, and to begin with he was allowed to live in the rectory house until the prior and convent should provide him with a 'competent mansion'. Whether this implies that the living accommodation was above or below the requisite standard is not clear.[27]

The Radcliffe living instantly declined in status and income. According to Thoroton it was worth £8 while the prior of Thurgarton was patron, less than half of the value of the original living assessed at £20 in 1291. Allowing for some inflationary trends, even this may have been an over-estimation in real terms.

Between 1377 and 1473, eight vicars were appointed to Radcliffe. (A list of clergy appears on p. 250.) Probably they were all canons of Thurgarton as stipulated, but only four are so listed in the records. It was the last of these, Canon John Ackworth, who saw the start of the Tudor dynasty in 1485 when Henry VII defeated Richard III at Bosworth in Leicestershire. As the new era dawned and the Wars of the Roses ceased, it must have seemed inconceivable that centuries-old traditions should come to an end. Warning signs, however, already existed, Around the time that Radcliffe's living had been changing from rectory to vicarage, John Wycliffe, the rector of Lutterworth in Leicestershire, was attacking the Papacy, the clerical hierarchy, and the doctrine of transubstantiation, while advocating individual access to the scriptures by the translation of the bible from Latin into English. These heretical views were supported by his followers known as Lollards. Although their significance was never widespread, there were still a few sympathisers in Henry VII's England, and Wycliffe's ideas were eventually to have greater impact when taken up by Martin Luther in Germany.[28]

Case study 1

FIVE GOOD AND TRUE MEN

Although the Lancastrian Henry VII had defeated Richard III at the battle of Bosworth in 1485, the Yorkists had every intention of regaining the throne. In 1487 their leaders were the Earl of Lincoln and Francis, Lord Lovel, whose local estates had included the manor of Stoke Bardolph and, as heir of the Deyncourts, a manor in Radcliffe. They used a pretender, Lambert Simnel, to masquerade as the Earl of Warwick, the nephew of Richard III. After arriving in Ireland, Simnel was crowned in Dublin as Edward VI. The rebels then landed in Furness with Irish supporters and some German mercenaries. Joined by a small English force they moved towards York where they were refused entry. They next turned south towards Newark.

Henry Tudor as a young man

In the meantime, Henry was informed of the rising, gathered a force under the command of the Earl of Oxford, and moved swiftly from his current position at Kenilworth. Various accounts and interpretations of his movements and of the subsequent battle exist, but his itinerary and a herald's report clarify the initial events. Marching via Coventry, Leicester, Loughborough and Ruddington before picking up reinforcements at Nottingham, the royal army spent the night of 15th June 1487 encamped alongside the 'Luyng' at Radcliffe. (Radcliffe Lings appears on O.S. maps near to Saxondale.) The anonymous herald who chronicled the march reported:

> *There was a great skyr[mish]e which caused many cowards to flee; but the Earl of Oxford, and all the nobles in the forward with him, were some in a good array and in a fair-battle, and so was the king, and all the very men that there were... I hear of no man of worship that fled but rascals.*

On the following morning, Saturday, the 30-year old king rose early and heard two masses for which his Secretary of State, Richard Fox, Bishop of Exeter, sang the 'ton'. It was then decided that local knowledge was needed to guide the royal army towards the enemy.

> *...the king had five good and true men of the village of Ratcliffe which knew well the country, and shewed where were marres [morasses or boundaries] and where was the river of Trent, and who shewed his grace the best way for to conduct his host to Newark, where were villages or groves for [am]bushment; or straight ways that the king might conduct his host better, of which guides the king gave two to the Earl of Oxford to conduct the forward, and the rema[i]nant retained at his pleasures.*

Two of these unnamed local heroes would have been with the Earl of Oxford's force when, after covering a dozen or so miles, in 'good order and array' it encountered the 'enemies and rebels' before 9 o'clock that morning near East Stoke, 'a large mile out of Newark'. Any obligation to Lord Lovel, as a former manorial lord, would have vanished when tenants were faced with the authority of the king in person.

The three-hour battle was allegedly bloody, and the rebels were routed. (Red Gutter on the site is said to be a reminder of the carnage, although the scale of the defeat is now questioned.) The Earl of Lincoln was killed and Lord Lovel disappeared, his estates having been already confiscated to the crown. As befitted his humble origins, Lambert Simnel was made a scullion in the royal household. So ended the last major battle of the Wars of the Roses, even though the Yorkist threat continued to haunt Henry VII throughout the rest of his reign.

By the time of his death in 1509, the king had acquired a reputation for miserliness, but his chamber accounts, in which he initialled each payment, show that he generously rewarded those who had served him, including musicians, dancers, gift bearers and guides. Unfortunately few payments are recorded during the disrupted period immediately before and after the battle of East Stoke, but there is no reason to suppose that the five men of Radcliffe who showed him the way were not similarly rewarded.[29]

THE EARLY TUDOR SQUIRES

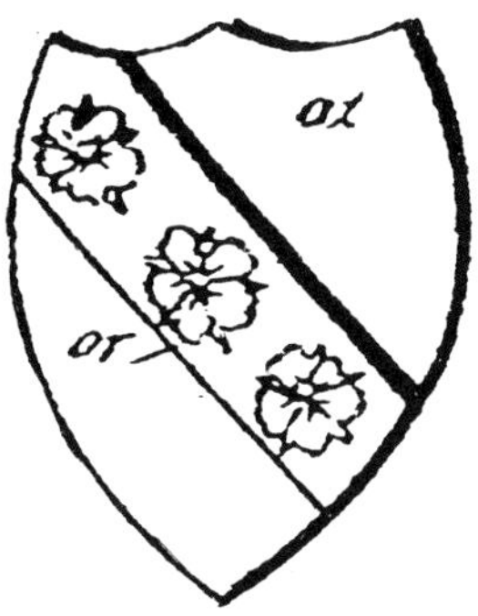

Rosell shield - azure field with a gold bend carrying three roses

The Rosell family provides one of the few consistent strands in the history of Radcliffe in Tudor and Stuart times. Probably originating from Rosel in Normandy, they held land at Denby in Derbyshire, as well as a manor at Rempstone and property at Cotgrave (the latter close to Radcliffe) in Nottinghamshire during William the Conqueror's reign. The first Rosell linked to Radcliffe was Robert, who is found in documents between 1395 and 1422. The Rosells improved their status in the 16th century, met ill fortune in the 17th, and left Radcliffe as the Stuart period came to a close. While they were never the only major landowners in the village, they were the only resident squires of the period, the visible representatives of gentry authority at a time when the absentee landlord was commonplace. Great political or social heights eluded them, but they provided an element of stability in a changing world.

Thomas Rosell and his family

The first Rosell of whom any picture emerges is Thomas who died in 1507. He was the son of John, recorded as a coroner in 1471, and his wife, Margaret. Thomas grew up to marry Agnes, the daughter of John Bingham of Car Colston in Nottinghamshire, probably around the mid-1460s during the time of the Wars of the Roses. This dynastic struggle between York and Lancaster was played out sufficiently far from Nottinghamshire to have had little impact on the fortunes of the newly married couple. The first of five sons was born around 1467 and named John after both his grandfathers. The second, Robert, is probably the man who became chamberlain of Nottingham in 1515-16, and sheriff in 1518-19. When he drew up his will in 1522 he asked to be buried in St Mary's in Nottingham. Ralph, the third son, took holy orders and in April 1505 was installed at nearby Adbolton church, where his father was patron of the living. He became vicar of Gonalston in 1507, the year of his father's death, and died in 1511. Thomas's fourth son, another Thomas, appears fleetingly in the Nottingham records as 'Thomas Rosell the younger, gentleman'. On 13th September 1503, he strode into the Guildhall where the mayor and two aldermen were 'sitting upon the Bench' and claimed that one of them was biased in a case that was being heard. He may have had legal training, for he appears as 'attorney' on behalf of George Bredon and his wife when they acquired land and property from the Radcliffe vicar in 1506. (Thomas senior was one of the witnesses to the transaction.) The youngest son, William, went into trade in East Retford, Nottinghamshire, where he prospered. He died in 1524.[30]

Thomas was head of the family when Richard III left Nottingham Castle in the summer of 1485 to meet his death at Bosworth, and when Henry VII came through the village two years later before routing the rebels at East Stoke. His sympathies on either occasion are not recorded. Only one reference to him in the first decade of Henry's reign has been found - in 1493 when he took his oath in Nottingham at the Inquisition on the possessions of Henry Eland who had recently died. (There was soon to be a marriage between the two families.) Thomas's main interests, traditional for his class, would undoubtedly have been his lands.[31]

Even in the early Tudor period, landowners with an eye to greater efficiency and profit, often at the expense of tenants and labourers, were interested in enclosing open fields. Although Nottinghamshire lagged behind the movement in general, a number of enclosing landowners in the county were particularly active in the decade between 1501 and 1510. The Rosells were amongst them. Thomas may not have been personally involved, for it is his son John who is named as encloser of 4 acres of land in Lamcote in 1504/5. (As the Enclosure Commissioners were carrying out their enquiry in 1517, however, it is possible that local memory was faulty about the date, and it may have occurred after Thomas's death.) There is no record of local unemployment as a result. In contrast, at nearby Holme Pierrepont Sir

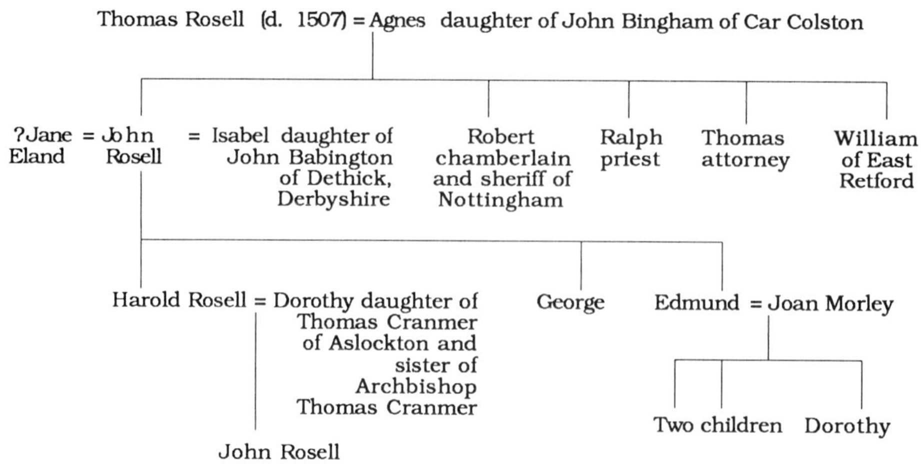

The Rosell Family - early Tudor period

William Pierrepont demolished two houses, left six others in decay, and made tenants homeless and unemployed after enclosing 80 acres. The only other village encloser in the early Tudor period was Richard Grey who in 1513 enclosed 2 acres of arable land and turned them to pasture. In 1518 the government ordered the destruction of these post-1488 enclosures, but judging by references to closes in later documents, particularly in connection with Rosell holdings in Lamcote, the order was ignored or superseded.[32]

If Thomas did witness the early enclosing in Lamcote, it was in the last years of his life. He died on 31st March 1507, and, as was customary with one of the crown's 'tenants-in-chief', an Inquisition took place six months later concerning the lands he held at the time of his death. Part of these holdings can be linked to the complicated story of Radcliffe and Lamcote's manorial history.

According to Thoroton, the Basily family had made piecemeal acquisitions of land in the old Deyncourt manor throughout the 13th century until they held most of it, although still under Deyncourt overlordship. In 1396 a fortunate marriage with a Basily heiress had ultimately brought these acquisitions to the Rosells, along with other property in Radcliffe. It was as a result of this marriage that the Rosells had come from Cotgrave to live in the village. They still did not hold the manorial title itself, however, for in 1452 John Slory (Slurry) of Old Laford in Lincolnshire claimed its reversion. In the meantime, the last Lord Deyncourt had died and his inheritance passed through the female line to the Lovels. As already seen, their direct descendant was Francis, Lord Lovel, who fought against Henry VII at the battle of East Stoke. As a traitor, Lovel had forfeited all his property to the king. The Slurry connection nevertheless continued, as shown by an Inquisition into the property of Richard Slurry of Uffington, Lincolnshire, in 1506. At the time of his death Slurry held this manor, then worth £5, from the unnamed heirs of William Deyncourt, sometime Lord of Granby. Subsequently, the Slurry family sold all their local possessions. From this time it is even less clear who had the manorial title, even though the Rosells held a number of Deyncourt lands.

After Thomas Rosell died in March 1507 the Inquisition into his possessions confirms that by the end of Henry VII's reign his family had acquired extensive lands locally, including a manor which would carry administrative and legal rights. Despite the description of holdings in the Inquisition document, it is unfortunately not possible to identify them with 20th century areas of land. Measurements are mainly in bovates (identical with oxgangs which were locally identified as 23 acres in 1271), and the legacy of the medieval system of suit and service is clearly still intact:[33]

> *Manor of Ratcliffe-upon-Trent called 'Rosyll Manor' and a messuage [house and outbuildings], 6 bovates of land, 6 bovates of meadow and 6 bovates of pasture in Radcliffe worth 5 marks, held of the Lord St John by 10s rent yearly.*

From later sources the Lord St John referred to as the manor's overlord can be identified as the Prior of the Hospital of the Knights of St John of Jerusalem whose possessions were scattered throughout England. It is possible that Deyncourt property acquired from the Basilys had been included in this manor.

The Inquisition then noted further local property:

> *8 bovates of land in Lamcote worth 53s.4d, yearly value 8s.4d, held of the Earl of Kent by a fourth part of a knight's fee. [i.e. the obligation to provide military assistance to an overlord, often commuted to a money payment by this date.] A messuage, a bovate of land, a bovate of meadow and a bovate of pasture in Radcliffe aforesaid, worth 10s held of the heirs of Lord Grey by a rent of 1 lb cumin. A bovate of land in Lamcote, worth 8s held of the hono[u]r of Tethill [Tickhill], parcel of the Duchy of Lancaster, services unknown.*

As well as the Radcliffe and Lamcote holdings, Thomas held lands in Oxton, Cotgrave, Epperstone, Adbolton and Sherwood Forest:

> *[A messuage], 4 bovates of land, 4 bovates of meadow and 4 bovates of pasture in Oxton, worth 40s held of the heirs of John Babington, knight, by suit to the court of Hockerton.*
> *A messuage, 4 bovates of land, 4 bovates of meadow and 4 bovates of meadow in Cotgrave, worth 100s held of Brian Stapleton, knight, by a rent of 1 lb of cumin.*
> *4 bovates of land, 4 bovates of meadow, 4 bovates of pasture and 40 acres of wood in Epperstone. The wood is held of the Lord Scrope of Bolton, services unknown.*
> *3 messuages, 5 bovates of land, 5 bovates of meadow, 6 bovates of pasture and 9 acres of land in Adbolton worth £4 held of the heirs of Strelley by a rent of a clove yearly.*
> *A wood called Sampson Wood in the forest of Sherwood, held of the same forest, services unknown.*

In connection with this last holding, Thomas had been one of a number who had taken part in a perambulation of Sherwood Forest on 26th August1505. Such walks were customary in order to clarify boundaries.[34]

John and Harold Rosell's obligations and dues

When Thomas Rosell died, his son John was said to be aged at least 40. He had married Henry Eland's granddaughter Jane, the heiress of half this prestigious family's properties, including a few parcels of land in Radcliffe and Lamcote. John is then listed as married to Isabella, the daughter of a Derbyshire squire, John Babington of Dethick. He had three known sons - Harold, George and Edmund - of whom at least Harold was born to Jane.

John's name appears only occasionally in the records. When his brother William, who had settled in East Retford, drew up his will in March 1524 he left him his best gown and best doublet. William also remembered John's son, Harold, leaving a chamlet jacket (made of fine material) to the young man. In the following year, along with Edward Ballard of Radcliffe, John attended an Inquisition in Nottingham into the property of Christopher Wode (Wood) gentleman, who had died in 1524. (Christopher, who held the manor of Burton Joyce, belonged to the family which eventually gave its name to Woodhall, another of Radcliffe's manors.) John was sworn again for a similar inquiry in Nottingham in 1530 after the death of Anne Fitzwilliam, and for an Inquisition at Ollerton a month later concerning John Williamson, one of his own Cotgrave tenants.[35]

The administration of lands still meant that old obligations had to be acknowledged. As some of the Rosells' Lamcote lands were part of the Honour of Tickhill within the Honour of the Duchy of Lancaster, suit was owed for these at a court which was held at Cropwell. The Rosells, however, like others of some social standing, regularly neglected to appear and were fined for their absence. The patchy records show, for example, that in 1536/7 John was fined 11d. (From the 1560s at least, later Rosells were regularly fined 12d for not attending another court where they owed suit - the Peverel Court.) The more prestigious the suitor, the less likely he was to put in a formal attendance.[36]

Two other obligations to the crown reveal the status of local landholders. When Henry VIII needed military support, he called on those owing him suit to supply it. Heading a muster list of some 25 villagers providing helmets (sallets), bills (pikes) and other pieces of equipment was John Rosell, who had to produce 'harness' or armour for himself. This muster roll is not dated, so it is uncertain when he was assisting the king, but as local squire he might well have led out the villagers when he was beyond the nominal age of 60. Henry's reign produced several occasions when service was needed against the Scots, the French, or against English rebels.

The second obligation was to help the crown in financial terms by paying subsidies. Henry VIII's ambitious foreign policy of the 1520s, masterminded by Cardinal Wolsey, led to regular demands for financial aid. In Radcliffe's case this is exemplified by the subsidy of 1524/5 raised from laity with more than £1 worth of goods, land or annual wages. John Rosell headed the 20 eligible names on the village list, being assessed for a hefty 20 shillings. (The humblest on the list paid 4d, but most villagers would be too poor to pay anything. See p. 82.) The more usual rate of a subsidy was much less, based on either land or goods. Subsidy rolls for the 1540s show that John paid 6s.8d on a land valuation of £10 in 1543/4, and 16s on a land valuation of £8 in 1545/6. This increase in payment, despite a drop in land value, was caused by the wars against Scotland and France at the end of Henry VIII's reign. The same sum was needed in the first year of the young Edward VI's reign as foreign problems continued. The exact date of John's death is not known, but by the time of these last two subsidies, he was perhaps beginning to hand over responsibilities to his son Harold, as the latter was asked to pay 12s and 10s on goods worth respectively £12 and £10. By this time the Rosells had considerably increased their status.[37]

The Cranmer connection

Thomas Cranmer (1489-1556)
born Aslockton, Nottinghamshire,
Archbishop of Canterbury.
Brother-in-law of Harold Rosell.
(Based on a contemporary
engraving)

It must have been in the 1520s that Harold had married Dorothy, daughter of Thomas and Agnes Cranmer of Aslockton. The marriage was to raise the fortunes and the prestige of the Rosells, particularly after Dorothy's brother, Thomas, became Archbishop of Canterbury in March 1533 as reward for the support he had given to Henry VIII in the matter of his divorce from his first wife, Katherine of Aragon, and his marriage to Anne Boleyn.

A second, but humbler, wedding in the Rosell family was that of Harold's brother, Edmund, to Joan Morley. When a daughter was born, he paid the Cranmers a compliment by naming the girl Dorothy. She was to be left a year-old calf and a featherbed in 1549 by her maternal grandmother. Dorothy seems to have proved wayward as she grew up, for when Edmund came to draw up his will in 1560 he was to impose some conditions on her inheritance. Provided she lived with and was ruled by her mother and friends until she was married, she could inherit half her father's movable and immovable goods. If, however, she refused to be so ruled, she would get only a third.[38]

While brother Edmund was coping with his daughter, Harold and Dorothy had at least four sons of their own to bring up: John (named after his grandfather), Thomas, Nicholas and Michael. Harold, who had himself probably been to Christ's College, Cambridge, was particularly concerned about the appropriate education for the second boy, Thomas, who seemed to have an aptitude for learning. Around October 1533 he approached his recently-elevated brother-in-law, Archbishop Cranmer, for advice. Possibly there was some thought of the boy, his uncle's namesake and perhaps his godson, making a career in the church. Despite the great man's concern with affairs of state, he still found time for his nephew's education. In an undated letter from Otford, his official residence in Kent, he wrote in familiar terms to Harold:

> *Brother Rosell, in my right hearty wise I commend me unto you, and in like wise to my sister your bedfellow etc. And where I understand that your son is very apt to learn and given to his book, I will advise you therefore that ye suffer not him to lose his time; but either that ye set him forth to school at Southwell, or else send him hither unto me, that at the least between us he utterly lose not his youth etc. Further I pray you, have me commended unto your father and mother. And thus fare ye well.*

Southwell, with its minster, and only some twelve miles from Radcliffe, would have been a convenient place for Thomas's education. Unfortunately, Cranmer's letter coincided with an outbreak of either 'sweating sickness' or plague - endemic throughout the period. The archbishop heard that it had reached Southwell and hastily wrote again to Harold on 12th October with an alternative suggestion:

> *... And whereof of late I wrote to you, that ye should send your son to school in Southwell, supposing at that time that those parts had been clear from sickness, so it is as I am advertised that they die there. In consideration thereof and forasmuch as I am credibly informed that Master Stapleton, parson of Bingham, hath by his provision set up a free school in his parish, of whose good name and conversation I hear much report worthy of commendation and praise; I will therefore advise you that forthwith you send your son thither unto school, to the intent the said Master Stapleton may have the governance of him, to whom I have written a letter in that behalf.*

It might seem surprising that the archbishop, writing from Otford, should have information on the state of education in Bingham, only three miles from Radcliffe, which the Rosells did not seem to possess. Presumably he had his own sources of local gossip through his family in Aslockton. At Bingham, Father John Stapleton, Cambridge educated, had been the incumbent since 1519. Cranmer's letter to him about young Thomas Rosell's schooling was written the same day as the second letter to Harold. It would seem that the 'bearer' of the letter collected Thomas *en route* and delivered him with the letter to Bingham:

> *In my right hearty wise I commend me unto you; signifying to the same, that I am right glad to hear such good report of you as I do, as well in that ye be so effectuously minded and given to see your pastoral cure discharged by your continual preaching and teaching, as also in confirming the same by your good conversation, example of living, and charitable behaviour towards your neighbours; whereunto I exhort you in Christ's behalf to go forward and proceed, as ye have hitherto right well begun. And where also I am advertised, that by your both good provision, and provident wisdom, there is a free school maintained with you for the virtuous bringing up of youth; I heartily require you, in as much as with this bearer I send now unto you my sister's son, named Thomas Rosell, apt (as I suppose) to learning, that ye will at this my attemptation and request do so much as to see him ordered and instruct[ed] in such doctrine as shall be convenient both for his age and capacity. And for those pains in so doing I will always be ready to show unto you like pleasure. Thus fare you well.*

Cranmer's letter, a mixture of flattery and *fait accompli*, depicts Father Stapleton as the ideal tutor for his nephew. Whether the boy ever benefited from the arrangements is not known.[39]

Monastic gains

Three years later, by the time of the dissolution of the monasteries, Harold was in receipt of the Archbishop's patronage as his Clerk of the Kitchen, responsible for the accounts of a key department of his household. The Cranmer connection, however, did not always produce results. In September 1535, Harold, his father-in-law and three other local gentry were granted the patronage of Granby church, which was held by Thurgarton Priory, and was at the disposal of the prior, Thomas Dethick. This grant, however, had little effect as, following the dissolution of the priory, the Granby patronage was transferred to others in January 1538. Moreover, the archbishop himself failed to acquire nearby Shelford Priory for Harold after its dissolution in 1536. (See p. 40.)

Nevertheless, the Rosells did benefit from land dealings which followed the monastic upheavals. Amongst these gains were lands in Radcliffe and Lamcote which had formerly belonged to the Priories of Newstead in Nottinghamshire and Dale in Derbyshire, collectively amounting to 50 acres of land, 20 acres of meadow, 40 acres of pasture, two messuages and two gardens.

In addition, in 1539 after Swineshead Abbey in Lincolnshire was dissolved, the Abbey's properties in Cotgrave and Kinoulton (including Cotgrave Grange, Harteswell Grange, and Broughton Grange, along with other manors and granges in those places), plus annual rents of 3s from Nottingham and 2s from Manchester were bought by Harold from the crown for £684.16s.8d. Their annual value was £38.1s a year. (As a Robert Rosell had given 14 acres at Cotgrave to Swineshead Abbey in the 12th century, there was some neat justice in this allocation.) Harold 'acquired' this property on May 1st 1539. Three days later he was granted a licence to 'alienate' (sell) Harteswell Grange in Kinoulton to John Constable and Joan, his wife. The rest was passed at the same time to a near neighbour, George Pierrepont and Elizabeth his wife, of Holme Pierrepont. Such rapid business transactions were typical of the speculation in former religious property. Nevertheless, the manoeuvre did not end the Rosells' interest in Cotgrave, for by the 1580s they were still credited with holding the manor and extensive lands there.[40]

The acquisition of Woodhall manor

The Cranmer and Rosell families were clearly on good terms throughout Harold's time. He and Dorothy were members of the Trinity Guild in Newark, associated with ensuring that prayers would be said for the dead to release souls from purgatory. In 1541 they contributed 16d to guild funds. Next on the list were Dorothy's parents, who contributed the same amount. Moreover, it was around this time that the wheels were set in motion for the Rosells to make what was probably their most substantial gain - Woodhall manor.

The history of this manor is linked to Henry, the last Lord Grey of Codnor, who died in 1496, leaving two bastard sons. To Richard, he left in his will manorial lands in Radcliffe and elsewhere. (Henry Grey's legitimate heirs through marriage, the Zouches of Codnor, did not give them up without a struggle: as late as 1599 they were claiming them as their right. 'How they ended their suits I have not found,' wrote Thoroton in the 17th century, but the Zouches' ruinous entanglements in this and other law suits could help to explain why they disappeared from Nottinghamshire.) The Greys had given their name to this manor: in a French document of 1446 it was referred to as 'Greys grang' or 'graner', and in another it was called 'Greysmaner'. From the 16th century it had gained an alternative title - 'Woodhall'. (Its site can be tentatively identified with Radcliffe Hall, now the Royal British Legion).[41]

This name probably came from the short-lived occupation of at least some of Richard Grey's property by the Wood (or Wode) family. According to information which Thomas Rosell subsequently gave to Thoroton, James Wood, gentleman, and his wife Elizabeth (the daughter and heir of William Burton of Burton Joyce) sold to Richard Grey in 1509 all their 'messuages, lands and tenements, rents and services' worth 43 shillings yearly, clear of all charges. By buying Wood out, Richard Grey restored his family's direct ownership of the whole manor until the middle of the century. He was the 'improving' landowner of 1512/13 who enclosed two of his Radcliffe acres and turned them to pasture.[42]

When the dissolution of the monasteries brought vast quantities of property onto the market, Thomas Grey, the son of the illegitimate Richard, was amongst those taking advantage of the situation. Wishing to acquire the former lands of Langley Priory in Leicestershire, he transferred Woodhall manor to Henry VIII in part exchange. Some sources indicate that Archbishop Cranmer had a persuasive finger in this pie in order to acquire Woodhall for his relations. After Henry VIII received the manor from Grey, it was reconveyed, along with other property, to Cranmer on 20th March 1547 in the early months of Edward VI's reign, and passed by him to his nephew, Thomas Cranmer, before coming to the Rosells.

There has been confusion about exactly when this occurred, for the marriage between Harold Rosell and Dorothy Cranmer was not the only link between the two families. Two generations on, another John Rosell was to marry Mary Cranmer, the daughter of the archbishop's great nephew. The Boun manuscript written about 1640-2 suggests that it was through this second marriage that Woodhall came to the Rosells, and later authorities have accepted this. An examination of Inquisitions Post Mortem into the properties held by the Cranmers, however, shows that they were not holding Woodhall in the mid-16th century. This implies that it had already gone to the Rosells at the time of Harold and Dorothy. According to Thoroton's approximation, it then consisted of 10 messuages, 400 acres of unspecified land, 200 acres of pasture and 30 acres of meadow. Apart from Radcliffe lands, the manor included possessions in Lamcote, Tithby, Burton Joyce, and in the town of Nottingham.[43]

Before the transfer, Thomas Grey had a fair copy of the Woodhall rental for 1545/6 drawn up to show its saleable value - £41.16s.1½d, approximately four-times the annual rental. (An assessment of the tenants and holdings just before they were acquired by the Rosells appears on pp. 99-100.) John Rosell, Harold's father, was already a freeholder occupying some of the Woodhall lands and premises, on which he was paying chief rent of 2s.1d plus a pound of cumin (or 3d?) for 'lands and tenements' in Radcliffe, and 14d for (close?) lands in Lamcote. The figures show, however, that he was a minor occupant before his son's takeover.

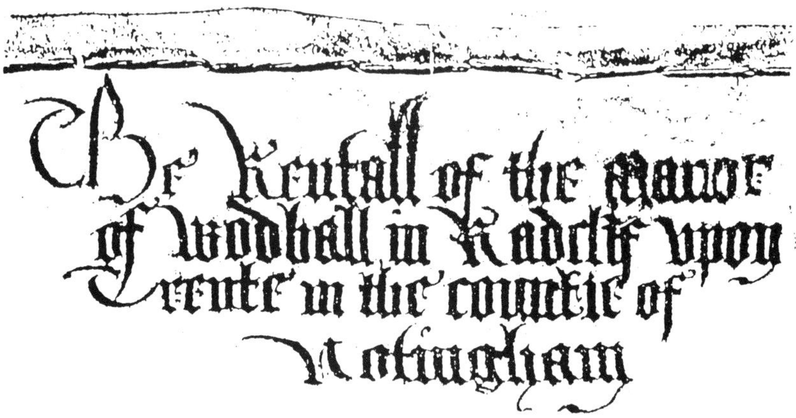
The Rentall of the Manor of Wodhall in Radclif vpon Trente in the countie of Notingham

The heading of the Woodhall [Wodhall] rental of 1545/6
(PRO Sc11/540 73/21)

It is clear that Woodhall manor was a major acquisition for the Rosell family. Thus, by the mid-16th century, thanks largely to the Cranmer patronage, they seemed poised for entry into the upper ranks of the county gentry.[44]

Epperstone wood

One estate problem was solved in his later years by Harold, together with his son, another John. This concerned the rights to a 40-acre wood in Epperstone. In 1507, at the time of the enquiry into Thomas Rosell's possessions, the wood was held from Lord Scrope of Bolton in Yorkshire, but the services due were not known. Since then the wood had been purchased by Sir John Chaworth of Wiverton, with the Rosells still in occupation, and with presumably even less certainty about rights or obligations than there had been fifty years before. Sensibly, rather than argue, it was agreed in 1556 that the wood should be divided between the two families. Even then it may have seemed more trouble than it was worth for the Rosells who were consolidating their holdings close to Radcliffe, and ten years later John disposed of it, along with Oxton and Hoveringham properties, reserving the right to repurchase, which was never taken up. Old traditions die hard, however, and Rosells' Wood is still marked on 20th century maps.[45]

Harold remained active throughout the 1550s as Mary's rule imposed unpopular religious and foreign policies on a nation suffering poor harvests and disease. The Catholic queen's condemnation and execution by burning of Archbishop Cranmer must have been a grievous blow to the family. From 1554 Harold regained the patronage of Adbolton rectory, held earlier by his grandfather Thomas. In the previous year he was called on to supervise the will of Edmund Cartwright (formerly of Kent but latterly of Ossington in Nottinghamshire). He was the husband of Dorothy's sister Agnes (Cranmer). Harold also regularly supervised or witnessed Radcliffe wills, and was modestly recompensed with legacies of 2s, 6s.8d and 7s.4d for his pains. Additionally, when Edmund Rosell drew up his will in January 1560, he left Harold a quarter of barley - a token from a younger brother who had had to make his own way in the world. (Mistress Jane and Mistress Mary Rosell were also left a ewe and a lamb each - perhaps they were Harold's daughters.) The date of Harold's death is not known but he does not appear again in the records.[46]

Case study 2

THE MUSTER

In the early Tudor period records of the musters survive from periods of national crisis. These calls to arms were organised on the basis of the wapentakes and counties in accordance with a custom which stretched back to Anglo-Saxon times. It was accepted that all adult men between the ages of 15 or 16 and at least 60 were expected to defend their county and, in the event of an enemy landing or a serious civil disturbance, to cross county borders, though not to be sent overseas. The men had to provide their own weapons according to wealth and it was assumed, perhaps optimistically, that they would be proficient in using them. Every man would certainly have carried his own dagger for cutting his meat, if not for war, and evidence from Radcliffe wills suggests that some were equipped with more than just a knife. For example, in 1519 Richard Bayley had been left a 'harness [set of armour] to go to the war with' and his brother Thomas - who does not appear in the muster document - a halberd in their father's will. A sword and buckler (shield) were left by John Grenhall in 1534 to his brother-in-law William Farnsworth.

There was one occasion during Henry VIII's reign when the bravest and best of Radcliffe's manhood, 24 men in all, were gathered together and their names and weapons recorded in some detail. As the date is unknown, it could have been in response to war with France or Scotland in the 1520s or to the Lincolnshire Rising and the Pilgrimage of Grace in 1536. Men from Nottinghamshire are known to have been involved in the suppression of the risings in that year. If it was the latter, the Radcliffe men would probably have assembled at Newark which was under threat, although the more usual place for a muster was in Castle yard, Nottingham.

The resulting muster return has a general heading which announces that: 'These be the names of those persons which be able to do the [king's suit]', indicating that only the able-bodied and perhaps those in a position to leave their homes and farms were enlisted. Under the sub-heading 'The Township of Radcliffe' the return shows that the village was led by Mr John Rosell who, as befitted a gentleman, possessed a harness for himself and either a mount or some extra weapon. (In 1536 he would have been aged about 69, but the Duke of Norfolk, in overall command of troops to suppress the Pilgrimage of Grace, was 63, subsequently serving in France in his 70s.) His son Harold was absent - perhaps he was away serving his time in Cranmer's household. The rest were armed for defence rather than attack. The most common piece of equipment was a sallet (helmet). John Dewsbury, John Franke, Richard Wright, Richard Good, William Fox, John Parr and Richard Bayley all had one (but the latter's harness is not mentioned). John Franke had splents (padded armour for the arms) as well, as did Richard Greene and William Sheppard. William Farnsworth (whose inherited sword and buckler were not listed), William Capendale, Thomas Bradley and Richard Goodall had bills (pikes), whilst William Wolley and Robert Darwyn had a 'jack' (leather jacket) and John Cowper and William Pare a gorget each (armour protecting neck and shoulders). Five of them could provide no weapons or armour at all - for they were a true cross section of society - not even Robert Grenesmyth who, as his name implies, was probably a blacksmith.

How much confidence these representatives of Radcliffe's manhood inspired in the old men and womenfolk watching them assemble before setting off, let alone their officers, can only be imagined. As they had to bear the expense of finding their own weapons and had to absent themselves from their farms during the muster, some were no doubt less than enthusiastic. For the high spirited, however, and those without responsibilities, the muster may have provided a welcome break from normal routine.[47]

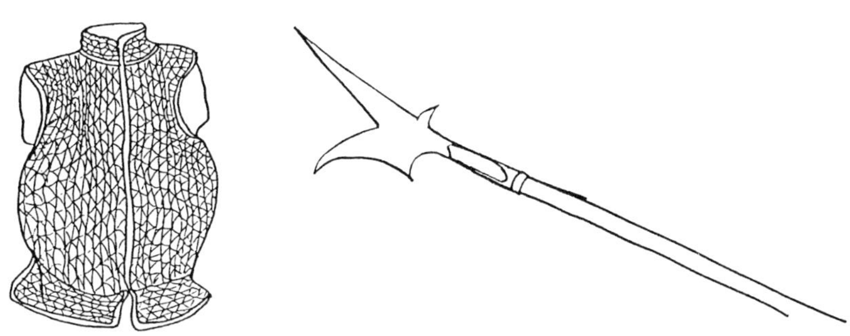

Padded leather jack (jacket) and bill hook (pike) - items mentioned amongst the equipment in Radcliffe's muster list

RELIGIOUS CHANGES 1485-1558

It is from the Tudor period onwards that more can be learned about St Mary's church and the religious practices of the community. Early 16th century wills and a church inventory refer to the font in the south aisle, a rood cross, an Easter sepulchre, and three bells in the steeple. By the 1580s a clock is mentioned. Thurgarton Priory continued to appoint the incumbents until the Reformation. Father John Ackworth was vicar from 1473 until 1504, witnessing the start of the Tudor dynasty in 1485, and Henry VII's arrival in the village some two years later when he heard two masses before the battle of East Stoke.

John Ackworth was succeeded by John Browne who ministered through the last five years of Henry VII's reign, and the first decade of Henry VIII's. Prebendary Edmund Lodge (Luoge), appointed in 1519, died within two years and was succeeded by Prebendary James Meynell in 1521. Father William [Car]Colston came in 1524 and was still in charge a decade later when the first rumblings of change reached the parish. In addition, there was a priest attached to the chantry chapel, the only known holder of this office being Thomas Smythe from at least 1519 into the 1540s. The wills of two of these priests have survived and give an insight into their personalities and concerns before the upheavals of the mid-century.[48]

John Browne 1504-1519

Buried at Radcliffe on 18th October 1519, John Browne might never have heard of Luther's protest two years previously against worldly church practices. A local man, Browne lived and died in the security of traditional belief. Predictably, this is expressed in the preamble to his will:

> *First I bequeath my soul to almighty God, our lady saint Mary and to all the holy company of heaven; my body to be buried in the churchyard of Ratcliffe near unto the body of my father and mother.*

After acknowledging his duty to pay a 'mortuary' (see p. 38), his first financial bequests were to local religious endowments: 2d to 'our Lady of Southwell'; 4d to 'the sepulchre light'; 8d to 'our Lady light'. The last two of these were perhaps to Radcliffe church and to the chantry chapel where prayers were said for the souls of the dead. Guilds also had religious functions, and to St Nicholas Guild in Lincoln he left his cloak. He also remembered the practical needs of his parish with '12d to the highways mending in Ratcliffe'.

His friends, including other clergymen, received the rest of his estate. He had relied on some cattle to supplement his livelihood, for two 'kyne' and 20 shillings were left to Robert B[resse?]. Fellow clergyman John Helmsley, who also supervised his will, received 12d, while Thomas Smythe, Radcliffe's chantry priest, was left another 12d along with his pet bird in a cage. As an educated man John Browne had a collection of unspecified books. These, along with his 'bonnet', he left to Richard B[or?]. He was musical too, for he left a harp to the parson of Holme Pierrepont, and a lute to John Thrave (Therafe). His remaining goods went to his friend John Jac(k)son, who was made executor of the will.

The overall impression of John Browne is that he was neither wealthy nor worldly, but a cultured, even a gentle, orthodox priest, whose vicarage house was a modest centre of music and learning, enlivened by the singing of a bird.[49]

Edmund Lodge 1519-21

John Browne's successor to the vicarage also left a surviving will, made the 3rd of August 1521 and proved some six weeks later. For so early a will, Edmund Lodge's preamble is surprisingly simple. He left his soul to God, with no mention of the Virgin Mary or saints, requesting burial in Radcliffe churchyard. His legacies, however, show complete devotion to Catholic practices.

Four bequests were made to the local Friars: 6s.8d each to those in Newark and Leicester, 3s.4d to the Austin Friars of Lincoln, and 12d to the Friars Minors of Nottingham. To a chapel he gave 16d. By far his greatest concern was for the soul of a dead priest, Henry Glaston of Glaston, perhaps in Rutland. He left the vast sum of

£10.6s.8d 'to an honest priest' to pray for Glaston's soul and to sing in Glaston church for half a year. (To a living priest, Lawrence Glaston, he left a Catholic book and 6s.8d.) For his own soul Edmund Lodge requested the saying of a trental - thirty requiem masses.

In his secular bequests, he remembered his family as well as friends. His father and mother received the second largest legacy - £1.6s.8d. A sheet, a pewter dish and a saucer went to a kinsman in nearby Shelford. A mattress, a coverlet, a sheet, a pewter dish and a saucer went to another in Muston. Further household possessions included his prepared sermons and a commentary on the gospels and epistles. These went to John Barlock. All his grammar books went to Henry Lees, a witness to the will, along with a blue gown, a shirt, a coffer and a cushion. Other beneficiaries received 5s and a gown (to a fellow priest); a gown, a pewter dish and 12d; and the sum of 13s.4d. John Longton, another priest, received the pick of the household bedding - a mattress, a featherbed, a pair of sheets and the best coverlet. He was also left 10s and any remaining goods which he was to dispose of 'for the health of my soul'. Outdoors, the vicar had kept no livestock apart from bees. Two beneficiaries shared his three swarms.

Once again, there is little hint of luxurious living or ignorance - charges frequently levelled against the clergy by reformers. If the most significant of Edmund Lodge's worldly goods were three gowns and a shirt, three pewter dishes, two saucers, a coffer in which to store things, a cushion to sit on, enough bedding for two beds and some books, then he must have enjoyed a simple existence in the vicarage house. He was succeeded by James Meynell until 1524.[50]

Lay piety before the Reformation

While religious orthodoxy might be expected in the wills of two priests, it is also found in the ten surviving wills of their parishioners dated between 1516 and 1534. Although four of these wills were witnessed by village clergy, there is no indication that this affected the nature of the bequests. All ten stress ceremony, good works and masses for the dead to reduce time in purgatory. There is no feeling of a restless community bent on reform along Protestant lines. (Only the religious content of wills is examined here.)

The preambles to all these wills contain only slight variations on the wording found in that of John Browne: souls were bequeathed to Almighty God, Saint Mary, and all the saints in heaven. Eight of the ten testators requested burial in the churchyard. Richard Bayley in September 1519 was very specific about being buried 'at the west end of the steeple'. Perhaps he had been a bell ringer, for he also left 3s.4d for the repair of the bells, and 3d for bread and ale for the ringers. To 'him that maketh my grave', he left 1d. Two parishioners wanted the status of being buried inside the church. Henry Caunt asked to lie 'in the south aisle near the font'. Richard Wright, perhaps of Scottish descent as he refers to the 'kirk', was cautious about spending his money even after death. Wishing to be buried in 'our lady aisle', he left 6s.8d for the 'sepulchure' there. (An Easter sepulchre was a recess with a tomb chest to receive an effigy of Christ. An elaborate version has survived at Hawton, near Newark.) Richard Wright's gift, however, was only to stand if 'the parishioners be content that I shall be buried in the Kirk', otherwise 'they shall not have the said money'. Records do not show whether his wish was granted. Lights were important when the deceased awaited burial, and some testators made specific bequests to ensure their presence. William Johnson and John Horne both left 3 lbs of wax to be burned around their hearses. John Webster specified the burning of two torches as well as 2 lbs of wax. Henry Caunt wanted to ensure a good attendance at his funeral:

> *To every man woman & childe that will come to church the day of my burial to have a loaf & drink withall.*

All was to be carried out by executors for religious as well as practical reasons, as William Johnson made very clear:

> *Executors shall do right & after my mind according to good conscience both for the well of my soul & of my children as they will answer afore god at the day of doom.*

Religious or semi-religious bequests to churches or churchmen were as common from the laity as they were from the two priests. Indeed, half of the wills contained more religious than secular bequests. Often the first item referred to the mortuary, in effect a tax paid to the priest on the death of a parishioner, as recompense for any unpaid tithes and dues. Before 1529, payment was normally of the second best animal, but eight of the nine Radcliffe wills before this date refer to the 'best beast'. Only the careful Richard Wright did not use this term, merely leaving to the vicar 'all that as right requireth'. (Perhaps a local custom ensured that the priest did not lose out when a parishioner had only one animal.) After 1529, all those leaving goods worth less than £30 were exempt from mortuaries. From £30 to £40 the rate was 3s.4d to 6s.8d. In 1534, John Sharp bequeathed to a new vicar, William Welbie 'being then my ghostly father 3s.4d', as his financial mortuary. In the same year, however, John Grenhall was still paying in kind, this time 'a ewe and a lamb & half a quarter of barley'.

Most religious bequests were for the benefit of St Mary's in Radcliffe or the local vicar, and were a mixture of crops, livestock and money - 6s.8d was a standard amount from the more affluent testators. Three wills show the range of these gifts. William Johnson was one of three testators who left 12d to the high altar 'for tithes forgotten'. He also left 10s and a quarter of malt to the church as a whole, and a bushel of barley for each of four 'lights' - those of the rood (a cross over the entry to the chancel), the (Easter) sepulchre, and special lights for All Hallows and Plough Sunday. A stone of hemp for 'bellstrings' completed his gifts to the church. John Horne left 8d to the altar, 6s.8d to the church as a whole and 'as much wax as will fund the Roundel of our lady the space of 2 years'. (The roundel was an iron ring for holding candles.) John Grenhall, perhaps primarily a sheepman rather than an arable farmer, not only paid his mortuary in stock, but also bequeathed a sheep to both the All Hallows and sepulchre lights, as well as two ewes and a quarter of barley to the church. Moreover he left three sheep to Thomas Smythe, the chantry priest, 'to the guiding of my son Thomas', although whether in spiritual or educational matters is not clear. He could afford a full trental to be said for his soul to be performed by Thomas Dewsbury, a priest who was the brother of villager William Dewsbury. (The latter had made do with half a trental, also to be said by his brother, for 5s.)

Eight of the ten surviving wills for the pre-Reformation period contain bequests to religious institutions outside Radcliffe. William Johnson and John Horne left grain to Shelford church, a bushel of barley to both Saxondale and Cropwell chapels, and a bushel of barley to both the White and Grey Friars of Nottingham. William Johnson additionally left a bushel each to the Leicester and Derby friars, as well as 20d to Cotgrave church. Richard Bayley's list was equally wide-ranging: a bushel of barley each to Gedling with Stoke church, Cropwell chapel, Saxondale chapel and Bassingfield church; a bushel of wheat and a bushel of barley to both the White and Grey Friars of Nottingham. Robert Dewsbury's half a quarter of barley went to Radcliffe, but he also left 6d to 'our lady of Southwell', as did William Dewsbury. The latter also remembered Shelford church and the Nottingham White Friars with a strike of barley each. Richard Wright left a quarter of malt to 'our lady light' of Bingham. Both orders of Nottingham friars did well from John Webster who left them four strikes of barley each, the same amount he left to the Radcliffe vicar. He also left a quarter of malt to the Newark friars. John Grenhall remembered the Nottingham friars with a bushel of barley each, Holme church with 3s.4d, and 'the brother' of Shelford Abbey with 6s.8d. Equally, testators elsewhere remembered Radcliffe in their wills. For example, William Brigs alias Cowper of Holme Pierrepont in 1526 left a quarter of barley to Holme church and half a quarter to Radcliffe. All such pious bequests were gradually to end as the Reformation took hold.[51]

The start of the Reformation in England

The revolutionary changes set in motion by Henry VIII had to be implemented at local level by three Radcliffe vicars: William Carcolston, William Welbie who died in 1549, and his successor Edward Sheppard. Also affected was the chantry priest Thomas Smythe. Although the king was an opponent of Lutheran ideas - in 1521 he had actually been granted by the Pope the title of Defender of the Faith for his book opposing Luther's views on the sacraments - his need for a male heir and wish to have his marriage to Katherine of Aragon annulled in order to marry Anne Boleyn caused him to clash with the Pope. When the latter failed to grant Henry's wish, the King went ahead with his second marriage, and forced legislation through Parliament which made him Supreme Head of the Church in England from 1534 and allowed him to seize church lands. Trends towards Lutheranism, however, were checked, and conventional Catholic doctrine was reinforced in 1539. It is perhaps significant that no Radcliffe will has survived from between 1534 and 1549 - years of great religious upheaval - so it is not possible to detect from preambles any immediate effect at parish level.

The dissolution of the monasteries

It was allegedly Thomas Cromwell who claimed that he could make Henry VIII the richest king in Christendom by confiscating the wealth of the church which no longer belonged to Rome. In January 1535 commissioners were appointed, drawn from bishops and local gentry, to make a nationwide enquiry into the true annual value of each ecclesiastical benefice and monastic house. In the following autumn the findings were presented in 'a fair book of the auditor's fashion', commonly referred to as the King's Book. In this *Valor Ecclesiasticus* William Carcolston was recorded as vicar of Radcliffe and his living was worth £4.12s.6d a year in taxation to the crown. An attack on religious institutions soon followed.[52]

Although Radcliffe had no monastic house, the village was affected by the fate of Thurgarton Priory which had held the lands on which the rectorial tithes were paid since 1379. As Vicar General, Thomas Cromwell sent out national commissioners from the summer of 1535 to 'visit, repress, redress, reform' the church's monastic bodies. The speed at which the commissioners worked has led to doubts about the validity of their findings, which were often of a scandalous nature. For such testimony to have been credible to contemporaries, however, the reputation of the religious houses could not have been high. The smaller houses were suppressed in 1536 and the greater had gone by 1540.

The royal visitors who inspected Thurgarton in 1536 were Richard Layton and Thomas Legh. Out of a comparatively small number of Augustinian canons there, they claimed that ten were guilty of unnatural offences, that the prior (Thomas Dethick) had been incontinent with several women, and that six canons had been incontinent with both married and single women despite the rule of celibacy. They also claimed that eight of the canons wished to be released from their vows. The Priory's annual income was given as £240.

Thomas Dethick resigned, and John Berwick was briefly elected prior in his place. A Latin document in the Public Record Office lists the numerous holdings and leases agreed in John Berwick's time on 27th April 1536. The details of the Radcliffe leases include the following:

> *And concerning £20 of the farm of the Rectory and house of Radcliffe-on-Trent...with all the tithes of hay and grain entirely produced there multiplying and growing within the town meadows, fields of the parish... with all the tithes of lambs and wool there together leased through John Berwick, lately prior, and the convent to Richard Whalley esquire....*

Richard Whalley of Screveton, in personal service to Henry VIII since 1524 and employed by Cromwell to visit some of the lesser monasteries, quickly acquired rights in Radcliffe and elsewhere. He was confirmed as holder of the above leases and tithes for forty years, on more favourable terms than they had been held before. While paying the prior, convent and their successors (shortly to be the crown itself) £20 annually 'at the feast of the Lord's nativity', he was to be allowed automatic leeway of fifteen days for default of payment, or thirty days 'if it is asked for'. In return, he was to continue allowing Radcliffe's chantry priest (Thomas Smythe) and his successors to occupy his house within the rectory as long as there was no 'disturbance or vexation' to Whalley or his assigns. Moreover, this house had to be 'supported and maintained with all repairs... And all other buildings of the aforesaid Rectory shall be sufficiently repaired & maintained by the said Richard Whalley & his assigns for the whole of the aforesaid term'. Wood was to come from

Remains of Thurgarton Priory
drawn in the 19th century

Thurgarton for such repairs. Richard Whalley would still have made a handsome profit from the deal as the income was now valued at £52.10s, while his outgoings only amounted to £20 with responsibility to maintain the buildings.

It was on 14th June 1538 that the surrender of Thurgarton to the crown was signed, but Richard Whalley was to retain the Radcliffe lease only temporarily, despite the 40 years of the agreement. In July 1539 the new prior was granted Fiskerton Hall and a pension of £40 a year. The sub-prior, a confessed adulterer according to the commissioners, was granted a pension of £6.13s.4d, and seven canons were given £5 a year each. The priory itself was acquired by William Cooper of London.[53]

Thurgarton Priory and the rest of the monastic institutions were suddenly no more, and the royal coffers were temporarily boosted. While there were those who objected to these changes, notably in Yorkshire and Lincolnshire where the Pilgrimage of Grace was crushed, many, like Richard Whalley, saw an opportunity to make money or to expand their holdings as ecclesiastical buildings and vast areas of land were suddenly released onto the property market. These new lay land-owners, or 'impropriators', acquired not only new lands which they could rent out, but the right to collect the tithes which had been paid to the monasteries. (Hostility to tithe paying became a national issue in the 17th century.) Along with the acquisition of lands and tithes went the right to appoint incumbents, which was transferred from patron to patron as different sections of land changed hands. It is not always easy to identify who obtained the rights of presentation in Radcliffe's case, although immediately after Thurgarton's suppression it passed jointly to Richard Molyneux of Hawton, near Newark, and John Shepharde, a yeoman from Balderton.[54]

The Rosells of Radcliffe were amongst those hoping to benefit when the nearby Shelford Priory was dissolved. (There Legh and Layton claimed that three of the Augustinian canons were guilty of unnatural sin, three of incontinence, while three others wished to be released from their vows. Moreover, the priory had spurious relics, including the girdle and milk of the Virgin, part of a candle which she carried at her purification, and some oil of the Holy Cross.) Archbishop Cranmer did his best to smooth the way for his brother-in-law (probably Harold Rosell rather than Edward Cartwright who was rewarded with Malling in Kent), when he wrote to Thomas Cromwell, the dissolver of the monasteries, on 25th March 1536:

> *...I commend me unto you; and as one that is bold many a time to trouble you with suits both for myself and my friends, which naturally, yea, and by the law of God, I am bound to do, in my right heartiest wise desire you to be so good master unto this bearer my brother-in-law, who is now the Clerk of my Kitchen, and for whom I spake unto you yesterday at the court, as to get him the farm or lease of the priory of Shelford, or of some other house of religion in Nottinghamshire, where his native country is, which now are by the Act of Parliament suppressed; and he shall find the king's grace sufficient sureties for the Payment of the rents and revenues thereto belonging.*

Even an Archbishop, however, had to be a careful suppliant to the mighty Cromwell. Moreover, patronage had to be carefully measured. Cranmer had another possible client, and he made it clear that he did not want a favour to his brother-in-law to jeopardise the claim of the other. On this occasion, however, his influence was to no avail. In June 1536 almost the whole of the manors, advowsons, and other properties belonging to Shelford Priory went for 60 years at an annual rent of £20 to Michael Stanhope, 2nd son of Sir Edward Stanhope of Rampton, and not to Harold Rosell. They were worth £100 a year. Before the end of Elizabeth's reign the Stanhopes had acquired the Radcliffe rectory lands too.[55]

Suppression of the chantry

The next stage in the plunder of the church began in the last years of Henry VIII's reign. The King, acting as his own minister after the execution of Thomas Cromwell, planned to augment his income further by suppressing the chantries - chapels financed by pious bequests for the saying of masses for the dead. In February 1545 commissioners carried out a survey based on the answers to eight questions. Radcliffe's replies throw light on a religious institution which was about to be eliminated.

It was claimed that the chantry had been founded 'for a priest to say mass there for ever for the Soul of Stephen Radcliffe'. (The latter had been the 13th century priest and benefactor of the village, whose wooden effigy rested along the south wall inside the church.) A 'copy of a writing thereof' was then shown to the four commissioners as proof. At the time of the *Valor Ecclesiasticus* of 1534-5 the priest had been paid an annual stipend of £4 by Thurgarton Priory. This had now (1545) increased to £4.2s.2d, from the 'Lands, tenements, and other possessions lying and being in Divers places within the said parish of Ratclif', which had presumably belonged to the dissolved priory. (A payment of 4d went to Nottingham castle.)

The current chantry priest was still Thomas Smythe - the recipient of the vicar's bird and cage in 1519, and of three sheep to pay for the 'guiding' of John Grenhall's son in 1534. According to the Woodhall rental of 1545/6, Smythe owned some land which he rented out to William Pare. This must have helped to supplement his modest income, but he had to pay a chief rent on it of 2½d to the manor. He also had to pay a rent on his garden of 12d a year.

From the commissioners' point of view Radcliffe must have been a disappointment. Although the chantry did not have to support an additional preacher, a schoolmaster, or relieve the poor, there was no 'mansion or dwelling place' belonging to it which could be rented out, and no lands, or yearly profits beyond what had already been noted as providing the priest's income. Moreover, it had no portable wealth - 'neither chalice, vestment, nor any other ornaments or movable goods... but only of the parish church cost' (i.e. what was provided by the church). Either the chantry was very poor, or anything of value had been removed before the commissioners arrived.

It is difficult to envisage the chantry arrangements. The commissioners described it as 'a Chantry within the parish church of Radcliffe'. There was, however, a house for the chantry priest within the rectory which, as is made clear when Thurgarton was dissolved, had to be maintained by the new holder of the priory's Radcliffe lands. Two other references offer a little further insight. In 1591 the lease of the parsonage house 'or chantry' with all appurtenances was left by William Roulstone to his widow, Jane. It was by then in the possession of the Rosells who held it from the crown. If Jane chose to surrender it, she was to have £120 'at agreed times' from Mr Rosell. An Inquisition Post Mortem into the goods of John Rosell taken on 23rd September 1607 refers to 'one chamber called the chantry of the vicar of Radcliffe, and a garden lying in Radcliffe, lately of the chantry of Radcliffe now dissolved'. Whether masses for the dead had been said within part of the church, or within a separate building is not really clear.

Henry was to die before the chantries could be suppressed, but they went early in his son's reign. Edward VI, aged only ten when he succeeded, had been brought up as a Protestant and in his name his ministers, with Cranmer continuing as Archbishop of Canterbury, pushed through an extreme form of Protestantism. The Radcliffe chantry was reassessed, but valued as in Henry's reign, although by this time Thomas Smythe, the chantry priest, had died, so the income automatically went to the young king. A cottage, occupied by Robert [Hempsell?] at an annual rent of 3s.8d, and village lands which had provided the income for the chantry (then rented by Richard Bayley, widow Isabel Pight and Richard Greene) soon became the prey of speculators. They were acquired in 1551, with many other lands, by Richard Monynges and Thomas Watton, two squires from Kent. As has been seen, however, by the 1580s the property was in the possession of the Rosell family.[56]

The imposition of extreme Protestantism

Still more religious changes were imposed by legislation in Edward's reign. Across England rood screens were destroyed, medieval wall paintings whitewashed, commandments written on the walls, and statues pulled down in the name of reformation. Inventories of all parish goods, plate, jewels, vestments, bells and other ornaments were demanded. Churchwardens Richard Bayley and Thomas Greene together with three Radcliffe 'Townsmen' (John Franke, Richard Greene and Richard Wright) drew up the village's inventory on 3rd September 1552. Two were tenants of the dissolved chantry lands and must have been particularly aware of the threat of confiscation. Their list reflected the ceremonial services which were now banned: a silver chalice with a paten (i.e. a shallow dish used for bread at the eucharist), a latten pyx (a vessel of bronze-like metal in which the host or consecrated bread was preserved) with a latten cross, a cross cloth of green silk, a vestment and cope of white satin, a vestment and cope of black worsted, six altar cloths, three towels, two brass candlesticks, two brass hand bells, two 'corpraxses' (communion cloths) with their cases, one holy water 'fate' (probably a vat) of brass, a basin and lavabo of latten, one sacring bell, a sanctus bell broken in the crown with trussing, three bells in the steeple, a surplice with two 'rachettes', and three albs belonging to these vestments.

It soon became apparent to the authorities that after being inventoried church possessions were often 'embezzled or removed'. Local commissioners - Sir George Pierrepont in Nottinghamshire's case - were therefore appointed in 1553 to 'take full view of all such goods, in whose hands soever they be, make an inventory and compare it with the former inventories remaining with the churchwardens or other keepers and make search for such as are found wanting...' Whether Sir George found the Radcliffe goods intact is not known, nor is their ultimate fate, although a silver cup and cover are recorded in the 18th century. (Perhaps significantly his probate inventory of 1563 reveals a quantity of miscellaneous ecclesiastical plate.)[57]

The new church services which underlay the rejection of ceremony were now conducted by clergymen who no longer had to be celibate despite being in full orders, and who from 1549 based them on Archbishop Cranmer's new English prayer book. By later standards this was a conservative attempt to cling to ancient forms, while removing what the reformers regarded as idolatrous elements. While this approach was broadly accepted, in the west country there were protests against, amongst other things, the use of English instead of the more familiar Latin. There is no record of how Radcliffe people felt, but as the deviser of this new work was the brother-in-law of the local squire, it was probably wise to accept it quietly. Less easy for traditionalists to accept was the second prayer book of Edward's reign, imposed from 1552, which removed all 'relics of popery', making it no longer possible to interpret the communion service in a Catholic way. Transubstantiation was now rejected. Communion became a commemorative act frequently celebrated at a table rather than at an altar, using ordinary bread, and the minister was no longer to wear special vestments or make devotional gestures. The emphasis was to be on the pulpit instead of the altar. All was to be enforced by an Act of Uniformity, and those who failed to attend church on Sundays could suffer ecclesiastical punishment, including excommunication.

Henry VIII would have been horrified at this extreme Protestantism, and doubtless Radcliffe people wondered at the changes to their church. As the traditional religious images went, many parishes substituted lay heraldry to emphasise continuity and tradition. It may have been at this time that Radcliffe chose to confirm its links with the great local families of the past - and with the fast rising Rosell family - by putting in place the colourful emblems which Thoroton noted in the 17th century. Pride of place went to the Deyncourt arms, displayed in the chancel window. In the north aisle were the arms of the Grey family, and in the south aisle were those of Strelley, and Rosell with Basily. All have long since gone.[58]

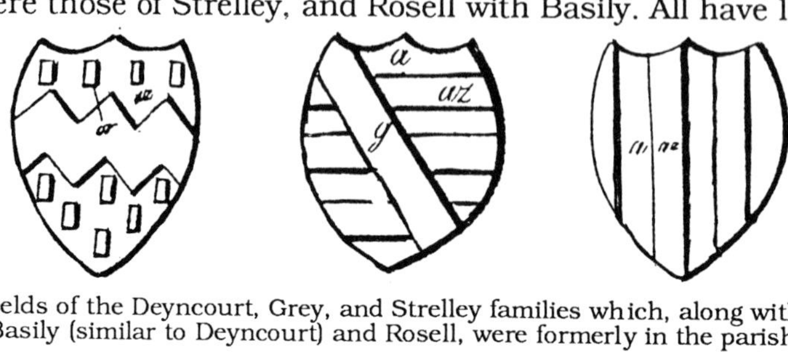

Shields of the Deyncourt, Grey, and Strelley families which, along with those of Basily (similar to Deyncourt) and Rosell, were formerly in the parish church

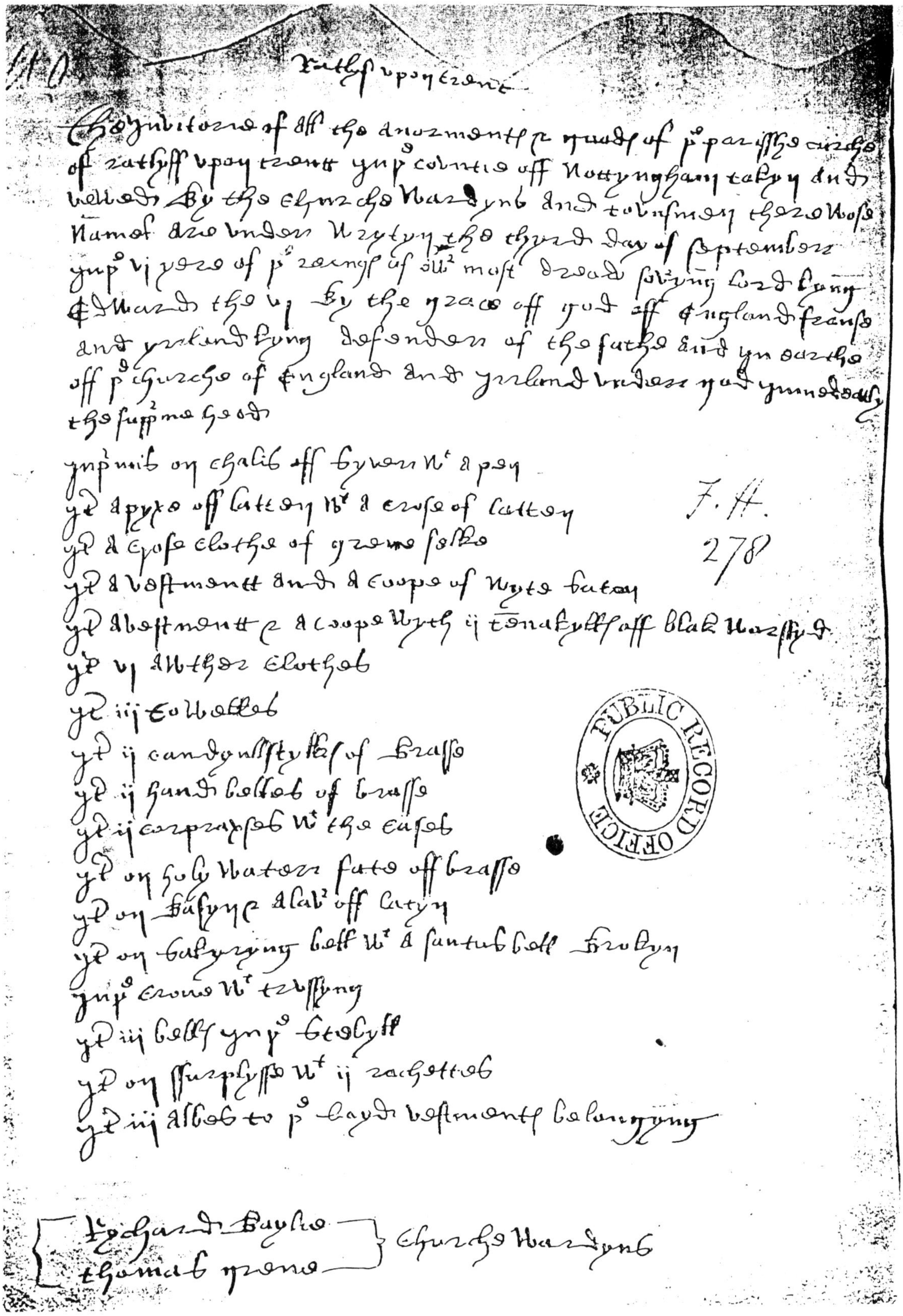

110

Ratclyf upon trent

The Inventorye of all the ornamentes & goodes of the parisshe churche of ratclyff upon trent yn the countie off Nottyngham taken and vewed by the churchewardyns and townsmen there whose names are under wrytyn the thyrd day of September yn the vj yere of the reigne of our most dread soveryng lord kyng Edward the vj by the grace off god off England frans and yrland kyng defender of the fathe and yn earthe off the churche of England and yrland under god ymmedyatly the suppreme hede

Inprimis on chalis off sylver wt a pen

It a pyxe off latten wt a crose of latten — 7. ff. 278

It a crose clothe of grene selke

It a vestment and a coope of whyte satyn

It a vestment & a coope wyth ij tonakylls off blak worsted

It vj alther clothes

It iij towelles

It ij candylstykes of brasse

It ij hand belles of brasse

It ij corprasses wt the cases

It on holy water fate off brasse

It on basyne & laver off latyn

It on sakeryng bell wt a santus bell broken

Inprimis crosse wt trussyng

It iij belles yn the stepyll

It on surplysse wt ij rachettes

It iij albes to the sayd vestmentes belongyng

Rychard Bayle
thomas grene } churchewardyns

Inventory of church possessions taken 3rd September 1552
(PRO E117/7/80)

The wills of William Welbie and five parishioners

Some indication of the way these changes affected the community can be found in the wills of a vicar and five parishioners made between 1549 and 1552. William Welbie had succeeded William Carcolston as priest sometime after 1534. He made his final will on 3rd April 1549, and had probably died by April 25th when Edward Sheppard was installed in his place. This was the time that Cranmer's first prayer book was being imposed on the nation.

Unusually, William Welbie specifically renounced earlier versions of his will, perhaps because they emphasised Catholic beliefs. The preamble of this version stresses imperialism and the supremacy of the monarch in spiritual matters:

> *I Wil[lia]m Welbie, clerk vicar of Ratcliffe a yond Trent in the County of Nottingham, being of whole mind and perfect memory Thanks be to God, The Third day of April in the third year of the Reign of our Sovereign lord Edward the Sixth by the Grace of God King of England, France and Ireland, defender of the faith and in earth next immediately under God, supreme head of the Church of England and Ireland, do make and ordain this my last will and Testament...*

More traditionally, he then bequeathed his soul to God and Jesus Christ, but all references to the Virgin Mary or saints in heaven were omitted. Masses for the dead having been abolished both doctrinally and practically with the suppression of the chantries currently taking place, he could only bequeath 2s to the minister performing his burial service 'in the honour of our blessed Sacrament'. He did, however, ask his executors, after all legacies, debts and funeral expenses had been paid, to bestow any remaining goods 'after their conscience and discretion for the health of my Soul'. He also asked to be buried within the church at the north end of the chancel.

Noticeably absent is the type of religious bequest found in earlier wills. Instead, William Welbie's 'good works' took the form of benevolence to the poor and to the public good of Radcliffe and five other local villages. There were a few personal bequests. He remembered each of his seven godchildren, notably William Ballard to whom he left 'one cow that is in the Custody of Thomas Godfrey in Shelford'. A kinsman, John Welbie of Norfolk, was left 20s 'if he be alive'. His four witnesses, John Franke, Robert Darwent (Darwyn?), Richard Wright and 'Mr John Rosell', received 12d each. Like his predecessors John Browne and Edmund Lodge, William Welbie seems to have enjoyed a simple lifestyle.[59]

The five other wills which have survived from Edward VI's reign confirm that the Protestant trends expressed by the vicar were reaching the laity, even though old habits had not entirely died out. The testators (or their scribes) all emphasised the religious supremacy of the monarch. Husbandman Edmund Taverey in 1548 played safe and left nothing that could be construed as having a religious connotation. Widow Alice Morley in 1549, harked back to the old ways, leaving 3s.4d to Radcliffe's high altar, and 2s to the high altar of Gedling church. Nevertheless, she was aware of the new thinking, and left 4d to the 'poor men's box'. Husbandman John Fuldiam and Joanna Taverey both left gifts to the new vicar - a strike of malt and 12d respectively - but no other bequests that could be construed as religious. The vicar was also left 12d to pray for William Wolley in 1552. The latter left someone else to decide between the spiritual and the secular by leaving 6d for either the church or the village boat.

Catholicism restored

The young king died in 1553 and was succeeded by his half-sister Mary. As the daughter of the rejected Katherine of Aragon, Mary was staunchly Catholic and was determined to bring England back to Papal doctrine and control. Although she was partly successful in this, her use of persecution to force conformity alienated many who would have accepted a return to the old ways, and made Protestantism a cause to die for. Of the 300 or so victims in her short reign, the most prominent was Thomas Cranmer. After recanting his Protestantism and then withdrawing his recantation, the 67 year-old former Archbishop was burned in Oxford in March 1556. The Radcliffe Rosells had lost both a kinsman and patron.

There is little evidence to show whether or not Radcliffe people in general returned to Catholic ways. Only four wills have survived from the two last years of Mary's short reign, but they show some rejection of Protestantism. Gone are the preambles rehearsing the imperial power and religious supremacy of the sovereign. In each will the Virgin Mary and saints are restored as recipients of the testator's soul, and some modest religious bequests are made. Typical were the wills of John Martyn and husbandman Richard Greene, both from October 1557. The former left 2 lbs of wax for his funeral, 12d for the high altar, and 10s to be spent in the church on the day of his burial. A small sum was left to the vicar Edward Sheppard, his 'ghostly father', to pray for him. Richard Greene not only left 2s to the high altar for forgotten tithes, but also 4s for a coverlet for the church. He was so anxious that the church should receive this gift that he made the proviso that if the money 'will not serve, then I will that my wife lay down at her discretion so much as will buy it'. John Franke in 1558 asked to be buried in the church. He wanted a 'p[ro]cession' at his funeral and the poor were to be given wheat. Richard Roulestone drew up his will on 16th November, the day before Queen Mary died. Of the four, he was the most generous to the vicar, leaving him 6s.8d, as well as 2s to the high altar.

While these Radcliffe testators appear to have accepted Mary's Catholicism, nearby there was opposition from two members of the powerful Pierrepont family. William, a younger son, had held the rectories of Holme Pierrepont and Widmerpool since 1527, well before the Reformation. As a supporter of reformed principles he had married. Now Mary's regime reimposed Catholic principles, including clerical celibacy. (The return to celibacy in the last years of Henry VIII's reign had also caused problems for reforming clergy, including Archbishop Cranmer himself.) Unable to subscribe to Mary's religion, William Pierrepont refused to answer the charges brought against him in May 1554, was deprived of his living, sentenced to penance, public apology and a profession of chastity in front of his wife. He ultimately submitted and was restored to his priestly functions. Another Pierrepont, Edward, preferred exile in Frankfurt by 1557 rather than conform to Catholicism. In contrast, some later members of the Pierrepont family were linked to Catholicism. (See p. 116.)[60]

In one area, Mary could not turn the clock back. She found it impossible to restore all the confiscated lands, now in the possession of lay owners, to the church. There were some exceptions, however, when they were in crown hands, or had belonged to attainted persons. For example, the lands which had formerly supported Radcliffe's chantry chapel had apparently come to the crown since their acquisition by two Kentish landowners, and in 1556 Mary granted them to the master and chaplains of the Savoy Hospital in London. This charitable institution had been founded by Henry VII in 1509 for the relief of a 100 poor people, but like the chantry had been suppressed in Edward's reign. It was now re-founded and endowed with many lands throughout the country. Similarly, Radcliffe lands were amongst those in crown hands which had belonged to the dissolved hospital of St John of Jerusalem. These were returned when the hospital was restored in 1558.[61]

Mary could also return to the church any advowsons (rights of presentation to livings) which were held by the crown. By the time of William Welbie's death in 1549, the Radcliffe patronage had passed to John Constable of Kinoulton, who appointed Edward Sheppard as the new vicar. By 1553, however, extensive Nottinghamshire lands and several advowsons, including Radcliffe's, had been acquired by John Beaumont, Master of the Rolls (soon to be disgraced for corruption). In that year he sold them to the crown. The Radcliffe advowson was consequently one of many in the diocese of York temporarily granted to the archbishop on 31st October 1558.[62]

Seventeen days later Mary was dead. However good her intentions, her reign was dominated by religious persecution, rebellion, foreign war, epidemics and poor harvests. Her half-sister Elizabeth inherited a ravaged country.

Case study 3

THE THRAVE FAMILY

The Thrave (Thuryff, Threve, Threaves, Threive, Treve) family is one of the oldest continuously in Radcliffe from Medieval to Stuart times. The earliest reference so far found is in the subsidy of 1332. From the early Tudor period the name is often followed by 'alias Long', an addition which continues into the 17th century.

An early land dispute

A dispute in the time of Mary Tudor provides information about the family as well as about landholding practices. The humble Thraves were prepared to stand their ground against their social superiors, and the case went as high as the Court of Chancery in London. Unusually, the judgement has survived.

Edward Ballard - referred to as 'gentleman' in the Woodhall rental of 1545/6 - and Henry Trent claimed that they were tenants in common, sharing equal rights to two leys of land on which a grange or barn had been built, and to six acres and one rood of arable land with 'appurtenances' which were 'bounded and butted' in Radcliffe's common fields. Denying their claim was William Thrave, who described himself as 'a poor, simple and quiet person... a man of great poverty', whose 'utter undoing' would follow if he lost the case. Perhaps William was exaggerating his poverty-stricken state to gain sympathy from the authorities. His family were holders of lands on which allegiance was owed to the Peverel Court, and also of lands within the Duchy of Lancaster in both Radcliffe and Lamcote. Moreover, while not amongst the highest tax payers, they had owned sufficient in goods to be on the subsidy lists of the 1540s.

A year or so after making no headway with their claim, Ballard and Trent took the case to Chancery during the time that Bishop Stephen Gardiner was Lord Chancellor (1553-5). They complained that 'divers Evidences, muniments and writings' concerning the 'premises' had casually come into William Thrave's possession, by colour of which he was aiming to disinherit them, and daily disturbed and molested their quiet and peaceable occupation. They had several times asked Thraves to hand over the documents, but he had refused. They did not know how many documents there were, nor in what they were contained, and were consequently without remedy under the common law. (Complaints about missing title deeds were frequent in such cases, and were sometimes an excuse to have rights defined in law.) They wanted Thrave to be subpoenaed to answer their charges.

Although the case for Ballard and Trent was clearly presented, they offered no support for their claim. In contrast, in his response William Thrave gave a detailed account of how he came to hold the disputed lands. He started with his grandfather, Thomas Thrave, alias Long, who held the barn and lands 'as of fee', which meant that they could be inherited. On his death, they passed to John Thrave, who broke the family pattern by having 'Gyford' as an alternative name! (Perhaps he was the John Thrave who was left Father John Browne's lute in the latter's will of 1519.) When John died, his elder son Thomas (alias Long) inherited, and on Thomas's death the lands and barn came into the possession of his brother, the defendant, William Thrave.[63]

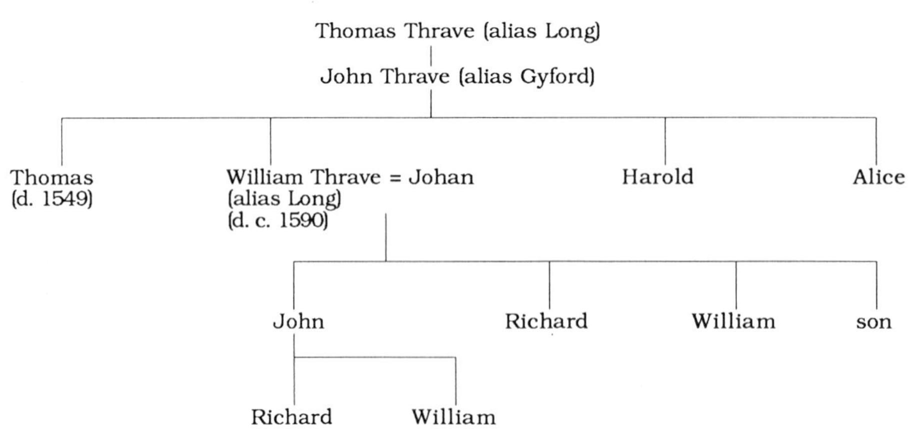

The Thrave Family

The casual reference to Thomas's death masked a tragic incident. A coroner's inquest held at Radcliffe on 16th March 1550 revealed what had happened:

About 3 a.m. on 12th June 1549, when Thomas Thrave alias Long intended to cross the River Trent in the fields of Radcliffe-on-Trent in a boat worth 10s, the said small boat went under the water through the force of the current of the river, whereby Thomas was drowned in the river. Thus he came to his death by misadventure by the force of the river and the small boat and not otherwise.

William had thus come into possession of his lands unexpectedly.[64]

No mention was made of any documents in William's evidence, but his detailed account of the family's long-standing occupation of the disputed lands carried weight with the court. It was judged on 12th November 1556 that Ballard and Trent had not proved that they had 'any good title or interest to the said lands and tenements' and their claim was dismissed from Chancery, to be determined by common law. It would seem unlikely that William would lose any further case, however, for the court ordered that Ballard and Trent should pay him the considerable sum of £6 in compensation for the costs and charges that he had 'wrongfully sustained'.[65]

William Thrave and his family

After successfully fending off the claim to at least some of his lands in 1556, William Thrave faded from recorded history for a number of years, and his everyday routine of farming, his marriage and the raising of a family has to be assumed. Records of the Peverel Court confirm his landholding status, and he rarely missed attending between 1564 and 1587/8. Although he was described as a husbandman in his will of 1589, he added to his farming interests over the years, and from at least 1575 he was also a 'common baker and brewer', more than once 'breaking the assize' - the statutory regulations for weights and measures - for which he was 'amerced' 4d by the Peverel Court. His wife, Johan, shared in this work, being independently described and amerced in the same way in 1578.[66]

Johan produced four sons, three of them still alive when their father died. Perhaps the growing children strained the family economy, for at some point William had to borrow 50s from Richard Howlyn, and though the debt was forgiven when the latter drew up his will in 1570, a condition was that William must give 6s.8d to each of his own boys - an indirect way of bequeathing a legacy.

William, however, was perhaps as much concerned with the problem of his brother Harold as with his children. (Thomas, his elder brother, had of course been drowned in the Trent.) In February 1573 Harold was brought before the church court at Mansfield for incontinence with Joanna Bird (Byrde) - a common enough charge. After investigation, the pair were summoned to West Bridgford in June, but failed to appear, so it was not until 16th July that the court pronounced judgement:

that the said Thrave was and is a lunatic and one on whom the said Bird could not lay the said crime...

Harold was consequently dismissed, but Joanna had to perform a penance, which she certified in September. The case may have been over, but Harold's plight must have been a constant worry for his family, perhaps along with that of an unmarried sister, Alice. The two were clearly William's overall responsibility, for in his will he allowed them the continued use of accommodation:

My will is that Harold my brother and Alice my sister shall have house room in the yard, as they have had, so long as they live using themselves honestly as they ought to do, and that Harold shall pay for his house room yearly during his life 6s and Alice shall pay for the house room yearly during her life 3s.4d...

The qualified nature of this 'legacy', particularly the use of the term 'honestly', suggests that William found both brother and sister something of a trial.[67]

Apart from family problems, at times William had trouble with other Radcliffe residents, in particular Robert Hall. The latter was one of the parish élite, and a substantial holder of land in Costock, Adbolton and Basford, as well as in Radcliffe itself. Both men were brought before the church court in 1577 for failing to attend Easter communion. This was not because of a lapse in faith, however, but the result of an unspecified quarrel between them. They gave their explanation on 30th April to the court in St Peter's, Nottingham, by which time any ill-feeling seemed to have waned:

... in consideration of a breach at the time they received not, but immediately after upon agreement they received [communion] the Monday fortnight after Easter.

As both men certified their conformity they were dismissed, but any reconciliation was only temporary. Early in 1578 they were before the Peverel Court for having been involved in an affray 'against each other'. For drawing blood from Hall, William was amerced 5s - a particularly large sum. (It was at the same sessions that Johan was amerced 4d!) Robert Hall was fined 3s.4d for his part in the affair. The cause of the quarrel is not stated. The situation was made worse by the presence of Hall's son-in-law, William Roulstone, who then turned on William and drew blood in his turn, so earning a fine of 3s.4d. There is no further record of the quarrel.[68]

By the beginning of 1589, William was 'sick in body' and drew up his will. His bequests indicate a modest agricultural household. (No inventory has survived to indicate the contents.) Apart from the arrangements made for his brother and sister, his main concerns were for his wife, sons, and two grandsons. Johan's status as supervisor of the household was to be preserved:

> *... my will and pleasure is that Johan my wife shall have her finding here in this house as she hath had heretofore during her natural life with the governance in the house and yard as she hath had.*

His son John, who temporarily took over as common baker and brewer, was to be William's executor, and to inherit any goods not specified in the will, once debts and funeral expenses had been paid. Specifically, he was left the draught (ploughing team) 'and all that belongeth thereto', as well as the hovels, longhouses and pales in the yard. These, with the exception of the draught, were eventually to go to John's son, Richard. The latter was to inherit immediately an iron-bound wain or wagon. Richard also acquired some brewing and baking equipment - a pair of querns for grinding corn, three tubs and a 'lead' or vat. When his grandmother died, he would inherit her brown heifer. His brother William was left a calf and a ewe hog.

William remembered his two other surviving sons. Richard was to receive a wether sheep for being supervisor of the will - his only legacy. He may have been well established elsewhere. William was left £6.13s.4d 'to be paid to him at any time within these 4 years next coming for his filial part'. Modest bequests of livestock went to Richard and Marie Walker and to Elizabeth Whittaker.

William Thrave's will was proved on 7th September 1590. It contained no reference to the right to hold the lands for which he had so tenaciously fought in Mary's reign. Nevertheless, he seems to have left his family quite adequately, if not generously, provided for - his son John was sufficiently well-to-do to be amongst those paying £3.8s on their goods when the queen needed subsidies in 1592/3 and 1593/4. Future generations of Thraves appear in the 17th century on both sides of the legal divide. The family as a whole, and William's records in particular, give a brief insight into the concerns of Radcliffe people in Tudor times.[69]

ELIZABETHAN LANDLORDS

The early Tudor Rosells had taken advantage of a fortunate marriage with Archbishop Cranmer's sister, and of the dissolution of the monasteries to increase their landholdings and their status in the county. They fitted the national pattern of rising gentry. To some extent the Elizabethan period saw the Rosells consolidating their position, but the seeds were sown of problems which arose in the early 17th century, partly because of sprawling family commitments. An attempt to give financial protection to junior and female members of the family was to ensnare the next generation.

John Rosell senior - a litigious squire

The pacific approach successfully taken over Epperstone Wood was not to be followed once Harold's son, John, was in complete control. Even allowing for the litigious nature of the age, he seems to have been involved in more than his fair share of disputes. Perhaps all were not of his making, but he gives the impression of being an outspoken, and perhaps difficult man.

Court actions were one way of maintaining the family prestige. Another was to make a good marriage, and John was to make two. The first was to Barbara (or Catherine) Sacheverell, from the prominent family based at Ratcliffe-on-Soar. A son, another John, was born as a result of this marriage, probably around 1560. John senior's second wife was Annora, daughter of Sir George Pierrepont - another distinguished bride for an ambitious man. Annora's dowry in practical terms, however, was not particularly generous if her father's will is anything to go by:

> *And I will that my executrix shall pay to my son in law --- Rosell who hath married my daughter Annora twenty pounds which shall be of my said daughter's portion and marriage money.*
> *And beside that £20 I will give and bequeath to the said Annora [an]other twenty pounds of my good will in full recompense and satisfaction of her child['s] part and portion.*

Three more sons came from this marriage - Gervase, Henry and Anthony - so there was no question of the line failing.[70]

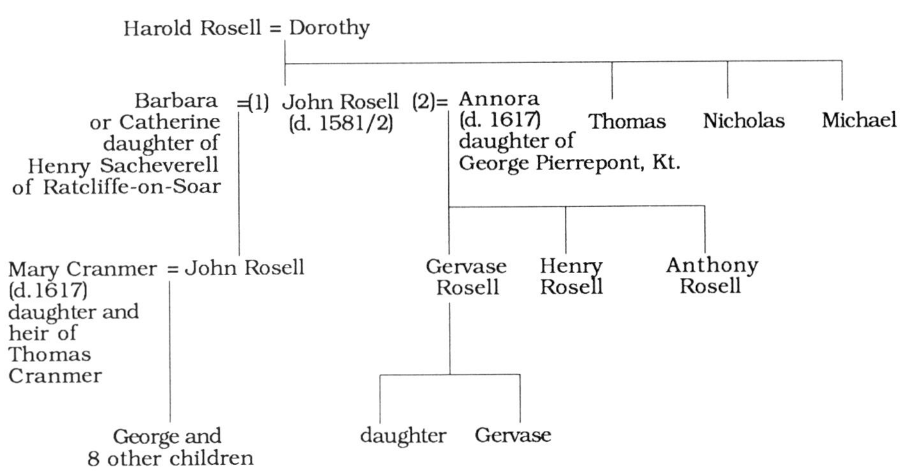

The Rosell Family - Elizabethan period

While relinquishing the more distant Epperstone, Oxton and Hoveringham properties in the 1560s, John maintained his status nearer home. Like his father he held the patronage of the rectory of Adbolton, appointing Thomas Wallys there in June 1564, a cleric who was subsequently linked with Radcliffe. He also had his toe on the county's administrative ladder when in 1568 he was the collector of the subsidy of fifteenths and tenths in Bingham Wapentake amounting to £82.10s.

(Although the Radcliffe figures have not survived for that year, the Rosells headed the village contributors throughout the 16th century.) This, however, seems to have been as close as the Rosells ever got to joining the administrative ranks of the county hierarchy for another hundred years.[71]

When it came to property, John made significant gains in 1564/5 when he bought the manor of Lamcote with fishing rights from George Pilkington of Croxton Kerrial in Leicestershire. (The latter had acquired the manor in Edward IV's reign via Agnes Marmion whose heir, her cousin Agnes, had married a Pilkington.) At the beginning of the century the Rosells had held no more than 9 bovates of land there, but their holdings now became substantial, and included 100 acres of 'land', 100 acres of heath, and 100 acres of pasture, as well as 20 acres of meadow, ten tofts, eight cottages, ten gardens, a windmill and some rents. Thoroton's comment that John Rosell 'suffered a recovery' of the Lamcote manor in 1565/6, when members of the Cranmer family 'claimed against him', is probably a reference to a legal device for breaking entails on property, rather than a genuine clash with the benevolent Cranmers. John Rosell was certainly in full possession of the Lamcote manor when he died. Moreover, three years after the Lamcote 'recovery', when Thomas Cranmer, the archbishop's nephew, was disposing of the rectory, church and patronage of Aslockton and Whatton, he passed them for a time at least to a Robert Brookesby, and to John's brother Nicholas and his heirs, confirming that good relations between the two families continued beyond the archbishop's generation.[72]

Rosell versus Hill

The Radcliffe squire, however, did have a knack of finding himself involved in controversy, both civil and ecclesiastical. On at least three occasions he was before the Court of Chancery during the time that Sir Nicholas Bacon was Keeper of the Great Seal (1558-1579). In one case he was the complainant, in the other two the defendant.

The undated case of Rosell versus Hill concerned a modest amount of property - 'one messuage with the appurtenances' in Radcliffe, and the 'issues and profits thereof'. That such a case could reach Chancery in London indicates the tenacity with which property disputes were fought in the later 16th century. John claimed that 'of long time now past' he had the right to hold the messuage as part of his demesne, but that the documents ('divers evidence, deeds and writings') had been lost - a common complaint in such cases - and fallen into the hands of one William Hill, who had consequently 'unlawfully entered' the premises, expelled Rosell, would not allow him to 'have and enjoy' the premises, and refused to hand them back. As a result John claimed that without the court's intervention he was remediless, and asked for Hill to be summoned by subpoena to answer the charge.

William Hill's reply was that he was 'a very poor man', that Rosell had brought the case 'only to vex, molest and trouble him', and that he was 'unjustly and wrongfully served and troubled' by the squire. Moreover, he had never had any evidences or writings concerning any messuage, had never secretly 'conveyed' or entered any premises, nor expelled Rosell. In fact, he did not have, or claim to have, any property in Radcliffe whatsoever. Nothing in Rosell's claim was true. Not only was he ready to answer in court, but he expected to be awarded costs for the charges he had wrongfully had to bear.

Whether the court made a judgement is not known. William Hill's denial seems so conclusive that it is difficult to understand John Rosell's motives in bringing the case, except as an excuse to establish his rights over undocumented property. No other reference to a William Hill has been found in Radcliffe sources of the period.[73]

Ballard versus Rosell

A second case that went to Chancery, probably from May 1566, was a reversal of the Hill affair and put John on the defensive. William Ballard, a substantial landholder from Wymeswold in Leicestershire, but with possessions in Radcliffe, had married Anne Hall as his second wife. (Her memorial brass is in Radcliffe church.) He accused John of plotting with Agnes Thomson, a Radcliffe widow, to deprive him (Ballard) of a substantial amount of property: a messuage, two cottages, three gardens, two outhouses, 50 acres of land, a ley of meadow, 30 acres of pasture, as well as 10s of rent, and appurtenances in both Radcliffe and Lamcote. This time, he specified that three deeds or 'evidences' had come into the hands of Rosell, who had then 'craftily devised and conveyed unto the said Agnes divers and sundry secret estates'. As a result, Agnes was collecting the rents and profits from the premises, without any just title. On several occasions, claimed Ballard, he had 'very gently' asked for the return of the three deeds, and to be allowed to occupy the premises, but had been refused. He admitted that he did not know the 'certainty' of the three deeds, nor in what they were contained - 'whether in bag ensealed, box enclosed or chest locked'.

William's vagueness about the three deeds again suggests that the case was being brought to define rights, but the amount of property involved indicates that there was genuine friction between two powerful men, perhaps pursuing their own vendetta. Moreover, the relationship between John Rosell and Agnes Thomson seems ambiguous. If she could collect the profits in her own right, it is surprising that neither she nor her former husband appear in other contemporary documents. (The only known references to a Radcliffe person of the same name occur some forty years later.) No judgement has been found, but the itemised property at stake is similar to that which William Ballard's widow Anne was to hold from the Rosells for her lifetime. (See pp. 53 and 125.)[74]

Hall versus Rosell

The third Chancery case in May 1571 was the most complicated of the three, and certainly reflected tangled claims and John Rosell's acquisitiveness when it came to land. The plaintiff, Robert Hall, described himself as a yeoman, perhaps to gain sympathy from the court against a more powerful neighbour. In fact, he had acquired manorial lands in Cortlingstock (now Costock), and owned lands and rights in Radcliffe and Basford, as well as half the manor and extensive lands in Adbolton, where he had also acquired the advowson of the church from the Rosells. In other documents he is described as 'gentleman'. Significantly, when it came to village feuds, he was the brother-in-law of William Ballard, the complainant in the previous case.

Robert Hall claimed that he could 'hardly have any right by ordinary trial in the Country' (i.e. county) as John Rosell was 'of great power' locally. At the heart of the dispute were two messuages with appurtenances, and 40 acres of meadow and pasture land in Radcliffe and Lamcote. (Hall's document erroneously gave the latter as Hurcote, which allowed Rosell's side the pleasure of some legal nitpicking.) This property had belonged to yeoman John Pare. In 1569, around the time of 'the feast of St Michael the archangel' (September 29th), Pare had sold it to Hall for £25. Having paid part of the money, Hall had then to sell cattle and stock 'to his no small loss' in order to raise money for the rest of the payments on the days agreed with Pare. Unfortunately for Robert Hall, Pare died before the conveyance of the premises could be completed. John Rosell 'who long time before had sought to prevent' Hall of his bargain, then by 'sinister counsel' and 'very crafty and indirect means' worked on Pare's son and heir, Barnard. The two obtained possession of the premises, having acquired all Hall's evidences and writings.

Robert Hall was undoubtedly unlucky in failing to complete his payments before John Pare died (the will was proved 15th September 1570), and may have deserved sympathy and perhaps redress. Although these accusations of Rosell's devious determination to acquire the property are difficult to substantiate, it may be significant that when John Pare drew up his will on 21st May 1570, some eight months after Hall claimed the agreement had been made, John Rosell was a witness. Barnard Pare was left all his father's land in Radcliffe and Lamcote (subject to some considerations for his mother). Whether John Rosell and Barnard Pare knew of the sale to Hall, and chose to ignore it in the light of the general terms of the will - as Hall's complaint to Chancery implies - cannot be proved. Alternatively, the two men could have acted in ignorance of the transaction, an interpretation which would fit John Rosell's response to Hall's charges.

John Rosell's evidence to Chancery was simply that by John Pare's last will and testament the lands were left to Barnard who lawfully conveyed them to him (Rosell). He could produce the deed for this. It was untrue that the premises had been sold to Hall, or that he (Rosell) had acquired any of Hall's documents, or had 'deceived' Hall of any 'bargain' made for the lands as was 'slanderously and untruly alleged'. He even hoped to receive 'costs and damages' for the 'wrongful vexation' he had sustained.

Unfortunately, the judgement of the court has again failed to come to light, but it seems unlikely that Hall would have had the courage to invent the transaction, as Rosell claimed. When Hall died a decade later, however, the Inquisition into his property showed that he held only one croft with appurtenances that had belonged to the late John Pare, and even this he held of John Rosell as part of Rosell manor. The messuages and 40 acres are not mentioned, so it would seem that John Rosell had come off the better. The case demonstrates the importance of territorial expansion to the rising gentry.[75]

John Rosell senior's last years

As if the land disputes were not enough to occupy him, John Rosell found fault with the parish curate in 1572. As a result, Thomas Granger brought a charge of slander against him, the case going beyond the Nottingham Archdeacon's Court to York to be considered. Another curate, John Alred, was publicly humiliated by the Rosells in 1579 after a clash over church attendance at Easter. (See pp. 62-4.)

Nevertheless, a local community automatically relied on their squire as a figure of authority. John Rosell helped to sort out the disputes of others, such as that over church seats in 1577 (see p. 63), or assisted with the drawing up of wills, just as his father had done. This last duty was sometimes quite profitable. For his trouble in witnessing and supervising the will of Robert Darwyn in 1574 he was left 20 shillings, and his wife, Annora, a further 6s.8d. The terms in which he is mentioned in the four surviving wills in which he officiated is never more than a respectful 'Mr John Rosell'. While he could look back on a life in which he had consolidated the gains of the Rosells, his financial position may not have been as secure as it seemed at first sight. Two wills suggest that he was beginning to borrow money. On 14th August 1579 yeoman William Rowe from Bunny listed John Rosell, amongst other debtors, as owing him 26s.8d. In the following July, Margaret Greene, a Radcliffe widow, ambiguously stated that £30 which her son, Harold, had paid to Mr Rosell was 'his own'.

John Rosell senior died in 1582, survived by his second wife, Annora, her three sons, and by John junior, his eldest son by his first wife. He left a nuncupative (verbal) will which has not survived.[76]

John Rosell junior's inheritance

The contrast between father and son is very marked. Wills drawn up after the young man inherited his estates suggest genuine affection as well as respect between villagers and squire. Phrases which occur in nine of the ten surviving wills in which he was mentioned between 1585 and 1599 include 'my well-beloved master' in two, 'my worshipful John Rosell esquire', 'my master', 'my landlord', 'my very good master', 'my loving Mr John Rosell', 'my very good landlord', 'my loving master'. Moreover, from his time there is little evidence of friction with villagers or neighbours over land, or with local clergy over their conduct of religious matters. The village was a quieter, if duller, place. This apparent tranquillity, however, masked a deteriorating economic situation after the 1580s gave way to the 90s. Bad weather and poor harvests nationally towards the end of the century - reflected in reduced bequests of crops in wills, and in local action to combat poverty - turned dullness into depression.

It is in this period that the first signs of Rosell decline occur, and yet, to begin with, John Rosell junior - 'minor' in contemporary documents - seemed set on following the 'upwardly mobile' route of his father and grandfather. When he married Mary Cranmer, the co-heiress of Thomas of Aslockton - the archbishop's great nephew - the links between the two families were reinforced. Moreover, when Mary's father died in 1578 the young couple acquired part of the manor of Aslockton and rectorial tithes of Whatton and Aslockton. There is evidence that they let out the Aslockton rectory lands, and doubtless the other lands too, but they were not to become a permanent part of John Rosell's inheritance, for there is no mention of them when he died. (In the long run they passed to the Molyneux and then to the Pierrepont families.) Such gains also carried responsibilities. Holders of rectory lands normally had to maintain church chancels. In June 1595 John Rosell and John Thorolde, as joint farmers of the rectory lands of Whatton, were presented before the church court at Newark for having failed to maintain the chancel of Whatton church which was 'in decay'. Neither man put in an appearance, but they presumably had to foot the bill for repairs in due course.[77]

Of greater financial significance, John junior's substantial inheritance from his father was already compromised. In April 1581, less than a year before he died, John senior had entailed the estates in an attempt to ensure their security for posterity. By an indenture they were conveyed to a group of gentry with estates in Yorkshire, Lincolnshire, Derbyshire and Nottinghamshire (including Thomas Ashton of Radcliffe) and their heirs, who were to ensure that the line of inheritance as laid down by John senior was followed. This was a common legal device. Understandably, John senior had secured the estates for his own use for the rest of his life. It was the arrangements he made for after his death that were to hamper his son. In general the line of inheritance was to descend via John junior and Mary to their male heirs. Should they fail, then the lines of John junior's half brothers Gervase, Henry or Anthony would be followed. Should all these fail, then the line from John senior's brother Michael would take over. (There was no mention of his scholarly brother, Thomas, for whose education Archbishop Cranmer had taken such pains in 1533.) There were sufficient exceptions, however, to reduce John junior's initial inheritance quite drastically.

In particular, provision had been made for John senior's second wife, Annora (Pierrepont). She was allowed the substantial lands of Woodhall manor, Cotgrave manor and three closes in Lamcote for her lifetime. John junior's half-brother Gervase Rosell was granted Radcliffe's old chantry lands for his lifetime, which he rented out to the Roulstones in Radcliffe. As both Annora and Gervase were to outlive John junior, he only ever had the use of just over half of the total Rosell estates: Rosell manor, Lamcote manor and some former lands of Newstead and Dale Priories in both Radcliffe and Lamcote. Excluding messuages, cottages and gardens, this roughly amounted to 700 acres. Annora held some 570, and Gervase about 110. In addition, some time before John senior died, the Ballards had acquired some Rosell holdings, which William's long-lived widow, Anne, was to hold for her lifetime. These comprised a cottage with appurtenances in Radcliffe, a second cottage and seven bovates of land, meadow and pasture in Lamcote, together worth 40s a year. As she survived until 1626, all this was also tied up beyond the foreseeable future.[78]

Advance of the Pierreponts

As John junior's curtailed inheritance coincided with a time of reduced yields through poor harvests and inclement weather, it is not surprising to find from two village wills of 1591 that, like his father, he owed money. William Capendale of Lamcote gave to the squire 'that which he oweth me', and William Roulstone, gentleman, gave 'forty shillings of that which he oweth me'.

A more substantial way of raising instant money was to dispose of some of the lands, although in the long run this would reduce income from rents. Despite the entail arranged by his father, John junior seems to have managed to do this. A clause in the indenture of 1581, by which the estates were handed to a group of gentry for administration, stated that the property was not to be alienated (sold) by John Rosell within 25 to 30 years. However, before the expiry of this time limit, probably around 1600 and certainly before the end of Elizabeth's reign, some of the Rosell lands came into the possession of the Pierreponts.[79]

As early as 1527 an Inquisition Post Mortem indicates that the Pierreponts had had some slight holdings in both Radcliffe and Lamcote. A later 16th century list shows that they were encroaching on a number of enclosed lands scattered through Lamcote:

First Mr Rosell's new close butting on the mill field - 6 leys at the east side
In Mr Rosell's Long Croft close - 6 leys at the west side
A new close bounding upon Moreland's yard's end - 3 leys
A hempyard & a close bounding upon Agnes Shep[par]d's yard end
Two hemp yards at the other side of the street over against
Moreland's house & Agnes Shep[par]d's house

Three little pingles [small pieces of land] between the little ditch & the Lane
Mr Rosell's west Crifting Close
A Close between both the Lands w[hi]ch Robt Darwyn doth occupy
A close upon the west side of the Land w[hi]ch belongeth to Holme milne
Mr Rosell's close bounding [next?] to Holme town meadow of the east side.

Pierrepont shield

Sir Henry Pierrepont's rental of September 1601, in a magnificently bound book in the British Library, confirms his family's expansionist policy. Not only is there specific mention of lands in Lamcote and Radcliffe bought from the queen, but also reference to lands 'lying in Ratcliffe bought of Mr Rosell'. When Sir Henry died in March 1615 his Radcliffe holdings amounted to four messuages, four cottages, 100 acres of land, 20 acres of meadow and 20 acres of pasture.[80]

One other Pierrepont gain around this time was also a threat to Rosell authority: the overlordship of the manor formerly belonging to the Knights of St John of Jerusalem, under which the Rosells held their own manor. Tenants had to attend its court, originally held in Shelford, and subsequently in Cotgrave, just as they had in medieval times. The Pierreponts also acquired the right of the lord to have tenants' wills and inventories proved in this court, rather than by the church. Radcliffe tenants paid fees for this obligation, but they benefited from the court's power to exonerate them from paying certain tolls on the carriage of goods. (Fuller coverage of this court can be found on pp. 75 and 178-80.)[81]

The significance of the Pierreponts' expansion in Radcliffe could not have been foreseen at the time. They helped to hamper the Rosell family's mid-16th century progress, and were to gain complete control in the 18th century. By that time the Rosells were in decline and had left the area altogether.

Stanhope gains

Stanhope shield

Another powerful local family, the Stanhopes, also helped to restrict any lingering Rosell ambitions. Prominent as Nottinghamshire MPs in the 15th century, they were loyal to the early Tudor kings, and Sir Michael Stanhope was granted the site of Shelford Priory with its numerous lands (including some in Radcliffe) after the dissolution of the monasteries. His brother-in-law was Edward VI's Protector Somerset, and when the latter fell from power, Stanhope was executed. Nevertheless, the local Stanhopes, headed by Sir Thomas, continued to make progress. While spending large sums on creating a fine house at Shelford out of their monastic windfall, they consolidated their estates in the area by taking over the Bingham inheritance of the Stapleton family when its male line failed, and by mopping up other smaller properties as they became available. Through a confusing series of transactions in Elizabeth's reign, members of the Stanhope family acquired not only the advowson and rectory lands of Radcliffe church, but also a manor in the village belonging to the Molyneux family of Thorpe near Newark. This may have been the same as 'Beaumont's manor' (forfeited to the crown by John Beaumont in Edward VI's time) which was granted to the Stanhopes by Elizabeth in 1602.[82]

A rental for 'Beaumont's manor' has survived from just after the close of Elizabeth's reign. This shows that in 1604 there were some 21 tenants, and the total annual value of the rental was £12.5s.5d. On the outside is written:

Henry P[arnham] must not fail to be at Elvaston the sixt[h] of October with the rents for I must send them to London on Monday following.

By this time Stanhope interests were divided between Shelford and Derbyshire estates at Bretby and Elvaston. Henry Parnham would have been the manor's rent collector. The manor house and the demesne were held by Henry Parr, at a rent of 40s. Other tenants included John Rosell junior and Thomas Dewsbury who paid 3½d and three peppercorns respectively for chief rents on their lands. An oxgang held by Henry Hall for 5s rent was still crown property for which the Stanhopes had to reimburse the crown 3s.4d. There are only hints as to where the lands lay.

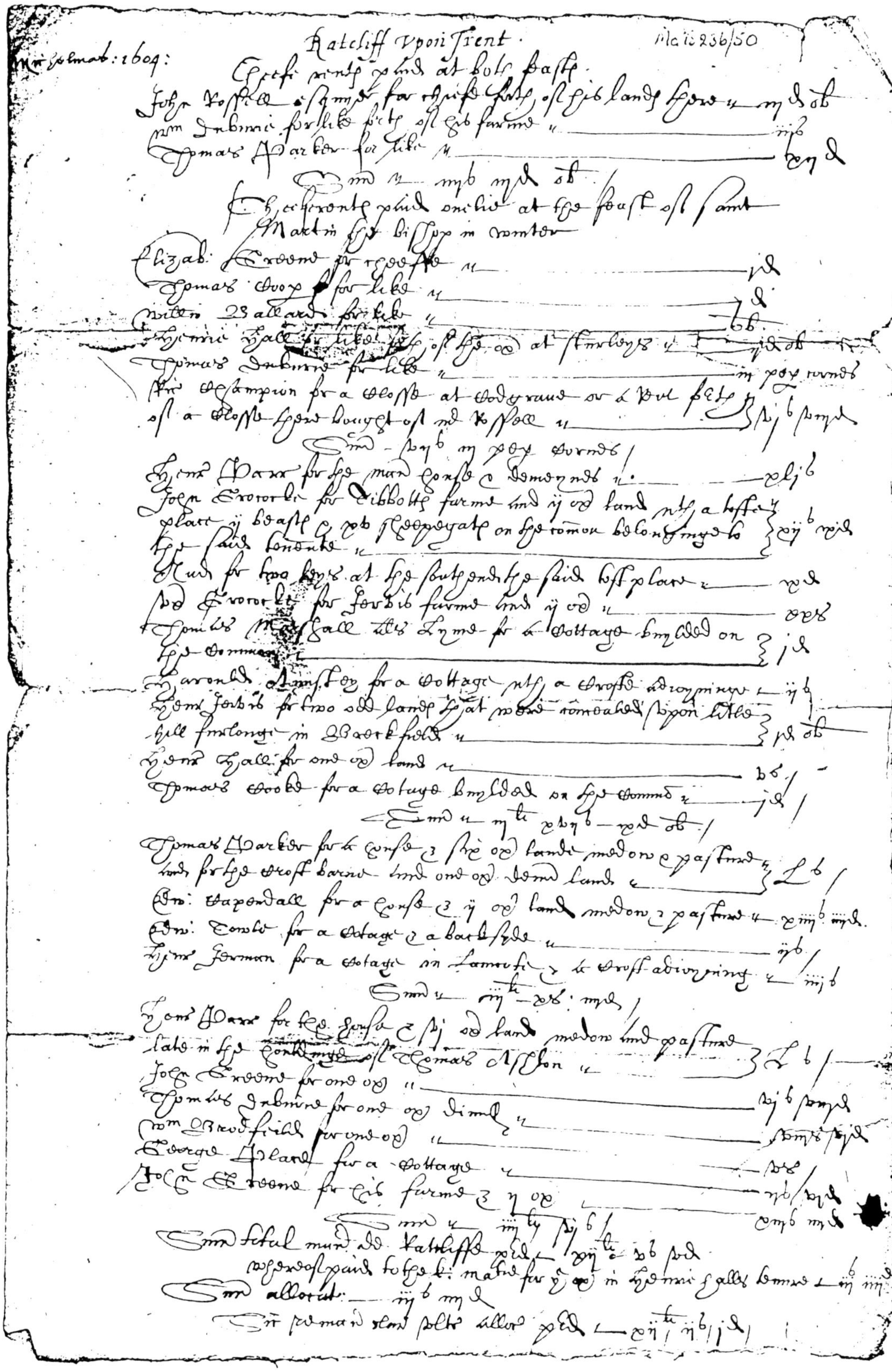
Ratcliff upon Trent

MaB 236/50

Extract from rental of Stanhope's manor (formerly Beaumont's manor) for 1604
(U of N Manuscripts Department MaB 236/50)

Henry Jervis paid 1d 'for two odd lands that were concealed upon little hill furlong in Breck field'. Henry Jerman paid 4s for a cottage in Lamcote, and two cottages had been built on the common. A document of 1668 refers to 'bye flats, back of ground isles or gravel beds' in the manor encompassed by the river Trent.[83]

The Rosells would almost certainly have wished to acquire these smaller properties to enhance their estates and confirm their position in Radcliffe in the best traditions of the rising gentry. Lacking the means to do so, however, and faced with what appears to be the aggressive expansionist policy of the Stanhopes (and Pierreponts) they had no choice but to acquiesce. Moreover, the intruding interests of these powerful neighbours provided potential for conflict and embarrassment when allegiances were tested. For example, John Rosell junior's stepmother was Annora, Sir Henry Pierrepont's half-sister. Sir Henry was married to Frances Cavendish, the daughter of the formidable Bess of Hardwick by her second husband. The granddaughter of Bess's fourth husband, the Earl of Shrewsbury, was to marry Sir Henry Pierrepont's son. Rosell interests must have been tested in the 1590s when tensions between the Shrewsbury family and the Stanhopes found expression in a dispute about rights on the River Trent. (See p. 58.)

Memorial to Sir Henry Pierrepont in Holme Pierrepont church from a drawing in Throsby's edition of Thoroton's *History and Antiquities of Nottinghamshire*

Sir Thomas Stanhope painted in 1572 (Private Collection)

John Rosell junior's last years

Until the end of his life, John Rosell junior was hampered by restrictions on his lands occupied by his step-mother, his half-brother Gervase, and Anne Ballard. Worse still, having been forced to part with some of his holdings, the Rosell estates were smaller at the end of his life than they had been at the beginning. (Woodhall manor lands were depleted by two messuages, five gardens, two cottages, 20 acres of land, 4 acres of meadow and 10 acres of pasture. Rosell manor lands had shrunk by two messuages, a dovecote, three gardens, 10 acres of meadow, 10 acres of pasture and 60 acres of heath.) While not all of these holdings necessarily went to the Pierreponts, a good portion of them did, at least for a while. With the Stanhopes also expanding, John Rosell was so hemmed in by his two grander neighbours, that there was no hope of him capitalising on the great strides made by his grandfather.[84]

While his income had been plummeting, his family increased. Mary (Cranmer), described in his will as his 'most loving and kind wife', had borne him at least nine children - two boys and seven girls. The Rosell manor house or 'capital messuage', occupied by his father and grandfather before him, must have been a bustling and noisy place. It is small wonder, with his estates so restricted, that he would express great concern about his children's welfare when he came to draw up his will.

The site of 'Rosyll manor' can be identified from a map of 1710, by which date it was a four-storeyed building on the village main street, later known as The Chestnuts, Rushleas and, by 1995, as Tudor Grange. The smaller 16th century wing can still be identified at right angles to the main frontage. Internal beams, some with sophisticated tooling, indicate the area of a main room or hall approximately 30 feet long and 15 feet wide.[85]

One other event contributed to the stress of John Rosell junior's last years. Uncharacteristically, he quarrelled with a village family, and brought a defamation case before the Archdeacon's Court on 12th April 1605. Joan, the wife of Michael Richards, was the abuser. Michael had been a 'common brewer and baker', fined 4d by the Peverel Court for breaking the assize in 1589 and 1590. In September 1601 he was renting a farm in Radcliffe from the Pierreponts for 20s, probably on ex-Rosell lands. Neither the cause of the quarrel nor the outcome has been found. Five months after the court case, however, John junior drew up his will, describing himself as being 'sick in body'. He was to survive until November 1606.[86]

Tudor Grange, once the 'capital mansion' of the Rosell family. The 16th century house was entered in the centre of the lower wing to the left of the main (17th century) front

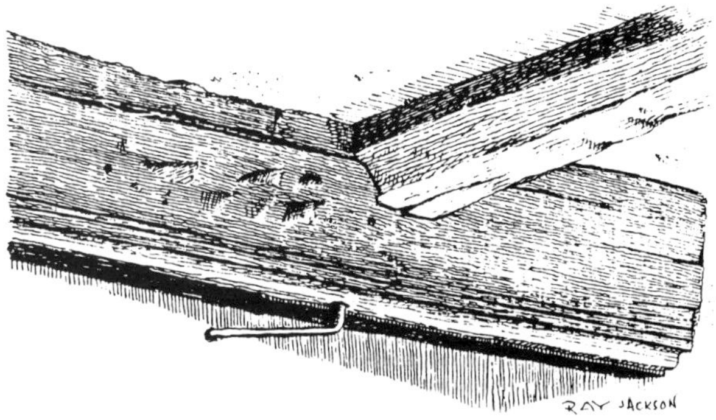

Portion of main beam in the former hall showing tool marks and decorative grooves

Case study 4

THE RIVER and Sir Thomas Stanhope's weir

In the 16th and 17th centuries the river remained as important to Radcliffe as it had been in medieval times. At some point there had been a dramatic change in its course. The Nottinghamshire Coroners' Rolls refer in 1541 to 'the old Trent' within the lordship of Shelford, and a 16th century map clearly illustrates the altered course at Radcliffe. This explains why part of the parish came to lie across the river, so that villagers had to drive their cattle across to graze on the other bank. (This area became part of Stoke Bardolph parish in the early 20th century.) It is therefore not surprising that between 1551 and 1594 five villagers left money in their wills for the 'reparations of the boat', and another in 1579 left 2s towards 'buying of a cable for the boat'. The river remained treacherous, however, and accidents occurred. Two were investigated by the coroner in 1549 (see p. 71). The land across the river was also liable to flood, so in 1580 Robert Hall bequeathed 3s.4d towards the making of a mound in Hesgang for the saving of cattle in floods. There were advantages. Not only did the river enrich the village's meadows, but it also supplied gravel and stone. Thoroton cited an anonymous writer of 1640: 'There are in the channel of the river divers hursts or shelves which in summertime lie dry, from whence the bordering inhabitants gather great store of these boulders as they have occasion'. Moreover, there were fishing rights attached to both Lamcote and Woodhall manors. (Christopher Fisher leased the latter's fishing for 6s in 1545/6, and William Fisher of Colwick paid 26s.8d to the Pierrepont estate for Lamcote fishing rights in 1591.)[87]

Sir Thomas Stanhope's weir

The concerns shared by villages such as Radcliffe, where livelihoods were to some extent dependent on the river, are well illustrated by a dispute which came to a head in the 1590s and resulted in a case being brought before the Star Chamber. This quarrel, between Francis Fletcher of Stoke Bardolph and Sir Thomas Stanhope of Shelford, had long been smouldering and also involved the well-recorded enmity between Sir Thomas and the powerful 7th Earl of Shrewsbury. Behind it lay quarrels over property rights, but the erection of a weir by Sir Thomas some time previously was the pretext for a complaint by Fletcher. He said that the passage of certain boats up the river was almost discontinued, and barges that could previously have been drawn by three or four men could now not be drawn by six or seven strong men. Moreover, boats and barges were locked in the weir for a long time to the detriment of the boatmen. In addition, Stanhope, by putting 'nets of such unmeasurable greatness in the mouth of the said stream', was destroying 'the salmon running upstream to spawn from the Trent Fall to Nottingham'. Finally the banks were flooded and worn down.[88]

Sir Thomas Stanhope's works on the river had involved erecting the weir, diverting the river to a stream on the Shelford bank and building two locks. He was also alleged to have built corn mills on the stream and, by breaking up private mills and hand querns, had forced the people thereabouts to use only his mills. The effect on the neighbourhood was such that a petition by 500 inhabitants of 39 villages was forwarded by Chief Justice Lord Willoughby to the Privy Council, with a note saying that he thought 'the informations are partly true'. On 3rd July 1592 the Council reprimanded Stanhope, claiming that

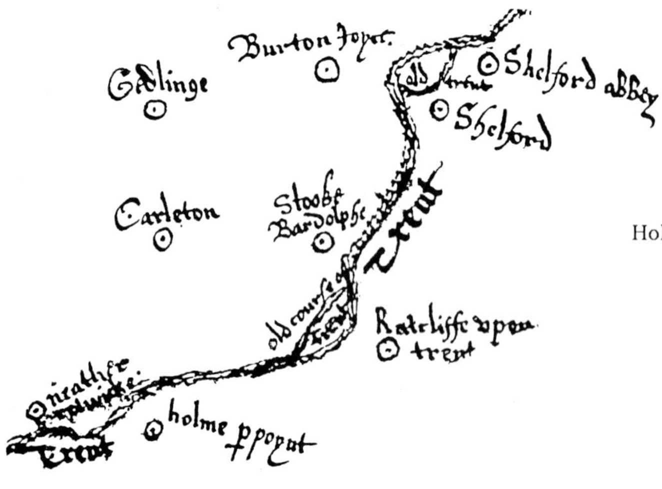

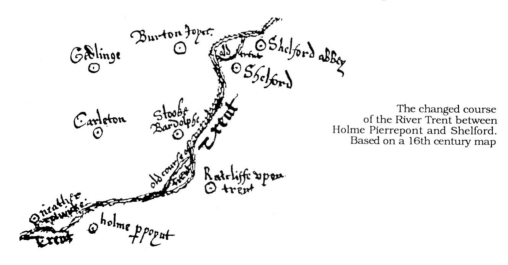

The changed course of the River Trent between Holme Pierrepont and Shelford. Based on a 16th century map

the trade of fishing is greatly decayed whereby divers poor men did get their living - that now are brought to great poverty and the passages of the river are so straightened that divers of them, as they allege, have lost their boats and themselves often times endangered and put in hazard of their lives..

After a number of disturbances in the neighbourhood Sir Thomas wrote to Sir John Puckering, Keeper of the Great Seal, on 10th April 1593 expressing fears that his weir might be 'plucked down', and claiming that it brought positive advantages to the river, including easier navigation and increased catches of salmon now averaging 18 score per year. His fears about damage to the weir were justified. The Earl of Shrewsbury's men - some four or five hundred of them, mainly on horseback and arrayed in 'warlike manner' according to Stanhope - destroyed the weir on 14th April 1593. He ordered it to be rebuilt and organised a small band of armed men, mainly drawn from Bingham, to defend it under the leadership of his bailiff. Now the whole dispute had been turned into a matter of law and order and it was brought to the attention of the queen herself who took it 'very offensively'.[89]

The quarrel had revealed deep divisions among the county magistrates, some of whom were very hostile to Sir Thomas Stanhope. When the justices proposed to investigate the matter on 10th May at Nottingham, the sheriff ordered the sessions to be held at Newark instead, where the erection of the weir was condemned. Sir Thomas's views were not heard because he had attended at Nottingham as originally arranged. He complained bitterly about his treatment to Sir Robert Cecil, the queen's acting Secretary of State, and added that the Earl of Shrewsbury's servants had threatened his workmen who were repairing the weir and had dug a trench which resulted in his mills running dry. The Council condemned both the weir and the trench as being unlawful, but appear to have been impressed by Sir Thomas's letter. As a result a message was relayed to the sheriff expressing Elizabeth's personal displeasure at the partiality shown against Sir Thomas, and at the sheriff's dilatoriness in proceeding against those who had destroyed the weir. This was to be 'left in the same state it was before the disorderly proceedings at Easter'. The trench was to be made up, the weir repaired and the watercourse turned again. No further actions were to be taken until the whole matter had been determined by law.[90]

Witnesses in court

The case came before the Court of Star Chamber and over 30 witnesses, including servants and tenants of the Stanhopes, were questioned on 29 counts as to what had occurred. Among them were four labourers from Radcliffe (for the family had by this time acquired Beaumont's manor in the village) - Edward and Robert Towle, Robert Close and George Place. Their interrogation took place on 27th December 1593 in the Shire Hall at Nottingham before justices of the court of Star Chamber and must have been an alarming experience for

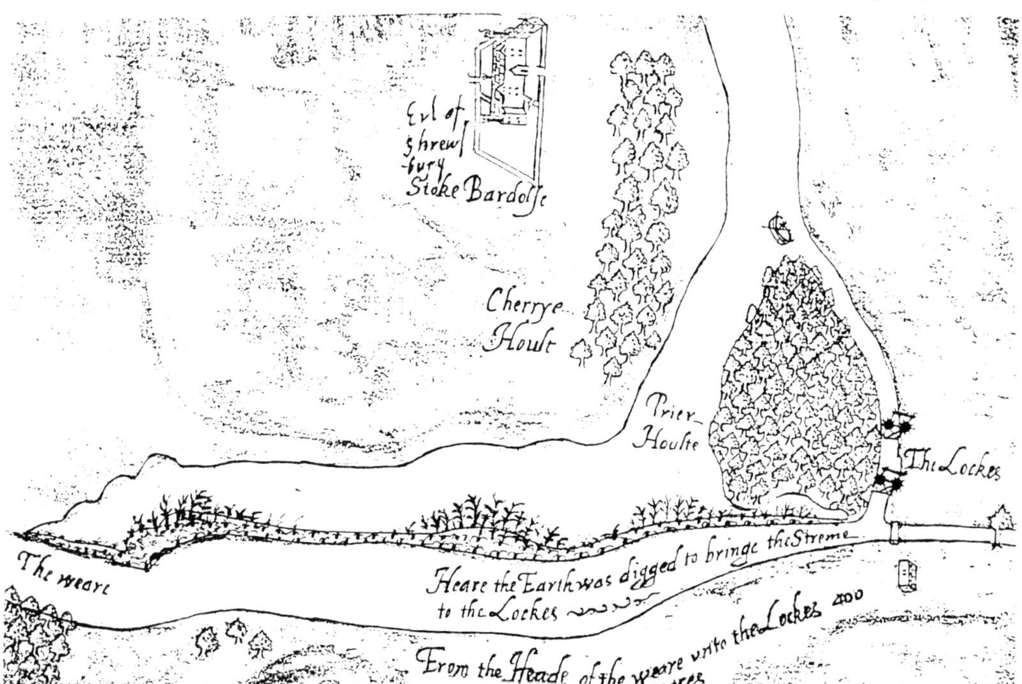

Part of a map showing Sir Thomas Stanhope's weir on the Trent (PRO MPF 10)

them. Two other witnesses who showed particular local knowledge may also have been from Radcliffe: the names of Grococke and Greene appear in 1604 on a rental of Stanhope's manor in Radcliffe and a Francis Grococke kept an ale-house in the early 17th century with a record of being in trouble.[91]

The four Radcliffe labourers were interrogated and insisted that they, along with two others from the village who were not questioned, had only been employed to repair the weir and not to act in its defence. Nor had they carried weapons, only the tools of their trade. They managed to evade answering the most awkward questions; whereas Francis Grococke, if he was Sir Thomas's tenant, exhibited a rare degree of independence, not to say courage. He said he was not sure whether the stream had existed before the building of the weir, but he was sure that boats used to pass where the weir now stood and that they could no longer pass so freely. He had heard that even when the water was high, boats and barges could not pass, though they had at other times, both by day and night. Moreover, he had also heard that two boats had sunk and he said that 'the carriages of commodities up and down the river is not now so much used as before the erection of the weir'.

He then made a direct reference to the effect the building of the weir had had on Radcliffe. The village had a ford 'of ease' for its own use to reach the pastures on the other side of the river. But now it was

> *deeper than it was before the erection of the said weir - men cannot go over there with their carriages unless they swim their cattle.*

He told of the disaster which befell William Pilkington, one of the townsmen who, when 'attempting this last summer with his wain and oxen to [fetch] hay forth of Radcliffe meadow, did drown three of his oxen'. Admittedly this had occurred after the weir had been pulled down, but he implied that the river was dangerous enough when the waters were high and the erection of a weir could only make it worse. As for fishing, he had seen nets laid and had heard that 'they have caught there half a dozen salmon in a week and he thinketh they do take the greatest store about Michaelmas'.

A more favourable witness for the Stanhope cause was William Porter from Stoke Bardolph who gave the most detailed account of fishing at Shelford. Usually a net to catch eels was set about Michaelmas and at some other time in the year, twice in the month. The net would hold eels of a size valued at two or three to the penny and he had known some nights when they had caught eels and other fish to the value of 5s, some being sold and some used by Sir Thomas's household. He added that '...the narrowest mesh of the said cod net that is used about the said weir is an inch or thereabouts and the narrowest mesh of the draught nets is about an inch and a half'. He thought that there had been a general decline in fishing the river both for salmon and for other fish, but not, as far as he knew since the building of the weir.

William Porter was a valuable witness for in the past he had helped the bargemen haul their vessels up the river and had acted as a workman and watchman on the weir. The only passage was now through the locks, but he denied that this involved any delay: in fact it was safer. Two boats which had sunk, had done so while the weir was being mended. In high water the boats (like the fish) could pass over the weir and the bargemen needed no more help than before. Francis Grococke had implied that there had been some loss of firm ground, which the bargemen would have used, when the locks were built. Porter acknowledged that the ground near the weir was wasted, though whether because of the weir or not he did not know. On the other hand, the pastures and meadows close by had not, he felt, deteriorated by being 'over-sanded'.

The depositions given by these men have to be read with the understanding that they all had reasons to keep the approval of Sir Thomas Stanhope. Francis Grococke's evidence about the loss of William Pilkington's oxen and the deepening of the ford since the weir had been built, is therefore all the more significant. Whatever the truth of the allegations made against Sir Thomas (and the final outcome of the dispute is not certain), the witnesses draw a lively picture of the interaction of the river with their lives and the feuds of their landlords.

Later problems

Although there were no further disputes on this scale, the river continued to provide problems as well as benefits. Maintaining the banks was a burden for local landowners and many a labourer from Radcliffe must have spent long hours working on them. As will be seen, the 'considerable sums of money in Waterworks' which were needed to repair the frequent breaches in the banks contributed to the financial problems of the Rosells in the later part of the 17th century. The creation of weirs at a gravel bed known as Knight's Holt was one solution, and a deed of purchase of 1720 included an agreement concerning the repair and support of these weirs 'to prevent [the] stream of river breaking down banks at or near the same weir and forcing a new Channel into the same'. The Pierrepont manuscripts of the early 18th century confirm that repairs were often necessary to curb the encroachments of the Trent.[92]

Elizabeth was the daughter of Henry VIII and his second wife, Anne Boleyn. She had been brought up as a Protestant, but, while eschewing the Catholicism of Mary, she preferred to tread a more moderate religious path than her brother. By her religious settlement she became Supreme Governor, rather than Supreme Head, of the English church, and services were based on Cranmer's first prayer book. Protestant exiles returned and, although injunctions were issued which swept away any remnants of Popery from Mary's reign, Catholics were not at first persecuted provided they outwardly conformed. This broad church could embrace many in the nation, but there were those at either extreme - Catholics and Puritans - who respectively felt that the Reformation had gone too far, or had not gone far enough.

Effect of the Elizabethan church settlement

Not surprisingly, the preambles to the 35 surviving Elizabethan wills from Radcliffe show little religious consistency after the turmoil of the three previous reigns. The first two wills, those of husbandman Richard Wright and Edmund Rosell, the squire's kinsman, kept to Catholic terminology, calling on Saint Mary and 'all the holy company of heaven'. Not until husbandman Richard Bayley's will of December 1561 does the first clearly Protestant preamble appear with its emphasis on faith or 'trust' in being saved through God's 'glorious merit'. Only ten of the wills were introduced with the queen's full titles, but even these did not always refer to her as Defender of the Faith, and in none did she appear as Supreme Governor of the church. It seems that the aggressive enforcement of state religious authority found in Edward's reign was softened.

There was, however, still scope for individuals to express their own real piety and concern for the afterlife in their wills. In September 1597 John Hempsall, a tailor, was one of several concerned with doctrinal niceties. His preamble took up nearly half the length of his will:

I do yield &.... bequeath my soul into the hands of the almighty God my maker & unto Jesus Christ his son my only redeemer and saviour assuredly believing that the lord my god for the son['s] sake will be merciful to me & forgive my sins & receive my soul to himself not for the worthiness that is in me but for the worthiness of Christ Jesus the son, my only saviour, Jesus Christ, that he will raise up [my body?] at the last day not as it is now vile and corrupt but at all points he will make it like to his own body...

A third of the testators specifically requested burial in Radcliffe churchyard. Five asked to be buried in the church, while Robert Hall, 'gentleman', in 1580 asked to be buried either in the church or in the churchyard at the chancel head, 'as it shall please my wife'. The rest who mentioned burial left the choice of site to their friends or executors.

Despite these pious concerns, religious bequests were thin on the ground in Elizabeth's time. Money for forgotten tithes was perhaps the commonest item. Occasionally some grain or a small sum of money was still left to the church. Husbandman Robert Darwyn, for example, provided 3s.4d for 'the mending of the decayed places of the church' (1574). Two parishioners remembered the bells: Edmund Rosell left 12d (1560), and Elizabeth Darrenton 6s.8d (1579) 'towards the mending of the great bell'. The earliest mention of the church clock appears in Robert Hall's will (1580). He left 6s.8d for its 'reparations' - the sort of item which the 18th century churchwardens were to record repeatedly. The meagreness of such bequests compared with those in pre-Reformation wills is very noticeable.[93]

Early examples of church discipline

Parishioners who failed to comply with official religious practice and morality could be presented before the archdeaconry courts held routinely in the main Nottinghamshire churches. (See also p. 75.) Between 1570 and 1575 discipline was rigorously enforced throughout the diocese by the Archbishop of York, Edmund Grindal, but there is no evidence of nonconformity (of either Catholic or Puritan persuasion) in Radcliffe in the early archdeaconry records. The villagers presented in the first five cases were typical of many parishes: a quarrelsome woman (Agnes Chadwick) and those accused of sexual incontinence - of concern to parish officials, not just on the grounds of immorality, but through fear that an illegitimate child might have to be maintained at the community's expense. Johanne Patterson's incontinence with George Swinsdale of Cotgrave was punished in December 1570 by penance on three Sundays or Feast days in their local churches. The spectacle of Johanne in penitential white garb confessing her sin before the whole Radcliffe congregation would be a warning to others as well as a humiliation for herself. Three similar cases between February 1573 and February 1574 were less typical. In the first, Harold Thrave was summoned for incontinence with Joanna Bird, but, as has been seen (page 47), eventually evidence was produced that Thrave was a lunatic against whom Joanna could not lay a claim. She was absolved after performing a penance. When in June 1573 Robert Greene and Margaret Bordman were cited (unusually in West Bridgford church) for the same offence, they claimed that matrimony had been intended. The court ordered them to marry by 9th August. In the following February at a court held in Mansfield, William Noden and Agnes Cowe both pleaded not guilty to the charge of suspected incontinence. Noden maintained his plea throughout. Agnes was certified 'non-compos-mentis' and warned not to consort with Noden except as the law allows.[94]

Thomas Granger - a curate in trouble

It is not known when Edward Sheppard died or resigned as vicar of Radcliffe. He had been appointed in 1549 in succession to William Welbie, and still held the living in November 1558 when he witnessed a parishioner's will. He may have continued for many years longer, for the next reference to a vicar is to Thomas Wallys in a will of 1570. (The latter had already been appointed to the rectory of Adbolton in June 1564 by John Rosell - Harold's son - who held the patronage there.)[95]

About 1572, however, Thomas Granger was appointed curate, and soon proved that the church courts could curb the activities of the clergy as well as the laity. To begin with, in February 1573 he was summoned in Mansfield - a discreet distance from Radcliffe - for failing to minister divine services and other sacraments at an opportune time. Having been instructed to perform services appropriately, he was summoned again in the following July on a different charge, failed to appear, was pronounced in contempt of court, and summoned again a fortnight later. This time he turned up and was accused, with a William Clerke of Tuxford, of taking out of Walkeringham church around the previous Christmas time 'a linen towel of twenty yards long'. Thomas Granger denied the charge, and the court decided to summon the Walkeringham churchwardens to prove their case against him.[96]

The outcome is not known, but in the meantime Granger was involved in an intriguing libel case which went to higher authority in York. Perhaps his unconventional behaviour had caused disquiet in Radcliffe, and the current squire - John Rosell senior - seems to have expressed himself forcefully. As a result, Granger had dared to bring a case against the squire, a man well used to court appearances on secular issues. In June 1573 Martin Grococke, a Radcliffe husbandman aged 36, was a key witness in the case. He testified that he had known the curate for some six years (although the latter had only been in the parish for about twelve months), and that he had known John Rosell for twelve years. On leaving church after evening prayers on the previous Candlemas Day (2nd February), he was in the churchyard when he heard John Rosell, in the presence of William Braisfield and John Grococke and others, call Thomas Granger 'amongst other words knave'. Of this he was sure, but uncertain whether John Rosell had used the term 'scab[be]d knave' or not. Grococke spoke up for the curate, declaring that he was 'of honest life and of good name and fame and also very well beloved within the parish of Ratcliffe'. Perhaps not wishing to give offence to either party, Grococke then said that he did not believe that the words impaired the curate's 'good name and fame', that he was 'indifferent who have victory in this cause'. Nevertheless, he claimed that John Rosell had actually confessed to using the word 'knave'.

Not surprisingly, John Rosell remembered the churchyard scene differently. The words he used were not opprobrious or injurious to the curate. He had simply said that Thomas Granger's 'doings were not honest nor agreeable to his calling'.

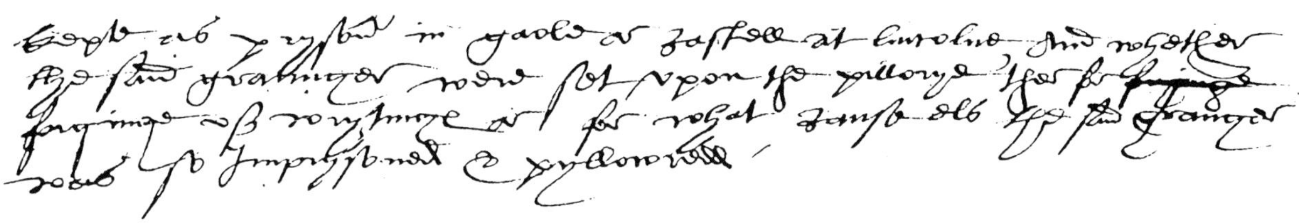

Extract from the questions concerning Thomas Granger's past as to whether he was 'kepte as prysn[or] in gaole or castell at lincolne And whether the said graunger were set upon the pillorye ther for [------] forginge of wrytinge or for what cause els th said Granger was so Imprysoned & pyllowredd'

(Borthwick Institute, York, CPG 1654)

Who won the case is not revealed, but the curate's standing cannot have been improved, for the investigation stirred up some muddy waters.

In an associated document questions were asked as to whether Granger had been imprisoned in Lincoln gaol at some time in the previous six years, or 'set upon the pillory there for forging of writing or for what cause else...' Questions were also asked about his wife Anne, as to where she was born, and whether she had once been the wife of one Swynburne, 'and whether the said Swynburne be yet living or no'. It seems unlikely that a curate linked with irregular religious practices, accused of theft, suspected of having served a gaol sentence, and of having a possibly bigamous wife would have lasted long in a small community.[97]

Discipline in 1577

Discipline was again tightened with the appointment of a new Archbishop of York, Edwin Sandys (1576-88). On the 30th April 1577 alone there were four village cases before the court in St Peter's church in Nottingham.

Poor Joanna Humbee was the accused in the first, driven to 'cursing and banning' after her husband, Richard, had sold their possessions. She confessed that she had 'bade God's curse of their hearts' who advised her husband to sell their goods 'and to waste them ...by such means'. In a second case Robert Hall, the wealthy landowner, and William Thrave were summoned for not receiving holy communion at Easter. This, however, was not a case of nonconformity but 'a breach at the time' between them. They proved that they had received communion two weeks after Easter and were dismissed. (See p. 47.)

The main problem brought to the April court's attention was the need for repairs to the church and churchyard, complicated by the fact that the previous churchwardens had not surrendered their accounts. Both sets of churchwardens were therefore separately summoned, and by-mid June a sitting at Ordsall was assured that the accounts had been extracted and the necessary repairs carried out.

In the meantime, a quarrel between John Greene and Robert Greene, who had been 'contending for their seats in the church', was sufficiently serious for both to be presented to the court. Sensibly, it was decided that the allocation of seats was an issue best decided by the community. The village élite, comprising John Rosell, Thomas Ashton, Robert Hall and Thomas Parker, were deputed to determine the matter.[98]

Two more curates and the Rosells

Two more Radcliffe curates were in trouble for irregularities. John Alred first appears in Radcliffe records as witness to Robert Darwyn's will in 1574 - soon after the Granger affair - and was presented at Newark in September 1577 'for serving without license'. He had been given authority only verbally, but on payment of a fee to the court registrar his case was dismissed. A month later, curate John Parker was excommunicated for not appearing at a recent synod at Southwell. He was subsequently absolved. Whether these men had sole charge of the parish, or served under a vicar is not clear as the records are either imprecise or missing.[99]

John Alred, however, was only temporarily replaced and appears again in Radcliffe records. In 1579, described as clerk, he was linked with both Holme Pierrepont and Radcliffe. Like Thomas Granger he fell foul of John Rosell senior, at whose instance he was suspended, and pronounced in contempt of court in May. The cause of the quarrel is not known, but it was to deepen when Mistress Rosell was presented to the court on 16th July for not receiving communion at Easter, perhaps at Alred's instigation. The affair backfired on the cleric, however, for he was presented with 'a schedule' - a court order that he was to ask the forgiveness of John Rosell and his wife. Initially he ignored the order, but the court absolved him on condition that he complied the following Sunday, or whenever the Rosells 'shall be in the church' - a public humiliation for Alred at the hands of the squire.[100]

John Alred was to survive this confrontation. On 30th January 1580 he was presented by the crown as vicar of Radcliffe, on the death of the last incumbent - perhaps Thomas Wallys. He also became vicar of Granby in 1586. Probably he was the same man as the William Alred who appears as Radcliffe's vicar in a Gedling tithes case in early 1583. (The court scribe perhaps confused him with the puritanical William Alred who was a Cambridge graduate and rector of Colwick from 1569 to 1627.)[101]

Discipline and morality 1579-1589

The quarrel between John Rosell and John Alred in 1579 coincided with another contentious case, which combined issues of church conformity with morality. The squire presented Alexander Scarboroughe to the church court in the May, for being a 'chider and inconvenient talker in the church'. Moreover, neither he nor his wife had received communion at Easter. On failing to appear, Scarboroughe was excommunicated and forbidden to enter church in June. In July the court ordered him to receive at the next communion and to live 'in love and charity with his neighbours'. In a separate case John Pight was presented as a 'suspected person with Alexander Scarboroughe's wife'. Unusually, this was the only village morality case in the first period of Archbishop Sandys' primacy.[102]

A villager who was one of a number disciplined in the 1580s was William Wheatley. In November 1585 he was suspected of fornication with his wife's sister. Pleading guilty he said 'that he would marry the same woman'. (Presumably he was a widower.) As marriage with a deceased wife's sister became legal only in the 20th century, the court understandably would not allow this and ordered Wheatley to perform a penance. When he had not done so by 23rd December he was excommunicated. Fifteen months later he was involved in another case, this time with Agnes Daye, described as a fornicatrix and excommunicate. Although Wheatley 'absolved' her, she was sentenced to perform her penance at the discretion of the Radcliffe vicar. (Other contemporaries were having to perform penances in Nottingham market place as well as in their local churches.) This leniency was 'because it was alleged that the same Agnes was very lame'.[103]

The churchwardens in the 1580s had concerns other than the morality of the parishioners. The incumbent's failure to read the queen's religious Injunctions more than twice in the previous year, the disrepair of the churchyard wall again (1587), the fence round the vicarage, and the 'decay' of the chancel (1589) were amongst them. The latter was the responsibility of Sir John Zouch, as impropriator of the rectory lands since 1577 which he had for £20 a year from the crown. (The parish was only responsible for the upkeep of the nave.) Whether or not Sir John paid for the repairs is not known, but some two years later in April 1591 the rectory lands were transferred by the Queen from him to the Stanhopes.[104]

A conforming parish

The appointment of John Piers as Archbishop of York (1589-94) was followed by a visitation in 1590 and a series of Injunctions in the following year, the fifth of which ordered nonconformists to be brought to court. This could have had no marked effect in Radcliffe where evidence of nonconformity has not been found at this period. The only unorthodox case concerned Christopher Bosworth early in 1594, who was 'informed to have baptized a child at Basford being a layman' for which he was eventually excommunicated. Other matters that brought villagers before the church courts between 1590 and the end of 1594 were modest in number and kind. They included a licence for marriage 'during a prohibited time', two cases of sexual impropriety, a long-running 'libel' case concerning breach of promise of marriage (see p. 67), another action for matrimony which does not seem to have been pursued, and a disputed will involving Thomas Ashton 'gentleman'.

Wills had to be proved before ecclesiastical authorities. In 1590, Alice Pinchbeck of Hawton challenged Thomas Ashton in the church court over a legacy from Margery Thorpe, a Radcliffe widow. According to Alice, Margery had been living in the house and care ('in domo et custodia') of Thomas Ashton at the time of her death. She had possessed up to £10 in good and legal English money, as well as goods and chattels, which Ashton had disposed of. In his response, Ashton rejected all Alice's claims as untrue, and in return said that he believed that Margery Thorpe had died intestate. Whether he managed to hang on to any acquisition, if the money and goods had indeed existed, is not known.[105]

Religious Articles

Matthew Hutton succeeded John Piers as Archbishop of York from 1595 to 1606, and a tolerant attitude to Puritans was followed until the accession of James I in 1603 when action against nonconformity was again taken. Nevertheless, routine checks on parishes were maintained through Religious Articles - sets of questions to be answered by churchwardens - which were regularly amended. Unfortunately the surviving Articles and the Radcliffe responses never quite coincide. Nevertheless, the range of questions - often over 40 in number - is clear. They covered the state of the church building, the service used, the sacraments and other ceremonies, the conduct of the minister, the churchwardens' accounts, and the behaviour of the parishioners themselves.[106]

A typical response, but without the questions, has survived for May 1596. The churchwardens declared that all was well with regard to the first eight articles, but the chancel - now the responsibility of Sir Thomas Stanhope - was again (or still) in need of repair. In response to article 24 they reported that some of the seats 'be not sufficient'. To the 35th article they stated that Michael Richards had not given 'a just account for certain timber'. (Perhaps he was a supplier for church repairs.) It was their response to article 16, in a section headed 'The laity', that suggests that, as in the time of Thomas Granger and John Alred, there was tension between the Rosells and the church authorities. Along with a John Shutt, 'Mr John Rosell esquire' junior and his wife, Mary (Cranmer), were presented for not receiving communion the previous Easter. It is not possible to deduce whether there were religious scruples behind the omission.[107]

In times of crisis, the church could revert to its pre-Reformation role as supporter of the poor. The appalling weather, crop failures and disease of the 1590s caused the authorities to issue special Articles to alleviate suffering. In February 1597 in response to these Articles, the vicar, George Cotes, and his churchwardens testified to encouraging fast days, and to having collected money from every husbandman for the relief of poverty. (See pp. 77-8.)[108]

Some church court cases 1598-1603

Court cases involving Radcliffe parishioners followed a familiar pattern in the last years of Elizabeth's reign. Sexual morality - or the lack of it - was the prime concern in at least five cases. A double case in 1602 linked both Henry Pare and Henry Jervis with Alice Frith. Alice pleaded guilty to incontinence with Jervis, but not with Pare. Henry Jervis bought his way out of performing the usual public confession by paying 20 shillings, a formidable sum, to the churchwardens for the use of the poor. Although the court books often indicate that a penance had been performed, only one certificate, signed by the vicar, has survived from these years: Elizabeth Pare, perhaps related to Henry, performed her penance dressed in penitential garb at morning prayer on the 13th November 1602 for having sinned with John Bell of Orston.[109]

There were other Radcliffe matters before the courts at this time. In November 1598 George Goodwin sued a Cotgrave couple for a legacy of £3 from the will of widow Elizabeth Darwyn of Radcliffe. The Capendales occupied a good deal of court time between 1597 and 1602. Widow Margery Hallam, alias Capendale, brought an unspecified case in October 1597 against Edward Capendale. In June 1600 John Capendale, was charged with 'not paying a mortuary due by him to be paid to the church of Ratcliffe' - a fee still payable out of the estate of a dead parishioner. William Capendale was charged with failing to attend church in July 1602. In the same year, there was yet another complaint about the chancel - this time concerning the decayed state of its windows. A Book of Homilies was also needed.[110]

The Book of Homilies

The book which had to be provided was first published in 1562, and consisted of twelve homilies, or sermons, to be read in churches. Their titles sum up the intention of the Protestant establishment to impose uniformity of moral and spiritual teaching from the pulpit:

I	*A Fruitful Exhortation to the reading of Holy Scripture*
II	*Of the misery of all Mankind*
III	*Of the Salvation of all Mankind*
IV	*Of the true and lively Faith*
V	*Of Good Works*
VI	*Of Christian Love and Charity*
VII	*Against Swearing and Perjury*
VIII	*Of the Declining from God*
IX	*An Exhortation against the Fear of Death*
X	*An Exhortation to Obedience*
XI	*Against Whoredom and Adultery*
XII	*Against Strife and Contention*

The Book of Homilies was still being used at the end of the Stuart period. By then the volume needed in 1602 had had to be replaced with an edition published in 1713. This copy still survives, inscribed on the inside cover: 'This book belongs to Radcliffe-upon-Trent Church & in the Care of the Vicar'.[111]

From at least 1593, perhaps following the ministry of John Alred, Radcliffe's spiritual welfare had been in the hands of an unpredictable incumbent, George Cotes. His story, however, belongs more to the Jacobean than to the Elizabethan age.

Case study 5

ISABEL DEWSBURY'S BREACH OF PROMISE

For a few months from August 1592 Isabel Dewsbury (Dewbery, Deubery, Dusbery etc) appears on the historical stage in a breach of promise case which provides an insight into how Elizabethan marriages could be arranged. She was the unmarried daughter of Thomas Dewsbury, a Radcliffe yeoman, perhaps acting as his housekeeper. She had four sisters - Margaret, Joan, Elizabeth and Margery - who were already married, and two brothers, Richard and William, aged 46 and 36 respectively. From this it seems likely that in 1592 Isabel was above the usual marrying age. (The family may be commemorated by Dewberry Hill and Lane near today's Golf Club, the area being known as Deuberhowe in Elizabethan times.)

A will and an arranged marriage

On 23rd August 1592 Thomas Dewsbury drew up his will. He left each of Isabel's four sisters only 2s and a 'half-quarter' of barley, with an additional 2s and an ox calf to Joan's son, Philip. (Presumably they had received their 'portions' when they married.) The bulk of Thomas's property was to go to Isabel's two brothers. Richard, the elder, was a husbandman living at Southwell. He was to inherit Thomas's dwelling houses, barns, stables, necessary buildings, orchards, gardens, enclosures and arable land - some of which had been bought by Thomas and the rest having 'descended' from his own father. Richard was also to inherit a cottage in Narrow Lane (now Water Lane) with its querns, pales, hovels and other appurtenances. William, like his brother, was a husbandman, but he still lived in Radcliffe probably in his father's house, and appears to have gone on doing so with Isabel even after Richard had inherited the main part of the property. He was to have the timber lying in his father's yard, the long table standing in his hall, and the rest of his goods, cattle and corn in his fields and stores.

Isabel, as the unmarried daughter, was to have all her father's household stuff (such as bedding, pewter, chests, coffers and brass), with the exception of the long table. In addition, until she married she was to share land leased from Sir Thomas Stanhope with her brother William. If she married, it would go to William, who would compensate her with £6.13s.4d over four years. Isabel, therefore, came from a family of some standing, and with possessions of her own once her father died. These would pass to her husband should she marry. In the meantime, she would be her brothers' responsibility.

The exact date of Thomas Dewsbury's death is not known, but it would seem to have been soon after drawing up his will in the August, although it was not proved until 17th January 1593. (The lack of parish registers for this period prevents greater certainty.) Before the end of September 1592 a suitor for Isabel's hand in marriage appeared on the scene. This was a Richard Harmston from Lincolnshire. The Dewsburys had not known him long - between two and three months by early November. Moreover, his marriage negotiations were carried out by a go-between, Leonard Thompson, a 38-year-old yeoman from Doddington in Lincolnshire. (Thompson was to deny in court that he was paid for his services.) Whether the Dewsbury brothers had initiated the match to avoid responsibility for an unmarried sister is not clear. Whatever the circumstances, the outcome was unexpected. It was Richard Harmston who sued Isabel for breach of promise of marriage.

The suitor's evidence

The case came before the Archdeacon's Court in the autumn of 1592, and initially Richard Harmston must have felt that he was on firm ground. He even expected Isabel's brothers to appear as witnesses on his behalf. According to Harmston's evidence recorded by the court scribe, his proposal of marriage had been well received. (For clarity, the evidence has been set out in dialogue form.)

> *"Isabel, can you find in your heart to love me above all other men and to become my wife?"*
>
> *"Yes," said she, "that I can, and I am willing so to do so that you provide for me a homestead to dwell in, for I understand you want [i.e. lack] one, and I would be very loth to marry and not to have a house of mine own to dwell in."*
>
> *"It is true," (said he) "I want a house for you, and now seeing that God hath made me able (I thank him for it) I will provide and take one for you, and such home I hope as shall be to your liking, and I thank you, for this is in good will."*

To comply with Isabel's wishes - understandable in the light of her comfortable background - Richard Harmston had taken a farm at Westborough, about a mile from Doddington, and had suggested that she should send some trusted friends to view it on her behalf. Three or four days after Michaelmas (29th September), her brothers duly went over to Westborough, then conferred with Leonard Thompson, before returning with Harmston to report back favourably to Isabel. They did suggest, however, that Isabel should be guaranteed the lease of the farm in case Richard Harmston should die before she did.

> *"At your request" (quod he the said Richard) "I am willing so to do."*
> *And then forthwith the said Isabel said unto her brethren, "As you like, I like, and what you do I am contented withall."*
> *And then the said Richard in the presence of the brethren of the said Isabel said unto her, "Seeing that your brethren like well of all things, can you now find in your heart to take me to your husband?"*
> *"Yes," (quod she) "that I can..."*

At this point, Leonard Thompson, the marriage 'broker', allegedly confirmed the arrangements with her. Taking her by the hand he asked whether she would take Richard Harmston as her husband. Isabel then 'contracted herself in matrimony' with Richard, saying to him:

> *"Seeing that you have so well provided for me, I will be your wife and I take you to my husband."*
> *And then forthwith the said Richard answering said unto her again. "I will be your husband, and I take you to my wife", and thereupon in the presence of the said parties kissed her...*

Richard then gave his future bride a gold angel (a coin worth perhaps 10s by this date, often pierced and used as a token), which she apparently gratefully accepted. News of the intended marriage was published in both Radcliffe and Westborough.

Isabel's terms

According to Richard Harmston's account, Isabel had seemed a docile girl, prepared to marry provided her brothers approved the terms. Holding property in her own right, however, which she could lose to her husband when she married, she seems to have used her docility to mask a certain financial shrewdness. The basic scenario described by Harmston was not disputed by other witnesses, but the details were. According to other evidence presented to the court, Isabel had stopped short of the agreement to marry. She had also expected to visit the farm at Westborough herself, Leonard Thompson having failed to keep a promise to fetch her.

Thompson's own account of the events mentioned a further condition. As well as wanting the lease on the Westborough farm, Isabel wished to retain control of the five nobles a year for four years (£6.13s.4d) she would receive on giving up the shared lease of Sir Thomas Stanhope's land to her brother. Should she die before her prospective husband, she wanted to be able to bequeath the money in her will. To this Richard Harmston had agreed. Thompson then asserted that as Isabel's brothers liked 'well of all things', she had indeed been willing to be Richard's wife.

She had even added:

> *"I pray you make all things ready against Martinmas [11th November], for betwixt this and then I will be married."*
> *"Will you come then so soon?" said Harmston.*
> *"Yea," quoth she, "if I live so long."*

It was at this point, according to Thompson, that Richard Harmston kissed Isabel. This whole last episode had occurred before noon 'without the door' of Isabel's late father's house in Radcliffe.

If Richard Harmston had expected the Dewsbury brothers to support him in court, he was quickly disabused when they gave their evidence. Perhaps under pressure from Isabel, they could only be described as hostile witnesses. Richard (Dewsbury) threw doubt on whether Harmston had fully agreed to all Isabel's terms about the lease of the Westborough farm. He had wanted to know

> *...if he [Harmston] married his said sister she might have an assurance of the farm in case she happened to survive him for the tenure of her life, which Harmston refused to yield unto, but was contented to assure it unto her for certain years.*
> *Whereupon the said Isabel... said, "Brethren, as you like I like, but I will be bound to no man till I come to the church and till the living be sure, and I will see it to[o]."*

When it came to the episode of Leonard Thompson's taking Isabel's hand and asking if she could love Harmston, Richard Dewsbury suffered a lapse of memory: 'What she answered he cannot, as he sayeth, call to mind'. Nor could he remember anything given or taken between the couple.

William Dewsbury (unlike his elder brother who could only sign his testimony with a mark) appended a firm signature to his evidence. He refuted the versions of Richard Harmston and Leonard Thompson about the favourable impression of the Westborough farm. When he and his brother had gone to see the house

> *they found [it] to be but a cottage, and after their return he...himself told the said Isabel that they had seen the said house and liked it not and she answered again and said, "I have put it to you my friends, and if you like, I must needs do so, because my word is past."*

Although in this version Isabel's wording does not greatly differ from that remembered by her suitor and his go-between, the implication is that as her brothers did not like the house, then she need not like it. If she had ever seriously intended to marry Richard Harmston, she had changed her mind.

Having gone to the trouble and expense of leasing the house for her, Harmston had decided to sue for breach of promise of marriage. The case came before the archdeaconry court between 19th October and early November, the evidence being heard either at Newark or in the North Muskham Prebend's house at Southwell. On 10th November in St Peter's, Nottingham, the court gave judgement in Isabel's favour. At once Harmston's counsel gave notice of appeal, and the matter was to be resolved before Christmas. The date of appeal was fixed for 14th December and the hearing was to be in the house of David Watson, the East Retford bailiff. There is no entry of further proceedings, so either Richard Harmston gave up his suit, or the matter was settled out of court. It has not proved possible to discover whether he or Isabel ever married.[112]

Impression of a gold angel, bearing the image of St Michael, the coin allegedly given as a love token to Isabel Dewsbury by Richard Harmston

CONTROLS AND OBLIGATIONS IN THE TUDOR PERIOD

The Tudor villager was subject to a complex system of controls. As today, the central government imposed political and social legislation which was enforceable at local level by a system of civil and criminal justice. In addition, religious legislation and moral sanctions were largely in the hands of church courts, while manorial courts were entitled to enforce their own obligations and customs. (For the well-to-do, if local courts could not settle a dispute, there was recourse to central courts such as Chancery. John Rosell senior's three cases (pp. 50-1) show that this sort of ultimate authority was regularly used.) Less structured were the obligations to assist the church, the community as a whole, or the poor in particular, which were felt in varying degrees throughout the period. Whatever the authority or obligation, initial enforcement was implemented by local officials such as constable, bailiff, thirdborough, churchwarden or overseer of the poor. Continuous data for all systems does not exist, but the patchy surviving records of coroners' inquests (available for the early Tudor period only), the courts of the Honours of Tickhill and Peverel (for 1536-1544 and from the 1550s respectively), the archdeaconry court (from 1569), and wills provide glimpses of the concerns and tragedies of 16th century village life.

I Cases Before the Coroner's Court

Three murders

Although little evidence about the enforcement of law and order at either local level through parish constables or at county level can be found for the 16th century, some early Tudor cases before the coroner's court show one aspect of legal control of the community. Between 1518 and 1555 three village cases of violent death were judged to be murder by the county coroner and a jury. The inquests were held in Radcliffe or Lamcote, probably in an inn close to the scene of the crime, as they were in later times. The jury of between 12 and 15 men was chosen from the village and nearby areas.

William Federston was the victim whose inquest was held at Radcliffe on 11th June 1518. Two days earlier he had been assaulted by Robert Parker, a labourer, who had wielded a staff (worth 2d) in both hands, breaking the left side of William's skull 'so that his brains flowed out'. William had died on the day of the inquest. As some Radcliffe property belonged to the Order of St John of Jerusalem, the alleged murderer had instantly fled to a house held of the prior and brethren, and sought sanctuary. (The right of sanctuary still existed for up to 40 days, despite some limitations imposed in 1486. It was to be drastically curtailed by Henry VIII between 1529 and 1540.) The instant sanction of seizing Parker's property was impossible, since on the day of the murder he was found to have 'no goods, chattels, lands or tenements'. He is last recorded on 17th October 1519, when he was outlawed - the equivalent of conviction - in the county court at Nottingham.

A more premeditated assault occurred about 10 o'clock at night on 15th November 1543. Two labourers, George and Thomas Brokhouse, armed with staves and daggers, lay in wait for John Bacon in the 'broke furlong' (ploughed ground), at Lamcote. They beat, ill-treated, and wounded their victim with their daggers (worth 10p) which they held in their right hands. John fell to the ground and immediately died from his wounds. His body was found by 10-year-old William Jervis, a boy of 'good reputation and standing'. Like Robert Parker, neither of the Brokhouses had any possessions which could be seized. They were outlawed in the county court on 6th December 1546.

In both these cases the murderers, and perhaps their victims, were poor men, and they belonged to the locality. In the third case, Radcliffe merely provided the venue for a crime involving strangers, and female strangers at that. Phyllis Phanthazious and Joan Pryggmaryon, two spinsters from Glamorganshire, at about 10 pm on 2nd June 1555 killed an unknown woman in Radcliffe's 'wheat furlong' near the common highway, and subsequently fled. The victim's body was discovered by Richard Wright, a man more accustomed to serving on inquest juries than giving evidence before them. Perhaps because the identity of the murdered woman could not be discovered, the inquest was not held until 25th August. Not surprisingly, the two alleged murderesses were said to have no possessions, and there is no record of their having been caught.[113]

Although there is no evidence that in any of these cases the culprits were hanged for their crimes, it seems that provision for such a sentence was close at hand. The map showing Sir Thomas Stanhope's weirs on the River Trent c. 1592 has a sketch of gallows situated on the outskirts of Radcliffe at Malkin Hill. The tradition of a site of local execution is thus established, and today an area is still known as Hangman's Hill.[114]

Sketch showing a body hanging from a gibbet on Malkin Hill on the outskirts of Radcliffe from a Tudor plan of the area (PRO MPF 10)

Three accidental deaths

On three recorded occasions between 1534 and 1550 sudden death struck down local men. On October 3rd 1534 John Sharp went into the 'Westfield' in Radcliffe to catch a bay-coloured mare (worth 5s) to pull his plough. The mare, however, struck him on the forehead with her hind feet, causing a wound four inches long, two inches wide, and one inch deep. John died on 6th October, the day before the inquest. The verdict was that 'the mare slew John'. A criminal case then developed. Normally any 'goods' involved in a coroner's inquiry were placed in the keeping of a county official - the general deputy almoner. On this occasion, however, the mare was kept by William Farnsworth (Ferinworth), Radcliffe's constable, and was apparently never handed over to the almoner. The wheels of justice turned extremely slowly. Eventually he was summoned to answer for the mare before the court of King's Bench, and was ultimately outlawed in the county court at Nottingham on 22nd September 1544, almost ten years after John Sharp's accident.

The other two accidents occurred when the victims were crossing the river in the summer of 1549. The force of the current was noted in both cases, suggesting an unusually wet season. The case of Thomas Thrave alias Long, crossing in a boat (worth 10s) about 3 am on 12th June, has been mentioned elsewhere (see p. 47). The inquest was held in Radcliffe the following March, indicating a long delay before the body was found by John Heron and Thomas Hoton. Robert Peas was the second man drowned in 1549. On 30th August he was fording the river at Radcliffe while riding in a wagon. The force of the current overturned the wagon, and he was suddenly thrown into the water. The inquest was held at Shelford, some three weeks after the accident, again indicating that it was some time before the body was found, this time downstream. The wagon (worth 8s) was recovered, and stated to be the cause of Robert's death. Both the wagon and Thomas Thrave's boat were placed in the keeping of William Ottye, the general deputy almoner.[115]

II The Manor Courts in Tudor Times

Tenants' obligations

The majority of people living in this part of England were tenants on a manor, and regular appearances at the manorial court were a permanent feature of their lives. There the tenant had to pay homage to the lord of the manor or his deputy and submit to the jurisdiction he held. This varied from manor to manor. It was at the court that rents were paid, tenures regulated and any changes in ownership recorded. The manorial court was also the arena where complaints could be aired and in some places minor infringements of the law dealt with. The presiding steward protected the lord's rights within the manor and guarded against negligence in maintaining the water courses and highways. Officials such as the constable and pinder (responsible for stray animals) were sworn in and arrangements about managing the common fields were made. Tenants also had an obligation to form the jury which presented culprits and recommended amercements (fines). From this it will be seen that where the court was regularly held and efficiently conducted, its influence in the community could be very great. More people probably attended a manorial court on a regular basis than ever appeared in a civil or ecclesiastical one. Many of its functions were, however, gradually being taken over by other agents, such as parish vestries or common law courts, especially where, as in Radcliffe, no single lordship dominated the parish.

As has been seen, in Radcliffe the Rosells possessed two manors by the mid-16th century - Rosell manor initially held of the Knights of St John of Jerusalem and Grey's manor or Woodhall, part of the Honour of Peverel (an Honour being a group of many manors under one lordship). There were three manors in Lamcote, which lay partly in the parish of Holme Pierrepont (the larger part) and partly in Radcliffe. One of these, Lamcote manor, came into the hands of the Rosells in the early years of Elizabeth's reign. Another, in the possession of the Pierreponts, lay within the Honour of Tickhill, itself part of the Duchy of Lancaster. Some of the lands of the manor of Holme Pierrepont lay within Radcliffe's boundaries as well. Many tenants held land in several manors so that they would find themselves answering to more than one manorial court, as well as to the courts of civil law and the church. From a 20th century standpoint it appears to have been a complicated world, but those who grew up in it understood its rules and customs well enough.

Attendance at court was such an important part of village life, continuing over so long a period, that it must have produced many records: but from only four of the manors which held land in Radcliffe have any court records been found - the Lamcote manor in the Honour of Tickhill, Woodhall in the Honour of Peverel, the Knights of St John of Jerusalem, and the manor of Holme Pierrepont.

The court of the Honour of Tickhill

This court was held at Cropwell Butler at Easter and Michaelmas for those manors belonging to it which lay in this area. A representative would pay the common fine (in the sense of dues) from each manor and present those who were the free tenants who owed suit at the court. In the few surviving records, between 1536 and 1544, John Moreland of Radcliffe declared that John Rosell, Thomas Long, Edward Ballard, William P(are) and two priests - Thomas Somer of Thurgarton Priory and Thomas Smythe, Radcliffe's chantry priest - were all bound to pay homage to the court. So also were some unnamed people from Newton. In 1536/7 a stray ewe with her lamb had been impounded and would be held until the following Easter, but their fate like everything else about this manor is unknown.[116]

The court of the Honour of Peverel - Woodhall or Grey's manor

Heading of Peverel court roll for April 1579
(U of N Archives Department Mi Mp 36)

For most of its history this Honour was in the hands of the crown. An 18th century commentator explained the system this way: '... there is for all the manors but one Court yet they are Quasi several and distinct Courts'. Woodhall or Grey's manor belonged to it, but in the Peverel records it was simply known as the manor of Radcliffe-on-Trent, suggesting that these were local names given to distinguish it from the Rosell manor. For many years its lords, the Greys of Codnor followed by the Rosells in the 16th century, were obliged to pay homage at the court. So too were the other tenants who had to travel to Nottingham or wherever the court was being held. The Curia Magna or Court Baron and View of Frankpledge was held twice a year at Easter and Michaelmas to settle the business of the manors within its jurisdiction. In the earliest days the court was held in a chapel in what is now St James's Street in Nottingham and for some time in the Basford mansion of the Eland family, who held land in Radcliffe. The Willoughbys eventually succeeded them as bailiffs and in Elizabeth's reign the court was held in Nottingham castle.[117]

Its jurisdiction, to modern eyes, appears to have consisted of a strange mixture of peacekeeping, sanitation control and acting as moral watchdog. Although by the late 16th century manorial jurisdiction was in decline, the Peverel court had long had the right to exclude the sheriff's writ from those areas which lay within the Honour and it tried to protect what was a potentially lucrative privilege. The main concerns of the court were to ensure that free tenants appeared and paid homage or sent their excuse (their essoin), that the common 'fine' or charge for each manor was paid, and to protect the rights of the lord. It controlled the quality of ale and bread sold within its jurisdiction (the assize), dealt with minor breaches of the peace and the collection of debts.

Attendance at the court at Easter and at Michaelmas was no doubt, like many of the burdens placed on villagers in feudal times and on parish officials under the Tudors, a mixed blessing - an occasion for grumbling about the time and trouble it took, a break in routine, an opportunity for meeting up with friends, for gossip and for the quaffing of ale. The freeholders were led by their decennarius, thirdborough or headborough who reported anyone breaking the rules or causing trouble (in some places he was synonymous with the parish constable). These titles hark back to pre-Conquest days when every man had to belong to a tithing which would act as security for him. At one time they had reported to the hundred court, but over many years the jurisdictions had been transferred to manorial courts such as Peverel. About 39 manors in Nottinghamshire belonged to the Honour and at a conservative estimate some 200 tenants or 'common suitors' would have gathered on a court day. The court's organisation may well be imagined - the clerks sitting at their tables, the lines of men waiting to pay homage and make their presentments. The procedure is suggested by the survival of a small bundle of scraps of paper held together with a pin and dating from 1637 and would have been the same for the Tudor period. Each slip concerns a different manor. The one dealing with Radcliffe reads in very small writing: 'Presentments made by the thirdborough of Radcliffe at the Court for the Honour of Peverel held at Wollaton the 6 October 163[7] by Gervis [Gervase] Par[r] of Radcliffe upon Trent. Present[ed] Jo Hilton, Robert Dardin for breaking the assize of bread. Gervis Par[r]'. It seems likely that the thirdborough dictated his presentments to a clerk who wrote them on the scraps of paper to be handed to another, who entered them in rough on the court roll (already prepared with spaces for each manor, the judgements and fines), to be copied in a fair hand on parchment at some later date. There may have been other clerks who collected the common fines and handed out receipts. Finally the steward of the court, with the help of jurors drawn from among the freemen, gave judgement on any cases brought before him. After a long day there would be the journey back home on horseback or on foot with all the latest news from Nottingham to tell the neighbours.[118]

Those who failed to appear at the court to pay homage or failed to send an excuse were amerced (fined) not in relation to the amount of land they held but according to status. The ordinary freeholders were fined between 4d and 12d a time and if they were unable to pay their goods could be impounded. The gentry and aristocracy were listed separately in their degrees at the end of the court roll with fines ranging from 12d to 3s.4d. Among them were many who were great landowners in their own right. They neither came personally nor sent an excuse and the same names appear year in year out with the appropriate fine written 'over their heads'. Fining the absent gentry would be lucrative for the Honour and the gentry probably obliged by sending in their fines, for there are no records of any arrears accumulating. As manorial lords themselves they would have had an interest in maintaining the system.

Evidence from the Peverel rolls

Apart from a few references preserved from medieval times which indicate that the court was active and which confirm that Radcliffe belonged to this Honour, the series of rolls only begin in earnest from 1551/2 when Radcliffe sent its thirdborough Richard Wright to pay the common fine of 3s, which was levied on the whole manor and was paid only at Easter. Other manors paid anything between 6d and 24s, and some were allowed to pay in two parts. The Woodhall rental of 1545/6 shows a number of tenants-at-will (who would not have had to attend the court) and 14 freeholders, but no copyholders. In the early years of Elizabeth's reign complete lists of freeholders were not made, but those that appeared in the court records amounted to no more than half a dozen at a time. The Rosells had acquired the lordship, but the records do not make clear exactly when. The first reference to Mr Rosell is found towards the end of Edward's reign in April 1553 when he 'withheld the 3s by year'. He may have baulked at the arrangement whereby Radcliffe paid in one instalment. He soon conformed, however, and though in the early years of Elizabeth several tenants (including William Ballard) were fined for not coming to court, from 1564 onwards discipline seems to have been tighter. Two years later the court clearly decided that John Rosell senior belonged to the ranks of the gentry. He was listed with them and like the rest of his rank he paid his personal fine and stayed away.[119]

The real work was performed by the thirdborough. Richard Wright held this office for about four years; after that, with a few exceptions, Thomas Ashton took over until 1588. In 1580 Radcliffe (and a number of other places) failed to send its 'officer as according to ancient custom' and was fined 6d. In 1585 Thomas Ashton sent in a message to say that he was sick but that he sent the common fine. Thereafter he frequently did not appear personally, but invariably reported that all was well and that there were no further presentments to make.[120]

Life in Radcliffe was not without incident, however, for in 1578 Thomas Ashton reported a breach of the peace - '...that Robert Hall and Wills Thrave make affray mutually and that the aforesaid William Thrave drew blood from Robert Hall'. William Roulstone (related by marriage to Hall and, like him, of gentry status) now probably came to the rescue of Robert for he engaged with William Thrave, also drawing blood. William Thrave was fined 5s, the other two 3s.4d. (See p. 48.) This must have been considered a serious incident - perhaps there had been a history of brawling between these men - for the fines were severe. In 1619 a general rule was recorded that fines for an affray should be 12d and for bloodshed only 3s.4d.[121]

The most common presentment in all manorial documents was that for breaking the assize of ale and bread, that is for selling goods that were sub-standard or in short measure. A note was made in 1610 of the charges levied on brewers and bakers 'not sufficiently licensed, every offender 12d, and for every one licensed 4d'. William Thrave (alias Long), and sometimes his wife, were common bakers and brewers. There were others, such as John Milner and Michael Richards in the 1580s, who plied these trades which were useful by-employments to fall back on in difficult years, and there were probably many more who avoided presentment at court. Not all were local men: John Browne of Nottingham was fined 4d in 1580 because he was 'a common baker and sold bread within the town against the assize'.[122]

The court also enrolled land transactions among its freeholders, though these occur so rarely it may be that they were normally entered separately in documents which have now disappeared. The entry for 6th April 1561 explains how Thomas Parker came to the court and showed a deed whereby Thomas Close had given him one messuage in Radcliffe and one in Lamcote. He appeared at the court and paid homage so that he and his heirs might take possession of the inheritances and holdings. This appearance by Thomas Parker could have been in response to pressure from the Honorial court upholding its rights, for on the same occasion an order was made that tenants from Stapleford and Watnall, said to be between 17 and 21 years of age, were required to pay homage, and at the same time an enquiry was ordered into the age and holdings of one John Hugo in Radcliffe.[123]

Straying animals were a great nuisance in an open field village and their owners would have to pay a fine to have them released from the pinfold. In Radcliffe three sheep were impounded some time before the feast of St. Michael in 1568 and were being held in the meantime by John Rosell. Three years later two others, a 'wether hog and a ewe hog' were also rounded-up. It seems unlikely that these were the only animals to have been found straying over all these years; their appearance in the court rolls was probably because their ownership was in question. If no one claimed them the lord would confiscate them. What became of the black hen which was found wandering on the 1st August 1589?[124]

The court of St John of Jerusalem

The lands of the Knights of St John of Jerusalem were dispersed widely throughout the country. In the Middle Ages they had been divided into commanderies (those in Nottinghamshire being centred on Ossington) and bailiwicks. Lands in Radcliffe were held under the bailiwick of Shelford, so the court was sometimes referred to as Shelford St John's.

The court's property had come to the crown at the Reformation. When Henry VIII's Catholic daughter Mary became queen she intended to restore the confiscated lands to the Order, but her early death thwarted this plan and it remained with the crown. In 1558 four local men are listed as renting the Radcliffe lands of this manor. John Rosell senior occupied the largest holding for which he paid 10s. Edward Ballard paid 2s, William Pierrepont 12d, and Henry Inman 4d. Not long afterwards the Pierreponts acquired the lordship of the whole manor with its court, now moved to Cotgrave. The records in their estate papers survive mainly from the Interregnum and show that there were tenants from ten parishes in south-east Nottinghamshire attending the court but none, surprisingly, from Shelford itself.

Tenants of this manor had an obligation over and above that of most. Because of an ancient privilege of the lords dating from medieval times it was to this court that their executors would bring their wills to be proved, rather than to the church courts. For this reason, receipts for the fees charged for proving wills at 1s.8d a time turn up among these manorial papers. There were, however, also rights attached to this manor which benefited tenants until the 19th century. They included freedom from payment of 'Toll, Pontage, Piccage, Murage, Pannage, Stallage, Passage and Carriage for their Goods, Chattels and Cattle in all Fairs, Markets and other places throughout the whole Kingdom of England'.[125]

III The Church Courts

Evidence from the Archdeacon's Court records has survived from 1569 onwards. Examples of the way they affected individuals in Radcliffe appear in the chapters on the church as part of the evolving story of the parish. A summary of the general trends here, however, illustrates the extent to which the church controlled community behaviour. The courts were held every fortnight in Nottingham, in Retford each month, in Newark several times a year, and occasionally at other localities including West Bridgford, Mansfield or Southwell. Radcliffe people would most likely have to travel the five or six miles to Nottingham to answer charges at St Mary's or eventually at St Peter's church.

The discipline imposed undoubtedly had a considerable impact on villagers' lives, whatever their status. While concerns about the church fabric could have hit the pockets of some, and the unorthodox activities of clerics provided a source of village gossip, most parishioners could be affected in their routine behaviour. In particular, sexual transgressors, those who failed to attend Easter communion, those who committed misdemeanours on church property, and those accused of slander could be reported by churchwardens or vicar to the court. Fines might be exacted, but punishment in immorality cases was also implemented in the local church. The penances performed by Johanne Patterson and Elizabeth Pare (see pp. 62 and 65) were normal for sexual incontinence before marriage. Specifically, the guilty parishioner had to stand on a stool before the full church congregation, dressed in a white sheet, bare-headed and bare-footed, carrying a white wand, and make a full confession of his or her sin. Failure to comply with the court's sentence meant excommunication.

The rigour with which the system was imposed locally undoubtedly depended not only on the character of the incumbent, but on the attitudes of the current archdeacon and archbishop. For example, Edmund Grindal, Archbishop of York from 1570 to 1575, not only enforced the state's anti-Catholic policy, but tightened up on general discipline in the diocese. In the twelve months before his primary visitation only 29 disciplinary cases were initiated in the Nottinghamshire church courts, but there were 52 presentments immediately after. When Edwin Sandys, another committed reformer, took over as archbishop from 1576 to 1588 he encouraged preaching and study groups for the less learned clergy, but was opposed to the extreme Puritans. Supporting them in Nottingham was John Lowth, a lawyer and clergyman, who served as archdeacon from 1565 until 1590. A staunch advocate of the new theology, it was under his administration that Puritanism first became established in the county.

From July 1569 until the end of Elizabeth's reign in March 1603, information about some 47 known Radcliffe cases which came before the Archdeacon's Court can be found in the court books, presentment bills, penance certificates and so-called libel actions. (The records are incomplete, and most cases involved more than one person.) At least 21 of these concerned fornication or sexual incontinence - about 45%. It is probable that two of the three unspecified cases also dealt with sexual transgression. High as this total may seem, it was probably slightly below average. Rough comparisons with other areas can be made, even allowing for differences in the periods and range of documents studied. For example, between 1566 and 1600 sexual cases in Bunny were 72% of the whole, while for the same period in Beeston they were only 32%. At Retford in the 1590s they were 58% of the total. Local factors, such as the number of other types of case, the vigilance of individual churchwardens or the character of the parish, could account for these variations.

Occasionally other kinds of troublesome behaviour were curbed by the court: being quarrelsome, 'cursing and banning', contending seats in church, and chiding and talking in church landed four villagers in court. The last case was combined with failure to receive Easter communion. Four other cases (two involving the Rosell family) concerned this particular breach of religious conformity. Three villagers also breached church discipline by failing to pay a mortuary to the minister, by not resorting to their parish church, and by baptising a child despite being a layman. The clergy themselves were not immune to criticism. Three Radcliffe curates were before the court for failing to administer services at an appropriate time, for serving without a full licence, or for not appearing at a synod. (One was involved in a case which went to the Archbishop of York, but which cannot be found in the archdeaconry records.) As vicar, one was reprimanded for not obeying a court order, and was subsequently involved in a tithes dispute. Churchwardens - normally the presenters of others - were in court themselves on one occasion for not carrying out repairs to the church fabric, their predecessors having failed to make up the accounts. The Radcliffe squire, as lay owner of Whatton rectory, was charged with neglecting the fabric of Whatton chancel. The remaining four cases involved two breaches of promise and two disputed wills. No significant conclusions can be drawn about the greater likelihood of men or women being presented, nor about their social status. While the court could not always force those who came before it to comply, no one could escape its overall authority.[126]

IV Obligations to the Poor and Community

The problem of poverty undoubtedly increased during the Tudor period, evidenced by the growth of legislation to deal with the matter. At the start of the century manorial lords were legally responsible for the relief of the poor, but in practice various religious bodies - the local church, the monasteries or the mendicant friars - also contributed, although perhaps not on so great a scale as was once thought. The moral obligation on the individual to contribute either to church bodies or to the welfare of his fellows was considerable.

Early Tudor bequests to the poor

Any evidence in Radcliffe's case comes from surviving wills. As already seen (page 38), parishioners gave generously to the various orders of friars. Seven out of 12 wills before 1536 contained such bequests, usually in kind, principally barley, with some wheat and malt. Only Edward Lodge, the vicar, in 1521 left money rather than grain to the friars in Newark, Lincoln, Leicester and Nottingham. To what extent this form of almsgiving eventually benefited the poor is unclear.

After the dissolution of the monasteries between 1536 and 1539, however, a main source of relief, particularly in the form of hospitality to itinerants, was removed. Legislation against vagabonds was severe, but help was to be provided for those unable to work by a law of 1536 which ordered clergy and churchwardens to 'gather and procure voluntary alms with boxes every Sunday and holiday'.[127]

The first mention in Radcliffe of the poor man's box or chest is found in a will of 1549, when William Welbie, the vicar, left 12d to each of the 'poor man's chests' in Radcliffe, Cotgrave, Holme (Pierrepont), Shelford and Saxondale. Three others in the early Tudor period left money to the poor man's box: 4d from widow Alice Morley (1549), 12d from husbandman John Fuldiam (1551), and 12d from William Wolley (1551). The latter also left to 'every one of poor folks a peck of corn at the sight of my executors'.

Early Tudor bequests to the community

William Wolley's will provides an example of another type of charitable bequest, this time to the community as a whole. He left his executors to choose whether the church or 'the Boat for the reparations' should receive 6d. The state of the town boat - essential for a riverside community - was also in the mind of widow Johan Taverey when she drew up her will about the same time as William Wolley. She unequivocally left 6d for its repairs.

This sort of benevolence is found throughout the early Tudor period. For example, five testators left money or gifts in kind for mending the highways at Radcliffe. John Horne in 1517 was unusual in specifying that his 12d was to be spent on the highway between his house and the church. In 1521 two gifts of 6d for Thurlbeck Bridge, which was presumably in disrepair at the time, were made by husbandmen Robert and William Dewsbury. (Thurlbeck dyke crosses the present Radcliffe-Nottingham road just east of Holme House.)

Occasionally, testators bequeathed money to the parish without specifying the use to which it should be put. Richard Bayley in 1519 left 12d for 'common works', while in 1549 the vicar, William Welbie, left the considerable sum of 20s to the parish of Radcliffe 'for their commonwealth'.

Elizabethan bequests to the poor

Information about attitudes to the poor in Elizabethan Radcliffe can still only be gleaned indirectly. It is clear, however, from wills that private benevolence continued until the later stages of Elizabeth's reign. Of 22 wills from the first 30 years, over half the testators still gave alms to the poor. Seven of the bequests were of money, such as William Roulstone's 2d to any cottager in Radcliffe (1558), husbandman Edmund Franke's 2s to the 'poor folks of the town' (1586), or John Mylner's 12s to the 'most poor of the parish' (1587). Five bequests were in kind. In 1558 John Greene willed that 'xx [i.e. 20] dozen of wheat bread should be given to poor people on the day of my burial'. The rest were in grain: a bushel of barley for the poor from husbandman John Franke (1568), 'a strike of barley for the poor men's box' from yeoman John Pares (1570), Richard Howlyn's peck of corn in the same year to 'all such cottagers as [have] but one cow or none at all' (in addition to 2s.6d to the poor man's box), and widow Margaret Greene's peck of malt 'to any cottager' a decade later.

In the later years of Elizabeth's reign from 1588 to 1603, however, only one testator out of 15 left alms to the poor - yeoman William Brodfield who bequeathed 2s in 1598. (There were occasional windfalls as, for example, when Henry Jervis after repeatedly failing to perform a public penance for fornication, was dismissed after certifying on 17th July 1602 that he had paid 20 shillings to the church-wardens for the use of the poor.)[128]

Legislation on poor relief

There are several possible explanations for the fall in private benevolence in the last years of Elizabeth's reign. To combat the increasing problem of poverty, the office of overseer of the poor was created in 1572 and parishioners were ordered to contribute to a poor rate. (In practice many did not do so until the 1660s.) From 1576 any who refused to do so could theoretically be forced to pay double the assessment. By the same act, materials were to be provided for the employment of 'every sick, poor and needy person... able to do any work' in their own parishes, for which they were to be paid. Refusal could result in being sent to a House of Correction. Anyone who was granted poor relief and then went begging was to be whipped and burnt through the right ear. At the third offence they could be hanged. The death penalty for all forms of vagabondage was abolished in 1597. With officialdom now taking responsibility for the poor, private gifts inevitably declined. At the same time, inflation, bad weather and poor harvests in the 1590s reduced the surplus wealth of the population, so exacerbating the situation.

So bad was this crisis, that the church authorities issued special Articles to alleviate suffering. In February 1597 the vicar, George Cotes, and his churchwardens testified to encouraging fast days, and to having collected money from every husbandman for the relief of poverty:

> *Whereas according to the articles read us in Church concerning fasting and relieving the poor according to the same direction we have done our endeavour herein.*
> *And have collected money of every husbandman for the same. And I have bestowed it as need did recognise.*
> *And everyman was willing according to his ability to distribute it to the Collector w[hi]ch ... gave it p[re]sently after he had it.*
> *And all the rest of the Articles are likewise observed and kept*
> *To the w[hi]ch we have upon our oaths set down according to truth.*

Evidence from other responses confirms the difficulty of the times and the importance of the church as a means of administration. Husbandmen were generally contributing between 1d and 4d to help those in difficulty, and fasting from flesh was to be enforced on Wednesdays as well as Fridays (fish days). Holme Pierrepont's return stated that

> *no man doth absent himself in this time of dearth from his own house......our minister resident keeping hospitality after his power... We are exhorted to charity, liberality and other works of mercy and also to patience and confidence in God his p[ro]vidence and goodness.*

This stoical acceptance of God's providence was typical of the period.[129]

At national level, two further acts rationalised existing legislation and made additional arrangements for children. The act of 1598 confirmed at parish level the responsibilities of overseers of the poor and churchwardens in collecting rates and providing work. They could also apprentice children whose parents were unable to maintain them. The act of 1601 additionally empowered churchwardens and overseers to build houses for the impotent poor paid for out of the rates. Responsibility for ensuring that parish officials carried out this legislation was placed in the hands of the magistrates at Quarter Sessions rather than the church authorities.[130]

Elizabethan bequests to the community

State legislation had little effect on other forms of benevolence. Despite the passing of the Statute for the Mending of Highways in 1555, which laid down that two surveyors should be appointed annually in each parish to oversee the repair of highways leading to any market town, there were eleven bequests for road repairs in and around Radcliffe in Elizabeth's reign. Roads to Cotgrave and Shelford were also mentioned. The gifts were usually of money, ranging from 6d to 10s, but barley, wheat and malt continued to be donated. Robert Darwyn in 1574 showed particular concern for the villagers whose unpaid labour was required for the repairs. He requested that 'at the next mending of the ways belonging to the bounds... of Radcliffe and Lamcote after my decease, my executors shall bestow five shillings in bread and as much ale as a bushel of malt will make to be bestowed upon the labourers thereof'.[131]

As in the early Tudor period, money was left for the maintenance of the town boat: 2s by widow Elizabeth Darrenton towards the 'buying of a gable [i.e. cable?] for the boat at Radcliffe' (1579), and 5s by Steven Palmer, labourer (1594). The substantial landowner Robert Hall (1580) left 6s.8d for repairing the boat, as well as 6s.8d for the church clock and 3s.4d for 'the making of a mound in Hesgang for saving of men's cattle... [in] floods'. Such gifts to the community were to peter out in the early 17th century.

Case study 6

THOMAS PARKER - a bailiff at odds with his landlords

Around the time that Sir Thomas Stanhope was battling to save his weir and Isabel Dewsbury was charged with breach of promise of marriage, two other villagers were involved in a dispute which went to the Court of Requests. Although based in Westminster, this court was able to hear evidence in the provinces. The case is of interest as it not only highlights the complicated terms on which land might be held, but also demonstrates the way landlords, in a period of inflation, tried to increase rents when leases fell in. Moreover, the apparent ease with which the participants - albeit people of some substance - could move about the country refutes the conventional view that travel in the 16th century was difficult. As so often with court documents, the final judgement has not come to light.

Terms of Thomas Parker's landholding

The main village protagonist was Thomas Parker, a yeoman of some standing in the community: a regular witness to wills, one of the parish élite chosen to settle a dispute about church seats in 1577, an occupant of lands owned by the Honour of Peverel (to which he owed suit and service), and from 1592/3 to 1599/1600 wealthy enough to appear on the subsidy rolls. (He was consistently taxed at 8s for having goods worth £3.)

He and another villager, Edward Carpenter, occupied some lands owned between 1579 and 1588 by a John Russell of Little Malvern in Worcestershire through his second wife, Jane Lumley. How she came to have a life interest in Radcliffe lands has not been discovered. Moreover, although the name Rosell was sometimes corrupted to Russell, no connection between these Worcestershire Russells and the Radcliffe squires has been found. Of these lands, Thomas Parker held the greater share, variously described as consisting of three plough lands, beside meadow, pasture and common pasture, and several messuages or tenements and hereditaments. Edward Carpenter held only one plough land, along with a farm house and appurtenances. The terms on which Thomas Parker rented his lands were complicated. There was no written agreement, for the letting was 'by word', and John Russell's terms were for twenty years if his wife lived so long. For each five-year term of the twenty years Thomas Parker was to pay a £20 entry fine (other witnesses claimed it was £15) and £5 of rent annually, payable in two equal portions at the 'feasts of Pentecost and St Martin [the] Bishop in the winter' (i.e. Whitsuntide and 11th November). Edward Carpenter was to pay a £5 entry fine for a five-year term and 28s.8d annually in equal parts at the same feasts. In addition, Thomas Parker had been appointed to act as bailiff on these lands, to look after his absentee landlord's interests and to produce the rents when due.

Executor, widow and young husband

The dispute between the Radcliffe tenants and the Worcestershire Russells arose some time after the death of John Russell in London on St Andrew's day (30th November) 1588, although it took nearly four years before much of the evidence was heard by the court - from April to October 1592. Henry Russell, John's brother, was executor of his will, and pursued one line of grievance against Parker and Carpenter since he claimed that back rent was owing to the estate from before John died. A parallel dispute occurred because of the change of ownership of the Radcliffe lands. On John Russell's death they had initially reverted to Jane, his widow, since she held a life interest in them. She was not left to grieve long, however, for on 3rd February 1589, just over two months after her bereavement, she remarried. Her second husband, 26-year-old John Walwyn, therefore acquired the ownership of the lands during Jane's lifetime, since married women's property automatically passed to a husband. It was the imposition of fresh terms by this young new landlord which provoked further friction. An approximate sequence of events can be pieced together from the court evidence of the various witnesses.

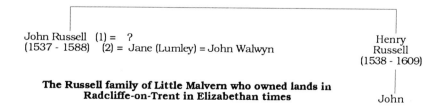

John Russell (1) = ?
(1537 - 1588) (2) = Jane (Lumley) = John Walwyn

Henry Russell
(1538 - 1609)

John

The Russell family of Little Malvern who owned lands in Radcliffe-on-Trent in Elizabethan times

After marrying the widowed Jane, John Walwyn rode over to Radcliffe with 76-year old John Pearte from Little Malvern to 'enter' into his wife's lands around All Hallows-tide (1st November) probably in 1589. They went to Thomas Parker's house where they met Edward Carpenter as well as Parker himself. The two Radcliffe men pleaded with Walwyn that he would 'take the like course with them' as John Russell had done, and 'that he would be no worse unto them in his grant' - that is, continue the terms of the lease as they were before. In fact, John Walwyn considered that the lands had been undervalued. He claimed that they were worth over 100 marks more than the existing joint rents of £6.8s.8d (a mark was 13s.4d), and that rents were low because of the entry fines, and because the right to the holding could cease on the death of Jane - or of her husband. In Parker's case Walwyn chose not to increase the rent, but he raised the entry fine to £30, with no repayment should he (Walwyn) or his wife die within the term of five years. Carpenter was presumably unable to find more than his existing entry fine of £5 - Sir Thomas Stanhope pleaded on his behalf - so Walwyn doubled his 28s.8d rent instead. Although the specific circumstances of these rents and entry fines may not be typical, the general inflationary trend for such short-term leases was. Whilst the landlord was protecting himself against rising costs and prices, this was not necessarily unjust if the tenant was making higher profits from the sale of corn or meat from those lands.

Thomas Parker's visit to Little Malvern

Whether or not such increases were justified, ill feeling on both sides came to a head over the non-payment of the back rents claimed by Henry Russell on behalf of his dead brother's estate. As bailiff of the Radcliffe lands, Thomas Parker was responsible for these. He clearly felt, however, that as his old landlord had died within the set term of five years, some compensation was deserved for not receiving the full value of the entry fines, and had consequently withheld the rents. Both John Walwyn and John Pearte gave evidence to the court that about Trinity Sunday eve (the week after Whitsun) in 1590 Thomas Parker had visited Little Malvern where they had met him in Henry Russell's house. For a 76-year-old, John Pearte gave a remarkably vivid account of his version of the conversation:

> *Mr Henry Russell demanded of the said Thomas Parker... what rent was behind and unpaid unto his brother John for his lands in Radcliffe before his death.*
>
> *The said Thomas Parker answered that there was one half year's rent behind and unpaid.*
>
> *Then said [Henry Russell]... "That I must have, for that I am executor unto my brother."*
>
> *Then answered Parker and said, "Nay, marry, not so, for I will keep and have that, and I would I had more in my hands to keep also in some recompense of my late fine paid unto my landlord your brother."*
>
> *Then replied [Henry Russell]... "Why, goodman Parker, did not my brother grant and set the living to you casually, that was if either my said brother or his wife died before your five years were expired that then his grant and your bargain and interest or hold therein was void?"*
>
> *Then answered Parker, "Yes, sir, I must needs confess that."*
>
> *Then said [Henry Russell]... "I must then needs have the rent due before his death or I shall know why I shall not have it. Therefore, Parker, if you will let me have it by fair means, so it is. If not, I must and will come by it as I may by law."*
>
> *Parker answered, "Sir, do your pleasure."*
>
> *Then Mr Russell said, "Parker, then look to hear from me shortly."*
>
> *Then said Parker, "On God's name, sir," and so parted.*

The current law case was the result.

Further accusations and the defence

Worse still from Thomas Parker's point of view, John Pearte had some additional information which he had picked up when he and Walwyn had been over to Radcliffe. He had talked to Edward Carpenter, also behind with six months' rent, who had implied that Parker had been less than honest in dealing with his (Carpenter's) entry fine:

> *... Moreover... when he [Pearte] was at Ratcliffe-upon-Trent in Nottinghamshire he... and the aforesaid Ed[ward] Carpenter walking together, the said Carpenter did [say] that he had paid to Thomas Parker a great part of his fine since the death of his late landlord, Mr John Russell, and was well assured that the said Parker had not paid the same, nor any part thereof, to any executor or assignee of his said late landlord deceased. Whereupon the said Ed[ward] Carpenter asked... whether he might not well sue the said Thomas Parker for that part of his fine so resting in Parker's hands, adding moreover that he minded to sue him for it.*

If Pearte is to be believed, Thomas Parker was not merely at odds with the Russell estate over unpaid rent, and with his new landlord over entry terms, but with his fellow tenant in Radcliffe for keeping hold of the latter's entry payment.

Henry Russell's argument to the court was that not only did Parker and Carpenter owe unpaid rents from John Russell's lifetime, but other rents up to the end of the last 5-year agreement after Russell's death. This withholding of money was all the more unjustified since they had had 'great commodity and profit by the said leases' as the lands 'were yearly more worth than the whole fines and rent' payable to John Russell 'in the whole term of five years end'. Henry Russell's principle, at a time when agricultural profits were generally rising was to extract as much as possible on behalf of his brother's estate. His concern, however, was not totally disinterested. John Russell had had no son, and though Henry could not inherit the Radcliffe lands, he could benefit if the back rents were paid.

While Carpenter and Parker agreed with the basic scenario, their explanation, as expressed by Parker, was that John Russell had died only some two years after the latest 5-year entry fine was paid. At that time, Parker was holding half a year's rent owed by himself and Carpenter. This he had kept as 'satisfaction' for part of the entry fine already paid. Three years' worth of this had been lost when Jane Russell (Walwyn) had immediately 'avoided the said lease' on the death of her husband. This he thought 'in right equity and good conscience he might lawfully do'.

The case therefore hung on whether the verbal agreement over fines and rents - Henry Russell admitted that he did not have any 'evidences or writings' - should continue for the full five years, or whether it was nullified by the death of John Russell and the tenants entitled to some remission. Whatever the verdict, it is clear that Thomas Parker's action was not unique, for it emerged from Henry Russell's evidence that two Yorkshire tenants in 'Alborrowghe and Colden in Holderness' were trying the same tactics. Who won this second contest is also unknown.[132]

THE TUDOR VILLAGE - a social survey

When Henry VII passed through Radcliffe on his way to the Battle of East Stoke, the village consisted of several manors with their tenants owing fealty and paying rents and fines to more than one lord. The inhabitants, however, would have seen themselves as one community. Together they farmed the great open fields where their strips were scattered and intermingled and together they decided how to manage them. There is no contemporary record as to how this happened, but co-operation there must have been, probably under the supervision of the parish constable as in the 18th century (see *Radcliffe-on-Trent 1710–1837* pp. 25–26). The villagers also shared responsibility for the upkeep of the highways and boundaries of the parish. As neighbours living cheek by jowl with each other they were bound together by common interests, lending, borrowing, helping each other out, worshipping together and at the very last witnessing each others' wills and testaments. There was little privacy in 16th century society, little that the 'towns-people', as they saw themselves, would not have known about each other.

The outside world also saw them as one community. Radcliffe's and Lamcote's inhabitants all belonged to the same civil unit, although those of Lamcote were in the ecclesiastical parish of Holme Pierrepont, which caused some confusion. They also belonged to one township in the eyes of the law, the tax collector and the muster returns officer who called on them to defend their country (see p. 35).

I Wealth and Status - the Early Tudor Period

Early Tudor subsidies

Taxation returns can help to provide an overall view of a community. Examples of subsidies from the early Tudor period date from Henry VIII's need for money for his foreign adventures in 1524/5 and 1543/4. These were levied on laymen only, on whatever yielded the most of an individual's land, movable goods of all kinds or wages over the value of 20s. The rate was on a sliding scale which changed from one subsidy to another. Being immensely unpopular, they were subject to much evasion. Whilst the returns cannot be relied upon to give very exact indications of wealth, they do show who were the most important inhabitants.

The subsidy of 1524/5 shows that much had changed since the lay subsidy of 1332 (p. 19): Radcliffe now with 20 taxable inhabitants (whose total assessment was £3.11s.4d - uncorrected total), had acquired a somewhat different character for it now boasted a resident landlord, John Rosell, squire of one of the several manors. He paid 20s on his goods and was far more prosperous than anyone else. The next most prosperous, paying 8s, was a member of the minor gentry, Edward Ballard, and below him widow Alice Bayley and John Webster assessed at 6s each. These four provided more than half of the total assessment. Six contributed between 2s and 5s each including Alice Bayley's son Richard. At the other end of the scale, half of those taxed paid less than 2s each, adding up to less than one sixth of the total and they included another son of Alice and one of John Webster. When allowance is made for the number who were too poor to be taxed, it is clear that Radcliffe had become a much more unequal society since the Middle Ages. However, no one in the return was taxed on wages, not even John Moreland, described as servant/labourer, which suggests that each still had some land to work.

Family names which were to play a large part in Radcliffe's history over many years appear amongst those taxed in 1524/5. Among the medium tax payers were the names of Franke and Dewsbury and among those paying the least were Parr, Darwyn and Greene. Richard How(e)lyn who paid 2s is the only one whose name can be traced back to the 1332 tax assessment, although it is possible that some of the others had equally long pedigrees, but that their names had changed over the years.

The number of those listed increased dramatically from 20 to 37 in the 1543/4 assessment (£2.9s.2d - uncorrected total). The tax threshold had been lowered and Radcliffe like the rest of England had probably experienced a rise in population. The seven wealthiest people, that is nearly a quarter, contributed three fifths of the total. John Rosell, grandson of the squire of 1524/5, was assessed on land rather than on goods, a sure indication of his pre-eminence in terms of wealth and status; his land was valued at £10 and he had to pay 6s.8d. However, two other men had to pay the same tax but on goods not land - Robert Darwyn and Richard Bayley. Some names, such as Ballard and Webster, had gone altogether and some new ones had been added. Among them was Richard Wright, probably a blacksmith, who paid 2s.6d on £8 worth of goods, and William Capendale who paid 8d on £4. The Greenes and the Parrs had begun that proliferation which was to become such a marked feature of their families. There were three Parrs, headed by Henry, who each paid 2s on £6 and four Greenes (besides Robert Grenesmith) headed by Thomas also paying 2s on £6. Both of these families appear to have gone up in the world since 1524.

1524/5 Tax paid by 20 people

1	@	20s		=	20s	
1	@	8s		=	8s	
2	@	6s		=	12s	
2	@	5s		=	10s	
1	@	4s	6d	=	4s	6d
1	@	4s		=	4s	
2	@	2s		=	4s	
6	@	1s	6d	=	9s	
3	@	1s		=	3s	
1	@		4d	=		4d
Corrected totals					74s	10d

1543/4 Tax paid by 37 people

3*	@	6s	8d	=	20s	
2	@	2s	8d	=	5s	4d
2	@	2s		=	4s	
6	@	1s	8d	=	10s	
9	@		8d	=	6s	
1	@		6d	=		6d
7	@		4d	=	2s	4d
7	@		2d	=	1s	2d
					49s	4d

* one taxed on land

Hereafter the Tudor subsidies only record those who paid the highest tax. In 1545/6 there were nine but only six in 1547/8. John Rosell was still taxed on land, its value reduced on both occasions to £8 from £10. His son and heir, Harold, now shared some of his wealth, however, being taxed on goods valued at £12 in 1545/6 and £10 two years later. Thomas Dewsbury and Thomas Thrave (a new family name in the Tudor lists but found in Radcliffe on the 1332 subsidy) were also taxed on land in 1545/6 but in both cases it was only valued at £1 and neither appear on the lists of 1547/8. In these later subsidies the same families as before emerge as the most affluent. Robert Darwyn, John Franke and Richard Wright were all among the highest tax payers, followed at a distance by Thomas Greene and Henry Pare.

Inexact as these figures are, they do confirm the presence of a group of families who were not gentry but who, through two generations, were among the most prosperous of the village. Because of their local knowledge and reliability their menfolk provided the members of the juries who sat on the Inquisitions or inquiries into local matters. Richard Bayley, John Dewsbury, Richard Howlyn, Richard Wright, William Capendale and several of the Greenes all performed this service. Moreover, at that most important moment of a man or woman's life, the making of a last will and testament, they were likely to be asked to act as witnesses.

Wills and some subsidy payers

There are few records which can match wills for the light they shed on individuals in an age when literacy was rare, and the richness of the material they offer will be given more detailed treatment elsewhere (see sections on Legacies and Farming below). They were, however, usually made only by the more affluent in the community, most people relying on the sanctions of local and manorial custom to safeguard the interests of their family. As a gauge of relative prosperity they have their failings. Some people may have arranged for the disposal of their goods among their adult descendants before they made their will. Moreover, the will shows only a given moment in time, not the testator's overall wealth, and therefore status, over a lifetime. The time of the year he or she died and the amount already invested in children in the way of apprenticeships and marriage portions could affect the amount bequeathed. In cash legacies the wording of wills was often ambiguous. Inventories are more precise but none have survived from Radcliffe before the 17th century. However, wills can be used to fill-out information from subsidy returns and as a basis for general conclusions about the 16th century community.

Twenty two wills are extant from the early Tudor period, three made by vicars, two by widows and six by husbandmen. The other eleven did not specify their status, although some appear to have been among the more comfortably off in the village. No one claimed to be a yeoman, but the wills and subsidies show that several might have been justified in doing so. Their wealth lay in their farms (though not the type of tenure by which they held them) and their stock, which gave them status and enabled them to survive adversity. The difference in housing and way of life between gentry and yeomen was not always so great at this period; it was birth and lineage which distinguished the two groups, although attitudes were more relaxed about such things than they were soon to become. Cash bequests in these wills were:

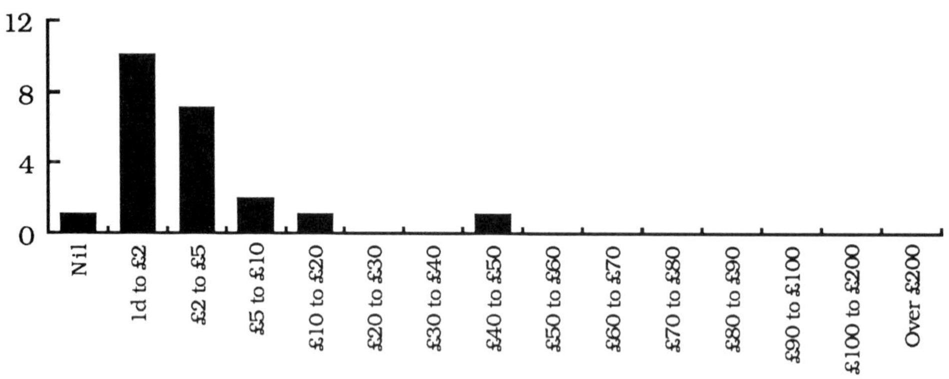

Some of these wills were made by individuals on the subsidy lists or by members of their families, so allowing comparisons to be made between the two types of record. Alice Bayley who paid 6s in 1524/5 and whose son paid 6s.8d in 1543/4 was the widow of Richard (unspecified) who made a will in 1519. He seems to have been prosperous, leaving over £7.15s in cash and going into some detail over his farm goods which were probably surplus to the main inheritance passed on to his sons. It is therefore not surprising that his family ranked so high in the tax assessments. He was able to be generous to a number of different churches, to his godchildren and to his two daughters. Fifty years later Alice's son called himself a yeoman.

Another high taxpayer was John Webster (unspecified, paying 6s in 1524/5) who made a will in 1527. He also was generous in his religious bequests and in gifts to friends or servants to whom he left a number of sheep and cattle. One son, Robert, paid 21d in tax. The other was referred to in his will as Sir Richard, indicating that he was a cleric. This would have involved a heavy investment in his education and may explain why he left only £2.6s.8d in cash. John Grenhall's will (1534) does not confirm the prosperity his place on the 1524/5 subsidy list suggests (when he paid 5s). He bequeathed a number of sheep to godchildren and to religious institutions, but not to friends, and he left about £3.3s.4d in cash; his children, however, appear to have been under age when he died, so he may have had little room for generosity.

Just below these in the 1524/5 subsidy was John Dewsbury who paid 4s. He was probably the son and heir of Robert Dewsbury who made his will in 1521 and who called himself a husbandman. Robert's will gives plenty of detail about farm goods including some old bound wheels and an iron-bound cart, which were status symbols in themselves, as well as some personal items of clothing, but he left only 12d in cash. He too seems to have educated one of his sons to the priesthood and he had three other sons and a daughter. Another member of the family, Thomas (probably John's nephew), paid 8d tax in 1543/4. The effect of sharing the family's goods among a number of siblings must have been to dilute a family's wealth.[133]

Hard times

Of the 22 early Tudor wills, 12 were made between 1516 and 1534 inclusive, ten between 1548 and 1558 inclusive, but none in between. This 13-year gap seems too long to be simply a reflection of a low mortality rate, but without parish registers there is no means of checking this. Were people perhaps suffering from a loss of confidence after the destruction of the religious institutions to which for generations their forebears had left legacies? The gap coincides with a period of economic hardship as well, which may be another reason for the absence of wills. Between 1544 and 1551 a series of debasements of the coinage drove up prices and contributed even further to the inflation already caused by Henry VIII's wars and a rising population. Repeated harvest failures in the 1540s exacerbated the situation.

II Wealth and Status - the Elizabethan Period

Though prices continued to soar (more than 60% in the reign of Elizabeth), by 1560 the coinage had been stabilised and this period saw a remarkable rise in the standard of living. The very conditions of price inflation and variable harvests which brought hardship to some, brought opportunities to others and made them acutely aware of their material possessions and their status. It would have been surprising if Radcliffe had not shared in these general conditions and in fact the records do show signs of this increasing prosperity.

Elizabethan subsidies and wills

Only eight subsidy returns have survived in a legible fashion and these are from 1592 onwards. Six inhabitants paid tax on each occasion, John Rosell junior (the first John Rosell's great grandson) always paying 20s on land except in 1593/4 when he paid 24s. Eight other families shared the burden, all paying 8s on goods - Thomas Parker and a member of the Parr family were always on the list. Henry Jervis and Edward Capendale (whose families had been on the 1543/4 subsidy list) and William Grococke (a newcomer) paid six times. John Franke, John Thrave and Richard Dewsbury, all from old families, paid twice each. There were, however, other affluent families living in Radcliffe at this time not on the subsidy lists, so some arrangement for sharing the tax burden may have been made between them.[134]

From the 45 years of Elizabeth's reign 35 wills have survived. There are gaps - one of five years between 1561 and 1566, two of four years and the rest approximately of two years, but nothing so large as in the early Tudor period. The greatest number were drawn up in the last two decades of the century; from 1558 to 1574, 12 men and women made wills, and 23 from 1579 to 1599. People were now much more status conscious. There were two gentlemen, five yeomen, ten husbandmen, four widows, two labourers, one cottager and three artisans, although eight of those leaving wills still did not specify their status. Except for Edmund Rosell, a younger son, none of the Rosells or the Ballards left a surviving will, but two other families, the Halls and the Roulstones, claimed to be gentry.

These wills clearly show that the inequalities seen in the 1524/5 and 1543/4 subsidies had greatly increased. The most startling aspect is the rise in the amount of money left by a minority if compared with the early Tudor period. Much of this can be accounted for by the debasement of the coinage and inflation, but also by the rising prosperity of some of the villagers. The amount of money left was:

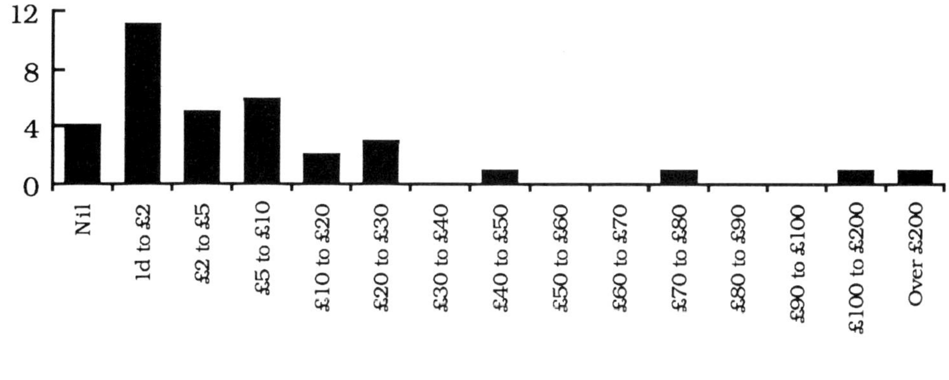

Minor gentry

The two gentry families who left wills were headed by men of property who were new to the village. Robert Hall made his will in 1580 and is first found in 1561 in the Peverel court records. As already noted he possessed the manors of Adbolton and Costock, the advowson of East Bridgford and was patron of the church of Adbolton. Richard Roulstone, who made a will at the very end of Mary's reign, left property in Rollestone, Staffordshire, from where he probably originated, but it was his son William who claimed gentry status in his will of 1591. He bequeathed the lease of Radcliffe's former parsonage house or chantry to his wife. Such families had taken advantage of the highly fluid land market which followed the dissolution of the monasteries and the confiscation of properties of traitors and felons under the Tudors. The Halls and the Roulstones were related by marriage as were both families to the Ballards. (The senior branch of this last family was based in Wymeswold in Leicestershire, but they held land in Radcliffe throughout the Tudor period.) They represented a small group of minor gentry, who can be viewed as below the Rosells in status and who had connections and interests beyond Radcliffe.

Their arrival in the parish and the growing presence towards the end of the century of powerful local landlords like the Pierreponts and the Stanhopes, which may have divided the loyalties of many of the tenants, point to a less stable community in the Elizabethan age. Neither the Halls nor the Roulstones appear to have stayed in Radcliffe more than two generations; by Charles I's reign they had both gone. The Jordans, an affluent yeoman family, stayed even less time after their first appearance in 1598.

It was these new families who left the largest cash bequests; Robert Hall nearly £300 in 1580, William Roulstone nearly £150 in 1591 and his father nearly £50 in 1558. In Richard Jordan's will of 1598 all his cash bequests amounting to £70 were to be disposed of some time after his death. The newcomers also showed their wealth in their possessions, Robert Hall in particular, whilst William Roulstone in 1591 lovingly disposed of the clothes of a gentleman. (See pp. 89 and 95.)

Two other men, one with claims to be a gentleman, were prominent in the Elizabethan period but disappeared from the Stuart scene - Thomas Ashton and Thomas Parker. They were both freeholders in the Peverel court, Parker serving as churchwarden, frequently acting as thirdborough as well as being bailiff to the Russells of Little Malvern. Their importance within the community may be judged from the fact that they both acted as arbiters in a quarrel over seats in the church which came before the Archdeacon's Court in the 1570s. (See p. 63.) In addition, Thomas Ashton was one of the trustees in an Indenture made by John Rosell senior in 1581 where he was called gentleman. He was a witness to just two wills - those of the widows Elizabeth Darrenton and Margaret Greene for whom he was also a supervisor. Thomas Parker, on the other hand, was witness to innumerable wills made by all sorts of people from Richard Roulstone (1558) to William Aynesley the cottager (1578). Although he was a yeoman, there was probably little difference between him and a member of the lower gentry like Thomas Ashton in terms of lifestyle. He died early in James I's reign but he was strictly speaking an Elizabethan and was among those contributing to the later subsidies of her reign.

Yeomen and husbandmen

Traditionally, it was during Elizabeth's reign that the yeoman came into prominence, his wealth enabling him to respond quickly to market conditions. The Bayleys had been important in the early Tudor period as subsidy payers and as jurors. Richard called himself a husbandman when he made his will in 1561 leaving £2.7s.8d in cash and a large amount of farm goods. His son, another Richard who made his will the same year, claimed to be a yeoman but bequeathed no cash and simply requested that his debts be honoured. Of the other three claiming yeoman status only Thomas Dewsbury's will (1592) revealed the sort of bequests in property and household goods which might be expected from a man of his status.

A number of husbandmen from the older families also left large cash bequests in their wills - Robert Darwyn (1574) and John Greene (1594) over £25 and Robert Parr (1595) £10. Another group, who bequeathed between £6 and £10, also had names familiar from the early Tudor period: Capendale, Wright, Parr, Thrave and Howlyn. Often acting as churchwardens, these older families had cultivated their friendships over many years. They showed it in their wills when they left bequests of both money and goods to each other and to their respective children. (See p. 88.)

Cottagers and Labourers

Cottagers and labourers left few records. Evidence from a wide area, however, suggests that their numbers were on the increase during the 16th century. The poorest were the landless day labourers, living in make-shift dwellings, and almost completely dependent on their wages for their livelihood, although they may have been allowed some common rights, perhaps to graze animals or gather fuel. The end of the century was a time of great economic stress for such people and many of them were driven off the land altogether, moving into the towns. It is not known if there were any of this category in Radcliffe, but the labourers commandeered by Sir Thomas Stanhope in 1593 to help in the repair of his weir may have belonged to it. (See p. 59.) Two of them, however, (Edward and Robert Towle) shared the family name of a cottager William Towle listed, along with seven others, on a rental of 1601. These cottagers were marginally better-off as they had a small plot of land attached to their homes. None had more than one acre, a far cry from the four acres which an Act of 1589 stipulated should be attached to every cottage when it was erected. However, there would almost certainly have been customary rights to pasture a few beasts and sheep on the common lands attached to their holdings.

By careful management of their animal stock some labourers and cottagers were able to improve their fortunes and there may have been little to distinguish them from the poorer husbandmen. The main difference would have been that the husbandman concentrated on working his own land, only hiring his labour out to others in hard times, whilst the labourer supplemented his income on a regular basis with seasonal wages and often some by-employment as well. Two labourers in Radcliffe made wills and the fact that they did so is an indication that they were not poor. John Skynner's (1598) is uninformative, but Steven Palmer's (1594) is revealing. He left over £25 and at least seven people owed him money. He seems to have had no family of his own and perhaps this was one of the reasons for his relative affluence. He probably held little land and would not, therefore, have had to invest his savings in a farm, although he left a few sheep (which would have been cared for by the common shepherd), and some household furniture to the children of friends. William Aynesley (1578) called himself a cottager rather than a labourer. He may have made a will to prevent family disputes over his much loved cows (see p. 102). Evidence of the hidden presence of many more labourers and cottagers in Radcliffe at this time than appears in general documents is revealed in Richard Howlyn's will (1570). He left a peck of corn to all cottagers owning just one cow.[135]

III Occupations

Radcliffe was within comfortable reach of the markets of Nottingham and Bingham and, with self-sufficiency in the home and the occasional visit from the pedlar and packman, the community's needs would have been easily met. In the 16th century almost everyone would have earned their living on the land and most crafts would have been those directly connected with agriculture. Of the 57 wills surviving from Tudor Radcliffe and Lamcote only eight testators specify an occupation, as against status. There were three clergy in the early period and one weaver, two tailors and two labourers from the end of the century. But internal evidence in the wills and other sources reveal a few more.

Richard Wright may have been a blacksmith for he left 'four tons of iron' to his son William in his will (1521), but there are no signs of any of the family practising the craft after him. Richard appears to have been prosperous, for he bequeathed silver spoons, pewter and brass. The Woodhall rental dated 1545/6 clearly shows Robert Greene to have been a blacksmith, for he rented a cottage with a smithy and an acre of land for 8s. He, or one of his family, may have been the Robert Grenesmyth who appeared on the muster return (but without any arms) sometime during Henry VIII's reign. (See p. 35.) By 1557 he had been succeeded by William 'otherwise called Smith' referred to in a will of that date. William Greene of Lamcote, though he did not state that he was a blacksmith, must have followed the family tradition, for in his will of 1585 he bequeathed the 'ironwork' to his wife and the tools in the shop to his two sons, the younger one of whom was to be bound apprentice to his brother. He may also have been a substantial farmer for he had a farm lease and a draught to leave as well as sheep and four heifers.

There was a windmill in the manor of Lamcote, part of the Rosell estate referred to in a document of 1582, but no miller was named in the Tudor period. There was, however, a fisherman (Christopher Fisher) who rented 'the water' for 6s in the Woodhall rental. This suggests that other villagers' rights to fish were restricted or non-existent. Thomas Smythe, the chantry priest named in the same rental, may have acted as a tutor to Thomas the son of John Grenhall who left him three sheep in return for his 'guidance' in 1534. It is very possible that he had more pupils and that other clergy throughout the period also taught in their spare time. One or two servants were mentioned in the wills, but this term could encompass a wide range of occupations from the purely agricultural - 'the servants in husbandry' or labourers, some hired by the day and some living in - to the domestic and the clerical or secretarial. The latter are more likely to have been employed by the gentry if only on an occasional basis. William Brownell of Stoke Bardolph may have been a clerk to Robert Hall as the latter left him 20s 'to do the inventory'. The names of two shepherds from Elizabeth's reign, Edward Coole employed by Robert Hall and Miles Cragge, have survived. There was also the lowly gravedigger who was left 1d for his pains by Richard Bayley in 1519.

The gentlemen and yeomen who graced the scene in Radcliffe during Elizabeth's reign would have created a demand for more goods and an opening for men who could use their skills to make a living. The tailor Richard Cowper made a will in 1595 leaving all his 'wool' to his children, 'half of the cloth which is middling, which is part spun and part unspun' to his mother with a pair of new shoes and another pair of shoes to his mother-in-law. Though he called himself a tailor, it looks as though he may also have spun and woven his own cloth and even perhaps have made shoes. Perhaps two tailors were one too many for such a small place as Radcliffe, for John Hempsall, the other tailor, made a will in 1597 which shows that he died owing money (7s.8d) to two people and quantities of peas to two others, including his landlord. He went into some detail over his household belongings (which included a great doubler, brass, a coffer and an aumbry) and mentioned 'the shop board and all things belonging to my occupation'. Hugh Bushy the weaver also bequeathed his 'shop with all the furniture thereunto belonging' in 1582. In addition, all these artisans left farm goods in their wills showing that they were not wholly dependent on their craft for a living.[136]

IV Social Relationships - Legacies in the Tudor Period

From the 57 surviving wills of the whole Tudor period something can be learnt of the relationships between the testators and their families, their kin and their friends. Although custom and law governed the disposal of real estate and movable goods, there was considerable latitude for the dying person to choose how to provide for the family, how to protect the weaker members and even how to control them from beyond the grave. These wills will be considered under five main categories: real estate and land tenure, bequests to wives and children, bequests to other relatives, miscellaneous bequests and debts.

Real estate and land tenure

Only one of the wills of the early Tudor period gives information on the inheritance of real estate; three do, however, state that rent, among other debts should be paid before the residue of the estate was distributed. Before 1540, real estate could not be disposed of by will but was passed on either under common law according to the laws of primogeniture (the eldest son inheriting), or according to the local custom of the manor. Primogeniture was most common in areas of open-field cultivation where agriculture was the main source of income, as in much of the East Midlands. The Statute of Wills of 1540 allowed for free disposal by a will in writing of any lands held in fee simple, (freehold land which was not subject to an entail). Copyhold land could not be devised by will until 1815, but a copyhold tenant could bequeath land by surrender to the use of (the terms of) a will, a procedure which would be recognised by the lord of the manor.[137]

The principal information about the type of landholding in Radcliffe in the early Tudor and Elizabethan periods comes from documents other than wills but some of this information can be tied to those wills which have survived. Both those paying chief rents and tenants-at-will were listed in the Woodhall rental of 1545/6. Richard Greene was a tenant-at-will who paid rent for a house, a close and 3 oxgangs of land. In his will of 1557, he mentions a wife and a son William, but he had no security of tenure so his family might not retain the property. (He may also have had freehold and/or copyhold land which would descend to his heirs.)

Edmund Taverey was shown as paying chief rent in the rental and he described himself in his will of 1548 as a husbandman. He appears to have had only one son who, with Edmund's widow, would inherit this freehold land. The widow would be entitled to one third for the remainder of her life. Robert Darwyn also appeared in the rental. He was a sub-tenant of Edward Ballard on land for which Ballard paid chief rent, that is freehold land. He also rented Burton yard, of which Ballard was a tenant-at-will, and other land and tenements which Ballard held in Radcliffe. No land is mentioned in Darwyn's will (1574) but he left 20s to Mr William Ballard, Edward's son, 'desiring him to be good to my wife'.

Richard Roulstone (1558) left a share of a family estate in Rollestone, Staffordshire, first to his wife for life and then successively to his three sons and their heirs. If all the sons died childless, then the land was to revert to his brother, who had been given the other half of the manor by their father (no primogeniture there, so they were probably younger sons). There was no mention by Richard of land in Radcliffe.

More of the Elizabethan wills give details of the devise of land. The most illuminating gentry will is that of Robert Hall (1580), who had accumulated a considerable estate in Nottinghamshire. He left his manor of Cortlingstock (Costock) and land in Radcliffe and Basford to his eldest son Henry, adjuring him to make no delay in moving to it. Henry had been occupying the manor of Adbolton and Robert left this jointly to his second and third sons, together with land in Radcliffe and Basford which he held on lease from the queen. Robert's widow Elizabeth was to receive an annual income from all these lands. His son-in-law William Roulstone was to occupy the manor in Adbolton until Robert died. William was then to leave it and live with his mother-in-law until her death. Robert may have been concerned that his widow and younger sons were cared for. After his mother-in-law died William could resume occupation of the Adbolton farm for the remainder of the lease, paying the old rent to Robert's heirs.

The primogeniture rule can be seen in operation also among those further down the social scale. In 1585 William Greene of Lamcote left to his wife the lease of his farm and a share of the draught during her life equally with his son John; after her death it was to go to John and his heirs and, if he had no issue, to son Robert. If neither sons had issue, two daughters were to inherit in equal shares as was customary when women inherited. Thomas Dewsbury, yeoman (1592), left his houses and land in Radcliffe, both inherited and purchased, including a cottage in Narrow Lane, to his eldest son Richard. His second son and his unmarried daughter Isabel were to share land leased of Sir Thomas Stanhope; if Isabel married, she gave up her share in return for £6.13s.4d paid over four years. (See pp. 67 and 90.)[138]

The fate of a widow who remarried, of her children and their inheritance was a matter of great concern at this period. Provision was, therefore, made for the devise of land under these circumstances. Richard Cowper, tailor (1595), left to his wife the lease of his house during her widowhood, but if she then married 'one who shall misuse her or her children', the supervisors of his will had authority to 'enter upon the said lease to the use and behoof of my son John and consider her at their discretion'. Restrictions were also placed on a wife or son selling the farm away from the family. Robert Parr, husbandman (1596), left half his farm to his wife during her life if she did not re-marry; she was to pay the rents and other charges due and make sure her half part was sown that year. She was not to sell or let her share except to Henry, their son - 'he giving her so much for it as shall be awarded and judged that it shall be worth by two indifferent [i.e. impartial] men'. If she died before the lease expired, her half share was to go to Henry's son Robert.

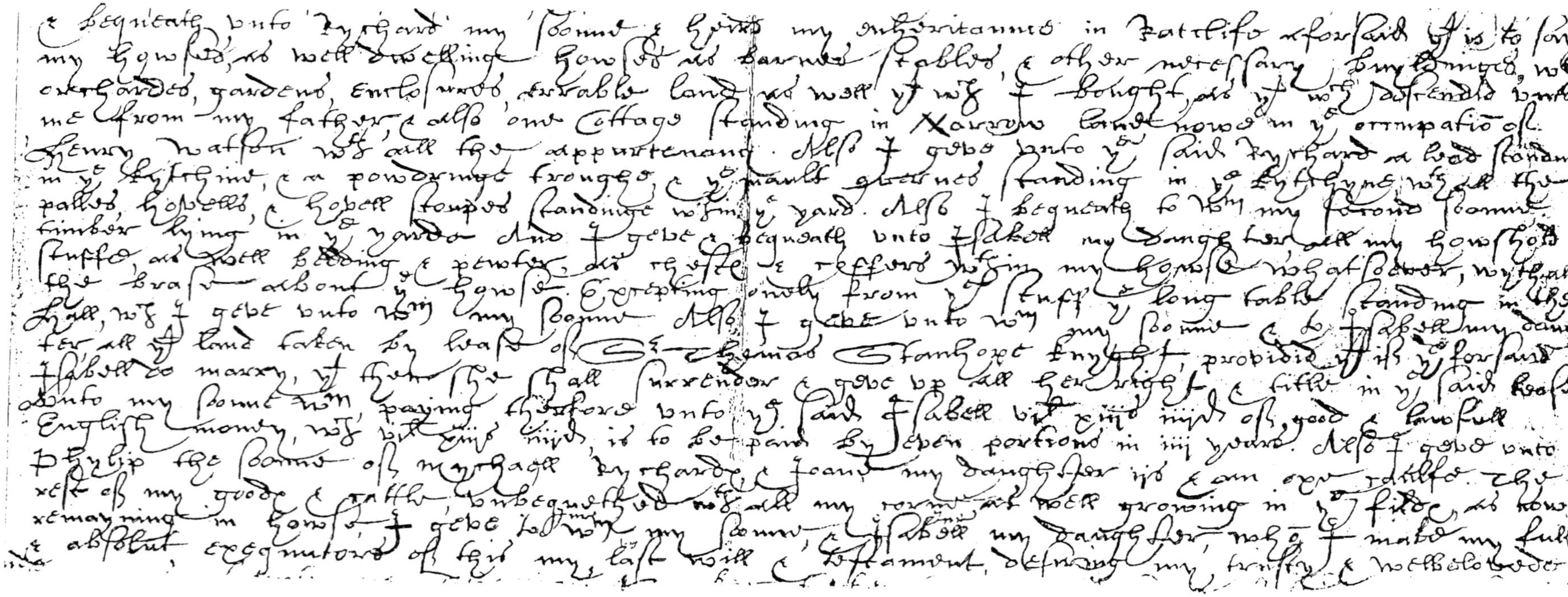

Extract from the will of yeoman Thomas Dewsbury (23rd August 1592) illustrating primogeniture inheritance.

His eldest son, Richard, is bequeathed the dwelling houses, barns, necessary buildings, orchards, gardens, enclosures, arable land, a cottage in Narrow Lane and equipment.

His second son, William, inherited timber, the long table, and shared some land with his sister Isabel, who inherited household goods

A son may have lived away from home until his father died and he could take up his inheritance. John Grococke (1589) left his whole farm to his wife for three years, after which time his eldest son William was to 'come home and have in every field an acre of land ploughed and sown for three years'. He was to enter on the whole farm at the decease of his mother. Yeoman William Brodfield and his son William had obviously had a difficult relationship. In his will of 1598, William the elder left his son barley and peas to sow the acreage of land he had already given him and

> *in consideration that I have many and sundry ways been an hindrance to my said son William, I make the larger regard of him and do give unto him in every field one acre of arable land which belongeth to my house to be sown for him of my own corn.*

William was the only son mentioned in the will and would inherit the whole farm on his mother's death. A William Brodfield was shown to be paying 20s rent for a farm of over 36 acres in a rental dated 1601 of lands acquired by the Pierreponts from the Rosells.[139]

Personal estate

Personal estate was distributed according to the common law rule of one third to the wife, one third to the children and one third freely disposable by the testator, the 'death's or soul's part' as it was called, after the payment of debts and funeral expenses. Stricter rules operated in Wales, the city of London and the ecclesiastical province of York, of which the archdeaconry of Nottingham was a part. Each child was due a competent portion whereon to live, unless he or she had been provided for in the lifetime of the testator. The widow's third, unlike a jointure, was hers to dispose of exactly as she wished and these provisions remained in force in the province of York until 1692. A jointure was customarily given to a wife as part of her marriage settlement, particularly among better-off families. It recognized the dowry that she had brought to the marriage and provided for her sustenance on becoming a widow and for the maintenance of any under-age children. She was, of course, always entitled to her third share and this could be augmented in the will, as will be shown later.[140]

The widow's third

Robert Hall's widow Elizabeth was to be paid £4 per annum by the eldest son 'for her jointure and dowry' and 26s.8d per annum by whichever son held the manor of Adbolton 'in full satisfaction of her jointure or thirds'. Lower down the social scale Richard Cowper, the tailor (1595), also referred to his wife's dowry. He left her 'all such goods as I had with her at the day of her marriage' together with all other goods in the house, excepting only his wool, plus a 'fat cow' for the payment of his debts.

The division of the personal estate into thirds can be seen in the early Radcliffe wills. John Horne (1517), Henry Caunt (1518) and Richard Greene (1557) all left one third to their wives and one third to their children, but they each chose to dispose of the remaining third differently: to be distributed by executors, the residue left to children, and the residue left to the wife. Edmund Wilkinson (1586) left his wife 'one half of my poor and little goods that God hath lent me'; William Wilkinson (perhaps his son) was to have the other half 'if he will be ruled by my wife, Mistress Hall and William Roulstone, or else not'. Both Robert Darwyn, husbandman (1574), and William Capendale (1591) made their wives residuary legatees of all their goods; both men had left money legacies to their children, William's being under legal age.

Widows were allowed to remain in the family home, often sharing this with one or more adult children, otherwise provision had to be made for them elsewhere. William Thrave, husbandman, set out specifically in his will (1589) how his farm was to be managed after his death. As has been seen (p. 48) his wife was to 'have her finding here in this house as she hath had heretofore during her natural life with the governance in the house and yard as she hath had'. (His son was residuary legatee of much of the farming equipment.) John, son of the blacksmith William Greene of Lamcote, was to share the lease of his farm and the draught equally with his mother; she was to have her 'part of the iron-work free without any manner of charge to her' (1585).

The children's portion

From the Radcliffe wills there is every indication that an equitable distribution of assets was made among the testator's children. The son who was to continue working the family holding did, as one would expect, receive equipment and animals to enable him to do so. This son may not, however, have been the eldest. Richard Bayley made two of his sons joint supervisors of his will (1519) and asked that they, with their mother, should guide the other three children. One of them, Robert, was left the best wain and gear, a plough and share and four 'work-worthy' bullocks. As the other two sons had children and therefore establishments of their own, it seems probable that Robert was helping his mother to run the farm. Where two-thirds of the farm had gone to the eldest son, as in John Pare's will (1570), it followed that he should also get all the farming equipment together with all pales and wood in the yard. He was to pay 20s to the second son, and the four daughters were to share the residue of the goods, John's widow having received her customary third of land and goods. Another Richard Bayley, husbandman, left farming gear to both his son Richard and married daughter, Alice Wood, in his will of 1561. She was the only daughter to receive a specific bequest of farming equipment.

The percentage of wills which bequeathed farm equipment, animals and household goods to children was roughly equal between the early Tudor and Elizabethan periods. Daughters received slightly more gifts of money, animals and household goods in the earlier period, but in the later period gifts to sons in all categories except household goods exceeded those to daughters. It should be remembered, however, that the term 'residue of my goods' (which was frequently bestowed on daughters) could contain effects in some or all of these categories.

Wills containing bequests of money to children rose from 25% in the early Tudor to 40% in the Elizabethan period. John Sharpe left his children £4 in 1534 - how many there were is not stated. His wife was made joint executor with his brother, so the children may have been young. Richard Roulstone (1558), after disposing of his real estate, left each of his three sons £3.13s.4d and each of his three daughters the same amount at age 20 or on marriage, whichever was the earlier, provided they married with their mother's consent. Robert Darwyn, husbandman (1574), left his son £6.13s.4d and his married daughter a piece of gold worth £3.10s. William Capendale of Lamcote left mainly money to his children in 1591. Each was to receive 40s 'at lawful age' with an additional 20s to his son William 'because he is lame'. In some wills one child might be singled out to receive a cash legacy. For example, Nicholas Jervis' son Robert, who already had three children of his own, was to have 40s in full settlement of his child's part (1568). Another son, however, had cereals and sheep and Nicholas' clothes, and three other children were to share one third of his goods and the residue of the testator's third.

Some wills contained no specific bequests of cash to children. In 1549 widow Alice Morley whose daughter Johane had married Edmund Rosell, left 40 of her best sheep for them to share as well as the residue of her goods. Her other five daughters each received five sheep and one of them, Marjorie, was also to have her best gown. Most legacies to children, however, were a mixture of bequests in the categories mentioned, and they also often had a share in the unspecified residue of goods.

Special arrangements could be made for unmarried daughters, setting aside an amount for their dowry either at full age or before, as in Richard Roulstone's will (1558). Robert Hall's daughter Agnes was even better placed; her brother Henry was to pay her £80 out of money owed to him and she was to receive £20 from her brothers George and William in consideration of the bequest to them of the residue of the farm animals (1580). In contrast a married sister, who would already have received her dowry on marriage, merely received £6.13s.4d and a hive of bees. As has been seen (p. 30), Edmund Rosell's will (1560) stated that his daughter should 'continue and abide with her mother until such time as she be married'. If she was content to be ruled by her mother she was to have half his goods, if not only one third. Another problem daughter may have been Richard Bayley's child Margaret, who was left 5 marks and his aumbry 'after her made content her mother's mind'.

It was quite common for married children living away from home with their own families to receive a special 'topping-up' legacy beyond the child's portion they would have received on marriage or perhaps on starting an apprenticeship. Such a bequest was sometimes said to be in full or final settlement of a child's part. John

Mylner and his wife died within three years of each other (1587 and 1589); both left a share of their goods to their children Robert and Elizabeth. Son Harold, who had probably left home, got a bay mare and foal from his father and a long chest and great pan from his mother. Their married daughter Barbara had a quarter of barley 'set out for her already' in full settlement of her child's part from her father and a great candlestick and two coats from her mother. Thomas Dewsbury, yeoman (1592), left his four married daughters 2s and half a quarter of barley each in final payment of their child's parts.

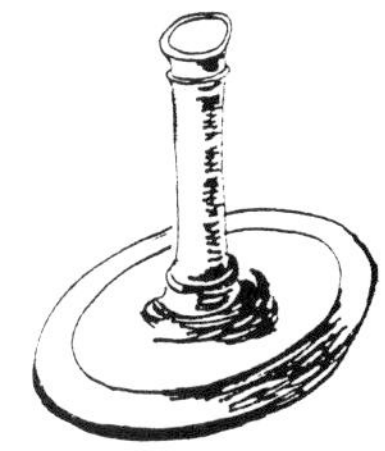

Sketch of Tudor candlestick

When payment of a child's part had not been made at full age or on marriage, an estate was burdened with these payments on a testator's death. Richard Jordan, yeoman, gave very precise instructions in his will (1599). His second son Thomas was to receive a black colt and £20 three years after his father's death; in the meantime Mr Thomas Markham 'my master' was to take care of the money for Thomas and 'dispose of it for his best commodity as shall seem best to his wisdom'. Within a year of the payment of £20 to the second son, the eldest son James, who inherited the farm with his mother, was to get £20 also. Daughter Susan was to receive £20 at age 20 and 'a feather bed with all that belong to it'. Within a year of their mother's death the eldest son was to pay both Thomas and Susan £5.

Very few of the testators died childless. Two who did were Hugh Bushy, weaver (1583), and Steven Palmer, labourer (1594). Hugh left to his wife the residue of his goods and his shop with all the furniture belonging to it 'to use to her best advantage during her natural life'; after her death it was to go to his brother. Steven left no wife or children. Although he left to his sister and her two children 10s each and his uncle 5s, the main beneficiary was his 'wellbeloved friend' Robert Browne, whom he made his executor and who was to collect over £7 owing to the testator.

An implied reference to an illegitimate child occurs in the earliest Radcliffe will, that of William Johnson (1516), probably a widower. He bequeathed to

> *John my son £3.6s.8d and the mother of the child to have the keeping of him and she to have every year of the same money 13s.4d for the span of five years and if that she can bring good surety that the stock shall be saved and kept to [i.e. till] the child comes to lawful age and can guide it himself then I will that my executors shall deliver to the child 5 [?marks].*

Two legitimate children shared the residue of his estate under the guidance of friends or relatives. There is only one overt reference to an illegitimate child and that not a member of the testator's known family. Robert Darwyn (1574) left 20s and a ewe and lamb to Elizabeth 'the bastard daughter of Martin Grococke'.

The weak position of women in the eyes of the law with regard to their children is well illustrated by the elaborate arrangements made in the will of William Roulstone, gentleman (1591), regarding his unborn child should his wife prove to be pregnant after his death. Although testators on the whole showed respect for their wives, usually making them an executrix of the will and giving them control of the children, widows had no automatic right to bring them up. In 1580 William Roulstone had been instructed in the will of his father-in-law Robert Hall to live with his mother-in-law Elizabeth until her death, and her influence was to prove significant. Whether William had had a first wife (perhaps the Geys or Joys (Joyce) Roulstone referred to in Robert Hall's will as his daughter-in-law) is not clear. The wife mentioned in William's own will in 1591 was called Jane, daughter of Mr Thomas Cockes and his wife and granddaughter of Mrs Cockes. After provision for Jane, William made his hoped-for child residuary legatee (he does not appear to have had any other children) and stipulated that Elizabeth Hall, whom he referred to as his mother, should bring it up, leaving her for the purpose £14.18s.8d owing to him and a further £24. If his wife should prove not to be with child, or if it died while in Elizabeth's care, the latter was to have the disposal of its goods. If Elizabeth died, however, his wife Jane was to bring up the child, receiving half its goods to enable her to do this, the other half to be kept until it was of lawful age. If the child died while under her governance, she was to have £20 and the residue to be divided equally among the testator's brothers and sisters. One suspects that Jane was very young and the marriage of short duration. The lack of parish registers at this period makes it impossible to know whether or not a child was born.

Two stepchildren were remembered in the wills. John Horne (1517) left his wife's son a great brass pot and a great brass pan with an aumbry. His own children had shared a third of his goods. William Wolley (1552) after providing for his own children, left his stepson a horse or a mare 'at the sight of the vicar and William Foxe'.

Sketch of a Tudor aumbry

Grandchildren

Animals were favourite gifts to grandchildren, ranging from a ewe lamb to a year-old calf or a cow. Richard Bayley (1519) left each of the children of his sons Thomas and Richard a ewe and lamb 'neither of the oldest nor of the youngest'. Alice Morley (1549) left her granddaughter, Dorothy Rosell, a year-old calf and a feather bed. Richard Bayley (1561) gave his only grandchild a black heifer, two silver spoons and a basin.

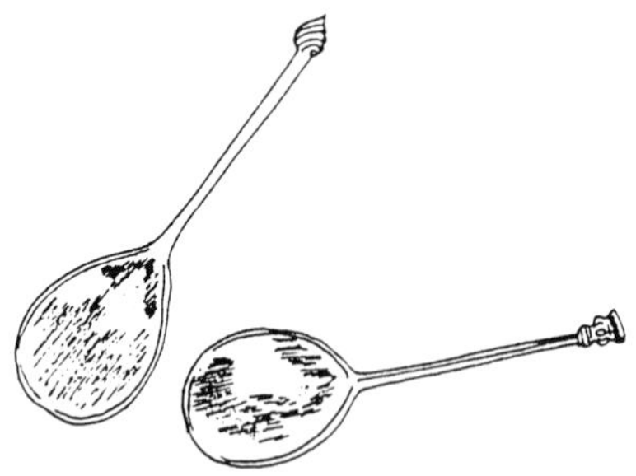

Tudor silver spoons

Robert Parr, husbandman, made substantial provision for the children of his only son Henry in 1596, perhaps hoping that they would stay in Radcliffe to work the family lands. Robert was to have his grandmother's half-share of the farm if she died before the lease expired, and in addition an iron-bound wain, two bullocks, two cows, 20 ewes and 20 lambs, ten ewe hogs and ten wether hogs. Thomas was to have a yoke of oxen, a cow, ten ewes with lambs and ten hogs 'of the middle sort'; Henry was left two bullocks, a cow calf, ten ewes with lambs and ten 'shere' hogs; to each of his granddaughters Isabel and Elizabeth he left two heifers and ten ewes with lambs. His unborn grandchild would get two cows. The usual proviso was made that if any of the grandchildren died before they married, the legacies were to be divided amongst the survivors.

Two widows left household goods to granddaughters: Elizabeth Darrenton (1579) left her linen, except apparel, equally to her 'daughters' daughters'; Margaret Greene (1580) shared linen and plates (doublers and chargers) among her granddaughters.

Godchildren

Godchildren received legacies in 11 of the 22 wills of the early Tudor period. If the gift was of money, this was either 2d or 4d, although Richard Bayley (1519) made a distinction between those within the 'town' who got 2d and those without the town who got 1d. Two testators left a ewe and lamb to each of their godsons, one a sheep to every godchild and one a ewe lamb for his goddaughter's education. William Welbie, the vicar, in 1549 left a cow in the custody of Thomas Godfrey of Shelford to his godson William Ballard and to each of seven other godchildren a hive(?). Gifts to godchildren decreased after the Reformation from 50% to around 30% in the Elizabethan period. Two testators gave animals: Edmund Rosell (1560) a ewe hog to each of his two godsons and William Greene (1585) a heifer calf each to a godson and his sister. Remaining Elizabethan legacies were of cash, ranging from 4d to 26s.8d, which Richard Howlyn's goddaughter Jane Dewsbury had 'to her marriage' (1570).

The wider family

Mention has been made of William Roulstone's bequests to his parents-in-law and grandmother-in-law. In the case of Mr Cockes, the gift was 'a sparkyall of 15s'. Two other wills contained legacies to parents or parents-in-law. Edmund Lodge, vicar of Radcliffe (1521), left 26s.8d to his father and mother. Richard Cowper, tailor (1595), left gifts of clothes and shoes to his mother and mother-in-law.

Only four of the early Tudor wills itemised gifts to brothers and sisters and their children, although relationships were not always detailed. William Johnson (1516) left sister Alice a ewe and lamb and a year-old calf, and sister Agnes one acre each of barley, peas, and wheat and rye. William Dewsbury (1521) made his brother, the priest Thomas, joint executor and overseer, leaving him a share in the residue of his goods, 5s for a trentall (30 masses) and an 'ambling foal'. Three other brothers were left a quarter of barley each. Richard Greene left his sister at harvest a peck of wheat and a peck of rye. John Martyn (1557) gave each of his brother's children a jacket.

Gifts to brothers and sisters and their children increased in the Elizabethan period: about 40% of the 35 wills contained such bequests. Robert Hall gave his brother William 'an old angel for a token between him and me' and his best hose, doublet and shirt. William's son was left 40s, his eldest daughter a hive of bees and each of his other children a ewe and lamb. Robert's sister was to have an angel and each of her daughters 6s.8d. William Roulstone forgave his brothers and cousin the money they owed him. A sister and various nephews and nieces were given sheep and a brother-in-law was left a 'pair of meane blades'. William Roulstone's gifts to his uncle conjure up his appearance: 'my white cuillyon [sic] doublet, my second cloak, my hose of same cloth, a green jerkin, better pair of netherstocks of blue'.

Husbandman's widow Margaret Greene (1580) was anxious about the well-being of her sister Agnes Shepperd for she wanted her to be given meat and drink and other necessaries by her son Harold Greene, as long as he stayed on the farm and she lived with him. If Agnes left, Harold was to give her annually a bushel of malt and a bushel of maslin. Without this provision Agnes could have been in a vulnerable position when the next generation received its inheritance. William Thrave, husbandman (1589), made similar arrangements for his insane brother Harold and sister Alice, so that both had a home for the remainder of their lives (see p. 47).

Friends and servants

Wills in the early Tudor and Elizabethan periods were particularly full of bequests to people other than immediate family; some can be identified by name as relatives, others were probably friends or servants. Animals and cereal crops figured in the bequests: a ewe and lamb, a cow and calf, sheep and steers, also barley, wheat and peas. John Grenhall (1534) left the woman's child at the windmill a lamb. Household goods and clothes were bequeathed too: in 1516 William Johnson left Jenett Willimott a violet jacket and a violet hood in addition to a stone of hemp and a little hog; Robert Halyday had his best doublet and William Worthyngton his motley jacket. John Webster (1527) gave Agnes Burton a cow, a pot, two pans and two pairs of sheets.

The wills of widows are often of interest, particularly if they did not have many close relatives. Anne Wright, for instance, who had made her son-in-law residuary legatee, had quite a long list of legacies in her will (1566), almost all to women who were perhaps her personal friends: to Johan Symson her best gown, best red kirtle and a tick bolster; to Isabel Pare a mattress, a bolster, a pot and her best cap and hat; to Anne Pare a sheet and Isabel Knight two couples of sheep, a calf at the 'stacke' and a meat board with trestles; to Agnes Knight two pewter doublers, a sheet with a seam, two pillowcases and a towel; and to Alice Poppell a pewter dish and a kerchief.

Man's jacket and doublet. Woman's open gown and kirtle

Servants were not forgotten. John Franke (1558) left a heifer, a pair of sheets and a kirtle to his servant Alice and a heifer and two sheep to his servant Kathryn. John Franke, husbandman (1568), left a bushel of barley and a ewe lamb to John his man, a strike of barley to Miles his shepherd and a bushel of barley to Isabel his maid. After bequests of an animal to four servants Robert Hall (1580) gave his shepherd 6s.8d and 'the furthest land in Lamcote field sown with barley'. In 1583 Hugh Bushy, weaver, left 13s.4d to his servant Elizabeth Parker if she dwelt with his wife and served her until the day of her remarriage or death. Perhaps Alice Bushy died before 1598 as an Elizabeth Parker, servant to William Brodfield, received 20s in his will of that year.

The clothes which William Roulstone left Henry Burden in 1591 suggest he was a servant: 'the doublet I wear, old freize jerkin, hose and netherstocks I have on'.

There were bequests, too, to gentry who were employers or landlords, apart from those they received as executors or supervisors of wills. William Roulstone (1591) left to Mistress Rosell, wife of his landlord, 'the best ewe and lamb that Miles Cragge did keep of mine in his flock'. Edmund Wilkinson (1586) gave Mistress Hall 'my best pan but one', William Roulstone one wether sheep and one pewter platter and Joyce Roulstone one pewter platter and one chafing dish. His wife had one half of his 'poor and little goods'! Steven Palmer (1594) left Mistress Barbara Rosell a wether lamb.

Debts

A new element entered the Elizabethan wills. Unlike the early Tudor wills, 13 of the wills of this period referred to debts, usually owing to the testator, and these occurred at all levels of village society. A frequent way of dealing with them was to stipulate that the debtor paid over all or part of the debt to a beneficiary of the will. Richard Howlyn (1570), for example, willed that Thomas Dewsbury, who owed him 50s, gave to his daughter Jane, Richard's godchild, 26s.8d 'to her marriage', the rest of the debt being freely forgiven. William (Thrave alias) Longe owed him 50s, of which he was to give his four sons 6s.8d each, the rest freely forgiven. The role of Steven Palmer, a labourer (1594), as a probable money-lender has already been noted (p. 87). His debtors included Richard Champion of Cotgrave £4, Michael Richards 14s, John Pight 11s, Henry Watson 20s, Mr Lea 8s and the vicar George Cotes 43s.1d. Moreover, Mistress Cotes (probably the vicar's wife) owed him for 15 lbs of wool; she was to pay herself 11s for 'two shirts which I had of her and a yard of cloth, the rest I freely forgive'. The debts were to be paid to Steven's executor, his friend Robert Browne, who would then distribute some of the money.

The gentlemen of the parish also lent money, largely to their own kindred and to those of the same or higher status. Robert Hall stated in his will (1580) that his eldest son Henry should have £160 which William Ballard, Robert's brother-in-law owed, but specified how it was to be distributed. William Roulstone, Robert's son-in-law, was owed a considerable amount of money: £13 by his brother Francis, £4.18s.8d by his brother-in-law Richard Parker, £11 by his brother-in-law Henry Hall, £5.6s.8d by his cousin Edward Ballard and an unspecified amount by his brother Edward. Some of these debts were to be settled in favour of other beneficiaries and some were forgiven the debtor. As has been seen (p. 52), even John Rosell senior was among the debtors, as was his son. William Capendale, status unknown (1591), appointed his master Mr John Rosell to be overseer of his will and in return forgave him 'that which he oweth me', asking him to be good to his wife.

V Household Furnishings

Though little is known about houses in 16th century Radcliffe, something about their furnishings can be discovered from the bequests made in surviving wills. A comfortable bed was highly prized and in the early Tudor period widows left most in the way of bedding. When a married man made a will, the bed with sufficient linen customarily went to the widow. John Pare, however, specifically left a feather bed to his wife in 1570, perhaps to ensure the widow received it unless it was in addition to the marriage bed. Along with two pairs of linen and two pairs of harden sheets, a mattress and a quilt, Alice Morley also bequeathed a feather bed in 1549. Much thought went into the will which the widow Johan Taverey made two years later. She carefully apportioned her bedlinen between three daughters, leaving none to her only son. Each girl received a pair of linen sheets, a pair of harden sheets, a hempen sheet and a boardcloth. Alice and Agnes were given a bedcovering and two towels each, but Bride only one towel. Bride and Agnes, however, were also given a pillowbere each. Agnes may appear to have done best out of these arrangements, but whereas Alice received a mattress and Bride 7s to purchase one, she was given only 6s.8d to buy one. (She also received less in the way of animal bequests probably because she was the only one of the three to receive a heifer from her father in 1548.)

The Elizabethan period was a time of rapidly improving standards of living, especially in homes and their furnishings. Bedlinen appeared in more wills (14 out

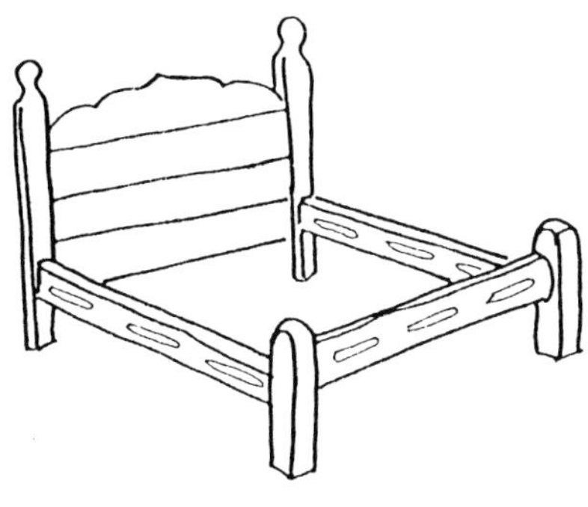

Tudor bedstock

of 35) and in greater quantities. The same materials were being used for sheets and in addition two pairs of corden, a pair of flaxen and one pair of 'midlinge' sheets were mentioned. Anne Wright in 1566 left a sheet with a seam, so perhaps it is safe to assume that most sheets were made in one piece. More pillowberes, a bolster with a covering and five feather beds (two from Robert Hall 1580) were among the bequests. A number of beds were also left, usually referred to as bedsteads or bedstocks. These terms give little idea of what they looked like, but they would have been free standing, usually with a post at each corner and laced with stout cords; on this base would be laid a thin rush mattress. Margaret Mylner (1589) left a trussle bed. Other signs of comfort appeared in Henry Pare's will (1569) where he bequeathed the hangings in the house (hall) and parlour. These could have been painted cloths hung on walls for decoration. Robert Hall (1580) left two cushions.

Dining and kitchen utensils were popular gifts in the early period, but only Richard Wright, the blacksmith (1521), left a silver spoon. Three people left pewter including six dishes bequeathed by Johan Taverey. Other bequests were a few brass pots or pans, a little skillet pan, a saucer, two pottingers (?porringers) and a spit. Many more silver spoons were bequeathed in the Elizabethan period than in early Tudor times: Robert Hall left 13, the widow Elizabeth Darrenton 12 and Richard Wright five. Robert Hall also bequeathed two silver bowls and one gilt goblet. Pewter, sometimes described as platter, chargers or as doublers, was left by five people and Richard Bayley, husbandman, left four 'tynen' spoons in 1561. Pots and pans, frequently with the prefix great or greatest, included Edmund Wilkinson's 'great kettle' and a chafing dish in 1586. An unusual bequest was that made by Nicholas Jervis (1568) of the irongates in the chimney. Equally unusual was the hair-cloth bequeathed by Robert Hall to his wife; this may have been a horse-hair cloth on which grain was laid to be dried in the malt kiln. Perhaps its ownership had been a bone of contention among the family.

The aumbries left by John Horne in 1517 and Richard Bayley two years later were the only pieces of furniture bequeathed in the early wills, but a number of the Elizabethans chose to give furniture as gifts. Anne Wright left a meat board with trestles and Nicholas Jervis 'the great chair at the board end' - a luxury item. William Greene the smith (1585) left a long table with its frame and two buffet stools. Three people left chests - two widows who perhaps kept their linen in them and Steven Palmer the labourer who acted as a money lender; he left two in 1594 perhaps to safeguard his coins. Coffers, however, which were usually wooden and covered with leather, were generally used for valuables and John Hempsall, the tailor, left one in his will of 1597. He also bequeathed three chests, an aumbry, a big table, a form and trestle and a little board.

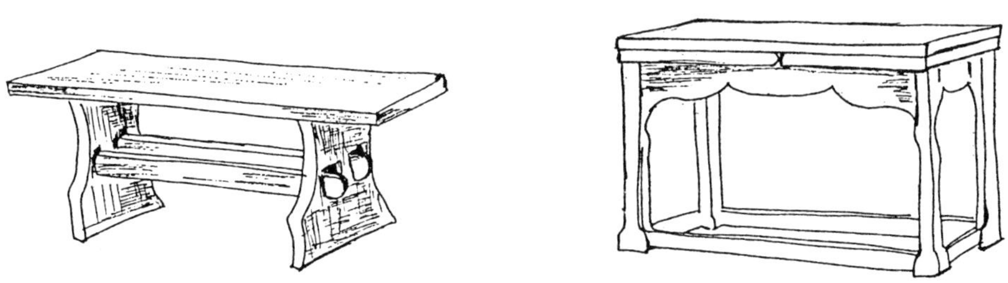

Sketches of two Tudor tables - boarded with trestle (left) and framed (right)

....from Nottingham to Belvoir all by champion ground in sight.

So wrote Leyland the great 16th century traveller in his *Itinerary* as he rode through the open, rolling countryside of the Trent Valley, unenclosed by hedges into small fields. The eastern half of Nottinghamshire was fielden country, showing some of the best examples of the classic common field system in which mixed husbandry flourished. The soils, mostly Mercian mudstone (Keuper marl), were suitable for the arable crops of barley (the main cereal), wheat, rye, oats, beans and peas, the latter often the largest crop of all. The farmers' lands were distributed across the open fields in strips according to changes made in earlier generations by exchange, sale or division. In rotation there were one or more corn fields, a peas field and a fallow field. The holder of a yardland in the open fields was entitled to common pasture in the permanent grazing land by the custom regulating the stint (the share). In this part of the world the stint could be for 30 sheep, two horses and 'a breeder', and three beasts and 'a breeder'. What constituted a yardland varied according to district and to the quality of the soil but it was usually about 20 acres in south Nottinghamshire. Evidence for Radcliffe can be gleaned mainly from Tudor wills and rentals.[141]

The open fields

There is a reference to the four open fields of Radcliffe in a rental of the manor of Woodhall dated 1545/6 when William Greene paid 12s.6d 'for an oxgang a croft and eight lands in four fields'. Using the names established by the time of the final enclosure of the Radcliffe and Lamcote fields in 1790, they were called Cliff Field stretching from the cliffs to the Syke drain, Breck Field across the drain, Stony Field on its southern edge stretching to the Cropwell Road, and Sunpit on the other

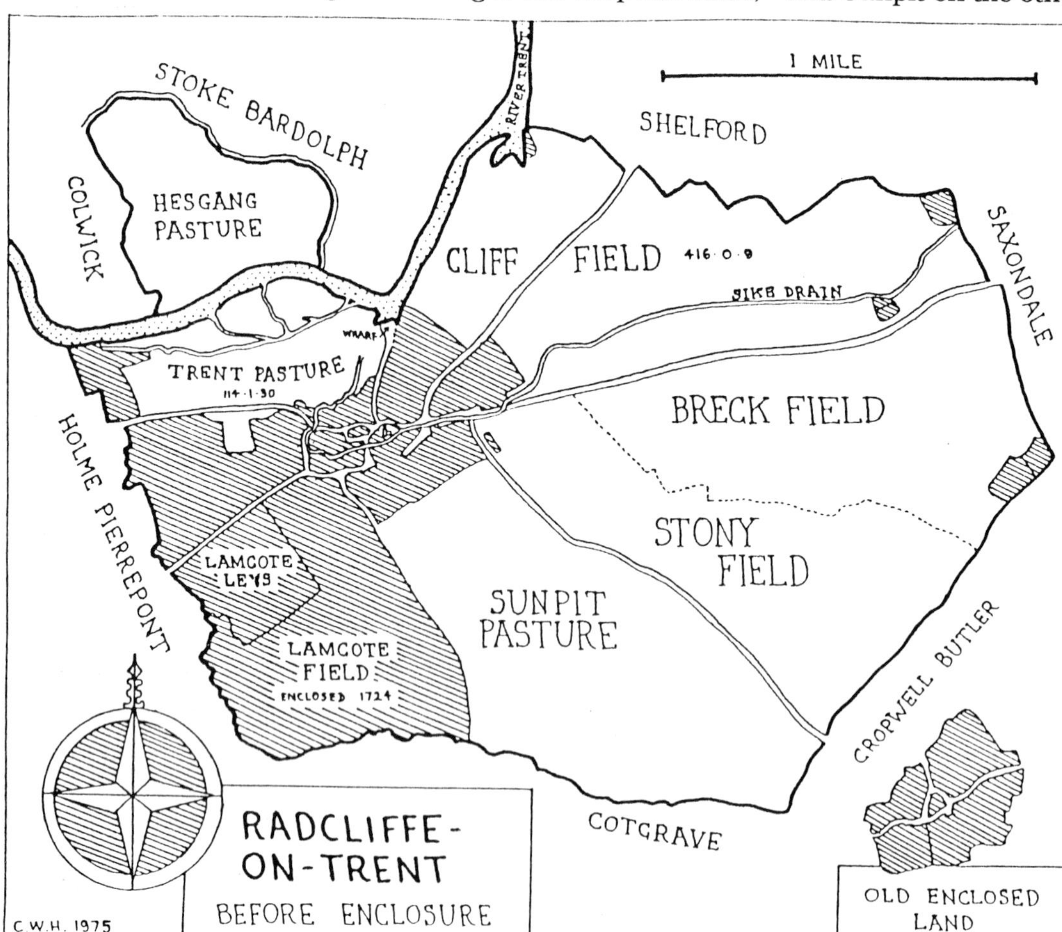

side of the road extending to the Lamcote fields. At some point Sunpit Field became known as Pasture, for it is so described by the late 17th century, implying that it had been taken out of the system of rotation to become permanent grazing. The older Trent and Hesgang pastures lay on either bank of the river in the low-lying flood plain where the Trent had changed its course at this meander over the years. The Trent Pasture on this, the Lamcote side, was coursed through by several streams and ditches draining into the river. This would have been a likely area for coppicing willow wands for basket and hurdle making and for gathering various reeds for roofing material. Evidence that flooding was troublesome during this period can be found in contemporary wills. (See p. 78.)

There were other pieces of pasture land within the three arable fields and these leys were ploughed up and cultivated again after one or more years' grazing - the more productive for the rest and the manuring. References to 'up and down husbandry', as it was called, became more common in the Midlands in 16th century documents. Among the tenants on the Woodhall rental was William Capendale, who 'holdeth two leys in Radcliffe' for 18d a year and 'for a ley in Lamcote [-] yearly 6d'. Usually the individual leys were scattered about the three fields and animals were tethered or folded whilst feeding on them to safeguard the field crop. Sometimes several farmers together left them untilled to become permanent pasture. The open fields usually had their adjoining meadowland fenced off from them with movable fences, locally called 'fleakes'. Robert Hall in his will of 1580 left half his fold fleakes to his wife with a hundred head of sheep. The meadows were compact blocks of land divided into doles or swathes between each farmer to give them crops of hay. Animals could also be pastured on whichever field was lying fallow for a year and on the meadowlands after haymaking until the Feast of Candlemas (2nd February) when they would be re-sown. Sheep could feed on the other fields on what they could find between the harvesting of the crops and their re-setting.

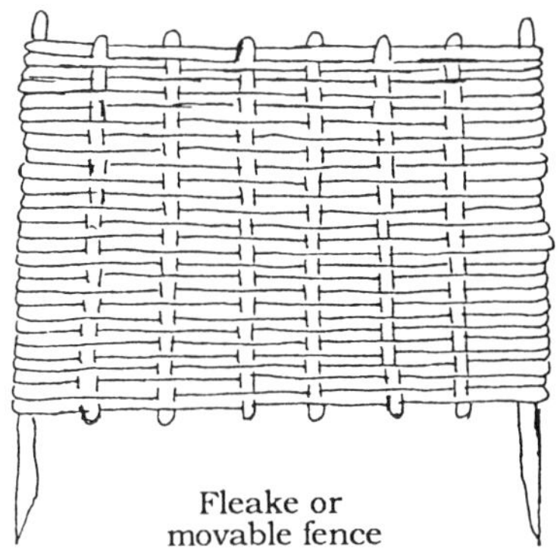

Fleake or movable fence

There are only two references in the wills which place the crops that were growing in any particular one of the open fields in Radcliffe or Lamcote. Robert Hall (1580) left his shepherd, Edward Coole, the 'furthest land in Lamcote field sown with barley'. William Roulstone, gentleman (1591), left to Thomas Walker and Edward Cowe 'a land of barley lying over Bingham gate furlong (in Cliff Field) betwixt Mr. Rosell's wong and the major [part of the field]'. Few measures of land were indicated. William Johnson (October 1516) itemised one acre, a separate half acre, and another half of wheat; Richard Wright in January 1558 bequeathed one acre of sown corn; widow Margaret Greene (July 1580) had among her bequests three acres of barley, two of wheat and three of peas.

The Woodhall rental

Rentals, such as that from Woodhall manor, provide information about the 16th century farmer, as the profits to be made from farming often depended on the type of lease the farmer held. Particularly vulnerable were the tenants-at-will, the terms and conditions of whose tenancies were at the discretion of the lord. They were usually occupiers of demesne land, part of the manor reserved for the use of the lord of the manor which he was no longer farming himself. This rental shows that in 1545/6 the absentee lords of this manor, the Greys, gathered over £10.15s a year from their tenants and that the 11 tenants-at-will brought in five times as much as the other 14 tenants. No copyholders were included; they would have held their lands on fixed rents and customary terms, protected by the manorial courts.

Rents were paid in two halves at Pentecost and on St Martin's Day (11th November). John Franke headed the list of tenants-at-will for he rented the manor 'place' itself and the demesne for £3.6s.8d; such a tenant frequently acted as bailiff for his master. Henry Pare paid 32s for a close and 2½ oxgangs of land. From the Greene family there were three tenants: William, Robert the blacksmith who rented his smithy with a cottage and an acre of land for 8s, and Richard occupying a house, a close and three oxgangs of land together with meadow for 33s. Echoes of medieval practice when rents were paid in kind can be found in Edward Ballard's rent for Burton yard, which was either two capons or 8d in money. The 6s that William Pople paid for his cottage and toft (a plot big enough to grow vegetables for domestic use) seems a large amount compared to these other rents. Some of the tenants, such as Isabell Cowper who paid 9s for an oxgang and meadow, rented only land. Thomas Smythe, the chantry priest, cultivated a garden for which he paid 12d. Woodhall Manor must also have included land near the river for Christopher Fisher, as already noted, appropriately paid 6s for his water (fishing) rights.

Other tenants in the rental were freeholders. Sir John Chaworth knight, Richard Samon esq and Symon Wodis, all non residents, held lands belonging to the manor which lay outside Radcliffe in Tithby, Burton Joyce and in the town of Nottingham. John Rosell whose family were soon to acquire the lordship was at this time just a tenant paying 2s.1d, a pound of cumin or 2d in money for lands in Radcliffe and 14d for lands in Lamcote. Five tenants sublet their lands - Edward Ballard to Robert Darwyn, Geoffrey Markham esq to Richard Todde and two priests Thomas Somer (of Thurgarton) and Thomas Smythe to William Sheppard and William Pare respectively. Another, William Fox, held land of Edward Ballard called Barrwithe 'in the narrow lane', now Water Lane near the church, for 2s.4 1/2d. (This was a passage into a field). No rent was for more than 6s.8d and the lowest was just 1d, charged to William Greene 'for the chief of his lands there'.[142]

Arable farming

Winter and spring corns were sown in the same great field. Spring corn, almost entirely barley, was due to be sown by Lady Day (25th March) and the whole area was called the Corn or, more usually, the Barley Field. The barley plots were spread with dung during April or May.

Winter corn, both wheat and rye, could be sown together in a mixture known as maslin (referred to in a will of 1580), and were sown by hand in September on freshly harrowed ground which would then be harrowed again. The field sown was the one prepared by lying fallow the previous year, which would have been ploughed over three times during that year turning in the dung of pastured animals. Sheep were often turned onto the rye in the spring to eat the shoots down and manure the strengthened crop.

Barley was the largest grain crop and as a less greedy feeder on the common field was very much the 'countryman's tillage'. Its chief uses were for bread making, malting and stock feed. Twenty-three Radcliffe wills of the Tudor period have barley by the acre, quarter, bushel, strike and peck, and malt by the quarter, bushel and strike. (A peck was two gallons, a bushel four pecks, and a quarter eight bushels.) There was a pair of malt querns (small grindstones) disposed of in the will of Richard Bayley (1519) who also made two gifts of a strike of malt. Thomas Dewsbury (1592) left malting equipment which included a powdering trough, querns and pails.

Tusser's *Five Hundred Points of Good Husbandry*, a contemporary work among several that were written to help the development of farming in the 16th century, states:

Peason and barley delight not in sand
But rather in clay or in rottener land

which suggests why barley and peas did well locally and that wheat and rye would have been sown where the fields drained well, on the hill slopes above Radcliffe village, away from the river.

There were several sorts of peas - white, green grey, black and innumerable local varieties. Seven of the wills simply disposed of 'peas'! In July 1580 Margaret Greene left separately three acres of peas which would be still growing in that month, but were the two separate acres of peas of William Johnson in 1516 still in the fields in October when his will was made? (He also bequeathed barley, wheat and rye in acreages besides quarters of malt, ten bushels of barley, and strikes of rye and peas.) The September will of Robert Dewsbury (1521) left three gifts of peas - a bushel and two quarters. The other four wills, with strikes and pecks of peas among their bequests, were all made in November. A specific reference to storage was made in one of them, that of Robert Hall (1580) with 'a hovel of new peas'. This meant that

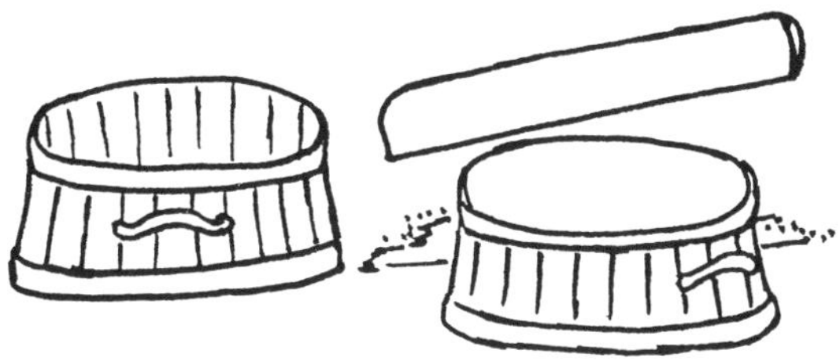

Stored peas were levelled in their containers by the bar' 'struck across the top - hence the use of the term 'strike'

the peas were stored hanging on frames, still drying, as they would not keep if closely packed. After poor grain harvests the authorities tried to discourage the storage of peas and beans for animal fodder. An Act of Privy Council, dated 6th November 1586, enjoined farmers of seven counties including Nottinghamshire to 'bring peas to markets' and prohibited them from feeding the same to sheep.

Although beans were not a named crop in these wills they may well have been set mixed with the peas. Peas and beans were sown broadcast and then ploughed or harrowed into the peas field which was the one that had borne the cereal crop the year before. Sown in January and February the work fell between the sowings of the winter and spring corn. The commonest beans at this time were small horse beans made into little ricks after reaping or mowing and, like peas, used to feed livestock and, in lean years, humans. There was also a domestic variety for sowing, with a dibber, in gardens.

Hemp would have been grown by many farmers, though not mentioned in any of the wills except as yarn or made-up into sheets. William Johnson in 1516 left two gifts of a stone of hemp - one to the church to make bellstrings. There is a reference, probably Elizabethan in date, to three hempyards bounding upon a yard and two houses in Lamcote, and there would certainly have been many more.[143]

Livestock

Breeding horses and geldings was a good proposition in arable areas close to towns. They were likely to have been bred in Tudor Radcliffe for village use and possibly to take to the horse fairs at Nottingham or Southwell. The typical workaday horse was able to pull a small cart, to be ridden or to carry a pack. Horses had gradually become more common for draught use from 1530 onwards and from that date more were actually mentioned in the village wills. Among others Richard Wright (1538) left a filly and a colt, John Fuldiam (1551) a one year old bay foal and Nicholas Jervis (1568) a bald foal. ('Bald' intimated a white streak on the face of horses or cattle.) Later in the period Edmund Franke (1586) had a black sorrelled colt (a young black and bright chestnut piebald horse) and Robert Parr (1595) a red filly, bay mare and bay colt.

These testators were mostly husbandmen. The gentry obviously kept superior horses. Robert Hall, gentleman, left a black gelding, another gelded horse and 'an elder stoned colt', a white filly, his elder mare, a bay nag and a 'little ambling mare'. This last animal would go at an easy pace, lifting two feet on one side together and then those on the other side. All these horses were passed on to his wife living on their Radcliffe estate.

Parishes such as Radcliffe on the banks of the Trent probably fattened more cattle in their meadows than did those in other fielden districts of east Nottinghamshire. Some farmers in this region kept 40 to 80 beasts, but none of the early Radcliffe wills give any indication of such large herd numbers. The animals described in the wills suggest a mixture of local cattle and cross breeds, not herds of particular breeds as on individual farms today. The will of Robert Hall, gentleman (November 1580), whose holdings in Radcliffe were part of a more widespread estate, was the richest. The animals he bequeathed included four oxen, two bullocks, ten kine and four heifers besides the several horses already described. There were greater numbers of cattle and sheep mentioned in this will than in any other until that of husbandman Robert Parr who left a similar number of oxen and kine in March 1595.

Just as many men kept an all-duty horse, so each household usually had a cow or two to give milk for butter and cheese. It was the practice to use cows that were not needed for producing calves or milk as draught animals. They laboured for some ten years before being fattened up for sale on hay, beans and peas and barley mash and were then butchered between July and September. The younger animals and the breeding stock were usually overwintered, not slaughtered, as there was seldom a shortage of fodder.

The affection in which these farming folk held the animals they tended breaks through in a number of formal documents. Many animals were specified according to age or condition and by their colour. Richard Bayley (1561) left four kine which he described - a red, a white backed, a black with a sterne (star) and a young black - and William Greene of Lamcote (1585) gave two heifer calves and a red and a bald heifer. Most touching of all in the will of William Aynesley (1578) were cows with names! He left Primrose and Cherry and a heifer called Brownie to be the shared responsibility of his son and daughters.

There is no indication that any particular breed of sheep was farmed in Radcliffe or Lamcote. Sheep were carefully tended through all stages of their growth. After the lambing season in early spring, the ewes and lambs were moved from the meadows to the rough stubble of the common fields. Shearing took place in the middle of June and the flock was culled at Michaelmas, only fattened animals being slaughtered except when the hay crop had failed. In winter the grass in the fields was supplemented with feed of hay and straw, dried beans and peas and with mashes of barley, beans or acorns. In spring the sheep were put out to graze on any tares grown or to nibble down the shooting wheat and rye. Ewes in lamb might also be fed on oats or peas. Four or five year old wethers, bound for the butcher, were taken to markets between December and May.

In open field areas such as Radcliffe the sheep were put into a common flock under the supervision of a village shepherd; in Elizabethan Radcliffe this was probably Miles Cragge. He would oversee the folding of the sheep between hurdles at night and the moving of their pens each day from one part of the field to another. It took many sheep to dung a part of the common field each night and the whole field needed to be manured before sowing. This could only be done on dry land, because of foot rot, so was often possible only from May to September. Sheep's dung was considered to be the best manure though all kinds were used including highly prized pigeon dung from the dovecotes. It was recognized that the better fed the animal the richer was the dung.

Testators were most particular about the age and condition of the sheep to be passed on to various family members and friends. A sheep or ewe hog described a young animal above a lamb in size (before its first shearing), but it is uncertain whether other bequests of hogs really meant swine, (animals under a year old, castrated and being fattened) or sheep. William Johnson (1516) made eight gifts of a ewe and a lamb and, as already seen, such bequests or sometimes a wether ram were favourite items to give to grandchildren, nephews and nieces, or godchildren throughout the century.

Several wills itemise small bequests of sheep. Richard Bayley (September 1519) bequeathed two sets of a ewe and a lamb, another two of a ewe and a lamb which were to be 'neither the youngest nor the eldest' from his sheep and 28 'workable taggs'. ('Taggs' or 'tegs' were sheep in their first winter.) Alice Morley left a number of sheep including three 'ewes great with lamb' in June 1549. Widow Johan Taverey (1551) made 16 gifts of a sheep and John Franke (1559) made 23. It is usually difficult to assess the size of an individual's flocks but two wills indicate larger numbers. On Robert Hall's farm in 1580 was a flock of 100 sheep and in March 1595 Robert Parr bequeathed three sets of ewes and lambs, ten individual wether hogs (castrated rams), 20 ewe hogs and 60 ewes with suckling lambs.

Very few pigs were mentioned in these early wills but this does not necessarily mean that few were kept, rather that they were of relatively little monetary value, so not much of a gift! This is perhaps borne out by the stipulation in the will of husbandman Richard Bayley in December 1561 of a *good* hog among other gifts of hogs and of three gifts, each of a *fat* hog, from the estate of Robert Hall, gentleman, in November 1580. Pig keeping had long been the peasants' standby when enough kitchen waste could be found. Renowned as 'the husbandman's best scavenger, the housewife's most wholesome sink' their flesh kept better than any other meat. However, pigs were less common in the cottage gardens of Tudor times than they became after the introduction of potatoes. Remembering that 'sheep hogs' confuse matters, there were only six swine hogs mentioned in the 16th century wills.

Little poultry was mentioned in these wills, even in those of women, but all but the poorest would have kept a few hens and chickens and sometimes ducks to be fed on any available grains. Included under 'all my household stuff unbequeathed' passed on to his wife Elizabeth by Robert Hall were the pigs and poultry, 'swine and pullen'. More hives of bees must have been kept than were mentioned. Edmund Lodge the vicar in 1521 left three beneficiaries a swarm of bees apiece and no other farm stock. Weaver Hugh Bushy in February 1582 left a swarm and a hive of bees standing next to 'Groc[oc]ke yard', his only livestock other than 'one lamb to be delivered at weaning time'. Three further hives of bees were bequeathed by John Greene in April 1594 and he too would seem to have kept only sheep besides. Robert Hall included amongst his many bequests two gifts of a hive of bees. Honey being the chief way of sweetening food on Tudor tables and the equipment being cheap, there would have been beehives everywhere, in this area made of long rye straw.[144]

Two types of Tudor beehive
woven (above)
thatched (below)

Farm equipment and buildings

References to ploughs and their equipment occur in six early wills. During Henry VIII's reign William Johnson (1516), Richard Bayley (1519) and William Dewsbury (1521) all left 'a plough with a culture and a share'. (A culture or coulter was the iron blade fixed in front of the ploughshare.) John Pare's will (1570) includes a plough and harrows. Many others mention draught beasts, both oxen and horses, showing that Radcliffe had areas of heavy and lighter soils. Richard Bayley (1519) bequeathed four 'work-worthy bullocks' and Robert Parr (1595) a 'yoke of oxen' (a pair). There are several references to yokes for coupling draught animals but it is not usually possible to tell if these were used to draw ploughs, harrows or carts. The wain left by William Dewsbury (August 1521) was bequeathed with the two oxen which drew it and their yoke and teams (chains). In 1561 Richard Bayley, husbandman, left 'a grey mare with a yoke and gear'. Whenever the term 'gear' was used it indicated all the equipment needed for the particular task involved.

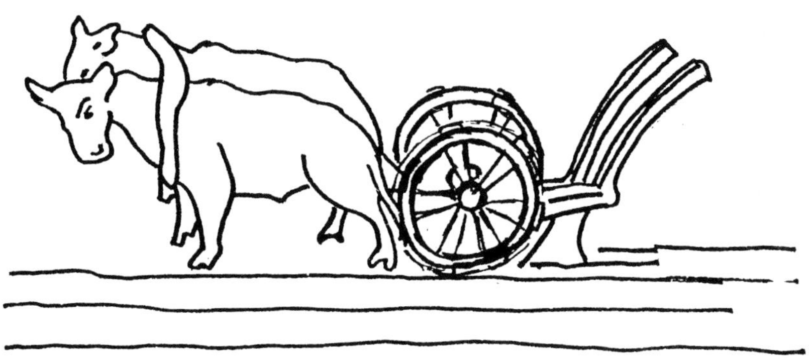

Oxen yoked to a plough based on a contemporary drawing

In the early Tudor period the better-off yeomen may be identified by their having more than one farm wagon and especially bound wagons. William Johnson (1516) left a 'wain unshod and an unshod cart'. ('Unshod' describes bare wooden wheels as opposed to iron-bound wheels.) It took six beasts to draw the 'best wain' left by Richard Bayley (1519) and at least one other was indicated. Robert Dewsbury, husbandman (September 1521), left an iron-bound cart, another with its gears and a pair of old bound wheels. From 1558 farming fortunes were improving and such equipment is much more commonly found. In June 1570 John Pare, yeoman, left a wain, ploughs, harrows, yokes and teams so his holding in the great fields must have been considerable, and since there were 'pales and wood in the yard', a farmhouse and outbuildings are indicated. Margaret Greene's will (July 1580) made reference to 'the farm' and this too was equipped with a substantial iron-bound wheeled wain and had been worked by 'great oxen' in yokes and teams (the requisite chains and leather harness). Robert Hall, gentleman, included an iron-bound wain with all the equipment needed to harness it to horses among his bequests in November 1580.

There are some interesting outbuildings mentioned on the premises of John Hempsall, the tailor, for even the craftsmen were also farmers if only in a small way. His will (September 1597) refers to stables, hovel, cowhouse, swine cote and well-frame. Animals housed here included 'my cow that is with calf' and a heifer.

At harvest time wheat and rye were reaped with sickle or hook and the barley, like the hay earlier, was mown with a scythe. No small tools such as these were mentioned in any of the wills although it is likely that each man had his own, fashioned by the blacksmith and put in good order beside the winter hearth to be ready at harvest time. Workmen's tools, however, were described by four labourers from Radcliffe in a court hearing over Sir Thomas Stanhope's disputed weir on 27th December 1593 (see p. 60). Edward Towle had a 'hatchet', Robert Towle and Robert Close each had 'a shovel, a hatchet and a pick' and George Place owned to a 'spade, a pick and sometimes a hatchet'. In addition John Cheater (it is not known where he came from) 'had there with him his usual working tools viz: a shovel, a headying bill, a hatchet and a hack'.[145]

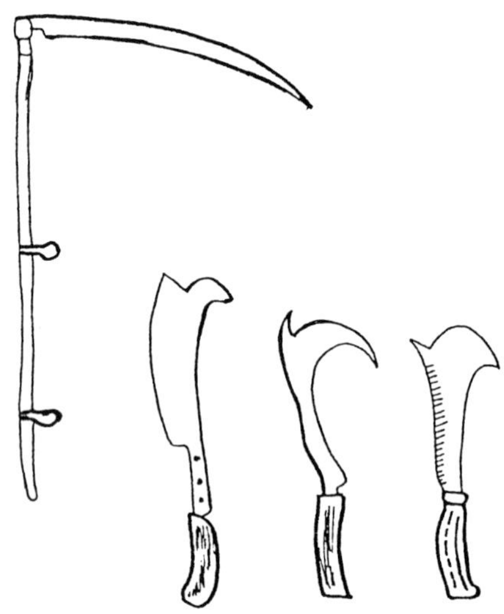

Tudor scythe and bill hooks

Harvest failures

Radcliffe was little affected by early enclosure from arable to pasture (see p. 27), which created heated debate in the 16th century, but it could not have escaped the hardships caused by inflation in the 1540s and harvest failures in 1545 and 1549-1551. Another run of bad harvests in the 1590s, which eventually halted the conversion of grain land to pasture, led to near famine. So little wheat had been grown between the years 1558-88 that pure wheaten flour was afforded by only the wealthy. Barley and rye breads were the staple fare on the boards of most yeoman and humbler households.

Something of these tribulations would seem to have touched Radcliffe. Even allowing for the effect of the Reformation on reducing the bequests of crops to the church, the 13 wills spanning the years 1549-1561 show a marked decline in the number and value of separate bequests of crops, (although there were no wills in 1545 and 1550, the poor harvest years of Edward VI's reign). In 1549 widow Alice Morley, who was wealthy enough to leave an iron-bound cart, over 50 sheep and at least one year-old calf, had no crops to bequeath separately. There were two wills made in 1551. Widow Johan Taverey in June had a wain, plough and draught, 16 sheep and five cattle to divide between her son and four daughters, but again no mention of any crops. John Fuldiam in July made bequests of sheep and a year-old bay foal, but just three strikes of malt.

There was a small recovery indicated by the bequests of crops made in years 1566 to 1599. Nearly all the 20 wills from the 1580s and 90s still contained far more of value in gifts of animals than of crops, sown or stored, and this situation continued well into the 17th century. Even Robert Hall's will of November 1580 mentioned very small quantities of grain and peas compared with the number and value of the animals he bequeathed. This may indicate that at this time crops were far too precious to be left as separate gifts away from the main beneficiary.[146]

Case study 7

THE JORDANS - recusancy and 'murder'

Richard Jordan's will

The Jordan family only features in village records for about 15 years, but they were years of incident, including charges of recusancy and murder. The family must have been the subject of much gossip and speculation among the neighbours. They first appear in the will made by Richard Jordan, yeoman, on 4th January 1599 which shows that he leased a farm in Radcliffe, the lease still having some years to run. This he bequeathed to his wife Katherine unless she remarried, in which case she was to share it with his elder son James, who would inherit it anyway after her death. Another son Thomas and a daughter Susan were to receive £20 each - Susan when she turned 20 and Thomas three years after his father's death. A year after Thomas received his £20, James was to have the same sum. In addition Susan was to have a feather bed and its accoutrements and Thomas a black colt, and they were to have £5 each from James after their mother died.

There was nothing remarkable about these legacies, but when Richard Jordan died about July 1601 he was a worried man, for this was a Roman Catholic family. Although the short preamble at the beginning of his will was couched in orthodox Protestant terms and gave no hint of his recusancy, there were other clauses which did. He showed that he had connections with the Markhams of Ollerton and Kirby Bellers in Leicestershire.

Kirby Bellers, the Markhams' house where Thomas Jordan was living in January 1599

From a letter in the Salisbury papers it is clear that he was serving Thomas Markham in the 1590s. Mr Thomas Markham, the head of the family, had children who converted to Catholicism during the last decade of the 16th century and he and his wife were also under suspicion. In his will Richard Jordan stipulated that Thomas's £20 should be paid to Mr Thomas Markham of Kirby 'desiring him that he will take care of it for him and dispose of it for his best commodity as shall seem best to his wisdom'. He also asked that Thomas's black colt should be delivered to him 'my said master to my said son's use'. It looks as if the younger Jordan son was under age and living in the household at Kirby Bellers at the time that his father made his will.

Richard went on to choose as overseers 'my young masters' Mr George Markham and Mr Phillip Vincent of Wilford. George Markham, Thomas's younger son, was a declared Catholic and would shortly inherit his father's estate because both his older brothers were in exile. Mr Vincent remains a mysterious figure; he would certainly have been a Catholic and, because Wilford is situated near to Clifton, perhaps connected with the recusant Lady Clifton, wife of Sir Gervase. He was also one of the two witnesses and probably the scribe, writing the will in a clear, literate hand. Richard desired the two overseers 'for god's cause to guide and assist my said wife and children'. The other witness was John Richmond, making his mark in a small nervous hand. He was perhaps a servant, the only person other than the Jordans who may have come from Radcliffe.

There is another link between the Markhams and the Jordans which may explain how the latter came to Radcliffe in the first place. Sir Henry Pierrepont had married Frances Cavendish (another Catholic gentlewoman), the eldest daughter of Bess of Hardwick and Sir William Cavendish. In 1592 a correspondent of the Earl of Shrewsbury, Bess of Hardwick's stepson, wrote that Mr Thomas Markham's wife Mary was 'chief companion to the young Countess when in Nottinghamshire'. The Pierreponts owned land in Radcliffe and Lamcote and the influence of Mrs Mary Markham could well have helped the Jordans obtain the lease of the farm mentioned in the will. It was exactly in this manner that Catholics would cluster around great houses where they might from time to time have heard mass in safety.[147]

Persecution

Richard's fears were justified. Since 1581 Catholics had been oppressed with

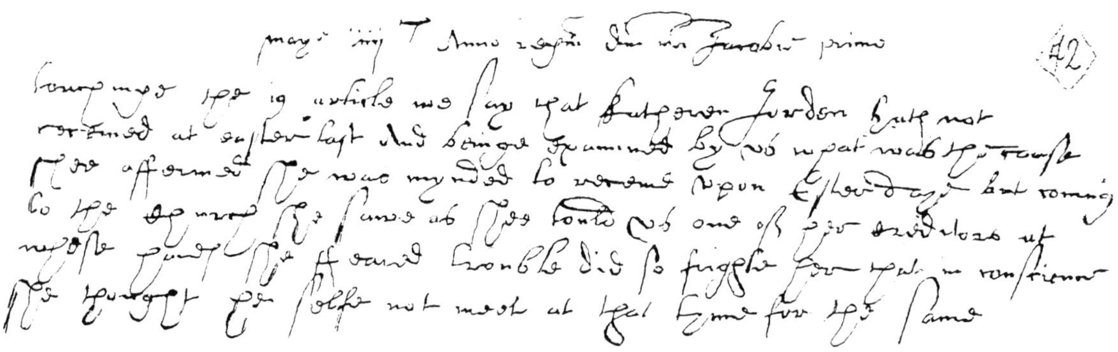

May iiij Anno regni Dni nri Jacobi primo 42
Concerning the which we say that Katherine Jordan hath not received at Easter last And being examined by us what was the cause she affirmed she was minded to receive upon Easter day but coming to the church she saw as she told us one of her creditors at whose hands she feared trouble did so fright her that in conscience she thought her self not meet at that time for the same

Katherine Jordan's excuse for not attending Easter communion as reported by the Radcliffe churchwardens
(U of N Manuscripts Department PB 293/6 f.42)

heavy fines - as much as £20 a month for not attending their parish church - and from 1593 they were supposed to remain within five miles of their domicile. Richard had already been presented by the Radcliffe churchwardens to the Archdeacon's Court in April 1598, for not having received communion at Michaelmas, Christmas, and Easter. After his death in 1601, his widow Katherine continued the family's Catholic stance and was reported for not receiving holy communion at Easter by the churchwardens in April 1602. In May 1603 they reported her again, along with two other men, for the same offence. This time they were given an ingenious excuse for her non-attendance:

> *...And being examined by us what was the cause she affirmed she was minded to receive upon Easter day, but coming to the church she saw, as she told us, one of her creditors at whose hands she feared trouble. [This] did so fright her that in conscience she thought her self not meet at that time for the same.*

Unconvinced by this, the churchwardens presented her again before the Archdeacon's Court in July. On 4th April 1605 she was yet again presented. The church court absolved her, ordering her to frequent the church at once, but as she had persistently refused to attend she was also brought before the magistrates at Quarter Sessions ten days later. Her punishment is not recorded, and this seems to have been her last court appearance. Perhaps she died soon afterwards.

Susan, the daughter, is not heard of again after her father's death, but her yeoman brother Thomas, Richard's younger son, openly continued to carry the Catholic banner in a period when anti-Catholic feeling ran high. (Although there had been some respite from persecution at the beginning of James I's reign, harsher legislation was enforced after the Gunpowder Plot of 1605.) Like his mother, Thomas found himself before the civil magistrates for his constant absence from church. He was listed with Catholic recusants from a number of places in April and July 1607, and again in the October, this time with the wife of William Wood of Radcliffe. In between these two court summonses, however, he was charged with murdering one Michael Eyre.[148]

Thomas Jordan's murder case

The incident took place on 10th September 1607 in Radcliffe, possibly whilst the men were working on the harvest. Two days later an inquest was held in the village by the coroner James Leek, gentleman, with the assistance of a jury of local men: five each from Cotgrave and Bassingfield, four from Cropwell Butler, three from Shelford, but none from Radcliffe. The dead man was identified and the course of events investigated. The jury was told how Thomas Jordan, leaping on Michael Eyre 'did strike and thrust' at his left side with a two-pronged pitchfork (valued at 2d), piercing him and inflicting a mortal wound 4 inches in breadth. Thomas was imprisoned to await his trial at the Assizes.

Despite this, he was also summoned to appear before the archdeaconry court for non-attendance at church in December 1607, and again in the following March. Although the court claimed fees which had to be paid a week later, the officials absolved him for his religious lapse, presumably recognising that he had hardly been in a position to attend church in recent months!

The Assize Court assembled on 11th March 1608 under the jurisdiction of two justices of the King's Bench. The next stage in the proceedings was known as 'Gaol Delivery'. A grand jury formed by the sheriff and his bailiffs from among local freeholders examined the calendar or list of prisoners to decide in each case whether a 'true bill' was found and the accused should be tried before the judges and another (the petty) jury. By this point some prisoners would already have succumbed to the harsh conditions of a 17th century gaol, but Thomas was young and able to attend the court in person. For this occasion he called himself 'gentleman', perhaps hoping it would help his cause and pleaded that he had acted out of self-defence, to avoid his own death and without any premeditated malice. The court heard the evidence of the coroner but they accepted Thomas's plea and he was discharged, the outcome of the Gaol Delivery being registered at Westminster. The cause of the quarrel was not revealed but there is a more than even chance that the young man was provoked to violence by taunts about his recusancy. The case illustrates very well the extent to which local people were involved in judicial proceedings and suggests that ill feeling against Catholics was not so strong that it was allowed to interfere with justice.[149]

The end of the Jordans in Radcliffe

Thomas was back in the archdeaconry court in May 1610 for not receiving Easter communion, and his last court appearance seems to have been on 11th July 1612 when he was excommunicated. His brother James, so far without a blemish recorded to his name, was accused by the same court of sexual incontinence in December 1613. Perhaps the lease of the Jordan farm ran out about this time, while the constant irritation of fines or court appearances caused them and other Catholics to conform or to move away, for in May 1614 the churchwardens could report that there were no recusants in Radcliffe.

If the Jordans stayed in Nottinghamshire, they probably took shelter with their former patrons, the Markhams. Lists of recusants recorded at Quarter Sessions show a Jacob (James) Jordan living at Ollerton in 1629 where the Markhams continued to profess their Catholicism defiantly. Throughout the years leading up to the Civil War George Markham, his wife, mother, son Thomas, and the latter's wife were all charged with recusancy. Nevertheless, George signed the Protestation in 1642 which condemned the apparently pro-Catholic policies of Charles I's government. 'Recusant' was written by his name. By this time Jacob Jordan had disappeared from Ollerton. As for Thomas, what more likely than that a young man with his past record should decide to seek his fortune abroad? Among those who arrived on the ship *Diana* at Jamestown, Virginia, some time before 1624 was a certain Thomas Jordan.[150]

Despite the social and economic progress the Rosells had made in the 16th century, by the start of the Stuart period in 1603 their position was by no means secure. The family was numerically outgrowing the estates on which they depended, and John Rosell junior, instead of enjoying the total inheritance of an eldest son, had been left in reduced circumstances by the generous terms granted to his relatives. Sales of lands to the Pierreponts, and the increasing power in Radcliffe of the Stanhopes had also affected the family's status in the village. Fortunately, although the early 17th century was a particularly vulnerable period for the Rosells, their two powerful neighbours were entering on less expansionist phases locally.

Sir Thomas Stanhope had died in 1596 (some three years after the river dispute) in the midst of an expensive building programme at his Shelford house. He had also left a rapacious widow, Dame Margaret, whose financial actions were challenged by his family until at least 1613. In 1606, his grandson Philip, then living at Bretby in Derbyshire, needed to raise money on the strength of a number of his lands, including the rectory and parsonage of Radcliffe, and the Radcliffe manor which had been acquired from the Molyneux family. He did this through a so-called 'perpetual lease', defined as 600 years in this case, to three landowners (Ralph Sneyd of Bradwell in Staffordshire, William Cooper of Thurgarton and Thomas Wright of Snellaston in Derbyshire) for an unspecified 'competent sum of money'. As acknowledgement that Sir Philip retained ownership of these lands, the three tenants had

> *to pay yearly on the feast day of St John Baptist one red rose flower if the same be lawfully demanded at the manor house of Bingham...*

A decade later his fortunes had sufficiently revived for him to find allegedly £10,000 to pay for his elevation as Baron Stanhope. (He became Earl of Chesterfield in 1628). Such expenditure must, however, have restricted the Stanhope family's activities in other directions.

The Pierreponts were led by Sir Henry until 1615. His son Robert, who rivalled the Stanhopes in the peerage stakes by being created Earl of Kingston-upon-Hull in 1628, was more concerned with the state of his health than with further aggrandisement in the village. The Rosells could therefore cope with their own problems relatively undisturbed.[151]

George Rosell's responsibilities

John junior died on 19th November 1606 aged about 48. His elder son, George, would then be about 26 years of age. In his will, John junior had recognised that there might be problems between mother and son over the dwindling inheritance. (During her lifetime Mary would be allowed the estates which she and John had jointly inherited under John senior's terms.) While leaving his wife a third of his goods, her 'widow bed' and two of the best cattle in the yard, he begged her to be 'good and favourable' to George by yielding up to him as much of her jointure as she could spare. Her sacrifice would allow

> *George thereby the better and sooner able to relieve his own estate, and in reasonable time be a stay and second father to all my children, which being performed by love I rest at quiet in my poor soul and conscience and think myself a very happy man.*

Along with the reduced legacy of lands and unbequeathed goods, therefore, John had left his son a heavy moral burden. This he emphasised by making him the executor of the will 'not doubting in my conscience but that he will perform the brotherly and secondly fatherly care of his poor brother and sisters (of whom I commit the tuition and government unto him the said George) in convenient and reasonable sort as God shall make him able'.

Poor George. Such responsibilities must have weighed heavily on a young man in his twenties. Elizabeth, Gertrude, Mary, Dorothy, Jane and Nicholas had all to be

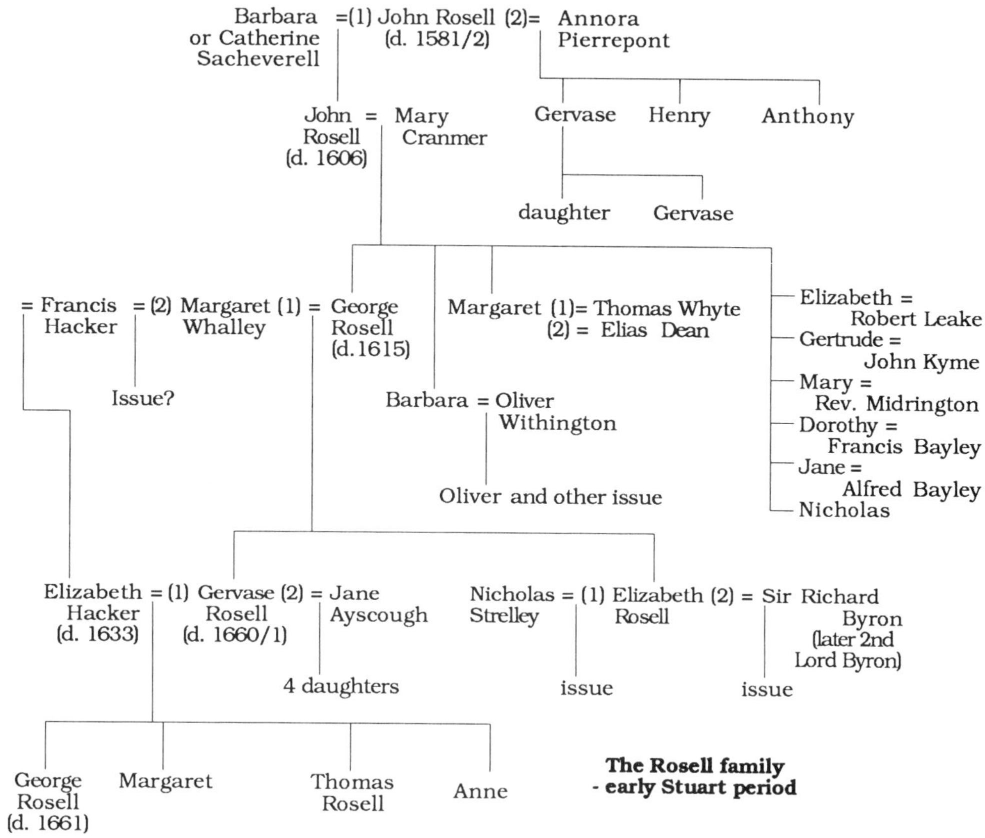

The Rosell family - early Stuart period

provided for. Moreover, George himself was already married when his father died. In July 1605 Margaret Whalley of Cotgrave had become his wife, and there were at least two children - Elizabeth and Gervase - to add to the bustling household.

Mercifully, another two of his sisters were already married. Barbara and her husband, Oliver Withington of Oxton in Nottinghamshire, whom she had married by licence in 1599, were merely left ten shillings each for (mourning) rings in John junior's will. Silver spoons were to go to each of their children. Sister Margaret had gone to London and a licence for her to marry Thomas Whyte, a London salter, was taken out for 1st May 1602. Either the marriage had never taken place or Margaret had been quickly widowed, for she was the wife of Elias Dean when her father drew up his will. Like the Withingtons, the Deans were each left 10s for mourning rings. Both sisters had thereby received their 'filial' portions, except in Margaret's case George was also to pay her some sums of money on the death of their father, which he had 'given his word for at London already'.[152]

The remaining terms of John Rosell's will confirm his concern for his relations, tenants and servants. His brother Gervase had already been generously treated with the chantry lands, and was now forgiven debts of £16 and £4 which John had paid on his behalf to a Mr Riggs and Mr Robert Cranmer respectively. Gervase's daughter was John's goddaughter, and he left her a silver spoon. Her brother, another Gervase, was left 2s.6d. Anthony Rosell, John's half brother, was remembered with particular affection. (He was to die at Adbolton in 1616. The Holme Pierrepont churchwardens were paid 5s by his wife Anne for his burial in the church there, and a year later she was to join him.) Described as 'kind and loving', he was left John's rapier and dagger, as well as five marks (£3.6s.8d) for a nag. George was specifically instructed 'to make good account of him and to trust him for an honest and just man'. The omission of such remarks about Gervase is striking. A kinswoman, Elizabeth Rosell, was remembered with 2s.[153]

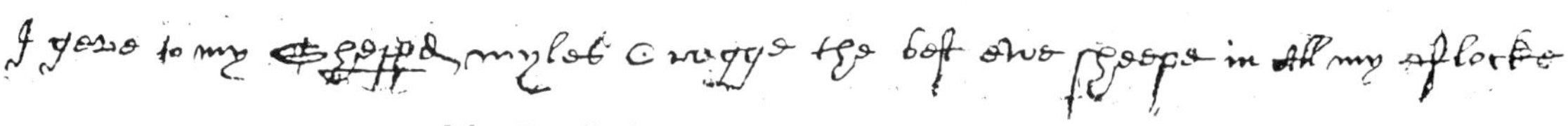

John Rosell's bequest to his shepherd (NAO PRNW)

George was urged 'according to his own ability to be good to all my tenants'. In particular he was to make much of Miles Cragge, the shepherd, who was to have the best ewe in the whole flock, and be 'very well dealt with' when his lease expired. Roger Campion (the parish clerk) was to have 2s.6d and a 21-years' lease of the house and yard, but not the orchard, occupied by Richard Hardy. John Tonge and his wife were to be provided for 'according to the speeches delivered both before the will and after' - John was left 2s.6d, his wife 2s. In addition, every servant in John Rosell's employment when he died was to receive 12d.

As executor, George had to see that all these terms were carried out, but two supervisors were also appointed - his uncle Anthony Rosell, and Sir Henry Pierrepont, his father's 'most kind and loving friend', prestigious kinsman, and the new owner of some of the Rosell estates. Sir Henry was left 10s for his pains. Both supervisors, along with Robert Pierrepont (Sir Henry's son) and Thomas Gamble from the village, witnessed the will.

A short-lived squire

George's own inheritance in the will is merely identified by John Rosell junior as 'All the rest of my goods, cattles and chattels whatsoever unbequeathed', debts, legacies and funeral expenses excepted. The estates were initially in a depleted condition, with both his step-grandmother, Annora, and his mother having claims on the use of them. (Anne Ballard, too, retained control of Rosell property in Lamcote and Radcliffe until her death in 1626. See p. 53.) His mother seems to have followed her husband's request about relinquishing her rights to her son. Although she outlived him, the estates were in his name in the Inquisition after his death. This suggests that Annora must have died by this date too. George, therefore, managed to keep the inheritance intact, and even regained the use of much that had been inaccessible. Confirmation that he was indeed worth more than his father comes from the subsidy assessments. John junior had been assessed on income from lands, beginning at £6 (1592/3) and was reduced to £5 (from 1596/7). In 1606 George was assessed at £10, a marked increase, even allowing for inflation, and was nominally back on the same income as his grandfather.[154]

Perhaps he inherited something of his grandfather's touchiness, for in January 1610 he found himself in the embarrassing situation of being before the Quarter Sessions magistrates, one of whom was his aging kinsman, Sir Henry Pierrepont. He had been in dispute with a Michael Jennings, and was ordered to keep the peace, particularly towards the latter. He had to find £10 on his own recognizances, and George Barratt of Thoroton and Thomas Hall of Costock (grandson of Robert who died in 1580) stood surety for him to the tune of £5 each.[155]

Nevertheless, he and his immediate family seem to have been sufficiently well-liked to be remembered in tenants' wills. Harold Greene, husbandman, who drew up his will on Christmas day 1613, left 6s.8d to 'my very good mistress' Margaret Rosell, and 'an ewe hog' (a sheep) to young Gervase. George himself witnessed the will and acted as supervisor, receiving 10s for his trouble. Humphrey Campion's will in 1614 confirmed him as 'my very good master'. He died in 1615 or 1616, aged no more than 34.

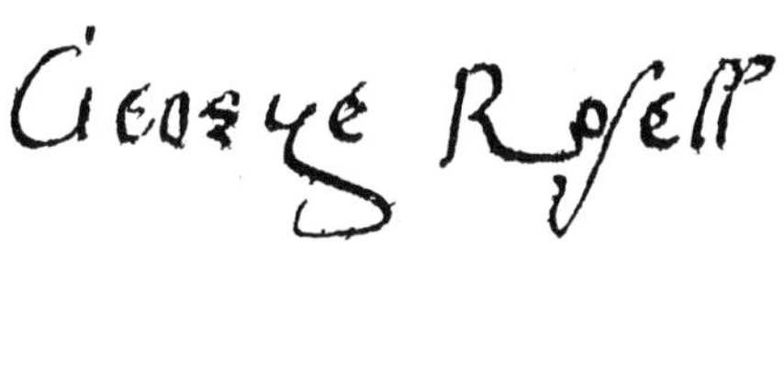

George Rosell's bold signature when witnessing William Greene's will in 1604 (NAO PRNW)

Mary Rosell's will

By the end of January 1618, George's mother Mary died - the second of the three women who had had claims on the Rosell estates. Mary had been born a Cranmer, but there is no reference to the Aslockton family in her will drawn up in September 1617. Nor is there any mention of George's wife and family, confirmation that she had long-since foregone on his behalf much that she could have legally claimed.

Her first request was to be buried in the church 'as near to my husband as I may'. Her bequests were all to her younger children, and largely of a domestic nature. Elizabeth, who was to marry Robert Leake in 1619, was left two pairs of linen sheets, one pair of 'midlin', a table cloth, a towel and a dozen linen napkins. She was also to have the 'great brass pot', and a year-old red calf. Jane, eventually to become the wife of Alfred Bayley, was supplied with an identical set of linen, plus another dozen napkins, and a trundle bed with its bed clothes. Her year-old calf was brown. She was also to have the best pot but one, and a pan. Perhaps closest in size to her mother, she was left Mary's best gown, her best petticoat and her best smock.

Shortly after the will was made, Dorothy was married by licence in December 1617 to Francis Bayley, a vintner from Cromwell near Newark, perhaps Alfred's brother. She was left the only other specific item of her mother's clothing - 'my petticoat I wear every day'. Otherwise a pair of linen sheets, a dozen linen napkins and a towel provided 'full satisfaction of her child's part'. Gertrude had married John Kyme of Nottingham, gentleman, in April 1616 when they were both aged 26. She was left an identical set of linen to Elizabeth, and an unspecified year-old calf. There is no mention of Mary, who had married the Reverend Midrington of Gotham, nor of the two eldest daughters, Barbara and Margaret, both married before their father died. They were, perhaps, no longer living. Oliver Withington, probably Barbara's son rather than husband, was remembered with a ewe and a lamb 'to be put forth for his profit'.[156]

Mary's second son, Nicholas, was to be her executor, and was left £10 'which is in Thomas Gamble's hand'. (Gamble was a witness to the will.) He was also left her 'jade' (her horse), and a third of her unbequeathed goods. He survived her by only five years. The other two-thirds of her remaining property was to be divided equally between Elizabeth and Jane, the two daughters who were unmarried at the time the will was drawn up.

There was a generous legacy of 20s for the poor 'to be given them in bread', and George Cotes, the vicar and one of the witnesses to the will, was left 10s. Overall, Mary gives the impression of being a loving wife and mother, concerned with the needs of her children and the personal running of her household.

Gervase Rosell's minority

After the time of George Rosell and his mother, it becomes much more difficult to assess the circumstances of the Rosells. There are no further Inquisitions into their estates, and the next surviving wills are not until the 1680s. The earliest parish registers (with their imperfect bishops' transcripts from 1625), along with marriage licences, and ecclesiastical and civil court records leave only a hazy image of their concerns.

It is not clear exactly how old Gervase was when his father died. According to genealogical information collected by Thoroton in 1662, he would have been born in 1603, but this was two years before George and Margaret Whalley took out their marriage licence on July 24th 1605, an unlikely irregularity at that period. It is possible that Thoroton was misinformed about the date, or that Margaret Whalley was a second wife. Whatever the explanation, Gervase would have been somewhere between 10 and 13 years of age at the time of his father's death and too young to administer his estates unaided.[157]

Margaret Rosell was not left a widow for long. On 23rd December 1617 she married Francis Hacker of East Bridgford, a widower and substantial landowner both there and at Colston Bassett, from a family comparatively new to Nottinghamshire. He already had a son, Francis Hacker junior, who was to supervise the execution of Charles I, and who was in turn to be executed at the Restoration. How many children Margaret now produced is unclear, but Francis senior had two other sons (both to become ardent royalists) and two daughters who were younger than Francis junior. It is therefore possible that young Gervase had half-brothers or sisters. When Margaret died is not known. (The Margaret Hacker whose burial is recorded in the East Bridgford parish register on 6th January 1627 was her mother-in-law.) She must have been comparatively young, however, for in November 1634 Francis Hacker buried a third wife, Elizabeth.[158]

It is from the subsidy lists for Radcliffe that something can be deduced about the administration of the Rosell lands while Gervase was growing up. Those for 1621, 1622 and 1625 are the first not to be headed by a Rosell. Instead, Francis Hacker's name appears, but assessed for only a nominal amount. Gervase's step-father was clearly in charge, though whether the boy had been made an official ward of court is uncertain. By the time of the next assessment in 1628, Gervase would have been over 21. He therefore heads the list in his own right, but the lands on which he was assessed were valued at only £2. (His father's assessment of 1606 had been for £10.) If Gervase was indeed a ward of court, this may explain the drop in the value of his lands. Administrators notoriously milked the estates of those in their care, and resentment against this abuse built up as Civil War approached. (The Court of Wards was abolished by Parliament in 1645/6.)[159]

The closeness of the Rosell and Hacker families was underlined on 19th January 1622 when a marriage licence was taken out between Gervase Rosell, gentleman, of Radcliffe and Elizabeth Hacker, Francis Hacker's daughter. Francis himself is described as of Radcliffe. (A reference to a former servant in the Quarter Sessions minutes confirms that Francis Hacker had temporarily lived in the village.) Gervase would be at the most 19 years of age, and possibly only 16, at the time of his marriage. Elizabeth may have been a daughter by a first wife, or an illegitimate daughter, thus accounting for the unusual description of her as Francis's 'natural and lawful' daughter on the licence. Francis Hacker had thus made sure that the benefits of the Rosell estates stayed within his own family by arranging a marriage before the minor had control of his inheritance - a common device by administrators. A marriage settlement could help to explain why the Rosell subsidy valuation was so low, even after Gervase had come of age.[160]

Meanwhile, Gervase's sister Elizabeth was married to Nicholas Strelley of Strelley, probably around 1616. There was one son, George, who died unmarried in France in 1680. After her husband's death she was to link the Rosells to one of the most prestigious families in the county, the Byrons of Newstead Abbey. As the first wife of Richard, 2nd Lord Byron, she was to produce ten children according to the monument in Hucknall church, and was the ancestress of Byron the poet. (She could not, therefore, have been the Elizabeth who was buried at East Bridgford in 1634, Francis Hacker's third wife, as has been suggested.)[161]

The young squire

The first reference to Gervase after his marriage comes from 1624 when the Lamcote husbandman, Robert Greene, left him 20s in his will. There is no reference to any Rosell child in the bequests. The early bishops' transcripts of the parish register record the baptism of Thomas in November 1627, and Ann in September 1628. The will of Miles Cragge in January 1635, however, indicates that there were two other children, presumably born before the survival of parish records or away from Radcliffe. These were George and Margaret. The two boys were left a ewe sheep each, and the girls one between them. By the time of John Stapleton's will of July 1639, only three children are mentioned who were left £15 to be divided between them. Margaret is missing and had presumably died.

Throughout these years there is no indication as to how the Rosells reacted to the increasingly arbitrary policy of Charles I. Ruling without parliament since 1629, with the aid of the 'thorough' policies of his ministers Archbishop Laud and the Earl of Strafford, the king was insulated from growing resentment in his cultivated but extravagant court. Short of funds, he irritated the county gentry by the collection of Ship Money. Although initially few withheld payment for long, the weakening of royal authority left the 1639 levy largely unpaid. When the imposition of the English prayer book on Scotland provoked rebellion, Charles had no option but to recall parliament to ask for funds to pay for an army. The stage was set for a clash between parliament and monarch which was to lead to Civil War.

In the meantime, Radcliffe's young squire must have cut something of a dash in the village. John Stapleton referred to him as Captain Rosell. He was an officer in the Nottingham trained band (volunteer militia men) from at least 1634. The force was made up of 407 men, 41 pioneers, 593 private arms, 60 horse and 50 attached clergy. Gervase was one of eight officers, none from above the ranks of the lesser gentry. As he was still known as Captain Rosell in 1651, it does not seem that he exhibited great qualities of leadership meriting promotion, despite the fact that the Civil War would allow him some experience of real soldiering.[162]

He was also known for his fox hunting - hunting in general being the sport of gentlemen, and a preparation for the rigorous horsemanship needed in battle. In March 1639 Sir Henry Pierrepont's son, Robert, now Earl of Kingston, and something of a valetudinarian, had an interesting use for Gervase's skill in the fox hunting field. Writing to his kinsman, Sir Gervase Clifton, he sympathised with

Lady Clifton who was indisposed, suggesting a remedy for breathing problems:

> *...Believe me, dear Cousin, I did require more than one of my serv[an]ts to send to my cousin Rosell for a fox lungs, that I might have sent the same by one of yours for my La[dy] Clifton. It now attends her La[dyshi]p and to mine understanding nothing can unto the lungs be more precious bec[ause]:it operateth ex proprietate. It is to be mingled with old Conserve of red roses & taken a little before sleep, suff[e]ring both the roses and it to melt in the mouth by long retaining them therein...*[163]

Apart from soldiering and hunting, Gervase had to see to the management of his estates, but little information about this has survived. Sheep on his pasture lands tempted Mary Huttam and Jane Cassam to steal wool from their bodies, for which in April 1629 the magistrates sent them to the Assizes. Gervase was summoned to appear to give evidence on pain of £20. Another incident occurred in 1641, after Gervase had turned out Richard Asby, one of his Lamcote tenants, presumably for not paying his rent. The court's ultimate decision was that he should be rehoused on Lamcote's 'waste', with Gervase's approval as 'lord of the waste there'.[164]

By this time, Gervase's personal life had radically changed. At some uncertain date his wife Elizabeth had died (in 1633 according to a genealogy of 1714), and in August 1638 he fathered a daughter, Marie, by his servant Abigail Smith. This produced an awkward situation for the parish's new vicar, William Creswell, as sexual indiscretions were a matter for church discipline. (See p. 135.) In January 1641 he regularised his life by marrying by licence the heiress Jane Ayscough of Hempshill in the parish of Nuthall, Nottinghamshire, which brought a welcome, if temporary, boost to Rosell holdings. By the time their first child was born, the Civil War had broken out, and the county was at odds with its own county town.[165]

Case study 8

THE WILL OF JEFFREY LIMNER

For a man whose name is still remembered in Radcliffe for the 'Jeffrey Dole', Jeffrey Limner (Limmer) proves to be an elusive historical figure. The family name, in whatever permutation of spelling, is unknown in the village except in the imperfect documents of the early 17th century. In the surrounding counties, only in Leicestershire is the name common. Jeffrey himself was a wheelwright, and he served as churchwarden in 1614. There is no record of his wife, but he had a sister (or perhaps sister-in-law), Alice Wheatley, whose name appears on the admonition bond after his death.[166]

He also had a son, William, and it is possibly because of William's early death that the legacy to the Radcliffe poor came about. William made his will on 25th March 1616, being sick in body, but 'whole in soul and of good and p[er]fect remembrance'. Unusually, he described himself as a bachelor. The lengthy preamble to his will suggests a man of deeper religious commitment than was common for his time:

> *First I bequeath unto Almighty [God] and wholly resign into his blessed hand my soul which I received of him being fully assured that the thing committed unto him cannot perish. And my body I commit unto the earth to be decently and Christianly buried within the churchyard of Ratcliffe not doubting but at the last day of my saviour Jesus Christ coming to Judgement I shall receive my body in its mortality to be united to my soul. And then my faith is that by the merits of Christ's blood I shall have for ever both body and soul in the glorious presence of God's ma[jes]ty in the heavens.*

Whatever his spiritual commitments, William seems to have been comfortably situated. He left all his 'houses, tenements, lands and hereditaments' to his father. It seems probable that he occupied them jointly with Jeffrey, for he mentions 'our servant', Elizabeth Wright, to whom he left a ewe and a lamb. He also left all documentation - 'writings, and evidences, rights and titles' - as well as his goods to his father, who was to be his executor. The vicar, George Cotes, who witnessed the will with Roger Jackson, was left 2s.6d, and 5s went to the church 'to make a prayer'. This last item was more reminiscent of pre-Reformation than Jacobean times. Finally, he left 5s to Radcliffe's poor. The young man was dead within a month, for Jeffrey dealt with his admonition bond on 25th April.[167]

Jeffrey Limner was thus left without a direct heir. A year later he was himself ill, and he drew up his own will on 17th April 1617. He seems to have shared his son's religious commitment, although the preamble to his will is not as lengthy as William's, and he, too, asked to be buried in Radcliffe churchyard. There is little indication of his wheelwright's craft in the will, beyond the bequest of 'a pair of my best wheels' to a Mr Jackson his executor. He also appointed an overseer to his will, Laurence Grimthorpe, to whom he left his mare. The vicar, George Cotes, and three villagers - Brian Barnes, Thomas Gamble and Robert Greene - witnessed the will.

The main bequests indicate a man of some substance, who remembered a close circle of acquaintances with a number of personal bequests or sums of money. His house in Radcliffe with its croft and rights in the common fields he left to Elizabeth Inkesall for her lifetime, along with 'one best pot and two hanging kettles'. After her death the house(s) and appurtenances were to go to John Wheatley's 'law daughters', and if they lacked heirs, then to Radcliffe church 'for ever'. Two special items indicating the wheelwright's hospitality were to stay with the house: 'My mind is that the board in the house and form shall stand as an heirloom'. Some of his clothes were specifically bequeathed: his old doublet to William Speed, his buckskin hose to George Richards, and a jerkin to carpenter John Wells. Like his son, he left the household servant, Elizabeth (Wright), a ewe and a lamb, and remembered that he owed her 42s, presumably for wages. Apart from the mare to his overseer, the only bequest of livestock was his 'swine hog' to Humphrey Drecot.

His remaining bequests were substantial but entirely financial. The vicar was to have £3.6s.8d 'to discharge the due to him', and Radcliffe church was to have £10 'to use at their discretion'. William Patchett was also to have £10, and his four sisters £20 between them. Another £10 went to George Capestake. The same amount was left to the poor:

> *I give to the poor of the town of Ratcliffe to be put forth at the discretion of the townsmen £10 that the clear profit may be paid them yearly from time to time and so to continue for ever.*

This was by far the largest recorded bequest to the village poor during the 16th and 17th centuries.

Jeffrey Limner had died by 8th August 1617 when Alice Wheatley swore to carry out his wishes. His substantial gift was managed by the churchwardens who lent out the money at interest. Other smaller bequests were made over the years, and it is clear from tallies appearing randomly in the parish registers that these were handled in the same way. The first surviving list is headed 'Legacies bequeathed to the poor of the parish of Radcliffe the Interest whereof is to be annually Distributed by the Min[iste]r & churchwardens'. It was drawn up by churchwardens between 1636 and 1669, and contained about sixteen names, some no longer decipherable, as well as details of borrowers. By then Jeffrey Limner's contribution was given as £8.4s, and was lent out to the squire, Gervase Rosell. Other names were added over the years, and the situation again summarised in 1714. Jeffrey Limner's amount had then dropped to £8 out of a total of £33. From this it seems likely that the invested money was not keeping pace with inflation, rather than that the original legacy was worth less than the £10 the wheelwright had intended. For this reason by 1718 the monies were invested in land in the open fields, and after these were enclosed in 1789 the poor were allocated land close to the centre of the village on Bingham Road. The profits from building leases on this land in Victorian times are still distributed annually. In 1885 a plaque was erected in the church to the memory of these early benefactors, headed by Jeffrey Limner, based on one of the lists in the parish register.[168]

Plaque in St Mary's church commemorating Jeffrey Limner's gift to the poor and other 17th century donors

CHURCH AND PARISH IN THE EARLY STUART PERIOD

Both Catholics and Puritans had hopes of sympathetic treatment when James VI of Scotland succeeded Queen Elizabeth as James I of England in 1603. Catholics looked to him to follow the traditions of his executed mother, the Catholic Mary Queen of Scots, while Puritans felt that his upbringing in Calvinist Scotland would lead him to favour their cause. In fact, both extremes of the religious spectrum were disappointed, and continued to feel the weight of state disapproval. Toby Matthew, who became Archbishop of York in 1606, was more concerned with eradicating Catholicism, than disciplining extreme Protestants. Nevertheless, it was during the early part of James's reign that such pressure was put on nonconformists by the authorities in the Scrooby area of Nottinghamshire that they moved first to the Low Countries in 1607, and subsequently to America in the *Mayflower*.[169]

Radcliffe villagers showed no sign of deviating from state religious policies in the direction of Puritanism, but there were those such as the Jordans (see pp. 105-7) who followed the Catholic faith, despite hostile legislation and heavy fines in the later years of Elizabeth's reign caused by the threat of Spanish invasion and Jesuit activity. The Gunpowder Plot of 1605 again aroused strong anti-Catholic feelings. The Jordans were not the only Catholics in Radcliffe, however. William Fox alias Wilson and Alice, the wife of William Wood, also refused to take communion and found themselves before church or civil authorities. Moreover, there were other Catholic families as near as Bassingfield, and perhaps at Holme Pierrepont Hall itself. One tradition suggests that Edmund Campion, the Jesuit priest, had spent Christmas 1580 with the Pierreponts, and this sympathy continued into the 17th century with Lady Frances Pierrepont. A committed Catholic, she conformed to Protestantism only after great pressure was put on her in 1626, a time of fierce anti-Catholic debates in the House of Commons. In the meantime, Radcliffe's Catholics had either moved away or conformed, for in May 1614 the churchwardens reported that there were 240 communicants and no recusants in the village.[170]

George Cotes c. 1593-1622

George Cotes was vicar in charge of Radcliffe while the Jordans were defying the authorities. Traditional sources (*Alumni Cantabrigiensis* and Godfrey's *Notes on the Churches of Nottinghamshire, Hundred of Bingham*) indicate that he ceded the vicarage of Radcliffe in 1622 on becoming rector of Adbolton in that year, having become rector of St Peter's in Nottingham in 1617. There he preached against Catholics and was a convinced Puritan. An inscription in St Peter's parish register testifies to his faithful ministry and a laudatory monument, described by Thoroton, was erected to his memory after his death at the age of 53 in 1640.

This pious image is at odds with what was known about George Cotes' career in Radcliffe, but further research has explained the discrepancy. Reference to him as a village cleric as early as 1593 has been found, so it is clear that he could not have been the man who became rector of St Peter's, since he would need to have been appointed in Radcliffe at the impossible age of six to fit the known age of death in Nottingham. Distinguishing in the sporadic documents of the period between two clerics of the same name (variously spelt) who chronologically overlapped and who both served in the Archdeaconry of Nottingham has been difficult. The incumbents' signatures on penances for Radcliffe and St Peter's have been compared with signatures on other documents, however, and this has helped to identify them with more certainty.

(Left) Traced signature of George Cotes vicar of Radcliffe

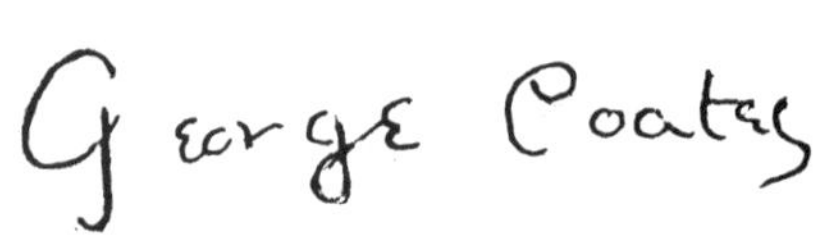

(Right) Traced signature of George Co(a)tes rector of St Peter's

George Cotes' early career

The earlier George Cotes was curate and then vicar of Radcliffe for the last decade of Elizabeth's reign, and for most of James I's reign, before moving to Adbolton in 1622. He disappears from the records there in 1628. Between 1593 and 1606, his behaviour suggests normal diligence in carrying out his duties. The first document which links him to Radcliffe concerns a charge of simony and usury against the vicar of Ruddington in 1593. As Radcliffe's curate (confusingly referred to as William Cotes at one point), he was one of four clergymen before whom the Ruddington vicar was to purge himself. He was one of those who featured in the will of Steven Palmer (1594), the Radcliffe labourer who lent out money. George Cotes owed him 43s.1d. Mistress Cotes also owed Palmer for 15 lbs of wool. Apparently she contributed to the household economy by weaving and making clothes. Out of Palmer's estate she was to pay herself 11s for a yard of cloth and two shirts she had produced for him. He waived the rest of her debt. Described as vicar in April 1595, George failed to put in an appearance at the Bingham deanery visitation, but this sort of absence was not uncommon, and his response to the hardship appeal of February 1597 was exemplary (pp. 77-8).[171]

Church discipline was routinely maintained during these early years. George Cotes certified penances for sexual transgressors in November 1594 and early in 1596, the latter case involving a lapsed churchwarden, Robert Greene, who had to perform his penance in penitential garb. Henry Pare, Henry Jervis, Alice Frith and Elizabeth Pare and the Capendales were others who had all faced the disapproval of the church courts between 1598 and 1602 (see p. 65), and there was certainly no relaxation after James became king. Harbouring women 'begot with child in fornication' broke religious Articles and could lead to a court appearance as John Taylor discovered in December 1604. As already seen, those suspected of Catholicism were equally in trouble, while in 1606 a tithe dodger, William Dafforne, was pursued in the church courts by George Cotes himself. A bonus for the vicar was the 3s.4d left by William Greene in 1604 'toward making a desk for the minister to read prayer in'. The parish seemed to be well supervised.[172]

Vicar and parishioners before the courts

There was a modest quota of sexual immorality cases sent to court in 1607 and early 1608, but eyebrows must have been raised when on 23rd April 1608 Elizabeth Chamberleyne appeared in the court held in St Peter's church in Nottingham and pleaded guilty to incontinence with Mr George Cotes, vicar of Radcliffe. She was ordered to perform a penance - an awkward matter since this was normally carried out in the presence of and certified by the parochial clergyman. Two weeks later, George Cotes himself was brought to answer the equivalent charge, and, not surprisingly, Elizabeth did not return with a certified penance. The vicar, still a married man, denied incontinence. Perhaps he was falsely accused, but he was nevertheless ordered by the court to purge himself at the hands of six clergy, and he was dismissed by the court on 28th May.[173]

Those whose penances for similar offences were supervised by George Cotes shortly after this episode must have wondered about the justice of their fate. Between April and July 1609 Anne Capendale, Alice Wilkington and Elizabeth Lanford had to confess their sins before the congregation in Radcliffe church dressed in white penitential habit. Robert Beardsley in December of that year had not only to appear in church in penitential garb on two separate occasions, but also to stand similarly dressed for an hour in the full Nottingham market on a Saturday and confess his sin. As a clergyman, George Cotes was treated leniently.

The cases of Anne Capendale and Elizabeth Lanford were in fact linked, as the churchwardens' presentment bill of 1609, unusually signed by the vicar himself, made clear:

> *We present Elizabeth Lanforde for a common bawd betwixt Edward Swinston [Swinscoe] and Anne Capendale as the said Edward Swinscoe hath certified to the Justices.*
>
> *And we present John Capendale upon common fame to be a bawd betwixt his wife and Edward Swinscoe.*

The Capendale family had not been unknown to the church courts a decade earlier (p. 65). The unconventional domestic arrangements of the household now became the subject of village gossip and were to keep the courts - religious and secular - busy for over four months. Initially, when Ann Capendale confessed in the Archdeacon's Court on 1st April 1609 to her incontinence with butcher Edward Swinscoe, the matter might have seemed to be no more than routine. She even performed her penance 'for the filthy crime of adultery' before the end of May. Unfortunately, Edward Swinscoe had in the meantime engaged in some unruly behaviour, apparently connected with the Capendale case, and on 24th April he found himself before the Quarter Sessions magistrates. Two butchers from Lincoln and Grantham stood surety for him to the tune of £10 each. It was presumably on this occasion that he revealed the complicity of Anne's husband and Elizabeth Lanford in bringing the couple together. The magistrates ordered the butcher to keep the peace and not to associate illicitly with Anne Capendale. (Two days earlier, the churchwardens had added religious fuel to the situation by reporting Anne and Edward Swinscoe for not receiving communion at Easter.)

The Archdeacon's Court then began to follow up the butcher's assertions. He was summoned to appear on a charge of fornication on 29th May, the day Anne was dismissed, having certified her penance. He did not turn up and was threatened with excommunication. By 15th June he gave in, appeared in court and was sentenced to perform a penance. There is no evidence that he did so. The court wheels continued to turn and on 15th July John Capendale and Elizabeth Lanford were separately charged with acting as bawds between the adulterous couple on the strength of Edward Swinscoe's evidence to the magistrates. John Capendale denied the charge, was ordered to purge himself, and was dismissed by 29th July. Elizabeth was also initially ordered to purge herself, but having produced no compurgators, she was sentenced to perform public penance in the usual penitential habit. When she returned with her certificate on 12th August, however, the court found that it was incomplete, and it was another week before she was finally dismissed.[174]

The Capendale scandal had scarcely died down when the villagers were distracted by the spectacle of their vicar in trouble again. Along with his wife Helen (or Elen), and two husbandmen - William Massey and William Cotes, perhaps a kinsman - he was charged with riot and affray, appearing on 2nd October 1609 before the Quarter Sessions magistrates, headed by Holme Pierrepont landowner Sir Henry Pierrepont. The cause of this intriguing case is not specified, but all four defendants were fined 12d each for their share in the brawl.[175]

Soon after this episode Helen Cotes must have died, for the vicar's licence to marry Margaret Goodwin of Kirkby-in-Ashfield was taken out on 28th November 1612. A Nottingham saddler, Henry Hawkins, provided the necessary £10 bond. The marriage was to take place in Kirkby, and it seems to have had a sobering effect on the vicar since he is not found before either religious or secular courts again.[176]

'Whores', sabbath-breaking, violence, bells and a bible

Despite the vicar's own failings, religious discipline continued to be exerted over his continually straying parishioners. Some familiar names appear in this period. Richard Gardam and Elizabeth Chambers in 1614 seem to have been continuing an affair which was first brought to the attention of the court some seven years earlier. Henry Jervis, having bought himself out of trouble in 1602 (p. 65), was presented in May 1610 for 'harbouring Elizabeth Lealand begotten with child' by Robert Beardsley. She was 'lodged in his [Jervis's] hovel... and went away without penance', and without churching. In May 1614 Henry Jervis was finally trapped and had to marry Joanna Smedley, his maid servant. In October 1618 Elizabeth Lammyn's case was dismissed 'for that she was slandered to be Richard Northe['s] whore'. In a second case that October, however, the epithet stuck. Jane Grococke was brought before the church court 'upon a common fame to be a notorious whore'. John Garton stood alongside, 'upon a common fame of adultery' with her. Her reputation lingered on, entrapping the prestigious Francis Linley of Skegby in 1621. He denied the charge of incontinence, wanting the restitution of his good name. The court warned him not to consort with her. Only four penance certificates signed by George Cotes have survived for the years 1616 to 1621, all for fornication cases.[177]

Other archdeaconry cases in this period throw some interesting sidelights on village life. An increasingly puritanical approach to secular activities on religious days, which cut across the needs of an agricultural community, occurred around 1612-13. (Only one previous case has been found when Henry Parr and Bartholomew Pilkington had been charged in 1604 with loading corn on St Bartholomew's day, 24th August.) In June 1612 George Bayley was reported to the court because

> *he yoked his horses the Sunday after May day either in Evening Prayer time or pretty [soon] after. [He] fetched a load of bedding or such like stuff from Trent [field].*

William Benet was charged with working in time of divine service on Lammas day in 1613, while William Morley and his wife were presented as they 'did teem a load of hay upon the Sabbath day' in October of the same year.[178]

Two cases of violence in church occur in this period. In May 1617 carpenter John Wells was ordered to perform a penance before six witnesses 'for pulling one out of a seat in the church in time of divine service wherein he had no right to sit but by kind p[er]mission'. The Wells' family were to have later brushes with the church authorities. A year later Anthony Franke was presented 'for disorder in the church by common fame', and admitted having laid violent hands on John, the servant of Robert Greene of Lamcote.[179]

Occasionally the churchwardens would have to approve a major purchase. At least one of the three bells noted in the inventory of Edward VI's reign (p. 43) was either recast or replaced in 1612, and a fourth bell was possibly added at this time. The inscriptions on these two bells read as follows : IHESVS BE OVR SPEDE 1612 and VIRGO . EST . ELECTUS . IONES. Sometimes the churchwardens were on the receiving end of court orders. Particularly significant was the instruction to Edmund Watts and Richard Richards in May 1618 to provide 'a bible of the largest volume of the new translation' by 1st August. This was the great Authorised Version of James I's reign, to be read in each parish church, its language imprinted on the nation for over 300 years.[180]

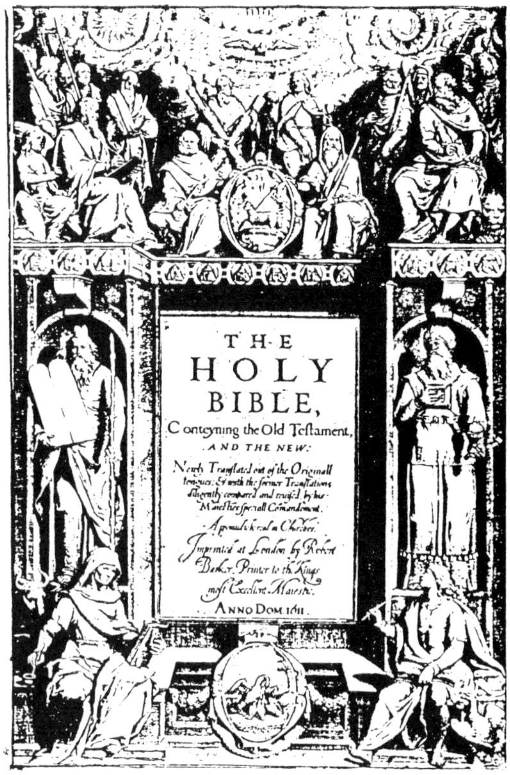
THE HOLY BIBLE,
Conteyning the Old Testament, AND THE NEW:
Newly Translated out of the Originall tongues: & with the former Translations diligently compared and revised by his Maiesties speciall Commandement.
Appointed to be read in Churches.
Imprinted at London by Robert Barker, Printer to the Kings most Excellent Maiestie.
ANNO DOM. 1611.

Title page of King James' bible which the churchwardens were ordered to purchase in 1618

Neglect of the chancel

Neglect of the church by the patron of the living was a regular problem. In April 1609 Sir John Stanhope was reported for not arranging special 'quarter sermons'. (As a non-graduate George Cotes would only be allowed to read from the Book of Homilies and not preach.) More often it was the state of the chancel, specifically the responsibility of the patron, which was a continual worry to the churchwardens. It had been in a state of decay since 1602. In 1612 its condition was reported to the church authorities, but as Sir John Stanhope had recently died, the wardens did not know who was then responsible. By 1620, they found themselves falling between the two stools of the next patron, Philip Stanhope, Baron Stanhope of Shelford, and the powerful tenant to whom he had let the former rectory lands:

> *We present Mr Leeming [of Derby] who is the farmer to our parsonage for not repairing our Chancel. It is betwixt My Lord Stanhope and him, and my Lord hath been made acquainted with it and he sayeth he is free therein.*

The matter was doubly irritating because over the previous two years Timothy Leeming had sued a sub-tenant, John Franke of Radcliffe, over payment of tithes on these lands. It must have seemed as if Mr Leeming wanted the benefits without the responsibilities of his holdings. Getting nowhere, the churchwardens, tackled Lord Stanhope on the matter, presenting him at the next visitation in November. In the following April they presented him again, this time for failing, like his father in 1609, to send someone 'to preach quarter sermon'. Although the decaying chancel was not mentioned on this occasion, it is clear that Lord Stanhope had done nothing about it, for in May 1622, soon after George Cotes' successor had taken over, the churchwardens were again complaining:

> *Nothing to present save that our Chancel is out of repair as heretofore reported but no reformation for which we present Mr Timothy Leeming.*

He was next reported in October 1623, specifically for the 'glass windows'. Perhaps something was at last done, for the chancel is not mentioned again until 1635.[181]

The last of George Cotes

George Cotes ceded Radcliffe-on-Trent vicarage around 1622, taking the rectorship of Adbolton instead - perhaps a profitable but undemanding living for his later years. The surviving Call Books (which list clergy and churchwardens twice a year) confirm his presence there until 1628. In the following year his Adbolton successor recorded the curious item that he had just received the archbishop's mandate for George Cotes' induction. Presumably this was a clerical error, although whether on the part of George Cotes or the archbishop's staff it is impossible to say. Perhaps he died at Adbolton, but the records have not survived to confirm this. Despite his disreputable escapades in Radcliffe, overall George Cotes seems to have been sufficiently well-regarded to be occasionally remembered in his parishioners' wills and to act as their scribe. Even in the imperfect records of his period, he emerges as an interesting personality.[182]

Richard Rumney 1622-1624

George Cotes' short-lived successor at Radcliffe, Richard Rumney, held a B.A. degree, probably from Oxford, where one of his name matriculated at Queen's College in July 1607 at the age of 16. He was instituted at Radcliffe in March 1622 under the patronage of Lord Stanhope. The few surviving documents from his period show only the continuing concern over chancel repairs outlined above, the certification of a marriage, presumably after sexual incontinence, and a longer-running case involving John Wells, the carpenter who had previously been in court for brawling over a church seat. On this occasion in October 1622 Wells was presented to the church court 'for misdemeanour in words within the church'. The man with whom he quarrelled was Richard Wilford who maintained that his allegation was the truth. He too ended up before the court. Four days later the subject of the 'words' was made clear when the Holme Pierrepont churchwardens presented Wells for adultery with Frances Barker, the wife of Richard Barker. Wells denied the charge. Some nine months later, however, he was back in court on a similar charge, Frances this time being described as 'his sister-in-law'. In some way, too, Richard Wilford was still involved in the case since he was also in court again. Initially excommunicated, Wells was not finally free of the court until January 1624 when he certified that he had performed public penance for his 'incest'.[183]

Daniel Willcockes 1624-c. 1632

Soon after the end of the Wells scandal, Richard Rumney died at the age of 33, and was succeeded by Daniel Willcockes. Like Rumney, Daniel Willcockes was a University man, a sign of the increasing standards of education for the clergy. Having matriculated sizar from Trinity College, Cambridge, in 1619, he took his B.A. in 1623-4, and his M.A. in 1632, shortly before he died. Allowing for early student entry into the universities at this period, he too would have died young, perhaps around the age of 30.[184]

General parish concerns

Daniel Willcockes' ministry is significant for three reasons. In 1625 two bells were replaced or recast, to complete the work begun in 1612. They bore the following legends: *I sweetly tolling men do call to taste on meat that feed the soul 1625* and *All men that hear my mournful sound repent before you lie in ground 1625*. The one surviving relic from Radcliffe's original church - the brass to Anne Ballard (see p. 125) - is also from his time, as are the earliest surviving parish registers.

Despite this additional source of information, evidence for the period remains sketchy. Nevertheless, some impression emerges of religious discipline and concerns in the parish. For example, the churchwardens were variously summoned before the Archdeacon's Court for failing to present their accounts or neglecting the repair of the churchyard fence. In 1630 they reported that the church needed a pulpit cloth, and a table of prohibited degrees of marriage. They were also short of a hood for Daniel Willcockes. George Parr and his wife were summoned for failing to pay their tithes, while Maria Dewsbury was sufficiently obstinate about not paying hers that the vicar brought his own case against her in 1631. In the same year Thomas Henfrie and his wife began a long-running case against Francis and Jane Grococke over a disputed inheritance. (See p. 127.)

The full weight of the court's puritanical displeasure was brought to bear on William Hutchinson, one of the village's churchwardens, for Sabbath breaking in 1629. He was sentenced to perform his penance in Radcliffe church after the end of evening prayers before Daniel Willcockes, the churchwardens and two neighbours. The clerk of the court had then to amend the order by crossing out the letter 's' of 'churchwardens' since Hutchinson could not confess his sin before himself! While he was spared the public confession and the humiliating garb of sexual sinners, he still had to make a full acknowledgement of his transgression. (See p. 122.)

As usual a number of parishioners, such as William Greenhall and his wife Anne Bird (Byrde), appeared before the court for having sexually anticipated their wedding. Ellen Taylor had an illegitimate child and was described as 'hawer' (i.e. whore) in the court records of 1631. There is no mention of marriage in the case of William Riley's incontinence with Anna Rye of Scarrington, and he was ordered in 1630 to confess and submit to penance in Radcliffe church dressed in full penitential garb. William Riley's penance certificate is one of only two which have survived for immorality cases signed by Daniel Willcockes. (See p. 122.)[185]

William Greene's defamation case

The constant concern with sexual morality meant that accusations could be made against the innocent as well as the guilty. Such was the claim of William Greene, a Radcliffe husbandman, presented to the church court for incontinence with Margerie Chester in July 1625. She, the daughter of a Langar husbandman, had been married by licence to John Chester, a Radcliffe tailor, in May 1614. By 1625, John Chester was sufficiently prominent to be made churchwarden, the only time he is so recorded. The case was therefore very embarrassing for both men.

William Greene strenuously denied the charge, producing four compurgators who testified to his good name (Roger Campion - parish clerk and frequent church-warden, Henry Pare, John Greene and William Rogers). He brought a defamation case against Gabriel Garton, the man whom he regarded as the perpetrator of the slander. Asserting that he was a man of good character, William claimed that vituperous, scandalous, opprobrious and injurious statements had been made about him between October and May by Garton. The latter had stated that he

> *did see Will[ia]m Greene.... and Margerie Chester the wife of John Chester together in a dike & that they were naughty together....*

In the 17th century the last phrase had much stronger connotations than it has in the twentieth! Not only did the term cast aspersions on William Greene's good name, but Gabriel Garton had spoken with as much violence as if Margaret Garton (presumably his wife) had been involved in the alleged misconduct:

Transcripts of two penance certificates (modernised spelling)

Penance enjoined to William Hutchinson of the parish of Radcliffe-upon-Trent to be performed by him as followeth viz:

The said Wm Hutchinson upon some Sunday after the receipt hereof is to be present in the parish church aforesaid after evening prayers ended, and then and there before the minister and the churchwarden and two others of his neighbours shall make this acknowledgement saying after the minister viz:

Good people whereas I Wm Hutchinson not having the fear of God before my eyes nor regarding the breach of his holy commandment did upon the Sabbath day teem and stack a load of barley. I am heartily sorry for this my misdeed beseeching Almighty God and all you that I have hereby offended to forgive me upon this my submission. And I promise by God's grace never to offend in the like kind hereafter. Which that I may the better perform I desire you that are here present to pray to God for me and with me saying our Father etc.

To certify 12th December 1629. Dated 17th October 1629.

[Note at bottom] Performed sixth day of December 1629.

Witnessed by

Daniel Willcockes minister there

George Franke churchwarden
[Hutchinson himself was the other churchwarden]

* * * * *

Penance enjoined to William Riley of the parish of Radcliffe-upon-Trent to be performed by him as followeth viz:

The said William Riley is to be present in the parish church aforesaid upon some holy day between the first and second lessons of morning prayers, and then and there, he being covered with a white sheet from the shoulders downward, standing barelegged, barefooted and bareheaded, holding a white wand in his hand, near to the minister's seat, a step or two high the better to be seen and heard of the congregation there assembled, shall in penitent manner and with an audible voice say after the minister as followeth:

Whereas I William Riley, not having the fear of God before my eyes nor regarding my own soul's health, have to the great displeasure of Almighty God, the danger of my own soul, and the evil example of others committed the filthy and heinous sin of fornication with Anne Rye of Scarrington. I am now therefore come hither to acknowledge my fault, and am heartily sorry for the same, beseeching Almighty God to forgive me upon this my submission and hearty repentance, and all you whom I have thereby offended, not only to forgive me and take example by this my punishment to lead a chaste and Godly life, but also to join with me in hearty prayers to the throne of the Almighty for the assistance of his holy spirit that I never commit the like offence again, saying as our Saviour Christ hath taught us in his holy gospel viz: our Father.....

To certify performance before ministers and churchwardens at St Peter's at next court. Dated 27th March 1630.

[On reverse] These are to certify that the order of penitence enjoined to William Riley was performed by the said William in the parish of Radcliffe according to the form prescribed.......

Witnesseth this

Daniel Willcockes minister

William Hutchinson
Henry Parr churchwardens

[The words] beinge spoken in anger, malice, or in upbraiding mann[er], and in such manner as the said Gabriel Garton did utter them....in common sense, understanding, construction, and use of speech did & do import, signify & mean as much as if he, the said Gabriel, had said that he did see Will[ia]m Greene & Margaret Garton committing adultery together, and so they who heard the same did take, interpret and understand the same words or speech...

Documentation from only William's side of the story has survived, and it is not clear whether the court ever gave judgement in the case. Perhaps there was no smoke without a little fire, however, for less than two years later in June 1627 William took out a licence to marry Margerie Chester who was by then a widow. Although both were still living in Radcliffe, they chose to marry away from gossip in Adbolton, where the rector was George Cotes, the former Radcliffe vicar, who had himself not been immune to such problems. They were to enjoy nearly thirty years of married life before Margerie died in September 1656.[186]

William Greene was not alone in being angered at the spread of rumours - even if there was more than a grain of truth in some of them. When in October 1631 Humphrey Fox, alias Wilson, was presented for sexual irregularities with Alice Duke of Holme Pierrepont 'as the fame goeth', he denied the charge, claiming that the 'fame' was 'first raised by his own wife Anna'.

Little of Daniel Willcockes' own personality emerges from the documents during his ministry, although the penance for his churchwarden over Sabbath breaking does suggest puritanical zeal. The early parish register gives one posthumous clue to his personal life with the burial in September 1633 of Frances, the daughter of Gartwright Wilcock[es], widow. There is no further indication of any possible family. Perhaps he was ill for some time before he died, for the Call Book for May 1632 shows that he had the assistance of a curate, John Dinons.[187]

Paul Sherwood c. 1632-1638

On Daniel Willcockes' death, the patron of the living (Philip Stanhope, now Earl of Chesterfield) appointed Paul Sherwood to take over the parish on 13th November 1632 and was instituted in June 1633. A contemporary of Daniel Willcockes at Cambridge, Paul Sherwood had matriculated sizar of St John's College at Easter 1620, been awarded his B.A. degree in 1623-4, and was ordained in November 1627, so he too would have been in his early thirties.[188]

Archbishop Laud's policy

Unfortunately for Paul Sherwood, his incumbency coincided with the appointment of William Laud as Archbishop of Canterbury. Laud's emphasis on order and ceremony within the church struck at Puritan ideals and contributed to the unjustified suspicion that Charles I's government was attempting to bring the country back to Catholicism. Moreover, repairs to neglected church fabric, the replacement of communion tables by altars at the east end of churches, or the erection of communion rails (separating clergy from congregation) all cost money which had to be found by local communities. Laud had a convinced supporter in Richard Neile, Archbishop of York from 1632, who reported in 1634 on the state of his diocese. The marked contrast in Radcliffe's presentment bills before and after this date shows how the policy of 'thorough' was enforced locally.

Between July 1626 and October 1629, the churchwardens had found nothing at all to report to the church authorities. After Neile's appointment (and Paul Sherwood's) they became busier. For example, in 1633 they reported two fornication cases, two cases of swine defacing the churchyard, and a case of neglect in repairing the churchyard fence. In addition, they seemed supportive of their new vicar in presenting Roger Campion, the long-serving parish clerk, for negligent attendance.

Towards the end of May 1634 Paul Sherwood and his churchwardens supervised the penances of two female parishioners, Margaret Watson and Alice Hutchinson, for fornication with Henry Whitacres and William Walker respectively. Neither man seems to have been available for punishment, but both women confessed their sins in full penitential dress before the whole congregation. Some nine months later, on 24th February 1635, the vicar performed Alice Hutchinson's burial service. Possibly she died in childbirth.[189]

A discordant year

1635 proved to be an eventful year. There was perhaps some touchiness in the parish. One set of churchwardens - John Clark and George Beely (Bayley?) - picked on the vicar when responding to the official probings of the new set of religious Articles:

> *Concerning the Clergy*
> *To the 14 Article we can present nothing saving we present Mr Paul Sherwood the Vicar for not wearing a hood.*
> *To the 3 Art[icle] concerning the church we can present nothing.*
> *Concerning the schoolmaster we have none.*
> *To the 1 2 3 4 5 6 7 & 8 Art[icle] we can present nothing.*
> *To the 9 we present Roger Lewis gent for a negligent comer to church on Sundays and holidays.*
> *To the [?] Art[icle] we can present nothing saving that we present Brian Greene for fighting, quarrelling & beating William Stenson in our churchyard.*

Later in the same year Paul Sherwood retaliated by presenting churchwardens, John Clark and Henry Gamble (the latter in disgrace for having had 'carnal knowledge' of his wife before marriage) 'for not giving a full information into the court of the defects of the chancel being out of repair'. He also complained that they had not repaired the bells, and there was a lack of other items, including a cloth for the communion table.[190]

Paul Sherwood's reference to a communion table rather than an altar, and his failure to wear full vestments by appearing without hood suggest that theologically he was more in sympathy with Puritanical than Laudian leanings. Perhaps this atmosphere of religious intelligence-gathering was too much for him. If Susanna Close, one of his parishioners, is to be believed, he preached and gave communion on the evening of Sunday 11th October while drunk. She spread this information at Bassingfield on the Monday or Tuesday following in the hearing of Elizabeth Leeson and Isabell Henfrie. In December he brought a defamation case against her.

With the vicar himself at the centre of one defamation case, his parishioners were treated to another which reached the church court at the same time. George Wells of Radcliffe had taken exception to gossip spread by Margaret Dewsbury the elder of Saxondale about himself and her daughter-in-law. She claimed that George

> *sat kissing of William Deswbury's wife of Ratcliffe...whilst he the said William sat by and that he the said William kept the said George Wells in his house to make him cuckold and further reported that Margaret the wife of the said William was a whore in the month of October last past 1635 & about the xixth or xxth day of the same month both in Ratcliffe & in Saxondale.*

No record of the outcome of either case has yet been found, but the latter end of 1635 was evidently a turbulent time in the village.

The atmosphere calmed down in 1636 when the churchwardens could report that 'All's well' and that church repairs had cost £7. In fact, the civil magistrates had detected a Catholic recusant in Radcliffe that year - Esther, the wife of Robert Bowman. As no other reference to a family of that name has been found, perhaps she was only a temporary resident. In 1637, apart from a parishioner's refusal to pay an assessment and a case of fornication, the churchwardens again claimed that all was well, only to add a criticism of Paul Sherwood whom they presented 'for want of prayers'. This apparent laxity by the vicar continued, and in 1638 the churchwardens again presented him to the Archdeacon's Court 'for that he did neglect the doing of divine service both at morning and evening upon the Lord's Day in November last'. Around July 1638 he resigned, leaving his successor to cope at local level with the collapse of religious control.[191]

Case study 9

THE BRASS TO ANNE BALLARD

In today's church, there is only one memorial that has survived from the original building. It dates from Daniel Willcockes' time as vicar and is a brass plaque to Anne Ballard, who died in 1626. Although she was one of the parish élite, comparatively little is known about her. In 1677 Thoroton mentions no other memorial to a Radcliffe worthy, apart from the medieval effigy of Stephen of Radcliffe, so Anne's brass is particularly significant. Reputedly the last brass to be created in Nottinghamshire, it depicts a lady wearing a kerchief on her head, a starched ruff, and a long gown with close-fitting sleeves. She is at a prayer desk covered by a fringed cloth. In her right hand she holds a book, and in her left a watch - a not uncommon emblem symbolising the transience of life. On the viewer's left is a shield bearing the griffin of the Ballard arms. On the right are the arms of Anne Ballard's maiden name. Nichols, the 18th century Leicestershire antiquarian, identified her as a member of the Hall family of Godalming in Surrey, but it has not been possible to prove this connection from Surrey records. The name, however, is tentatively confirmed by a will drawn up in 1580. In this the wealthy local landowner, Robert Hall, refers to his 'brother in law Mr William Ballard'. The term 'in law' is often used loosely in this period, but it does suggest that Anne could have been Hall's sister.

She was born about 1543, and became the second wife of William Ballard of Wymeswold in Leicestershire, whose family also held lands in Radcliffe. (Robert Hall held lands at Costock, across the Nottinghamshire border from Wymeswold, as well as in Radcliffe and Adbolton.) The date of Anne's marriage to William is not known, but his first wife, Isabel, was buried at Wymeswold in May 1570, having produced at least three sons and a daughter. In her turn Anne bore her husband six sons between 1575 and 1580. Their names are recorded on the brass: George, Adrian, Miles, Daniel, Bowett and Gabriel. The two last were twins who died young: Bowett in 1580 when about a week old, and Gabriel in 1583. Miles died in the previous year, aged about four. Of the remaining sons, Daniel is known to have survived to at least 1640, and to have become the father of a London goldsmith.

In March 1595 William Ballard drew up his will. After leaving money to the poor of a number of parishes, including 3s.4d to Radcliffe, he made provision for his children of both marriages. To Anne he specifically left half his linens, one bed 'with all the furniture thereto belonging' and all the goods and jewels she brought with her, presumably at her marriage. He also bequeathed to her all her apparel - technically a wife's 'possessions' belonged to her husband during his lifetime. Some two weeks later William Ballard died, and was buried at Wymeswold on 1st April 1595. It was perhaps at this time that she came to live permanently in Radcliffe, where both the Halls and Edward Ballard, her step-son, held property.

As it was usual for a widow to inherit a third of her husband's property for her lifetime, Anne would have been left comfortably off, despite the limited bequests in her husband's will. For example, in 1601 she was renting more than 115 acres from Sir Henry Pierrepont. Moreover, she enjoyed concessions on a farm of 5 acres and 2 roods in Radcliffe. In theory for this she paid Sir Henry £5 a year in rent. In practice, the special terms attached to this property meant that she held it for her lifetime while paying only an annual entry 'fine' - as Sir Henry's son sourly noted in the rental book years later:

> *My father never rec[eive]d any rent for Mrs Ballard's farm (it being her jointure) and by a lease he made in reversion thereof reserved only £3.6s.8d per annum.*[192]

Similarly she held certain Rosell property for her lifetime (identified in their Inquisitions as a cottage with appurtenances in Radcliffe, a cottage in Lamcote along with six bovates of land, meadow and pasture, valued at 40 shillings a year).

According to the brass Anne 'lived in good report' to the age of four score and three years, dying on 9th December 1626. She was interred near to the brass, which Thoroton implies was originally positioned in the north aisle of the church. Although parish registers have not survived for that year, a transcript sent to the bishop has, but her name does not appear on it.

The legend on the brass ends with a couplet which testifies to her piety and benevolence:

> *Aske how shee liv'd & thou shalt know her end*
> *She dyed a Saint to God, to poore a Freinde.*

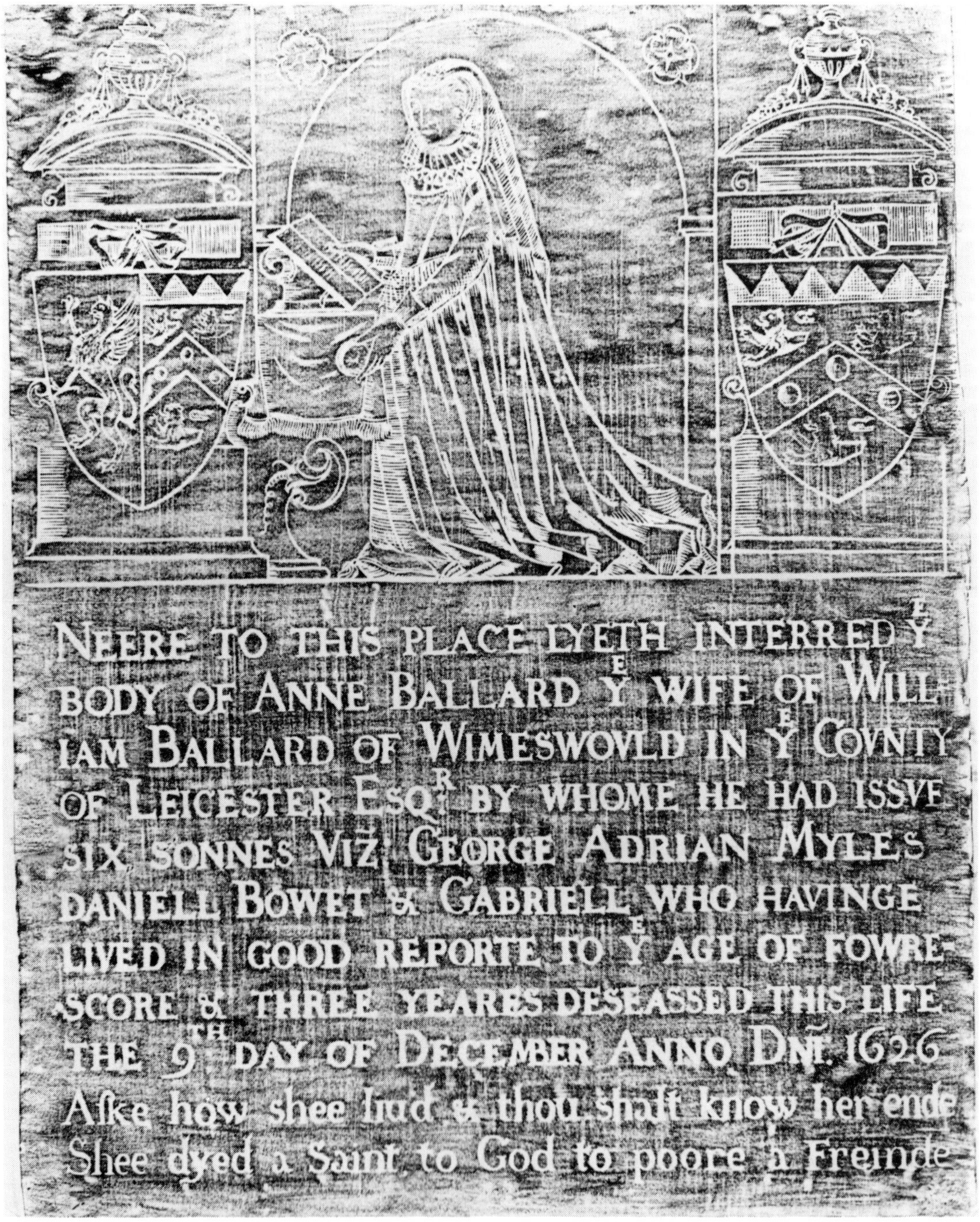

NEERE TO THIS PLACE LYETH INTERRED Y^E
BODY OF ANNE BALLARD Y^E WIFE OF WILL-
IAM BALLARD OF WIMESWOVLD IN Y^E COVNTY
OF LEICESTER ESQ^R BY WHOME HE HAD ISSVE
SIX SONNES VIZ GEORGE ADRIAN MYLES
DANIELL BOWET & GABRIELL WHO HAVINGE
LIVED IN GOOD REPORTE TO Y^E AGE OF FOWRE-
SCORE & THREE YEARES DESEASSED THIS LIFE
THE 9TH DAY OF DECEMBER ANNO DNI 1626
Aske how shee liud & thou shalt know her ende
Shee dyed a Saint to God to poore a Freinde

Rubbing of the memorial brass to Anne Ballard
in St Mary's church Radcliffe-on-Trent
(original size approximately 27½ x 22 inches)

Case study 10

ANNE BYRDE'S DISPUTED WILL

When it came to inheritance disputes, the humbler members of the community could be as tenacious as their financial superiors. With few exceptions, the ecclesiastical courts were the arbiters in such matters up to 1858. Anne Byrde's case concerns the terms of a written will, in conflict with a later verbal will - a rare occurrence. It offers yet another tantalising glimpse of interests and conflicts, both within the village and beyond. Her background can be briefly sketched-in from ecclesiastical and civil court records, and marriage licences, but the date of her birth is not known.

Anne's mother, Jane Whitworth of Eastwood, was left a widow and married Francis Grococke of Radcliffe around November 1619 at Radcliffe. At the time of the marriage Francis was described as a yeoman, but he was probably a former innkeeper, banned in July 1609 from following his trade by the justices 'for harbouring vagrants, vagabonds and suspicious persons'. In the following October he had been before the magistrates again for persisting in brewing ale despite the ban, and had been there again with others in October 1610 and January 1613 for respectively 'harbouring inmates' and for 'brewing without licence'. He was then described as a husbandman.[193]

The Grocockes seem to have been equally careless about conforming to the morality laws of the church courts. As early as September 1603 Francis himself had been presented for 'that he did harbour' Katherine Pettinger. Whether he was married or a widower at this stage is not clear, but he had a daughter, Jane, who was before the Archdeacon's Court in October 1618 'upon a common fame to be a notorious whore'. This was a year before her father married Anne Byrde's mother. Young Jane, however, was not inhibited in her activities by having a stepmother. In March 1621 she was named again in an 'incontinence' case with Francis Linley of Skegby. A year later her family may have been relieved when a licence was taken out for her marriage to William Dallewater, a Tuxford labourer.[194]

It might be thought that the Grococke environment would be uncongenial to Anne Byrde, but it seems that she was quite capable of leading the way in straying from the conventional path. When she married is unclear, but it must have been well before her mother's remarriage, for she was living in Radcliffe by December 1613 as Anne Byrde when she was charged with 'incontinence' with Jacob (James) Jordan and ordered to perform a penance in the following January. (It is also just possible that she was the Anne Byrde with whom William Greenhall was charged with fornication in December 1626.)[195]

From the subsequent dispute over her will, it is clear that she had a daughter, Elizabeth Byrde, who went to live in London. (Perhaps she was in service.) Anne herself was by now widowed, but was sufficiently affluent to be able to lend out money. Jane and Thomas Henfrie of Edwalton owed her £6, for example, but this was more than a business loan, for Jane was named as executrix when Anne Byrde drew up her will. Anne had also lent 50s to John Stevens of Eastwood - the village where her mother had lived before the Grococke marriage, and presumably where Anne had grown up.

In her will (which is only known through archdeaconry evidence), Anne wanted her goods to be used for the benefit of her daughter Elizabeth in London, and for paying any debts. After making these arrangements, however, Anne was betrothed to Robert Bowes of St Nicholas' parish in Nottingham (and subsequently of Bobber's Mill in Radford parish), around September 1630. The banns were called in both St Nicholas's and St Mary's Radcliffe. According to Robert Bowes, Anne gave him a letter of attorney to recover the 50s from John Stevens, along with a brass pot, said to be worth 3s.4d. He obtained half the loan and the value of the pot. Anne also at that time 'in the presence of divers witnesses' at Radcliffe, 'by word of mouth' willed to Robert all her 'goods, cattles, chattels and rights whatsoever', and these too he obtained. At the same time, when Henry Pare, a Radcliffe neighbour, suggested that the £6 owed to Anne by the Henfries should go to her daughter in London, Robert had agreed.

Before the marriage could take place Anne died, sometime in December or January 1630/1. By this time, Robert Bowes was in possession of her goods, but he seems to have tried to do the honourable thing. Anne had requested that he should be good to Jane Grococke, her mother, so Robert drew up a schedule of the goods and delivered them to the Grocockes in Radcliffe. However, he retained the loan money and the price of the brass pot. At this point Jane Henfrie of Edwalton, named as executrix in Anne's will, and her husband Thomas stepped in. They brought a case through the Archdeacon's Court against the Grocockes for having obtained the goods without legal authority, and against Robert Bowes for his share in the transaction. The latter was clearly confident of his rights, for there was even a suggestion in the subsequent investigations that he had laid a wager that the Henfries would not prevail against him.

The goods about which so much court time was taken in 1633, while probably not Ann Byrde's total possessions, suggest a modest standard of living:

Imprimis her purse, her girdle and her outward wearing apparell	*£2 10s 0d*
Item two coverlets and a bolster	*6s 8d*
Item three pairs of harden sheets, two smocks, two ruffs, ten quoifs, eleven cross cloths, one green apron, one flaxen apron, four hempen aprons, seven pairs of ear stays, a pair of gloves, a pair of ruffs, eight neck cloths, eight napkins, two hand towels and three binders	*£1 0s 0d*
Item one black cow	*£2 6s 8d*
Item five yards of woollen cloth	*12s 6d*
Sum total	*£6 15s 10d*

Jane Henfrie was not to be denied the arrangements of the original will, and the requisite document, with the seal attached of the Archbishop of York's Commissary of Exchequer, was produced in court to prove her rights of administration. While Robert Bowes at first appeared to have his side of the case accepted, the officials eventually decided against him. Thwarted, he was 'disobediently absent' from the final judgement on 4th July 1633. The court found nothing had been proved on his behalf to destroy the lawful right of Jane Henfrie to administer Anne's goods for Elizabeth Byrde - the verbal will was thus set aside in favour of the written will. Moreover, it was decreed that Robert had received 25s of the 50s owed by John Stevens and the 3s.4d value of the brass pot without legitimate authority. He was put under sentence of excommunication, was to be publicly denounced and had to restore the sum of 53s.4d to Jane Henfrie. (He did not pine long for his late betrothed. On 13th November 1631 - less than a year after Anne's death - he married Elizabeth Dring at Radford, Nottingham.)

Jane Grococke, fared no better than her daughter's would-be husband. Both she and Francis were condemned for having acquired the goods listed in the schedule 'without legal authority' and for having 'converted them to their own use in contempt of the law'. Even when requested to hand them over, they had delayed. Consequently, they too were excommunicated, were ordered to hand back the goods to the Henfries, and to pay their legitimate expenses. It is to be hoped that Elizabeth Byrde in London appreciated the lengthy efforts that had been made to ensure that she received her legacy.[196]

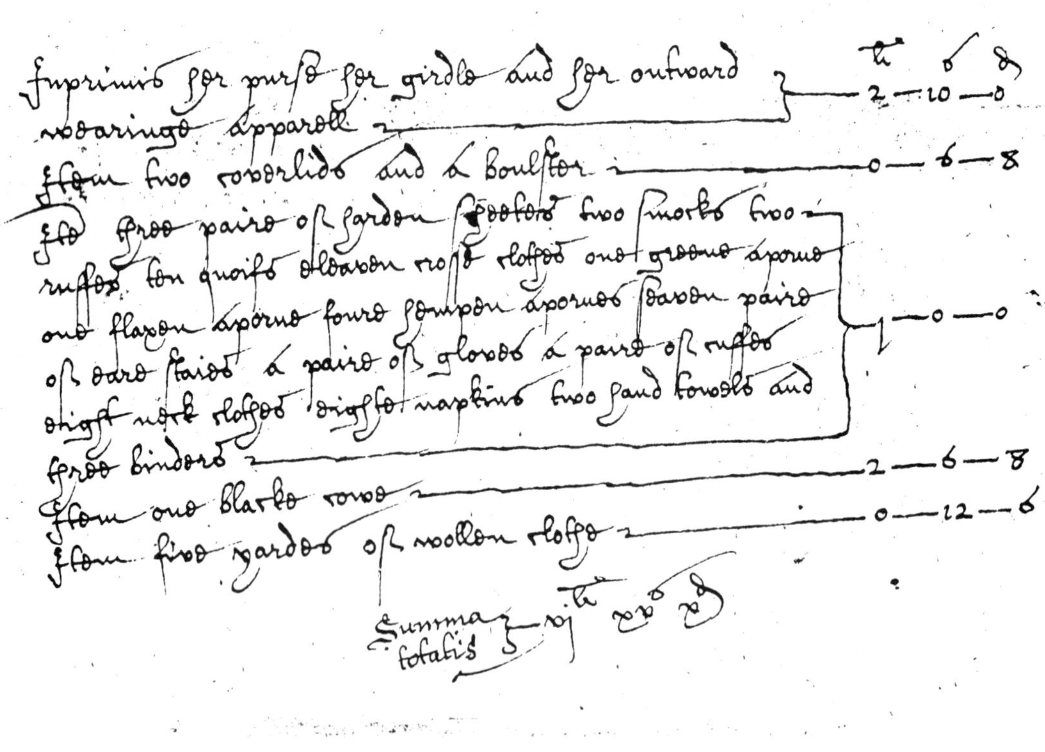

The inventory of Anne Byrde's goods
(U of N Manuscripts Department LB 225/5/7)

After 11 years of personal rule Charles I was forced to call a Parliament in April 1640 to ask for funds to put down a Scottish rebellion. When M.Ps refused his request and attacked his policies, he dissolved this Parliament after only three weeks. The subsequent Scottish invasion of England, which led to the humiliating defeat of royal troops, caused the king to summon a new Parliament. It was this 'Long' Parliament which removed traditional instruments of government and prepared to do battle with monarchy.

When Charles I raised his standard near Nottingham castle on 22nd August 1642, the Rosells, like many families, may have felt divided loyalties. Gervase's step-father and father-in-law, Francis Hacker, was agent to the Earl of Rutland who was a moderate Parliamentarian. (The earl's Belvoir Castle was takn by Royalists before it was successfully besieged by Parliament.) Two of Francis's sons, Thomas and Rowland, were to fight for the king, the former dying in a skirmish near Colston Basset in 1643. As already noted, their brother Francis supported Parliament and was to be labelled a 'regicide' for his supervision of the king's execution. For more than a decade he would seem to have chosen the safer course. Gervase's sister, however, provided further links with the Royalists as wife of Richard, the future second Lord Byron, one of seven brothers active for the king.[198]

Topographically, too, there were arguments for throwing in one's lot with either side. The village was close enough to Nottingham with its market for livestock and crops for allegiance that way to be wise. The town, however, was soon held for Parliament by John Hutchinson of Owthorpe, while the county with which Radcliffe shared so many other interests was largely loyal to King Charles. Small wonder that people left little record of their allegiances locally. Sitting between Parliamentary forces in Nottingham and Royalist forces in Newark and the Vale of Belvoir, Radcliffe could jeopardise its existence by overt action at the wrong time. Like the neighbouring Pierreponts, the Rosells may have tried to avoid committing themselves for as long as possible.

The Rosells in the 1640s

Prior to the outbreak of war, along with the rest of the male community over the age of 18, Gervase had signed the 'Protestation' of early 1642 in support of the Protestant religion, and against the King's seemingly pro-Catholic policy. (See p. 134.) So had an Edmund Rosell. (This was perhaps a clerical error for Edward who died in 1668, whose exact relation to Gervase is uncertain.) George and Thomas, Gervase's sons were too young to sign. The Protestation, however, was no real guide to Civil War loyalties since future Royalists and Roundheads alike are known to have signed.

From April 1643 Gervase's responsibilities increased when Elizabeth, the first of four daughters, was born to him and his new second wife, Jane Ayscough of Hempshill. Katherine followed in November 1644, and Dorothy in 1646 who died as a baby. Maria or Mary was born in 1647. (Presumably the illegitimate Maria of pre-war days had died.) These births recorded in the parish register indicate that the Rosells remained in the village during the Civil War period.

With his trained band experience it is unlikely that Gervase escaped action for long. One glimpse of him is found in Newark in February 1643 during an early attempt by Roundheads to take the town. A defender, Edward Twentyman, is recorded at that time as being 'ensign to Captain Rosell'. It therefore seems certain that Gervase fought as a Royalist.[199]

'Civil War artefacts'

In the summer of 1932 some large pieces of leather, bearing initials, and 109 staves were found when 'The Chestnuts', the large house near the corner of Wharf Lane (now Tudor Grange), was being re-roofed. As has been seen (p. 57) this building corresponds well with the main house on the Rosell estate map of 1710, and can be regarded as the basis of the family mansion. Although newspaper speculations at the time of the find were wildly inaccurate about 17th century activities in the village, experts who looked at the artefacts associated them with the Civil War

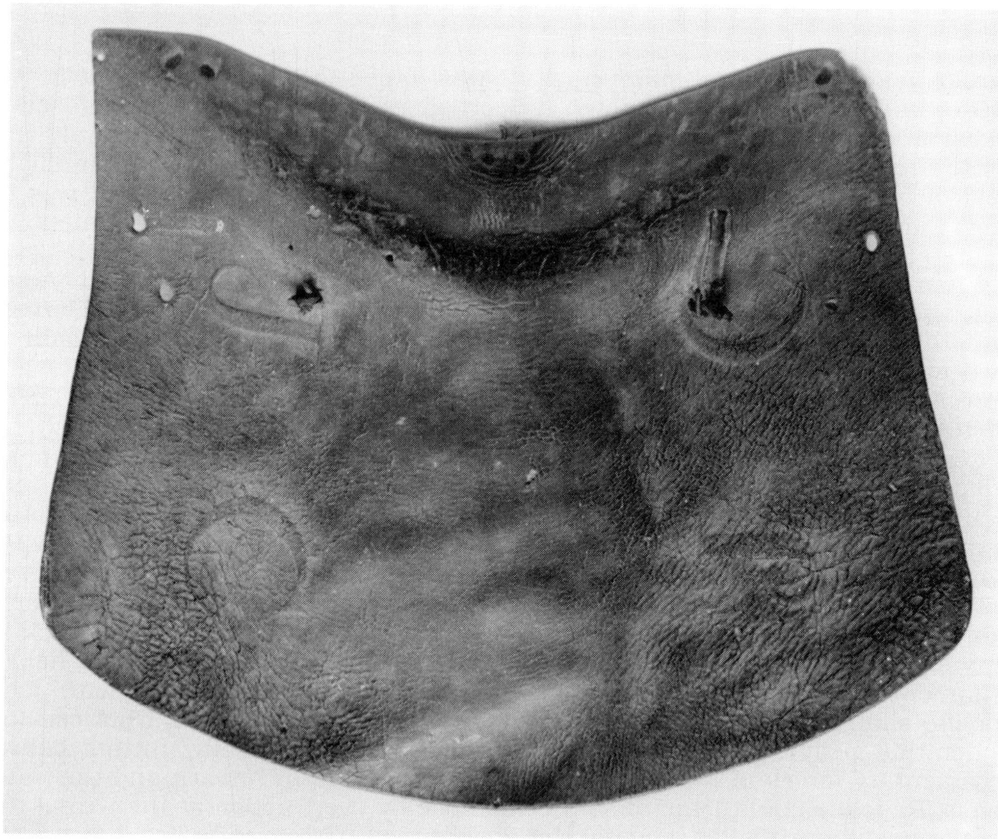

A piece of leather 'horse armour' allegedly from the Civil War period found in 1932 in the roof space of The Chestnuts (now Tudor Grange)

period. Current investigation has failed to prove this, but the tradition is well-established locally.

One of the leather pieces has been traced. It is thick, shaped, approximately 23 inches wide by 17 inches high, has five sets of paired holes and a leather strap 3/4 inches wide on the reverse. It bears the initials J. C. (The newspaper reports refer to another bearing the initials S. P. and contemporaries recall other pieces.) The ash-riven staves do not seem to have survived and are said to have been affected by woodworm. Experts in the 1930s suggested that the pieces were worn by horses, although leather 'armour' is not normally found in the 17th century. The lettering, too, may not be typical of the period. There are later episodes to which they could be linked, but there is as yet no certain proof that they are not Civil War artefacts.

While the J.C. cannot be associated with any prestigious name in Radcliffe during the Civil War, John Chaworth of Wiverton Hall was a staunch Royalist. He had become the second viscount Chaworth in 1639, had garrisoned his house for the king and was one of the king's commissioners at Newark at the start of 1644. Although he died in June of that year, the leather could have belonged to his troop of horse. In November 1645, nearby Shelford Manor was destroyed by Parliamentary troops. No quarter was given and 140 defenders were put to the sword. Wiverton was taken immediately after. Apart from Newark, which did not fall until May 1646, the Vale of Belvoir was cleared of Royalist garrisons. Those fleeing might well have hidden identifiable leather and staves in a sympathetic household to be used again when fortunes turned. Once there, they could have been forgotten as Parliamentary rule dominated for a generation. This interpretation and association with the Rosells can never be more than speculative without further evidence.

The additional find in 1951 of three hats, then identified as of the Cavalier period, in an inglenook ceiling recess in a 17th century cottage in Walnut Grove may provide further evidence of a time when it was safer to hide Royalist attributes. The present location of the hats is unknown (1995).[200]

The Pierreponts and the Stanhopes

While the Rosells were insufficiently prominent in the Civil War for them to be listed amongst those who had estates sequestered (confiscated) by Parliament, Radcliffe's two other main landowners suffered in varying degrees for their Royalist activities.

Robert Pierrepont, Earl of Kingston, had tried to stay neutral at the start of the war, pleading poverty when asked for a loan by the King. According to Lucy Hutchinson, he declared to a Parliamentary Committee in 1643, 'When I take arms with the King against Parliament, or with the Parliament against the King, let a cannon-bullet divide me between them'. This must have seemed a safe challenge to fate as a prognostication based on the hour of his birth - 10.30 a.m. on 5th August 1584 - had promised him 'no likelihood of violent death'. By July of that year, however, he threw in his lot with the king and was besieged at Gainsborough. Forced to surrender, he was put on a pinnace on the Trent in order to be sent to Hull. The boat was hailed by Royalist troops but failed to stop, and they consequently opened fire. Arriving on deck to stop the shooting, the earl was indeed cut in two by a cannon ball, fired by his own side.

Robert Pierrepont
1st Earl of Kingston

His sons were divided in their loyalties. The eldest, Henry, Lord Newark, who succeeded to his father's title and became Marquess of Dorchester, was a Royalist who subsequently became a Fellow of the College of Physicians. His brothers William and Francis supported Parliament. Recent research suggests that the Pierrepont allegiances were more a matter of principle than of policy. Nevertheless, when Henry 'compounded' with Parliament over his 'delinquency' in supporting the King, he was fined only about a tenth (£7,647) of his vast estates' value, rather than a third or sixth which many Royalists had to pay. Moreover, the fine was granted to his Parliamentarian brother William. Although it was to son George, whose allegiances are unknown, that the earl ('sick in body and much grieved in mind') had initially left his Radcliffe holdings when he drew up his first will in 1634, it is clear from later accounts that they remained with the main line of the family. The Pierreponts' local tenants would thus be little affected.[201]

Henry Pierrepont
Marquess of Dorchester

Philip Stanhope, Earl of Chesterfield since 1628, had no doubts about where his loyalties lay when the war broke out in 1642. He raised a regiment of dragoons and fortified Shelford Manor for the king. His house at Bretby in Derbyshire fell to Parliamentary troops in December 1642. Fleeing to Lichfield, he was again besieged, surrendered in March 1643, and spent the remaining thirteen years of his life as a prisoner on parole in London. All his estates were sequestrated (confiscated), and subsequently let for £1,005 a year. He also suffered a fine for delinquency of £8,698. Of his eleven sons, three paid dearly for their loyalty to the king. Ferdinando, his seventh son who was M.P. for Tamworth and a Colonel of Horse, was killed at West Bridgford in 1644 while doing 'a charitable office, in commanding assistance for the quenching of an house there on fire by accident'. Philip, the eighth son, was the stubborn defender of Shelford. 'I keep this garrison for the king and in defence of it

I will live and die,' he declared. In 1645 he was killed when the Parliamentarians sacked the house and slaughtered most of the garrison in one of the bloodiest Civil War episodes in Nottinghamshire. Michael, the tenth son, was killed during the second Civil War in 1648 at the battle of Willoughby Field.

The Stanhopes did not maintain their Radcliffe interests after the Restoration, and although some rebuilding took place at Shelford manor house, it was never more than a shadow of its former self. The family concentrated more on estates in Derbyshire, and many of their local holdings were sold. The nearby Pierreponts were to take advantage of the Stanhope misfortunes and eventually acquired their village concerns.[202]

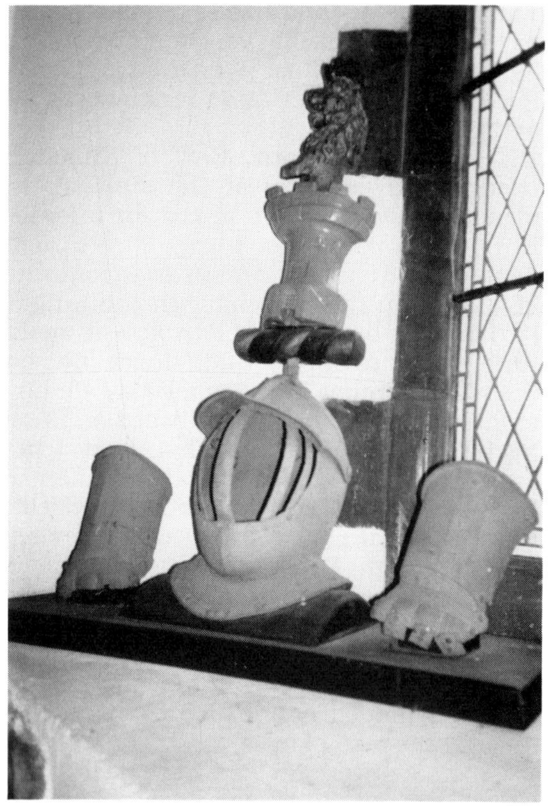

Funerary helmet and gauntlets belonging to the Stanhope family in Shelford church. One authority associates them with Colonel Michael Stanhope who was killed and buried at Willoughby in 1648.[203]

The families of Gervase and Anthony Rosell

During the Interregnum period, the surviving references to Gervase Rosell are particularly scanty. He was fined in 1650-1 a routine 3s.4d for his non-appearance at Holme Pierrepont manorial court where he owed suit for lands he rented from the Pierreponts. In the 1651 entry he is still referred to as 'Captain Rosell'. He was fined 7s for not doing his 'suit and service' in April 1660, just before the restoration of Charles II. In the four surviving wills of the Interregnum period, it is his children, not he, who are named. His elder son, George, was left 20s by widow Margaret Franke in December 1653. George's brother and sister were left 40s to be divided equally between them. These would be Thomas and Anne, aged 26 and 25 respectively, the other surviving children of Gervase's marriage to Elizabeth Hacker. Thomas and Anne were witnesses to Joane Needham's will of February 1658, and Thomas witnessed Anthony Franke's nuncupative will in August 1659. It seems that the next generation was taking on the traditional responsibilities of the squirearchy. Perhaps both Gervase and the elder son, George, were failing in health, for they died soon after the Restoration. Gervase was buried on 2nd January and George on 14th December 1661.[204]

It is during the Interregnum that another branch of the Rosells became active in the village. Anthony Rosell - the son of Edward Rosell, a tailor, who was buried in Radcliffe in 1668 - had been apprenticed on July 2nd 1640 to the Skinner's Company (dealing in skins and furs). Such apprenticeships for junior branches of the gentry were not unusual. For example, three years earlier Harold Scrimshire, from a prominent Cotgrave family with whom the Rosells were linked, had also been apprenticed to the Skinner's Company.[205]

The exact relationship of Edward and Anthony to the senior branch of the family headed by Gervase is uncertain, but an earlier Anthony, the son of John Rosell junior and his second wife Annora (Pierrepont), had died at Adbolton, and been buried at Holme Pierrepont in 1616 (p. 109). The Anthony who returned from his apprenticeship and settled in Radcliffe with his wife, Maria, during the 1650s was perhaps his grandson. In September 1650, a son, George, was born to the young couple. The baby was buried on 4th April 1652. Nine days later a second son was baptised, also named George after his dead brother. Three more children followed between February 1654 and November 1657 - Major, Elizabeth and Anthony.

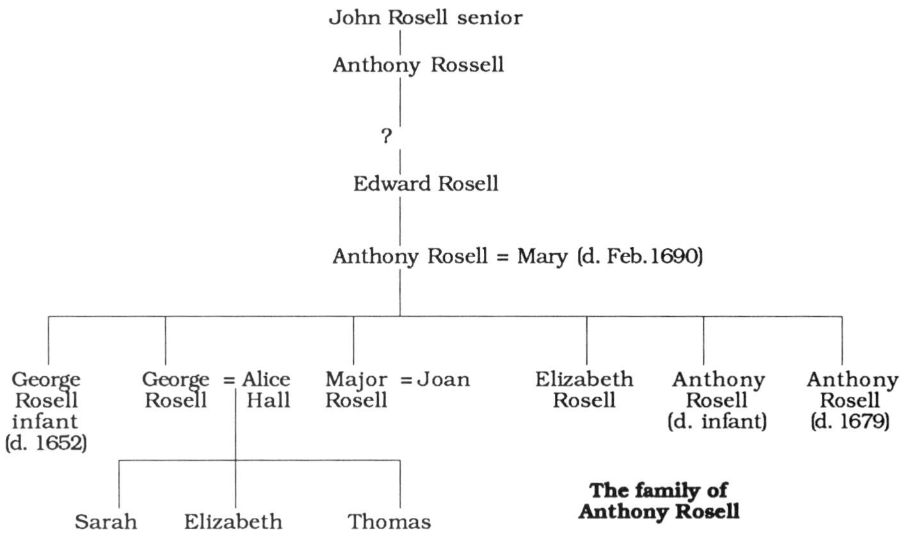

The family of Anthony Rosell

With the christening of a child 'Major', it is tempting to suppose that Anthony Rosell was in favour of Cromwellian ideals, and had been placed in Radcliffe to supervise the Rosell estates in place of his Royalist kinsman. (In the year after Major's birth, Cromwell divided the country into eleven districts, each ruled by a Major-General.) The explanation is probably less divisive. At Staunton, where the staunchly Royalist family had suffered severely for their loyalty, the heir to the ruined estates had been christened Major, a corruption of the old Staunton family name of Mauger. The naming of a son 'Major' by Anthony Rosell was possibly a compliment to the Staunton family, and the parish register there does contain a number of Rosell entries.[206]

After Anthony and his family left Radcliffe around the time of the Restoration, they settled in Arnold to the north of Nottingham, where they continued in trade, prospered, and began to look towards land again. Another Anthony was baptised there in August 1660, so their last Radcliffe son must have died. This second Anthony died when he was 19. Son George became a tailor, and at the age of 25 was married by licence at St Mary's in Nottingham in January 1678 to Alice Hall, an Arnold widow, some ten years his senior. They had three children born between November 1678 and January 1683, the first dying soon after birth. George served Arnold as constable, churchwarden or overseer of the poor. In 1681 he took part of Bestwood Park on a lease for nine years from Nell Gwyn, who had acquired it from Charles II. (George's brother Major had a son, another George, baptised in Arnold in 1690, but their occupations are not known.) Trade and a less rural lifestyle was not unprecedented for the Rosells. A century earlier this way of life had been adopted by branches of the family in Retford, and would be followed by other members of the Radcliffe line as their fortunes declined after the Restoration.

Case study 11

THE PROTESTATION RETURN

In early March 1642 a remarkable event took place in Radcliffe and in other places throughout the country as a result of unpopular government policies. These included Archbishop Laud's emphasis on religious ceremony which smacked of Popery, coupled with Charles I's own apparent sympathy for Catholicism. At the instigation of Parliament and because of the growing political crisis, all men over the age of 18 were required to sign what was known as the Protestation affirming their support for the Protestant religion and for the King in Parliament. (The traditional fiction of blaming the monarch's advisers, rather than the monarch himself, explains why support could be requested for the king.) The Protestation, it was hoped, would flush out the papists, the universal scapegoats in time of trouble, reveal them as traitors and rally popular support for Parliament.

The form of the oath was as follows:

I A.B. in the presence of Almighty God promise, vow and protest to maintain and defend as far as lawfully I may, with my life, power and estate the true reformed Protestant religion expressed in the doctrine of the Church of England, against all Popery and Popish Innovation within this realm contrary to the same, and according to the duty of my allegiance to his Majesty's royal person, honour and estate.

It was usually the duty of the local clergy to administer the oath - William Creswell in Radcliffe's case - supported by the church-wardens and other parish officers.

Ninety-eight men led by the two Rosells, Gervase and Edmund (or Edward), the only gentry present. lined up to sign or make their mark as they were able. The resulting Return is a unique document, showing as it does all the adult males living in the village at that time. Heading it is the statement:

None refused, but all will be as ready to perform as they were ready to vow whatsoever is therein contained.

Perhaps this hints at a lack of under-standing by at least some of the signatories. The Greenes with five members and the Parrs with four (one Pare) were the largest contingents. They were joined by members of other leading families - the Frankes and Thraves (two each, plus John Longe alias Thrave), Martin Grococke and John Wright. Roger Campion the long serving parish clerk and his son John were there among others from families who had probably arrived during Elizabeth's reign (about ten of them) including the Pilkingtons. There were about 11 from families who first appeared in the early Stuart period, such as the Hutchinsons and the Johnsons, and another 11 who had only recently arrived - including the Butlers, a prosperous family which was to become important in the village in the years to come, a new branch of the Halls (with four members) and the vicar William Creswell. A large number (about 20) have family names which are difficult to follow with any certainty. Then there were those, nearly a quarter of the whole, whose names occur nowhere else in the records or only seldom and sporadically. It is more than likely that these were apprentices, domestic servants or servants in husbandry originally from other villages and only serving their time in Radcliffe, just as many of Radcliffe's sons would have been doing elsewhere. They were probably brought by their masters to sign. Just how much choice they had and how much interest in political matters is open to question.

The signing may have taken place in an inn, a manor house, in the church porch or even the church itself as it was early in the year and likely to have been wet and cold. As the men waited for their turn, their women-folk, (excluded from the cere-mony) no doubt watched from the sidelines, whilst their children swarmed around. The solemnity of the occasion must have affected all, but few could have predicted the situation six months hence. Their world was about to be shattered and they were to endure all the deprivations of civil war. Some would leave their homes to join one of the contending armies. Those who remained were to be heavily taxed by both sides and their crops and cattle, farm gear and homes were liable to be impounded by whichever side had the upper hand in their neighbourhood at any one time.

As an assessment of literacy, Radcliffe's return is a disappointment since only a list of names, rather than original signatures and marks, has survived. As a guide to population figures the Protestation has some validity, but it must be viewed with caution. A crude estimate of 274 villagers can be made by doubling the total of adult males and adding 40% for children.[207]

THE BREAKDOWN OF RELIGIOUS AUTHORITY 1638-1660

The religious policy of Charles I and Archbishop Laud already outlined led to conflict with Presbyterian Scotland. The enforced use of the English prayer book in St Giles Cathedral, Edinburgh, had provoked a riot in July 1637, followed by the signing of a National Covenant in Scotland in March 1638 'to recover the purity and liberty of the Gospel'. After the General Assembly had abolished episcopacy and re-established Presbyterianism in the November, the king prepared for war in 1639 to reassert his authority over his northern kingdom. Lacking men and money to overcome the superior Scots, however, and reluctant to call an almost certainly hostile English Parliament after a gap of some ten years, he brought an end to the first Bishops' War in June 1639. It was only the beginning, and not the end of a deteriorating situation, and it was against this background that a new young vicar, William Creswell, performed the first full year of his duties in Radcliffe.

William Creswell 1638-1661

The son of yeoman Thomas Creswell of Longdon in Staffordshire, William Creswell had been sent as a boy to Queen Elizabeth's Grammar School in Mansfield, Nottinghamshire, then under the direction of Mr Poynton. Along with a local boy (John Westwood, the son of a Mansfield carpenter), he had gone to St John's, Cambridge - the third Radcliffe vicar in a row to be a Cambridge man, and the second from St John's. He was ordained in 1635, was awarded his M.A. degree, and was instituted at Radcliffe through the patronage of Philip Stanhope, Earl of Chesterfield, on 3rd August 1638. He was probably about 24 years of age.

There is no record of his marriage in the parish registers, but in January 1640 his wife is given as Elizabeth when their son John was baptised. A second son, Gervas(e), was baptised in March 1642, but lived only three weeks. A daughter, Ann, appeared in August 1643. and another child, William, is recorded in June 1650. There must, however, have been at least three more births for in the early 1650s William Creswell claimed that he had six children.[208]

William Creswell's first years

The young man had a lively start to his ministry, notably at the hands of John Wells and his son - another John. Only three weeks after officially taking over his parish, the vicar was forced to have them both brought before the Archdeacon's Court on August 25th 1638 in St Peter's, Nottingham. John Wells senior (a carpenter in court more than once when young), was presented 'for giving ill language to the minister presently after divine service in the church', and his son 'for being a common disturber of the bells on Sundays & holy days'.

Dealing with disruptive, but humble, parishioners was one thing. Coping simultaneously with the moral lapse of the squire must have required considerable tact as well as firmness from the new vicar. On 19th August he baptised Marie, the illegitimate daughter of Gervase Rosell and the latter's servant Abigail Smith. Matters were managed very discreetly, however. The father's name does not appear in the parish register which remained in the village, but only in the transcript sent to the bishop. Moreover, when the churchwardens reported on the state of the parish, they noted that Abigail Moore, alias Smith, had produced a child, but added 'with whom we know not'. When it came to church discipline, however, only limited concessions were made to the squire's status and to the fact that he was a widower. Gervase and Abigail were summoned to appear before a church court on 27th August. This was held in St Mary's, Nottingham, two days after humbler villagers had appeared at the court held at St Peter's. Gossip would have been kept to a minimum. The usual penalties were imposed, but no evidence has been found that the vicar publicly enforced them.[209]

More routine problems completed the year. Laurence Hall and Edward Swinscoe - a name familiar from George Cotes' time - allegedly refused to pay their offerings which they denied, while the churchwardens found themselves before the church court 'for that they have not the table of the degrees of consanguinity and affinity' -

the list of relationships which were prohibited in marriage.

Problem parishioners were still reported to the church authorities in 1639. Typical were two immorality cases. In May William Fox, alias Wilson, was charged with incest with the wife of his son, Thomas. Thomas and Isabella Pollard had to perform the modest penance of confessing at morning prayers on a Wednesday and Friday in their usual clothes for 'carnal incontinency before marriage'. (Their daughter Margaret had been baptised in April and was to die in November 1641.) Over a matter of unpaid dues, Henry Stokes, a newcomer to the village, was lengthily pursued from March 1639 to June 1640 by the churchwardens of Thoroton. Stokes had held 3 1/2 oxgangs of land in Thoroton on which dues were owed for the repair of the church. Although he produced witnesses as to when he had ceased living at Thoroton, the case turned on whether Stokes had to pay on crops he had sown when resident, but reaped and carried away after he had come to live in Radcliffe. The Thoroton churchwardens charged him 16d per oxgang - a total of 4s.8d.

The growing controversies of this period seem to have caused people to prefer discussing matters in the ale-house than listening to the vicar. Certainly, more parishioners were presented to the church courts for this reason in 1639 than in any other year. In May, George Taylor was presented to the court in St Peter's for having sat drinking with his wife in Laurence Hall's ale-house on a Sunday in the previous March. Laurence Hall, accused the previous year of not paying his 'offering' and no stranger to the civil magistrates, was also in court for having entertained him. Both men appear to have been fined 4s.8d. Laurence Hall was there again in August for having company drinking in his house on 'Sunday was fortnight' all day and almost all night 'drinking and quarrelling'. He was fined another 4s.8d, while Samuel Hutton was singled out for being present on that occasion and fined 2s.4d.

Whether public penances were also performed by all these men is not clear, but John Hutchinson, described as an 'aleman', certainly had to confess his sin in public for a similar occurrence. In November 1639 he was charged with having company drinking in his house on a Sunday during the time of evening prayers, and Francis Warde of Holme Pierrepont was charged alongside him as one caught in his house at that time. (Marion Close, a spinster, was similarly presented for having company in her house, or her father's house, on a Sunday during divine service.) On 13th December William Creswell signed that John Hutchinson had performed his penance after morning prayers, in the presence of himself and the churchwardens only. His confession was very specific in a time of growing religious nonconformity:

> *Whereas I John Hutchinson have been presented by the Churchwardens for having Company drinking in my house upon a Sunday in time of divine service, I do acknowledge that I hereby have greatly offended Almighty God by profaning the Lord's day and have been an evil example to others. And I desire Almighty God to forgive me and all others that thereby I have offended to take notice of this my submission And p[ro]mise to be more careful that I offend not in the like kind hereafter.*

Other parishioners in trouble included Margaret Taylor (the wife of 'aleman' John, not the drinking George above) who was sufficiently provoked by William Harrold to throw a stone at him 'which broke his head'. As the incident took place in the churchyard, she was brought before the church court in May 1639, rather than the civil magistrates. Another case suggests that William Creswell may not have been a particularly charismatic preacher. On August 20th Thomas Rippon and his wife were presented for being absent from the service the previous Sunday, while his wife was also charged with being a 'continual sleeper' in church.[210]

The collapse of church discipline

However closely William Creswell attempted to retain control in 1639, it is clear that this was becoming more difficult as the national situation continued to deteriorate. The 'Long' Parliament which the king was forced to summon in 1640 not only condemned his political acts, but introduced a petition to abolish the episcopacy and imprisoned Archbishop Laud. The whole religious edifice, built up over centuries, was being overturned in the turmoil.

It is small wonder that the archdeaconry records reflect national tensions at local level. While the only Radcliffe cases found for 1640 do not occur until December, they are particularly significant, suggesting conflict and questioning of traditional values. Both William Hutchinson and John Thrave, alias Long, were presented 'for chiding and brawling in the Church upon a Sunday after prayers'. At the same time, William Creswell had Robert Butler presented for making what must have seemed an outrageous statement:

> *for that he said in my hearing that the word of God was not true neither would he ever believe it.*

There would be an upsurge of such free thinking, both secular and religious, as censorship collapsed in the following year.

The two Radcliffe court cases for 1641 were traditional in subject matter. Richard Blanckley and widow Alice Barnsley were accused of fornication. William Creswell supervised Alice's public penance, performed on two Sundays in June, while Richard escaped more lightly with purging himself before three neighbours - William Hutchinson (hardly an example of rectitude after his own recent brawling in church), Henry Lindupp and Roger Campion, the parish clerk. The last Radcliffe case before the Civil War was that of Henry Wells, presented in August 1641 for fornication with Dorothy Pight, an Adbolton widow, 'as she hath confessed'. (With the prospect of an illegitimate child in Adbolton, the civil magistrates also ordered him to make financial contributions towards the child's maintenance.) Wells was ordered by the church officials to purge himself before three neighbours, but by this date he felt safe in flouting their authority. Over the next twenty months he was repeatedly summoned to reappear, until in April 1643 any pretence at effective court sittings was abandoned. Henry Wells and his kind must have welcomed the collapse of religious discipline.[211]

The Protestation, the parish register and plague

With the collapse of the church courts, a key source for understanding the role of the church in the community disappears and information on the Civil War period in Radcliffe is disappointingly thin. The Protestation of 1642 (see p. 134), supported by all adult males in the village, cannot provide evidence of religious attitudes to royal policy. (There were no refusals in other local parishes either.) Men were merely swearing to support what was the official religion. Despite Puritan fears, however, Protestantism had never been threatened by the king or Archbishop Laud. Moreover, many who had disliked the king's policies, both religious and political, sided with him at the outbreak of hostilities as the crown symbolised stability in a disintegrating world.[212]

The only other known source until the 1650s is the parish register in which the vicar and churchwardens continued to record the bare landmarks of parishioners' lives. The register is less legible and less well-kept from 1642 onwards, as if reflecting the disorder of the times, and transcripts for the bishop do not exist after 1641 - well before the fall of episcopacy in 1643. William Creswell's signature is not found after 1641 until 1646, when the wars locally were over. There is no reason to suppose, however, that he was absent all this time. His second surviving child, Ann, was baptised on August 8th 1643, but as no more of his children appear in the register until 1650, perhaps his wife was away from time to time to give birth to other children. In general, the registers show few abnormalities, although the 20 burials in 1642 was high for the period. (See p. 198.) There were no marriages in 1645 when the first Civil War was coming to a close, but this is not necessarily significant as marriages were not recorded in a number of other years either. The only unique entries are for August and early September 1645 when some eight parishioners, mainly from the Rogers family, died of the plague. (There were 19 victims in Balderton, and such were the fears in Nottingham that watch was kept to prevent people entering the town from villages south of the Trent. The county was even worse hit in 1646.) A comparative newcomer to Radcliffe, George Rogers was an ale-housekeeper, a vulnerable occupation when troop movements brought suffering strangers to a community. For the most part William Creswell doubtless continued performing his routine duties, acting as occasional scribe, and being present at the high and low points of people's lives as he did before and after the wars.[213]

The vicar's poverty

Whatever William Creswell's personal views on the collapse of ecclesiastical court discipline, civil war and the execution of the king in 1649, he should eventually have been financially better off. In the previous century the Stanhopes had acquired the advowson of Radcliffe and the lands formerly belonging to the rectory (held by Thurgarton Priory from 1379 until the dissolution of the monasteries) on which the great tithes of wool and lambs had to be paid. The glebe (also formerly held by Thurgarton) had come into the hands of Robert Pierrepont, Earl of Kingston, by the time of the Civil War. The Radcliffe vicar had only ten acres of land, the lesser tithes and some dues on which to maintain himself - a situation which could have changed little since the 14th century. The value of the living was consequently between only £5 and £10 a year.

As already seen, Philip Stanhope, Earl of Chesterfield, had been an active Royalist in the Civil War, and his estates including those in Shelford, Saxondale, Newton and Radcliffe had been sequestrated by the victorious Parliament. Amongst these possessions were Radcliffe's former rectory lands which Parliament decided to rent out to William Pilkington of Radcliffe for £160 a year, payable annually in two instalments. (As the lands could bring in £250 a year, Pilkington would still make a handsome profit.) Out of this rent it was agreed on 27th January 1648 that £50 should go to the Radcliffe vicar, despite suspicions that he was a Royalist, to augment his impoverished living. A Parliamentary Survey of church property, taken in August 1650, summed up the overall situation:

> *... the Impropriation of Ratcliffe upon Trent which is worth one hundred and sixty pounds per Annum in the possession of the State, sequestered from the Earl of Chesterfield. And the Glebe Lands which are worth thirty five pounds per Annum belonging to the Earl of Kingston. And the vicarage of Ratcliffe aforesaid which is worth five pounds per Annum, William Creswell Clerk the present Incumbent thereof who hath the Cure of souls there and receives for his salary the profits of the said Vicarage and fifty pounds per annum forth of the Tithes of the said Impropriation by way of augmentation. [He] preaches once and expounds every lord's day and sometimes preaches twice but is disaffected to the Parliament proceedings.*[214]

William Creswell's initial satisfaction at this improvement in his financial circumstances, which would benefit his growing family in difficult times, soon turned to frustration. In neither 1650 nor 1651 did any of the promised extra money appear from the Nottinghamshire sequestrators. Perhaps, like the commissioners who allocated the money, they suspected that at heart the vicar was a conservative who was out of sympathy with Parliamentarian government. More likely, their financial dealings were less than honest. The story of William Creswell's battle with stone-walling officials is told in a series of documents now in the Public Record Office, although their exact sequence is difficult to determine.[215]

By the late summer of 1652 the vicar was getting desperate. Orders from the Committee for Compounding in London, issued on 11th August and 8th September to the sequestrators in Nottinghamshire, confirmed that the arrears should be paid. Apparently these orders had no effect. On 12th October the vicar wrote to the London committee pleading for their help:

> *...The petitioner having a wife & six children; (and but £10 [sic] stipend) hath according to his duty; (& the best of his abilities) served the cure all the time that the Augmentation hath been withheld by the new sequestrators for want of your order.*
>
> *He humbly prays (on the behalf of the parish & himself) that this honourable Committee will explain their former order to the sequestrators. That so the Arrears which shall upon oath appear to be due... shall be paid out of such moneys as they have or shall receive out of the said Rectory for the use of the Commonwealth & to continue payment of the £50 so established as aforesaid.*

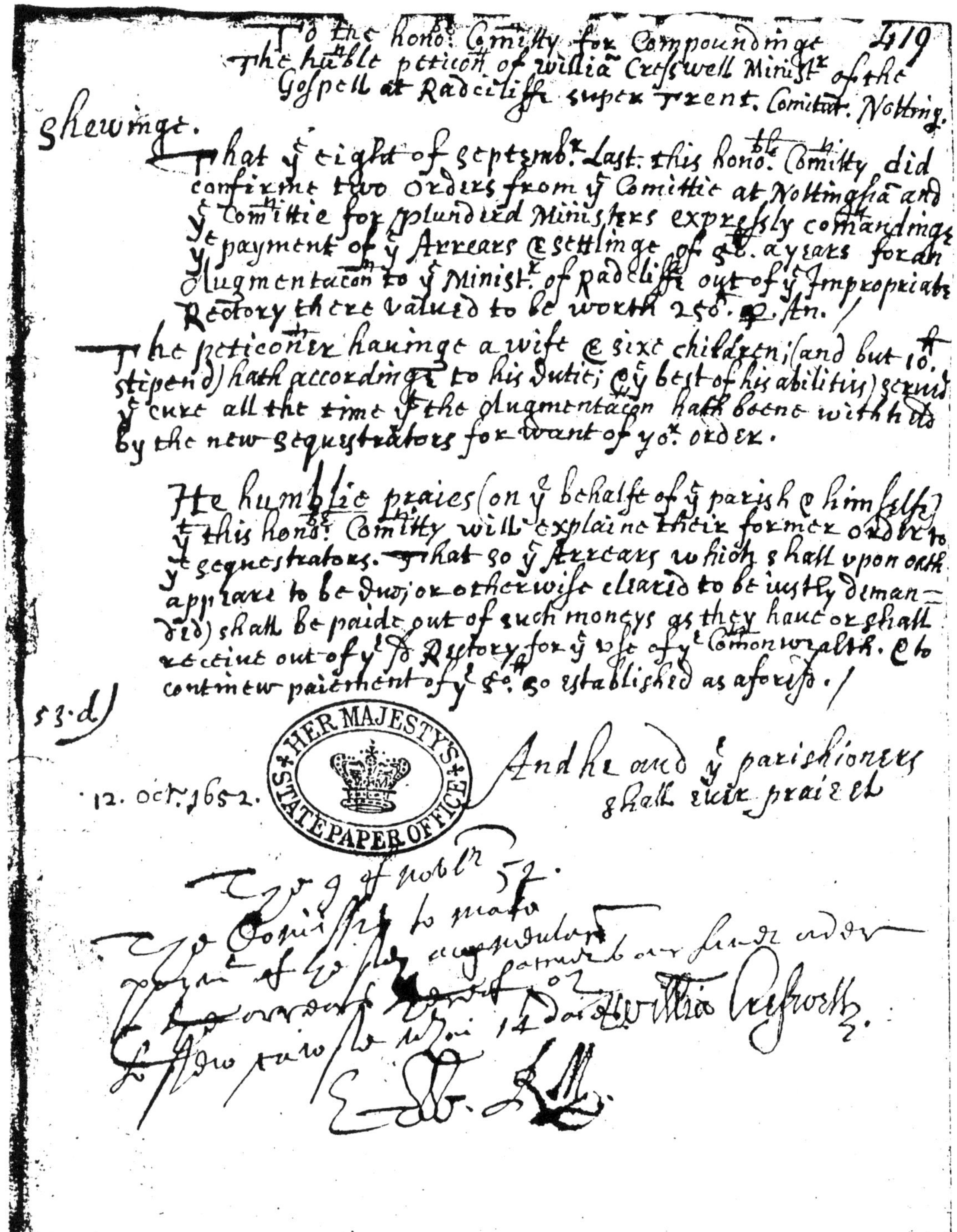
To the Hono[ble] Comitty for Compoundinge 419
The humble peticon of Willia[m] Creswell Minist[er] of the Gospell at Radcliffe super Trent. Comitat. Notting.

Shewinge.

That ye eight of Septemb[er] last this Hono[ble] Comitty did confirme two Orders from ye Comittie at Nottingham and ye Comittie for plundred Ministers expressly comandinge ye payment of ye Arrears & settlinge of 50li a yeare for an Augmentacon to ye Minist[er] of Radcliffe out of ye Impropriate Rectory there valued to be worth 250li p An.

The peticoner havinge a wife & sixe children (and but 10li stipend) hath accordinge to his dutie & ye best of his abilities served ye cure all the time yt the Augmentacon hath beene withheld by the new sequestrators for want of yor order.

He humblie praies (on ye behalfe of ye parish & himselfe) yt this Hono[ble] Comitty will explaine their former order to ye sequestrators. That so ye Arrears which shall upon oath appeare to be due, or otherwise cleared to be iustly demanded) shall be paide out of such moneys as they have or shall receive out of ye sd Rectory for ye use of ye Comonwealth, & to continew paiment of ye 50li so established as aforesd.

53.d

12. oct. 1652.

And he and ye parishioners shall ever praie &c.

HER MAJESTY'S STATE PAPER OFFICE

[illegible] William Creswell

William Creswell's plea to the Committee for Compounding in London for the payment of his arrears, 12th October 1652
(PRO SP 23/77)

Mr Brett and Mr Bland

On 9th November 1652 the Commission for Compounding in London, having read William Creswell's petition, formally ordered the Nottingham sequestrators to pay the augmentation with arrears, 'or certify cause to the contrary' within 14 days of receiving the notice. The vicar went in person with the notice to the two local officials, Michael Brett and Francis Bland. He found them with a ready excuse for the non-payment, as he explained to the London Commissioners when he was forced to write to them again for help on 12th January 1653:

> *...they answered that they was never unwilling to pay the Arrears due to the Petitioner. But having accounted them to the state, they durst not make repayment out of the moneys in their hands, or out of any other which should come into their Receipt without your express order assigning them from whence.*

In the same letter William Creswell refuted any suggestion of disloyalty to the new regime, while emphasising his dire financial plight made worse by debt:

> *There being no Incapacity in the Petitioner for doctrine, Conversation & fidelity to the Commonwealth as now established; he having constantly officiated at the Rectory during the detention of his...salary.*
>
> *Humbly prays that your honours will make valid your former orders, according to the Act & in charity to look upon his sad condition, having borrowed money to support himself, his wife & six children all the while. And that you will positively direct the sequestrators, how and from whence, the petitioner shall (by them) be paid, that which is his just due and so behind.*

In the light of what is known of Michael Brett and Francis Bland, their plausible excuse for non-payment - that they had already paid their moneys to headquarters and needed London guidance as to the source from which the Radcliffe vicar could now receive his income - is not convincing. Brett had served in the Parliamentary forces as an intelligence officer, and the pair had been appointed as Nottinghamshire commissioners early in 1650 in the hope of improving efficiency in collecting fines from royalist 'delinquents'. They complained about having met with opposition from 'many malignant spirits', but the smallness of the revenue they collected undoubtedly masked sharp practice. For example, on paper the Nottinghamshire sequestration money for 1649-50 should have been £9,260.14s.9d, but only £1,286 was paid in for the half year. William Creswell was not alone in writing to London to protest about their conduct and they were shortly removed from office. Their successors, Thomas Lindley of Skegby and Robert Brunts of Mansfield, were later warned by the London authorities not to follow the dismissed men's example: 'whilst you are guided by Brett & Bland we can expect nothing better...Take heed of them lest they put you to justify their unworthy actions.' Michael Brett, perhaps with an eye to the future, subsequently defected and took part in a Royalist rising in August 1659.[216]

In the meantime, despite an order that the money could be paid out of the Treasury, William Creswell was still struggling to get his money. In March 1653 he wrote again to the London commissioners over the withholding of payment, reminding them of his wife and six children, and humbly asserting that it was 'as proper for him to receive profit from the Rectory (where he did officiate) as any stranger'. He had also heard of a vacancy at Attenborough from which he hoped to benefit 'as satisfaction in p[ar]t of his arrears.' This time he took the precaution of getting proof that Brett and Bland had actually received rent from the rectory lands for 1650 and 1651 by getting William Pilkington, the tenant, to supply a certified copy. A look at the accounts confirms that the sequestrators had been less than honest, failing to pay in to headquarters £50 for an initial half-year's rental. As the vicar pointed out, the accounts clearly showed that

> *they [Brett and Bland] received £290 for the use of the Commonwealth & Mr Brett of late being tasked and questioned about the odd £50 made answer*

(with a Blush) that it's true he accompted not for it at first but hath now of late...

The London commissioners again ordered that William Creswell should be paid, but again nothing was done, even after the disgraced Brett and Bland had been removed. In the summer of 1653 the desperate vicar was once more painfully setting out his case, although by this time it seems that he and his parishioners had managed to get hold of £55 towards his arrears. There was, however, still £45 outstanding. He now specifically charged the sequestrators with obstruction and dishonesty, claiming that there had been seven orders from London about the payments owing to him. He reminded the commissioners of the proofs he had presented, showing

> *...that over and above the Rent there was £50 in Mr Brett's hand unaccounted for and concealed from the State. And £55 lay dormant in the Farmer's [i.e. Pilkington's] hand secured by the parishioners and your petitioner. The which moneys (thus discovered) was ordered (March ye 10th Last) to be paid to ye petitioner ....*
>
> *But Mr Brett, though he confesseth the money to be in his hand & hath oft promised payment yet (after 4 months chargeable attendance) your petitioner is still deluded, to the great hindrance of your petitioner from his calling.*
>
> *The parishioners (who are herein much concerned) & your petitioner having a wife & 4 [sic] children & but £10 per An[num] salary besides this Augmentation Humbly pray That he may no longer be put upo[n by] the sequestrator.*
>
> *But the Residue of his Arrears (£45) according to your order [of] Jan 12th may be paid him out of the Treasury. And that Mr Brett and Mr Bland may be sent for up to pay the £50 unaccounted for to the state; or be dealt withall as touching their Contempts...*

From this it would seem that the vicar was on good terms with his parishioners, who were supporting him in his fight. Brett and Bland were ordered yet again to pay what was due or appear before the London committee within fourteen days. Perhaps, having already been dismissed, they at last complied, for no further petitions from the vicar have been found. It had been a long struggle and according to his last letter his children had been reduced by two during the previous year. As their deaths cannot be found in the registers, perhaps they had simply left home.[217]

The parish in the 1650s

It was from 1650 that compulsory attendance at a parishioner's own church was abolished, provided that some place of worship was attended. Without the discipline imposed by the church courts, however, this requirement was impossible to enforce. Moreover, the Barebone's Parliament in 1653 in theory took away from clergy not only the custody of the registers, but the duty of solemnising marriages. The latter function was entrusted to justices, while a 'Parish Register', elected by all ratepayers and sworn-in by a magistrate, was to be in charge of the registers. In practice, the new rules were not always strictly adhered to, and the minister was sometimes elected as 'Register'. This seems to have been the case in Radcliffe, for William Creswell signed the register throughout the 1650s, and it seems that he, rather than a magistrate, conducted all ceremonies.

In 1654 a system of 'triers' and 'ejectors' attempted to secure the appointment of Puritan ministers to English parish churches, and the temporary rule of the Major-Generals from 1655 also helped to enforce some moral discipline, although their concerns were as much with law and order as the spiritual needs of the population. The fact that William Creswell remained in control of Radcliffe throughout this time suggests that wherever his sympathies had lain in 1650, he was prepared at least in part to adapt to the changing times. Nevertheless, he was clearly never a Puritan, and was perhaps lucky not to be turned out for showing sympathy to those who preferred more traditional ways. (The suggestion by Wood that John Penn, a Puritan, was ejected from Radcliffe-on-Trent after the Restoration seems to have been an error for Ratcliffe-on-Soar.) For example, between June 1654 and September 1658 he baptised 14 Cotgrave babies following problems in that parish with a new minister appointed under the Puritan policy of 1654. The first of these babies was Ann, the daughter of Thomas and Margaret Orgreave, and on this occasion William Creswell added an explanatory note in the Radcliffe register: 'Bendall their intruded Rector refusing'. (Mr Bendall is not identified in Cotgrave's own parish register. His extreme Puritanism is confirmed by the marriage of Reforme Bendall to John Jackson in 1656. Their daughter was named Livewell.)[218]

The Orgreaves had been married at Radcliffe in the previous July, indicative of the temporary dramatic change in the pattern of marriages under the religious legislation of the Interregnum. Normally, at least the bride came from the parish in which the couple were married, but there were always some exceptions to this if a special licence was obtained. In the decade from 1641-1650 only two couples from a total of 18 marriages are listed as coming from outside Radcliffe - both in 1650 - although the cleric Robert Heath who was married in Radcliffe in 1648 was also an outsider, being the incumbent of Shelford. In the decade of 1651-1660, 35 marriages are recorded. In nine cases the bride and groom came from two different outside parishes. In 11 other cases the bride certainly came from outside Radcliffe, and probably the groom as well. (All but one partner came from Nottinghamshire.) This freedom of movement was to disappear after the Restoration. Between 1661 and 1670 15 marriages are recorded - none between 27th November 1666 and 1st June 1671. Of these, only one was between non-Radcliffe people, and it took place at the start of the decade in February 1661.

Death of the parish clerk

From the 1580s the village clergy had been assisted by a long-living parish clerk, Roger Campion, who had also served as churchwarden from time to time. In 1657 the parish register records his death in unusual detail:

> *Buried Roger Campion the parish clerk aged 97 years at least having occ[upi]ed his afores[ai]d office in this parish eighty years September 29.*

The loss of this apparently permanent fixture in the village must have been all the more felt when his successor, Robert Dickinson, survived only five months, being buried on the following 25th February .

William Creswell and the Rustats

In 1659 the vicar's personal circumstances changed when his wife Elizabeth died. His last signature appears in the parish register in 1660. In June of that year he remarried at Holme Pierrepont, his bride being Alice, daughter of John Rustat, the rector there. A son, Thomas, was baptised in the following May, but the marriage was short-lived for on 14th October 1661 William Creswell was buried at Holme Pierrepont. In August 1663 his widow married Richard Hawis, her father's curate - one of a number of preachers called on to help out in Radcliffe in the early 1660s.

John Rustat, originally from Barrow-on-Soar in Leicestershire, had another daughter, Eleanor. In 1671 she married the Reverend Humphrey Perkins, also from Barrow and curate at Widmerpool, Rustat's second parish. (On her marriage licence Eleanor gave her age as 30, but according to the Widmerpool registers she must have been about 40!) Humphrey Perkins collected tithes for his father-in-law at Holme Pierrepont in the 1670s, was perhaps his curate there, and ultimately became rector on Rustat's death in 1680. Eleanor died childless in 1693, and in June 1697 Humphrey Perkins married Anne Cheswell at Holme Pierrepont. (It is tempting to speculate whether she could be a mis-spelt descendant of William Creswell.) A settlement was agreed to provide for her maintenance after his death, and in 1712 Perkins bought 65 acres of Gervase Rosell's estate in Radcliffe and ten acres from William Pilkington to fulfil the agreement. This second marriage was also childless, and the profits from the Radcliffe purchase were used to found the Humphrey Perkins School at Barrow-on-Soar after Anne's death in 1735.[219]

In the meantime, the death of William Creswell in the autumn of 1661 had brought to an end an incumbency which totally spanned a period when the world had been 'turned upside down'.

Case study 12

THE GAMBLES AND THEIR DAUGHTERS

It is rarely possible to discover when or how a new family moved into the village, but in the case of the Gambles the events which led to their departure can be traced. They probably lived in Radcliffe for not much more than 75 years, arriving by the later years of the 16th century. Thomas Gamble, who acted as witness to eight wills from 1586 onwards, was overseer of his father-in-law John Greene's will in 1594. Three of his sons - John, Henry and Harold - were mentioned in this will and at some time he had another son, Thomas. Thomas senior was also a witness to John Rosell's will in 1605 and probably to several others in the early Stuart period. Of the four sons, John and Henry appear to have been most active, displaying a casual, even aggressive, attitude to the law. Both held the office of churchwarden at least once and from 1621 they were both involved in a number of minor incidents which brought them before the magistrates and the church courts. In several of these offences they were joined by their relatives by marriage from the Greene family.

lease of the farm in Radcliffe which my brother Thomas Gamble did give unto me', with instructions that their father should receive 10s a year during the term of the lease. This lease may be the one which Thomas (together with Henry Parr) acquired from Lord Stanhope in June 1623. It consisted of three messuages, four cottages, 480 acres of land, 42 acres of meadow, 140 acres of pasture and common pasture in Radcliffe and Lamcote. It may also explain the events which took place immediately after Henry's death. On the 9th January 1637 Gertrude, Henry's widow, and Thomas were charged at Quarter Sessions with forcible entry and John with trespass. Perhaps the dispute was with Henry Parr who may have tried to take advantage of the widow and her very young son by not yielding up their share of the property. The cryptic judgement 'stay of restitution and fine' four months later is the sole indication of the outcome. Gertrude shortly consoled herself by marrying William Stapleton of Clipstone in June 1638 and she and Francis disappeared from Radcliffe.

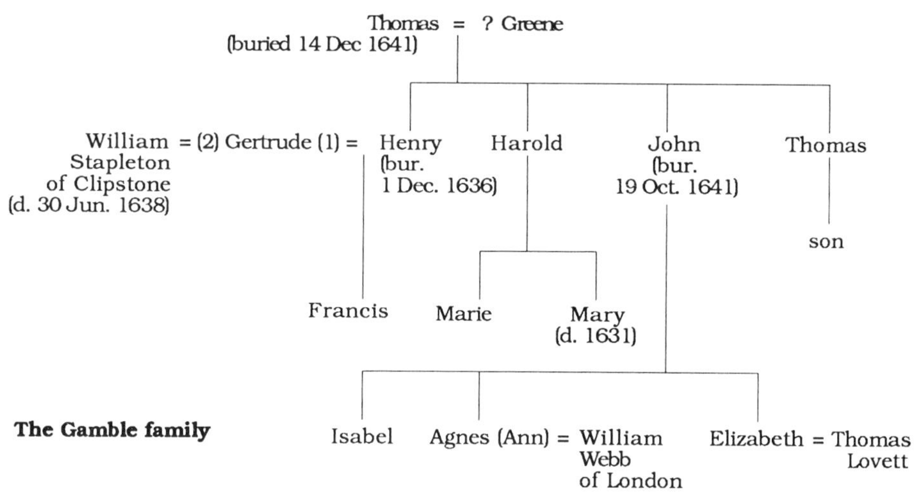

The Gamble family

Henry Gamble's will

In 1635 Henry and Gertrude his wife were cited for fornication before marriage and their son Francis must have been born about this time. Their marriage lasted less than two years, however, for Henry was buried on 1st December 1636. His nuncupative will shows that his father Thomas was still alive, that his brother Harold had a daughter Marie and had moved to Nottingham, that brother Thomas had a son and that John had three daughters. Henry left legacies of £3 or £4 to each of his nieces and nephew and to Harold, whilst he gave to John all that he owed him and made him guardian of Francis. To his wife and son he left an equal share 'of that part of the

John had a further brush with the authorities in May 1640 when he tried to avoid taking on the job of parish constable. He was clearly the most prosperous of the brothers for he paid the subsidy tax in 1628 and again in 1641. In October of that year he died and two months later so did Thomas (almost certainly his father). No will has survived for John but an admonition bond to administer his goods was taken out by Thomas Thrave of Gimerston, Lincolnshire, on a surety of £40. The name of John's widow is not known but she may have been the widow Alice Gamble who, only four months after his death, took out a marriage licence with a Thomas Thrave, this time of Radcliffe, yeoman and bachelor.

Three daughters

Three daughters were thus left to share John's freehold property. Their names were Isabel, Agnes (Ann) and Elizabeth. By 1650 Agnes had married William Webb a citizen and merchant tailor of London and the other two sisters had moved to Nottingham. On 19th June 1650 their inheritance was sold to Robert Butler who paid £300 to Agnes and William Webb and £150 to Isabel and Elizabeth Gamble. By this he acquired half a messuage in Radcliffe and the adjoining buildings, gardens and orchards with the meadows in the fields of Radcliffe and Lamcote (estimated as being 80 acres 'as yet undivided'). The sale also included half the arable and pasture (already divided) which belonged to the messuage and consisted of $3\frac{1}{2}$ oxgangs in Radcliffe and $\frac{1}{4}$ oxgang in Lamcote. (Of this Robert Butler was already the tenant, together with Joane Needham and John Campion). In addition he acquired two closes of three roods each, called Coafer Lane Close in Radcliffe (tenant John Hutchinson) and Lamcote Close in Lamcote (tenant William Morley). The bargain and sale was signed by William Webb and the three sisters - Isabel with a good signature, Agnes (signing as Ann) and Elizabeth with just a mark. Thomas Gamble, probably their uncle, was a witness. By the time the final concord was enrolled at the Court of Common Bench, Westminster, six months later, Elizabeth had married one Thomas Lovett. This sale to all intents and purposes marked the end of the Gamble presence in Radcliffe.

The Butlers

The remaining brother Thomas disappears from the records and there is just one reference to a Henry Gamble in 1679 who was perhaps his son. Subsequently the Butlers became an important family in the village, rivalling the Parrs and Greenes with the number of their sons and their family relationships. When Robert Butler died in 1654 the Gamble inheritance was passed to his second son William, with the exception of the land in Lamcote Field which went to the eldest, Richard. William died in 1698. Nearly 30 years later his widow and their only son William proceeded to arrange a series of mortgages of the property first to William Brown of Ruddington and then to John Plumptre of Nottingham, doctor in physic. Part of the documentation for these transactions includes a terrier, a survey setting out in great detail the lands scattered among the four fields of the village, the only one of this type known to have survived from Radcliffe. Covering two sides in a small script, it illustrates graphically the complexity of property transfers which required a minute description of each strip of land - no doubt a source of rich pickings for lawyers and their scribes![220]

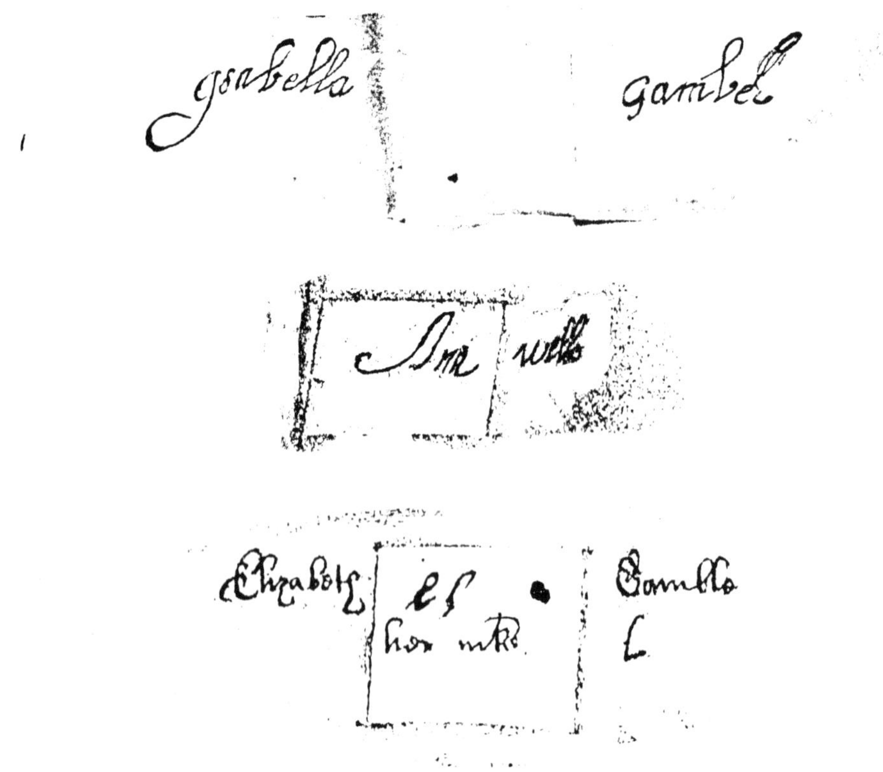

The signatures and mark of the three Gamble sisters
(NAO DD MM 72)

Case study 13

LAWRENCE HENSON - ship's carpenter

Many young men and women in Radcliffe would have spent their youth as living-in servants hired out by local farmers until they acquired a farm of their own or a cottage from which they worked as day labourers. Some would have gone further afield as apprentices to artisans and craftsmen in towns. Few details about them have emerged, so a probably inaccurate impression is left of a rather static population. The rare survival of information concerning one such apprentice, Lawrence Henson, adds a touch of adventure, even romance, to village history.

The *Royal Defence*

Lawrence's birth may have been too early for the surviving parish registers, but his brother John is recorded as the father of four children born to his wife Alice between 1648 and 1656. The three youngest were still alive when Lawrence died. It is because John acted as executor to Lawrence's will that his story has come to light.

He was apprenticed to John Chester, ship's carpenter of London, probably some time in the 1640s or 50s. If the latter were a kinsman of the John Chester in the defamation case of 1625 (p. 121) this could explain how Lawrence came to find such an apprenticeship. In 1657 he was at sea on the *Royal Defence* - an intriguing name for a ship during the Interregnum - under Captain John Cox.

A possible explanation can be found by examining the context of the times. The merchantman *Defence* was one of a number hired for use as men-of-war by the Parliamentary navy between 1649 and 1654. By 1657 numerous vessels had, in the words of a harassed merchant trader, 'gone to the enemy [i.e. the Royalists].... and assisted them like parricides'. Such ships worked out of Ostend and other continental ports, and it seems likely that the *Defence* was one of them, with *Royal* added to its name. (After the Restoration, a Captain John Cox was rewarded with commands and a knighthood. He died at the battle of Sole Bay in 1672.)

Lawrence Henson's will

By 1657 Lawrence must have completed his apprenticeship as he refers to his wages when making his will on 16th December in the presence of three shipmates. He was still on board 'this present ship', and must have died not long afterwards for the will was proved in London in the following April.

First he left to his master John Chester

> *all my wages that shall appear to be due unto me for my voyage in this present ship ...excepting five pounds which I do give and bequeath unto his daughter Mary Chester to be paid at the age of sixteen years but the same to be paid unto her father...*

John Chester was to receive them from the ship's captain. Perhaps Lawrence's hopes of being a master craftsman included marrying his master's daughter! If so, they were cruelly dashed by his premature death. His next bequest was of £5 each to his maternal aunt Dorothy Peet and the sons (Joseph and William) of his brother John. His aunt was to receive hers immediately and the boys when they reached the age of 21 years. To the poor of Radcliffe he left 20s and to his brother's daughter Mary 'all the linen that was given by my mother'. The rest of his 'goods, money, clothes' he gave to his brother John.

The Archdeacon's Court case

The probate shows that John undertook on oath the task of administering the will, implying that he visited London to do so. Time passed, however, and according to Aunt Dorothy, a widow, she never received her legacy. It was perhaps the long delayed arrival of Lawrence's apparel into John Henson's custody in 1667 or 1668, together with £15 or £16 from Master John Chester, which prompted her to press for her legacy and ultimately to take her nephew to the Archdeacon's Court - the church being responsible for the administration of wills. There she pleaded her case on the 18th September 1669. Lawrence's will was produced and she maintained that his goods and chattels had been sufficient to pay his debts and his legacies and that they had come, or could have come into the hands of his brother to administer. Indeed, she estimated that his estate amounted to as much as £180. Moreover, John Henson had in his possession the sum of £50, £40 or at least £30 which had been due to Lawrence 'being a portion given him by his father and w[hi]ch in the life time of him the said Lawrence and at the time of his death was unpaid to him.' She had asked John more than once - or at least once - for the £5 due to her, but he had not paid any attention and had refused to comply with her request - or at least he delayed more than was right. Dorothy appears as a confused plaintiff always qualifying her remarks, but if it were true that she had not received her legacy, she had every right to complain, for 11 years had passed since Lawrence's will had been proved in London. As so often happens in these cases, John Henson's defence and the final judgement have been lost. The parties may have settled out of court which would have been the happiest outcome.[221]

Case study 14

THE GENTRY, THE MILITIA AND THE COLONEL

The events of 1660 restored not just the king, but also the loyal gentry to their old positions of power in the county. In 1662 Parliament passed the Militia Act which renewed the county militia or trained bands of horse and foot. They were under the ultimate command of the king, but the lords lieutenant of the counties and their deputies (chosen from the more important local families) exercised considerable autonomy over them. Shaken by their experiences during the Civil War and the Interregnum, they regarded the county militia as a safeguard against anarchy on the one hand and the possible establishment of a standing army by the king on the other. The new political settlement rested upon the supremacy of the local gentry, and the militia was used to crush any opposition.

In Nottinghamshire the lord lieutenant was the Marquess of Newcastle commanding two companies of horse and six of foot. His Lieutenancy Book covering the years 1660-1677 reveals the atmosphere of suspicion and tension which marked this period. There were reports of risings being plotted, followed by house searches and arrests. These alarms touched Radcliffe in the early 1660s, for in its vicinity the rumours centred around Colonel John Hutchinson of Owthorpe, who had held Nottingham castle for Parliament and had been a signatory of Charles I's death warrant. Through the influence of friends, he had been lucky enough to escape a grisly death on the scaffold and had now retired to his estates. At last in 1663 his enemies managed to implicate him in the Northern or Yorkshire anti-royalist plot. Lucy Hutchinson, his wife, wrote in her *Memoirs* of her husband how late on 11th October the soldiers came to the 'Town' (Owthorpe) on

> *as bitter a stormy, pitchy, dark, black, rainy night as any that came that year*

and arrested him. He was taken to the Talbot Inn, Newark, put into a 'vile' room and guarded by two soldiers.

At the same time various seditious agents were reported to be at large in Nottinghamshire and the deputy lieutenant Sir Francis Leeke summoned two companies of foot to Newark, one from the villages of Thurgarton Hundred under Captain Palmer and one from those of the Bingham Hundred under the captaincy of Peniston Whalley. The latter force consisted of three sergeants, two drummers and 65 soldiers including five men from Radcliffe - Thomas Butler, George Bayler (Bayley?), William Hutchins, John Duke and John Wilcocke. They served in Newark for four whole days from 14th to 17th October, covering part of the time that Colonel Hutchinson was held there. Lucy Hutchinson wrote disparagingly of the troops:

> *And now what they ailed we knew not, but they were all seized with a panic fear, and the whole country [county] fiercely alarmed, and [they were] kept at Newark many days at intolerable charges, and I think they never yet knew what they were sent for in to do but guard Colonel Hutchinson...*

The ignorance of the men as to the purpose of their employment was perhaps a feature common to many soldiers everywhere. The deputy lieutenant in charge, Sir Francis Leeke, was almost equally scathing about them for hardly had they arrived in Newark than he was writing to the lord lieutenant with a request that they should be dismissed 'for they are of little service'. Newcastle agreed to send them home, 'because I desire not at all to put the Country to any unnecessary duty'. They were to be drawn up, the reasons for their being called up explained to them and dismissed with thanks. But 'the trained bands' troops [were to] be at an hour's warning to appear again when there shall be any occasion'.

The state of alert and the investigations in Nottingham and among the villages near Owthorpe continued for some time in 1664 and 1665. Anyone who had had any dealings with the Colonel was questioned. A tailor from Cropwell Butler admitted that he had put 'some clasps on a buffcoat' for him about five or six years previously, while Captain Philip Pendock of Tollerton insisted that his only correspondence with him had been over the buying and selling of horses. There was little evidence against Colonel Hutchinson, but he was removed to London, first to the Tower and then to imprisonment in Sandown Castle, Kent where he died less than a year later. It was his stepbrother Charles Hutchinson who was later to be one of the trustees appointed to manage the Rosell estates.

Colonel John Hutchinson

Captain Whalley's company

of foot was to feature again in the Lieutenancy Book, but with few details such as those given in 1663. About 1666 he was reported to have ten officers and 80 soldiers including 52 musketeers and 28 pikes. He and his men were paid when on active service or on musters; the captain received 8s a day, the lieutenant 4s and the ensign 3s. There were no more large scale plots, but there was a determined campaign against 'fanatics', that is all kinds of dissenters and Catholic recusants (many of whom lived at Colston Bassett), who were regarded as enemies of the state. Captain Peniston Whalley, who was also a magistrate, with his colleague Dr Thoroton, led a ferocious attack against Quakers in particular throughout the area. Whether Radcliffe's militia men were involved in the house searches and the arrests of these wretched people, who were imprisoned and heavily fined, is not known. They were not summoned to musters too often, however, for an account in the Lieutenancy Book notes that the bands were exercised and trained only 24 days between 1662 and 1674, whereas by law they could have been summoned for 14 days each year during the first three years and eight days each year for the remaining 11. The foot soldiers, it was revealed, had been paid at the rate of 1s.6d '(the 12d per diem allowed by Act of Parliament not being sufficient)'. Because of the infrequent summoning of the militia, it was noted that the noble marquess had saved his county the considerable sum of more than £7,261.13s.4d over 14 years.[222]

Militia men in the mid-17th century
(based on a contemporary illustration)

If the early Tudor period was one of expansion for the Radcliffe Rosells, and the early Stuart period a time of stagnation, the later Stuart age saw their decline and disappearance from the county. The reasons are complex - a combination of unexpected deaths, gross mismanagement and law suits. In addition, a lack of sons eventually brought an end to the main Rosell line altogether.

Thomas Rosell - the Restoration squire

Gervase, the captain of the Civil War period, was buried on 2nd January 1661. (See p. 109.) His unmarried elder son, George, was also dead by 14th December of the same year. It was left to 34 year-old Thomas, as yet a bachelor, to take on the responsibility of the estates. He soon found himself a bride - Elizabeth Wright, co-heiress of John Wright from Ripley in Derbyshire. Her parents were both dead at the time the marriage licence was taken out on 23rd June 1662. The times were still disturbed, however, and Parliament reinstated the county militias. Two months after his wedding Thomas is recorded as a volunteer in Viscount Chaworth's troop which mustered in Mansfield on 19th August 1662. Between May 1664 and April 1681 he and Elizabeth were to produce seven children - Gervase, John, Elizabeth, Thomas, Harold, George, and, after a gap of eight years, William. (John and Harold died young, the latter some three months before William was born. When Harold was buried in January 1681, the phrase 'late of Radcliffe-on-Trent' occurs in the parish register, so it is possible that the family, or at least Elizabeth, had been away for some time. No such phrase appears alongside William's birth.) Thomas also had an unmarried sister, Anne, and three unmarried half-sisters - Elizabeth, Katherine and Mary - and was thus the head of a large family.

Thomas gives the impression of being a dependable man, proud of his ancestry. It was he who produced so many documents and provided much information about his family, and about Radcliffe itself, for Robert Thoroton, the Nottinghamshire doctor and antiquarian. Already supervising tenants' wills before his father died, Thomas was the last Rosell to be consulted in this way. He witnessed six of the surviving nine wills from his time as squire, and two tenant farmers included his family in their bequests. In December 1669 George Franke left Thomas's wife, and his sister Anne 5s each to buy (mourning) gloves. Two of his children, Gervase and Elizabeth, were left ten shillings each. John Greene in January 1682 left 7s to each of the four surviving elder Rosell children, and 5s to baby William, then less than a year old.

Thomas was also one of the few Radcliffe Rosells known to have taken part in town business, and, if not one of the county élite himself, this brought him into contact with those who were. In 1663 he headed the list of 25 men sworn as jurors for the Assize Courts held in Nottingham. In 1671-2 he was one of the commissioners who enquired into Nottinghamshire lands and money for the relief of the poor, particularly Hanley's charity (£40 a year left by Henry Hanley of Bramcote for a hospital to house twelve poor people). On this body he served alongside members of the Pierrepont, Hutchinson, Sacheverell, Willoughby and other notable families. On another occasion, again in the company of county names such as Pierrepont, Byron, Chaworth, and Parkyns, he ventured close to politics. William Drury, a Nottingham corporation member suspected of disloyalty, was turned out from being a 'common council man' in January 1679 by the crown commissioners regulating corporations. He was also imprisoned on suspicion of instigating a riot. Thomas Rosell and his colleagues were prepared to certify to Drury's loyalty and to his innocence of factious and seditious principles.[223]

Thomas's main concerns, however, were his family and his estates. Apart from what he owned, he occupied lands on which he paid rents (including £15 a half year to the Pierreponts) or for which he owed the ancient obligations of 'suit and service'. As usual for a man of his status, however, he preferred to pay nominal fines of 3s.4d or 2s.6d rather than put in personal appearances before the manorial courts of Holme Pierrepont or St John of Jerusalem for his lands.[224]

Occasionally he was in conflict with the church authorities, the first time being on his wife's behalf. In 1664 Elizabeth had failed to receive the sacrament,

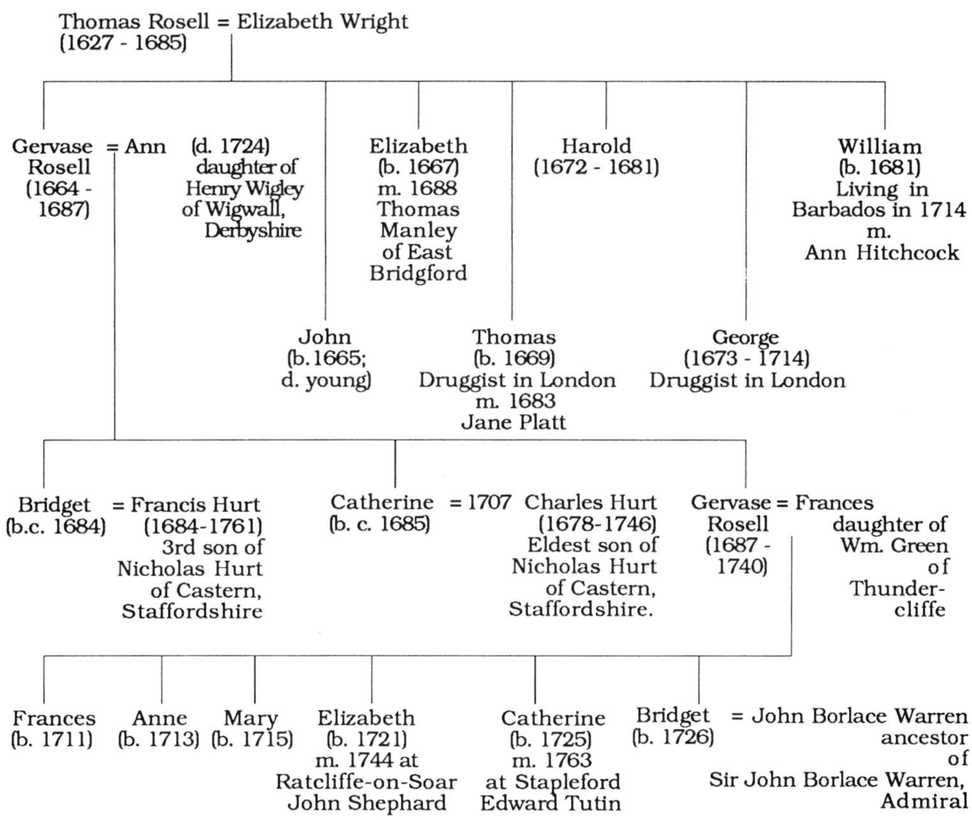

The Rosell Family - later Stuart period

apparently at Easter, when she would have been heavily pregnant. She was summoned before the Archdeacon's Court at St Peter's in Nottingham on September 17th. Thomas defended her, not because she had been pregnant, but on the grounds that the parish had had no minister. This was certainly the case (see pp. 169-70), but why this affected Elizabeth (and three other parishioners a few days later) rather than the whole community is unclear. Whatever the reason, the presence of the squire's wife in court would certainly draw attention to the unsatisfactory situation in Radcliffe. A year later she certified that she had received communion.[225]

The second occasion was a lengthy tithe dispute which began in the summer of 1675. (The full details are covered on pp. 167-8) From the ramifications of the case, which involved the method of paying tithes of wool and lambs on his flock in Lamcote Field, it seems that Thomas Rosell was ready to cut through customary procedures to gain his own ends, but on this occasion he came up against a man as obstinate as himself. Moreover he was disparaging of the humble witnesses who spoke against him.[226]

Sisters in dispute

Four years before Thomas was embroiled in the tithe case, a dispute came to a head about an inheritance involving his three half-sisters. The 16th century Rosell habit of pursuing matters as far as the Court of Chancery in London was revived, only this time a Rosell sued other members of the family, rather than outsiders.

In 1641 Thomas's father, Captain Gervase, had married as his second wife Jane, the daughter and heiress of Sir John Ayscough of Hempshill (Hempsall). This had brought much of Hempshill in Nuthall (held of the manor of Bulwell) temporarily under Rosell control, although the lands were run by trustees on Jane's behalf. After Gervase's death, his widow tried to ensure that these estates should pass to her Rosell daughters, rather than be absorbed in the main estates for the benefit of Thomas. In March 1664 she sold the trusteeship to William Byron and Robert Pierrepont, by then lords of the Bulwell manor. Thomas, with a Christopher Newton, also purchased some rights over the property from another Ayscough line.

After Jane died, her three surviving daughters - Elizabeth, Katherine and Mary - quarrelled over their inheritance, Mary eventually taking her claim against the other two to Chancery in 1671. At that time, they were aged 28, 26 and 23 respectively, living at Hempshill, were all unmarried, and remained so for the rest of their lives. Mary felt that she had been badly treated by her sisters, claiming that the 'capital messuage of Hempshill' and various properties in Hempshill and Bulwell ought by custom to descend to the youngest daughter and her heirs, and only then to all the sisters. She had been ignorant of this right as she had been under 21 until recently. (Under common law, all daughters or sisters would have inherited equally.) Furthermore, Katherine and Elizabeth, via three trustees, had been managing the profits of the estates on her behalf, the implication being that this was to her detriment. She now wanted to secure possession and benefits of the estates, and complained that her sisters and agents had 'contrived amongst themselves to suppress... her means of the recovery thereof'. Already she had taken her case to Robert Pierrepont and William Byron in order to obtain 'right and justice', claiming that by an act of Charles I they, as lords of the manor, rather than the common law had the power to decide the matter. The two men doubtless realised that whatever judgement they made would be highly unpopular with somebody, and declined to arbitrate. Mary asked Chancery to compel them to hold a (manorial) court for this purpose.

The widow of one of the men accused by Mary of acting on her sisters' behalf - a Catalina Eason - gave evidence which has survived. Her argument (or that of her legal adviser) was that there was no proof that Mary's father and mother were ever 'seized of' (i.e. owned) the property in dispute, and that Mary had not proved her own title to it. The Chancery judgement has not survived, but it seems that she lost her claim to the whole inheritance. In March 1673 William Byron and Robert Pierrepont declared that they held the Bulwell manor estate in trust for Jane Rosell's three daughters, one third part to each. Two weeks later, the complication of Thomas's claim was resolved when he and his partner released their indenture to the three women for £30. At least Mary's action had succeeded in increasing her control over her own third and in clarifying the sisters' overall rights.[227]

A few details have survived about the further history of the sisters, (and their half-sister). Although she was the youngest of the three, Mary was to die first - at the age of 42 in 1690. The date of Elizabeth's death is not known, but Katherine, who survived until 1713, became very close to her half-sister, Anne (Thomas's full sister.) Anne never married, lived at Linby, but was buried in Radcliffe on 3rd January 1698. In her will drawn up eleven days earlier, she left £20 each to Thomas's three surviving sons - Thomas, George and William - and twenty shillings each to the three children of her dead nephew, Gervase. Another twenty shillings apiece went to her niece Elizabeth and her husband, and to Sir William and Lady Stanhope for mourning rings. Apart from 20s to the poor of Radcliffe, and half a guinea to William Smith of Radcliffe, the rest of her estate went to her 'dear sister' Katherine, who was made her executor. Katherine herself lived in Nottingham, but asked to be 'decently buried' in Radcliffe when she drew up her will in August 1712. She left £5 to the poor of both Radcliffe and St Mary's, Nottingham. All the rest of her estate, including her 'bonds, bills, debts' she left to her niece (Thomas's daughter), Elizabeth. An inventory of her goods after her death suggests a spartan lifestyle, the result of over-generosity or moneylending. Her purse and apparel were assessed at £5, but, apart from 'some other odd things' valued at £1.10s.6d, she had no household goods of any note. Debts owing to her, however, and 'supposed to be good' amounted to £300.

Thomas Rosell's inventory

Long before his sister and half-sister came to draw up their wills, Thomas Rosell had to put his own affairs in order. Some impression of his lifestyle, centred on the 'capital mansion' occupied by his family since at least Harold Rosell's time in the reign of Henry VIII, can be gleaned from the inventory taken when he died in 1685. (As it provides the most detailed impression of local agriculture available, it will be assessed more specifically in the section on Farming, p. 236 et seq.) Apart from a brewhouse and dairy, the outbuildings included stables housing twenty horses, geldings, mares and foals. There was a bed in the stable for a stable hand, and an 'oven hearth'. Barns contained barley, rye and hay. There was malt and wheat in a 'little garnerhouse', and a chamber above the coalhouse contained barley as well as locks and 'teathers'. Peas and beans were stored in hovels. The yard was a busy, cluttered place with sacks, forms, shuttles, wagons, carts, wains and wheels. There were ploughs, harrows, cart and plough gears, bullock yokes and old iron, stone troughs and querns, wood and stone, plaster and a large quantity of bricks. Fourteen young beasts, swine and more crops were also in the yard. Thomas's bull was worth £1.13s.4d. Even though it was December, out in the grounds around the house were three horses, 35 bullocks, cows and calves with grass and hay. The rest of the stock consisted of sheep in Lamcote and Radcliffe fields, and at Holme. Wheat was already growing in Radcliffe and Lamcote fields. Elsewhere, barley stubble and 'clots' of ploughed land were ready for sowing. There was more stock at Bole, in the North Clay area of Nottinghamshire, and more crops and cheese were stored in two other villagers' homes. The whole picture is of a squire who was above all a working farmer. Out of the total inventory of £1,101.13s.8d (which did not cover the value of his house, outbuildings and other properties rented out), crops, stock, and agricultural implements were worth some £960. The contents of the house itself included some stored grain not included in this total.

The Rosells' house from the map of 1710

The room-by-room inventory of the house listed Thomas Rosell's furniture and utensils. The building was probably extended in the 17th century so that by the time of Thomas's death a high frontage had been added to the original house. A sketch of it appears on a map of 1710, by which time it was let to Thomas Knight. (As noted, this house was to evolve into 'The Chestnuts', and currently (1995) 'Tudor Grange'. See p. 57. Unfortunately, the rooms in the inventory cannot be safely identified with the 20th century layout.) The main room on the ground floor was the hall set out with five tables and two forms amongst other things. Fire irons and reckons (hooks for suspending pots over the fire) were by the hearth. Such rooms were still used for giving hospitality to tenants in the 17th century. The great parlour would be a more private room, again with its fire irons and reckons, but with only three tables, and with the greater comfort of a dozen chairs rather than forms. The contents here were worth £6.8s compared to only £1.12s.6d for those in the hall. Alongside the parlour was a little closet containing glasses and bottles and other items. There were more bottles and glass in the pantry, along with a table and a napkin press or cupboard. Down below was a cellar (now covered over) containing eleven hogsheads - large casks holding about 48 gallons of ale - and a thrall, or cold storage slab. In a second little closet was another table, and more glass and bottles.

The four assessors drawing up the inventory, headed by George Hacker who had supported Thomas in the tithe dispute, next went upstairs. In the nursery were two beds, a table, a press (cupboard) and other things. Up again was the garret with its cupboard, trundle bed and a quantity of cord. A little chamber at the 'stair head' contained the most valuable goods - linens in two chests, and a table. These were valued at £24.8s.10d. (The room with the next most valuable contents was the nursery at £9.17s.4d.) Three of the upper chambers were boldly coloured. The main bedroom was purple. It was comfortably furnished with a bed 'with the furniture' (its curtains, linen, pillows, blankets etc), a chest of drawers, three chairs, four stools, a fire shovel and tongs. It was presumably over the great parlour, sharing its chimney for heating the room. The little red chamber contained a bed 'with furniture', a chair, a table and a grate. In the green chamber was a bed and 'furniture', and, amongst other things, a livery cupboard. (In sleeping quarters, this was often used for bread and wine.) Two more chambers contained beds: the 'little lawther' (lower?) chamber which also held a table and two stools, and the chamber over the kitchen with its 'widow bed' - which was excluded from the valuation - and unspecified goods worth £6.7s.2d. The chamber over the hall was used for storage, the main items being corn and two stills.

Downstairs again, and on the way out towards the yard, was the kitchen, its pewter, brass, pans etc being worth a substantial £18.15s.7d. Next in order came the brewhouse with its brewing vessels, the dairy with churns and milk vessels, the little garner house, and the coalhouse containing coal (perhaps from Wollaton), with its chamber already mentioned.

Luxury items were few. Apart from silver plate worth £8, there were some unspecified books and a 'stonebow'. This was a crossbow for firing stones, a hunting relic from a bygone age. Thomas Rosell's 'purse and apparel' were valued at a standard £10. The household was spacious enough to provide privacy for its occupants, a luxury enjoyed by some 17th century households in contrast to those of the 16th century when communal sleeping arrangements were usual at even the highest levels of society. While Thomas and his wife would have shared the purple room, at least three of his five surviving children had a bedroom to themselves. Two may have shared the nursery if the 'widow bed' was left unused. The trundle bed in the garret was likely to have been used by a servant, but most servants must have slept out. (There was the additional bed in the stable.)

The other main luxury which was becoming more common by the 17th century was the improved heating supplied by hearths and chimneys as opposed to central unflued fires. When the hearth tax was collected in 1664 and 1674, Thomas Rosell headed the village list with 7, (assessed at 2s a hearth in 1664). The inventory specifically mentions four grates or sets of fire irons in the house (including those in two bedrooms) and a hearth in the stable. The kitchen and at least one other room would have provided the comfort of additional warmth. However grand such a household may have seemed to the rest of Radcliffe, it was modest compared to that of Thomas's prestigious county neighbour, Henry Pierrepont, Marquess of Dorchester. In 1674 he was taxed at Holme Pierrepont on 62 hearths.[228]

Family and finances 1683-1685

By the 1680s, Thomas Rosell was having to give thought to his children's future. John had died young, but Gervase, Thomas and George were growing up. Harold had died at the beginning of 1681, shortly before the birth of William in the April of that year. There was also Elizabeth for whom provision had to be made.

The heir to the estates, Gervase, lacked his father's solid character. He gives the impression of being more like his grandfather, Captain Gervase - more interested in hunting for sport than in the practical running of a farming enterprise. Moreover, while Thomas as a younger son had not expected an inheritance, and had not married until he had come into the estates at the age of 35, Gervase was just turned 19 when he married. His bride, Anne Wigley, came from his mother's county, Derbyshire. She was one of three daughters of Henry Wigley of Wigwall near Wirksworth. (Their only brother, Henry, was to die in 1690 at the age of 13.) The young couple were married some few miles away at Bonsall on 8th October 1683. There were to be three children of the marriage. (When the eldest, Bridget, came to marry by licence in 1701 she gave her age as 22, putting her birth in 1679, but it is more than likely that she exaggerated her age and was in fact only about 17.) In theory, the terms of the marriage were satisfactory to the Rosells, for Anne was to have £800 as her portion. The Wigleys, however, failed to pay up at the time of the marriage. Less than three months later Henry Wigley died, his three daughters subsequently putting up a church monument to his memory. His widow Mary was to marry John Slack, a Wirksworth attorney, after which there was even more difficulty in extracting the money.[229]

One means of providing for a family was brought to Thomas's attention in 1685 when he was approached by his cousin William, Lord Byron, to help with a similar problem concerning the latter's three daughters - Elizabeth (Rigmayden), Catherine, and Juliana - for whom he needed to provide either marriage portions or annuities, as well as to raise money to pay off debts. He used his estates as security and on 2nd June mortgaged them 'for 1,000 years' to Thomas Rosell and Edward Burdett of Gray's Inn, Middlesex. A peppercorn rent, if demanded, retained the Byron interest, and the two mortgagees were to pay the portions and debts out of the estates.[230]

Perhaps with this example in mind, and some doubts about the reliability of Gervase, Thomas made his own financial arrangements in July 1685. In the past, there had been restrictions on the way the estates could be inherited, and Thomas wanted a free hand, so that Gervase would not automatically get everything to the detriment of the rest of the family. Whether the young man realised his father's intentions is not clear, but he was a party to the variant of a legal device which Thomas used, known as a 'recovery', for the 'docking, cutting of, and barring all estates tail and remaindered' which limited the disposal of his lands. They could then be held in 'fee simple', so that the property could be disposed of freely.

On 2nd July 1685, this was effected by a fictitious sale. For 5s, William Cooke of Wymeswold in Leicestershire acquired the manors of Lamcote and Radcliffe, the latter 'commonly known as Graisen manor or Woodhall manor' with their rights and associated lands. Cooke now became the 'perfect tenant' or vendor of the property. John Eyre of Ripley in Derbyshire was then to acquire the property as 'demandant'. The normal procedure was for the freehold tenant (Cooke) to appear in court, and then, instead of defending his title, to call on a third party, known as a 'vouchee', to do this for him. Often, this was the court crier, but on this occasion, the Rosells themselves acted as vouchees. When a demandant asked for leave to confer with the vouchee, this was granted, but the vouchee would fail to return to court. As a result, the court would give judgement to the demandant, who then acquired the property. The purpose of the charade in this case was made clear in the agreement (a tripartite indenture). Eyre was to acquire the premises 'to the only proper use and behoof of... Thomas Rosell his heirs and assigns for ever and to none other use intent or purpose whatsoever'. The transaction, allowing Thomas to dispose of his property as he wished, was to be effected before the end of the following Michaelmas term - December 21st.

This legal document is of particular interest as the late 17th century Rosell property is itemised in some detail. An outline is given below:

Capital messuage with appurtenances - occupied by Thomas Rosell or assigns.

Several parcels of arable, meadow & pasture land in Lamcote - occupied by Thomas Rosell - 26 oxgangs.

Several closes and parcels of land in Lamcote and Radcliffe:- Lamcote Field, Lamcote Leys, Lamcote Meadow, Escung (Hesgang) Meadow, West Close - all occupied by Thomas Smith.

Two Lirpat Closes - occupied by William Smith.

Another Lirpat Close - in possession of Thomas Simpson.

Great Long Croft, Little Long Croft and Pingle, Marshawbottom, Great Hillicky Close, Little Hillicky Close, Holme Close, Pond Close, Little Criftin adjoining the Coneygrey Close, Thorney Close, Bailey Close, Great Criftin - all in possession of Thomas Rosell.

Little Criftin - in possession of William Smith.

In Radcliffe - 4 oxgangs - occupied by Thomas Rosell or his assigns.

Windmill in Radcliffe - occupied by Thomas Rosell.

Messuage and homestead with land & appurtenances - 3 oxgangs - occupied by William Needham or assigns.

In Lamcote - Pares Close, Hookin Pasture Close, Messuage and Pools Close. In Radcliffe - land - 2½ oxgangs - formerly in possession of Thomas Hardy, now occupied by Thomas Rosell or assigns.

Messuage & homestead in Radcliffe - in possession of John Greene.

Land in Radcliffe - 3 oxgangs - in possession of John Greene or Thomas Rosell.

Square Close in Lamcote - in possession of Robert Oliver.

Several cottages in Radcliffe and Lamcote with appurtenances - occupied by William Morley the elder, Thomas Smith, John Wilford, William Parr, Henry Pare, Widow Campion, Thomas Simpson & Robert Oliver or assigns.

A summarising document gives a clearer idea of the total acreages of the estates:

> *... the Manors of Radcliffe-on-Trent and Lamcote with appurtenances, and of 20 messuages, 11 tofts, one windmill, one dovecote, 20 gardens, 400 acres of land, 50 acres of meadow, 100 acres of pasture, 200 acres of furze & heath, and common of pasture for all cattle with the appurtenances in Radcliffe-on-Trent, Lamcote and Holme Pierrepont, and in the parishes of Radcliffe-on-Trent and Holme Pierrepont.*

Allowing for some changes in quantity or use over the years, this summary corresponds fairly well to the combined holdings of Woodhall, Rosell and Lamcote manors found in the Inquisitions of 1581/2 and 1608. The distinctions between them were perhaps becoming blurred by this date.[231]

Thomas Rosell's will

Thomas then drew up his will on 8th July 1685. As far as he was concerned, he was merely sorting out his affairs in a practical manner, and had no immediate thought of death, for, unusually, in the preamble he stressed that he was 'in health of body' as well as 'of sound and disposing mind and memory'. His first thoughts were for his 'dear wife' Elizabeth, who was to choose as much from the household goods as would 'furnish her a convenient Lodging Room' - a modest allocation which she subsequently overrode. His 18-year-old daughter Elizabeth was to have £800 as her portion when she married, or reached the age of 21 - the same amount that the Wigleys were supposed to pay to the Rosells for her sister-in-law, Anne. Until that time she was to have £20 a year for her maintenance. Her three younger brothers (Thomas, George and William, aged 16, just 12, and 4 respectively at the time the will was made) were each to have portions of £600 when they reached 21, but up to £100 out of this was to be spent in placing them as apprentices. Until they came of age, they were to be allowed £12 a year each for maintenance. Should any of these four children die before the portions were paid, their share was to be divided equally between all the surviving children, including Gervase.

The estates were to be kept intact, but Thomas was not prepared to risk leaving Gervase with the responsibility of carrying out the terms for the maintenance of the younger children. Consequently, all his 'manors, messuages, lands, tenements and hereditaments whatsoever' in Radcliffe, Lamcote, Holme Pierrepont and elsewhere in the county were passed 'upon special trust and confidence' to Thomas's friend Charles Hutchinson of Owthorpe (half-brother of the Parliamentarian John, governor of Nottingham Castle in the Civil War whose mother was a Stanhope), and to Lemuel Low, a yeoman from Bilborough, and their heirs. The contrast between the lack of trust between father and son in this case, and the confidence felt by John Rosell towards his son George in similar circumstances in 1605, is very marked. (See p. 108.) After paying Thomas's debts and funeral charges, Hutchinson and Low were to raise the money to pay the portions and maintenance of the four youngest children out of the 'rents, issues and profits' of the estates, or by leases or mortgages. Only then were the manors, lands and premises to go to Gervase and his heirs. As the youngest son was aged only 4, the time needed to raise this on-going money could be considerable, but then Thomas had no immediate expectation of dying, so any gap between the time of his death and Gervase coming into his own need not have been long. Even Thomas's plate, household goods, cattle, chattels, and personal estate (unless already taken by his wife as her legacy), were to be sold by the trustees and his wife for the 'better and more speedy raising and paying' of the necessary money. (It was to emerge later that Thomas's personal estate came to well over £2,000 which would include the £1,101.13s.8d of the inventory of his goods.) His 'heir at law' - a cold term to use of an eldest son - was to have only what was left unsold. It would be interesting to know if Gervase was told *all* the terms of his father's will at the time it was drawn up.

There were also some personal bequests for which the money had to be raised. Charles Hutchinson was to have £5 to buy a ring. Thomas's sister Anne, and his three half-sisters were also to have £5 each to buy mourning. His loyal servant, the shepherd William Smith (d. 1689 or 90), who had given evidence on his master's behalf in the tithe dispute a decade before, was to have 40s. The remaining servants were to have 5s each. The poor of Radcliffe were remembered with 40s. All these small bequests were to be paid within six months of Thomas's death. To recompense Lemuel Low for his trouble in carrying out the terms of the will, Thomas left him £5 a year for six years.

There was one other outstanding matter which had been on Thomas's mind - the unpaid portion for Anne, his daughter-in-law. On 3rd July, the day after the 'recovery' document was drawn up, and five days before he signed his will, Thomas had put these terms to Gervase: if his mother-in-law Mrs Wigley, now a widow, paid over Anne's £800 marriage portion to the executors within a year of Thomas's death, then Hutchinson and Low, or their heirs, were to settle as much on him (Gervase) from the estates as would produce an income of £200 a year. The matter, without specific details, was incorporated into the will. (As Gervase would benefit if the portion was paid, he would have had every incentive to put pressure on his wife and mother-in-law to produce the money. Unfortunately, his mother-in-law remarried some six weeks later. In 1689 she and her new husband - the Wirksworth attorney John Slack - had still not produced the money, claiming they were 'no way obliged so to do'.) The trustees and Thomas's wife were made executors of his will.[232]

Two unexpected deaths and an inventory

Despite the fact that Thomas was confident about the state of his health in July 1685, he was dead by early December at the age of 58. Although this was before the end of the legal Michaelmas term, there is no evidence that the 'recovery' was not fully completed, or that the terms of Thomas's will were therefore invalid. Nevertheless, both Gervase, the new squire now 21 years' old, and his mother were to ignore many of its terms. They were sufficiently in sympathy to go together in the following September to see the York Exchequer Court officials about producing the inventory and will, both signing their names on the relevant documents. Moreover, at some point Gervase was lent £49 by his mother to help him through his immediate financial difficulties.[233]

In theory it was now up to Elizabeth, Charles Hutchinson and Lemuel Low to implement the terms of the will. In practice, mother and son ran things their own way, and in trying to circumvent an unreliable heir, Thomas had unwittingly sown the seeds of his family's downfall.

On the face of it the restrictions in the will had their effect. An inventory of the young squire's household and stock made after the latter's death some 15 months later totalled only £422.15s.3d compared to Thomas's £1,101.13s.8d. A walk round the house and yard, however, would have revealed changes that Thomas had not intended. Gervase's mother was, of course, to be given accommodation, but the hall area of the house on the ground floor, the cellar, the chamber over the hall and the heated red chamber upstairs, the little chamber at the stairhead, the garret at the top of the house, and the outside coalhouse, are all missing from Gervase's list. (Other areas appear under different names.) This was far more than the 'convenient Lodging Room' envisaged by Thomas, and the contents also exceeded any traditional 'widow's third'. It seems that a vertical slice of the whole house, from cellar to garret, had been acquired by Elizabeth and presumably her younger children, although the latter may also have used sleeping accommodation in Gervase's part.

Gervase retained the parlour. It still contained 12 chairs, but one of the three tables had been moved out, and the fire irons and reckons had gone from the grate. Now, however, there were curtains at the window. The little closet by the parlour, the pantry and another little closet were listed as the buttery and two little larders, and still contained a collection of bottles, pots and glasses, as well as some kimnels (tubs used perhaps for curing bacon or washing butter). The nursery with its two beds, presumably used for Gervase's two young daughters, also housed new flaxen cloth, 13 pairs of sheets, ten table cloths, napkins and other things. These were the sort of items formerly in the little chamber at the stairhead, which was no longer in Gervase's territory. The table and 'press' (cupboard), formerly in the nursery, are not mentioned, but the value of the room's contents had still increased by nearly £3. Upstairs, the main bedroom - the purple chamber - had lost its chest of drawers, three chairs and two of its four stools. There is no mention either of its fire irons. Like the parlour, however, it had gained window curtains. Overall, the value of the contents had been reduced from £9.18s to £4. The little ('lawther') chamber retained its bed, had lost its table, but gained the livery cupboard from the green chamber. The latter, still with its bed and bedding, had acquired a table and four stools, as well as a luxury item - a looking glass. Perhaps Gervase's sister slept here. The chamber over the kitchen still contained its bed and bedding.

The kitchen below revealed the change in character between the old squire and the new. It still contained a quantity of pewter and brass, now reduced in value, but specifically including a warming pan and two candlesticks. In addition, however, it housed two guns and two cases of pistols. There is no mention of Thomas's stonebow, or of his books. The silver plate is not mentioned either, perhaps sold

	li s d
Imps his Purse and Apparell	10-00-00
In the Parlour one Grate twelve chaires two Tables window Curtains other small things	05-17-04
In the Kitchin Chamber one Bed & Bedding	05-00-00
The little Chamber one Bed and Bedding one livery Cubbord, Pan and Stoole	01-10-00
In the Nursery Chamber two Bedsteads and Bedding new flaxen cloth 13 paire of sheets 10 Tablecloths Napkins and other things	12-15-00
In the Green Chamber one Bed and Bedding one Table 4 stooles one looking Glass & other things	04-15-00
In the Purple Chamber one Bed and Bedding window Curtains two Stooles	04-00-00
In the Brew-house two Coppers Brewing vessels Querns and Barrels	10-00-00
In the Buttery Bottles	00-09-00
In two little Larders Kimnels Pots & Glasses	00-14-00
In the Deary milk vessels	01-00-00
In the Kitchin Pewter and Brass one warming Pan. 2 Candlesticks two Gunns two case of Pistols two brass Potts old iron other small things	13-06-08
In the chambers Wheat, Malt and Blend corne	06-12-00
In the Stable one Bed	00-06-08
In the Stable Ten Horses Mares and Geldings	67-10-00
In the Beast house four oxen	14-00-00
Plows and Harrows Horse Gears yokes & Teames	04-00-00
In the yard one Waggon one Cart two waines Eight Beast Cribbs one Fann	12-00-00
In the Hovels and yard 14 Beasts old & young	32-00-00
Two Sows and Piggs two Brawns & a little Shoat	05-00-00
In the Grounds and Stable Six Saddle Horses & Mares one Cart Mare one Foale	50-00-00
In the Fields Eighty six Sheepe fold, Fleaks and Cribbs	49-10-00
18 qters of Barley and Pease Sowne and Wheat Sowne and Fallows to Sow	85-00-00
Hay in the Grounds	15-00-00
In the yard Manure	05-00-00
one Pack of Hounds	05-00-00
one Settinge Bitch and other small things	01-10-00
Sum totall	422-15-08

Inventory of Gervase Rosell's goods and chattels taken 29th March 1687
(The Borthwick Institute, York)

under the terms of Thomas's will or more likely acquired by Elizabeth. The brewhouse had two coppers, querns and barrels added to its brewing vessels, thus increasing the value of its contents from £2.11s.4d to £10. While an increase in the brewing of ale may be one explanation, the fact that the cellar was not part of Gervase's property must have meant that items normally stored there had to be housed elsewhere. The dairy still contained milk vessels, and two 'chambers' housing wheat, malt and blend corn (a mixture of wheat and rye) can probably be identified with Thomas's 'little garner house' and coalhouse chamber.

The yard and lands, too, revealed some changes. In particular, Gervase had acquired a pack of hounds worth 5s and a setting bitch. Even with his sporting interests, however, he had been reduced to having only ten horses, geldings and mares in his stables, compared with the twenty of his father's time, although in the grounds and stable were another six saddle horses and mares, a cart horse and a foal. (Those that Thomas had had out at Bole, along with much of the other lands and stock, should have been in the hands of the trustees.) Nevertheless, Gervase still had enough stock and equipment to provide him with a comfortable living: this included four oxen in the beast house, 14 old and young beasts in the hovels and yard, two sows and piglets, and a collection of ploughs, harrows, horse gears, as well as a wagon, a cart, two wains, beast cribs, and manure. All he had in the fields, however, were 86 sheep with their folds and cribs worth £49.10s; 16 quarters of barley, and ground sown with peas and wheat as well as some lying fallow, together worth £85; and some hay in the grounds worth £15. Direct comparisons with Thomas's time are difficult to make when it comes to farming, but the latter's sheep in Radcliffe and Lamcote fields alone were worth £110.13s.4d. Whereas (excluding stored items in the house buildings) the total value of Thomas's stock, crops, and equipment had come to some £960, Gervase's equivalent amounted to less than £340. Even allowing for the consumption of fodder and stores between a December inventory (Thomas's) and one made in March (Gervase's), this is still a considerable drop. Nevertheless, Gervase was probably left with more than Thomas had ever intended.

The extent to which Thomas's will had been ignored emerged later. Elizabeth had acquired the whole of Thomas's personal estate, along with enough of his lands to bring herself an income of £100 a year, claiming this as her jointure. Gervase had then taken over all the rest of the lands, keeping the profits for his own use. The allowances to the younger children were not paid. All Thomas's careful planning had come to nothing. The revised inheritance, however, was not enough for Gervase's needs. In October 1686, less than a year after his father's death, he mortgaged the messuage and farm lands known as Greene's farm (by then let out to Thomas Campion) to raise £150, interest being liable on £100 of this sum. In the following January he raised another £100 on the same property.[234]

Some two months later he was dead at the age of 22, surviving his father by only fifteen months. The sporting interests revealed in his inventory - the guns, pistols, hounds and setter - may help to explain his end. A descendant of the Rosell family in the 1990s recalls an undated family tale of a young Radcliffe squire killed while on horseback after being struck on the head by galloping into the branch of a tree. If this is what happened to Gervase, he was not killed outright, for a short will was drawn up for him by a Hugh Cartwright (a name associated with the Kelham and Southwell areas) to which he was only able to add his initials. That was on 17th March 1687. He was buried two days later.

Gervase Rosell's will

For a young man of pleasure, the preamble to his will seems out of character. After the conventional acknowledgement that he was 'sick and weak of body' but of 'sound memory and perfect understanding', Gervase bequeathed his 'soul into the hands of almighty God, the Author and Creator thereof, hoping through the merits of Jesus Christ his son to obtain everlasting life'. There had been no reference to religious belief in Thomas's will. The start of Gervase's could have been written a century before. Perhaps it was the scribe at his bedside who took this way of helping a dying young man into the next world.

The terms of the will were simple. After the payment of his debts and funeral expenses, he left his estates to his 'beloved wife' Anne and the children 'that I had by her or may have'. (Two children, Bridget and Catherine, were already born, and Anne was expecting the third - another Gervase - at the time of her husband's death.) The lands and hereditaments were to be settled 'as Counsell learned in the law shall advise' to provide Anne with a 'competent jointure' during her lifetime, and for the education and 'portions' of the children. Charles Hacker (his father's friend) and John Brough, both of East Bridgford, were then empowered to arrange the jointure, the portions, and see to the maintenance of the children during their minority. The faithful Rosell servant, William Smith, who witnessed the will with his mark, was rewarded with another 40 shillings. Mary Rouse, perhaps another servant, was left a similar amount. Anne was made executrix but did not witness the will. As an afterthought, 40 shillings was left to the poor of Radcliffe. (According to the 'accounts' of money left to the poor in the parish register, Gervase had borrowed some £14 from this fund, including Jeffrey Limner's legacy and the two sums of 40 shillings bequeathed by his father and grandfather. His own bequest is not listed.)

The appeal to the Master of the Rolls 1689

Gervase's will did not override the terms of Thomas's, which had already been broken. Moreover, there was now a second widow, Anne, who was determined to look after her own interests, and those of her posthumous son. The original trustees - Charles Hutchinson and Lemuel Low - were either unwilling or incapable of carrying out Thomas's wishes and renounced their executorships. Thus the two widows, it was alleged, were able to

> *combine together to divide amongst them not only the personal estate of the said Thomas Rosell but also the rents and profits of his real estate.*

As a result, Thomas's children had not been paid their maintenance or portions when due and in June 1689 they brought an action against their mother (Elizabeth), their sister-in-law (Anne), Low, Hutchinson, and John and Mary Slack (Anne's mother and step-father).

Leading the complainants was Thomas's daughter, Elizabeth. She had been living at East Bridgford the previous September when a licence was taken out for her marriage with 22-year-old Thomas Manley of East Bridgford, gentleman. They married at Shelford in the October. On the grounds of both marriage and age she was entitled to her portion of £800 but, she claimed, the defendants pretended that this sum could 'no ways be raised for her', and that Thomas's personal estate would only pay for his debts. To the court, however, her mother professed willingness to pay the legacies out of what remained of Thomas's personal estate, but pointed out that she had been maintaining her younger children since the death of her husband, and asked the court to make her an allowance for this.

Anne (Gervase's widow) took a bolder line against the plaintiffs. She alleged

> *that the said Thomas never made any such will and that all the lands the said Thomas Rosell died seized [i.e. possessed] of descended to Gervase, her late husband as his son and heir, and he being dead the same are descended to... Gervase, his son, who being an infant, she possessed herself of part of the said premises and [has] taken the profits thereof to her son's use...*

Moreover, Gervase had died 'much more indebted than his personal estate would pay', and having taken over his 'premises' she 'could make but little profit thereof by reason of the said Trust'. She also claimed that neither Thomas nor Gervase had made any provision for her maintenance, or for the maintenance of her children. She hoped the court would allow her a reasonable subsistence out of the estate. In fact, both men had assumed that there would be property for their direct heirs, and Gervase's will contained specific arrangements for Anne's jointure. It seems that the terms of Gervase's will, like his father's, were either ignored or were incapable of being carried out because of the impoverished nature of the inheritance. Neither Charles Hacker nor John Brough, who were supposed to make these arrangements, were mentioned in the action of 1689, nor does Gervase's will seem to have been produced. Anne had been made sole executrix, but as she could only make her mark when the will was proved, she was presumably incapable of reading its terms and seeing that they were properly carried out. With her mother and step-father still refusing to pay the £800 promised as her marriage portion, she emerges as a young mother trying to protect the interests of her children, ill-equipped by her lack of education, and surrounded by grasping relatives.

The basic aim of the complainants, led by Elizabeth Manley, was simply to get their legacies paid as laid down in Thomas's will. Hutchinson and Low, his ex-trustees, were called on to testify. They believed that Thomas had indeed made the will, and had died possessed of sufficient real and personal estate to pay his debts and the annual allowances claimed by the petitioners 'with an overplus'. They denied they had ever 'meddled' with any of Thomas's personal estate, but said they were willing to make leases or mortgages as necessary, and then begged to be excused from 'further meddling therewith'. They had proved poor friends to Thomas.

With the information at its disposal, the court made its judgement. One of the Masters of the Court, Mr Methroyne, was to pay Thomas's legacies and maintenance to his children out of what remained of his personal estate now in his widow's hands. She was, however, to be allowed the £49 which she had lent to her son, Gervase. Any shortfall was to be made up from Thomas's real estate. Anne's infant son was to be allowed £80 a year out of the estates, payable to Anne as his guardian, and a similar payment made to any subsequent heir in the event of the boy's death. If Low and Hutchinson refused to do more than raise mortgages and leases to carry out these arrangements, then the Master would appoint other trustees, who could claim reasonable charges and expenses from the estates. In fact, Hutchinson did take up the burden of trusteeship again.[235]

Three apprenticed brothers

At last some payment of Thomas's legacies began. The first to benefit was his daughter Elizabeth. Her husband, Thomas Manley, signed a receipt for her full portion of £800 in June 1689. Two of her brothers on reaching 21 also signed that they had received all that was due to them. On 20th February 1691 Thomas, who became a druggist in London, was paid £400 by his mother and Charles Hutchinson. He had already been paid £100 by his mother, and another £100 by Hutchinson. In October 1692 he was admitted to the freedom of the Grocers' Company (one of two companies responsible for druggists). This was by redemption (purchase) through an order of the Court of Aldermen in the previous month. He was recorded as a druggist, still living in London on a genealogy drawn up in 1714.

His brother George was also admitted to the Grocers' Company in London and apprenticed to a John Chapman, citizen and mercer, by indenture of 19th August 1687 for seven years. On 25th September 1690 his apprenticeship was turned over to Thomas Pead, citizen and grocer, for the remainder of the term of seven years. Although his name does not occur in the records after 1690, he too was described as a druggist in a family genealogy. He received the final instalment of his £600 on 21st May 1695. Apart from £80 laid out for his apprenticeship, his payments were staggered over some fourteen months: £100 in April 1694, £80 in June, £40 in September, £50 on 9th April 1695, £250 on 30th April, and the final £30.5s on 21st May, which was interest on the outstanding money. Charles Hutchinson was again responsible for the payments, this time with John Brough of East Bridgford, one of the men who should have made arrangements after Gervase's will.[236]

For the youngest brother, William, life was more complicated. He had been less than 5 years old when his father died, had then lived with his mother until her death in 1693, after which he had gone to live with his married sister, Elizabeth Manley. At the age of 16 he too was sent to London as an apprentice. As far as he knew, his mother, then the Manleys, and then he himself from the time of his apprenticeship, had regularly received the £12 a year allowed by Thomas's will (which he never actually saw) paid via Charles Hutchinson or Charles Brough (assistant to the trustees) until October 1701. When he became 21 on 29th March 1702 he was paid only £100 as part of his remaining portion. Claiming that he was still owed £304.16s out of the £600 left by his father, William found that he was unable to procure it from Brough - probably because the estate lacked reserves for such substantial payments and had to wait for moneys to come in. As he was 'intending to go beyond seas for promoting and advancing his fortune', and without the money was unable 'to put himself into business', William decided to appeal to his relatives for help. His brother George, by then a druggist, and his brother-in-law Thomas Manley (both having long since received their dues from the will) duly loaned him the missing sum, raising the money from Charles Hurt of Derbyshire (the future husband of Bridget Rosell) in order to do so. William, 'not doubting that [they] would in a little time be reimbursed with interest', transferred his claims on the estate and made arrangements for them to be paid by a deed of assignment dated 3rd June 1703.

Unfortunately, the transaction went sour. Whether out of frustration at finding themselves unable to recover the money, or out of malice, is not clear, but brother-in-law and brother subsequently brought a court action against William. From the latter's defence it is clear that their sister-in-law, Anne, (Gervase's widow) had also helped to muddy the proceedings. Her assertion that she did not know that George and Thomas Manley had ever advanced the money, and that only William had the power to claim it from the estate was refuted by William, anxious 'not to hinder' the complainants in recovering their money. More seriously, any suggestion that he had received any money out of the estate after he had made the deed of assignment was hotly denied. He pointed out that no receipts existed to prove the charge. Indeed, William was certain that the complainants had actually received a year's interest on the £304.16s.

Attached to William's evidence are details of what was paid to him, with interest, after the first £100 in March 1702. The payments were made piecemeal as the estate administrators gathered in their dues: a substantial sum (perhaps £90) from Mr Brough, £72.6s.6d in two sums from James Wright, £46 and £20 by bills 'on Mr Egleton', and £8 from Mr Waterhouse - still leaving the £304.16s outstanding. This confirms the impression that the Rosell estates were existing on a hand-to-mouth basis, and that there were no reserves on which large sums could be drawn. It seems unlikely that Thomas Manley and George could prove that William had extracted money that was no longer due to him from the estate. They must have been reimbursed for their funding by 1706, for in April of that year Thomas Manley assigned the £304.16s in trust to Charles Hurt, who had backed the original loan. By then, too, William had probably married Ann Hitchcock at St Dunstan's in Stepney, London, and he had certainly achieved his ambition of going abroad. In the same year as a merchant in Barbados he signed a petition about paper credit. In 1714 he was recorded on a genealogical tree as still living there, but nothing further is known of him.[237]

Provision for Anne Rosell 1694

In the meantime, the position of William's sister-in-law Anne appeared to improve too. Not only had her young son been granted £80 a year out of the estates, but it seems that by 1694 her marriage portion, or at least £600 of it, had at last been paid. Admittedly, it had been laid out towards discharging her late husband's debts by his administrators, Charles Hacker and John Brough, but ultimately she was to have two farms (currently occupied by William Needham and William Smith), and a cottage and lands (held by William Stone) worth altogether £60 a year as her jointure. When young Gervase, then aged 6 or 7, reached the age of 21, the grant of the farms and cottage would be confirmed. Within a year of that time, too, Gervase would pay portions of £400 to each of his sisters, Bridget and Catherine. If either died before that time, the survivor was to inherit a further £200, the rest of the money being 'sunk'. (In fact Gervase was aged about 31 before he was able to discharge this obligation!) He was also to convey to his sisters through a mortgage some Radcliffe lands worth £80 a year. On the face of it, Anne's personal position was now secure, and her children's future provided for. Hacker and Brough failed, however, to raise any money out of the estates for the maintenance of the girls in the meantime. Consequently the financial problems of the family continued, doubtless exacerbated by the payments to her late husband's younger brothers and sister out of declining and incompetently administered estates.[238]

Maladministration and a draft Act of Parliament 1701

As matters grew worse, a desperate Anne had an Act of Parliament drafted in 1701 on behalf of young Gervase, still under fourteen years of age. It presents a catalogue of neglect and maladministration since the death of Thomas in 1685.

While the outgoings on the estate (to comply with Thomas's will and the hard won benefits for Anne and Gervase) were predictable, there were also erratic but heavy maintenance costs on lands close to the river for which the estate was financially unprepared:

> *And whereas the said lands adjoin to the River Trent and without constant care of the banks of the said river it is often requisite to lay out considerable sums of money in waterworks for defence of the same against the rapid force of the stream frequently making breaches in the banks, and washing away the same. For the raising of which sums, though sometimes absolutely necessary, there is no provision made by the wills of Thomas Rosell or Gervase Rosell...*

Significantly, after the Duke of Kingston acquired the estates in the 1720s he was to covenant to cover expenses in the event of the river breaking down banks at a weir and forcing a new channel in an area then known as Knight's Holt.[239]

Worse still was the negligent way the estates had been administered. When Charles Hutchinson had ultimately acted as trustee for Thomas's will, he had taken up 'at interest and disbursed several sums of money towards the discharge of the said trust' which were still outstanding. Moreover, Thomas's naive assumption in his will that his friends would gladly act as his trustees was further undermined when it came to their heirs. As the draft Act stated:

> *... the said Charles Hutchinson is since dead, and Thomas Hutchinson his son and heir is since dead, and left Julian his brother his heir, who is young and unfit to manage the said Trust and takes no care of the said estate nor demands the arrears of rent or takes account of the profits, but has actually released the said Trust, Estate, [sic], so that the debts upon the said estate must daily swell and grow bigger by the perpetual increase of interest and other incident charges, and the said estate be in a short time quite swallowed up and the children of the said Gervase Rosell deceased will be inevitably ruined for want of support and maintenance unless they may be relieved by the assistance of an Act of Parliament...*

The draft is full of gaps for names, dates or sums of money to be inserted, but the general intention is clear. Part of the estates were to be sold to raise enough money to pay off any debts and legacies remaining from the wills of Thomas and Gervase, including whatever Charles Hutchinson had mortgaged at interest. The £400 allowed to both Anne's daughters, Bridget and Catherine, was confirmed, and was to be paid when the girls married. Anne was also confirmed in the property that was bringing her £60 a year. Out of this she would provide for the maintenance and education of her daughters until they received their portions. If Anne were to die before that time, then the girls were to be allowed £20 a year out of the estates. An unspecified sum was to be allowed for the education and maintenance of young Gervase. A new departure was that up to £200 was to be raised 'for the placing out the said Gervase, the infant, as apprentice'. In the past only younger sons had been found apprenticeships. Even to suggest that the inheritor of the Rosell estates must find an alternative livelihood indicates the rapid decline in the family fortunes.

To make the most of what remained, money should be raised from time to time during Gervase's minority 'for the defending [of] the said banks of the said river as often as there shall be occasion'. Bailiffs and managers of the estates could be sued for rent arrears from tenants going back several years, or unaccounted for since the death of Thomas Rosell some 16 years previously. Goods could be distrained for rent and sold, according to an Act of Parliament passed some ten years before. Arrangements were also to be made to pay Anne her costs for having the Act drawn up, and for the payment of other expenses.

No evidence has been found that the Act was ever passed by Parliament. If it was not, then the existing situation of muddle and incompetence must have continued for a number of years more. No reference to an apprenticeship for Gervase has been found either, and he was left to maintain himself from his blighted inheritance.[240]

Two 'portionless beauties'

His descendants were left with an abiding impression of this decline. Anne Hurt, born in 1752, and married to Thomas Waterhouse of Beckingham Hall in Nottinghamshire, recalled:

> *The History of my Great Grandfather Rosell was very tragical and would be tedious to detail - suffice it to say that he was trepanned out of a fine estate and by a premature death one of the most ancient and opulent families of Nottinghamshire became extinct.*

Anne Hurt was the granddaughter of Bridget, one of the two daughters of Gervase and Ann and sister of the final Radcliffe Gervase. She described these sisters as 'two portionless beauties'. (In theory, they were not quite portionless, as they had been allocated £400 each, but in practice the sums do not seem to have been paid until June 1718, long after both girls were married and had reached the age of 21.) Despite their poverty, they attracted the attention of two brothers, Charles and Francis Hurt of Alderwasley and Wirksworth in Derbyshire, and of Castern in Staffordshire.

Catherine at the age of 22 married by licence Charles, the eldest Hurt son, in December 1707 at Laxton in Nottinghamshire. Within four years his father had died and he inherited the considerable Hurt fortune. He was High Sheriff of Derbyshire in 1714. Catherine produced six daughters who died unmarried, five sons who died young, as well as one daughter and two sons who married.

Bridget, the elder daughter, had the poorer bargain in financial terms. In December 1701 she married by licence Francis, the youngest surviving Hurt brother, at St Peter's Nottingham. According to her granddaughter, Anne Hurt, the younger Hurt brothers 'had nothing for their portion but a few shares in the lead mines'. The couple's financial situation could not have been improved by the size of their family. Bridget was to die in childbirth of her nineteenth child. (Ten children lived to adulthood - nine girls and Charles, who became an apothecary.)[241]

Sale of the Radcliffe lands

The Derbyshire links were increasing. Already the girls' mother, Anne Rosell, had her Derbyshire connections around Wigwall and Wirksworth. From the death of her brother in 1690, she and her two sisters - Bridget, the wife of Sir John Statham, and Mary, the wife of Michael Burton - had been the co-owners of the Wigley lands, with at least some also held with their mother, Mary Slack. Perhaps through the influence of John Statham, preparations were made from 1700 to divide the estate into three parts. This was accomplished by September 1702, with the Stathams having Wigwell Grange and its appurtenances as their third. The division meant that Anne now had property in her own right which she could dispose of as she wished. This would ultimately benefit her son, Gervase. Perhaps this partly explains why the 1701 Act of Parliament never came to fruition.[242]

Gervase, the last Rosell squire in Radcliffe, had his Radcliffe and Lamcote lands administered by his mother until he came of age. Additionally, her name appears in the surviving Pierrepont rentals for 1694. By this stage the Pierrepont estates were held by Evelyn Pierrepont, the 5th Earl of Kingston. In his rental book Anne is described as 'widow Rosell, relict of Mr Rosell'. She paid rent on over 20 acres of common field land, a little close called Butler's pingle, and over 8 acres of meadow - all in Lamcote Field. She also rented over 6 acres scattered through the four great open fields in Radcliffe, which had formerly been rented by Thomas Stone, and were also in the control of the Pierreponts. The total rent amounted to £18, and there was another £60 to pay on contentious tithes of corn, wool and lambs that were still due on the Lamcote holdings. Occasionally, there was something back from the Pierreponts. For example, chief rents surviving from 1705-1707 show that 'Mistress Anne Rosell' was regularly paid 6s.8d out of the farm rented to Richard Musson. In December 1708, this chief rent was paid to Gervase, for by then he was aged 21.[243]

One of his earliest decisions after coming of age was to have the administrative terms of his grandfather's will set aside. In May 1709 Thomas's trustees or their descendants (Lemuel Low and Charles Hutchinson's sons, Francis and Julius) claimed that they had performed the trusts of the will 'in all or most part'. In return for 5s, the original sum, they released and conveyed the manor and premises to

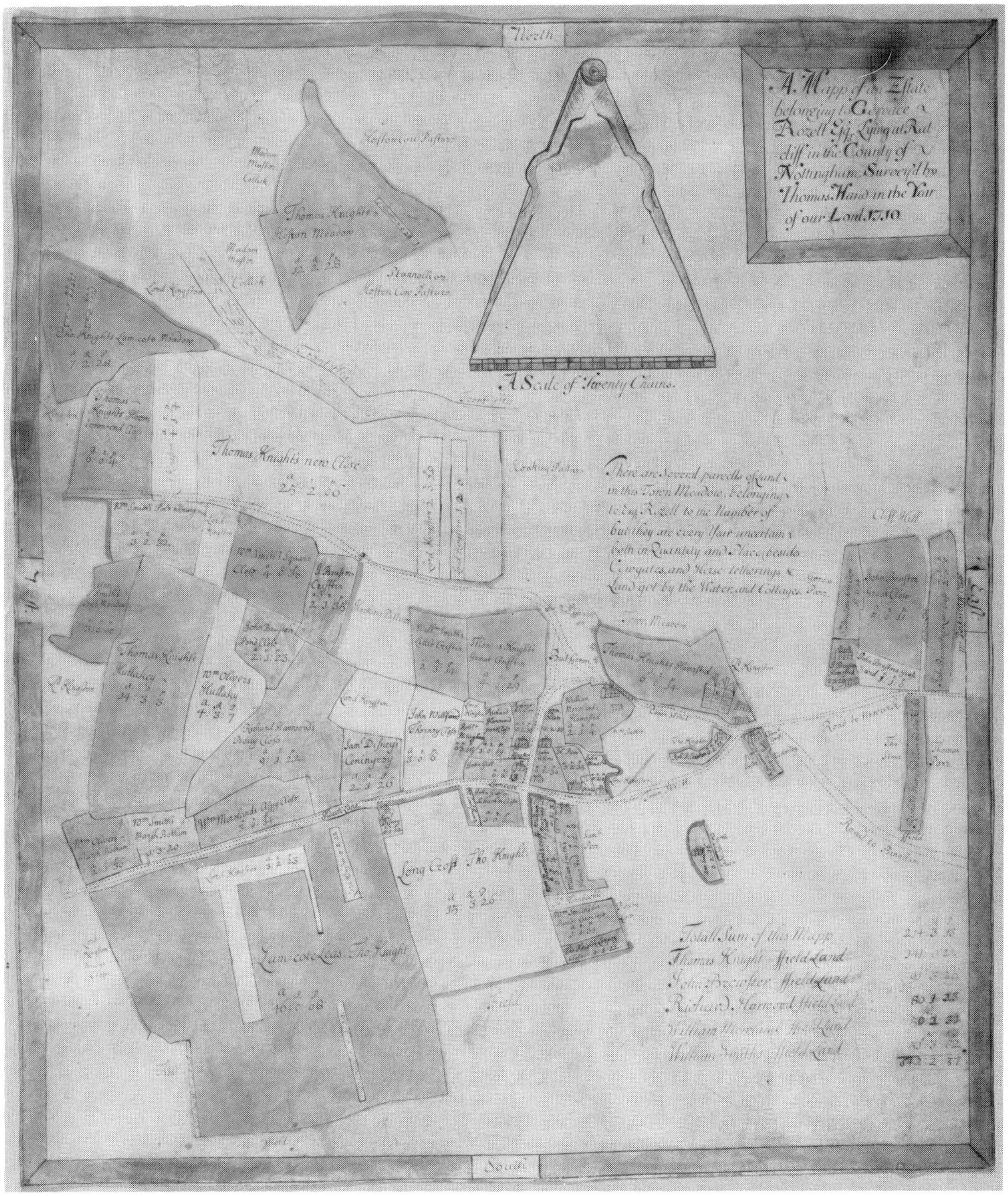

The estate map of 1710 drawn up for Gervase Rosell
in readiness for the sale of his local lands
(U of N Manuscripts Department Ma 2P 115)

Gervase, still subject to any trusts. It was perhaps around this time, too, that Gervase made an advantageous marriage. His bride was Frances, daughter of William Green of Thundercliffe Grange in Yorkshire, and she brought with her a handsome marriage portion of £1,300. The couple were eventually to have six daughters. Probably in 1710, Gervase decided to sell up his Radcliffe lands. In that year, he asked a Thomas Hand to draw up a map indicating the names of his tenants, the amount of their holdings, and, in many cases, the field or close names. (See p. 163.)[244]

The map names and places show some similarities with the 1685 list (p. 153), but changes over 25 years make exact comparisons impossible. It is surprising that the tenant with the most extensive holdings in 1710 was Thomas Knight, a name with no long-standing links with Radcliffe. He and William Smith seem to be the main tenants of the lands formerly farmed personally by Thomas Rosell. The map shows that Knight also held some other Radcliffe land, which was not part of the Rosell estate. It also confirms that Evelyn Pierrepont, 5th Earl of Kingston, was by now a significant independent landowner in the village, as well as a tenant on Rosell lands. The earl's latter holdings are remarkable in the way they trivially, but consistently, invaded the main Rosell fields, now occupied by Thomas Knight. It is as if the Pierreponts, having established a foothold in the village, were poised to take over the rest.

Evelyn Pierrepont
5th Earl of Kingston

As Knight was the occupant of the grandest messuage or homestead on the map (today's Tudor Grange), it seems that the Rosells had already left Radcliffe for Wirksworth in Derbyshire. Nevertheless, Gervase voted with the Tories in the election of 1710 on the strength of his Radcliffe lands. The waiting Pierreponts were supporters of the Whigs and soon found favour with George I when he succeeded to the throne in 1714. A year later Evelyn Pierrepont was rewarded with a dukedom.[245]

In the meantime, Gervase Rosell set in motion the sale of his lands, amounting to 642 acres, 2 roods, 37 perches according to the map (a fall in total acreage since 1685). On September 15th 1711, two months before his first child was born, he placed an advertisement in the *London Gazette*. According to this, the estate lands were worth about £300 a year in rents. The farms were described as well-tenanted and in good repair, and could be bought together or in parcels.

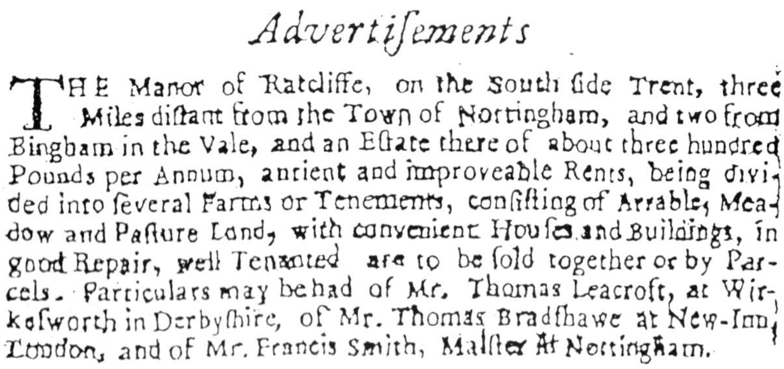

Advertiſements

THE Manor of Ratcliffe, on the South ſide Trent, three Miles diſtant from the Town of Nottingham, and two from Bingham in the Vale, and an Eſtate there of about three hundred Pounds per Annum, antient and improveable Rents, being divided into ſeveral Farms or Tenements, conſiſting of Arrable, Meadow and Paſture Land, with convenient Houſes and Buildings, in good Repair, well Tenanted are to be ſold together or by Parcels. Particulars may be had of Mr. Thomas Leacroft, at Wirkſworth in Derbyſhire, of Mr. Thomas Bradſhawe at New-Inn, London, and of Mr. Francis Smith, Malſter at Nottingham.

The advertisement for the sale of Gervase Rosell's Radcliffe estates which appeared in the *London Gazette* on September 15th 1711

In fact, initial interest does not seem to have been very great. Only five purchasers of piecemeal sales have been found between March and November 1712. With few variations the property corresponds with areas on the 1710 map, and in all cases Gervase is given as joint vendor with his wife and mother. The terms of the sales throw some light on rights in the open fields, and on the nominal survival of old manorial customs:

Details of five piecemeal sales between March and November 1712

March 28-29 John Butler	Close of meadow in Lamcote in tenancy of John Wilford. 1d annually to Rosell at Michaelmas as chief rent if demanded as suit of court to Manor of Radcliffe.	4 acres £87
May 28-29 Jonas Bettison of Holme Pierrepont, butcher	Close of meadow or pasture called Holme Town Ends close lying next Holme Green (tenant not named).	6 acres £140
May 28-29 Richard Musson, jun. of Radcliffe, yeoman (Sold to Bettison within 4 months)	Cottage or tenement in a close; close of meadow called Orish meadow in Lamcote in tenancy of Ann Smith. Liberty to drive and re-drive goods through Mercy Bottom close and Great Hillocky close to Orish meadow. Liberty to come with men and horses to take away hay that should grow thereon or lead [or take] thorns and manure at seasonable times. Common pasture for 2 cows and one follower and all other commons belonging to one cottage to be taken at all commonable times and in all commonable places and fields of Radcliffe and Lamcote. 1d annually to Rosell at Michaelmas as chief rent if demanded as suit of court to Manor of Radcliffe.	3 acres £85.10s.9d
May 28-29 Matthew Simmons of Nottingham	A close in Lamcote called Dickinsons Close.	1 acre £65
Nov 1 Rev Humphrey Perkins of Holme Pierrepont (later? of Barrow-on-Soar in Leics and left to Barrow school)	Messuage or tenement and Home close or croft. Arable land belonging to above 2 closes called Aspey. Meadow lying in the New close enjoyed by the tenant. 10 cowgates. Houses, outhouses, barns, yards, gardens, orchards, let grass, commons etc in tenancy of William Mor[eland].	2 acres 60 acres 3 acres £538.18s.6d

These five early sales amounted to only a small part of the acreage on offer, and Gervase may well have been disappointed at the poor response. In 1713 some stop-gap measures were taken to protect not only his own interests, but those of his wife whose financial input had been considerable. Through the agency of Charles Hurt (his wealthy brother-in-law), of a Thomas Smith, and of Gervase and his wife, there was a settlement of the manorial estates which passed to Smith's control. Within these holdings, the lands occupied by Thomas Knight on the 1710 map for £130 a year were set aside to Gervase and to Frances, as her jointure, for their lifetimes. Gervase retained the right to revoke any clauses about the use of his estates.

Details of one other sale has been found for 1716. Around Easter of that year, Gervase and his wife sold some 130 acres, a messuage, outbuildings and other property along with rights in the common fields to Katherine Wood for £120, a surprisingly low price, working out at less than £1 an acre. Perhaps this was because of Gervase's clause of revocation which a legal adviser of the time described as 'the most unaccountable clause I ever saw'.

Details of a sale around Easter 1716

Katherine Wood	1 messuage, 1 barn, 1 stable, 1 garden, 1 orchard	
	land	100 acres
	pasture	10 acres
	meadow	20 acres
	common pasture for every kind of cattle with appurtenances.	£120

Although the quantities cannot be exactly equated with the 1710 map, the messuage and lands are associated with the forerunner of Radcliffe Hall (now the British Legion). At the time of the 1710 map Richard Harwood was the occupier. The purchaser, Katherine Wood, was the daughter of Montague Wood of Woodborough. If Radcliffe Hall did indeed evolve from Woodhall manor as has been suggested (p. 32), perhaps the wheel had come full circle, and property which the Rosells acquired in Tudor times had returned to a Wood descendant at a bargain rate. Katherine died unmarried in 1738. Although she had five brothers and sisters, none left issue, and the Radcliffe lands passed to a second cousin, Jane Wood, who married James Taylor about 1720. (Her second husband was William Edge whose family also had interests in Radcliffe in the 17th and 18th centuries.) Jane's son, John Taylor, settled in Radcliffe and his descendants lived at Radcliffe Hall until 1905.[246]

The terms of the 1713 settlement were eventually revoked. The mortgage taken out by Gervase's impecunious father on Greene's farm in 1686, which had passed through several hands in the intervening time, was redeemed, and in September 1721 the bulk of the Rosell inheritance passed to Munday Musters of Colwick for £6,000. He did not retain the Radcliffe lands for long, however. In 1724 they were acquired by the Pierreponts for the same amount, but with another £455.8s.9d for Knight's Holt by the river. Their control of the village was to last until 1920.[247]

The end of the main Rosell line

Having left Radcliffe, Gervase and Frances Rosell were to have six daughters - Frances, Maria, Anne, Elizabeth, Catherine and Bridget - born between 1711 and 1726. All six girls were baptised at Wirksworth in Derbyshire, the new heart of Rosell interests, compounded by Gervase's purchase of lands around Alderwasley and Castern from the Hurt family in 1711-12 and 1728-9 (his sisters having married two Hurt brothers), perhaps with the proceeds of his Radcliffe sales.

The Nottinghamshire connections, however, were not entirely forgotten. His daughter Anne came to Holme Pierrepont Hall as housekeeper where she was ultimately paid £25.12s a year. The accounts for her last illness there between October 1st 1794 and 6th May 1795 have survived, including her surgeon's bill, her wine bill, and payment for dressing the feathers of the bed on which she died.[248]

Gervase lived until 1740, being buried at Wirksworth on 4th October of that year. The main male Rosell line had ended. Apart from the names of Gervase (d. 1660/1) and Thomas (d. 1685) on the list of Jeffrey Dole charity benefactors in the parish church, there are no reminders in Radcliffe today of the squires who for several hundred years had presided over the village.

Case study 15

A MAJOR TITHES DISPUTE

Around 1675 a complicated dispute over the payment of tithes came to a head. These tithes were not those due to the local incumbent, Peter Titley, but payments both in money and in kind for lands in lay hands which before the Reformation had belonged to Thurgarton Priory. At the heart of the dispute were John Walker of Nottingham and Thomas Rosell, Radcliffe's squire. The case is of interest for the insight it provides into local tithe customs and the personalities involved.

John Walker's tax bills

Although in this period the Pierrepont and Edge families owned the former rectory lands, John Walker of St Mary's parish in Nottingham was a long-term occupier of at least some of them, collecting tithes from the user. His problems began over the payment of ancient dues to the church hierarchy. During the Civil War and Interregnum, when bishops had been abolished, such payments had lapsed. After episcopacy returned at the Restoration it was difficult to know exactly who was liable for what. So far, John Walker had not paid any dues.

Around 1675 both the Archdeacon of Nottingham and the Dean and Chapter of York caught up with him, and demanded unpaid taxes going back to 1661. Walker protested that he had not paid the 10s annual pension (a sum set in 1379) to the Dean and Chapter 'because he is not bound by Law thereunto he believeth'. The Reverend Vere Harcourt, Nottingham's Archdeacon since 1660, was as unsympathetic as the York authorities. He presented Walker with an itemised bill for fourteen years' procurations at 7s.6d a year, payable at Easter, and fourteen years' synodals at 16d a year, due at both Easter and Michaelmas. Walker failed to pay these sums and was still being sued by Vere Harcourt some five years later in May 1680. Moreover, Walker's successor on these lands, Mr John Tuffin, also failed to pay his procurations and was similarly in trouble with the church court in September 1686. Eventually responsibility for such payments came to rest at the door of the *owner* of the rectorial tithes, rather than the occupant of the lands. By the early 18th century these dues are recorded in the papers of the Pierrepont estate.[249]

Thomas Rosell's sheep

In the meantime, perhaps because he was being financially harassed by the church authorities, John Walker became more than usually particular about his own rights. Occupying some of his lands in Lamcote was Thomas Rosell who had to pay Walker rectorial tithes in the form of wool and lambs. In 1675 Walker objected to the way the squire paid his dues and had him summoned before the Archdeacon's Court. The case became ever more complicated as it unfolded over a period of some twelve months.

Apart from some discrepancies in the number of sheep that Thomas Rosell was alleged to have kept, there was general agreement about the basic circumstances of the case. As Thomas Wilford, a weaver who was also parish clerk, explained:

> *...the land upon which Mr Thomas Rosell's sheep and lambs ...did depasture and feed is Lamcote field, and is a field kept in tillage, there are some other husbandmen who hold lands lying in the same field, and keep it in tillage as Mr Rosell doth and some part of this field is in the p[ar]ish of Holme Pierrepont, and the rest is in the pa[ri]sh of Ratcliffe...and [so is] some of the enclosure when the said sheep did depasture and feed in the winter time....*

The parish clerk had put his finger on part of the problem - that the field was in two ecclesiastical parishes. Unfortunately, the sheep did not recognise any distinction and, as Thomas Rosell himself put it, they fed and their lambs were 'gotten, Eyned [weaned?] and Nourished... promiscuously'; that is, they wandered across the parish boundary. It was on these sheep and lambs that Thomas Rosell had to pay his tithe to Thomas Walker in the summer of 1675, but somebody had also to pay a tithe to the Rector of Holme Pierrepont as the animals roamed on his domain too.

Witnesses in court

An approximate sequence of events can be pieced together from the claims of both Walker and Rosell, and the evidence of their witnesses. Francis Hacker, a 43 year-old gentry friend of Rosell, the Reverend Humphry Perkins, son-in-law of the Rector of Home Pierrepont, Robert Jennison, a 43-year old Holme Pierrepont churchwarden, William Smith, Rosell's own servant and Thomas Wilford, the Radcliffe parish clerk all spoke on Thomas Rosell's behalf. Supporting Walker were William Hutchinson and another John Walker from Radcliffe whom Thomas Rosell disparaged as of

> *small or little estimation credit or reputation, poor people, and such as are for the most part and so have been labourers, servants and workmen of, to, for and with the said John Walker.*

Moreover, they were indebted to Walker, the implication being that their evidence was being bought.

While Walker acknowledged that Hutchinson did owe him some money, it was 'not so much, [so] that he can... pay when he pleaseth'. In another document he said the debt was 'the value of 2 or 3 brewings of malt...' The men, he claimed, had also been employed by Rosell himself at times. Rosell's own servant, William Smith, confirmed that the two men merely worked 'for daily wages' but described them as 'honest', adding that William Hutchinson also kept an ale-house. Nevertheless, they certainly carried less social weight than Rosell's witnesses.

The tithe of fleeces and lambs

Events began in June and July 1675 when Thomas Rosell had his sheep sheared. From his 185 sheep he had 177 fleeces which were 'wound up', and he also had 108 lambs. (Initially Walker claimed that Rosell had 240 fleeces from 240 sheep, and 120 lambs. Other witnesses confirm Rosell's figures.) On 'Friday last before Lammas Day' - 1st August when the tithe was due - John Walker and the Rev Humphrey Perkins, acting as agent for his father-in-law at Holme Pierrepont, went to Thomas Rosell's house. Witnesses agree that Rosell led them to an upper chamber in the yard and showed them his wound-up fleeces and said that he was ready for the tithe. He also took them into his barn and showed them his lambs, also ready for tithing. Provided Walker and Perkins could agree about the distribution of the tithe 'he [Rosell] would be glad to be shut of them'. Unfortunately, Walker demanded the whole tithe, while Perkins claimed that a third part should go to the Holme Pierrepont rector. (Witnesses indicated that this division of payment had been agreed some years previously.) This third part, however, was not normally paid in kind, but commuted to a money payment of 30 shillings. Robert Jennison, the Holme Pierrepont church-warden, confirmed that Thomas Rosell 'doth pay church levies for some of the land towards the reparation of the p[ar]ish church at Holme Pierrepont & he...being churchwarden there hath received such money of the s[ai]d Mr Rosell'. Perhaps because of the financial pressures from the Archdeacon and Dean and Chapter of York, John Walker was reluctant to lose this 30 shillings. Consequently, he and Perkins could not agree, and the tithe was not 'set forth' at that time. John Walker subsequently claimed that Thomas Rosell had refused to set forth the tithe, and witnesses were divided between denying that Rosell had refused, or agreeing that he had, but only after Walker had declined to pay the money to Holme Pierrepont.

Irritated by this turn of events, Thomas Rosell decided to act independently. He summoned Thomas Wilford, the Radcliffe parish clerk, and Robert Jennison, the Holme Pierrepont warden, to carry out the tithing, which they did between 11 a.m. and one o'clock on the appointed day. Two lambs had not been brought up with the rest, so those two stood for Rosell's first choice, 'it being the manner of tithing lambs there for the owner to choose two and then the Titheman chooseth the third for his tithe lamb'. Eleven lambs and 18 fleeces were picked out for the tithe in this way. Each fleece was worth 1s.8d and each lamb 4s. On Rosell's orders, Thomas Wilford took the 18 fleeces and laid them in the church porch where they were to be watched over till nightfall. The 11 lambs were collected by the pinder and put in the pinfold. Thomas Rosell then sent his servant, Thomas Smith, to find John Walker, who happened to be at John Leeson's house in Holme Lane, and tell him what had been done so that he, Walker, 'might go or send to these places and take what was his due.'

While Thomas Rosell might have thought the matter was finished with, Walker had other ideas. He was furious at Rosell's proceedings, declaring that they were 'contrary to the custom & manner of such tithing in that p[ar]ish'. Consequently Walker 'took no more notice of that tithing'. Moreover if Rosell 'did send to give notice it was but to make or cause some difference or controversy betwixt him [Walker]...& the pr[e]tended agent for Holme with whom [he does not] conjoin nor have any thing to do'. Walker claimed that he ought to have seen the skins and the lambs to assess their value and choose for himself. Even Thomas Wilford, who had acted as Rosell's tithing man, had to acknowledge 'that it is not the custom within the p[ar]ish of Ratcliffe... for any one to set forth his tithe of wool and Lamb except when the farmer [of the tithes] or his agent or agents be present...' Rosell, complaining of 'great prejudice and loss', regarded Walker as 'malicious and envious' in bringing the case against him. Whether or not the court agreed is unclear.[250]

Whatever religious toleration was offered by Charles II prior to his Restoration in 1660 was not followed through by those elected to his first Parliament. They were intent on returning to the old ways, and if the Puritans would not conform, then they were to be excluded from the Church of England by a series of laws known collectively as the Clarendon Code. Although they might worship in small groups, they could not take part in official life or be educated at the universities. Such Protestant nonconformists, however, were regarded with somewhat less suspicion than Catholics, whom the new king seemed to favour.

The parish in the 1660s

In some respects, putting the clock back after the Interregnum highlighted old problems and led to a period of slack clerical control in the village. Before the Civil War Radcliffe had been a poor parish, but the £50 a year eventually extracted out of the confiscated rectory lands by William Creswell must have made the living almost comfortable. With the fall of the Commonwealth government, however, the rectory tithe lands again came into private hands, being bought by Mr James Seele and Mr Ralph Edge, the latter obtaining his half from the Earl of Chesterfield in 1661. William Pierrepont already possessed the glebe land, and in 1668 he acquired James Seele's share of the tithe land. The Edge and Pierrepont interests continued jointly until 1742. With the income from the old rectory lands once more under lay control, the Radcliffe living reverted to its old vicarage value, and remained impoverished until the mid -18th century.[251]

While enjoying the profits from the rectory lands, the new impropriators were, of course, again responsible for the upkeep of the chancel and for the appointment of a clergyman. Short of giving away their profits, however, they were unlikely to attract a vicar for such meagre rewards, and it may not have been for want of trying that a permanent incumbent proved difficult to find after William Creswell's death. In October 1663, churchwardens John Parr and William Needham presented 'Mr Ralph Edge and Mr Seeles... for not providing a Minister'. The Call Book for April 1664 has only a gap alongside the word 'curate' - an indication that the parish was to be effectively downgraded, and the wardens again complained 'that they have no minister'. This does not mean that services were abandoned in the village, but they were clearly haphazard and dependent on the churchwardens acquiring assistance as best they could. For example, in 1664 out of what should have gone to a vicar, churchwardens John Parr and William Needham paid £1.13s.4d to Mr Heath, the Shelford incumbent, five shillings to 'A travelling Minister', and £7.12s.4 1/2d to Mr Hawis, the Holme Pierrepont curate who had married William Creswell's widow (Alice Rustat). Richard Hawis served as Radcliffe's curate until at least 1666, while continuing to assist his father-in-law at Holme.[252]

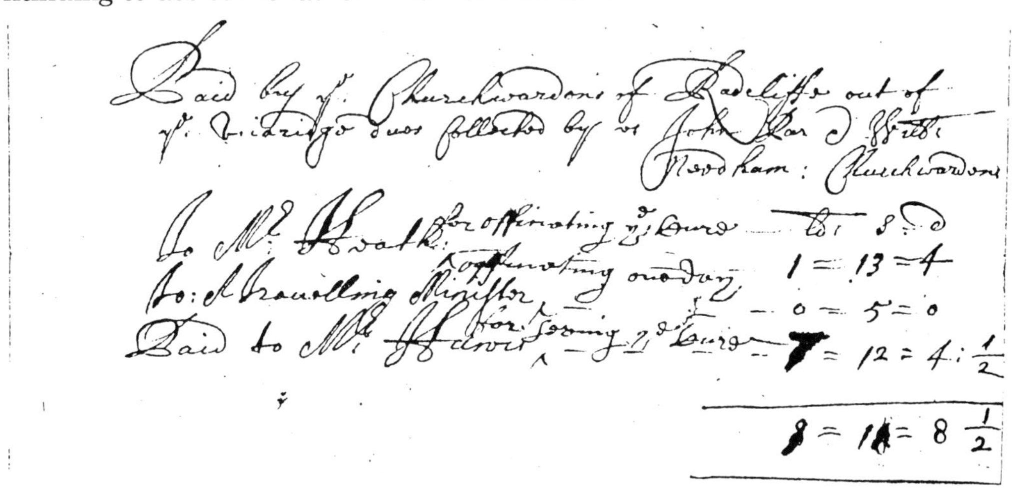

Churchwardens' payments for visiting preachers in 1664 when the parish lacked a minister
(U of N Manuscripts Department LB 229/2/15)

Religious discipline was revived when the Archdeacon's Court began holding sessions again from February 1662. Radcliffe's first case before the restored court occurred in September 1663. Joanna Batting (alias Pattin) was presented at St Peter's 'for having a bastard child'. She was there again in January 1665 when 'whore' was written alongside her entry in the Act Book. The pre-war pattern of bringing sexual offenders to court was re-established.

Other parishioners were slack about church attendance and payment of dues, but the wardens were not prepared to turn a blind eye, particularly at a time when Parliament was stressing the need for conformity. In September 1664 widow Jane Butler was presented to the court for refusing to a pay a 'mortuary' - at 6s.8d a heavy legacy from a bygone age. In the same month the churchwardens presented four parishioners for not receiving the sacrament the previous Easter. As has been seen, one of them was Elizabeth Rosell, the new squire's wife. Thomas Rosell protested on behalf of his wife, pointing out the obvious:

> *that they have no mi[ni]ster in their parish nor had at Easter last any neither doth he know when any communion will be administered in their parish.*

On the face of it, churchwardens Parr and Needham were being unreasonable, and the court merely ordered Elizabeth Rosell to receive the sacrament the next time it was administered. (The other non-receivers were given similar instructions.) It was a year later, in September 1665, before she certified that she had done so. Routine presentments by the churchwardens became less common after this time.[253]

Joseph Hawkins 1667-1671

By November 1667 Richard Hawis was replaced as curate by Joseph Hawkins. The only known church court cases from his ministry are three defamations from 1669 and 1670. Details of two - blacksmith George Squire against Richard Butler, farmer, and William Morley of Holme Pierrepont against Elizabeth Alcock of Radcliffe, which ended in agreement - have unfortunately not survived. The third, dealing with the claims against John Henson's administration of his brother's estate, is covered elsewhere. (See p. 145.)

Little else is known of Joseph Hawkins' initial short period in Radcliffe beyond the fact that he increased his income by being simultaneously curate of Shelford. He left Radcliffe by May 1671 and in 1672 he felt obliged to bring his own defamation case against a Shelford parishioner - Anne Miller, wife of George Miller - who had called him 'a whoremaster and the arrantest whoremaster in a Country or County'. Despite this reputation, he, or a man of the same name, returned to Radcliffe in 1699, to serve again until 1710. (See p. 174.) His intervening career - combining curacies at Shelford and Kneeton, replacing the latter with the vicarage of Burton Joyce in 1694 - indicates that pluralism was a necessity for many impoverished clergy in the 17th and early 18th centuries.[254]

Peter Titley 1671-1683

It was another curate, Peter Titley, who was to provide greater continuity in the village by serving for some twelve years after Joseph Hawkins left. It is difficult to be sure of his credentials. Perhaps he was the Peter Titley who matriculated from Magdalene College, Cambridge at Easter 1641 and was ordained deacon at Peterborough 1642-3. While struggling in a poor living, Peter Titley must have been irritated by the long-running dispute before the church courts about the profitable main rectorial tithes of the parish to which he was not entitled. (See p. 167.)[255]

The religious census 1676

While this tithe case was attracting attention locally, at national level more fundamental issues were at stake. The period of Peter Titley's curacy coincided with a mood of fierce Anglicanism in Parliament. The Clarendon Code was already restricting nonconformity, and attempts by Charles II to issue edicts of toleration -

which would encompass Catholics - were received with hostility, culminating in the Test Act of 1673. By this, officeholders were to accept communion according to the Church of England. When prominent figures, including Charles' brother James, the heir to the throne, were forced to resign from office and acknowledge their Catholicism, a national crisis occurred, with a move to exclude James from the succession. It was in this atmosphere of religious suspicion that the church authorities decided in 1676 to discover the leanings of people throughout the country.

In Radcliffe it was Peter Titley's job to answer the three questions concerning the number of people old enough to receive communion, the number suspected of Catholicism, and the number of other dissenters who absented themselves from communion. Of local parishes, Radcliffe emerges as the most conformist:[256]

Parish	Number of communicants	Number of Catholics	Number of Dissenters
Bingham	326	0	10
Cotgrave	269	0	54
Holme Pierrepont	70	3	4
Radcliffe	183	0	0
Shelford	171	0	14

Irregular records and clandestine marriages

The conformity of Peter Titley's parishioners indicated here is largely confirmed by the Archdeacon's Court records. Few immorality cases were presented at this time, and only one penance signed by Titley has survived - performed in May 1673 by 'paupers' John and Elizabeth Carrington for fornication before marriage. Peter Titley's era, however, is marked by a number of irregularities in other ways. A comparison between the parish registers and the copies sent to the bishop shows that records were not accurately kept. For example, between 19th March 1671 and 23rd February 1674, six baptisms appear in the parish register which are not found on the bishop's transcript, and between July and October 1679 three burials are missing. Such discrepancies may simply have been caused by transcription errors, perhaps by the parish clerk. (From around 1674 Thomas Wilford, according to the call books, was the first of two men of that name to hold the office.)

When it comes to the recording of weddings, the inaccuracies are considerable. Between 17th April 1673 and 14th January 1676, four are recorded in the bishop's transcript which have not been found in the parish register. Moreover, from the archdeaconry records, it is clear that many weddings at this time were occurring in a haphazard fashion, and often went unrecorded. After the freedom of the Interregnum period it was proving difficult to re-establish the traditional restrictions on the time and place for nuptials. Along with many of his contemporary clerics, Peter Titley was quite prepared to marry couples at 'unseasonable times', with or without banns or licence. The fees would have been a useful addition to his meagre income, while the bride and groom could avoid tiresome questions and regulations. In spite of the disapproval of the church authorities, 'clandestine' marriages were still valid. (In due course, after some cases involving under-age heiresses and unscrupulous fortune hunters, the Hardwicke marriage act was introduced in 1754 which insisted on the proper recording of banns and the recording of marriages in bound volumes of specially printed forms.)

The Radcliffe churchwardens did their best to be vigilant in such matters. In the Autumn of 1670 they reported John Campion and 'his supposed wife' Anne, for being 'married without Banns publishing'. The couple were dismissed by the Archdeacon's Court in the January when they produced evidence that they had been married at Eagle in Lincolnshire in the previous April. Similarly, in November 1672 John and Ester Henson were before the court because of their clandestine marriage conducted at Dale Abbey in Derbyshire on 7th October.[257]

Although Peter Titley was not involved in these two cases, it was not long after his arrival in the village that he was before the church court charged with irregularities. On 26th March 1672 he confessed that he had conducted the marriage of William Smith of Radford and Margaret Leeson of Lenton in Radcliffe church without licence or banns. (This marriage has not been found in Radcliffe's register.) As he voluntarily sought absolution, on this occasion the case was dismissed. When it came to marrying Alice Janner and John Fry(ery?) of Basford, the court took a less lenient view. The chosen venue was Eleanor Hutchinson's eating and tippling house ('edilius cauponule') in Radcliffe, she being present at the time, so the court was informed in March 1678. (The Hutchinsons were good baptismal customers of Peter Titley at this period.) This unconventional venue was perhaps to Peter Titley's liking. Some three years earlier in April 1675 the churchwardens had felt obliged to report him to the authorities 'for being drunk upon the Lord's Day'. The wedding in the Hutchinsons' ale-house is not recorded in the Radcliffe register and led to the curate being temporarily suspended from his duties. He proved incorrigible, however. and was again before the court in September 1678 for celebrating an unspecified clandestine marriage, and on 24th October was once more suspended.

By the autumn of 1681 the patience of the authorities was running out. Peter Titley was further charged with failing to publish banns in four cases involving individuals from St Mary's in Nottingham, Cotgrave, Plumtree and Stathern in Leicestershire. In 1682 a Bingham couple, John and Anna Turner, were brought to court for having been married as long ago as 1677 by Titley - not their own minister - without banns or declaration of place and time. The last case against him was brought in February 1683. In a Latin document the court summed up the charges: that while under three years' suspension he had celebrated matrimony without licence, or banns being called on three Lord's days publicly in the parish church where the parties lived: that marriages should not have been performed in unsuitable places or have been conducted outside the hours of 8 a.m. and 12 noon, but only in a sanctified church or chapel at a time previously published: that obstinately and without fearing for the safety of his soul between 1678 and 1682 in Radcliffe and several neighbouring parishes he had fanatically conducted clandestine marriages against the canons of the Anglican church. On this occasion he was specifically charged with improperly marrying two couples who came from four outside parishes - Cotgrave, Kinoulton, Lowdham and Tithby. It is shortly after this time that Peter Titley's curacy came to an end.[258]

Josiah Redford 1683-1686 and Peter Laycock 1686-1698

Peter Titley signed the bishop's transcript of the parish register in March 1683, but was replaced by Josiah Redford in December of that year. The latter was appointed as vicar, not curate. According to his induction mandate, he was presented by William Pierrepont, 4th Earl of Kingston, and Ralph Edge of Nottingham, who shared the advowson. His appointment was because of the death of the last incumbent, but no burial record for Peter Titley appears in the parish register.

Josiah Redford's time as vicar was brief, for in April 1686 Peter Laycock appears in the call book as curate. In March 1687, however, the latter signed the bishop's transcript as vicar, but subsequently as curate, while a call book, probably for May 1691, notes that he had been made deacon in 1682, and describes him as vicar or curate. From then on he appears in the Call Books as vicar until May 1696 from when he is again described as curate until his departure in 1698. His status in Radcliffe is therefore unclear, but his financial situation improved during his last four years in the village by his additional appointment in 1694 to the parish of Laxton over 20 miles away.

This would have meant frequent and tiresome journeys on horseback, but by then Peter Laycock would have been glad of this extra security, for on 20th June 1688 he had married by special licence Elizabeth Eyre of East Bridgford. He was then aged 30 and she 28. They soon had a large family to provide for: Walter was baptised in April 1689, Elizabeth in September 1690, Mary in September 1692, Peter in February 1694 and William in March 1696. (Ann was born in 1698 after the family moved to Laxton.) To begin with, Peter Laycock's income from Radcliffe dues had been comfortably supplemented by his Pierrepont patron at least. In December 1685 the Pierrepont estate accounts record a handsome payment to him of £17.10s for the half year - the same amount as had been paid to Josiah Redford retrospectively in December 1685, and perhaps on other occasions. Gradually, however, the half-yearly amount was reduced: to £16.5s on Lady Day 1687; to £15 from Michaelmas 1687 to at least May 1692. The book for Lady Day 1690 makes it very clear that any payment was the result of the earl's generosity and not an obligation. The £15 paid at that time

> *being half of what the Tithe of Ratcliffe is now Let for, being the Free Gift and Bounty of his Lo[rdshi]p To the vicar of Ratcliffe during his Lo[rdshi]ps pleasure only...*

The 'gratuity' was cut to a mere £10 a year by August 1697 in the time of Evelyn Pierrepont, the 5th Earl. It was to be reduced still further for Peter Laycock's successor.

The cuts must have added to Peter Laycock's financial difficulties as his young family was growing up. Small wonder that in the ill-kept parish register accounts of money left to the poor, which was loaned out by the churchwardens at interest, Peter Laycock is noted as borrowing the legacies of Joseph Pilkington and John Parr, amounting to £3. To further supplement his income, he rented lands from the Pierrepont estate from which he perhaps hoped to make a profit from selling crops or stock. For example in 1695 he was renting four pieces of land: Gilmore Breach, technically in the parish of Holme Pierrepont but probably in Lamcote, for £3.5s the half year; two pieces in Radcliffe at £3.10s the half year each; and a plot formerly held by Ester Henson for £1.5s the half year. Whether the curate ever made a profit on his outlay of £23 a year seems doubtful. As early as Michaelmas 1696 his name appears in a list of 'arrears'. It was there again for Lady day 1697, his total rents owing on both occasions. By the autumn and spring of 1697-8 only the money on Ester Henson's old plot seems to have been outstanding. As the estate was now having to pay taxes on land rented out (14s.3d in Laycock's case), and £7.2s a year on 'Pensions, Procurations, Synodalls & Annual tenths' on the impropriated Radcliffe lands, the Pierreponts were not likely to feel particularly sympathetic to a hard-up curate, and may have felt justified in cutting his 'gratuity' to compensate for the outgoings.[259]

Religious discipline prior to the Revolution of 1688

Peter Laycock's arrival in Radcliffe coincided with the appointment of a new parish clerk, William Bacon, who succeeded Thomas Wilford the weaver, a witness in the Walker versus Rosell tithes case. Another person referred to in that case, Thomas Whittle, the husbandman who had watched over the fleeces in the church porch, was mentioned again in the church court in July 1686. This time it was because of his wife Joan who, along with Anne, the wife of husbandman John Campion, was charged with not receiving communion at Easter. This suggests that the parish had once again the occasional nonconformist, although none had been present at the time of the census ten years earlier. Joan and Anne, however, were two of 120 named individuals called to appear at the church court in St Peter's on 2nd July. Most were on a similar charge. From August to December of 1684, throughout 1685 and the summer of 1686 abnormally large numbers of people were presented. The pressures put by Charles II on corporations to ensure the election of conformist M.Ps. followed by the unpopular pro-Catholic policy of his brother James II from 1685 had caused the archdeaconry authorities to emphasise conformity to the Anglican church. Matters came to a head in 1688 when James, insisting on trying to force through a policy of toleration for Catholics, provoked opposition from Whigs and Tories alike. He and his baby son were driven into exile, and his Protestant daughter Mary and her Dutch husband William were invited to take the throne. While there is no evidence of specific opposition to James II in Radcliffe, other clerics were more outspoken, and the village could not have been oblivious to the fact that Nottingham became one of the centres of this comparatively bloodless 'Glorious Revolution'.

Reported cases of sexual immorality were rare in the twelve years of Peter Laycock's ministry. In April 1687 William and Grace Whitby performed their penance for fornication before marriage in normal apparel before him and his churchwardens. (Their daughter Anne had been baptised in the previous November. Another daughter, Grace, was baptised in February 1688. The mother, and a new-born son, William, were both buried two years later.) No Radcliffe penance certificate has been found for Thomas Blatherwick, a bodice maker, who committed fornication with Mary Hancock, a West Bridgford spinster in June 1688. Alongside her name 'incarcerate' is written, for she and Thomas were handed over to the civil authorities when it was discovered they had tried to conceal the birth of a dead baby. (See p. 192.) Not for another six years, in May 1694, were there any similar presentments. In that year, the churchwardens, William and Thomas Parr, seem to have clamped down on immorality and brought three cases to court: labourer Richard Wilson and his wife Mary for fornication before marriage; labourer John Henson and Ann his wife for fornication and marrying clandestinely; and Mary Webster for having 'a bastard child'.

One other case from Peter Laycock's ministry is of interest. When Thomas Campion, a Radcliffe farmer, was excommunicated in 1689 for withholding his church dues from the churchwardens, he turned the charges against his accusers William Alcock and Thomas Butler. In October 1690 Campion put his case before the court and charged the two wardens with malpractice in their accounting:

> *That several sums of money in the said accompt mentioned to be paid, were not really and bona fide paid, and several other sums mentioned also in the said accounts to be paid are not allowable by law nor ought to have been paid...*

The wardens were to show their accounts, and keep copies. Unfortunately, the validity of the accusation cannot be checked as the account books have not survived for this period, and the outcome of the case is not known.[260]

Joseph Hawkins again 1698-1711

It was around 1698 that Peter Laycock left Radcliffe to take up residence in Laxton. He was replaced as curate by Joseph Hawkins who remained until his death in 1711. He had left the village in 1671 (shortly before bringing his defamation charge against a Shelford parishioner), continued at Shelford and had held Kneeton too from 1672 to 1694, in which year he became incumbent of Burton Joyce instead. During his absence from Radcliffe he had not proved the most conformist of clerics for in September 1684 he had been reported to the Archdeacon's Court by both his parishes of Kneeton and Shelford for not reading prayers on Wednesdays and Fridays, and for not reading from the pulpit a statute against swearing. His second spell in Radcliffe coincides with a period of chaotic entries in the parish register, but he was clearly prepared to enforce conventional morality. Out of eleven surviving cases presented to the church court from his time, seven dealt with couples who had committed fornication before marriage, and two concerned adultery. (Four penance certificates have survived for these cases.) One other case concerned the failure of the churchwardens in 1708 to repair the churchyard fence.

Little is known of Joseph Hawkins' personal circumstances, but as a pluralist he would have been financially more comfortably off than some of his predecessors. He certainly had little comfort from Radcliffe, for the Pierrepont estate reduced his gratuity from the £10 a year of Peter Laycock's last years to a mere £5 a year. He had at least two married daughters by the end of his life as they were his executrixes and received his last gratuity after his death.[261]

John Hagger 1712-1731

His successor, John Hagger, Radcliffe's curate from 1712 to 1731, was also granted the miserly gratuity of £5 a year at least until the 1720s, but he had additional income as incumbent at Cropwell, and eventually Sneinton too. (His interesting ministry is covered in the study of the 18th century village.) A terrier has survived for 1714 which gives a clear picture of the assets of a Radcliffe clergyman at the end of the Stuart period:

A Terrier of the Vicarage of Ratcliffe upon Trent in the County of Nottingham

Imprimis the Vicarage House containing two Bays of Building. Item, the Garden & Foreyard containing about a Rood of Ground. Item Easter Dues viz: Each Communicant's offerings 2d, Each Dwelling House 6d. Item For servants' wages 5d per £. Item Each Tradesman pro manu 4d. Item Lammas dues, viz: every new Milch'd Cow 2d, Every strapper [dry cow] 1d, Every Mare & Foal 2d, Every swarm of Bees 6d. Item, Small Tithes, viz: Pigs, Chickens, Pigeons, Apples & other Fruit etc. Item for Marriage after Banns published 3s.6d - with Licence 5s. A woman's churching 1s. A Burial 1s. Mortuaries are paid in the Parish: For £50 Personal Estate 13s.4d, for £40 - 10s, for £30 or £25 - 6s.8d.
Item, Paid by her Majesty at the Audit £1.10s per Annum.
Item, Given by the most Noble Marquis of Dorchester [i.e. Evelyn Pierrepont, formerly 5th Earl of Kingston] £5 per annum.

Such fees and lesser tithe payments helped to boost the value of a poor living so that by the early 18th century the parish was assessed as worth £10. Nevertheless, it was still amongst the poorest in the country, and the 'decayed' state of the vicarage house until its rebuilding in 1777 discouraged the residence of incumbents. Such fees had changed little by the time of a terrier for 1777.[262]

Rectorial tithes and obligations

The lands associated with the main rectorial tithes had been in the hands of lay landowners since the Reformation, but it is not until the later Stuart period that a real idea of assets and outgoings emerges. As already noted, at this time the rectorial lands and advowson were shared between the Edge and Pierrepont families, but the Pierreponts additionally held glebe land. The evidence comes from the Pierrepont records only.

The main regular outgoings were the dues to the church hierarchy, but there were other random payments. For example, in March 1707 the Pierrepont estate's half share for Joseph Shilcock's repairs to the chancel came to £5.1s.6d. The glazier, Bryan Borse, was paid 1s.6d 'for mending the choir windows' in November 1710, and the windows were again in need of attention in 1714 when Joseph Shilcock was hired once more for a total of £1.14s.11½d, of which Mr Edge paid 17s.6d.

One other payment was shared in this way in 1705 when substantial repairs were made to the tithe barn - a rare reference to what must have been a key landmark in the village which was soon to disappear. (From the map of 1710, it would appear to have been in the area of today's Orford Avenue.) Joseph Barker was paid £16.5s for carpenter's work, timber, stone, laths and nails.

Tithe barn from the map of 1710

Although they cannot now be located, the exact acreage of the impropriated lands is made clear from a survey made for the Earl of Kingston in 1694. In this it is clearly stated that 'All the Glebe and half the tithes belong to the Earl of Kingston'. Such tithes, payable in the survey by Mrs Rosell (mother of the last Gervase), were of corn, wool and lambs, similar to those paid by Thomas in 1675.

Enclosed areas, including a house and homestead of 3 roods and 8 perches, half the tithe yard, two closes ('Anslow Crosse close' and 'Glebe close below Spellow hill'), and another house and homestead came to 6 acres and 27 perches. In the four great fields of the village - Cliff, Breck, Stony and Sunpit - the land amounted to 87 acres 2 roods and 19 perches:

in Cliff field	31 acres 2 roods 16 perches
in Breck field	17 acres 0 roods 5 perches
in Stony field	11 acres 0 roods 36 perches
in Sunpit field	27 acres 3 roods 2 perches

In addition there were three pieces of meadow amounting to 3 acres 1 rood and 34 perches, and there were 12 beastgates (right of pasture) in the Eastgang (Hesgang) field across the river. All this was rented out and brought in a comfortable income. An undated paper in the archdeaconry records, probably from the 1680s, gives the value of these lands: £35 a year in rent from the Pierrepont half of the rectorial tithe lands; £10 a year from the glebe land, owned entirely by the Pierreponts.[263]

The dues payable by the Pierreponts on these lands had been initiated in 1379, and were similar to those John Walker was arguing about in the 1670s. (See pp. 25 and 167.) In February 1706 the equivalents were paid to Mr Thomas Sanderson, who distributed them to the appropriate authorities. They included two pensions of 10s for the Archbishop of York, due at Pentecost and Martinmas (Whit Sunday and 11th November); two pensions of 5s for the Dean and Chapter of York due on the same dates; procurations and synodalls to Dr Peirson, Archdeacon of Nottingham, amounting to 8s.10d; two synodalls and two 'nonaccompts' to the Archbishop of York at 4s.8d. Each payment required a receipt or 'acquittance' of 4d (20 pence altogether). In addition there was a tithes payment of 9s.3d due to the queen at Christmas, paid to a Mr Nicholas Suger, with a further acquittance for 4d and 'portaridge' amounting to 12d. (Before the Reformation this payment would have been paid to Rome as 'Peter's Pence'.) Altogether these ecclesiastical taxes and expenses came to £2.16s.1d a year, which made only a small dent in the income of £35 on the impropriation rents. Presumably there would be similar income and outgoings on the other half of the rectorial lands held by Mr Edge. The divided state of the rectory and advowson continued until 1743 when Evelyn Pierrepont, 2nd Duke of Kingston, acquired total control by purchasing the Edge holdings.[264]

The contrast between a vicar's income and the profits to be made by lay landlords from former church lands helps to explain the hostility to tithe-paying, particularly by nonconformists from the 17th century onwards. In Radcliffe's case, tithes were abolished at the time of enclosure in 1789.

Artist's impression of Radcliffe church in the early 18th century based on a sketch on the enclosure map c. 1787 (prior to the fall of the steeple) and a painting of the 1840s

The multi-layered nature of authority was as evident in the early 17th century as it was in the Tudor period. As in Elizabeth's reign, matters which would today be dealt with exclusively by the civil or criminal judicial system were often also handled by the manorial or ecclesiastical courts, so that the guilty might be punished by more than one body. This is particularly the case with regard to the poor laws and religious non-conformity (mainly Catholicism in Radcliffe's case.) Whatever court was involved, it was usually the official at parish level - constable, thirdborough, churchwarden or overseer of the poor - who initiated the process.

I Manorial Sanctions

The Rosells' manorial court, indicated in the estate sales of 1712 (p. 165), has left no records, but some evidence survives from three other courts which would affect Radcliffe and Lamcote people in the 17th century.

The Court of the Honour of Peverel

Seal of the Peverel Court from Charles I's time

There were no changes in procedure at the Peverel Court with the coming of the Stuarts. The Bailiff was Sir Percival Willoughby and the court was now usually held at Wollaton. The records clearly show, however, that discipline was neglected in this period, perhaps as a result of Sir Percival's own personal and financial difficulties (including a spell in the Fleet prison). At the beginning of James I's reign the office of thirdborough in Radcliffe was held by Richard and then by William Dewsbury, the brothers of Isabel in the breach of promise case of 1592. (See p. 67.) From 1610 until 1618 one of the village's two Henry Parrs took over. After this until 1641 when John Parr and William Hutchinson held the office in turn, the records are sporadic and demonstrate the decline of the court's authority, for on many occasions several manors failed to appear or arrears in the payment of fines accumulated. On at least seven occasions Radcliffe did not send its thirdborough to the court and many of the rolls were not completed.[265]

Like other manorial courts, it also issued general orders from time to time about keeping highways and watercourses clear, fences mended and animals under control. After the Poor Law Act of 1601, the court targeted those harbouring pregnant women; although only one place received a warning (Trowell), the rule against this would have applied to all. Few details are recorded for most manors, Radcliffe included, and it must be assumed that a good deal of business was conducted on the spot in each place, the local official, the thirdborough, administering a rough and ready sort of justice. It would not be in the interests of the tenants to bring too many cases to court. The reality for the less affluent who failed to pay their fines may be judged from a note written about one tenant in 1610 (the manor he belonged to is uncertain):

> *one brass pan and a candlestick of the goods of Christopher Levis were priced by the Jurors at this Court to the sum of 4s which goods the Bailiff seized by distress [force] for Amercement imposed upon the said Christopher.*

As an ultimate threat there was the debtors' gaol.[266]

As might be expected the Civil War brought the records of manorial jurisdiction to a temporary halt and, as Crown property, the Honour was later confiscated by Parliament. The new regime brought with it changes of title for whereas on 3rd October 1648 the documents were headed '...his Majesty's great Court Leet holden for his said honour at Wollaton', a year later this was changed to '...the Keepe[r] of the Liberty of England by Authority of Parliament's Great Court Leet and Court Baron.' In 1655 it became 'his highness the Lord Protector's great Court Leet and Court Baron' and in October 1659 it was held once more by authority of Parliament.[267]

When the records resumed in October 1647, Radcliffe was found to be in arrears for the common fine to the tune of £8.6s.6d. Of this, £5.7s.8d was paid into the court, but unfortunately for Radcliffe, the clerk's arithmetic left something to be desired for he then judged them to be £3.3s.4d in arrears. Over the next few sessions, the tenants endeavoured to pay off the debt, but in 1649 the total they owed had risen to £3.10s.6d. During the 1650s up to seven common suitors per session were presented for non-appearance, a negligence on the part of the tenants not seen in the earlier records. Of brewers of ale and bakers of bread there were plenty - six of them broke the assize in 1651. One of them was John Taylor, the local fisherman, who was also fined 'for fishing within unlawfull [ingress]' in 1653. The task of collecting the arrears and making tenants come to the court had clearly become a thankless one and in October 1655 the 'township', along with 16 others (out of the 39) was fined for 'want of a thirdborough'. There was, however, an attempt at clerical efficiency unknown in earlier records, for in 1656 the manors were listed in alphabetical order with their thirdborough. In Radcliffe this was William Butler; he paid the 3s fine and presented Gervase Parr who was sworn in for duty for the following year; he in turn presented John Walker in 1657.[268]

As in the Civil War period the business of the court may have lapsed in the last years of the Interregnum, and after Charles II resumed lordship in 1660 only lists of fines and miscellaneous documents have been preserved. Neither the Rosells nor the other tenants thought it worth their while to attend the court. In 1665 six brewers, including two widows, were fined 2d each, and William Sands, who was also a baker, 4d. The court was unable to establish who the heirs of William Dewsbury were and they headed the list for non-attendance, as they had done during the Interregnum, and were fined 6d. Two years later they had still not appeared, nor had five other tenants and a fine of 6s was demanded of 'the Inhabitants of Radcliffe-upon-Trent for that their thirdborough did not appear at this Court'. The truth is that manorial jurisdiction in general was by now an anachronism and could no longer command the respect it demanded. It became increasingly difficult to find enough tenants present at the court to form a jury. Parish administration, the upkeep of the highways, care of the poor, the maintenance of law and order were better dealt with by other agencies. The functions of the court of Peverel over the next 150 years were to dwindle to collecting fines for non-appearance at court, to jailing debtors, and to holding tenants' dinners.[269]

The Court of the Knights of St John of Jerusalem

The Court of Shelford St John's, in contrast to the Peverel Court, seems to have retained effective powers even in the later part of the period, perhaps because the lord was local. The Pierreponts owned both this manor and the manor of Cotgrave, so the same steward presided over both courts which were held on two consecutive days at Cotgrave. Between 1705 and 1708, this was Richard Roe and on each occasion he was paid 12s.6d for his work. Tenants were obliged to have their wills proved at the court and would have enjoyed the same rights to freedom from tolls which existed in earlier times. (See p. 75.) The Court House in Cotgrave was known as 'Brumby House' or St John of Jerusalem's House, and in 1704 nearly £7 was spent on repairs to it.[270]

Seal of the Court of St John of Jerusalem from a sketch by W.L. Ashmore

Surviving court records date from 4th April 1651 and continue throughout the 18th century. During the late 17th century up to 14 tenants from Radcliffe appear on each occasion, but not all came every time. Over a ten-year period to 1661 a total of 36 men and women were named. When one of their number died they reported this to the court. For example, on 4th April 1673 the clerk recorded the death of William Leeson, adding 'son and wife in the house'. In April 1685 'Radcliffe men present[ed] the death of Thomas Rosell' and two years later that of Gervase. New tenants were also noted such as Robert Butler who in October 1663 did 'make suit to this court'. After 1683 this was expressed more formally in Latin. Sometimes a son or a widow succeeded a deceased father or husband, as when Ester Henson in 1685 was admitted tenant with the use of the cottage occupied by her late husband. Sometimes an entirely new tenancy was created, as when William Jervis (Gervas) in April 1685 acquired the cottage lately occupied by widow Ellen Hutchinson. In 1691 William Marshall was charged with 'not doing suit [and service]' to the court, but after this date the records become less detailed. Apart from one occasion, the type of tenancy and the rent to be paid was omitted. In October 1675 the clerk listed 'Chiefes [freehold rents] given in by ye Bailiffs'. Mr Thomas Rosell paid 10s for Lamcote, although it should have been 12s (as shown by a note in the margin about a receipt for the purchase of the manor of Radcliffe). William Pilkington paid 3d, John Campion 3s, Widow Buxton 1s and Thomas Smith a pound of pepper.

Lists of tenants and the juries formed from them take up a good deal of the records. Jury service was every man's right and duty. In 1669 five men from Radcliffe were fined 12d each for absenting themselves and failing to make their presentments, but on one occasion the court clerk was fined for not including a particular individual on the list. It was a task to be taken seriously, especially when matters concerning the tenants' own 'township' were discussed. (For example, in 1674 there was a case of a man being fined for 'divulging the secrets of the jury'.) No one was immune from prosecution by the jury, not even the lord of the manor, the Earl of Kingston. He was admonished in 1697 'for setting down posts to [denvill] the highway against the house of Paul Simon and if not removed before the next court day [he would be fined] £1.13s.4d'.

As with other manorial courts, presentments for breaking the assize of ale and bread appear with the most regularity. Up to 1675 the same family names recur among the brewers of ale - the Hutchinsons and the Taylors (alias Fisher), one of the Greenes, and, for a while, Edward Swinscoe a butcher and Robert Barr the brick-maker. Sons took over the business from their fathers and widows from their husbands. John Hilton and Robert Vardin sold bread. All these people also appear in the Peverel court records of the same period. Other families took over after 1680 - the Hensons, Jervises, Bacons and Walkers and many who appear only once or twice. This must have been a steady source of income for the lord and was also a means of controlling the number of ale-houses. Moral censure appears in the occasional indictments for keeping disorderly houses and for harbouring beggars.

Most of the regulations, with the fines incurred for disobeying them, were included with the Cotgrave presentments, but many would have applied to tenants from all areas. They show how communal arrangements were made for farming the open fields, some being repeated many times throughout the period. Tenants were required not to tether their horses and cattle on the stubble before the corn was 'led away' (1653) and not to 'break the stubble fields with sheep' without a general consent of neighbours (1654). Consent had to be obtained before any man could plough 'betwixt Lord and Lord and likewise betwixt freeholder and Lord' (1653). In addition every farmer had to leave 'a footbalk betwixt Lord and Lord either at summer stirring or at sowing of peas in all the fields' (1656). Sheep which died of the 'wood evil' and 'carrion or infectious cattle that die' were not to be thrown on the highway but buried (1655). Swine were to be ringed at the age of ten weeks before they were put in the fields after the harvest (1673). Most frequent of all were injunctions like those of 1656 and 1663: 'if any inhabitant neglect the common work he shall forfeit for every day 6d' and 'all those that shall neglect common work with their draughts 5s'. Such regulations would have applied on the St John's Radcliffe lands.

Sometimes specific charges of infringing the rules were made against Radcliffe tenants. The fines imposed on them may have reflected the seriousness of offence, but the circumstances of the accused may also have been taken into account. Oliver Henson broke the lord's pound in 1651 and was fined 1s; so was William Morley in 1655 for keeping sheep in the cornfield. Thomas Wilford 'for tethering his cows in the cornfield after Lamas' was fined 3s.4d in 1675 and 5s in 1685 for keeping his mare on the 'commons'. Joseph Taylor appeared in 1670 for putting horses upon the common 'having no right of common' (fine 3s.4d) and William Littleton for 'oppressing the common', that is putting more than his stint there in 1703 (fine 5s).

A Mrs Brightman allowed her swine to trespass in Great Johnson Close and had to pay 1s in 1671. In 1668 Thomas Wilson was fined 2s 'for breaking the custom of our town in mowing of grass after the corn was gotten' and a man of the same name in 1702 'for mowing meres in the stubble fields in Radcliffe' was fined 1s.

A good deal of time was taken up with ensuring that watercourses and highways were kept clear and footpaths and bridges maintained. In 1655 the court ordered 'that John Fisher shall take up the stoops and rails about a spring at his house door which is very annoying to the highway between this day and this day fortnight' or forfeit 10s. One order in 1668 was directed against Radcliffe men 'that ploughs down upon the King's highway on Breck Furlong' (fine unknown). In April 1657 it was ordered that

> *there be a footbridge laid down in Radcliffe syke [drain] at the charge of Radcliffe or Lamcote and Cotgrave before the first day of August, for neglect hereof they shall forfeit to the Lord of this manor 6s.8d.*

From then on there were frequent charges for neglecting it. In 1697 Radcliffe and Cotgrave forfeited 10s between them for not repairing it and the dike itself was often not sufficiently scoured as in 1695 when Thomas Parr and the rest of the inhabitants (of Radcliffe) were fined 15s. Other ditches and watercourses within the village caused trouble: in April 1671

> *the common issue betwixt Spello[w]-bottom and the Plate Close, that if it be not scoured betwixt this and Whitsuntide we present the town for their neglect 10s.*

In 1702 the reference is simply to 'the common issue', its exact place not specified, for neglect of which William Needham and Joseph Taylor were fined 2s.6d. Boundaries, whether between fields or parishes, were also of concern: John Brewster and John Whittle were fined 10s 'for breaking up a mere called Hungerhill mere leading from Hungerhill to Fowl sike'. A warning was issued on 22nd August 1715 to all persons

> *that doth not make their parts in the [-] field fence good betwixt now and the first day of May... this fence lying betwixt Radcliffe and Shelford and belongs, both hedge and ditch, to Radcliffe.*

Officers, such as the thirdboroughs, were appointed at the court and there are references to an overseer for common work, a pinder and a neatherd, though none from Radcliffe is recorded. It is possible that the separate manors within Radcliffe shared some of these officers. This is indicated in 1711 when the jury imposed a fine of 2s.6d on Robert Scrimshaw of Cotgrave 'Cryer of Holme Court for not giving time by notice to the Neighbours of Radcliffe for ye Su[i]tering ye same of Radcliffe', a reference to the tenants' obligation to make fealty to the court. The manor of Holme was also under the lordship of the Pierreponts.[271]

The manor of Holme Pierrepont

The Pierreponts at Holme had long owned small pockets of land in Radcliffe and Lamcote, but when towards the end of the 16th century they began purchasing lands from the Rosells, it seems likely they absorbed them into their manor of Holme Pierrepont. Records of this manor only survive from the Restoration period and regulations issued between 1662 and 1704 show the same concerns as the St John's court. Tenants were allotted a section of the dykes to keep clear, these dykes lying on the west side of the village where Radcliffe and Lamcote bordered on Holme Pierrepont. In 1662 John Hutchinson was to scour up a 'piece of great Mucklin Ditch betwixt this and Martlemas next' on pain of a fine of 5s. In 1696 the tenants were warned that 'if any person turn the waters down from the over end of Mucklin by the street [hooke] or Catternes ditch' they were to pay 10d. 'Ratcliffe men' as a whole had been fined 7s.6d in 1679 for doing this. Also important was the management of animals: Henry Parnham and William Dewsbury were fined 1s for allowing the pinfold to go out of repair in 1660. Not only was good farming practice at stake, but peace within the community also had to be maintained, hence the severity of the order: 'If any person put any loose cattle horses beast or sheep into Holme Lane (being a detriment to the neighbouring Closes) [he] shall forfeit twenty shill[ings]'. Robert Doubleday was fined 1s in 1695 for taking his sheep onto 'home pasture' and for not repairing his fences. A much more serious offence was cutting Widow Randay's willows for which he was fined 2s.6d.

The manorial system embraced a multitude of functions. It did not exist just to bolster the privileges of the lord, but its customs also safeguarded the rights of its tenants and offered protection to the weak. What must have been an appeal to the court for charity was settled in 1704 when it was recorded that:

> *We agree that Holme Lane shall be given to Widow Duke only to eat [graze livestock?] and we do present any other person twenty shillings that shall put any goods into the same, and we appoint and desire Mr Coall to see the charity performed.*[272]

II The Archdeacon's Court Before the Civil War

Details of individual court cases of the Stuart period appear in the appropriate church sections. In assessing their overall pattern, as wide a range of documents as possible has been examined, but not all were currently accessible. In the 39 years of the reigns of James I and Charles I up to the cessation of proceedings, offences were similar to those of Elizabeth's time, the predominant concern again being sexual morality. (Where couples were presented jointly - the majority of occasions - they have been counted as one case. More than one appearance was often required, contributing to the nuisance of having to walk or ride the six miles to Nottingham.)

Out of some 147 cases so far found, 59 (about 40%) deal directly with issues of sexual morality - a slight drop from Elizabethan times. (Figures for Retford in the 1630s show a substantial drop to 29% from the 58% of the 1590s.) They include one case of sexual impropriety with a sister-in-law and another with a daughter-in-law. Both vicar (1608) and squire (1638) are found among the transgressors. A further ten cases are also closely linked to sexual morality: two women were said by 'common fame' to be whores; a man and a woman were charged with being bawds in connection with another case; three men were charged with 'harbouring' women who were either suspected of fornication or who had had an illegitimate child; three cases concerned irregularity in marriages - a couple being married without banns or licence, the court requiring assurance of another couple's marriage, and a clandestine marriage linked to one of the incontinence cases. Of eight unspecified presentments it is probable that three are also connected with sexual morality. Only occasionally was the charge denied, and the usual forms of penance were regularly imposed (i.e. confession in normal apparel, perhaps at a weekday service, for couples who had married after the offence, and confession in front of the whole congregation dressed in white for those who did not or could not marry).

Local church officials were regularly summoned before the court. Apart from the incontinence case included above, one vicar was presented for not wearing a hood (1635) and failing to perform divine service (1638). This was during the period that Archbishop Laud was attempting to impose order and ceremony in church services. The same vicar also brought a case for defamation or abuse over a charge of drunkenness (1635). (There were six defamation cases altogether, including one brought by the squire (1605) and two concerning sexual irregularities not included above. Two charges involving a disputed will were also brought.) Churchwardens appeared in court on 11 occasions. The causes, not always specified, included failure to complete their accounts (three times); failure to provide a bible (1618); failure to provide a table of degrees of consanguinity and affinity (1638); allowing the churchyard fence to fall into disrepair. The parish clerk (also at times a church-warden) was charged with negligence in attending the minister (1633).

More often, officials were the ones who drew attention to deficiencies, sometimes the result of people not paying their dues. Three disputes over tithes have been found, two brought by Radcliffe vicars and one by the farmer of the rectorial tithes. In their turn the churchwardens charged the farmer of the rectorial tithes on two occasions with neglect of the chancel, for which he was responsible, and with failure to provide the preacher of a quarterly sermon. (Two Radcliffe farmers of Burton Joyce tithe lands were presented for neglect of that parish's chancel.) The churchwardens also presented two parishioners for not repairing their share of the churchyard fence, and two for not paying their 'cessment' or 'offerings'. A case of a disputed bill of reckoning might also have related to church rates. (Another Radcliffe resident was pursued by the Thoroton churchwardens for dues on crops grown on lands he had occupied there.)

When it comes to other aspects of discipline, the most striking increase in charges since Elizabeth's time concerned failure to attend church or receive communion at Easter, particularly in James I's reign. Nevertheless, incidences are difficult to quantify as several summonses could relate to one lapse, and by no means all cases related to Catholicism. Overall, 14 separate cases have been identified, with members of the Jordan family - already known Catholics before the end of Elizabeth's reign - being presented on five occasions between 1603 and 1612. Of the other names which occur, Wilson, Wright and Wood might also be associated with recusancy. The Capendales and Swinscoes led irregular lifestyles which may have accounted for absences from church. The religious beliefs of Richard Ashbie (1614), Richard Palmer gentleman (1620), Roger Lewes gentleman, 'a negligent comer to church' on Sundays and holy days (1635), and of Thomas Rippon and his wife (1639) are not known. (As already noted, the latter slept when she did come.) Only one open denial of religious belief has been found (1640).

Occasionally Sabbath breaking was prosecuted. Four cases between 1604 and 1614 involved working during the time of divine service or on holy days. Activities included loading corn, yoking draught (oxen or horses), and 'teeming' a load of hay. The fact that the climate and agricultural needs could not wait on religious priorities was not always recognised. A penance certificate has been found for one such case. As authority of all kinds was being challenged in the years prior to the Civil War, another type of Sabbath breaking was prosecuted. In 1639 seven Radcliffe cases of illegal drinking or entertaining in ale-houses on a Sunday came before the church courts. Again, a surviving certificate confirms that the penance was performed in at least one of these cases.

Disorder on church premises also increased in the 1630s. In James I's reign (1603-1625) three cases had been reported: one parishioner pulling another out of a seat in church, one laying hands on another's servant, and one misdemeanour in words within the church. Between 1634 and 1640, however, eight such presentments occurred: two for allowing swine to damage the churchyard, three for fighting or brawling in the church or churchyard, one (a woman) for breaking a man's head with a stone in the churchyard, one for disturbing the bells on Sundays and holy days, and one for ill language to the minister after divine service.

Altogether 19 penance certificates have been found, only two for non-sexual offences. (Two examples are given on p. 122.) It is clear that by no means all those brought before the courts completed their penances, but it has not proved possible to quantify with accuracy the proportion who did .

As in the case of the manorial courts, church authority broke down with the onset of the Civil War. The last pre-war Radcliffe case in the court books concerned Henry Wells who was charged with fornication. (See p. 137.) Presented in August 1641, he was ordered in October to purge himself before three neighbours but failed to do so. As the powerless court continued to meet he was regularly cited again until 11th April 1643. During this time no new cases were presented and sittings were then abandoned until after the Restoration.

The breakdown of this form of religious discipline is summed up at the start of the Archdeaconry Act Book 48. There it is made clear that for a while the churchwardens of St Peter's in Nottingham refused to allow the court to continue in their church. It had instead to go to St Nicholas's, but was back at St Peter's on 19th April 1642 until its abandonment a year later. A further note reads:

> *That during most part of the years 1641 & 1642 no Proceedings in the Eccl[esiastical] Court were of any avail; almost all offenders set the Eccl[esiastical] Authority at Defiance, as the grand Rebellion drew on; & all that the Eccl[esiastical] Judge c[oul]d do was to keep up a seeming Face or*

shew of a Court & continue all Causes in Statu quo as Die in Diem in hopes of better Times...

The writer would have been relieved when the Restoration took place.[273]

III The Archdeacon's Court in Later Stuart Times

It is often assumed that the power of the church courts was permanently destroyed by the Civil Wars. The evidence from Nottinghamshire shows that this was not the case. They reconvened early in 1662 and made every effort to regain their former authority. By the following year the number of cases being dealt with was exceptionally high, and at the court held at St Peter's in Nottingham on 15th September 1663 there were 75 presentments from the Bingham Deanery alone. These included nine from Cotgrave and four from Shelford. Radcliffe, however, seems to have had an above average standard of conformity and morality on this occasion since only one case came from the village - that of Joanne Batting 'for having a bastard child'.

The diligence of the village churchwardens reflected in their twice-yearly presentment bills accounted for many routine cases. There were long periods, however, when they had 'nothing to present'. For example, between October 1665 and April 1673, they presented only one case. Other local matters dealt with by the courts such as defamations (two cases) or disputed wills (two cases) were raised by the individuals concerned.

In all, some 51 cases have been identified. Twenty (about 40%) covered sexual impropriety - fornication, incontinence, or illegitimacy - the same proportion as in the early Stuart period, and most named both partners. Occasionally people occur in more than one case: Joanne Batting in the 1660s and Ann Weaver in the 1700s. In the more relaxed Restoration period penances for sexual aberrations were performed in normal apparel (five certificates have survived from between 1663 and 1699), but in the six certificates surviving from 1701 to 1711 the full penance of white sheet, wand, bare head, bare feet, and bare legs can again sometimes be found. (As late as 1763, the date of Radcliffe's last surviving penance certificate, Ann Day had to appear in full penitential garb.) Other cases which can be indirectly linked to sexual aberrations, include a failure to perform a penance, and a marriage without the banns being published.

This last charge was independent of the five cases relating to clandestine marriages, mainly conducted by the vicar Peter Titley in the 1670s. He was also accused of being drunk on the Lord's day. One other incumbent was instructed by the court 'to exhibit orders'.

As in earlier times, not only the vicar but also the churchwardens could occasionally find themselves before the courts. In the 1690s there were linked cases in which they presented Thomas Campion for withholding his dues, while he in turn charged them with negligence in keeping their accounts. In 1708 their failure to present whoever was responsible for not repairing the churchyard fence also led to an appearance in court.

Occasionally, the churchwardens presented the patrons of the living for their neglect. In the 1660s this was for not providing a minister for the parish. On two occasions, the impropriators of the lands that went with this duty and with responsibility for the chancel were simply named in court, presumably to establish with whom such responsibilities lay.

In addition to the Campion case referred to above, three cases concerned failure to pay dues: refusal to pay a mortuary, refusal to pay a levy of 8d, and refusal by a Holme Pierrepont man to pay a 'lay' or levy owed to Radcliffe. Two cases concerned failure to pay what was owed by the farmers of rectorial tithe lands. The more significant of these involved John Walker in an escalating dispute with the Archbishopric of York, the Archdeacon of Nottingham, and Thomas Rosell, Radcliffe's squire. (See pp. 167-8.)

Although the ecclesiastical authority's proceedings were dominated by cases of sexual transgression, in the 1660s and again in the 1680s there were a number of cases concerning failure to come to church or to receive communion at Easter. Eight individuals, but including two married couples, were presented for such lapses in the later Stuart period. (The first was Elizabeth Rosell, the squire's wife in the 1660s, who certified her attendance only on her sixth summons to court.) Purges of nonconformity in 1684, 1685 and 1686 led to long lists of people summoned. In the last of these years two Radcliffe women were among 120 before the court for not receiving Easter communion.[274]

IV Law Enforcement Before the Civil War

The parish constable

Although justice administered by the parish constable is not recorded at parish level until the 18th century, the minutes of the county magistrates give some insight into his role from the early Stuart period. In some areas the office rotated annually among the more prestigious villagers, but in Radcliffe the constable seems to have been chosen by lot. The office was unpaid, and not until 1662 was the holder entitled to claim expenses from ratepayers. He was expected to ensure the upkeep of the stocks, inspect ale-houses, deal with vagrants, apprentice pauper children, look after militia requirements, convene meetings and collect taxes locally. He was subject to official reprimand if he performed his duties inadequately, and abuse from his neighbours if he performed them well. Not surprisingly, those chosen did not always welcome the responsibility.

In 1614 George Bayliff (Bayley?), a husbandman who was constable for that year, found himself before the local magistrates for not punishing vagrants. (This would normally be by whipping.) Three years later Richard Long was fined 2s.6d for allowing a prisoner to escape. The constable in 1637 was on the receiving end of drunken abuse from Arthur Taylor alias Fisher of Newark. When he called on Taylor's Radcliffe kinsman, George, (probably an ale-house keeper) to assist, the latter refused. Eventually the constable got both men before the magistrates. Perhaps the job was becoming particularly difficult at a time when authority was being questioned prior to the Civil War. In May 1640 the chosen constable tried to avoid the duty altogether and as a result found himself summoned before the magistrates:

> *[John Gamble of Radcliffe-on-Trent] being chosen Constable there by lot this year who hath hired one John Long alias Thrave to execute the office of Constable in his room, whom the Court is informed is for divers reasons unfit to serve being quarrelsome.*

The court ordered that as John Gamble was able, fit, and lived in Radcliffe he should execute the office 'and not hire any other to do it for him'. (Gamble may not have been as fit as the magistrates thought for he died in October 1641.)[275]

One of the constable's many duties was to set a watch in the parish. Normally watching was only compulsory from Ascension Day to Michaelmas, but a watch could be set at other times and every able-bodied man was bound to take his turn, properly weaponed, or find a substitute. In 1631 Thomas Symon refused to watch and was fined 6d. Three years later there was wholesale failure of the system and three labourers - Robert Shipman, George Parr and John Henson - along with William Pilkington's servant were charged with neglect of the night watch.[276]

Justices of the Peace

It was to the magistrates that the constable took the village offenders. Justices of the Peace originate by tradition from 1362, but in Nottinghamshire their records only survive from the early 17th century. They were appointed by the crown from the landed gentlemen of each county, and until 1906 a substantial property qualification was required for holders of the office. By Tudor times this amounted to 'lands and tenements worth £20 a year'. The full bench of justices, sitting with a jury could theoretically hear all cases short of treason. In practice, however, the most serious cases, such as the Jordan murder case (pp. 106-7) went to the Assize judges. As time went on, the justices were also given increased administrative functions, such as setting the price for bread or grain, or licensing ale-houses.

The justices met four times a year in what became known as Quarter Sessions - an important opportunity for local gentry families to exchange views and news, as well as administer justice. The Pierreponts of Holme Pierrepont and the Stanhopes of Shelford were amongst the local families who generally had representatives on the bench in the early Stuart period. Sessions were routinely held in Nottingham, Newark and East Retford. Special sessions were occasionally held elsewhere, for example at Burton Joyce in 1611 because of plague in Nottingham. Radcliffe's business was normally dealt with at the Nottingham sessions which covered the wapentakes of Bingham, Broxtowe and Rushcliffe.

Surviving records of the proceedings are mainly in minute books, which begin on 9 January 1603/4. Like the manorial and church courts the Quarter Sessions were interrupted by the Civil War. On 7th October 1642 an entry reads:

> *Here the Wars between the King and Parliament began and interrupted all legal proceedings.*

Records resume on 4th October 1652 until 11th April 1659 when they suddenly break off, doubtless because of the uncertainty of the times after the resignation of Richard Cromwell in May 1659 and before the restoration of Charles II. From then on the records are imperfect. The earlier minute books appear to be a fair copy of the court's proceedings, rather than the clerk's rough notes made at the time of the hearings. Frustratingly, they do not always give details of offences or punishments.

Compared to some other places in the county, Radcliffe had few cases brought before the Quarter Sessions. The village may have been a particularly law-abiding place, but it is also likely that many petty offenders were dealt with by justices locally. An Order in Council in 1605 provided for the appointment of Divisional Justices to meet between Quarter Sessions to deal mainly with statutory offences. It is likely that a local magistrate, perhaps of the Pierrepont family, dispensed justice at unrecorded monthly sessions in the locality .

In the Quarter Sessions minutes, Radcliffe cases fall into three main categories: robberies and misdemeanours, miscellaneous breaches of community laws, and poor law enforcement. (The latter will be dealt with in a separate section, p. 187.)

Robberies

Robbery and larceny of goods over 12d in value were amongst the capital offences (homicide, arson, burglary and rape being others) for which the accused could be sent to the Assizes for trial after hearings at the Quarter Sessions. In four cases of serious theft involving Radcliffe people, villagers were more likely to be in court as witnesses or victims than as the accused. In 1618 two men from Orston and Thomas Cartwright, gentleman, of Radcliffe were bound in the sum of £20 each to give evidence at the next Assizes against Gervase Stannyland, who was in gaol accused of stealing part of a mill spindle, mill picks, a javelin and other goods belonging to Hugh Kerchiver, gentleman, and harrow teeth owned by Thomas Cartwright. In 1620 John Humfrey was bound in the considerable sum of £40 to give evidence against Henry Mawson, in gaol on suspicion of stealing a horse belonging to a person unknown. There were two cases in 1629. In the first, Radcliffe's squire, Gervase Rosell, was bound in the sum of £20 to appear against Mary Huttam and Jane Cassam, both of them in gaol charged with stealing wool from the bodies of his sheep. The second case involved Edward Alcock, a Newton labourer, and Roger Campion, a Radcliffe husbandman who was also the long-serving parish clerk. They were bound in the sum of £10 each against Joan Laughton, formerly of Shelford, who was in gaol accused of 'burglariously' breaking into the house of Alcock and stealing one candlestick. If found guilty at the Assizes, all the accused in these cases could be hanged.[277]

Petty larceny

In contrast, several Radcliffe residents were found guilty of petty larceny in the early part of the period. The punishment was a spell in the stocks, after which the offenders were stripped to the waist and whipped until the blood flowed. This was carried out by the parish constable on a Sunday after divine service when most of the community would be present. The justices ordered Richard Strickland, a labourer, and his wife, Jane, to be punished in this way in 1609. The length of time in the stocks could vary, even in the same case. In April 1614, Helen Beardsley was sentenced to an hour in the stocks for petty larceny, but Elizabeth Lamyng, an accessory after the fact, was given three hours, as was Robert Key. The women, both unmarried, and Key were then stripped and whipped. Two labourers, Humphrey and Thomas Willson, were given the same treatment in 1623, but this form of punishment was shortly afterwards replaced by a spell in the House of Correction at Southwell. In 1627 the magistrates ordered Thomas Ganne, who had been labouring in Radcliffe and confessed to larceny, to spend a month there before being sent back to Drayton in Shropshire which he said was his home village.[278]

Misdemeanours and breaches of community law

The justices also dealt with various misdemeanours. As has been seen, the vicar, George Cotes, and his family were not immune because they were fined 12d each for riot and affray in 1609. Nor was the squire, George Rosell, in the following year when he was bound in the sum of £10 for a breach of the peace. (See pp. 118 and 110.)

In 1620 William Willson, labourer, was fined 18d for contempt; William Hutchinson, yeoman, fined 10s for trespass in 1630; and Thomas Johnson, labourer, presented for wandering at night in 1636. The magistrates' summoning in 1609 of Edward Swinscoe, the butcher with an irregular lifestyle, followed the ecclesiastical court's probing into his activities, demonstrating the powers of overlapping authorities. (See pp. 117-18.)[279]

The orderly running of ale-houses was a constant concern of the justices. There are several instances of Radcliffe people brewing without licence, refusing to sell ale according to the assize (the price officially set), keeping a disorderly house, or allowing people to drink in an inn on the Sabbath - the latter also the concern of the church authorities. Francis Grococke, a husbandman who also brewed ale, was a persistent offender. In 1608 the magistrates discharged him from keeping an inn because he had been harbouring vagrants, vagabonds and suspicious persons. Later that year he was presented for brewing without licence after being discharged, and in 1612 for again brewing without licence. (He had also been presented for 'harbouring inmates' in 1609 - taking in lodgers who might become a burden on the parish.) Richard Gardam, another frequent offender, refused to sell ale according to assize in 1609. Two women victuallers, Juliana Linney and Elizabeth Taylor, who were before the bench in 1633 for disorder, were almost certainly running the 'tippling house' in which three labourers (Robert Hough, Robert and James Byrd) behaved in a disorderly manner. Juliana - probably the daughter of George who was similarly charged in 1605 - was referred to as 'alias Hutchinson', although it was not until the following year that she married John Hutchinson, labourer and ale-man. Presumably she was already living with him. True to form, they were jointly charged with 'disorder' in their house in 1641. Elizabeth Taylor, probably a widow, belonged to a family (alias Fisher) with a similar history of irregular behaviour.[280]

At times the justices used 'informers' who made presentations and laid information on various matters, particularly relating to trade. The noxious effect of flax-washing led to a ban on this activity anywhere that animals might drink. In 1621 50 named persons from 11 villages were each fined 6d for washing flax in the Trent. Four came from Radcliffe: three yeomen (John Humfrey, John Gamble and Henry Pare) and the smith (Robert Greene). Roger Campion, the parish clerk, was similarly charged in 1629. On this occasion Henry Parr was the informer.

Between 1625 and 1634 four lists occur of people presented for engrossing grain (buying the whole stock to sell at monopoly price). The clampdown was partly the result of the Books of Orders issued by Charles I's government, particularly after poor harvests in the 1630s, to encourage the effective enforcement of statutes. A number of Radcliffe yeomen were amongst those summonsed for trying to corner the market in this way: William Hutchinson, Henry Gamble (twice), John Gamble, John Longe, William Leeson, William Pilkington and John Thrave. John Greene, another yeoman, was charged with extortion.[281]

Other concerns of the justices included the maintenance of roads: Lady Frances Pierrepont was fined 12d in 1619 because Holme Lane (between Radcliffe and Holme Pierrepont) was in decay. On occasions, the powers of manorial court cases could be reinforced at the Quarter Sessions. For example, when John Long alias Thrave was fined 12d for an unspecified cause in July 1620, he paid the money to the lord of his court leet. Wages and employment were further matters which came under the justices' control. In 1634 yeoman William Pilkington (the engrosser above) was presented for not paying a herdsman his wages. John Long senior, a carpenter, and John Long junior, a weaver, were jointly charged in July 1640 with 'seducing' Robert Tong from the service of widow Anne Sutton. At the same sessions William Grococke was charged with refusing to carry saltpetre - extracted from nitrogenous waste in stables and used in the making of gunpowder. (The case coincided with troop movements during the time of the Bishops' Wars with Scotland, the prelude to Civil War in England.) Additionally, the justices could approve the collection of money throughout the county for specific uses. For example, in 1636 they collected £11 from the wapentakes of Bingham, Broxtowe and Rushcliffe for the repair of the 'decays and ruins' of St Paul's Cathedral in London, and the 'beautifying thereof', then being planned by Charles I and his architect Inigo Jones.[282]

V Poor Laws and Charity in Early Stuart Times

It is largely from the Quarter Sessions minute books that some information can be gleaned about the enforcement of the poor laws which took up a great part of magistrates' time. At parish level those who had fallen on hard times could theoretically be catered for out of rates collected by the churchwardens or overseers of the poor. (The Radcliffe accounts do not survive before the 19th century.) In practice, the burden on the ratepayers was often resented, and responsibility evaded. In the pre-Civil War period the government was increasingly concerned about the problem of the poor, and local magistrates were regularly urged to carry out their duties effectively. For example, in July 1636, a 'time of infection', magistrate Sir Thomas Hutchinson wrote to the Assize judges, assuring them that the Privy Council's instructions for dealing with the poor had been carried out in large parts of Nottinghamshire, including Bingham hundred, in which Radcliffe lay. He stressed that hardly any rogues were now to be seen wandering, apprentices had been placed, and disorderly ale-houses suppressed. Moreover, 'We are careful to see the poor relieved in their several parishes, shelter in their several parishes to be provided'. The government's encouragement of these measures may explain why the minuted information for this period is fuller than for any other. The issues raised in the letter are reflected in the Radcliffe cases brought before the magistrates.[283]

Settlement laws

The problem of the mobile poor was one such topic. As no parish wished to pay out more than was absolutely necessary in poor rates, laws about settlement were strictly enforced. Only those resident for more than two years could expect help, and anyone else who was likely to become a liability would be moved on. Vagrants were punished, usually by whipping, before removal to their place of birth. As has been seen, failure to punish vagrants led to Radcliffe's constable being brought before the magistrates in October 1615. Similarly, those 'harbouring' non-resident 'inmates', who might become a charge on the parish, were also likely to find themselves before the magistrates (as Francis Grococke and Richard Gardam discovered in October 1609, and John Long alias Thrave in October 1620).[284]

When parishes were in dispute over who was responsible for an individual, the issue was settled by the magistrates. In January 1624 the village of Broughton Sulney forced Judith Howett, a spinster living with her uncle, to come to Radcliffe because of her poverty, 'pretending it is her birthplace'. The magistrates thought otherwise, sent her back, and ordered Broughton Sulney to find work for her or provide her with relief. Radcliffe lost a similar case in April 1640 by breaching the two-year residence rule. The parish tried to be rid of labourer Thomas Wyat, his wife and son by sending them to Bramcote. Bramcote, however, refused to accept them on the grounds that Wyat had lived in Radcliffe for two years and three months. The family had 'intruded' into the house of Thomas Brooke without the approval of either the community or Brooke, 'and thus might become a charge on Bramcote'. The justices consequently ordered the Wyat family to be returned to Radcliffe and put to work.[285]

Housing the poor

Usually, cases were far more complicated than these, and involved other issues, such as the provision of housing. There is no evidence from this period that Radcliffe provided houses for the permanent use of generations of poor, and any obligations of parish or landowner to provide accommodation did not go beyond the needs of any individual family. Some five disputed cases ended up before the magistrates, and the details provide fleeting insights into the lives of those struggling against adverse circumstances.

In July 1610, the magistrates gave permission for Henry Watson 'being poor and incapable' to build a new cottage at Radcliffe for himself and his wife on land belonging to Sir Henry Pierrepont. (He was on the bench at the time.) The cottage was to serve as a dwelling only while Henry and his wife occupied it. Presumably it could then be demolished, and Sir Henry would be under no further obligation.

The churchwardens and overseers were ordered in January 1628 to 'find a convenient habitation' for Gervase Steele 'so that he may not become a vagrant'. He had lived in Radcliffe for seven years, having formerly served in the house of Francis Hacker (the East Bridgford squire who had administered the Radcliffe estates of his under-age stepson and son-in-law, Gervase Rosell). Despite the order, and Gervase Steele's service to a prestigious family, the Radcliffe officials were dilatory in finding him accommodation, and in the following April the magistrates issued a warrant against the overseers (husbandman Martin Grococke, and yeoman John Davell), and against the churchwardens (Roger Campion and Thomas Pare). As the matter does not appear in the magistrates' records again, it seems that the warrant speeded officialdom into action.

Less than three years later the justices found that the parish officers had been unreasonable in their treatment of John Sheppard, Radcliffe's miller, his wife, and Elizabeth Carrington, his elderly, blind mother-in-law. In July 1628 the parish had allowed the miller a piece of land on which to build a house for himself, his wife and Elizabeth Carrington, 'on condition that he kept and maintained' the latter 'who otherwise would have to be maintained by the parish'. John Sheppard had then built his cottage for £3, and kept his mother-in-law at his own expense as agreed. The parish officials subsequently broke their side of the bargain and 'discharged' the miller from the cottage. The injustice was more than set right by the court. Not only did John Sheppard get back the £3 he had spent on erecting the cottage, but also reasonable expenses for having maintained his mother-in-law. The Radcliffe officials were either to allow him to live quietly in the house he had built, or provide suitable maintenance for Elizabeth Carrington. Their attempt to take advantage of the miller's efforts must ultimately have cost those paying poor rates far more than if they had kept to the original bargain.

A case before the magistrates in January 1640 involved both settlement and housing issues at a time when poverty was increasing. Robert Close occupied a new cottage built on the 'waste'. About six weeks previously Robert's daughter, Mary, had married Thomas Wade, a labourer from Chilwell. Instead of taking his new wife to Chilwell, Thomas had moved into his father-in-law's home. Radcliffe residents complained at this, since in time they feared his 'becoming a likely charge on the parish, being already burdened with a great number of poor people'. The magistrates decided that Thomas and his wife should be sent to Chilwell and put to work, unless the Earl of Chesterfield, the lord of the waste on which the cottage stood, should decide otherwise. No record of his decision has been found.

The last housing case before the Civil War was the most complicated. Between July 1641 and April 1642, decisions had to be taken about how Richard Asby, his wife and family should be housed. The underlying problem regularly surfaced, and was caused by Lamcote's obligations being divided between Radcliffe (geographical) and Holme Pierrepont (ecclesiastical). The minutes explain the confused situation:

> *... it appeared to the court that one Richard Asby, being a poor man, dwelt in a house in Lamcote in the parish of Holme Pierrepont, but within the constabulary of Radcliffe-on-Trent, and was tenant to Gervase Rosell of Radcliffe, gent., and that to Holme all assessments and payments for the poor from those grounds where he dwelt were usually paid, though Lamcote be reputed to be parcel of Radcliffe...*

All would have been well had not Gervase Rosell turned Richard Asby out of his house, and the latter been too poor to provide himself with another. Clearly he was a candidate for relief out of the poor rates, but whose - Radcliffe's or Holme Pierrepont's? The magistrates 'were divided in opinion whether Holme or Radcliffe ought by law to provide for him now in distress'. Whatever they decided was likely to cause local offence, so they evaded their responsibilities and left the matter to be sorted out by the visiting judges at the next Assizes. Both sides, representing Radcliffe and Holme Pierrepont, were to put their case, and neither place was to be prejudiced by where Asby settled in the meantime.

Some three months later the magistrates received the Assize judges' decision and issued their orders accordingly:

> *At this Sessions it is ordered that the churchwardens [and] overseers of the poor of Holme Pierrepont shall immediately take order for the building of a house for the habitation of Richard Asby, with his wife and family, upon the waste of Lamcote in the parish of Holme, by and with the licence and consent of Gervase Rosell, gent., lord of the waste there, which this court expects he will willingly and readily do, for that the said Asby hath long dwelt there and is now both poor and aged and without habitation, and not in any way able to provide himself an habitation, which house so to be erected shall and may continue for the only habitation of the said Asby during their lives and no longer...*

Holme Pierrepont, the ecclesiastical parish, had thus to honour its obligations, because church officials collected the poor rates. The fact that Lamcote was part of Radcliffe village had no effect. While Richard Asby waited for his house to be built, the Holme overseers of the poor were to provide him with some 'convenient habitation' and see that he and his family 'starve not for want thereof in the meantime'. As in the case of Henry Watson in 1610, however, the house was to be pulled down after the death of Asby and his wife 'unless the lord of the waste do buy it'. Such caution against the continuation of ephemeral housing was partly through fear of breaching an Elizabethan statute c. 1589 against the erecting and continuing of cottages.[286]

Pauper children

When there was the prospect of a child becoming dependent on the parish, particularly in the case of illegitimacy, the officials were anxious to exact payments. While the Archdeacon's Court might condemn the parents on the grounds of immorality, the civil magistrates were needed to take action for a child's maintenance, especially if the alleged father appeared to be evading his responsibility. From 1575-6, however, the mother, too, was expected to make a financial contribution to her child's upbringing or risk punishment. A small number of cases involving Radcliffe people between 1610 and 1642 show how the system worked.

A man named as the father of an illegitimate child, such as husbandman Richard Gardam in 1611 (already before the magistrates in 1609) could be given 'time to clear himself' if he denied the charge. In Richard Gardam's case, if he could not convince the authorities, he would have to bring up Frances Clark's child 'at his own expense', and indemnify Car Colston - her parish. Similarly, in 1619 labourer George Allen was ordered to bring up his child by Anne Jenkinson at his own expense and indemnify Radcliffe of any expenses. The disappearance of a father caused the parish further problems. When Nicholas Innocent fled, leaving Joan Ward pregnant and unprovided for, but leaving behind 'certain goods' at Radcliffe, the justices decided in January 1619 that she should take possession of the goods for part of her maintenance, and the churchwardens and overseers were to provide her with a suitable dwelling 'so that she does not become a vagrant'.

There could be some flexibility in arrangements, depending on circumstances. Ellis Ward, a Radcliffe labourer, was ordered in 1635 to pay £3.6s.8d to the parish officials of Burton Joyce towards the keeping of Frances Tompson's bastard child. (The sum was covenanted by James Holmes, a Lowdham husbandman.) In addition, Ellis Ward had to pay 10s a year in two instalments from the birth of the child until it was old enough to be apprenticed. The mother had to pay 6s.8d a year in two equal portions. If she failed to do so she was to be sent to the House of Correction.

A mother who was given no choice was Dorothy Pight of Adbolton. As already noted, she had a child by Henry Wells of Radcliffe. As soon as she 'recovered her strength, now in childbed', the justices ordered in October 1641 that she was to be sent to the House of Correction to be set to work, receive punishment, and stay there as long as the law appointed. Henry was ordered to pay 8d a week, in monthly instalments, towards the upkeep of the child until it reached the age of seven. Husbandman John Gamble and carpenter John Wells stood surety for him to the tune of £10 each, and Henry Wells himself was bound for £20 until the next sessions. The magistrates' heavy cautionary sums were perhaps influenced by Henry Wells' current defiance of the Archdeacon's Court over the same matter. By the following January the surety sums had been reduced by half, with labourer Christopher White replacing John Gamble, who had died about a fortnight after the original hearing. The latter's death contributed to Henry Wells' problems, however, for Gamble had been his employer and he was still owed back wages, without which he could not pay his 8d a week. The magistrates consequently ordered the executors of John Gamble's estate to pay the arrears, so that Wells could immediately pay the Adbolton officials. If the executors did not produce the back wages, then the sureties undertaken by Gamble and John Wells would be seized. Whether Adbolton was able to extract its 8d a week for seven years is not known. As Henry Wells defied the church court until the system collapsed with the outbreak of Civil War, it is possible that civil payments were difficult to extract too once the war came. No further records exist for over a dozen years.[287]

Private benefaction and charity

While the state system now provided the main safety net for those in difficult circumstances, private donations for the welfare of the community and the poor did not completely stop in the early Stuart period, although they were much reduced. In 1613 husbandman Harold Greene left 3s.4d 'to the making of a shade in Hesgangs', (the pasture on the north bank of the river where perhaps some protection was needed for livestock or men working there.) This is the last gift of this kind so far found for the rest of the period studied - a surprising decline after the modest but steady record of such gifts in the Tudor period. There were, however, occasional donations to those who appealed for help away from the locality. Money collected for these 'briefs' was normally recorded in churchwardens' accounts. These do not exist at this period for Radcliffe, but references in the archdeaconry and magistrates' records indicate that the village did contribute to this form of charity. In either 1612 or 1613 the village donated 20d and 2s.4d in two separate collections to assist St Albans. The reason is not given. Nearby Cotgrave contributed 2s.6d on both occasions. In March 1613 12d was collected to help Prague in Bohemia, then suffering as a result of a religious power struggle. (Cotgrave and Bingham gave 4d and 6s.8d respectively.)[288]

As well as a decline in gifts to the local community, a reduction in individual bequests to the poor is found in the early 17th century. Out of 21 surviving wills, only five testators left anything to the poor. Of these, two bequests were of 5s, and one was of 20s. In addition, Mary Rosell, the widow of squire John Rosell junior, left 20s in 1617 to be given to the poor in bread. The most substantial bequest, however, was £10 from Jeffrey Limner (Limmer or Lymber) in the same year, the proceeds from which still benefit the village in the 20th century. (See pp. 114-5.)

VI The Poor and Law Enforcement in the Mid-17th Century

Because of the disturbed times during the period of the Civil War and Interregnum, legal processes were interrupted, and records were badly kept or not preserved. Consequently, evidence concerning crime, civil disputes or poverty is slight, but by the 1650s it is clear that there was a tightening of control. A levy was raised on the county in April 1655 from which £50 was to go towards the completion of a new House of Correction at Southwell. Bolts, locks and shackles were to be provided 'necessary for the punishing of offenders'. (A new wing was added in

1707/8.) There was again government anxiety around this time about the increase in the number of vagrants. Major General Whalley, in charge of five Midland counties including Nottinghamshire from 1655, expressed concern in January 1656 about delays to plans for 'depressing of rogues' and 'providing for the poor'. Soon the prisons were so full of rogues, that he recommended sending them beyond the seas, and on 21st April 1656 he boasted to John Thurloe, the Secretary of State:

> *This I may truly say, you may ride over all Nottinghamshire, and not see a beggar or a wandering rogue; and I hope suddenly to have it so in all the counties under my charge, if it be not already...* 289

Although the wandering poor may have been eradicated from the county, parishes still had to cope with their own, and any collecting of poor rates often had to be supplemented by private charity. Of the five surviving Radcliffe wills for this period, two testators left money to the poor: widow Margaret Franke left 40s in 1653 to be added 'to the stock of the poor' and distributed by the minister (William Creswell) and churchwardens; and Robert Butler left 20s to be similarly dealt with in the following year. From the tallies of money in the parish register it is clear that both amounts were added to Jeffrey Limner's bequest of 1617, and lent out at interest. These register lists show that other parishioners, whose wills have not survived, also remembered the poor in their wills, but there is no accurate chronology in the order of the names, so it is not easy to know when the gifts were made. Nevertheless, from burials in the parish register between August 1641 and November 1651, William Grococke, Thomas Pare (Bare?), Henry Stoakes, William Hutchinson and John Campion can be identified as leaving money which was similarly lent out. (All contributed £1, except Thomas Pare who left 4s, and all were described as husbandmen with the exception of William Hutchinson, who as a yeoman had greater status.) This anecdotal evidence shows that private benevolence did not decrease during these troubled times.

Apart from a charge of brewing without licence against Edward Swinscoe in 1652, and a fine of 12d on George Derry in April 1653 for ringing bells on the Sabbath day - a sign of the puritanical times - only one example of official action has survived concerning the village from the Quarter Sessions records. In July 1655 John Hutchinson complained that the churchwardens and overseers had recently placed with him a poor boy, another Edward Swinscoe, as his apprentice in husbandry until the age of 21. The officials, however, had refused to provide the lad with 'convenient apparel'. Hutchinson had consequently had to pay out more than 28s to clothe the boy. The court agreed that it was unreasonable to expect him to bear such costs, and the officers were ordered to repay the money. The old system was clearly still in place, even if largely unrecorded, and the reluctance to spend poor rate money was not necessarily a reflection of hard times.290

VII Poverty and the Law in the Later Stuart Period

Although there was an apparent return to normality at the Restoration, the information in Nottinghamshire's Quarter Sessions' minutes is limited, so that evidence of how law was enforced, including the poor law, is slight and anecdotal. Private benevolence, however, continued to supplement the official system.

Bequests to the poor

Evidence from surviving wills shows that bequests to the poor were more common between the Restoration and 1688 (the time of the Glorious Revolution) than it had been in the late 16th and early 17th centuries when the impact of the Poor Laws was first felt. Nine out of 18 testators left money to the poor. Six were yeomen or farmers, all but one leaving 20 shillings, and the other 10 shillings. There was another 10 shillings from shepherd John Yardley in 1664. In addition, in 1685 squire Thomas Rosell left 40 shillings to be paid to the poor within six months of his death. From the parish register accounts, it is clear that this was immediately borrowed by his unreliable son, Gervase, along with much of the other money bequeathed to the poor. Whcn Gervase unexpectedly died in 1687, an afterthought to his will allocated another 40 shillings to the poor, but there is no specific mention of this sum in the ill-kept accounts in the parish register.

In the last third of the 17th century a prolonged period of low food prices adversely affected the farmer, while the burden of poor rates generally increased threefold. This may have led to a drop in bequests to the poor in the reigns of William and Mary, and Anne. Only three such gifts are found in the 14 surviving wills. These occurred in 1693, 1697 and 1699, years of particular distress for the poor caused by bad harvests and high food prices.[291]

From names in the parish register 'accounts', however, it is clear that there were some additional gifts to the poor in wills which have not survived. In 1714 all the bequeathed money, from Jeffrey Limner's time onwards, amounted to £33. It continued to be lent out at interest until it was invested in land some four years later.

Settlement and illegitimacy cases

The Quarter Sessions records have not survived from 1661 until April 1674, after which year it is recorded that the Nottingham magistrates met at the Shire Hall, alias King's Hall. The minutes subsequently confirm that the problem of settlement continued after the Restoration period. In fact, the system by which the parish of birth, or of residency for at least two years, was the area responsible for maintaining a pauper, was tightened in 1662. Any strangers could be removed by the justices except those who could pay £10 in rent for a dwelling, or provide security in case they proved financial liabilities to the new parish. When only a temporary stay was expected, as at the time of harvest, a certificate had to be brought from the parish of origin, indicating agreement to take back the newcomer if necessary. In practice, such settlement certificates were issued to many who did remain.

Three Radcliffe cases came before the magistrates in the reigns of James II and William III. In October 1687 the removal was ordered of Thomas Blatherwick, a bodice-maker, from Radcliffe to West Bridgford, the last place of his legal settlement. It seems that he did not go, for Radcliffe is still given as his parish in the following July when he was sent for trial at the Assizes. The charge was serious. Not only was he the father of Mary Hancock's stillborn child (she too was by then in gaol), but he had been present at the birth and had allegedly advised her to conceal the baby. The Assize judgment is not known.

In the 1690s Radcliffe appealed to the magistrates in two settlement cases. The first was in 1696 against the settlement of Richard Strawthorne and his wife in the village, although their parish of origin is not given. The second was in the following year against the parish of Flintham from where the magistrates had ordered Richard Scotter to be removed to Radcliffe. When Flintham officials failed to put in an appearance at the appeal, the magistrates reversed their original decision, and returned Scotter to be provided for by the Flintham overseers of the poor.[292]

The only record of those who came to Radcliffe with undisputed settlement certificates is found in the parish register in a list drawn up between 1703 and 1717. (See p. 193.) Twelve names appear on it, and at least two - George Sparrow and George Duke - became permanent residents, flourishing as headstone carver and wheelwright respectively.[293]

The other major concern of officials in this period - the cost to the parish of bringing up children without paternal support - is found in three cases, two of them related. In 1689 William Mantle, a Radcliffe labourer, was ordered to pay 12s to the overseers of the poor of Bassingfield and Holme for the maintenance of Mary Leeson during the month of her lying-in - a payment not found in the pre-Civil War period. He also had to pay 12d a week until her baby reached the age of seven (8d a week was typical in the 1640s), and then 20s towards putting the child forth as an apprentice. William must have disputed being the child's father, for the record states 'he should give good security to perform this order unless it appear that Richard Leeson [Mary's] ... husband was living at the time of the getting of the child'. The records do not show whether this fact was established, but the justices' views are clear since Mary was sent to the Southwell House of Correction for a year.

Ann Weaver was at the heart of two other cases. In April 1701 she had been ordered to perform a penance by the Archdeacon's Court for fornication with John Henson alias Hall. The civil authorities had then stepped in and the magistrates had ordered Henson to pay to the Radcliffe overseers 10s to cover the cost of Ann's

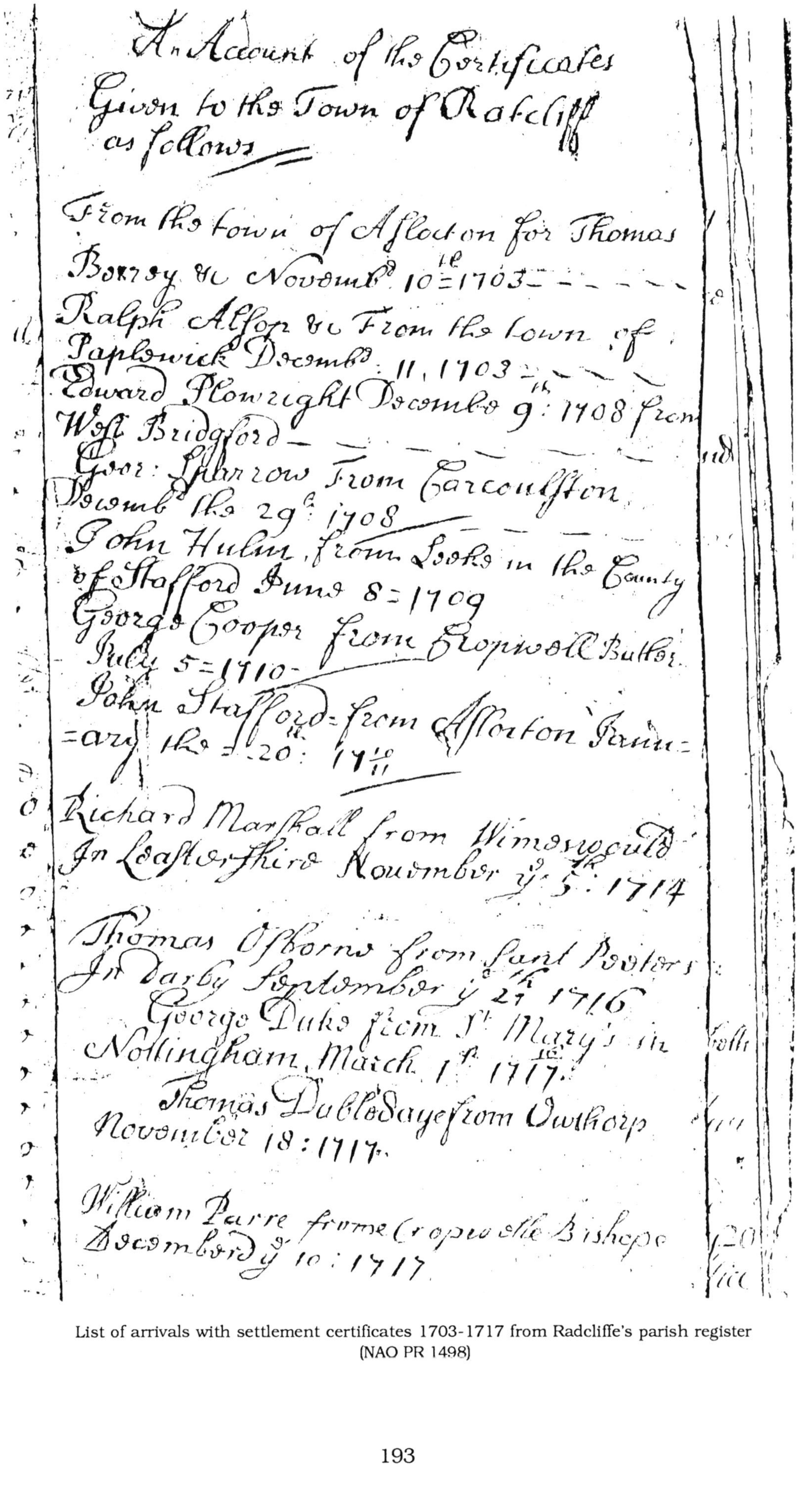
An Account of the Certificates Given to the Town of Ratcliff as follows

From the town of Aslocton for Thomas Berrey &c November 10th 1703

Ralph Alsop &c From the town of Paplewick December 11, 1703

Edward Plowright December 9th 1708 from West Bridgford

Geor: Sparrow From Carcoulston Decemb the 29th 1708

John Hulm, from Looke in the County of Stafford June 8 = 1709

George Cooper from Cropwell Butler July 5 = 1710

John Stafford = from Aslocton January the 20th: 17 10/11

Richard Marshall from Wimesyould In Leasterrshire November ye 5th 1714

Thomas Osborne from Saint Peeters In darby September ye 21th 1716

George Duke from St Mary's in Nottingham, March 1st 1717

Thomas Dubbledaye from Owthorp November 18: 1717.

William Parre frome Cropwelle Bishope December ye 10: 1717

List of arrivals with settlement certificates 1703-1717 from Radcliffe's parish register (NAO PR 1498) lying-in, and to pay one shilling weekly towards the maintenance of her baby daughter until the child should be seven years old. Another £3 would then be due for the child's apprenticeship. (Sureties of £20 were required from Henson, and £10 each from Richard Wilson and widow Hester Needham.) Before the time the child reached apprenticeship age John Henson had acquired a wife (with whom he was presented before the church court in May 1705, presumably for sexual impropriety before marriage) and he reneged on his responsibilities. In April 1707 the justices ordered the Radcliffe overseers to sell any of his goods and chattels in their possession towards the maintenance of the child.

In the meantime, Ann Weaver had pursued a colourful career. The Archdeacon's Court found her guilty of fornication with Robert Walker in 1705 and with farmer John Markham in 1710. At one point the church court scribe noted 'gone away' by his name, which may account for the civil magistrates intervening in April 1711 and ordering him to appear at the next sessions, with the considerable recognizances of £40, as the father of Anne Weaver's latest child.[294]

Miscellaneous disputes

However imperfect the records, it is clear that the administration of the poor law took up much of the justices' time, their work often still running parallel with that of the Archdeacon's Court. By comparison, other matters seem subsidiary. In April 1678 Thomas Wilford and Peter Beeston were indicted for 'surcharging the common', and indictments for non-attendance at church were frequent concerns of magistrates in the 1680s as well as churchwardens. Radcliffe inhabitants were charged with not repairing 'Icom ditch' in October 1687. The magistrates sorted out a wages dispute on 16th April 1694. Having heard the evidence from John Henson senior against his grandson, another John, they gave judgement for the latter and his wife. John senior had to pay them £4 for wages by 30th April. In July 1700, Radcliffe was presented for having put up an 'unlawful fence' between the village and Shelford. (Five years later the Court of St John ordered its tenants to mend a fence between the two villages (p. 180). It seems there was conflict between the two authorities.) The final case in the Quarter Sessions records returns to a familiar theme with the constable, Thomas Knight, in court in January 1712 for neglecting his duty.[295]

Case study 16

THE PILKINGTONS AND THEIR SONS

There are occasional references to the Pilkington family in Elizabethan records and one William Pilkington rented a farm for 52s a year in 1601, part of the lands bought from the Rosells by the Pierreponts. It was during the early Stuart period that the family came to prominence in the village as yeomen farmers and a William of that time was prosperous enough to be a subsidy payer in 1643.

William senior and junior

This William, who signed the Protestation in 1642, was known as 'senior', the tradition of calling the eldest son William being well established. He was a churchwarden on at least four occasions during the 1620s and 1630s. He and his wife Elizabeth had three or four daughters, the first being born in 1625, and at least three sons - William (born in 1633), Joseph and George. In 1661 William entered into a bond for the marriage licence of his son William the younger to Elizabeth Towne of Braceby, County Lincoln, spinster, daughter of a gentleman. This was a good match and the link with the minor gentry must have been the reason why from time to time contemporaries added the prefix 'Mr' to William junior's name and to that of his son, yet another William. The family, however, persisted in calling themselves yeomen.

By 1664 when the Hearth Tax was levied, William senior's three sons were about 31, 24 and 19 years old respectively. He and his married son may have had separate establishments or they may have divided the family home, for he paid tax on two hearths whilst William junior paid on four.

William senior died in 1670 and on the next Hearth Tax return of 1674 Mrs Pilkington, now described as widow, had four hearths and Mr William junior six. Whether this involved new building or enlarging of existing buildings is a matter of conjecture, but it is certain that the Pilkingtons were prosperous. They did not escape tragedy, however, for on 29th January 1679 William buried his youngest son Thomas (baptised a year before) and on the same day he drew up his will; eight days later when he was only about 46 he too was buried. His will referred to eight children, including five sons, the eldest William being 16 years old. He left £500 between his seven younger children, asking their appointed guardians, his brothers-in-law, to sell the farm known as Capendale's (which lay in Stanhope's manor) to raise the money. William also left 20s to his married sister (Trowman) and 20s to the poor of the parish, but he made no specific bequests to his wife and son William, who by the law of primogeniture would have succeeded to his lands. His will was witnessed by William and by squire Thomas Rosell, and was signed by all three of them.

Bachelor William and soldier John

Elizabeth was now left to raise the family on her own and it was probably not an easy task. Her mother-in-law had died in 1677 and her two brothers-in-law lived elsewhere - one in Nottingham and the other in Braceby, Lincolnshire. The three daughters were in due course married and so was one of the sons, John. This son John and his wife presented her in 1698 with a grandson William to carry on the family name. John may have seemed a steady

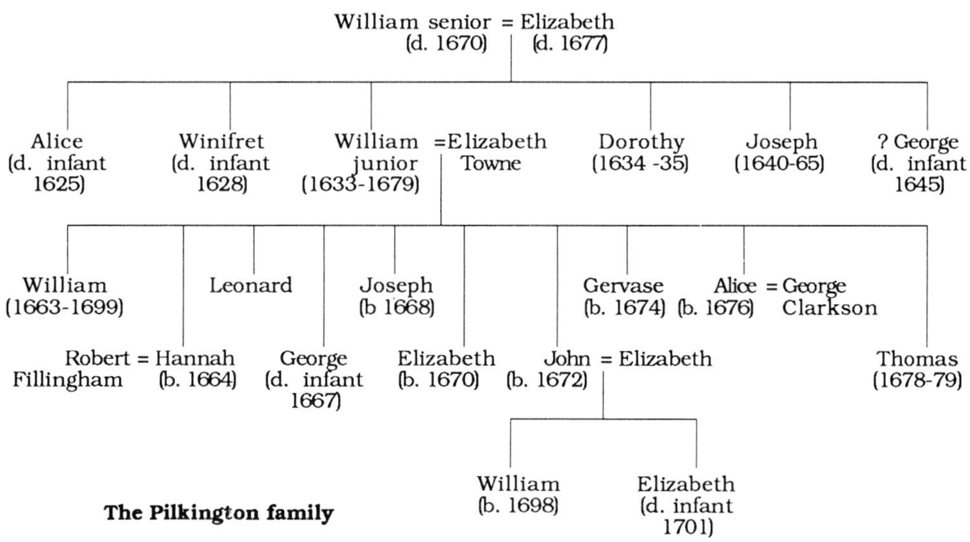

The Pilkington family

individual at this stage, but was to prove anything but in the long run.

William, the eldest, appears to have remained a bachelor. Despite the position of his family in the village, there is no record of him holding any parish office, though he was chosen to be a juror at Quarter Sessions on four occasions. When he died in 1699 he left all his properties in Radcliffe and elsewhere with their rents and profits to his 'dear and loving' mother. Thereafter, the remainder of the estate was to pass first to his brother John and his heirs, and if he had no surviving issue, to his brother Gervase and his heirs. His cash bequests totalled £110 and included gifts to his sisters and their children, his trustees being instructed to sell or mortgage part of his land to pay these legacies after the death of his mother. He was about 36 when he died and though his signature on his father's will had been confident, 20 years later he could only make an initial on his own.

William's inventory is one of the shortest from Radcliffe, but also one of the most interesting because the goods appraised hint at the sort of man he was. Their total value was only £19.3s.6d, his purse and apparel accounting for £5.10s and he had debts of £8 owing to him. His only furniture was a table, two presses and a trunk. The one heifer and four sheep in the inventory do not suggest a busy life as a farmer and it is possible that his health was not good enough to allow him to practise as one. Living off the rents from his properties, he must have passed his time pleasurably enough with a little hunting and fishing - for included in the inventory was a gun worth 6s and his fishing tackle and nets worth 10s. There was also a jack valued at 10s - this could have been a mechanical device or a protective coat, but in William's case was more likely to have been a leather bottle. There were no other goods in the inventory (not even a horse) befitting the tastes of a gentleman, though the appraisers called him one. Clearly, he preferred the simple life. He may have lived in lodgings, but if he lived in his mother's house, she must have claimed all the household goods and the farm stock (if there was any) as her own.

Although William's mother survived him, she did not live long enough to witness the deterioration in the family's fortunes. In his will, William had exhorted his trustees (his uncle John Towne and Robert Cole) to make the conveyances of his property in such a way that they 'shall not or may not be sold by my said brother John nor the remainders or Reversions thereof defeated or destroyed'. A note appended to the will in an 18th century hand, however, states that after the mother's death, his brother John

> *entered on the Estate and being a wild silly fellow went for a soldier and whether he had any ancient Deeds relating to the title is not known, but there are none now to be found save this will, but the Estate has been in the name for many Generations.*

A series of mortgages was then listed. The first in 1701 was made by John and the trustees to Elizabeth Smith, widow of Nottingham (probably William's sister), for £89.10s. In 1709 younger brother Gervase '(the said John Pilkington being then gone for a soldier)' and the sister with her new husband John Thompson of Lincoln mortgaged the premises to John Markham for £100; then to John Nevill of Nottingham in 1711 for £137.16s and to Joseph Booth of Brewhouse Yard in 1715 for £136.10s.10d. In 1721 the son of brother John (another John) had acquired the estate and mortgaged it to Anthony Clarkson of East Bridgford (perhaps a relative through the marriage of another of William's sisters) for £400, with another £100 raised two years later. Whatever ambitions the earlier William Pilkingtons may have had for founding a landed family were not achieved in the village. Their legacies had been wasted in debts.[296]

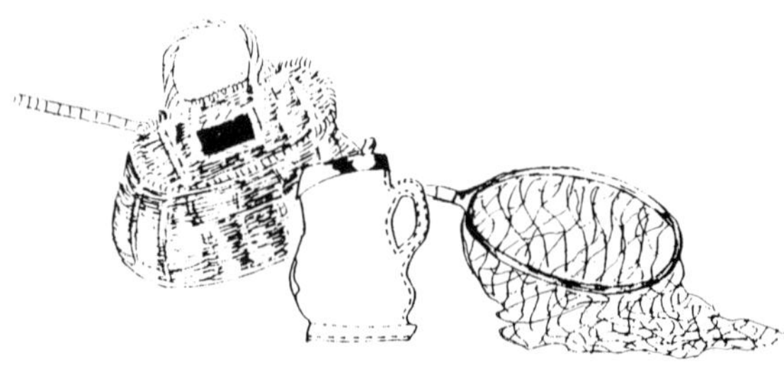

Fishing tackle and (black) jack - mentioned in William Pilkington's inventory. (Based on a contemporary illustration)

THE STUART VILLAGE - a social survey

I Population

Between 1530 and 1600 England's population probably grew from something like three millions to over four millions and by 1700 to over five and half millions. The greatest increases occurred down to the 1630s after which there were only slight rises before the 1740s. The pattern of growth in the East Midlands was in line with the national trends, although the evidence for Nottinghamshire in particular is less certain. Growth seems to have been steady until the 1670s when it was checked and did not fully recover until well into the 18th century. A rough estimate provides figures for the county of 56,250 in 1545, 71- 89,000 in 1670 and 85,145 in 1701.

Two ecclesiastical 'census' documents in 1603 and 1676 record the number of communicants and non-communicants in much of Nottinghamshire, and these have been used for estimating population. Comparison between the two dates is possible in 138 parishes, only 38, including Nottingham and some of the market towns, showing an increase. Radcliffe's return for 1603 has not survived, but in 1614 the churchwardens recorded 240 comunicants, one non-communicant and no recusants. In 1676 only 183 communicants and no dissenters were reported. From these figures a rough estimate of the village population can be made by using Dr Wood's formula of adding 60% to the total to allow for those too young to be communicants. Some authorities consider this figure too high, however, and add only 40% to produce a more accurate total.

The only other 'census' documents for Radcliffe in the Tudor and Stuart periods are the Protestation Return of 1642 and the Hearth Tax of 1674 (the tax return of 1664 being considered too deficient to be usable). The Protestation was signed by all males over 18 and the usual method of arriving at a population estimate is by doubling the number to allow for women and adding 40% of the total to allow for children. The Hearth Tax was based on households (not houses) and probable under-recording makes population assumptions uncertain. Household size is assumed to have been low - 4.25 persons per household is suggested - but there were bound to be local variations and an alternative estimate would be 4.5 persons per household.

Apart from the 1614 return, the figures shown below for Radcliffe and nearby villages are derived from published data using the methods described above. (Holme Pierrepont has been omitted as it is sometimes joined with Adbolton.) They do not take into account local conditions which might affect the total and the results can only be regarded as rough estimates. Figures are to the nearest whole number.

	1614 Communicants		1642 Protestation	1674 Hearth Tax		1676 Religious Census	
	+ 40%	+ 60%	Return	x 4.25	x 4.5	+ 40%	+ 60%
Radcliffe	337	386	274	319	338	256	293
Bingham			484	497	527	470	538
Cotgrave			468	463	491	452	517
Shelford			266	153	162	259	296

A further source for estimating the village population is the parish register, particularly the marriage entries. Radcliffe's original registers have survived from 1633, and some contemporary copies (transcripts sent to the bishop) from 1625. (A summary of trends is presented in the graphs on p. 198.) Apart from problems of legibility, there is no certainty that the records were accurately kept and discrepancies have been found between the bishop's transcripts and the local registers. There are several periods when no marriages appear, and entries late in the period, particularly between 1699 and 1704, are erratically recorded. During the Interregnum a number of couples with both partners from outside the village were married in Radcliffe. (It is possible, of course, that Radcliffe couples similarly married elsewhere.) Some doubts also surround the period of Peter Titley's incumbency (1671-82) as he was renowned for conducting clandestine marriages. (See pp. 171-2.) Moreover, marriages of some villagers living in Lamcote may be included in the Holme Pierrepont records. In making calculations the registers have

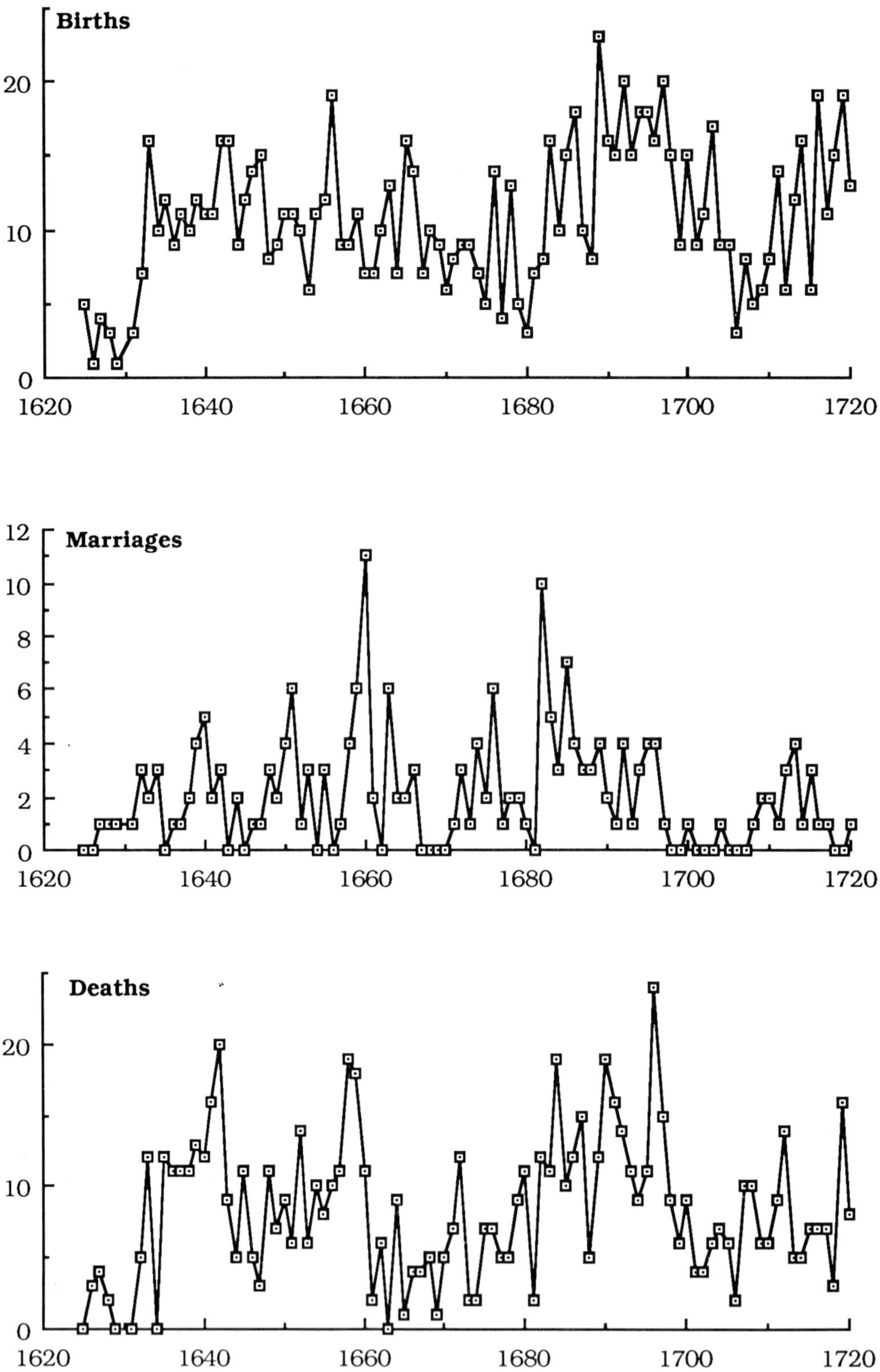

Graphs showing births, marriages and deaths in Radcliffe-on-Trent between 1625 and 1719 based on parish registers and bishops' transcripts. The findings should be viewed with caution because of illegibility, damage and erratic recording of entries, particularly for the years 1625-33, 1645 and 1699-1704. New style dating has been used.

been taken at face value, and no compensation has been made for irregularities. Any conclusions must therefore be viewed with caution.

Razell's method has been used by which the mean annual number of marriages is multiplied by 125. Marriages have been assessed in ten-year periods beginning in 1633 and ending in 1722. The totals are again rounded to the nearest whole number.

Years	Number of marriages	Estimated population
1633-1642	23	288
1643-1652	20	250
1653-1662	30	375
1663-1672	17	212
1673-1682	29	362
1683-1692	36	450
1693-1702	14	175
1703-1712	10	125
1713-1722	14	175

Whatever the deficiencies of Radcliffe's registers they reflect the overall, if unsteady, trend of rural population decline by the early 18th century. The 274 based on the Protestation Return corresponds reasonably closely with the 288 of the 1633-42 marriage records, and the 1674 Hearth Tax estimates of 319-333 are only a little lower than the marriage figures for the 10-year period of 1673-82 (362). The 1676 religious census figures, however, are lower still - at odds with both the hearth tax and the marriage registers - perhaps suggesting that the irregularities and inaccurate record-keeping of Peter Titley referred to above may indeed have had an effect for at least part of this period. Further research in nearby parishes is needed to account for other erratic trends.[297]

II Wealth and Status 1603-1660

On 21st April 1603 the town of Newark welcomed King James I on his progress to London for his coronation and, two months later, a similar ceremony took place in Nottingham for the queen and her two eldest children, Henry and Elizabeth. It is more than likely that among the crowds in both towns there were men and women from Radcliffe, although nothing about these stirring events appears in the village records. In the 17th century there would have been some who never travelled beyond their parish boundaries, but many others would have been accustomed to visiting Nottingham and Newark to attend the civil and church courts and the markets and taverns, where they could find entertainments such as bull baiting and cock fighting. Documents from the last quarter of the 16th century and up to the Civil War show that villagers married or had contact with people from a wide area. Besides Nottingham itself and villages in the immediate vicinity of Radcliffe such as Cotgrave, Cropwell Butler and Owthorpe, they came from as far afield as Trowell, Southwell and Langar in Nottinghamshire and from Grantham in Lincolnshire.

During the last years of Elizabeth's reign, large amounts of land in Radcliffe had changed hands and many villagers would have found themselves with new landlords. As already seen, the Stanhopes had acquired the former rectory lands and a manor in Radcliffe, and the Pierreponts had also made inroads into Rosell property in both Radcliffe and Lamcote. These two gentry families ranked high in the county hierarchy and had a wide sphere of influence. Moreover they lived near enough to be a forceful presence, unlike the more distant lords of previous times. The court case examining the dispute over Sir Thomas Stanhope's weir at Shelford shows how tenants could become involved in local politics through their landlords (p.58-60). Whether their new masters were of the 'improving' kind, imposing harsher terms with regard to their rents and leases, as did the Worcestershire landlords of Thomas Parker and Edward Carpenter (pp. 79-81), or were lenient in this respect, is not known. The power a landlord could exercise over his tenants, when they had no security of tenure, is illustrated by John Rosell's will of 1605. In it he asked his son and heir to deal generously with three of his tenants (p. 110.)

Two rentals, one of 1601 (Pierrepont) and one of 1604 (Beaumont or Stanhope) show some of the tenants who were among the most substantial inhabitants and who bridge the period of change from Elizabeth to James I. The Pierrepont rents, which include eight farms and eight cottages, total £23.2s.8d a year. The tenants with the largest holdings and known to have been resident in Radcliffe are Mrs Anne Ballard, Henry Pare and Robert Greene with more than 115 acres, 51 acres and 40 acres each respectively. The Beaumont rental is of less value, amounting to £12.2s.1d. Out of 21 tenants, at least nine are freeholders bringing in nominal rents. They include John Rosell, William Ballard, Thomas Parker and William and Thomas Dewsbury. The tenancies of the others are uncertain, but a Henry Parr appears twice, paying the highest rent of 50s for a house, meadow and pasture and also renting the manor house and the demesne for 41s a year.[298]

The disappearance of some of the more colourful and affluent Elizabethan gentry families such as the Ashtons, Halls and Roulstones left something of a gap in the village as far as polite society was concerned. The Rosells remained, of course, but during Gervase Rosell's minority from 1615 or 1616 only his guardian Francis Hacker Esq., who was a temporary resident, seems to have had pretensions to gentility (apart from Anne Ballard who died in 1626). Some other notable families also disappeared in the Stuart period. The will of Thomas Parker, yeoman (1603), showed that his only son was now farming in Bradmore. Richard Dewsbury, husbandman (died 1610), left property in Southwell as well as Radcliffe. After the death of his son William in 1637, his descendants disappear from the records though a family of their name is recorded later in the century. Henry Jervis, also a husbandman, made a will in 1612 showing that he had no sons to succeed him.

Early Stuart subsidies and the leading families

The changing fortunes of the leading families can be seen in the lists of those who paid subsidies during the early Stuart period. The subsidy payers, being the most affluent, were the men who were likely to be asked to act as security for bonds or to form the juries at Quarter Sessions, so they would have had some influence in the village. Three returns have survived from James I's reign and five from Charles I's. George Rosell heads the list in 1606 paying 5s.4d on £10 worth of land. After his death his son's guardian, Francis Hacker, paid 2s.8d on 40s worth of land. During Gervase's minority, however, Henry Parr was perceived as the most affluent man in the village. In 1622, the last time he was listed, he paid the highest tax of 5s on £5 worth of goods. In 1628 Gervase Rosell, now of age, replaced Hacker and was still taxed on land assessed at only £2, but this was at a time of economic stress. Other families were assessed on £3 or £4 worth of goods (though the rate sometimes varied), Henry Jervis for the last time in 1606, Anne Ballard in 1625 and William Dewsbury in 1629. John Greene paid the subsidy three times in the 1620s.

The Greenes and Parrs, together with the Frankes and the Thraves, none of whom were subsidy payers after the 1620s, were the most enduring families in Radcliffe and often linked by marriage. They could look back to at least early Tudor times for their origins in the village. A visitor to 17th century Radcliffe might well have remarked on the number of Greenes and Parrs. The Greenes had at least ten heads of families in the first half of the century, though not all would have been as affluent as John Greene the subsidy payer, who held a farm from the Stanhopes in 1604 for which he paid 13s.4d a year. There appear to have been three main families among the Parrs at the beginning of the century, one headed by Robert, who married Isabel Greene in 1604 and the other two by a Henry, one of whom had married Isabel, the daughter of the yeoman Thomas Parker in 1592. John Franke, a yeomen who died in 1626, was connected by marriage with the Greenes. He left one son George, who died childless after the Restoration, but he may have had a brother from whom later members of the family descended. They were very prosperous - in 1653 the inventory on the goods of John's widow Margaret was valued at more than £330, the highest from the whole 17th century apart from the Rosells. John Thrave claimed the status of yeoman in his marriage licence with Edith Richards in 1617 though he worked as a carpenter. These families represented elements of continuity and stability during a period of increasing population mobility.

In the last years before the Civil War they were replaced by the Grocockes and Gambles and then the Hutchinsons, Pilkingtons and Butlers as subsidy payers. The Grocockes first appear in village records in the middle years of Elizabeth's reign and William Grococke regularly paid the subsidy during the late 1590s. The 1604 rental shows that John Grococke held 'Tibbott's' farm for 12s.9d rent and widow Grococke paid 20s for Jervis' farm. No one in the family, however, was wealthy enough to pay tax in the first subsidies of James' reign but in those of 1628, 1629 and 1641/2 another William Grococke paid on £3 worth of goods. The Gambles seem to have arrived in Radcliffe about the same time as the Grocockes, but it was not until 1628 that the first member of the family, John, paid the subsidy on £4 worth of goods. He was on the list again in 1641/2. Four brothers were around in the early years of the century and they seem to have been very assertive, all except one being variously charged with engrossing grain, forcible entry or trespass. (See pp. 143-4).

The first reference to the Hutchinsons was in 1628 when William paid the subsidy tax on £4 worth of goods. He was a husbandman who also faced a number of indictments for engrossing grain and trespass. Just before the Civil War two other families, the Pilkingtons and the Butlers, appear on the subsidy returns both being taxed on £3 worth of goods. William Pilkington, yeoman, whose family became prominent in this period was also accused of engrossing grain. Perhaps the risks these families took with the law is linked to their rising prosperity. Little is known of the Butlers in this period, as they appear at a time when most records ceased.[299]

Wealth and status in wills 1603-1660

Twenty six wills have survived for the early Stuart period and the Interregnum. They were made by one gentleman, four yeomen, seven husbandmen, four labourers, one wheelwright, four widows, two bachelors and three unspecified. Some of these inexact terms disguise the true occupations of the testator - one of the labourers was Miles Cragge the shepherd. Admonition bonds were drawn up to empower relatives to administer the goods of a deceased person; 13 applications were made for people for whom no will has been found. No wills have survived from the Civil War years 1642-48, but there are five from the Interregnum 1649-60.

On the whole larger sums of money (as opposed to real estate or goods) were left than in the Elizabethan period, a reflection perhaps of inflation. The median was about £13. No one in these years, however, could aspire to the wealth of Robert Hall who in 1580 had bequeathed nearly £300. Those leaving more than £60 before the Civil War were Jeffrey Limner (£65.10s in 1617), Robert Greene (£76 in 1624) and one of the subsidy payers Richard Dewsbury (£120.12s in 1610). Others, who had paid tax and might have been expected to leave large sums of money, were Thomas Parker (1603) who left £14.6s, John Rosell (1605) who left just under £27 and Henry Jervis (1612) who bequeathed no money at all. Those who made wills during the Interregnum avoided any expressions which might be construed as royalist and, despite the recent disturbances, some of them showed that they had enjoyed considerable material comfort. Robert Butler (1654) left well over £200 and property in Radcliffe. Margaret Franke (1653) divided nearly £100 among her three daughters, their husbands and children. William Greene (1657) left over £10 in cash, but in Anthony Franke's will (May 1659) there were no details of any money or goods. He was a bachelor who died during the brief period of Richard Cromwell's rule. A summary of the sums of money bequeathed by all testators is shown below:

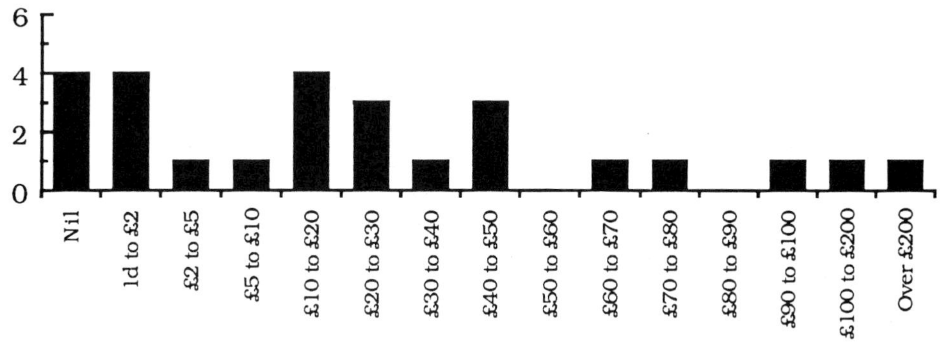

Inventories

In addition to wills, three inventories of goods have survived from between 1603 and 1660. Anne Byrde's modest inventory, totalling £6.15s.10d, has only survived because of a church court case (pp. 127-8). In contrast, Margaret Franke's made in 1653 totalled £330.16s.4d, confirming the affluence indicated by her will (p. 231). Still suggestive of a reasonably comfortable lifestyle, was the inventory of Joane Needham made in 1658, which was valued at £144.15s (p. 203). She had a house (hall), a parlour, two chambers and a brewhouse, but no details were given of their contents. They must have been simple, however, for her household goods were worth no more than £8.5s. In her will made the same year she left only just over £4 in cash, and a pewter dish and salt to her granddaughter Mary Needham. William Greene drew up his will in 1657, but his inventory, totalling £123.12s.8d, was not made until after his death in 1663, and properly belongs to the Restoration period.

III Wealth and Status - 1660-1714

The Hearth Tax

Hardly had the cheering for the restoration of Charles II died down than the country found itself presented with a new tax - this time on hearths, fixed items, easy to assess. The advent of 'the chimney men' was naturally unpopular and added to the burdens of the petty constable. He had first to make the assessment by questioning each householder or by entering the premises along with two substantial householders, and then to collect it - 2s for each hearth every year in two instalments. The best returns are those from 1664, when it was levied by the sheriffs, and 1674 when it was levied directly by county receivers and their sub-collectors, still using petty constables but bypassing other local officials. Even in that year, when the level of evasion seems to have been reduced, it is possible that under-registration in parts of Nottinghamshire was as high as 40%.

				Numbers of Hearths											
	Total	Charged	%	1	2	3	4	5	6	7	8	9	10+	Not charged	%
1664															
Radcliffe	66	55	83	48	5	-	1	-	-	1	-	-	-	11	17
1674															
Radcliffe	75	51	68	30	16	2	1	-	1	1	-	-	-	24	32
Bingham	117	95	81	39	35	15	2	2	1	-	1	-	-	22	19
Cotgrave	109	78	72	48	19	7	-	-	1	2	-	-	1	31	28
Shelford	36	26	72	11	9	6	-	-	-	-	-	-	-	10	28

The 1674 tax returns are generally regarded as the more accurate, those of 1664 being in many cases (including Radcliffe's) damaged. In both years the number of village family names was about 47, the most prolific being the Butlers with six heads of household, the Parrs with five and the Greenes with four. Comparisons between the two returns must be treated with some caution because different procedures were used, especially with regard to assessing those considered to be too poor to be charged. Only two families, the Rosells (with seven hearths) and the Pilkingtons (with six and four), had more than two hearths in both years. In 1674 they were joined by William Parr and William Markham, both with three hearths.

Of those with two hearths, as many as eight or nine can be identified as having acquired an extra hearth or moved to another house. The husbandman William Cooke was one of those who had a second hearth by 1674. His wife Mary and one of his sons had recently died, leaving him with a son and a daughter, Alice. Though both were under 12 years of age, his son could soon be apprenticed and his daughter could help in the house, so he would not have been overburdened with family

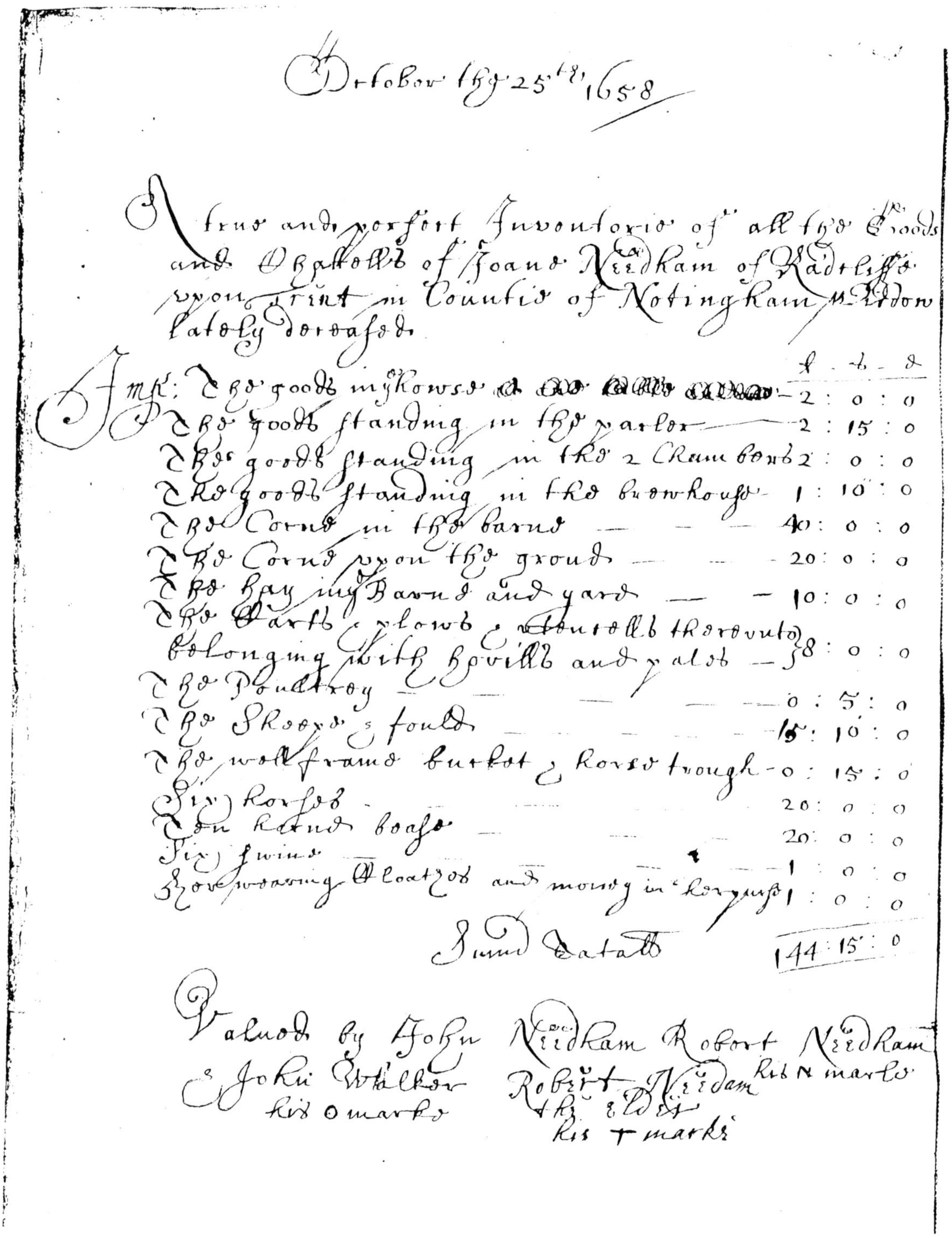

October the 25th 1658

A true and perfect Inventorie of all the goods and Chattells of Joane Needham of Radcliffe upon Trent in Countie of Notingham widdow lately deceased.

	£	s	d
Imp: the goods in house ~~[illegible]~~	2	0	0
The goods standing in the parlor	2	15	0
The goods standing in the 2 Chambers	2	0	0
The goods standing in the brewhouse	1	10	0
The Corne in the barne	40	0	0
The Corne upon the ground	20	0	0
The hay in the Barne and yard	10	0	0
The Cartts plows & ~~[illegible]~~ thereunto belonging with hovills and pales	8	0	0
The Poultrey	0	5	0
The Sheepe & foule	15	10	0
The woll frame bucket & horse trough	0	15	0
Six horses	20	0	0
Ten horned beasts	20	0	0
Six swine	1	0	0
Her wearing Cloathes and money in her purse	1	0	0
Summ totall	144	15	0

Valued by John Needham Robert Needham his X marke
& John Walker his O marke Robert Needam the elder his + marke

Joane Needham's inventory 25th October 1658

This inventory from the Interregnum period is one of the earliest to survive from Radcliffe. It shows that most of Joane's wealth lay in agriculture (NAO PRNW) responsibilities and could afford to make improvements. In his will of 1682 only Alice is mentioned and his inventory amounted to £108.10s.4d. William Needham (sometimes a husbandman, sometimes a yeoman) also increased the number of his hearths from one to two. In 1670 he was a churchwarden, an important position in the village, and he does not appear to have had more than two children, neither of them surviving infancy. His wife died in 1671 and soon after he paid his first instalment of the 1674 tax he married a widow, Emmot Bosworth of Ruddington. They were able to enjoy their two hearths together for another eight years before William himself died.

The group who were considered too poor to pay at all had more than doubled - an illustration perhaps of the growing gap between rich and poor. These increases, however, could have arisen because a more sympathetic constable made the assessment in 1674; or because a number of people had retired or been widowed and moved into separate accommodation between the two dates. Whatever the reason, the percentage of poor households - 32% - was high. Except for Radcliffe, those places in Bingham Hundred with less than 70% of households paying tax did not have more than 24 households altogether. The extra work to be found by villagers along the river banks and at Holme Pierrepont Hall (as evidenced by payments for labour shown in the Pierrepont estate papers) might have encouraged younger sons to stay on as labourers, or even attracted newcomers into the village. Whilst some prospered (no less than four labourers' wills have survived from the later Stuart period) they would always have been vulnerable to changing economic conditions and liable to become dependent on the parish.[300]

Money bequests - the later Stuarts

There are 32 wills surviving from this period (1660-1714) distributed fairly evenly throughout, except after the turn of the century when only three wills have survived. They were made by two gentlemen (the Rosells), seven yeomen, three husbandmen and three farmers (judged as one category), four labourers, one widow, three shepherds, one mason, one cordwainer, one blacksmith and six unspecified. Everyone left money and there was more to leave. The lowest total amount was 1s left by shepherd Matthew Simmons (1688) and the two highest totals were William Pilkington's £502 (1679) and the £2,629.5s of Thomas Rosell (1685) - the latter's amount being projected and not all cash in hand. Excluding the exceptional amount left in the Rosell will, which is untypical of the community as a whole, the median amount of money bequeathed was about £30 - some £17 more than in the earlier part of the Stuart period. The gap between the rich and the poor generally can be better appreciated if it is realised that Thomas Rosell was not, as gentlemen went, particularly wealthy (he had only seven hearths) and Matthew Simmons (who also had a cottage) would have been considered lucky to have had anything to leave at all. Including Thomas Rosell and William Pilkington the broad amounts of money left and numbers of testators are shown below and may be compared with the pattern for the 1603-1660 period on p. 201, and with the Tudor findings (pp. 84 and 85):

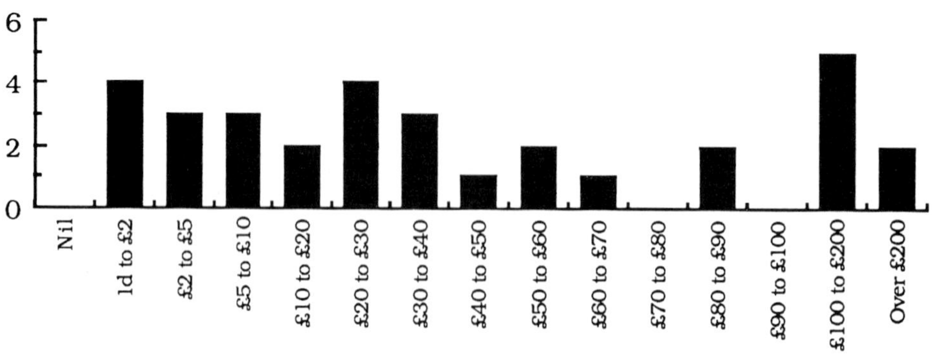

Apart from the husbandmen, the testators' position in the social hierarchy was reflected in the median amount of money they left:

	£	s	d		£	s	d
Yeomen	110	0	0	Labourers	22	7	8
Husbandmen and farmers	20	0	0	Shepherds	13	1	0
Artisans	30	2	0	One widow	1	12	0

Inventories

Inventories (supposed to be made on estates with a value of more than £5) provide a rich source of information about village life in the late 17th century. The appraisers were drawn from among the legatees, the creditors, the deceased's next of kin or two other honest persons. They had to be knowledgeable about the current market value of the goods they were viewing, but it was usually in their interests to keep the value of the inventory as low as possible. Most of those whose inventories have survived were primarily farmers and the total would depend very much on the time of year the inventory was taken and the local conditions then prevailing. It is impossible to discover the reason for their haphazard survival, but it is clear that many have been lost.

Although only three inventories have survived from 1603-1660, there are 31 from the post-Restoration era - 17 of them accompanied by wills. Yeomen, husbandmen and farmers, a labourer and craftsmen, two widows and an unmarried woman are all represented. This is in contrast to some villages like Norwell, near Southwell, where the community was largely made up of husbandmen, small farmers of comparable prosperity. Radcliffe and Lamcote villagers, however, were not well-off if compared with those of Clayworth in north Nottinghamshire, where 17 inventories made between 1670 and 1712 have been studied. This shows that six of them (excluding one gentleman and the rector) had totals above £150 and of those three were above £274. In Radcliffe 29 inventories of all groups except gentlemen (the two Rosells) made after 1660 show a different pattern:

Under £10	-	4	£100 to £150	-	4
£10 to £20	-	4	£150 to £200	-	3
£20 to £50	-	8	over £200	-	1
£50 to £100	-	5			

Although the range within the status and occupational groups (where known) was wide, on average the inventories of yeomen were worth more than those of the husbandmen and farmers, and the latter worth more than the inventories of the shepherds, the 'occupations' (comprising one labourer and four artisans) and the women:

		Range of totals							Median		
		£	s	d		£	s	d	£	s	d
Yeomen	5	19	3	6	-	167	7	6	110	10	0
Husbandmen and farmers	6	6	16	0	-	222	2	6	80	15	3
Shepherds	4	10	19	0	-	62	10	8	22	12	4
Occupations	5	6	11	0	-	41	14	0	29	0	4
Women	3	6	17	0	-	32	2	0	13	10	8

The inventories of the yeomen show that they had more invested in their agricultural goods than the husbandmen/farmers (a median of 90% as against 74%) a reflection of the larger farms they would have worked. They tended to have a higher value in their purse and apparel as well. The husbandmen/farmers had a higher proportion of their wealth tied up in household goods, however sparse their furnishings (an average of 16% as against 8% for the yeomen.) None of them had loans or wages owing to them, as did some in the other groups. They worked for themselves but, as the wills show, they had less money to leave their dependants than the yeomen, and would have found it more difficult to keep family farms, with their stock and equipment, intact. (At either end of the scale within these groups there are atypical examples such as the affluent farmer Richard Musson (1712) who had an inventory totalling £222.2s.6d, and the bachelor yeoman William Pilkington (1699) who had only £19.3s.6d worth of goods. (See p. 196.)[301]

IV The Parish Elite

Office holders 1603-1660

The churchwarden and the constable were the most important parish officers. Neither post was very popular, though some might have welcomed the opportunity to influence parish affairs. In Radcliffe the constable was chosen by lot but it is not known whether this was the case with the churchwardens - they could also have been elected or served in turn by houserow. All who held this office (two a year) would have been rate-payers and as they were responsible for money levied on the parish, they were likely to have been of some standing in the village.

The list of churchwardens is almost complete from the late 1580s. (See p. 250.) Between 1603 and 1620 George Bayley, a member of an old local family, served in the office at least three times. Representatives of the Greenes and the Grocockes were also prominent. During the next 30 years men who were subsidy payers like Henry Parr, William Hutchinson and William Pilkington held the office several times; so did several of the Greenes, the Parrs, George Franke and in 1634 George Bayley again. Roger Campion's name (also the parish clerk) recurred frequently. Richard Richards, though a labourer, also held the office, but his will of 1629 shows him to have been relatively well-off, for he left pewter, brass and over £10 in cash. The farming interest predominated; only three are known to have been craftsmen, John Chesters the tailor (1625), John Long the weaver (1636) and William Greene the blacksmith (1648). Those whom it is possible to identify fit into the accepted idea of the churchwarden being one of the village élite, reasonably prosperous, more often than not from one of the older families and therefore considered to be dependable.

The same could be said about the constables, although only five of their names have been found from this period - George Bayley (1614), Richard Long (1617), William Pilkington (in the 1630s), the reluctant John Gamble in 1640 (p. 184) and John Henson (1642). John Davell and Martin Grococke jointly held the relatively new office of overseer of the poor in 1628 and Roger Campion ten years later.

Office holders 1660-1714

The names of only four constables have come to light in this period - John Brewster in 1704, Thomas Parr in 1705 and 1707, William Butler in 1706 and Thomas Knight in 1712. In contrast, a complete record of churchwardens exists from 1662 showing in all some 45 different family names. Not surprisingly the Parrs are represented most often (13 times), the next often being the Greenes (ten), and the Butlers (nine). This list shows that in this period the office was clearly not the preserve of the most affluent, nor of the older families, because some men whose records give little indication of wealth served a number of times. Peter Beeson was one of these; the baptism of his son (also Peter) in 1657 is the first sign of a family which was to have a long association with Radcliffe. In 1690 Peter Beeson senior rented a house and homestead with three beastgates in the Eastgang pasture and his son, a house and homestead with three 'rows common', both from the Pierrepont estate. Unless they held greater holdings elsewhere, they could never have been very well-off. In 1708 widow Anne Beeson was judged too poor to pay a fine to the court of Quarter Sessions. Yet Peter senior was a churchwarden in 1671 and 1691 and his son in 1692. On the other hand, certain men who appear to have been prosperous rarely, if ever, took their turn. Affluent newcomer William Browne (see p. 228) instantly held office, but only once before dying in 1689. By 1690 Richard Musson had taken over Browne's house and homestead and in 1695, with a partner, he held lands of the Pierreponts worth £24 rent a year and more besides. Despite his wealth (his goods were valued at £222 on his death in 1712) Richard was churchwarden only twice - 1705 and 1706. Thomas Stone, servant to John Greene, married Miriam the daughter of Widow Dickinson. He too prospered, renting land from the Pierreponts in both Radcliffe and Holme; by the early 18th century his holdings included 'the Parsonage Land' at £7 a year, a farm at £10 and 'Townend Close' at £1.10s. He was nevertheless churchwarden only twice - in 1709 and 1710. (He died in 1711, his headstone in the churchyard distinguished by being the earliest signed by George Sparrow, one of two local carvers admired for the quality of their work.)

From the 1690s to the end of the period several men whose families do not seem to have been in the village long emerged as office holders, so perhaps elections were sometimes 'arranged'. In the case of Mr James Wright this rapid integration is not surprising as he was a gentleman. He is first recorded in Radcliffe in 1693 and three years later became a churchwarden. Thomas Knight also won easy acceptance. First mentioned in the parish register in 1710 with the baptism of his daughter Martha, by 1712 he was constable, albeit a negligent one (p. 194). He appears on the Rosells' map of 1710 as their main tenant leasing over 280 acres and occupying their manor house. Richard Harwood, who held over 93 acres from the Rosells, first appeared in the registers in 1707. These two men were also churchwardens after 1714.

It was in this period that the Brewsters moved into the village and their presence was to be an influential one, lasting almost to the 20th century. John aged 34 had married 23 year old Mary Richmond of East Bridgford in 1689 and two daughters and a son followed in quick succession. He was a churchwarden in 1692 and 1713, a constable in 1704 and an overseer of the Jeffrey Limner Dole in 1709. Initially he was a blacksmith, for so he declared himself in Richard Foster's will in 1695, of which he may have been the scribe. On the administration bond of Thomas Parr's estate (1708), however, he called himself a farmer and it was as farmers that the Brewsters flourished during the 18th century. The map of 1710 shows that John lived in a house on the Shelford Road now known as Old Manor Farm. Some years later the family moved to Thomas Knight's house (the Rosell manor house) and by 1732 the family had the largest holding of Pierrepont lands in the village.

Nearly all these office holders were farmers; many, like Richard Musson, now calling themselves with some pride 'Farmer' rather than husbandman. A few office holders can be identified as craftsmen or tradesmen. William Foster the blacksmith was churchwarden for three years from 1696 to 1698. Fisherman George Taylor held the office in 1696 and John Collishaw, appointed in 1710, was a weaver. These men, too, were farmers at least in a small way.[302]

The end of an era

Thomas Rosell appears to have fulfilled the role of squire and head of the leading family in the village. He was present at many a death bed, probably giving his advice to these unsophisticated people as best he could. But his death, followed so quickly by that of his son Gervase in 1687, left the village without a natural leader. During the long minority of Gervase's son until 1708, the only gentleman recorded as having settled in the village and become involved in village affairs was Mr James Wright who, as has been seen, became a churchwarden. Though many of the local farmers were prosperous, none appear to have been exceptionally so and thus able to dominate the community. Such men were conservative, continuing to farm the open fields in the old ways.

V Occupations

Crafts and trades 1603-1660

Radcliffe was never a centre of trade in the same way as Bingham, a market town standing near the junction of two highways. It was, therefore, unlikely to have offered as wide a range of goods and services, but parish and court records reveal a variety of craftsmen and tradesmen. The chance survival of such information makes it impossible to judge whether there had been any significant increase in their numbers since Tudor times.

Central to village working life was the blacksmith - a position held from at least the beginning of the 16th century by a branch of the Greene family living at Lamcote. Another essential craft was that of the wheelwright and Jeffrey Limner of Jeffrey Dole fame showed how profitable this occupation could be. Also recorded are two millers, Nicholas Ayre in 1604 and John Sheppard in 1630. In 1610 Radcliffe had a butcher, Edward Swinscoe (the first time this occupation is mentioned) and two tailors, John Chester in 1614 and Robert Dickinson, described by the Latin term 'scissorem', in 1642. Although weaving never became a dominant domestic industry, some may have practised this craft besides the two recorded - John Long junior in 1642 and James Randay in 1659. It was an occupation which went well with farming as it could be practised during the slack months. The presence of a brickmaker, Charles Barr in 1637, suggests that houses were being improved, made more comfortable or safer. There were also at least two carpenters to assist him.

There would have been many more brewers of ale than appear in the records. At the top end of the scale was the innkeeper who catered for the gentry and more respectable members of society, providing accommodation for passing travellers of quality. The village inn (perhaps with one of the more permanent signs which were becoming fashionable hung outside it), may also have been used for meetings of the parish officers, visiting magistrates and coroners' inquests. Francis Grococke claimed in 1609 and 1613 to be an innkeeper, although he was charged with harbouring vagrants, which makes it seem more likely that he was an ale-house keeper. An ale-house might also provide accommodation, but to those of lower status, travelling journeymen or seasonal labourers. These houses were likely to have been centres of village recreation, for wedding and christening feasts, entertainments such as ninepins, bowling and morris dancing. Many combined brewing with other occupations, putting up their alestake (a pole with a brush hanging at the end) when a brew was ready and inviting the locals to come with their buckets to buy. The records of the manorial courts of Peverel and later of St John are full of indictments for brewing without licence; one in 1651 was against John Taylor, the fisherman, and in 1635 the Quarter Sessions magistrates charged Edward Swinscoe, probably the butcher, with the same offence.

As has been seen (p. 186) magistrates' anxieties about unruly behaviour among the lower ranks of society centred around the ale-houses and the same names recur in court records, such as Juliana Linney alias Hutchinson and Elizabeth Taylor, for keeping houses where disorderly drinking took place. Brewing and baking were the only occupations in Radcliffe which women were recorded as having practised. (It was rare for unmarried women to sell ale, for the authorities frowned on them doing so.) Usually women followed their husbands' trade or continued it after they had died; many only came to brewing in their widowhood as an escape from poverty.[303]

Crafts and trades 1660-1714

This period was a time of increasing opportunity for craftsmen and tradesmen, with houses becoming larger and farms better equipped. Those whose names can be gleaned from documents of this period were probably only a few of the total number. Craftsmen's inventories are of particular interest because of the details they sometimes give about tools and equipment, but the three from Radcliffe - those of a blacksmith, a brickmaker and a shoemaker - show that they did not prosper more than the shepherds or labourers.

Smiths at work based on a mid-17th century woodcut

Blacksmiths continued to be represented by a branch of the Greene family (evidence of the importance of their craft to the community) and they were joined by the Fosters, who first appear in the registers with the baptism of Richard and Mary's daughter in 1662. In the Hearth Tax of 1664 Richard paid for one hearth and 10 years later for two. More surprising is the low value of the inventory made on his goods in 1695, given as £23.18s.4d. He had a five-roomed house, the only one among the inventories to include a larder and he had a kitchen besides. The house included a feather bed, a livery cupboard in his parlour and eight pewter dishes. The tools of his craft - 'one handmill, one pair of bellows, two anvils, two hammers, pair vices and odd things' were assessed at £7.6s.8d, a quarter of his total assets, but a good deal of his shop equipment would not have been subject to valuation. He also possessed 15 sheep and a cow. His frugal lifestyle enabled him to be generous to his grandchildren who received over £30 between them. His son William, who inherited his business and his property, paid £6.10s rent a year for land in Holme. His home, with a barn and orchard, was probably located at today's 1 Water Lane which still has evidence of a former forge area. (This was opposite where the wheelwright George Duke was to set up business soon after he came to Radcliffe in 1717.) William's work extended beyond Radcliffe for he was paid 'for shoeing and other work' and for 'mending a stove' by the Pierrepont's steward at Holme in 1705 and 1707. Blacksmiths appear to have been a close knit group. William's sister married one - Samuel Hemsley of Gedling - in 1682, and the witness to his father Richard's will was John Brewster, who also signed the bond, calling himself blacksmith.

Members of the Barr family continued to work as brickmakers. Robert Barr had an inventory made on his goods in April 1680 which showed that the occupation brought him little wealth for it came to only £6.11s, his purse and apparel amounting to just 5s. His household goods consisted of a table and a cupboard in the hall, a bedstand and bedding in the parlour and another bedstand and a chest in the chamber. With the lead and other things in the kitchen, these totalled £3.6s.8d and things seen and unseen 3s.4d. The phrase in his inventory 'all in the chempe' probably refers to a 'champ', a form of container in which material for brick-making could be crushed or pounded. On this occasion the appraisers found it contained nothing of any value. In the Hearth Tax of 1664 and 1674 Robert Barr was charged on only one hearth, for the kiln would have been exempt from tax. Like many he also brewed and sold ale. His inventory shows that he had £2.16s owed to him in wages, for he would have made his living not just from making bricks, but as a bricklayer as well.

Few names of shoemakers have survived, but they were certainly around. In 1667 the churchwardens of Holme Pierrepont paid 'the Shoemaker of Radcliffe for Leather to hang the bell 1s'. No doubt he supplied shaped leather wherever it was used for agricultural and domestic implements in both villages. Robert Oliver, cordwainer or shoemaker, had four rooms in his inventory of 1692 (a house, dairy, parlour and chamber) which totalled £34.8s and he probably used one of these rooms as his shop, or workroom. He owned but two beds and two chairs besides some brass. Most of his resources were invested in 20 beasts which were valued at £30.10s or over 90% of the whole. By 1714 another family which was to have a long history in the village, the Chamberlains, were working as shoemakers.

The marriage of William Fillingham to Marie Needham in 1668 brings to light the presence of a chandler. His son Robert, ironmonger, proved useful in more ways than as a supplier of goods. His large untidy signature appears on five wills and he acted as scribe for four of them. He was also one of the appraisers and probably the scribe for four or five inventories and he acted as bondsman for three testators. His first wife was Hannah, the sister of William Pilkington, an affluent member of the village community. He combined his trade with farming, renting land from the Pierreponts and appearing as a freeholder at the Peverel Court.

One of the many Parrs - Bryan - was a ploughwright. His craft combined some of the skills of the blacksmith and the woodworking expertise of the wheelwright, for he would have made edged tools such as hoes and spades besides ploughs. Perhaps he had been the apprentice of Harold Plowright whose widow (left with a small son) he married in 1687, two years after Harold died. Typically, he also had a small holding and a few beasts, for he rented a house and homestead from the Pierreponts (1690) which entitled him to three beastgates in Eastgang (Hesgang) pasture.

There was also a glazier or general builder in the village. In the Manvers estate papers there are accounts for paying Joseph Shilcock for repairing Radcliffe chancel in 1707 and in 1714 for 'glassing' the windows. Carpenters were represented by John Thraves in 1672 and Joseph Baker in 1705, while Thomas Pare, who made a will in 1679, was a mason. The family of butchers, the Swinscoes, seem to have disappeared about this time, but the farmer George Franke referred to his nephew John Greene as a butcher in 1672 and Gervase, the brother of the yeoman William Pilkington, was a tanner. There are also references to other craftsmen during the last 30 years of the Stuart era, if only brief ones: to George Sparrow, who was a cooper and gravestone carver; to the Roulstones who were to be basketmakers in the village for several generations; to the weavers William Bacon and John Collishaw; and to the tailors William Morley and Samuel Parr. The bodicemaker Thomas Blatherwick might never have been heard of if he had not been associated with the concealment of a stillborn baby in 1688. (See pp. 174 & 193). The first appearance of a framework knitter was in 1700 when John Henson signed a bond stating this to be his occupation.

By-employments were common, especially for those who had little land to farm, and brewing was still the favoured option. Though inventories show that cheese was made, there is no evidence that this was on a really substantial scale, but some farmers' wives would have made enough cheese and butter to take the surplus to market. Combing and spinning, turning fleece wool into thread, would have been an occupation in most farmers' and labourers' households. Spindles and spinning wheels would have been so commonplace as to have been included unidentified amongst 'the other things' in many inventories, but direct reference to 'wheels' occurs in three of them. Only one of them provides evidence of weaving - that of John Yardley the shepherd (1664) who had two looms.[304]

Women

The very real contribution that women are known to have made to the rural economy as the wives and daughters of farmers, craftsmen and tradesmen is for the most part hidden in these village records. It is probable that Radcliffe, like other places, had its midwives and nurses, their unrecorded work as essential to the community as anyone else's. Contemporaries recognised that husbands and wives worked in a partnership and in widowhood many women were able to make a living on their own.

VI Social Relationships - Legacies 1603-1660

Much can be learned about social relationships from legacies in the 26 wills of this period. As well as personal goods, both freehold and leased property was bequeathed, but the number of wills devising land and houses is slightly less (40%) than in the Elizabethan period (45%).

Real estate and land

Although only one will referred to the traditional widow's third in this period, a widow's right to dower for life from her husband's real estate continued until 1833. Squire John Rosell's widow Mary (1605) was therefore secure in her jointure in law but was asked to give up a portion of it voluntarily to help her son George. (See p. 108.) Anxiety about how the family and their inheritance would fare in the hands of a stepfather, should the widow remarry, was again a recurring theme. For example, husbandman Harold Greene, who had inherited his farm from his mother Margaret in 1580, left equal shares of the farm to his wife Agnes and to John, probably his eldest son in 1613. He was concerned that the property should stay intact with his heir, for he stipulated that during Agnes' life she was not to let or pass on her share to anyone but John and not to marry or let anyone come into the house 'to use it for her to be a disturber of the said son'. John in return was to 'order and use her part for her for a reasonable rate at the sight of the supervisors'. John was also to have the use of one oxgang of land in Radcliffe for two years, 'the corn to be brought him home to the house where he now dwelleth'. He was obviously not living with his parents at the time of his father's death. Should Agnes die before the end of the lease, her share was to go to John. Three other sons were left equal money legacies.

Robert Butler, yeoman, was concerned with dividing his real estate equitably. In his will of 1654 he left land to both his eldest and second sons. (See family tree p. 217.) His first son Richard and his heirs were to have

the messuage in which I now live with all appurtenances and the cottage house commonly called Barraughes house with all lands and commons belonging to the same messuage and cottage to be entered upon by him at age 18. Richard was described as a freeholder in the Peverel Court roll of 1669 and the Butler family had also had land in Langar, for Robert's father and brother are described as 'of Langar' in the will. Robert's second son William was left the land purchased of the heirs of John Gamble, except for the land belonging to it in Lamcote field which was to go to Richard. (See p. 144). The youngest son Robert was to receive £100, half of which was to be paid him by William out of Gamble's land and the other half by the executors out of personal estate at age 21. If eldest son Richard's land descended to William, Robert was to have a further £50 and the same if William's land went to Richard.

The Parker and Drecot families did not have the problem of providing for several sons. Thomas Parker, yeoman (1603), left all his lands to his only son, Richard Parker of Bradmore. After bequests to his two married daughters, he willed that his unmarried daughter Marjorie should have 'the house in which I now live' at a rent of 12d per annum. If she married (provided she did so with the consent of her brother and the two supervisors of the will) she was to have the choice of either staying in the house at the same rent or leaving it and receiving 20s a year for the rest of her life from brother Richard. William Drecot, labourer, made a nuncupative will in 1629, and appears to have had no children. He left to his wife Sislie

> *all my goods within doors and without and the house wherein I live during her life and, after her decease, my will is that my friends shall have the one half of my said house and the other shall be disposed of by my said wife.*

The friends are not named. Whether Sislie obeyed William's directions is uncertain. In her own will of 1634 she left 'all rights in the house in which I now live, with all appurtenances and all commons and common of pasture to the same belonging' to William Campion of Cotgrave and his heirs, but there is no further mention of real estate. Whether William Campion received only half her house, and his father John - Sislie's executor and residuary legatee - disposed of the other half, is not known.

Personal estate - the widow's share

Married women had no right to dispose of goods during their husband's lifetime, as shown by the will of widower William Greene (1657) who left to his younger son 'all those goods in the house given him with my consent by his mother late deceased'.

Of the other wills, where there was a surviving wife and children, five made the widow the sole residuary legatee and four left her a half share. In the first group two testators had left under-age children; the ages of the children in the remaining three wills are uncertain, but some at least may have been young or unmarried. In four of these wills, overseers were appointed to assist the widow. Of those who left the widow a half share, Thomas Pare and Harold Greene have already been mentioned in the previous section. In the latter case and in the will of Robert Greene (1624) the eldest son was to act as his mother's 'husbandman'. Henry Gamble (1635) left his wife and very young son a share of the lease of a farm, but appointed his brother to be guardian of the child.

The children's portion

Unlike the Tudor wills, there were only two specific bequests of farm equipment to children. Harold Greene (1613), always worrying about the possible dispersal of his property after his death, gave his son John the henge houses, hovels and pales which were not to be 'taken up or stirred during the lease'. Richard Dewsbury's only son William was left various indoor and outdoor goods and a horse and cart in his will of 1610. Animals continued to figure as bequests to children, often along with a money legacy. The main difference from the Tudor wills is the increase in substantial bequests of money to children, but it must be borne in mind that a proportionally smaller number of wills has survived for the early Stuart period and this may distort the picture. The testators who did leave cash to children, however, covered the social groups from yeoman to labourer. Richard Dewsbury left his eldest daughter £40 for her portion and his other four daughters £20 each and his house and land at Southwell during the life of their mother (1610). Robert Henson, yeoman, who had made his wife residuary legatee (in 1628), wished her to keep the three children until the age of 18. If she re-married they would receive £15 each at the age of 12, otherwise this sum would be paid when they reached 21.

Harold Greene, husbandman (1613), left £10 to three of his sons, but staggered the payments in a manner which must have added to the workload of his sole executor (his son John) and the three overseers. Richard would have £5 at the next-but-two feast day of St Martin in winter and £5 at Martinmas four years after that; Harold would have his first £5 at Martinmas next and the other £5 four years later, and George would be paid his first £5 at Martinmas next-but-three and £5 four years after that. George in addition was to have a black steer and a heifer. There may have been a number of reasons for these arrangements; to ease the burden on the estate or to provide a young man who might have used his legacy unwisely with another opportunity to be more sensible. Robert Butler (1654), perhaps to protect his daughter from a suitor who might take advantage of her youth, curtailed her freedom to choose her own husband. She would receive her legacy of £100 on her marriage day, provided her choice met with the approval of his executors. If she remained unmarried until she was 21, she would receive it then.

A son-in-law was often treated as a member of the blood family. Richard Richards (1629) coupled his son-in-law and daughter together in his bequest of £3. Margaret Boweker, Harold Greene's daughter, and her husband Richard each received 3s.4d 'in full satisfaction of their filial portions' (1613). Thomas Parker, a widowed yeoman (1603), treated his two sons-in-law generously. Apart from the Rosells, he was the only testator to leave silver. He bequeathed to his daughter Isabel two silver spoons and to her husband Henry Pare £10 in money, a feather bed, 'the middlemost brass pot' and £10 in goods within a year of his death. He also gave his daughter Ellen two silver spoons and £3 within a year of his death, while her husband Martin James was left two horses, the best saddle and other riding gear, together with his sword, dagger and best cloak.

Grandchildren

The percentage of wills containing legacies to grandchildren remained roughly the same in the early Stuart period as in the Elizabethan. John Rosell left to each of his Withington grandchildren a silver spoon worth 6s.8d (1605). Three testators left animals; each of the three grandchildren of labourer Richard Richards received a ewe and lamb and 20s, the money 'to be put forth to the use and behest of the children' (1629). In addition, the two granddaughters were to have his 'best brass pot but one' and two pewter dishes. Henry Jervis, a widower (1612), left neither money nor animals to his grandchildren. Instead, nine of them were to get a pewter dish and napkin each and in addition one granddaughter was given a little tin candlestick and another granddaughter a pewter candlestick. One Bayley grandson was given all his best apparel and another two old pans.

The most substantial legacies were made by widow Margaret Franke (1653).

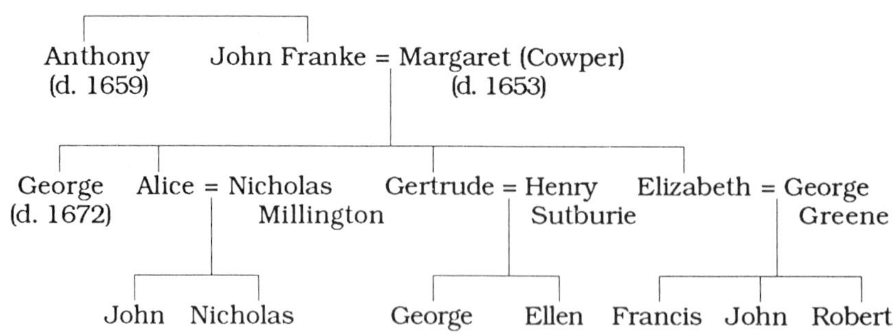

The Franke family

She left £6 'now in the hands of their father Henry' to her two Sutburie grandchildren and £20 'now in the hands of their father Nicholas' to her three Millington grandchildren. Of her three Greene grandchildren, Francis was to have £10, John £3 plus £5 to be paid at 21, and Robert 21s at age 21.

Godchildren

As with the grandchildren, the percentage of wills containing legacies to godchildren remained the same as they had in Elizabethan times. These wills, however, all occurred in the years before the Civil War and such bequests ceased altogether from 1640 to 1714. Gifts continued to be mainly of money or animals: William Greene's godson (1605) was to have a swarm of bees four years after his death and each of John Stapleton's four godchildren a ewe hog (1639). Humphrey Campion, labourer (1614), who had died childless, left his two godchildren 12d each. John Rosell's goddaughter and niece fared much better, as one would expect. She was left a silver spoon.

The wider family

The closeness of family ties was again reflected in these wills; 40% of the wills containing bequests to brothers and sisters and their children. For example Richard Dewsbury (1610) appointed his brother and brother-in-law supervisors of his will and left them and their children 12d each, and William Morley (1626) gave his two married sisters a ewe lamb each. Robert Butler's will (1654) contains an interesting legacy to his father, John Butler of Langar, of 'one load of coals to be laid down at his door yearly during his life, he paying for them at the pit'; he also received 'money due to me by bond'. In addition Robert left 40s to his brother William of Langar.

The labourer Richard Richards (1629) who lived in Lamcote bequeathed his tableware to his two nieces, though exactly how it was to be shared was a problem he left to his executors:

> *the best brass pot but one that I have and two pewter dishes whereof the one of them to be a charger equally to be divided betwixt the said two daughters.*

They would have faced a further dilemma with two other bequests; he left his 'best suit of apparel' to his older brother Richard and 'my best suit of my apparel' to the older brother of his godson. Humphrey Campion (1614), also a labourer of Lamcote, who left neither wife nor children, wished that 'all my goods undivided which came by my father and mother shall remain to Margaret Campion my sister to take as her right'. He appointed her executrix and left her the residue of his goods after debts and other legacies had been paid. He gave to William Campion alias Wright, his sister's son, £6 to be paid him at 18 years of age, and

> *if his mother to marry before then, he that shall marry with her shall be bound to my supervisors for the payment of the same to the use of the said William at the time aforesaid and ... I give unto him one brass pot.*

William was probably Margaret's illegitimate son, although this is not specifically stated in the will.

Friends and servants

On the whole, the wider distribution of gifts among friends and the children of friends that was seen in the Tudor wills does not occur in the wills of the early Stuart period. An exception was Jeffrey Limner, wheelwright (1617), whose only son had died two years previously, and who named no blood relatives among the beneficiaries in his will. (See pp. 114-15.)

Bequests to known servants included 12d 'to every servant with him at his death' from John Rosell (1605), the Limner bequests to their servants (1615 and 1617) and half a crown to each of his servants by Robert Butler (1654). Miles Cragge, labourer and shepherd (1635), left 5s to his servant, and widow Joane Needham (1658) gave her cousin Robert Needham 'who is now my servant' 10s.

As has been seen, bequests continued to be made to the local squire and his family, apart from those given in return for acting as executor or supervisor. Harold Greene (1613) left 6s.8d to his 'very good mistress' Margaret Rosell and a ewe hog to Mr Gervase Rosell, son of George. Robert Greene, husbandman (1624), left 20s to Mr Gervase Rosell. Miles Cragge, John Rosell's shepherd, generously left one ewe sheep each to 'Mr George Rosell, Mr Thomas Rosell, Mrs Margaret Rosell and Mrs Anne

Rosell' (1635). Widow Margaret Franke (1653) left 20s to a later George Rosell, gentleman, and 40s between George's brother and sister. John Stapleton, husbandman (1639), left the three children of Captain (Gervase) Rosell £15 between them - the same amount he had bequeathed to the only relatives mentioned in his will, his brother and niece!

Household goods and clothes

As has been seen, these early 17th century testators still wished to be remembered by their families and friends through the personal and often useful items they left them, such as pewter and brass dishes and the salt left by Joane Needham in 1658. Thomas Parker (1603) bequeathed to his son Richard 'a little coffer bound about with iron', in which he could keep objects of value and documents, as well as a silver pot with six silver spoons and a fire iron. He also expressed a desire to keep as much as possible of the family's household goods together, for although he left money, it was on condition

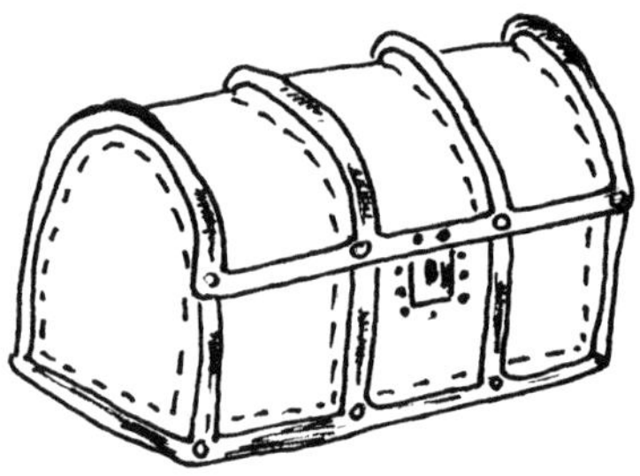

A 'little coffer bound about with iron'

> *always that there shall be no goods stirred or taken for the payment of these [a]for[e]said legacies within my now dwelling house so long as there is either corn, cattle or any other goods without doors sufficient to make payment for the same.*

The will of the childless widow Sislie Drecot (1634) gives an insight into what possessions were prized by an ordinary woman. She distributed her goods among members of the Campion family, of whom she may have been a member prior to marriage. She gave each of her three sisters a hive of bees. The sons, daughters and grandchildren of her residuary legatee John Campion received household goods and animals, each of the girls receiving one of the following items: a green blanket, a pillow case, a pewter doubler, her best brass pot, best coverlet and one linen sheet; the boys shared a ewe and lamb and a ewe sheep among them. Isabel Drecot of Aslockton, perhaps her sister-in-law or niece by marriage, was given a mattress, a bolster, a pair of harden sheets, a hempen sheet, a blanket, a coverlet, a brass pan, her hat, a russet safeguard and a waistcoat. Members of the Scrimshawe family, perhaps relatives too, received other gifts: Margaret a hive of bees, William son of Robert of Cotgrave a table, form and chest, and John a brass pot. Although her husband had been described in his will as a labourer, he had a house to leave as did Sislie herself, and she left a small amount of money: 10s equally between Isabel Kirkling's children of Long Clawson, and 12s each to the two supervisors of her will.

Examples of mid-17th century dress

Clothes were favoured items in these wills; at this period they were still being made of heavy durable materials, including leather. Thomas Parker (1603) would seem to have cut something of a fine figure when mounted for, as already noted, along with horses, best saddle, bridle, girth, stirrups, boots and spurs, he left a sword and dagger and his best cloak! Robert Henson (1628) simply left all his wearing apparel to his three children, one of whom was a daughter. Details of clothes usually appeared only in wills made by those who had no direct descendants, so it seems likely that they normally went to the children of the deceased. Humphrey Campion (1614) though he died childless, had a fair number of kin. To Roger Campion the parish clerk, who may have been his brother, he left his linen shirt and to Roger's son 'my best doublet and my best hat'. Richard Marbid of Cotgrave was to have a pair of leather breeches. John Stapleton, also childless, left to Humphrey Ward 'my green doublet', to Henry Smith 'my grey coat', 'all the rest of my apparel' to his brother Rowland and to the fortunate Roger Campion 'my best hat' (1639).

Debts

There are again a few references to debts in the wills of this period including those owed to John Rosell (p.109). Harold Greene (1613) asked that his brother Robert should have 'a land of barley to be sown for him at the springs and a land of peas to be sown for him at 'Ravensaker' in satisfaction for all reckonings betwixt him and me'. Jeffrey Limner's will (1617) settled his debts of 42s to his servant Elizabeth, probably for wages, and £3.8s.8d to Mr Cotes (the vicar). John Stapleton (1639) instructed that two legatees have 9s 'in the hands of Thomas Rippon'.

VII Social Relationships - Legacies 1660-1714

The wills from the late 17th century (30 excluding two prestigious Rosell wills) are very different in character from those of earlier periods, both in the type of legacies made and the choice of legatees. Gone is the detail about household goods and other possessions. Only five specify household furniture and utensils and only three mention clothes. Again only five include farm goods but all leave money, whereas in the Tudor wills the position was reversed. More now left property of some kind, but only one bequeathed artisans' tools or materials. Although the wills represent only a minority of the villagers, these facts indicate a very changed world, at least for some members of the community. The 16th century testators whilst making their wills had dwelt with some pleasure on the few goods they had to bequeath. By the late 17th century many had become accustomed to having better-furnished houses. Farm gear which had been accumulated slowly over generations could now be found on many well-equipped farms. Bequests of money instead of goods, usually by the more prosperous, were often made in order to avoid splitting up the family farm and its equipment.

In addition, whereas the earlier wills were full of bequests to godchildren, friends and servants, besides any number of religious institutions in pre-Reformation times, now the emphasis was very much on the testator's immediate family, with only 13 making bequests to their wider kin, 11 to friends or their children and three to servants. Two left something to members of the landlord's family, none to the minister or godchildren and ten to charity, usually the poor of Radcliffe. The Tudor community was based on shared interests; in a harsher world people were more dependent on each other. The later Stuart family which was affluent enough to leave a will, had less need to lean on other people in hard times, for example by borrowing tools or equipment. Such people probably did not feel it was necessary to repay favours with gifts or ensure support for their families in the future. This in itself would have exaggerated the gap, which was widening at this time, between the well-off and the poor.

Real estate

Of these wills, 14 (including those of Thomas and Gervase Rosell, 1685 and 1687) refer to the handing on of real estate, where the terms of the testator's tenancy allowed him to do so. In some cases the widow was to hold the property jointly with a son or daughter. John Hutchinson, yeoman (1671), shared his land between his wife and son, his wife receiving the customary third. Robert Oliver, cordwainer (1692), also left the residue of his estate jointly to his wife and son William, but his wife could dispose of his house 'at her will'. Richard Foster, blacksmith (1696), laid down what share of the land surrounding his house should go to his widow: 'two quarters and half the orchard, a cowgate and a little barn'. She would share the house itself with son William, the residuary legatee, and on her death the property was to pass to him entirely.

In others the son or daughter would not succeed to any property until the mother's death. For example, John Parr, yeoman (1666), ultimately left that part of his dwelling house, together with three oxgangs of arable and two closes which he had purchased of his father Henry Parr, to his son Robert, but the young man could not inherit in his mother's lifetime. William Parr was John's eldest son and in the 1664 Hearth Tax they were each taxed on one hearth, which suggests that William had already been provided with a property during his father's lifetime. In his will, therefore, John Parr was ensuring that the younger son, Robert, would have a home after his mother's death. Matthew Simmons, shepherd (1688), also provided for the devise of his house after his widow's death. The cottage with one croft and four acres of arable and all appurtenances was to go first to his son-in-law Thomas Fletcher for 10 years and thereafter to his own son, also Matthew, and his heirs forever.

John Walker, labourer (1670), would seem to have had two houses. The one he was presumably occupying when he made his will is not mentioned, although he is shown in the 1664 Hearth Tax paying tax on one hearth. In his will he left his wife his 'cottage house now in the possession of Will Alcock with all the appurtenances, commons and common of pasture thereunto belonging'. In the Hearth Tax, Alcock pays on one hearth and would probably continue to pay rent for this cottage to Walker's widow.

Three wills make provision for the sale of real estate to pay debts and legacies. Two of these wills were made by the Pilkingtons (see pp. 195-6) whose money was obviously tied up in their land. John Pare (1697), whose status was unspecified, was also a man of some substance. His cash bequests totalled £100.15s and his inventory was valued at £66.4s.10d. He instructed his wife and brother to sell land and goods to pay his debts. In contrast to the Pilkington and Pare wills, squire Thomas Rosell (1685) optimistically assumed that the rents and issues from his lands and the sale of household goods would be sufficient to meet debts and legacies, without needing to sell land.

The widow's inheritance

The widow's right to a third of her husband's chattels remained in force in ecclesiastical law in the Province of York only until 1693. Pressure from the community to treat the widow fairly, however, probably ensured that the tradition was maintained and there is no evidence that it ceased. As shown in the previous section, a widow continued to be allowed to remain in the family home, either singly or jointly with a child, when her husband was able by the terms of his lease to pass on his property. Where no right to such property is mentioned, one can assume that her position would depend on manorial custom. Four wills of this period made the wife sole residuary legatee of personal estate where there were surviving children. In only one case, that of yeoman William Parr (1693) were the children under age. William left his goods and chattels to his wife Mary 'to bring up my children' with the assistance of two trustees.

In nine wills the wife was either joint residuary legatee, with a son or daughter, or received a share of the goods when a child was appointed residuary legatee. John Hutchinson's widow was left all the goods in the house in addition to a third of the land, the son John being residuary legatee and executor (1671). Richard Foster's wife, who, as already mentioned, was left a share of the land surrounding their cottage and her widow's bed, was also to receive £4 a year from her son William, the residuary legatee, and one load of coals per annum for the term of her life (1696). The remaining seven wills left no specific bequests to the wife, but in two wills the disposition of the family home after her death presupposed that she would remain in occupation until then. In the other five wills, the wife was appointed sole executrix with power therefore 'to pay all debts and legacies' as William Alcock's will stated (1696); John Greene's widow Dorothy was given 'full power to dispose of my estate as seemeth fit' in 1682. In both these families, the children were minors and trustees were appointed to look after their interests.

The children's portion

In addition to the specific bequests of real estate mentioned in the first section, all later Stuart testators left money to their children, even if only implicit in their appointment as residuary legatees. The amount ranged from £800 to Thomas Rosell's daughter in 1685 either at 21 or on the day of her marriage (which proved hard to extract), down to bequests of a shilling. As there were a number of these, it would seem that they may have been token legacies, rather than expressions of parental displeasure, because the children concerned had already received their portions. Several sons-in-law were given this amount, as were sons and daughters by blood. Richard Musson, farmer (1712), for example, left his son and daughter and his daughter's husband 1s each, despite the fact that his inventory was valued at over £220. His children, however, would almost certainly have received their portions already, and though his wife was residuary legatee her estate would ultimately be shared between them.

Eleven of the testators left children who were still minors, and these were carefully provided for, consistent with their fathers' circumstances. Two members of the extensive Butler family left under-age children. In his will of 1676 Richard Butler (son of the Robert who had moved from Langar) left his land and personal estate jointly between his wife Ann and son Robert, the latter to take up his share at age 18. One daughter was to have £80 at age 21 and the other £60 at the same age, and if either died before 21, the survivor was to receive £110.

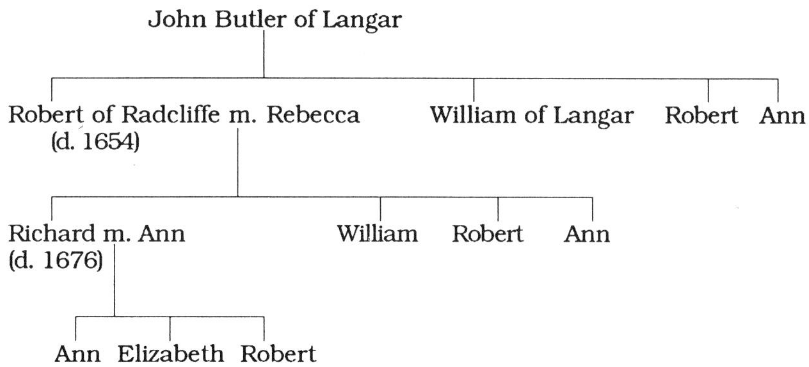

The Butler family, originally from Langar

Another Robert Butler, a husbandman whose relationship to the Richard who died in 1676 is obscure, made his will in December 1689 and died less than two months later. He was married twice, firstly to Margaret Greene by whom he had a son Richard, and secondly to Margaret Smith, by whom he had two daughters, Ann and Elizabeth, born in 1686 and 1688 respectively. Robert left his house and lands to Richard, requesting that when he entered into them he should pay £15 to his half-sisters between them, and in addition £10 to their mother when they were 16 and £5 to each sister at age 18. Margaret Butler died in 1691 long before the girls reached the age of 16. After her death the probate court appointed Richard as tutor/curator of his half-sisters until they were 21 or should marry. He had to promise to 'honestly educate and bring them up with sufficient meat, drink, clothes and all other necessaries during their minority', for which he entered into a tuition bond for £100.

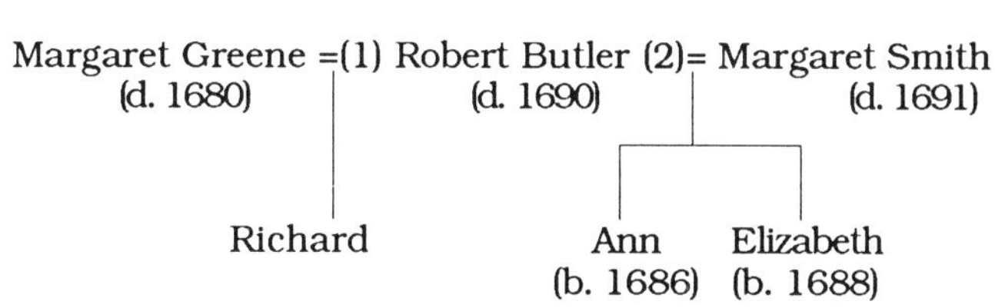

Robert Butler's family

The burden on the eldest son to provide for younger siblings could be considerable. William Parr, yeoman (1693), left all his goods and chattels to his wife Mary to bring up his children, but if she died before they received their portions, the eldest son Thomas was to continue to bring them up and pay their portions as follows: William (aged 13) £30, youngest son John (aged 6) £40, Elizabeth (aged 11) £20 and Mary (aged 9) £40: perhaps the difference in the amounts was a reflection of what had already been spent on them in terms of education, setting them up as apprentices, servants in husbandry or domestic servants.

Trustees could be appointed from outside the immediate family to oversee the bringing-up of minors. Although John Grccnc's widow Mary was given full power to dispose of his estate (1698), the four children's uncle and a friend were appointed trustees 'for my poor children', each child to receive £5 at age 21. William Alcock, shepherd (1696), left two under age sons, who were each to receive £24 at age 21, and two trustees were appointed to assist their mother. Almost three years after William's death, one of the trustees entered into a tuition bond, similar to that for Ann and Elizabeth Butler, to educate and bring up one of the sons, the other perhaps having reached the age of 21 by that time. No mention is made of his mother having died, but either this was so or she had remarried and it was preferable for the boy to stay with someone he knew rather than a strange stepfather.

Household goods, which made the earlier wills so interesting, are rarely mentioned as being given to children in this period: they include a flaxen sheet, a chest, and gifts to William Cooke's daughter Alice of a feather bed and bedstead, one new blanket and a pewter dish (1682). Moreover, there are no specific bequests of farming equipment and only two gifts of animals to children. One daughter was to have two sheep. Bartholomew Webster's son Bartholomew was left 'a ewe and lamb the best that he will choose at May Day following', in addition to £18 within one year of his father's death (1669). Bartholomew the elder, a labourer, shared the tools of his trade between his two sons. The will stipulates that the widow (referred to as 'my now wife' so probably a second marriage) should take a groat a day (4d) out of Bartholomew the younger's wages when he ate at her table, but not when he ate at his own table. It seems likely that he was her stepson and that she was employing him from time to time to help her.

Grandchildren

Bequests to grandchildren continued to be a mix of money, farm animals and some household goods. The most substantial gift of money was made by Richard Foster, blacksmith (1696), whose inventory was valued at £24.3s.8d. He left to his two daughters the token 1s each, but their seven children, three children of his son William, and another five children (possibly grandchildren or nephews and nieces) were given 40s each, a total of £30. John Yardley, shepherd (1664), left one granddaughter £3 and two other grandchildren 'a little heifer between them'.

The wider family

Thirty percent of the wills of this period contain legacies to brothers and sisters and/or their children. The more substantial gifts occur in the wills of those testators without surviving wives or children, as one would expect. Farmer George Franke, who died childless, inherited the residue of his mother Margaret's estate as her only son, and also all the estate of his uncle Anthony Franke, a bachelor. In 1669 he left £15 to his sister Gertrude to be shared equally with her son and £15 to her daughter. To three nephews he left 20 nobles (a noble was worth 6s.8d) each to be paid within two years after his death. A note was inserted in the will, apparently at a later date, that one of the nephews was dead and so 30s of the 20 nobles was to go to that nephew's son and the remainder to another nephew, John Greene, George's executor and residuary legatee. These nephews and nieces had already benefited from their grandmother Margaret Franke's will several years before.

The remaining bequests to relatives consist of amounts of money varying from 5s to £5. A brother-in-law was left 5s to buy gloves and Thomas Rosell left to his sister and half-sisters £5 each to buy mourning (1685). Some clothes continued to be distributed as legacies: John Greene, farmer (1682), left to his brother his best suit of clothes, as did John Pare to his brother (1697), but Isaac was to have 'my worst suit' - perhaps John Pare had only two suits worth passing on! Simon Chadburn, labourer, left all his clothes to be divided equally amongst three friends in 1681.

Landlords and servants

The Rosell family benefited from two of the wills; George Franke (1669) left to his landlady, Mistress Elizabeth Rosell, and to her sister-in-law Mistress Ann Rosell 5s each to buy (mourning) gloves, and 10s each to Elizabeth's children - Gervase and Elizabeth. John Greene, farmer (1682), gave to the four elder children of his landlord, Mr Thomas Rosell, 7s each and the youngest son 5s.

John Greene also remembered his two servants leaving them 2s.6d each (1682), but there are few such bequests compared to earlier times. John Pare (1697) left 5s to his maidservant and Thomas Rosell left 40s to his principal servant, William Smith, and 5s each to his remaining servants.

Debts

There are only two references to debts owed to the testator in the later Stuart wills. In 1689 Thomas Smith the shepherd forgave his son-in-law John 36s which he owed him. John Alvey in 1687 agreed to pay his mother Rebecca 20s and give her yearly at Christmas two strikes of wheat and three strikes of barley 'in consideration of four lands formerly due to her upon an agreement made betwixt her and me'.

More information about debts owing to the deceased comes from the inventories. William Pilkington junior (1699), had £8 owing to him; Thomas Smith (1690) £9 and Robert Barr, brickmaker (1680), £2.6s.6d for wages and a further unspecified 9s.6d. Edward Holmes, labourer (1664), had loans of £10, £2 and £3 out on bond, his total inventory being valued at £41.14s. John Hutchinson, a bachelor or widower living in lodgings, (whose inventory was valued at £21 in 1701) also lent £10 on specialty i.e. in bonds and £10 without specialty. All those who had money owing to them were either labourers (including the brickmaker) or men who had little farm stock and did not, therefore, have to invest any surplus money back into the land. In most cases, too, their family commitments were relatively light.

In contrast was Thomas Parr, husbandman (1708), who owed the very large sum of £80 and funeral charges of £1. His executors would not have been able to repay these debts by the sale of his goods because his inventory was only valued at £43.10s.2d. No will has survived for him, so his marital state and family are unknown.

VIII Houses and their Furnishings 1603-1714

Evidence from the early Stuart period

In Radcliffe there is little written evidence about the sort of houses people lived in before the first inventory of 1653. Any attempt to reconstruct them must draw heavily on general studies of vernacular building in the region. The pattern of development is clear, however, for a side effect of the rise in living standards in the 16th century was a revolution in housing from the later years of Elizabeth's reign. For the less wealthy this would have taken the form of improvements rather than of new houses, such as the division of houses to cope with a growing family. The hall might be partitioned into two rooms, with a fireplace dividing them and a new brick chimney stack usually built on the axis of the house (rather than at the gable end or on the side as in some regions). In this way a parlour was acquired. A third room, perhaps a service room such as a kitchen (which was not used for cooking) or a milkhouse, or a chamber over the hall or parlour would then be added. The alterations would be agreed between the tenant and the landlord's steward when the lease came up for renewal, the tenant often supplying the labour and the landlord raw materials from his estate. The purpose was not so much to gain privacy, a notion largely foreign to those of lesser status in the early 17th century, as to provide more space for the increasing amount of household goods. Higher yields from farming also required more rooms for processing and storing foods, such as butter, cheese and bacon. In the East Midlands the number of single-roomed cottages was decreasing by 1635, and there had been a substantial growth in the number of houses with more than two rooms.

Eight cottages were noted in the rental of 1604. These were probably no more than one or two-roomed units and quite likely still made of the poorest materials; mud and turf for the walls and untrimmed timbers for the roof. A cottage, although it usually had a garth or garden, rarely had any farm buildings of any description. There was one, however, belonging to Edward Towle, which had a backside. This backside was singled out for special notice in the rental and so may have been a farm building or even a service room added on to the back of the house. Such cottages continued to be built for many years yet. Notes written by an inhabitant in 1877 recorded:

The Green has been very much altered since first I knew it. Many of the houses were formerly partly of mud and partly of stone and thatch. They were built in the 17th century or thereabouts.

In 1610 the magistrates at Quarter Sessions, who guarded against the unchecked proliferation of cottages, allowed Henry Watson 'being poor and incapable' to build a new cottage for himself. In 1630 it cost John Sheppard, the miller, only £3 to build a cottage for himself, his wife and his mother-in-law.

Traditional methods of building persisted and there was little use of brick for the building of humbler homes at this stage, except for the insertion of chimneys. (In Radcliffe the first reference to a brickmaker is in 1637). The roof would be thatched with wheat, rye or barley straw which the farmers could put on themselves, or reed thatch which required a professional craftsman. Floors were usually of earth even in better houses and upstairs boards were often kept loose to make it easier to get bulky items into the chambers. A feature of the East Midlands was the use of gypsum plaster laid on reeds and joists for flooring. Renovations to the court house of the manor of St John of Jerusalem in Cotgrave in 1704 included making these floors. Bills were paid 'for Ground Sealing' and 'to the masons for shooting the floor, Burning the Plaster and under drawing the floor', which with the purchase of deals, nails, and lime and plaster amounted to £6.9s.4d. Floors of this type may be found in some of the older houses in the village today, for its use continued to be popular into the 19th century.[305]

Inventories provide an invaluable insight into houses, their size and their furnishings. As the appraisers worked, they often noted down the room they were in, building up a picture of the deceased's home (though they may of course have left some rooms out). The inventory made on the goods of the affluent widow Margaret Franke in 1653 only indicated a hall, kitchen, with no implements for the hearth in it, and an uncertain number of chambers. She probably shared her house, however, with her son and perhaps her nephew, both bachelors and may not have been in possession of the whole house. Widow Joane Needham's house, as outlined in her inventory of 1658 (p. 203), was typical of the more prosperous husbandman's, with its hall, parlour, two chambers and a brewhouse.

Later Stuart houses

The restoration of the monarchy in 1660 brought a renewal of building activity, which had been largely interrupted by the Civil War and the Interregnum. A map (not covering the whole of Radcliffe) made to accompany a survey of land held by the Rosells in 1710 (p. 163), with small drawings of houses on it, provides some evidence of the sort of housing in the village in the early 18th century. There are six cottages on Butt Green with chimneys, probably occupied by squatters without legal rights because they are sketchily drawn. In addition there are 15 two-storeyed houses, some with outbuildings within the homesteads and all except one close to the main street of the village. Ten of these have two bays mostly with one axial chimney stack. Four houses are divided into three bays, one with one chimney and three with two. Gervase Rosell's manor house with its three bays, four storeys and three chimneys and a number of outbuildings stands out as being by far the grandest.[306]

Rooms and their uses

More inventories survive from this period, not just from Radcliffe, but from all over the country. Houses everywhere were growing in size; there were now more with five to seven rooms, many of these being different kinds of service rooms. Parlours were frequently described as 'new'. In the East Midlands the parlour was still being used as a bedroom rather than as a sitting room, chambers were still used for storage, and cooking was still done in the hall (often called the house), for this was an essentially conservative region where traditional patterns of family life remained unchanged.

The record of housing in Radcliffe from inventories fits this general picture. Details of rooms were given in 20 inventories made after 1660 (excluding those of the two squires Thomas and Gervase Rosell, 1685 and 1687, which are untypical and are fully dealt with on pp. 150 and 155).

Houses	Rooms	Householder's occupation
1	8	Yeoman
1	7	Unknown
3	6	Yeoman, unknown (2)
7	5	Yeoman, husbandman (2), shepherd, blacksmith, fisherman, unknown
2	4	Cordwainer, widow
5	3	Husbandman (2), shepherd, brickmaker, widow
1	2	Labourer

There was always at least one parlour. Four people had an extra parlour and they distinguished them one from another by adding the prefixes little, over, upper. The appraisers of two inventories referred to the nether parlour, indicating that the original parlour unit had been divided and that one was reached by going through the other. Others referred to the netherhouse and to the nether chamber. Edward Holmes the labourer, who had only two rooms, had a nether parlour in 1664. All the parlours (except two which were extra ones) were still used for sleeping in, though five of them also contained dining furniture. All the houses had at least one chamber, three had two and one had three; one inventory referred to 'Above Stairs', confirming that a staircase was in fact used and that the room or rooms in this case were not simply boarded-in lofts reached by a ladder. Most of them contained mainly beds and bedding and storage for clothes and linen, but in one there was nothing recorded but barley and five also contained bacon flitches and cheeses.

Eleven houses now boasted a kitchen, but only one appears to have been used for cooking. The gallowbalks (gallowtrees), hooks, reckons or ratchets by which cooking pots and pans were hung over the open hearth were still found in the halls. In one there were two spits. Kitchens, however, may well have been used for food preparation because in them were to be found all manner of barrels, tubs, and leads with the occasional table. There was a dairy in seven houses and one milkhouse, but two of these households kept their cheesepress in the kitchen and one kept the churn there. Four other kitchens also contained a cheesepress. The dairy was more often than not a store for the pewter and brass, perhaps because it had the best facilities for washing up. Tubs, planks, shelves and milk vessels were also to be found there, but never cheeses. A ripening cheese was thought to be harmed by being in a room with moist ingredients such as milk, so the cheeses themselves were variously stored in the kitchen, a parlour or the chambers. William Butler (1699) kept 15 cheeses in one of his chambers along with bedding for the unfortunate member of his family who slept there! One household kept two bacon flitches in the dairy, but in four other cases they were scattered around the house like the cheeses. Two houses had a buttery, normally a cool room where brewing might take place; one contained four cheese vats and various items of food preparation and one was used for storing three wheels (for spinning) and three leather bottles. There is a solitary reference to a larder where brass and pots and pans were kept and a cellar, but whether fully below ground was not specified.

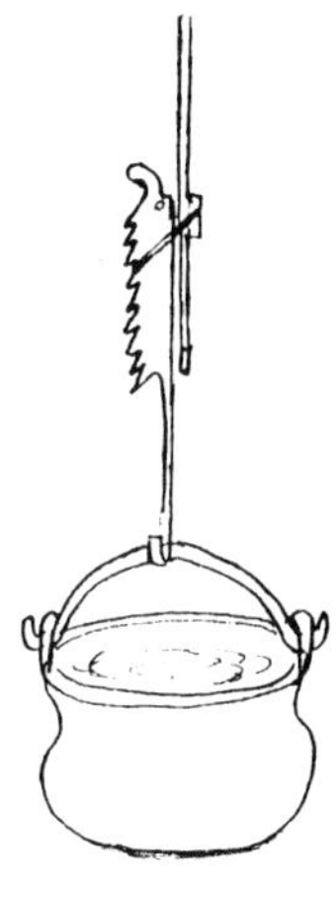

Ratchet (reckon) with cooking pot

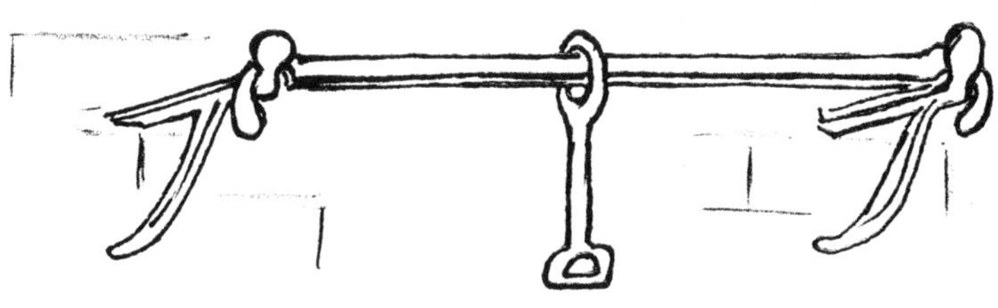

Sketch of 3 feet wide iron gallowtree (gallowbalk) balanced on supports with suspended ring for hanging a pot over the fire (perhaps from a reckon). It survives (1996) in a late Stuart Radcliffe house

Surviving buildings

Radcliffe is no different from many other Nottinghamshire villages in that any remains of Elizabethan and early Stuart phases of building have been largely overlaid in later times. Only buildings occupied by the more affluent and built of substantial materials have even partially survived, although some 18th and 19th century houses in the village may have older foundations and remnants of a previous house within them. As already noted (p. 57), Tudor Grange has developed from the Rosells' manor house. The building opposite the church, known as the Manor House, has a 17th century core, while 17th century beams, ingle nook fireplaces and fittings can be found in the much altered Old Manor House near Lamcote corner. These last names suggest that the sites were occupied by earlier manorial houses.

In 1995 at least two Stuart houses retained much of their original structure - 37 Water Lane (see pp. 225-7) and 1 Walnut Grove. The latter house probably dates from the later 17th century as it was built of brick and was not timber framed. Its high pitched roof suggests that it was formerly thatched, and remnants of thatching found in the roof, where some of the early timbers may have survived, confirm this. The ground plan of this house is similar to that of 37 Water Lane, with the main entrance opening from within its own grounds into a cross passage between the hall and a second room (kitchen or parlour). The two rooms shared a back to back ingle nook fireplace, beyond which was a staircase to an upper floor. The ground floor dimensions are 17 feet deep throughout with the kitchen or parlour 9 feet 4 inches long from the passage to the outside wall. The length of the hall is 15 feet 4 inches into the ingle, and a third room beyond is 10 feet 6 inches long. These downstairs rooms have ceilings with chamfered and end-stopped main beams. The upper floor has been changed too much for a reconstruction of the original plan to be possible.

House furnishings

Some examples of household goods have already been mentioned in the analysis of wills above. Inventories also provide information about furnishings, but those of the late 17th century are less rich in detail when compared to earlier examples which have survived from other parishes. (None of those made in Radcliffe, for example, give descriptions of the deceased person's clothes, nor what was found in their purse, but only supply their combined value). Inventories were made on movable goods, the interpretation of the term 'movable' being at times unclear. In William Greene's inventory of 1663, for example, four doors were valued at 3s.4d. They were, perhaps, not fixed, but items such as window glass, floor boards or wainscoting were also in an ambiguous category as they could be taken to a new home.

When drawing up an inventory, assessors may not have included all items of furniture. For example, the widow's bed and a convenient storage chest were customarily excluded, as were items regarded as heirlooms which should not be moved from the house. Some people, such as the widowed or the single, may have been living with relatives or in lodgings so not all the furniture in their rooms was their own. It is also possible that the deceased had disposed of a good many items in time to avoid their inclusion in the inventory.

The furniture itself was rarely described in any detail. Rough estimates demonstrate that, as far as household goods were concerned, people put most of their resources into their beds and bedding and their table linen. Two inventories specify mattresses, but only two houses possessed a feather bed and two a cradle. Three people had a set of hangings and one a set of curtains which would have hung from a tester or canopy above the bed. Only Gervase Rosell's inventory of 1687 mention window curtains. Pillows, bolsters, pillow-beres, mattresses, blankets, coverlets, a hilling and sheets, rather than just bedding, are detailed on several occasions. Nearly everyone had a table or boards (which would be placed on trestles or frame), but again their description is lacking. Twelve households had chairs, most of them between one and six, but one man, William Browne, had 23. No type of seating is mentioned in eight inventories, but in others there were forms and stools and in two houses a settle - a bench with a high back and arms at each end. The buffet stool (a dining stool) or form was to be found in three houses and one had a framed stool.

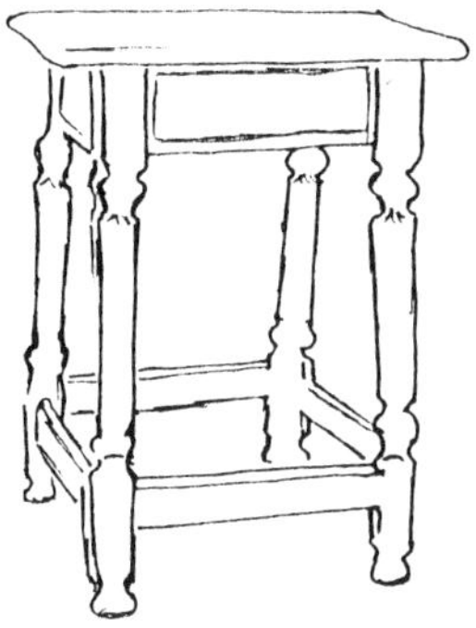

Sketches of 17th century buffet stool and settle

The main rooms of the well-to-do could be lined with decorative oak panelling. An example from about 1680 can be found in Radcliffe now incorporated into a chair in the possession of the church. The two main panels bear diamond shapes, decorated with diamond patterns. There are also two border lengths, one decorated with meandering scrolls with central spiral bosses, and the other with chip carving. It is not known if the panelling originally came from a local house.[307]

Examples of late 17th century panelling now incorporated into a chair which is kept in the village

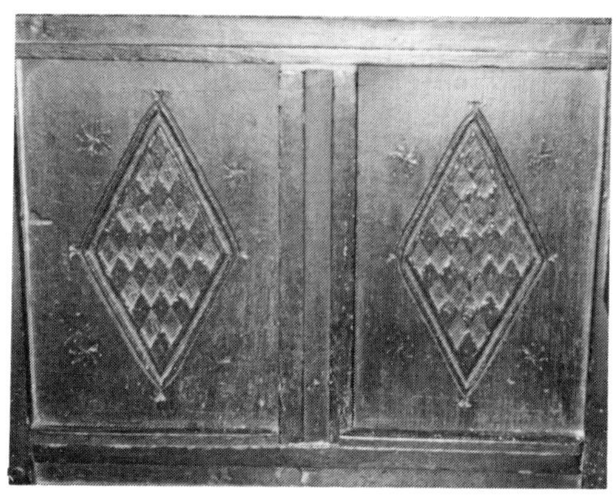

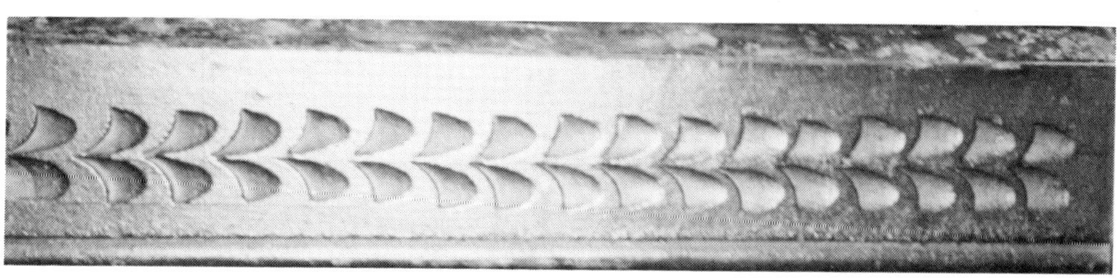

Cushions were itemised in two houses - four in one and six of turkey work in the other (a pile carpet material, possibly made at home by knotting and trimming thick woollen threads through a woven canvas backing). Most of the houses had a cupboard, although only two contained the more convenient press in which clothes might be hung rather than folded. Two people had a livery cupboard which they kept in the parlour; it would have been used for bread and drink to while away the long dark winter nights or for storing clothes. Cupboards, however, were far outnumbered by chests (often for storage of clothes and linen), boxes, whose use was not specified, and trunks (wooden boxes usually with domed lids and covered with nail-studded leather) for storage or travelling. The coffer, which occurred in five inventories, was more likely to be used for documents and other valuables. One household had two arks and another 'an old ark' - a wooden chest or bin, often suspended, for dry stores.

Pewter and brass were universal. In only three inventories is there a reference to the old fashioned wooden ware (treen) or wooden dishes and trenchers, but it is likely that not being of great value, they were usually subsumed under the general item 'other odd things'. Three households possessed flagons and one a tankard. Spoons were sometimes referred to, but no other form of cutlery; the relatively large number of napkins some households possessed being an only too necessary item in the absence of forks, not commonly used until well into this period. Only two testators are recorded as having towels, but no doubt napkins had many uses! Although the wills of the Rosells and of Thomas Parker earlier had indicated that silverware was not unknown in Radcliffe, there were no signs of such luxury among the inventories of the later Stuart yeomen.

Household utensils and vessels were covered by general terms such as porringers, pots, pans and frying pans, but twice a kimnel, which could be used for kneading dough or for dairying, was noted. There were a number of pestles and mortars and querns, and Richard Foster had a handmill - whether for malt, mustard or other grains is not stated. One salting trough is specifically mentioned but other troughs could have been used for this purpose. References to brewing vessels occur in only four inventories, but there were so many other utensils which could be used for brewing, such as leads, barrels and tubs, there is no doubt that home brewing, at least for domestic use, was widespread. The same is true of vessels used for making cheese and butter, but firm evidence that dairying was practised comes from 12 of the households. There is little indication of by-employments, such as weaving, only three households possessing equipment such as wheels or looms, cloth or wool. A copper found in one house would probably have been used for washing clothes.

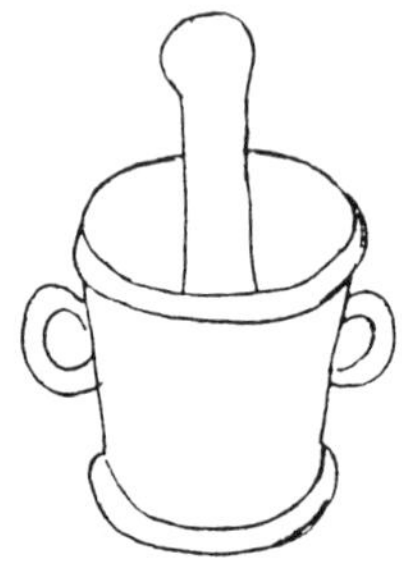

Sketches of 17th century pestle and mortar (above) and metal porringer (below)

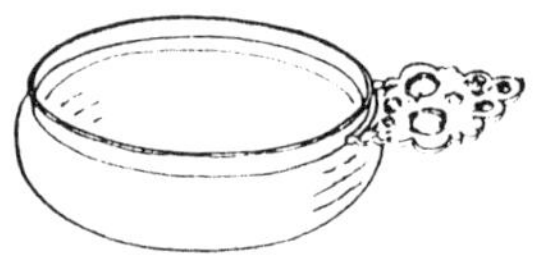

A 17th century table with flagon, tankards, drinking vessel and pipe

Case Study 17

A SEVENTEENTH CENTURY HOUSE - 37 Water Lane

Traditionally the oldest surviving house in Radcliffe, 37 Water Lane is said to date from 1637. The recent renovations have revealed the original timber frame construction typical of the 17th century. This building also illustrates the manner in which houses were being improved during the period studied, as a date of 1709 has been found on rendering near a small upper window, now filled in, probably marking the time when brick infill replaced the wattle and daub. The original roof timbers have not survived and the courses of brick visible above the wall timbers date from a later renovation when the upper storey was raised and the original thatched roof was replaced with tile. The current thatch therefore, although it is probably of the same pitch as the original, does not come down as far or have as low an overhang as it did in the 17th century.

Roadside view of house on Water Lane

The house is built lengthways directly on Water Lane (known at various times as Back Lane and Narrow Lane, but a part of the main route through the village). Originally there was no entry to the house from the street. The overall dimensions of its ground plan are approximately 40 feet by 18 feet - excluding extensions on the south side and recent additions on the west.

The main entrance is away from the road, facing the homestead's land. This leads into a short cross-passage nearly 10 feet long, with a doorway to the left into a room which was most probably used as a parlour. To the right another doorway leads into the main room (the hall or house) which originally measured about 16 feet by 16 feet at its widest point. These two rooms had ingle nook fireplaces, back to back, in line with the house main door. The ingle nook in the main room survives in good condition. The original staircase would have been situated on the street side of the fireplace. Within the ingle nook recess to the right of the fire is a spice cupboard which still retains its 17th century hinges. The main central beam of this room is 11 inches wide, excluding the chamfer which ends in pyramid stops, dating the beam as 16th century. It has been suggested that this beam came from an older building and was reused for the house in the Stuart period. The end nearest the fireplace shows (1995) charring from rushlights or candles which had been hung there. The present clearance between beam and floor is 5 feet 8 inches.

From the hall a doorway opposite the cross-passage leads into a further room, measuring approximately 16 feet by 13 feet. A second doorway (bearing a wooden latch and metal staple which are probably original), also leads to this room on the street side of the house. At one time this gave onto a narrow passage-way which extended across the street-side length of both rooms (from the original stair foot in the hall to the end wall). The floor level of this former passage way was slightly lower than the level in these adjacent rooms. A recently demolished screen, made of some six upright posts with lath and plaster infill of varying widths, but averaging 8 inches, divided this passage from the main part of the end room and probably continued across the hall to the staircase. Until recent alterations were made this passage contained a cool shelf or thrall towards the north east end, perhaps used at one time for storing dairy produce or for brewing vessels.

Although extensive alterations to the upper floor make it difficult to reconstruct the original lay-out, it seems that the 17th century rooms (probably three) led one from another without an independent passage. The external beams (recently uncovered on the street side of the house) were visible internally on the present staircase and upper wall, but are now partially plastered over.

The head of the household in the later Stuart period was Samuel Parr, one of the parish élite who served as churchwarden. Although he was not a tenant of the Rosells, his name appears on the 1710 map of their estate as the occupant of land adjacent to their property - the site still occupied by the house. Samuel was still there in 1725 when he drew up his will, referring to his 'present House and Homestead'. An inventory made on his goods in the same year itemises a hall or 'house', a parlour, three chambers, a dairy and a brew-house. His second son, Richard, inherited the house. Whether Samuel Parr's forebears built it in the first place is not known, but whoever did must have been one of the more prosperous members of the village community at that time.[308]

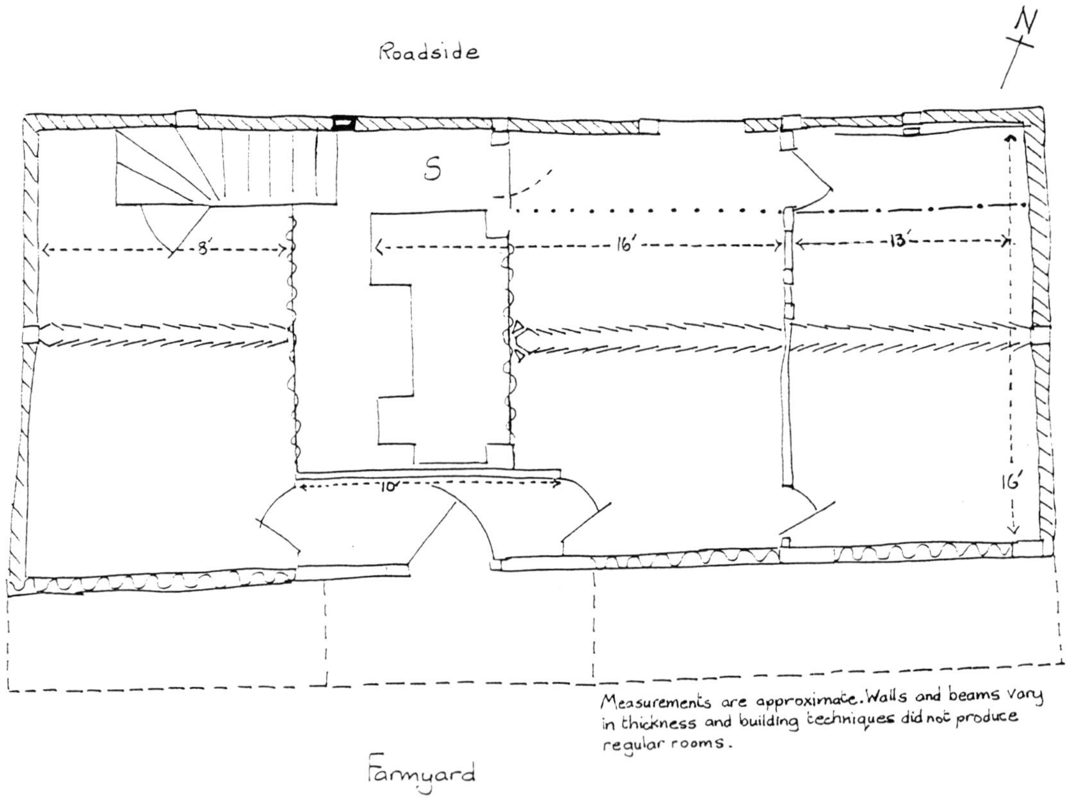

Ground floor plan of 37, Water Lane before internal alterations and 1995 extension.

Most important upright timber at head of stairs once held cross timbers and roof braces.

Exterior walls originally of lath and plaster replaced by rubble and brick infill 1709 and showing position of timber frame uprights uncovered in 1995.

Original wall removed at ground floor level except around main entrance door.

Ground floor extension line.

Position of pyramid stops. Main ceiling beams.

Lath and plaster wall removed in 1995

Change in floor level

Walls from ceilings to top of inglenook openings.

S position of original stairs

Spice cupboard in ingle nook to right of fire.

Ceiling of 'hall' showing main and cross beams

Pyramid-shaped end to main beam

Beams showing wooden pegging

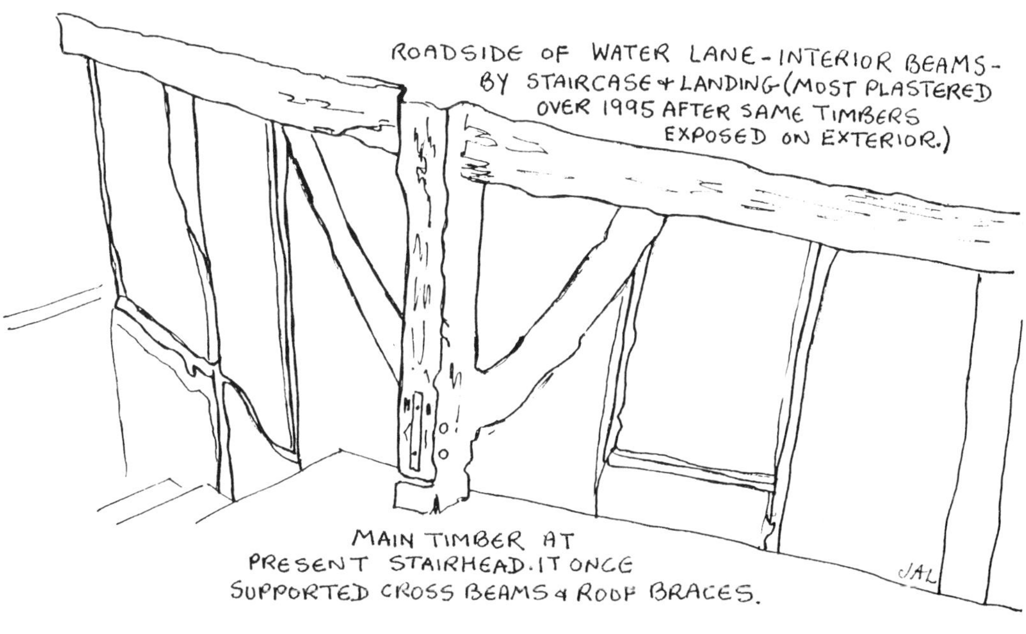

ROADSIDE OF WATER LANE - INTERIOR BEAMS - BY STAIRCASE & LANDING (MOST PLASTERED OVER 1995 AFTER SAME TIMBERS EXPOSED ON EXTERIOR.)
MAIN TIMBER AT PRESENT STAIRHEAD. IT ONCE SUPPORTED CROSS BEAMS & ROOF BRACES.
JAL

Case Study 18

SOME 17th CENTURY HOUSEHOLDERS AND THEIR INVENTORIES

Village history tends to be dominated by the gentry because so many of the surviving records concern them. Occasionally, however, there is enough information to build up a more detailed picture of families of lower status. Some of these stand out because there is something of particular interest in their homes, as shown in the inventories made on their goods, or in their family circumstances.

Two yeomen

William Browne farmed over 91 acres of land on the Pierrepont estate and his inventory, made in July 1689, totalled £191.6s.10d. His family had not been in Radcliffe for long and it is not certain where they came from, but he was married with two very young children. His farm goods comprised 77% of the total and he was clearly among the more prosperous farmers in the village for he possessed good stocks of horseflesh and cattle (including a bull). At the same time he was able to provide a comfortable home for his family, whose tastes appear to have been more genteel than some of their neighbours. Their lifestyle suggests that he was a yeoman, though his status is not given.

His inventory is the only one in this period (except for the Rosells') to show any departure from the traditional patterns of domestic life with regard to where the cooking was done and where people slept. The hall in his seven-roomed house had a fire iron and 'frog' in the hearth where some cooking may still have taken place; but the gallowtree 'and other things' in the kitchen indicates that it was mostly done there. No other inventory had such implements in the kitchen. In the hall were a table, ten chairs and a stool, (but no forms) - too much furniture for his small family, unless the household was larger than is recorded. Perhaps he was particularly hospitable. His main parlour, unlike those of other village farmers, had no bedding in it, but was furnished as a smaller dining room with eight chairs, a table, a form and two buffet stools, no doubt for family use. Someone (perhaps a wet nurse) was still sleeping downstairs, however, for in his little parlour there was 'a cradle and a little rug belonging to it' as well as a bed and bedding. Upstairs the Browne family had a 'best chamber' furnished with a bed and bedding, a chair and table, two chests and a trunk. Three other beds with their bedding, eight pairs of sheets and ten pillowberes were in the nether and little chambers and in one of them there were six turkey work cushions, perhaps worked by Mrs Browne herself. There were altogether seven chests, trunks, coffers or boxes variously distributed among the chambers, but only one cupboard. For the table there were two dozen napkins and five tablecloths, but only one towel. Even William Browne apparently had no silver or plate, only pewter, brass, brewing and milk vessels being itemised. A web of flaxen cloth and one of woollen cloth with wheels and other lumber suggest that his family was engaged in spinning or even weaving.

The cradle with its little rug must have belonged to his daughter Ann who had been baptised on the 7th June 1689. The parish register, which described her father as being lately deceased, was perhaps written-up some time later, for his burial took place on 20th July. His son George had been baptised only about 18 months previously. His death would have left his widow and two young children in a vulnerable position, despite the value of the inventory. As he left no will to assist in placing him socially, little else is known about him, apart from his once having served as churchwarden. His family seems to have left the village, Richard Musson taking over his land.

When Thomas Campion died in 1690 he was living in the largest house, apart from Rosell manor, for which there are surviving details. Despite this, the value of his inventory at £110.10s was low for a yeoman and 90% of it was absorbed by his farm stock. He had eight rooms, though they show few signs of comfort, for the emphasis was on service rooms rather than living rooms and the latter were sparsely furnished. There was only £1 worth of goods in the hall including a fire iron and gallowtree and one table. He must have slept in the parlour where his bedstead and bedding sheets were found and valued at £2.10s. He also had three chambers; one over the parlour, one over the hall and one called the cheese chamber, but

Sketch of 17th century cradle

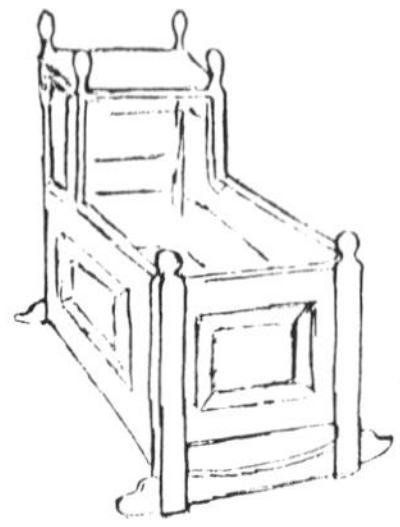

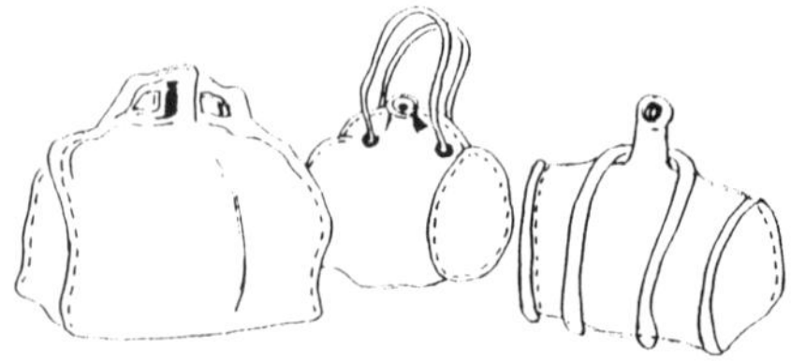

Three 17th century leather bottles

between them they contained only a bedstead 'and all other things' together worth £1. He had a dairy where the pewter was kept, a kitchen where brewing had taken place and a buttery where three leather bottles and three wheels were stored. (There were no cheeses or bacon flitches, nor any spun yarn stored in any room.) Thomas was probably the churchwarden charged with failing to present his accounts in October 1690, but he may have been already ailing for he was buried on 19th December. The following February his daughter Mary was entrusted to the care of William Nicholls of Cotgrave by the church court because her mother Sarah was dead. Sarah's death and Mary's baptism were not recorded in the parish registers, which suggests that Sarah may have returned to her parents (who presumably lived in another parish) before she died, perhaps for her lying-in. This could explain the emptiness of the Campion house when the inventory was taken.

Husbandmen

William Greene, who made his will during the Interregnum but died in 1663, had an inventory valued at £94.6s.4d, 76% of it in farm goods. Although it makes no mention of any rooms, it does give details not often found in other inventories of what is usually covered by the term 'bedding'. There were three bedsteads with two mattresses and a feather bed to go on them. There was enough linen for each bed to have two sheets, a bolster, a pillow with a pillowbere, a blanket and a coverlid. He also had a warming pan.

A 17th century warming pan

The beds and bedding together with a press and four cheeses were the most valuable of his household goods (£8.10s). One board, cupboards, tables and the fire irons were worth £7, but three pans, two pots, two candlesticks, two flagons, 12 spoons, the rest of the brass and five pewter dishes were worth only £2.2s. It was William Greene who possessed the four doors which were valued at 3s.4d and the household goods formed a relatively high proportion of the total value of the inventory (15%). Besides this, he had two bacon flitches and his was one of the few inventories to note the lease of his house valued at £5.16s, though the reason is not known. His wife had recently died and he had two sons of uncertain age.

William Alcock, sometimes called a shepherd and sometimes a husbandman, may have been in a transitional phase between one status and another. He died in 1696 and his goods amounted to only £19.8s. In 1670 he was renting a house from John Walker, labourer, with all 'the commons and common of pasture thereunto belonging' and had invested in livestock - two cows, 18 sheep and one swine, 63% of the inventory total. His status in the village is vouched for by the fact that he had been a churchwarden in 1690. He had only a three-roomed house with one hearth in 1674, but one of his three beds had a set of hangings and he kept six pewter dishes in the hall. His modest inventory indicates a life of frugality, but it allowed him to leave £24 to each of his two sons, both of whom were well under 21, when he died.

Shepherds

Two other shepherds left a will and an inventory. They both appear to have been more affluent than William Alcock, but were not called husbandmen. Matthew Simmons, whose inventory was made in 1689, had livestock and farm goods of a similar value to William Alcock, but they amounted to less of the total value - 42% of £25.16s, for his purse and apparel was worth £2.10s as against William's 6s.8d and he spent more on his household furnishings (but in his will he left no money to his next of kin). He had a second chamber and a buttery and slightly more furniture than William - five chairs, a table and two buffet forms. Matthew had only two beds but more details were given of his linen, which included six napkins and two tablecloths. Both shepherds had five or six pewter dishes, standard ware now even in humble households, but Matthew also had two candlesticks, a tankard, six pewter

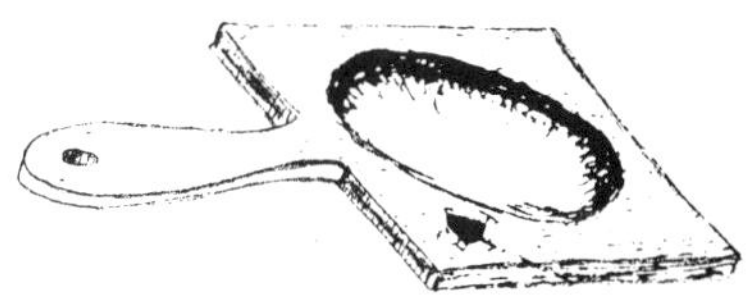

A wooden trencher with salt hole

spoons, a variety of bowls and tubs, a salt, one dozen trenchers and two pancheons. He also had a smoothing iron and a coolen. In the 1674 Hearth Tax he had one hearth.

The family of Matthew Simmons illustrates the way status could rise over several generations. In 1622 Matthew's father William, a labourer, acquired a cottage with one croft and one acre of land in every field in Radcliffe, with their commons, from Thomas Gamble, yeoman. When Matthew, the shepherd, made his will in 1688 he left the property to his son-in-law for ten years after the death of his widow and then to his son another Matthew. The inventory made in September 1689 values 'the fallows and the clots' at 18s.4d and includes crops of cereal and peas. In 1712 the son, now referred to as 'of Nottingham' bought a one acre close in Lamcote, called Dickensons Close, from the Rosells for the sum of £65. An abstract of the title to his estate was drawn up ten years later. He had sold his house and the close to the Duke of Kingston and a cottage to George Duke, the wheelwright. This time, however, he was referred to as 'Mr Matthew Simmons'. He had left the village and taken the first steps towards gentrification.

John Yardley, a widower, was one of those who drew up what might be described as a more 'old fashioned' will in 1664 (a nuncupative one) in that he left gifts of money of over £24 to the poor and a friend, as well as to his immediate family - a son and daughter who were both married, and three grandchildren. His inventory was valued at £62.10s.8d of which £30 was surprisingly accounted for by his purse and apparel. The number of rooms in his house is unknown but the household goods (12% of the total) show the contemporary emphasis and relatively high value given to the bedding - he had three bedsteads or beds, five blankets, four coverlids, three pillows and a bolster, two pillowberes, five pairs of sheets and a towel. All these with four cushions were valued at £4.4s. His furniture included the usual fire implements (he had one hearth in 1664), and only one chair. He had no table, but his ten boards and three forms provided the rougher furniture of more humble households and were no doubt used in a number of ways. These came to £1.4s.2d and, considering his chair was valued at only 6d, it is clear he preferred to spend money on bedding, despite its expense. His vessels and utensils are itemised more carefully than in some inventories. They included a kit and a 'soe' (a large tub) two pewter dishes worth 2s and four brass pans and a pot valued at 10s. Wooden dishes and trenchers were worth 1s.6d. John had worked as shepherd for the widow Margaret Franke - she left him 10s in 1653 - and probably for others as well. He had a number of sheep of his own (33) and his inventory provides rare evidence of wool being woven. Two looms are mentioned, as well as seven yards of woollen cloth valued at 18s. In addition, there was raw hemp and hempen yarn worth 12s.

Bachelors and widowers

Three inventories were made on the goods of solitary men who possessed so little in the way of household goods that they appear to have been living as lodgers, or in a house shared with a relative. One was William Pilkington (see pp. 195-6.) Another, John Hutchinson, probably the son of a yeoman, may have been a bachelor and the appraisers clearly stated that he lived in lodgings. His two nephews were his administrators. When his inventory was drawn up in 1701, his purse and apparel were valued at nothing, he owned no furniture except his bed which was worth £1 and he had no farm goods of any kind. However, he had capital to spare, for money lent out on specialty came to £10 and money lent without specialty 'hoped to be good debts' worth £10, bringing the total of the inventory to £21.

The simple life of a shepherd is clearly revealed in the inventory of the third man Thomas Smith senior, made in 1690 and totalling £10.19s. His wife Elizabeth had died a few years before him and all his children were grown up, but he had at least seven grandchildren (two of them were Ann and Elizabeth Butler, soon to be orphaned when their mother died in 1691. (See p. 217.) His inventory did not mention any rooms and appraised his clothes at 10s, one bedstead and bedding at £1, a brass pan and a brandiron (a stand for a kettle) at 4s, and

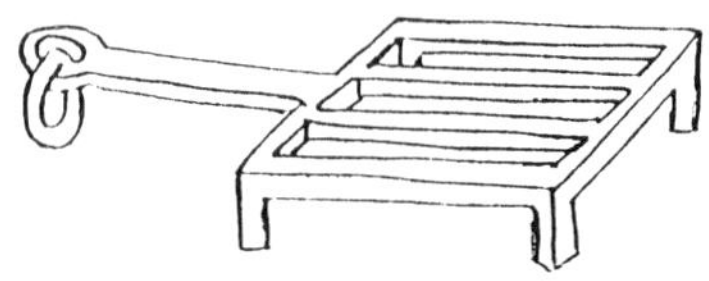

A brandiron

a sheep hog and a theave at 5s. He bequeathed them all to his grandchildren in his will of 1689 with £7 in money and a trunk, which seems to have escaped the eyes of the assessors. These bare necessities sufficed him and the fact that he was also owed £9 suggests either that he was lending money in a small way or that he was owed a good deal in wages.

A labourer and a fisherman

The only labourer with an inventory (made in 1664) was Edward Holmes. He had one hearth in the tax of that year. Although, he and his first wife Grace may have had other children, his will only mentions his son Roger (who would have been 27 years old and who was married with children), his daughter Elizabeth aged 23 and Thomas aged 18 years. In August 1663 just six months before his death Edward, by now a widower, had married Elizabeth Musson a widow of Bingham who had a daughter Ann. In his will he left all that he had to his son Roger together with one flaxen sheet and 12d for himself and his children. The younger son Thomas was to receive 20 marks within one month of his father's death and his sister Elizabeth 20 marks within three months. Besides this, his daughter was to have 'all that bay of building before the entry to make her a house on whilst she keeps her[self] unmarried without paying any rent'. These arrangements show how customary it was to divide a house into separate parts especially where, as in Edward's case, there may have been some grounds for concern about the relationship between his wife and his daughter or perhaps his daughter and her step-sister Ann Musson. (It is less likely that his eldest son Roger and his family shared the house as, in general, it was not usual for different generations of married couples to do so in this period.) He made no provision for his widow, although she was his executrix, but she may have brought an inheritance from her first marriage. There were only two bedsteads in his inventory (valued at £41.14s), but he was well supplied with bed linen, including eight blankets and five coverlids. In the hall were three chairs and he had two arks and a cupboard as well. All his pewter came to £1.10s and all his brass to £2. He also had hemp yarn in his possession valued at £1, perhaps because he was a part-time weaver and £15 was owing to him on bond, which accounted for the relatively high value of the inventory. His investment in agriculture was slight; hay, wood, coals and peas in the barn and three cows - a mere 25% of the whole.

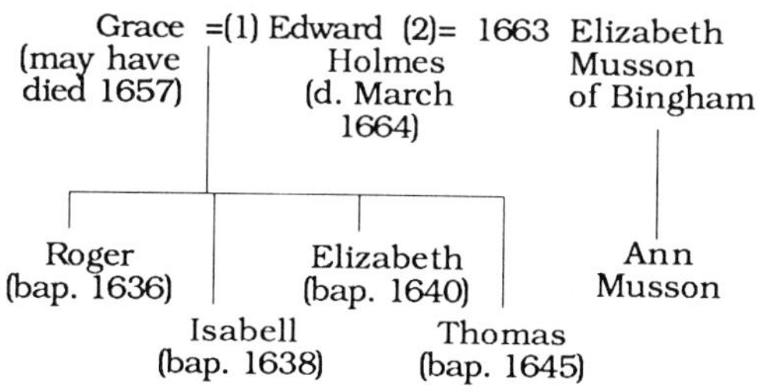

The family of Edward Holmes

The fisherman John Taylor was one of several of his family who made their living from the river; they were often referred to as alias Fisher. He and later his widow Deborah were also among the brewers who appeared so frequently in the manor courts for breaking the assize of ale. He had one hearth in the tax of 1664 and his inventory made the same year came to £29.0s.4d with household furniture accounting for 72% of it. 'All the implements' worth 8s could include his fishing gear. The three tables, forms, chairs, settles and stools, besides the usual fire irons, in the hall would have been just enough to furnish a small ale-house. He also had a considerable collection of cooking and tableware including a brass pot,

Sketch of 17th century brass pot

four brass pans and a frying pan, seven pewter dishes, four flagons, three butter plates, two cups, two muster (mustard) saucers, two salts, one basin and three candlesticks. It looks as if all these were kept in the hall along with two chamber pots and a smoothing iron. The parlour also contained a table and linen, perhaps for the family to eat privately, as well as two beds. His was the only inventory, apart from the Rosells', to include a cellar where he kept seven barrels with all their implements, so his brewing was on a a fairly large scale. In his kitchen he also had a lead, two tubs and a pair of querns (used for grinding malt or mustard). As did many other people, he stored food - in this case two bacon flitches - in the chamber. There was also wool and yarn worth £2, a cow and a sow, indicating some by-employment in the off seasons. His son (John) had been buried in 1650 on the same day as his baptism. There do not seem to have been any other children.

After John's death in 1664 George Taylor, probably a relative, became the local fisherman, paying the Pierreponts for the 'water' and a house and homestead with three beastgates in Eastgang (Hesgang) and other land. In 1704 the steward paid him 10s for 'putting two dozen of small pikes into fish ponds 4d and for fishing the Trent by My Lord's order and for waiting of his Lords[hip] to Haselwood ferry'. As a boatman he had many opportunities for making a living, for he also worked as a labourer repairing the river banks. To these activities he added the family tradition of brewing.

Two widows and an unmarried woman

Margaret Franke's inventory made in 1653 affords a view of the living standards of one of the most affluent families in the village. It totalled £330.16s.4d (including her purse and apparel £6.13s.4d) - the highest for the whole period (the Rosells excepted). She had married John Franke, yeoman, in 1599 and had been widowed in 1626. By the time she died all her children had grown up and had families of their own, except her only surviving son George. He was unmarried and was her main beneficiary. If he was still living with her, as seems likely, then Anthony Franke, her husband's brother and another bachelor could have been in the house too, because in his nuncupative will of 1659 he left all his estate to his nephew 'with whom he lived'. The inventory shows no rooms, but it is obvious that Margaret had ruled a large household, keeping considerable stocks of linen and bedding, perhaps in the hope that her son would bring home a wife to inherit them (he died unmarried in 1672). There were 20 blankets, nine mattresses, 14 bedhillings, one 'poogge', three feather beds, eight bolsters, 12 pillows, 18 pairs of sheets, seven pillowberes, seven bedsteads, but only one warming pan to warm them all! For entertaining she had four board cloths and two dozen napkins with 20 dishes of pewter, 12 pots and pans and a flagon. All the linen was, no doubt, carefully folded away in four chests, a press and two cupboards, but the only other piece of furniture was a chair, which suggests she took her meals at her son's table. Perhaps she occupied just a part of the house which she made comfortable with a pair of curtains and six cushions. She was, however, still mistress of some utensils in the kitchen, which included one lead, three tubs and a cheese press. She also owned extensive farm stock and equipment accounting for 86% of the total value of her inventory.

Alice Dickinson had married Robert, 'scissorem' or tailor in 1642 (he was also briefly the parish clerk). When she made her will in 1690 she had been widowed for many years, because he had died in February 1658, five months before her second son Robert was baptised. Life must have been a struggle for her but she never remarried. There are no further records of son Robert, but she had another son John, who may have been the labourer buried in January 1680, for she mentioned no sons in her will. Witnessing her will was Frances Boot who made his or her mark. This is the first time this family (of Jesse Boot fame) appears in the village records. Of her four daughters, three were married and she had four grandchildren. Her entire legacies consisted of small sums of money totalling 32s. Her inventory of 1691, valued at £6.17s shows that, like Margaret Franke, she must have kept most of the bedding which had been in use when the whole family was at home, for she had four beds with 'all things belonging thereto' which, with a chest, came to £3. Her pewter and brass was valued at £1, whilst the fire iron frogs and everything else in the hall came to £1. In her kitchen she kept milk vessels and a cheesepress, perhaps making cheese and butter for sale from milk provided by others (for she had no cows) or from the five sheep she kept. With her daughter Ann, (still unmarried at the age of 43) she had enough resources to support herself for she had been charged for one hearth on both the Hearth Tax returns.

Elizabeth Chadburn was only 20 years old and still unmarried when she died in 1691. She was one of several children of the labourer Simon Chadburn and his first wife Elizabeth Greene, the only one, however, to be mentioned in his will of 1681. (The two older daughters must have died for he calls her his only daughter). She would have been about 10 years old at the time, so it is surprising that he appointed her as full executrix with his second wife Isabel (previously Elizabeth Walker - she appears to have changed her Christian name on her marriage). After making his will Simon told his wife that he wished Elizabeth to receive £30 when she turned 17, the interest on the money in the meantime to go to her stepmother for 'the full bringing up' of his daughter. Isabel was anxious that these arrangements should be made public and after her husband died, 'out of my well intentions', she had a line inserted into the will stating the amount Elizabeth was to receive. In a statement later tagged on to the end of the will she explained that since, 'upon advice of friends and finding it not lawful, the same was struck out again' - as may still be seen today. Thomas Rosell was witness to both the will and the statement added afterwards, perhaps being one of the 'friends' or advisers in question.

Sketch of 17th century chest

In January 1683 Isabel Chadburn married Thomas Whi(t)te. Elizabeth almost certainly lived with her stepmother and her new husband, for when she died her inventory was appraised by Thomas and Isabel White. A member of her mother's family, John Greene, acted as bondsman. She had no furniture and her only possessions were a pan valued at 10s and a chest worth 3s, her clothes worth £1.4s and two shoes worth 5s. But she still had the legacy of £30 from her father, perhaps stowed away in that chest to be her dowry.[309]

Elizabeth Greene 1665 =(1) Simon Chadburn (2)= 1674 Elizabeth (Isabel) Walker

Ann (bap. 1667) | Sarah (bap. 1668) | William (bap. 1669) | Elizabeth (bap. 1671; d. 1691)

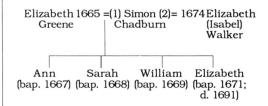

The Chadburn family

FARMING IN STUART TIMES

I Farming 1603 -1660

The appalling weather conditions of the last decade of the 16th century gave way to exceptionally good harvests in the early years of the next. But the fluctuations in crop yields and market prices proved to be as hard for the small farmer to cope with as the former blight; and the good years were soon followed by hardship, especially from 1619 to 1623. Although Radcliffe was well-placed to receive supplies brought up the River Trent, it would not have escaped distress altogether. The subsidy returns, recording tax paid by some of the more wealthy families in Radcliffe and which survive for a number of years, show that a low point was reached in 1622 when the total amount collected was 16s.8d as against 39s the previous year and 46s.8d in 1625. Between 1630 and 1633 the harvests again failed (as they were to in the late 1640s and in the 1690s). From this time on, however, the effects of such crises were mitigated by the fact that the rise in population, which had been so dramatic during the second half of the 16th century, gradually stabilised while improved farming techniques and better marketing began to cope with demand.[310]

Rentals and tenancies

The Pierrepont rental (1601) and the Stanhope rental (1604) show the tenants and the farms or cottages they rented, although the holdings were not necessarily the only ones that they occupied or worked upon. The largest holdings on the 1601 rental were 116 acres 1 rood against the names of John Pickering 'with widow Morris' and 115 acres 2 roods held by Mrs Ballard. A close in Lamcote was among Henry Parr's holdings together with over 8 acres in Lamcote and Radcliffe for which he paid 6s.8d yearly. Five other tenants held between 13 and 52 acres. Two cottagers had an acre apiece, paying 10s a year for them and three others rented 2 roods each. Perhaps because of varying land quality, John Lamminge paid 13s.4d for his, whilst Thomas Towle and widow Elizabeth Cowper paid only 5s each for their half acres. The other three persons renting cottages had one rood of land each. Discrepancies between these rents might be accounted for by differences in the condition of the cottages, the quality of the landholding or the terms of the leases.

Some of the entries in the 1604 rental give quite detailed pictures of what comprised the tenancies. John Grococke paid 12s.9d a year for Tibbott's farm and two 'oxlands' with a toft place, and grazing for two beasts and 15 sheep on the common 'belonging to the said tenancy'. Two leys at the south end of this toft place were rented for a further 9d. Similarly, John Greene paid 13s.4d for his farm and two orchards whilst Edward Capendale was charged 14s.4d for a house, two oxlands, meadow and pasture. When it came to humbler dwellings Thomas Marshall, alias Lynne, and Thomas Cooke each paid only 1d rent for their cottages built on the common. Harold Anstey paid 2s as his cottage had an adjoining croft, as did Edward Towle, probably because his cottage had a 'backside'. George Pare's cottage cost him 2s.6d and Henry Jerman's in Lamcote, with an adjoining croft, was worth 4s.

Four single oxlands were rented by other tenants and the sums paid annually for these varied - presumably reflecting the lands' condition, or perhaps because the tenancy agreements had been drawn up some time apart with different terms. Henry Hall and William Brodfield each paid 5s per annum but John Greene's oxland rental was 6s.8d and that of Thomas Dewsbury 8s.6d. The average value of land calculated from these four 1604 rents was 6s an acre. Henry Jervis was charged just 1 1/2d for two odd lands 'upon a little hill furlong in Breckfield'. Two men farming on a larger scale each paid 50s a year. Thomas Parker's tenancy included renting a house and six oxlands, meadow, pasture lands, and, with the croft barn land, another oxland tenement. As indicated earlier (p.79) Parker had also been a tenant of landlords in Little Malvern, Worcestershire, who owned land in Radcliffe.[311]

The fields

The terms of John Grococke's tenancy in the 1604 rental outlined above show that the system of open field farming continued as it had done in the previous century. By this farmers tilled their allotted lands in the great fields and grazed the animals to which their measures of land entitled them on the common pasture. Some light on local practice is shed by a transaction which took place in August 1622. Thomas Gamble, yeoman, conveyed to William Simmons, labourer, a cottage and a house in Radcliffe with its yard and backside and its entitlement or stint on the commons 'according to the custom of the manor of Radcliffe-on-Trent'. This was given as commons and pasture for two cows and one follower (or young beast) and 15 sheep, and one acre of arable land in every field belonging to Radcliffe with its 'meers and hades'.[312]

Arable farming

Crops, whether growing or stored, were seldom recorded in the wills of this period, even when bequeathed to the main beneficiaries. Of exceptional interest, therefore, is the December 1613 will of husbandman Harold Greene. He left lands in two of the great fields, one of barley to be sown at the 'springs' and one of peas to be sown at Ravensaker - and also 3s.4d to make a shade in the 'heygouys', or Hesgang Pasture across the river. His son John was to have one oxgang in the field of Radcliffe called 'the hall oxgang ploughed, ordered and sown to his own proper use and behoof for two years'. Robert Greene of Lamcote, husbandman, a tenant-in-chief on the Pierrepont estates with a farm in Radcliffe of just over 40 acres, also left instructions in his will of April 1624 about the cultivation of the land. Robert's son William was to till and sow Edmund Wattes' land for his sole use for the coming two years, providing his own seed, but using his mother's plough and draught animals. In return he was to stay with his mother as her husbandman. He was to have the whole crop of corn growing at the time of the will on two oxgangs of land. Four strikes of barley were left to nephews.

Two inventories drawn up during the Interregnum recorded all the crops growing and stored on the farms being appraised. In that of widow Margaret Franke (December 1653) the wheat growing in the fields was valued at £15 and the fallow was also valued at £15. There was £100 worth of corn and hay within the barns around the yard and Margaret must also have rented or borrowed a bay in Dewsbury's barn, which was filled with her barley, and a bay in Gamble's barn, which was filled with her corn. In October 1658 widow Joane Needham's inventory (p. 203) itemised corn in the barn worth £40, corn on the ground at £20 and hay in the barn and the yard at £10. There is no mention of malt in these inventories or in any of the early Stuart wills.

The frequent presence of flax and hempen linen among the legacies in many of the wills of Stuart times and in the inventories from 1653 onwards, suggests that these threads continued to be spun and woven within the household as they had been in Tudor times. Flax or hemp was grown in some of the closes adjoining the village farm houses and cottages. This was a usual practice in Midland or southern counties, where these fibrous plants grow best on rich alluvial soils. Cloth woven from hemp fibres was long lasting, thick and strong. In addition hemp seed was very good for feeding poultry. On 30th September 1621 four Radcliffe men were among 50 persons from 11 villages arraigned before the Quarter Sessions magistrates for washing 'lin et canas', that is flax and hemp, in the River Trent. It was necessary to steep the plants before beating the stems to loosen the fibres, but it was an offence to do this at a place in a river where the animals might drink. Perhaps it made them sick or tainted cows' milk; it was certainly very smelly and the water would have been polluted.[313]

Livestock

Quantifiable evidence about livestock is lacking, but sporadic information is found in wills and inventories. For example, some interesting legacies of horses, mares and foals were made in the period up to the 1640s, after which individual bequests of both horses and cattle thinned to almost none. Yeoman Thomas Parker (1603) left two geldings, one of an iron grey colour along with his best saddle and other riding tackle. A roan horse featured in Richard Dewsbury's will of 1610, a grey gelding in that of Harold Greene of 1613 and a yearling foal in Richard Greene's of 1624. Margaret Franke's inventory made in 1653 included 12 mares, geldings and three colts.

The cattle in the same inventory consisted of oxen, ten dairy cows, 13 young beasts and four calves. Equipment for managing this stock and the 15 horses was worth £15. There was also £1.10s worth of dairying equipment, which included a cheese press. In Joane Needham's inventory of 1658 were ten horned beasts worth £20 but no cows or dairy equipment. Bequests of cattle in wills, were often quite specific as to the animals' age and quality. Harold Greene (1613) left a heifer that was to be kept until it was four years old to Agnes Boweker. Two other cattle, a black steer and a heifer that was standing in the cow hovel, were to be kept for son George until the next Michaelmas. Lamcote husbandman Robert Greene (1624) bequeathed a red cow calf 'at the stake'. This could mean that the animal was tied to a stake or otherwise penned on one of the great field pastures, or was merely grazing on the allotment (the stake) of pasture belonging to the farm holding.

A ewe and a lamb continued to be a favourite bequest as in the Tudor period. Lamb hogs, sometimes specified as ewes, were also frequent gifts, but wethers have disappeared from wills of this period. In 1654, the year when Robert Butler made his will, a ewe and a lamb were worth 7s. He left a bequest of this value - 'about a noble' - to Mary, wife of John Jervis. Margaret Franke's inventory (1653) listed '4 score sheep and 12 odd' (i.e. 92) valued at £16, and equipment for their management, including hurdles, worth £22. With other equipment valued at £2 was a sheep 'tat', and there was a reference to 'fleakes herds'. She employed a shepherd, John Yardley, to whom she left 10s in her will. Included in widow Joane Needham's inventory of October 1650 were sheep and folds together valued at £15.10s.

There is a single reference to swine in the early Stuart wills. Jeffrey Limner the wheelwright left a swine hog in 1617 to Humphrey Drecot. When inventories become available from the 1650s, pigs a-plenty are revealed - 19 swine were counted on Margaret Franke's farm and six on that of Joane Needham. Of Margaret's animals, 12 were being fattened for slaughter and seven were younger swine. These widows had also kept poultry, a housewife's prerogative, valued in Joane Needham's inventory at 5s. (Poultry were not mentioned in the wills of the early Stuart period.)

Bees were given as legacies in two wills of 1604 and 1634. In the first William Greene left two swarms of bees, one to a daughter Ellen and the other to be given to his godson in four years time. Sislie Drecot bequeathed her best hive of bees in the yard and three others to her 'sisters' in the Campion family, and a swarm of bees to John Yardley's children.

Farm equipment and tools

There is no mention of stabling or of cattle sheds as such among the outbuildings referred to in the wills of this period. The hovels in Harold Greene's will of 1613 would have been open-fronted sheds that could have sheltered cattle or horses or been used as store places. They were not the tumble down shacks suggested by modern usage of the term, but were well-floored to suit standing animals or to raise drying crops of beans and peas off the ground. The henge houses in the same will and in that of Richard Dewsbury (1610) were similarly substantial out-buildings, in this case with hinged doors and so closed against the elements. The only cart referred to, one with iron-bound wheels, was also in the will of Richard Dewsbury, which mentions more equipment than does any other of the period. Besides pales or poles (usual spelling), which could be either stakes or fencing made of stakes, there were mangers, querns, a lead and a salting trough. Ploughs, harrows and other such implements were not mentioned in any will.

The two inventories provide more detail. Widow Margaret Franke (December 1653) kept two wains and three other carts with harness on her farm as well as ploughs, gear for horses to pull a plough, yokes and frames (wooden shafts) for coupling draught oxen, five harrows and three sets of leather harness. Except in this inventory, all mention of fleakes has disappeared. There was a plough with 'utensils thereunto' in Joane Needham's inventory of October 1650, as well as a horse trough, and a well-frame bucket.

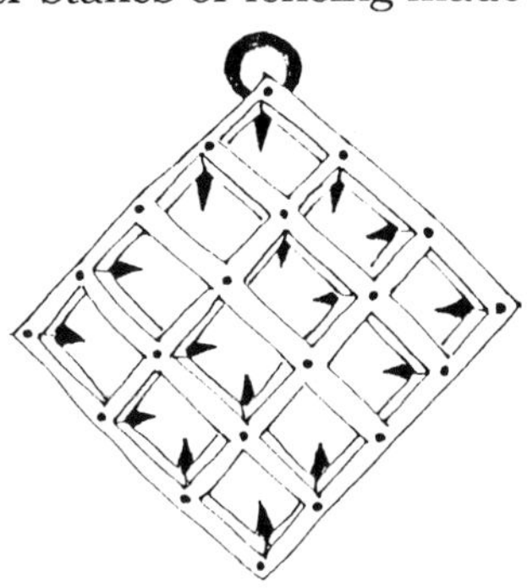

A 17th century harrow

II Farming 1660-1714

The fields

The tradition of open field farming continued in Radcliffe into the 18th century and its strength is well attested in records of the manorial courts which include directives for managing the open fields (see p. 179). Estate documents of the period refer to the open fields, the commons and beastgates. A survey was made in 1690 for the Earl of Kingston (the Pierrepont estate) covering those lands held by him in Radcliffe. It sets out very clearly the holdings of 27 of his tenants (six of them widows), each of them divided between the four fields - Cliff, Breck, Stony and Sunpit (sometimes Lamcote) - and Radcliffe and Eastgang (Hesgang) meadows. Robert Greene, for example, besides his house and homestead with just over one acre of land, held over 32 acres of arable and leys in the four fields, referred to as common field land, with seven and a half roods in the meadow and five beastgates in the 'Eastgang'. In addition he held just over an acre of pasture in 'Plate Close'. Not all tenants held arable land; 14 of them were listed just for their house and homestead with the number of beastgates (usually three or five) or 'rows common' they were entitled to in the meadow. Some like William Parr, who had a house and homestead on the glebe, were not entitled to any. The main evidence about farming practice in this period, however, comes from the inventories because few individual gifts of farm produce, animals or equipment were made in the wills. 314

Arable farming

Haymaking c. 1668

The inventory of squire Thomas Rosell's estate gives the most comprehensive picture of farming in this period and, not surprisingly, the goods and livestock appraised in the document far outstrip all others in value. The inventory was made on 9th December 1685 when his wheat growing in Lamcote field was valued at £48 and that in Radcliffe field at £66. Barley gathered into barns was valued at £53.6s.8d and in one barn was £6.8s worth of rye. (This is the only mention of rye in any Radcliffe inventory or will of the period.) Stored in How's barn was wheat worth £39.12s. More peas, barley, hay and wheat with other things in the yard (presumably the stack yard) totalled £81.19s. The barley stubble (of value for grazing), which was waiting to be ploughed up and sown, was worth £18.6s.8d, whilst the land in the fields already ploughed - 'the clots ready to sow' - was worth £95. Ripened grain could then be processed in the local mill. (Brief references to the Rosells' mill and millers occur in both the 16th and 17th centuries. See, for example, pp. 88 and 208.)

Crop totals of other farmers were considerably less, none amounting to more than £62. Several give details of types of grain and pulses and the condition of the 'oxlands'. In November 1687 John Campion had wheat and barley in barns valued at £40, hay in barns and stackyard at £8, wheat sown in the fields at £4, fallow manured ready to sow at £18, barley stubbles at 2 guineas and peas and beans on hovels at £10. (This inventory was the only one to name beans other than that of Thomas Rosell, which had 'upon hovels peas and beans £56'.) Husbandman Robert Butler (February 1690) left corn in the yard valued at £8, crops stored under the hovel (here a shed) at £1.10s, wheat in the ground at £1.5s, barley fallows worth £2.13s.4d and peas baulks worth £1.10s. Yeoman Thomas Campion (December 1690) had £24 worth of corn in his barns, yard and sheds and hay in the yard at £8, whilst the wheat in the ground and the clots to be sown were together valued at £20.

Ploughing c. 1668
from John Worlidge's
Systema Agriculturae

In December 1685 Thomas Rosell's farm had £10 worth of hay and grass 'in the grounds', which perhaps meant near the house, but not in one of the farmyards. Whether or not this was new autumn sown grass is not known. More hay and grass was appraised at Holme with 31 sheep, totalling £17.6s.8d. Two years later there was £15 worth of hay in the grounds on the March 1687 inventory of his son Gervase. Malt and hay were valued at £20 on yeoman William Parr's inventory of February 1697. A quantity of hay would have been needed to feed a number of his breeding horses, store cattle, a flock of sheep and swine (all valued at £57). Hay and peas were worth £5 on the inventory of John Pare in January 1698; his livestock, similar to William Parr's but fewer in number, was together worth £30. These crops would have seen them through the winter.

The only references to malt occur in the Rosell inventories, apart from that valued with the hay in William Parr's. Small quantities from Thomas Rosell's estate in 1685 had been brought into the house or its immediate farm buildings ready for use in brewing. There was corn with stills and other things in the hall chamber and two 'quartern' of malt and six strikes of wheat valued at £3 in the little garner house. Wheat, malt and blend corn worth £6.12s were recorded in the chambers of the household in Gervase's inventory in 1687. Brewing vessels were also to be found in several other households.

It is not possible to calculate any mean prices for particular crops (especially when two or more were appraised together) because no acreages or weights were given and the inventories range over every month of the year. Only one inventory indicates quantities - a quarter of corn was valued at £1.6s.8d in April 1663. On two inventories the term 'loads' was used; fisherman John Taylor had loads of hay worth £2.6s in February 1664 and Matthew Simmons in 1688 had three loads of hay, two of barley, three of peas and one of wheat. In July 1664 an amount of old hay was considered to be worth only 10s when appraised amongst shepherd John Yardley's goods.

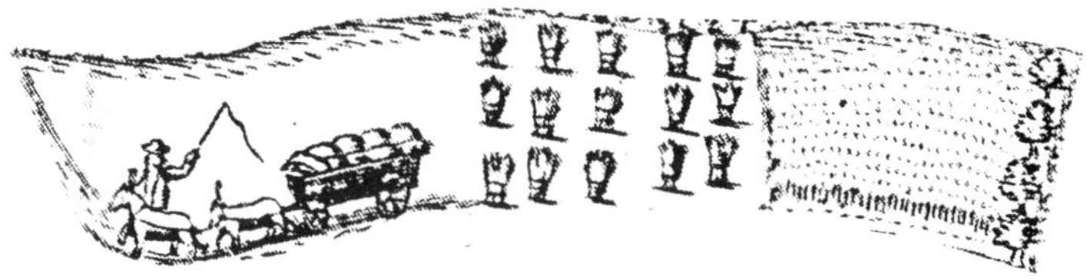

Harvesting c. 1668 from John Worlidge's *Systema Agriculturae*

Willows were grown beside the Trent, as references in the manorial courts show. For example, Robert Doubleday was accused of cutting Widow Randay's willows in 1695. The Roulstone family, who moved to Radcliffe in the later Stuart period, were to make their living as basket makers for many generations. An early Pierrepont rental (1591) describes the cultivation of ash trees and osiers for use in river bank maintenance on 34 acres of land in Holme Pierrepont (termed the upper and nether Hogholmes) providing employment for the Pierrepont tenants, many of whom came from Radcliffe. One of these was George Taylor, the fisherman (see p. 231). Wood from throughout the village would also have been put to good use in making agricultural equipment, woven hurdles and all manner of stakes used in husbandry, hedging and ditching.[315]

Livestock

Horses were prized at least as much as in the preceding century and a half and their monetary value is made clear in the assessments. The descriptions of the animals show that they were being bred and reared for sale as well as used about the neighbourhood for all-purpose mounts, pack horses and pullers of carts and farm implements. The finest horse flesh was doubtless that on the Rosell estate. In 1685 (besides two geldings and five mares held on property at Bole in North Clay) there were three horses worth £12 in the grounds and 20 horses, geldings, mares and foals worth £95 in the stables. Some of these animals would have been among those itemised on Gervase Rosell's inventory in 1687. Ten horses, mares and geldings valued at £67.10s were in the stables then. Elsewhere in stables or in the grounds were six saddle horses and mares with a cart mare and foal together worth £50. It is interesting that on both the Rosell inventories there was a bed in the heated stable. A comfortable stable hand was likely to be more concerned for his charges and could prepare their mashes as well as food for himself at the oven hearth. Some of Gervase Rosell's saddle horses were probably used when he was out hunting with his pack of hounds (worth £5) and his setter, a bitch (worth £1.10s). No other dogs feature in the inventories or wills of this or the earlier periods.

The next most valuable horses were on William Browne's estate in July 1689. From the descriptions he seems to have been breeding and rearing the animals. There were three fillies valued at £6, three mares and foals at £14, three barren mares at £12 and two colts at £10. Mares were itemised on eight other inventories and four of these have foals and/or colts with the dams. William Cooke, husbandman (November 1682), had six horses and mares. (The two hoof files on his inventory could have been for use on them or his five cows and two young beast cattle.) Three further inventories include other horses. Sixteen inventories do not mention horses but several of these were broadly drawn up. Just one horse was individually priced, a filly valued at £1.10s, the only horse belonging to Daniel Oliver in March 1707. The term 'filly' was used on only one other inventory - that of William Browne in 1689. The classification 'geldings' is found on the inventories of the Rosells and John Campion. In November 1687 the latter had eight mares and geldings worth £32 'in the stable and field'. Stables were otherwise only mentioned in the Rosell inventories and that of husbandman Thomas Parr in April 1708.

The leading horse-keepers were also the foremost cattle farmers in Radcliffe during this later period. Thomas Rosell (1685) had 35 bullocks, cows and calves worth £75.16s.8d in the grounds and 14 young beasts worth £21 feeding off hecks in the yard. Of particular importance was a bull valued at £1.13s.4d. Two years later this animal did not feature on Gervase Rosell's inventory which listed 14 beasts, young and old, in the hovels and yard assessed at £32. However, in his beast house were four oxen worth £14 which would have been used to pull ploughs and harrows through larger acreages of heavier soil in the great fields. Bullocks were also used to draw wains and other heavy carts.

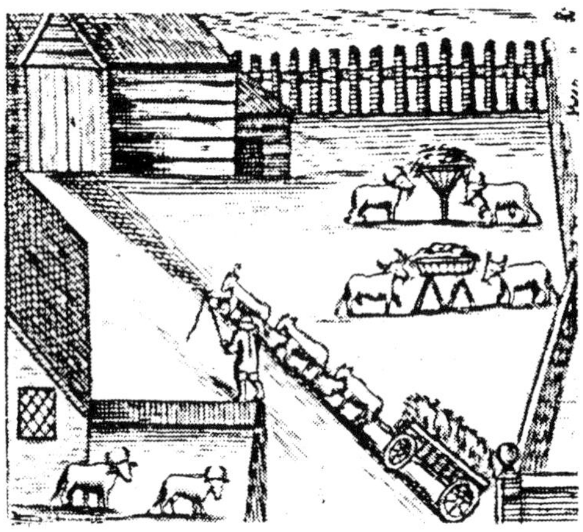
A farmyard c. 1668

The only other bull was on William Browne's farm, assessed with eight cows at £17. There were also five calves worth £2 and ten young beasts worth £11. Yeoman William Butler (February 1699) had £60 of his estate in his crops, £29 in horses and £24 in a small dairy herd, which consisted of six milk beasts, three two year-olds and three one year-olds. Husbandman William Cooke (October 1682) had five cows and two young beasts worth £10, with crops valued at £40 in his barns and £20 worth in horse flesh. In all these households there is evidence of cheese making.

Robert Oliver, a shoemaker whose inventory was drawn up in December 1692, kept only dairy cattle - eight valued at £16, eight heifers at £12 and four calves at £2.10s (perhaps they provided him with leather in due course) and 92% of his estate was in this livestock. John Greene (May 1698) had kept a full range of farm animals including a smaller herd than that of Robert Oliver. His seven cows, three calves and four young beasts were worth £20.10s, and he had a well-equipped dairy and a cheese press in the kitchen. Fourteen other inventories listed cattle, seven with between one and three cows, which were probably kept to meet only the households' needs.

The greatest number of sheep were kept by the Rosells and after them by the leading yeomen and husbandmen in the village. In the summer of 1675 a tithe dispute revealed that Thomas Rosell had between 185 and 240 sheep and between 108 and 120 lambs in Lamcote field alone (see p. 168). At the time of his death in December 1685 his inventory showed that his total sheep in the Radcliffe and Lamcote fields were worth £110.13s.4d. Even on a basis of 6s.8d per head, which is high for the period (see below), this indicates a flock of 332 sheep. It may have been much larger. He also had a further 31 sheep out at Holme worth, with hay and grass, £17.6s.8d. Only 86 sheep remained to be recorded on his son's inventory in 1687. Sheep folds and cribs were included in their valuation of £49.10s. John Campion (November 1687) would have had more than 70 animals as, together with their hurdles, they were valued at £19. Matthew Simmons (September 1689) had prospered as a shepherd attending other's flocks. His messuage entitled him to stints in the great fields and his fallow land that was already ploughed was worth 18s.4d. He also had his own sheep; the number is not clear as dairy cows were evaluated with them, but there were possibly 11 sheep. The inventory of another shepherd, John Yardley (July 1664), showed him to have been of even more substance with a total estate valued at £62.10s.8d compared to Simmons' £25.16s. In addition to three cows, he had kept 33 sheep and 15 lambs which, with their wool, were worth £16. Out in the yard was a sheep crib and a stone trough worth 2s.

A shepherd and his sheep
c. 1668 from John Worlidge's
Systema Agriculturae

Where sheep were assessed separately from other items of farm stock, considerable variations in their value are shown. William Browne's 57 sheep were worth £13 in 1689. The month was July so these sheep would have been shorn and were not yet in lamb, so the price per head was understandably less than for those appraised in either November or April. (He also had 30 sheep-folds and cribs on his farm.) Yeoman William Parr (February 1697) had three score sheep valued at £15, making the price per animal 5s, slightly higher than William Browne's. This value of 5s was given on several occasions; on William Greene's inventory in April 1663, on William Cooke's (November 1682) and on John Greene's in May 1698. These three husbandmen kept flocks of 20 sheep each. In January 1698, however, John Pare's 16 sheep were valued at only 3s.9d per head. The highest valuation was on William Butler's 30 sheep, both 'good and bad' in February 1699. They were appraised at £10 at an average of 6s.8d, so there must have been some very good sheep indeed! Probably most were in lamb and in good condition. In contrast, in April 1708, Thomas Parr's 30 sheep, described as young and old, had a very low valuation of £2.10s. As he was in debt, perhaps they had been neglected or the assessors were trying to keep the valuation down in order not to add to the financial burdens of his estate. (See p. 219.) Eight inventories did not mention sheep at all.

There is more information about swine-keeping in the inventories than in the wills of any period; of the 31 later Stuart inventories 15 itemised swine. Two of the others recorded bacon flitches in store, suggesting the earlier keeping and fattening of pigs. Two more did not specify the kinds of animals being raised. Whenever the term 'pig' was used it meant piglet (a word not found on any of these inventories although used in interpreting them). When the swine were placed on the farm they were either in the yard or in a barn, never in the grounds or further afield. The greatest numbers were kept on the Rosell estate. In 1685 Thomas Rosell's swine were worth 17s, whilst the hogs in the yard were worth £8. Two years later only £5 worth of swine was left in the Rosell barn, made up of two sows with pig(let)s, two boars and a shoat (a young weaned pig). In July 1689 husbandman William Browne had two sows and two shoats, valued at £3, suggesting that the boars on Gervase Rosell's inventory had been assessed at about £1 each. All the swine young and old on yeoman Thomas Campion's December 1690 inventory came to £3.10s. The numbers and value of swine kept by other farmers were lower, ranging from £2 for unknown numbers down to 10s for Margaret Butler's single swine in September 1691. The one sow that had belonged to fisherman John Taylor (February 1664), set at 16s, was likely to have been in pig at that price. The swine in the yard of husbandman Thomas Parr (April 1708) were a sow and three pig(let)s worth 16s.8d.

William Browne's inventory included six hives of bees, and Margaret Butler had two hives of bees (the only mention of bees in this period) valued 'with everything else' at 10s. Geese, ducks and hens are not specifically mentioned in Radcliffe documents in this later period, although they are occasionally found in inventories from elsewhere in Nottinghamshire.

Manure

Manure was a valuable resource and it featured in five inventories. In March 1687 Gervase Rosell had manure in the yard worth £5; on others its value (for unknown quantities) ranged from 10s to £4. Land that had been manured and was ready for sowing was also specified and accordingly appraised. The manure and the work involved in applying it made the land that much more valuable. The lands on which sheep had been turned to nibble down the first shoots of grains were given a further top dressing of manure in this way.

Farm equipment

As would be expected Thomas Rosell's estate in 1685 was well equipped. The wagons, carts, wains and (presumably spare) wheels in the yard were valued at £24. There was £7 worth of ploughs and gear for using these and the carts. This gear would probably have included horse harness, for bullock yokes were listed separately. Fourteen young beasts in the yard were feeding off hecks, and stone troughs were also mentioned. One framed hovel was valued at a guinea and would either have been a new open-fronted store place or, more likely, an empty frame on which to build a rick of peas or beans. The ploughs and the yokes reappeared on Gervase's inventory in 1687 together with harrows, horse gears and teams. In his yard was a wagon, a cart and two wains, eight beast cribs and a fan. This last piece of equipment was a winnowing fan used to waft chaff from grain after threshing and was mentioned only in this one instance. Hovels included in this inventory were for housing beasts.

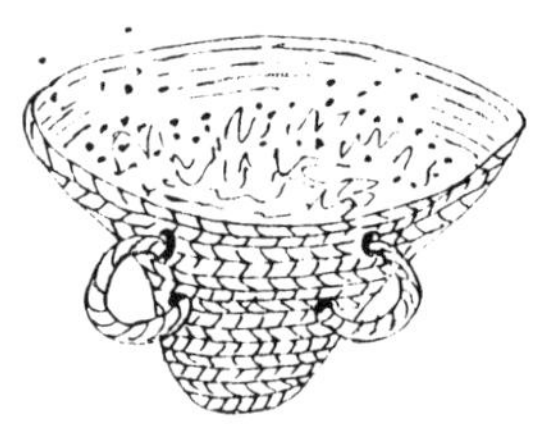

A winnowing fan

Hovels as either rick frames or open sheds appeared in several wills and inventories spelt in various ways, but not so as to differentiate between the two meanings or uses. Yeoman William Butler's inventory of February 1699 placed one framed hovel in the over (upper or top) yard and another in the nether yard (lower or back yard). Shepherd John Yardley (July 1644) had a 'hovel with pales about it in the yard', valued at £1. Perhaps these pales or stakes were ready to support a stack, as such a valuation suggests the hovel would have been an empty frame. There was also a sheep crib and a stone trough. On the inventory of husbandman William Greene (April 1663) there was the only reference to 'mangers'; together with racks and fleakes these were worth £1. Two hovels, pales and stoops were valued at £3.6s.8d. There were also horse gears, plough timber with the coulters and shares altogether worth £2.

Carts were itemised on 12 more inventories besides those of the Rosells. Ploughs appeared on 11 of the 12 and harrows on eight of these, testimony to the growing self-sufficiency of these farmers whose forefathers would have shared many of these items. Unusually three carts valued at £4 and two ploughs and two harrows at 10s were itemised on William Marshall's inventory of May 1692 without the listing of any harnessing equipment or horses. However, there were nine beasts on the list so a pair of these could have formed a team. With hecks, a hovel and old wood, there was also the only roller to be mentioned, altogether valued at £2. There was a fuller description of the items on the 1697 inventory of John Pare. Two carts, two ploughs, two harrows and 'other things for husbandry' were set at £6 and with the usual gears occurred the sole use of the term halters, together worth 13s.4d. Troughs for watering farm animals featured in many of the inventories. That of yeoman William Butler (February 1699) specifically had one horse trough and two troughs for swine.

The tools of a hired labourer, Bartholomew Webster, were listed by him in his will of January 1669. He left half of them to his second son Bartholomew so that he might similarly earn his living. These were named as axes, wimbles and 'farrows' (possibly harrows). The first two of these suggest working with wood, coppicing perhaps and using the wood to fashion agricultural structures such as hurdles, frames or farm buildings. 'Wimbles' could be braces or boring tools or, more likely in this instance, devices for twisting straw or hay bonds.

A wimble for twisting straw or hay bonds

Case Study 19

LITERACY IN TUDOR AND STUART TIMES

In 1533 Thomas Cranmer, Archbishop of Canterbury advised his brother-in-law Harold Rosell to send his son Thomas to a school at Bingham. There were also grammar schools at Nottingham, Southwell and Newark. Harold, however, would have been among a very small minority in Radcliffe able to educate their children. There is no sign of a school in Radcliffe in this period, so young Thomas had probably initially received tuition at home from one of the local priests. Others, like John Grenhall in 1534, entrusted their sons to their guidance, and Robert Dewsbury (1521) and John Webster (1527) both had sons who became priests, probably receiving their earliest education in the village. Elizabethan gentry such as the Ballards, Halls and Roulstones and yeomen such as the Parkers may also have found someone locally for their children, although the decline in the number of clergy in this period, especially the well-qualified, would have made this more difficult.

In 1633 the churchwardens reported to the church authorities, who licensed schoolmasters, that there was no school in Radcliffe and no evidence of one has been found until the late 18th century. It is not surprising therefore that, apart from the pre-Reformation priests, no one from the Tudor and Stuart periods bequeathed a book in any of the surviving wills, and only Thomas Rosell's inventory mentioned any books. This was despite the fact that there were many incentives to learn to read and write. Parish officials were presented with an ever-increasing number of documents to draw up or sign and affix to the church door. Litigation was a favoured pursuit of the age, even among the less well-off and the practice of making a will was becoming more popular. Even the most humble could gaze every Sunday on biblical texts painted onto the white-washed walls of the church.

The Protestation Return of 1642 required all the men in the community to sign or make their mark. Unfortunately only a copy of the return from Radcliffe was sent in, but of 49 parishes in Nottinghamshire where the lists bearing signatures and marks have survived, 76% could not write their names - the lowest literacy rate out of 25 assessed counties. Those who could sign at least showed a desire to learn as well as some aptitude, even if this does not prove that they were wholly literate.

In the early Stuart period Roger Campion, a husbandman who had a very characteristic firm signature, also acted as parish clerk. Substantial families like the Gambles, the Pilkingtons, the Markhams and the Frankes appear to have been literate, but as late as 1705 an affluent farmer like Richard Musson, whose inventory amounted to over £200, could only make a rudimentary mark in the parish register. In 1650 two of Henry Gamble's three daughters were able to sign. Perhaps Elizabeth, who made a mark was less able, but she may have received less schooling than her sisters. (See pp. 143-4). The diary of the 17th century Essex clergyman Ralph Josselin shows that some of his children received more schooling than others.

From the end of the Civil War more documents from Radcliffe have survived - wills, bonds, inventories and the church-wardens' signatures or marks in the parish registers. Just over 40 individuals showed they could sign their names as against about 50 making their marks, but the evidence would be tilted in favour of the literate, who were more likely to be asked to act as witnesses to wills. Two of them were women - Ann Rosell and Elizabeth Pilkington, wife of William Pilkington and a gentleman's daughter. Many of the marks were stereotyped so that, for example, there is little difference in the 'R' used by Richard Butler and Richard Marriott or between innumerable 'Ts' and 'Ws'. There were others who tried to make their style different like Thomas Butler in 1682 and Mary Greene in 1697. The widow Isabel Chadburn was required to make her mark twice within the same month in 1681. On the second occasion she gained courage and added some extra flourishes, perhaps discovering in herself hidden aspirations! She had another opportunity when her stepdaughter, Elizabeth, died in 1691. She and her new husband, Thomas White, were the assessors of the girl's inventory, but her mark on this occasion was a little more restrained. Assessors did not have to be literate and Thomas White could also only make a mark, but Elizabeth left so little it was probably not too difficult to check on what the scribe was recording.

After the Restoration artisans and shopkeepers become more prominent. The parish clerk John Dickinson was a tailor and probably the scribe of George Franke's will in 1669. Eight of this group were signing bonds (four of them being relatives of the deceased) guaranteeing the honest administration of wills, particularly from about 1690 and several of them also acted as scribes and witnesses for wills and inventories. All were able to sign their names. William Oliver, cordwainer, and William Foster, blacksmith, made good signatures, as did John Henson a framework knitter, Samuel Parr, tailor, John Brewster, another blacksmith, and at the very end of the Stuart period George Sparrow, a cooper and gravestone carver. The most familiar hand in these late documents, however, was that of Robert Fillingham, an ironmonger who acted as bondsman five times and as a scribe for several inventories and wills. The need to be able to read and write was more compelling for craftsmen and shopkeepers than for farmers, or perhaps their occupations attracted a certain type of man in the first place. Their skills and their place in the village community were to become increasingly important in the years ahead.[316]

Examples of signatures and marks

1. Mark of Joane Needham 1658

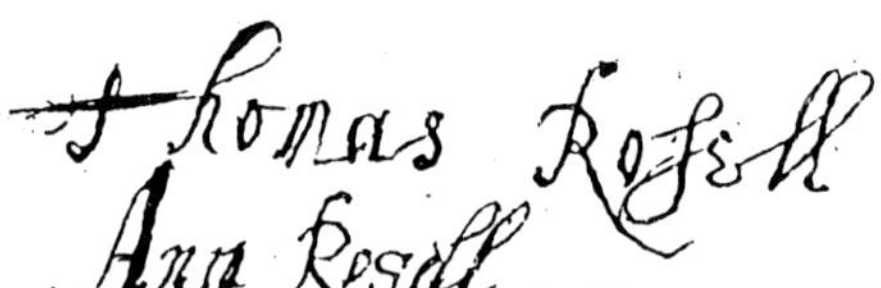

2. Signatures of Thomas and Ann Rosell 1658

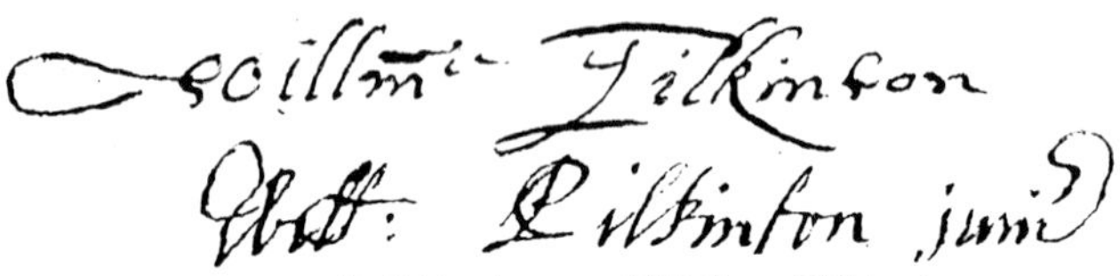

3. Signatures of William Pilkington senior and junior 1664

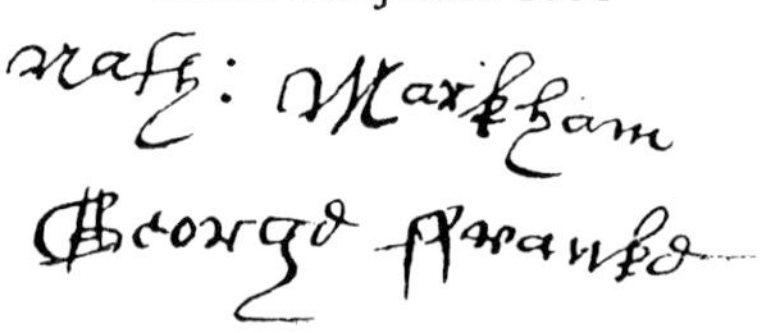

4. Signatures of Nathanial Markham and George Franke 1664

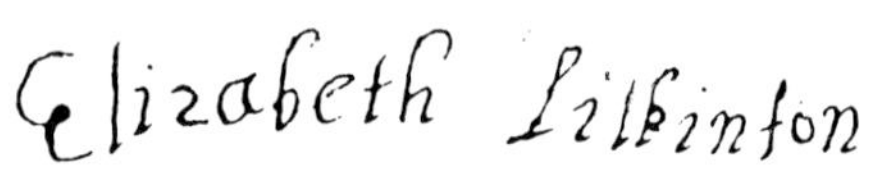

5. Signature of Elizabeth Pilkin(g)ton 1670

6. Signature of William Markham 1681

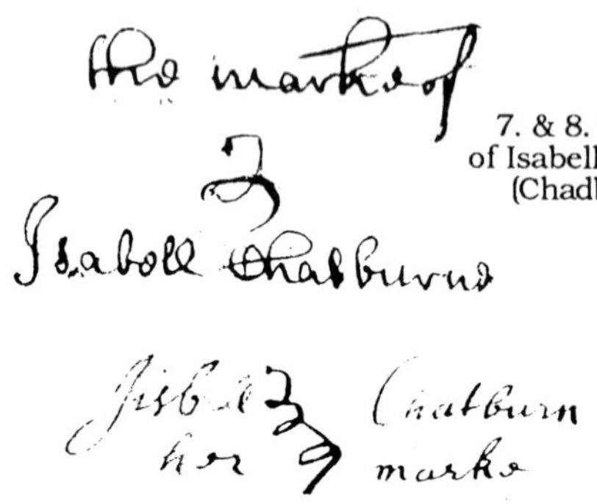

7. & 8. Two marks of Isabell Chatburn (Chadburn) 1681

9. Mark of Thomas Butler 1682

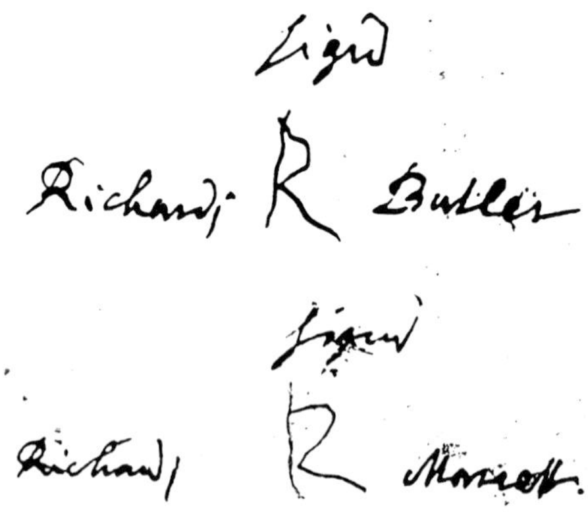

10. Marks of Richard Butler & Richard Marriott 1691

11. Signature of Samuel Parr, tailor, 1693

12. Signature of John Brewster, blacksmith, 1696

13. Signature of Robert Fillingham, ironmonger, 1697

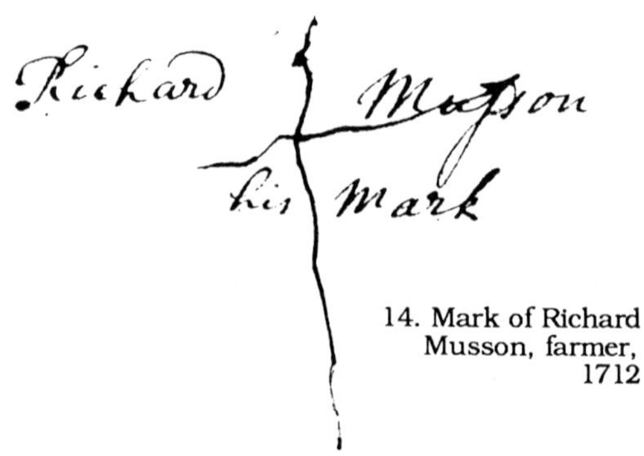

14. Mark of Richard Musson, farmer, 1712

APPENDICES

WILLS

Dates used in the text refer to when wills were made and not when they were proved.
The modern dating convention is followed.
The spelling of names has been standardised.
Status and occupations in square brackets [ ] are derived from sources other than wills.

The third column (**) indicates where the will is held:
Y = Borthwick Institute, York — N = Nottinghamshire Archives Office
P = Public Record Office — J = Court of St John of Jerusalem, Nottinghamshire Archives Office
I = inventory

Testator	Occupation	**	Will	Probate	Burial
William Johnson	Unspecified	Y	25 Oct 1516	6 May 1517	
John Horne	Unspecified	Y	5 Mar 1517	28 Apr 1518	
Henry Caunt	Unspecified	Y	15 Dec 1518	25 Jan 1519	
Richard Bayley	Unspecified	Y	6 Sep 1519	13 Oct 1519	
John Browne	Vicar	Y	18 Oct 1519	24 Jan 1520	
Edmund Lodge	Vicar	Y	4 Aug 1521	18 Sep 1521	
William Dewsbury	Husbandman	Y	18 Aug 1521	11 Oct 1521	
Richard Wright	Blacksmith	Y	22 Aug 1521	11 Oct 1521	
Robert Dewsbury	Husbandman	Y	17 Sep 1521	15 May 1522	
John Webster	Unspecified	Y	1527	30 Aug 1527	
John Greenhall	Unspecified	Y	2 Apr 1534	30 Apr 1534	
John Sharpe	Husbandman	Y	9 Oct 1534	24 Apr 1535	
Edmund Taverey	Husbandman	Y	24 Oct 1548	16 May 1549	
William Welbie	Vicar	Y	3 Apr 1549	25 May 1549	
Alice Morley	Widow	Y	23 Jun 1549	9 Oct 1549	
Johan Taverey	Widow	Y	28 Jun 1551	9 Jan 1552	
John Fuldiam	Husbandman	Y	3 Jul 1551	8 Oct 1551	
William Wolley	Unspecified	Y	1 Jan 1552	12 May 1552	
Richard Greene	Husbandman	Y	16 Jun 1557	6 Oct 1557	
John Martyn	Unspecified	Y	23 Jul 1557	6 Oct 1557	
John Franke	Unspecified	Y	12 Nov 1558	19 Apr 1559	
Richard Roulstone	Unspecified	Y	16 Nov 1558	19 Apr 1559	
Richard Wright	Husbandman	Y	11 Jan 1559	19 Apr 1559	
Edmund Rosell	[Gentleman]	Y	22 Jan 1560	9 May 1560	
Richard Bayley	Yeoman	Y	23 Sep 1561	23 Apr 1572	
Richard Bayley	Husbandman	Y	8 Dec 1561	22 Apr 1562	
Anne Wright	Widow	Y	9 Apr 1566	10 Oct 1566	
John Franke	Husbandman	Y	12 Aug 1568	12 Oct 1568	
Nicholas Jervis	Husbandman	Y	7 Nov 1568	14 May 1569	
Henry Pare	Husbandman	Y	19 May 1569	12 Apr 1570	
John Pare	Yeoman	Y	21 May 1570	15 Sep 1570	
Richard Howlyn	Unspecified	Y	3 Oct 1570	23 Apr 1572	
Robert Darwyn	Husbandman	Y	1574	12 Apr 1576	
William Aynesley	Cottager	Y	15 Apr 1578	9 Oct 1578	
Elizabeth Darrenton	Widow	Y	24 Apr 1579	12 Oct 1579	
Margaret Greene	Widow	Y	5 Jul 1580	30 Nov 1580	
Robert Hall	Gentleman	Y	21 Nov 1580	9 Nov 1581	
Hugh Bushy	Weaver	Y	4 Feb 1582	10 Oct 1582	
William Greene	[Blacksmith]	Y	4 Aug 1585	11 Feb 1586	
Edmund Franke	Unspecified	Y	29 May 1586	19 Jan 1587	
Edmund Wilkinson	Unspecified	Y	31 Jul 1586	13 Oct 1586	
John Mylner	Unspecified	Y	10 Jan 1587	11 Aug 1587	
William Thrave	Husbandman	Y	28 Jan 1589	9 Oct 1589	
John Grococke	Husbandman	Y	1 Mar 1589	9 Oct 1589	
Margaret Mylner	Widow	Y	31 Mar 1589	9 Oct 1589	
Benyt Ward	Unspecified	Y	4 Apr 1590	7 Sep 1590	
William Capendale	Unspecified	Y	17 Apr 1591	7 Oct 1591	
William Roulstone	Gentleman	Y	29 Nov 1591	12 Jul 1592	
Thomas Dewsbury	Yeoman	N	23 Aug 1592	17 Jan 1593	
John Greene	Husbandman	Y	2 Apr 1594	22 Jun 1594	
Steven Palmer	Labourer	Y	20 May 1594	10 Oct 1594	
Richard Cowper	Tailor	Y	28 Jul 1595	16 Jan 1596	

Testator	Occupation		**	Will	Probate	Burial
Robert Parr	Husbandman		Y	12 Mar 1596	7 Aug 1596	
John Hempsall	Tailor		Y	7 Sep 1597	11 Jan 1598	
William Brodfield	Yeoman		Y	28 Nov 1598	24 Mar 1599	
Richard Jordan	Yeoman		N	4 Jan 1599	29 Jul 1601	
John Skynner	Labourer		Y	30 Mar 1599	3 May 1599	
Thomas Parker	Yeoman		N	3 Jun 1603	11 Jul 1607	
William Greene	Unspecified		N	30 Jan 1604	3 May 1604	
John Rosell	Esquire		N	12 Sep 1605	1 Jul 1607	
Richard Dewsbury	Unspecified		N	21 Mar 1610	3 May 1610	
Henry Jervis	Husbandman		N	2 May 1612	20 Jul 1615	
Harold Greene	Husbandman		Y	25 Dec 1613	13 Jul 1614	
Humphrey Campion	Labourer		Y	31 May 1614	19 Jan 1615	
William Limner	Bachelor		Y	25 Mar 1615	25 Apr 1616	
James Dunington	Husbandman		N	10 Aug 1616	15 May 1617	
Jeffrey Limner	Wheelwright		Y	17 Apr 1617	8 Aug 1617	
Mary Rosell	Widow		Y	17 Sep 1617	21 Jan 1618	
Robert Greene	Husbandman		N	19 Apr 1624	13 Oct 1625	
William Morley	Unspecified		N	16 Aug 1626	12 Oct 1626	
Robert Henson	Yeoman		N	31 Jan 1628	8 May 1628	
Richard Richards	Labourer		N	5 Nov 1629	3 Aug 1631	
William Drecot	Labourer		N	13 Dec 1629	22 Apr 1630	
Sislie Drecot	Widow		N	8 Apr 1634	4 May 1637	22 Jun 1636
Miles Cragge	Labourer		N	29 Jan 1635	22 Apr 1635	29 Jan 1635
Henry Gamble	Husbandman		N	30 Nov 1636	19 Jan 1637	1 Dec 1636
John Stapleton	Husbandman		N	11 Jun 1639	31 Jul 1639	17 Jun 1639
Thomas Pare	Yeoman		N	16 Dec 1639	18 Sep 1640	18 Dec 1639
Margaret Franke	Widow	I	N	5 Dec 1653	27 Oct 1660	14 Dec 1653
Robert Butler	Yeoman		P	13 Jun 1654	22 Nov 1654	24 Jun 1654
William Greene	Husbandman	I	J	13 Aug 1657		
Joane Needham	Widow	I	N	19 Feb 1658	31 Dec 1660	18 Oct 1658
Anthony Franke	Bachelor		P	22 May 1659	13 Aug 1659	24 May 1659
Edward Holmes	Labourer	I	J	16 Mar 1664	1 Apr 1664	20 Mar 1664
John Yardley	Shepherd	I	J	5 Jul 1664	30 Sep 1664	6 Jul 1664
John Parr	Yeoman		N	29 Dec 1666	8 Mar 1667	2 Jan 1667
Bartholomew Webster	Labourer		Y	30 Jan 1668	3 Jun 1668	
George Franke	Farmer		N	29 Dec 1669	20 Apr 1672	25 Mar 1672
John Walker	Labourer		N	16 Dec 1670	21 Jun 1672	17 Apr 1672
John Hutchinson	Yeoman		N	14 Jan 1671	10 Dec 1675	7 Oct 1675
Richard Butler	Unspecified		N	23 Nov 1676	26 Feb 1678	19 May 1677
William Pilkington	Yeoman		N	29 Jan 1679	28 Jul 1679	6 Feb 1679
Thomas Parr	Mason		N	16 Dec 1679	13 Sep 1680	17 Dec 1679
Simon Chadburn	Labourer		J	2 Feb 1681	8 Apr 1681	4 Feb 1681
Nathaniel Markham	Husbandman		J	13 Apr 1681		
John Greene	Farmer		N	28 Jan 1682	19 Jul 1682	
William Cooke	Husbandman	I	J	31 Oct 1682		2 Nov 1682
Thomas Rosell	Esquire	I	Y	8 Jul 1685	Sep 1686	3 Dec 1685
Gervase Rosell	Esquire	I	Y	17 Mar 1687	Apr 1687	19 Mar 1687
John Alvey	Unspecified		Y	27 Aug 1687	Mar 1688	
Matthew Simmons	Shepherd	I	N	29 Sep 1688	25 Mar 1690	15 Sep1689
Thomas Smith senior	Shepherd	I	N	6 Sep 1689	20 Feb 1690	1 Dec 1689
Robert Butler	Husbandman	I	N	18 Dec 1689	7 Jan 1691	30 Jan 1690
Alice Dickinson	Widow	I	N	14 Sep 1690	24 Jun 1691	23 Mar 1691
Robert Oliver	Cordwainer	I	N	8 Dec 1692	8 Feb 1693	19 Dec 1692
William Parr	Yeoman	I	N	4 Mar 1693	9 Mar 1697	1 May 1696
Richard Foster	Blacksmith	I	N	3 Feb 1696	1 Apr 1696	5 Feb 1696
William Alcock	Unspecified	I	N	18 May 1696	12 Aug 1696	
John Pare	Unspecified	I	N	1697	9 Mar 1698	26 Jan 1698
John Greene	Unspecified	I	N	16 May 1698	1 Sep 1698	18 May 1698
William Pilkington	Yeoman	I	N	5 Jan 1699	25 Jan 1699	19 Jan 1699
William Butler	Yeoman		N	24 Feb 1699	19 Apr 1699	
William Needham	Yeoman		N	26 Apr 1700	15 May 1700	30 Apr 1700
Daniel Oliver	Unspecified	I	N	14 Feb 1707	2 Oct 1707	27 Feb 1707
Richard Musson	Farmer	I	J	29 Sep 1712		1 Oct 1712

The will and inventory of Anne Byrde (p. 127) are known only through archdeaconry evidence. The will of Lawrence Henson (p. 145) is excluded as he was not resident when it was drawn up.

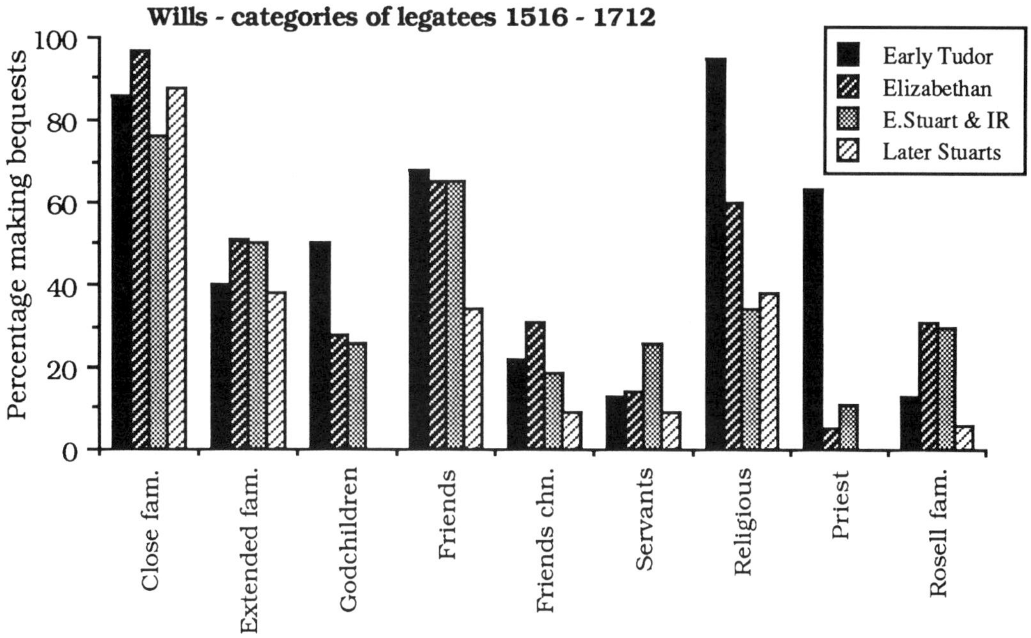

(chn = children; fam = family; Religious includes charities; Priest includes vicar)

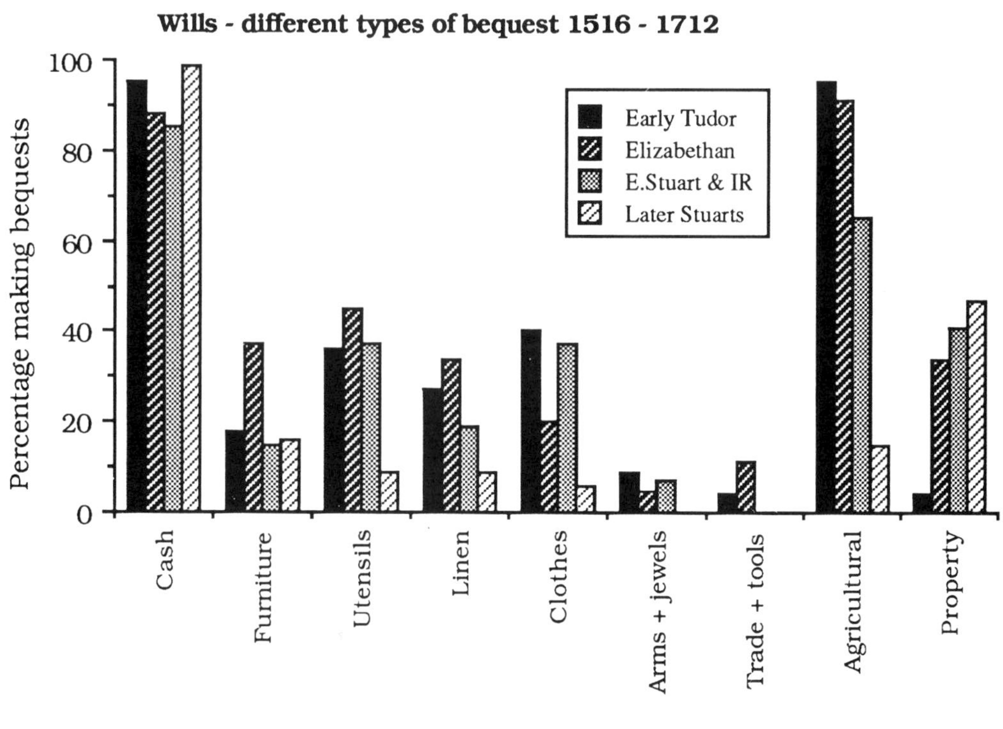

SUMMARY OF INVENTORIES

	Name and occupation	A	Date of inventory	Total £	s	d	Purse and apparel £	s	d	B	C	D	Houshold items of note, tools, etc
1	Margaret Franke Widow	J	19 Dec 1653	* 330	16	4	6	13	4	8	86	2+	Fire irons, 20 pewter dishes, 2C blankets, 18 pairs of sheets, 6 cushions, 3 feather beds, 9 ma resses, board & frame, cheese press.
2	Joane Needham Widow	J	25 Oct 1658	144	15	0	1	0	0	6	94	5	Brewing vessels.
3	William Greene Husbandman	J	23 Apr 1663	* 123	12	8	3	6	8	16	77		5 pewter dishes, brass, 2 flago feather bed, brewing vessels, 4 doors, lease of house.
4	John Taylor Fisherman	J	Feb 1664	* 29	0	4	3	6	8	72	14	5	Gallowtree, hooks, tongs, fire shovel, brass, 7 pewter dishes, settles, 2 chamber pots, bacon flitches, brewing vessel
5	Edward Holmes Labourer	J	25 Mar 1664	41	14	0	1	0	0	35	25	2	Pewter, hemp yarn, weaving sheets, 2 arks, coals, bonds.
6	John Yardley Shepherd	J	4 Jul 1664	62	10	8	30	0	0	12	39		2 pewter dishes, brass, woode dishes & trenchers, 7 yards woollen cloth, 2 looms, hemp, hemp yarn.
7	Robert Barr (Brickmaker)	J	1 Apr 1680	* 6	11	0		5	0	51		3	'All in the chempe', 1 chest, wages owed £2.16s,
8	William Cooke Husbandman	J	10 Nov 1682	* 108	10	4	1	0	0	9	95	5	Reckons & hooks, 2 chests, 1 coffer, pewter, brass, brewin vessels, 2 barrels, salting trou
9	John Campion (Husbandman)	J	13 Mar 1683	6	16	0		5	0	41	51	3	One bed.
10	Thomas Rosell Gentleman	Y	9 Dec 1685	* 1100	10	0	10	0	0	11	86	17	Silver plate, pewter, brass, glass bottles, press, chest of drawers, livery cupboard, trundle bed & cord, books, stonebow, 11 hogsheads, thra brewing & dairy vessels.
11	Gervase Rosell Gentleman	Y	29 Mar 1687	422	15	8	10	0	0	14	84	7	Pewter, looking glass, window curtains, livery cupboard, new flaxen cloth, brewing & dairy vessels, guns.
12	John Campion Unspecified	J	3 Nov 1687	* 189	14	0	2	0	0	10	88	6	Reckons, hooks, pewter, brass livery cupboard, kimnel, cheesepress, woollen yarn.
13	William Browne Unspecified	J	8 Jul 1689	* 191	6	10	2	13	4	21	78	7	Gallowtree, pewter, brass, cradle, 23 chairs, 6 turkeywor cushions, web of flaxen cloth, web of woollen cloth, brewing dairy vessels, bacon, coals.
14	Matthew Simmons Shepherd	N	27 Sep 1689	25	16	0	2	0	0	43	42	5	Gallowbalk, the hooks, pewter smoothing iron, tankard, salt, 3 pancheons, 1 dozen trenche 4 'cheesefats', coals.
15	Thomas Smith sen Shepherd	N	8 Feb 1690	10	19	0		10	0	11	2		Bedstead, bedding, brass pan brandiron, debts owing to him £9.
16	Robert Butler (Husbandman)	N	9 Feb 1690	36	13	4	1	10	0	18	73	3+	
17	Thomas Campion Yeoman	N	23 Dec 1690	110	10	0	1	0	0	8	90	8	Gallowtree, hooks, pewter, 3 leather bottles, 3 spinning wheels, brewing vessels.

	Crops in store	Crops on ground	Fallow grounds	Husbandry Sheep	Swine	Beasts	Horses	Equipment and items of interest
1	Corn, barley, hay.	Wheat worth £15.	Worth £15.	92	19	27	15	Wains, well-frame. Poultry.
2	Corn, hay.	Corn.		[60]	6	10	6	Carts, ploughs, folds. Poultry.
3	Corn.	Corn worth £56.		20		7	4	Plough timber with the coulters and shares. Manure.
4	Hay.				1	1		200 pales.
5	Hay, peas.					3		
6	Old hay.			48		3		Sheep crib, trough, 3 forks, a spade.
7								
8	Wheat, barley, peas hay.	Wheat.	Barley & peas 'ready to sow'.	20	2	7	6	Harrows, hoof files.
9						[2]		
10	Barley, rye, peas, corn, malt, beans, wheat.	Wheat, hay, grass.	Barley stubble, clots ready to sow.	231	[18]	50 with a bull	30	Waggons, carts, wains & wheels, bullock yokes & old iron, stable & barns.
11	Barley, malt, wheat, blend corn.	Hay, peas, wheat.	Fallows ready to sow.	86	5 with a boar	18	18	Winnowing fan, beast cribs. Manure.
12	Wheat, barley, peas, beans, hay.	Wheat.	Manured ready to sow; barley stubble.	[80]	[3]	13	8	Horse gears, hovels, plough timber, barns.
13	Unspecified, but worth £50.0s.0d.			57	4 plus piglets	24 with a bull	11 plus foals	30 fleake folds, 6 hives of bees.
14	Hay, barley, peas, wheat.			11		4		
15				2				
16	Corn.	Wheat.	Barley fallows, peas baulks.	[10]	[2]	[6]	[2]	One cart and 'all under the hovel'. Manure.
17	Corn, hay.	Wheat.	Clots to be sown.	[30]	[7]	[12]	[6]	Barn, sheds, yard carts, gears, ploughs.

	Name and occupation	A	Date of inventory	Total £	s	d	Purse and apparel £	s	d	B	C	D	Houshold items of note, tools, etc
18	Elizabeth Chadburn (Unmarried)	N	21 Jan 1691	32	2	0	31	9	0	2			One pan, one chest, 2 shoes.
19	Alice Dickinson (Widow)	N	26 May 1691	*6	17	0		10	0	77	9	4	Fire iron, 'froggs', pewter, brass, cheesepress.
20	Margaret Butler Widow	N	10 Sep 1691	13	10	8	1	10	0	36	50	3+	Cupboard, fire irons, beds & bedding.
21	William Marshall (Yeoman)	N	6 May 1692	64	16	4				9	92		Pewter, brass, wooden ware, cupboard, 2 tables.
22	Robert Oliver Cordwainer	N	26 Dec 1692	34	8	0	1	0	0	5	92	4	Fire iron, hooks, 2 chests, coal 'things in the dairy'.
23	Richard Foster Blacksmith	N	10 Feb 1696	*24	3	8	1	0	0	38	57	5+ shop	Gallowbalk & hooks, 8 pewter dishes, 2 flagons, salt, copper, 2 porringers, stone trough, feather bed, set of hangings, warming pan, bellows, anvils, hammers, vices.
24	William Alcock (Shepherd)	N	22 Jul 1696	19	8	8		6	8	37	63	3	6 pewter dishes, 2 chests, 3 bo set of hangings.
25	William Parr Yeoman	N	4 Feb 1697	125	10	0	10	0	0	10	82	6	Gallowbalk & fire iron, 5 chests, 2 boxes, pewter, brass, cupboard, 2 bacon flitches.
26	John Pare Unspecified	N	27 Jan 1698	66	4	10		5	0	8	92	5	Gallowbalk, cupboard, coffer, pewter, cradle, framed stool, 4 barrels, 2 tubs & other woodware, '1 viles & a reales'.
27	John Greene Unspecified	N	24 May 1698	*91	15	2		5	0	9	90	6	4 pewter dishes, bed hangings cupboard, buffet stools, coppe 2 tubs, 2 barrels, cheesepress.
28	William Pilkington (Yeoman)	N	16 Jan 1699	19	3	6	5	10	0	7	17		Jack, gun, fishing tackle & nets.
29	William Butler (Yeoman)	N	6 Feb 1699	*167	7	6	1	10	0	13	86	5	Fire iron, reckons, 6 pewter dishes, flagon, brass, trunk, 2 boxes, curtains, long settle, 1 doz pancheons, cheesepres copper, brewing vessel.
30	John Hutchinson Unspecified	N	25 Jun 1701	21	0	0				5			'the bed in his Lodging', mone lent without specialty £10, on specialty £10.
31	Daniel Oliver Unspecified	N	6 Mar 1707	8	10	0	4	0	0		53		
32	Thomas Parr Husbandman	N	8 Apr 1708	*53	0	2		10	0	8	74	5	Fire irons, reckons & hooks, pewter, brass, cushions, an old ark, 4 barrels, cheesepress, churn, funeral charges £1, debts £8
33	Richard Musson Farmer	J	2 Oct 1712	222	2	6							

	Crops in store	Crops on ground	Fallow grounds	Husbandry Sheep	Swine	Beasts	Horses	Equipment and items of interest
18								
19				5				
20	Corn, hay.			[5]	1	2		Two hives of bees.
21	Barley.	'the crop' worth £18.			2 plus piglets	21		Cart, ploughs, harrows and a roller. Manure.
22						20		
23				15		1		
24				18	1	2		
25	Wheat, barley, peas, malt, hay.	Wheat.	Barley fallows, peas stubbles.	60	3	[15]	6	Two carts, ploughs, harrows & gears.
26	Hay, peas.	Wheat.	Barley fallows, peas ground.	16	2	8	6	Two carts, ploughs, harrows & halters.
27		Corn worth £30.		20	10	14	9	Two carts .... 'other things for husbandry'.
28				4		1		
29		'crop' worth £60.	'Fallowing in the field'.	30		12	6	Over & nether yards, horse & swine troughs. Manure.
30								
31				[12]			1	
32	Wheat, barley, peas.	Wheat.		30	4	13	6	Cart & plough gears in the stable.
33								

Notes to this table

Column A — Wills held at: N = Nottinghamshire Archives Office; J = Court of St John of Jerusalem, Notts Archives Office; Y = Borthwick Institute, York

Column B — Household goods (percentage of total)

Column C — Agricultural goods (percentage of total)

Column D — Number of rooms

( ) = occupation uncertain * = corrected total of inventory

[ ] = number estimated from value

CLERGY AND CHURCHWARDENS

Sources: Thoroton, Godfrey, Torre mss, Archdeaconry Presentment Bills and Call Books, Parish Registers and Bishops' Transcripts.

Rectors

fl. 1208-09	Gerard de Radcliffe
-1226	Stephen de Radcliffe
1227-40	Gerard de Radcliffe
1240-90	William de Shenendon
1290-	Hugh de Goushill
-1340	Hugh de Goushill
1340-65	John de Kyneton
1365-67	Robert de Alyngton
1367-72	William Dalby
1372-77	John Caldewell
1377-c.79	Robert de Hanley

Vicars and Curates

c.1379-1404	John de Thurgarton
1404-10	Walter de Elmeton
1410-25	John Herle
1425-	Thomas Wryght
-1426	John Merehall
1426-42	John Mydleton
1442-73	Robert de Elynor
1473-1504	John Ackworth
1504-19	John Browne
c.1516-c.47	(Thomas Smythe chantry priest)
1519-21	Edmund Lodge (Lorge)
1521-24	James Meynell
1524-	William Carcolston
-1549	William Welbie
1549-	Edward Sheppard
fl. 1570	Thomas Wallys
c.1572-c.74	Thomas Granger (curate)
c.1574-77	John Alred (curate)
c.1577	John Parker (curate)
1579-c.93	John Alred (curate) (vicar from 1580)
c.1593-1622	George Cotes (curate & vicar)
1622-24	Richard Rumney
1624-32	Daniel Wilcockes
c.1633-38	Paul Sherwood
1638- c.62	William Creswell
1662-c.66	No regular minister
1666	Richard Hawis (curate)
1667-71	Joseph Hawkins (curate)
1671-83	Peter Titley (probably curate)
1683-86	Josiah Redford
1686-c.98	Peter Laycock (curate)
c.1698-1711	Joseph Hawkins (curate)
1712-31	John Hagger (curate)

Churchwardens

1586-87	William Franke William Dewsbury
1587-88	Robert Parr Thomas Parker
1588-89	Henry Jervis Richard Parker
1589-90	Robert Greene Michael Richards
1596 May	Henry Parr William Grococke
1596-97	Henry Parr Edward Capendale
1598	Robert Greene Richard Dewsbury
1598-99	Thomas Parker William Jenkinson
1601	Thomas Carson William Parr
1602	Michael Richards Henry Jervis
1602-03	Brian Barnes John Greene
1604	William Jenkinson
1607	Henry Greene Bartholomew Pilkington
1608-09	John Franke Brian Barnes
1609-10	James Dunnington John Greene
1610-11	William Grococke George Bayley
1611-12	Adam Pight William Drecot
1612-13	George Ballard Robert Hall
1613-14	Henry Pare Jeffrey Limner
1614-15	Henry Pare Richard Thrave
1616-17	George Ballard John Greene
1617-18	William Grococke William Morley
1618	George Bayley Richard Richards Edmund Watts
1620	George Bayley
1621-22	William Grococke Roger Campion
1622-23	Henry Pare John Greene
1623-24	William Hutchinson William Dewsbury
1624-25	Thomas Gamble William Pilkington
1625-26	William Moreley John Chester
1625-26	John Humphrey Roger Campion
1627-28	Roger Campion Thomas Parre
1628-29	John Parre William Hutchinson
1629-30	George Franke William Hutchinson
1630-31	William Hutchinson Henry Pare
1631-32	George (Robert) Greene John Henson

1632	John Greene
	John Gamble
1633-34	William Pilkington
	William Grococke
1634-35	John Slack (Clarke)
	George Bayley
1635-36	Henry Gamble
	John Slack (Clarke)
1636-37	John Long
	William Greene
1637-38	Martin Grococke
	John Campion
1638-39	John Parr
	William Symons (Simmons)
1639-40	William Pilkington
	George Greene
1640-41	George Franke
	John Hutchinson
1641-42	William Greene
	Henry Stoakes
1642-43	John Slack
	Thomas Rippon
1648-49	William Greene
	Gervase Parr
1649-50	John Parr
	William Needham
1662-63	Robert Greene
	George Parr
1663-64	William Needham
	John Parr
1664-65	John Hutchinson
	Robert Greene
1665-66	Richard Butler
	Robert Butler
1666-67	Nathaniel Markham
	William Needham
1667-68	William Pilkington
	John Henson
1668-69	Robert Greene
	George Marriott (Marrott)
1669-70	George Franke
	John Watts (Whittle)
1670-71	William Cooke
	Peter Beeston
1671-72	John Henson
	Joseph Taylor
1672-73	Fran(ke) Hall
	Will Butler (sworn late in August)
1673-74	William Parr
	William Greene
1674-75	William Greene
	Thomas Pare (Parr)
1675-76	Nathaniel Markham
	John Campion
1676-77	Nathaniel Markham
	George Taylor
1677-78	John Hutchinson
	George Marriott (Marratt)
1678-79	John Hornbuckle
	Robert Oliver
1679-80	William Marshall
	Richard Gibson
1680-81	Robert Greene
	John Campion
1681-82	Robert Greene
	William Bacon
1682-83	John Parr
	Thomas Topley (Copley)
1683-84	William Parr
	John Wilford
1684-85	Robert Greene
	Thomas Smith
1685-86	Robert Butler
	John Walker
1686-87	Matthew Simmons
	William Pare, junior
1687-88	William Browne
	Bryan Parr
1688-89	Robert Greene
	William Alcock
1689-90	William Alcock
	Thomas Butler
1690-91	John Watts
	John Cooke
	John Parr
1691-92	Peter Beeson, senior
	John Parr
1692-93	Peter Beeson, senior
	John Brewster
1693-94	Thomas Parr
	William Parr
1694-95	William Butler
	Thomas Whittle (Whittal)
1695-96	Henry Smith
	George Taylor
1696-97	James Wright (Mr)
	William Needham
1697-98	William Sutton
	William Foster
1698-99	William Foster
	William Morley
1699-1700	William Whitby
	William Morley
1700-01	William Whitby
	William Oliver
1701-02	William Moreland
	John Gibson
1702-03	John Moore (Morley)
	John Parr
1703-04	Jonathan (Samuel) Parr
	Richard (Robert) Buxton
1704-05	Thomas Parr
	Joseph Buxton
1705-06	Richard Musson
	John Walker
1706-07	Richard Musson
	John Walker
1707-08	Robert Greene
	William Vaus
1708-09	Samuel Hand
	John Collishaw
1709-10	Thomas Stone
	John Collishaw
1710-11	Thomas Stone
	John Collishaw
1711-12	Joseph Shilcock
	Joseph Shelton
1712-13	Robert Brewster
	John Butler, senior
1713-14	William Butler, junior
	John Whittle
1714-15	William Butler, junior
	John Whittle

SELECT CHRONOLOGY

Year National and international events

1485 Battle of Bosworth: Henry Tudor defeats Richard III and becomes Henry VII.
1487 Yorkist rebellion. Battle of East Stoke.
1492 Columbus' first voyage to the New World.
1497 John Cabot discovers Newfoundland.
1502 James IV of Scotland marries Margaret Tudor.
1504 Guilds placed under supervision of crown.
1507 Pope Julius II issues indulgence for rebuilding of St Peter's in Rome.
1509 Accession of Henry VIII and his marriage to Katherine of Aragon.
1513 War with France. Scotland declares war on England. James IV killed at Flodden. Infant James V succeeds.
1515 Archbishop Thomas Wolsey made Lord Chancellor. Francis I becomes king of France.
1516 Mary Tudor born. Sugar imported from New World.
1517 Beginning of Reformation in Germany.
1518 Enclosures made since 1488 to be destroyed.
1519 Leonardo da Vinci dies aged 67.
1520 Henry VIII and Francis I meet at the Field of the Cloth of Gold. Martin Luther excommunicated.
1521 Henry VIII given title 'Defender of the Faith'. Luther condemned at Diet of Worms.
1522 England at war with France (until 1525) and Scotland (until 1526). First circumnavigation of the world completed.
1524 Peasants' Revolt in Germany.
1525 New Testament illegally published in English by Tyndale.
1527 Cortes completes conquest of Mexico. Sack of Rome.
1528 Severe outbreak of plague. Thomas More appointed Lord Chancellor after Wolsey's fall.
1530 Wolsey arrested as a traitor and dies at Leicester in November on his way to London.
1531 Appearance of Halley's comet causes panic.
1533 Thomas Cranmer consecrated Archbishop of Canterbury. Henry VIII's marriage to Katherine of Aragon formally annulled; Henry marries Anne Boleyn. Elizabeth Tudor born.
1534 Henry VIII becomes supreme head of church. Thomas More & Bishop Fisher executed for treason.
1536 Suppression of smaller monasteries led by Thomas Cromwell. Anne Boleyn executed. Henry marries Jane Seymour.
1537 Edward Tudor born. Queen Jane (Seymour) dies. Coverdale's Bible.
1538 Mandate by Thomas Cromwell concerning the keeping of parish registers.
1539 Suppression of the greater monasteries. Great Bible in English. Act of Six Articles.
1540 Henry VIII marries Anne of Cleves; marriage annulled. Cromwell executed for treason. Henry marries Catherine Howard.
1542 Catherine Howard executed. Mary Stuart born and succeeds to throne of Scotland on death of James V.

Year The Midlands - including Radcliffe-on-Trent

1485 Francis Lord Lovel supports Richard. Sir John Byron supports Henry.
1487 Five men from Radcliffe act as guides for Henry; Lord Lovel defeated at East Stoke and disappears. Sir Henry Willoughby supports King.
1489 Birth of Thomas Cranmer at Aslockton.
1503 Sir Gervase Clifton, Sir Edward Stanhope and Sir Henry Willoughby escort Princess Margaret through Nottinghamshire to Scotland.
1504 John Browne succeeds John Ackworth as vicar (RoT).
1507 House of Observant Friars established at Newark by Henry VII. Death of Thomas Rosell.
1513 Nottingham High School founded.
1516 Radcliffe's first surviving will.
1517 Enclosure inquiry in Nottinghamshire.
1518 Report of epidemic in Nottinghamshire. Murder of William Federston (RoT).
1519 Edmund Lodge appointed vicar (RoT).
1521 James Meynell appointed vicar (RoT).
1524 William Carcolston appointed vicar (RoT).
1525 Henry FitzRoy, natural son of King, created Earl of Nottingham.
1528 Failure of harvest; grain imported from Germany.
1530 Wolsey stops at Newark on way to York in April.
1531 Thomas Magnus endows a free school at Newark. Act for erection of gaols in different parts of Nottinghamshire and Derbyshire.
1534 (Sweating) sickness in Southwell about this time. John Sharp killed by horse (RoT).
1536 Shelford Priory dissolved. Granted to Michael Stanhope and his wife Anne. Lincolnshire Rising and Pilgrimage of Grace against suppression of monasteries. Henry Norris, lord of manor of Stoke Bardolph, executed for undue intimacy with Anne Boleyn.
1538 Prior of Lenton executed for high treason Thurgarton Priory and Welbeck Abbey dissolved.
1539 Newstead Abbey dissolved (acquired by Byron family).
1540 Harold Rosell is granted manor of Cotgrave et al with license to pass to George Pierrepont. Leyland visits Nottingham.

Year	National and international events	Year	The Midlands - including Radcliffe-on-Trent
1543	Henry VIII marries Catherine Parr. War with France. Copernicus states that earth revolves round sun.	1543	Murder of John Bacon (Lamcote).
1545	French enter Solent and land on Isle of Wight.		
1547	Accession of Edward VI. Somerset appointed Lord Protector. Chantries to be suppressed.	1547	Archbishop Thomas Cranmer is granted manor of Woodhall. It is subsequently passed to Rosells.
1549	Act of Uniformity authorises the first book of Common Prayer. Earl of Warwick (Northumberland) replaces Somerset as Lord Protector.	1549	Newark receives first charter. Edward Sheppard succeeds William Welbie as vicar (RoT). Drownings of Thomas Thrave (alias Long) & Robert Peas in Trent.
1551	Thomas Cranmer's 42 Articles published.	1551	Sweating sickness at Newark. Suppression of Radcliffe's chantry.
1552	Ale-houses to be licensed. Second Act of Uniformity abolishes mass. Execution of Somerset.	1552	Inventory of church goods drawn up 3rd September. Execution of Sir Michael Stanhope.
1553	Edward VI dies. Lady Jane Grey proclaimed Queen, but deposed and succeeded by Mary I. Mass revived.	1553	Sir Henry Willoughby dies trying to find north-east passage to Cathay. Plague at Newark.
1554	Mary marries Philip of Spain. Lady Jane Grey executed. Serious food shortages.	1554	At least 13 local incumbents deprived of their livings because they refuse to put away their wives.
1555	Parishes made responsible for upkeep of roads.	1555	Murder of unknown woman (RoT).
1556	Archbishop Thomas Cranmer burnt at stake for treason and heresy.	1556	Rosell Wood in Epperstone divided between Sir John Chaworth and the Rosells.
1557	War with France. Scots invade England.		
1558	French capture Calais. Mary dies; succeeded by Elizabeth I. Mary Stuart marries French Dauphin.	1558	A 'marvellous tempest of thunder' at Nottingham. Nottingham elevated to episcopal see.
1559	Acts of Supremacy and Uniformity restore Protestantism. Dauphin becomes Francis II of France.	1559	Report of sickness in Nottingham.
1560	Francis II dies.	1560	Edmund Rosell dies.
1561	Widowed Mary Stuart returns to Scotland.	1561	Grant of arms to borough of Newark.
1562	First English participation in slave trade. Start of French wars of religion.	1562	Sir Henry Pierrepont marries Frances Cavendish, eldest daughter of Bess of Hardwick.
1563	20,000 die of plague in London. Le Havre seized by Warwick.	1563	Troops raised in Nottinghamshire.
1564	William Shakespeare born.	1564	Sir George Pierrepont dies.
1565	Mary Stuart marries Darnley. Tobacco introduced.		
1566	Mary Stuart's son, James, born.	1566	Chancery case of William Ballard v. John Rosell sen.
1567	Darnley murdered. Mary marries Bothwell, but is forced to abdicate in favour of her son, James.	1567	Separate sheriffs for Nottinghamshire and Derbyshire.
1568	Mary Stuart flees to England and captivity.	1568	Nottingham has its own sheriff for the first time.
1569	Northern earls revolt in support of Mary Stuart.	1569	Thomas Wallys referred to as vicar of Radcliffe.
1570	Pope 'excommunicates' Elizabeth.		
1571	Ridolfi plot to depose Elizabeth. First compulsory Poor Rate. Massacre of St Bartholomew in France.	1571	Chancery case of Robert Hall v. John Rosell senior.
1573	Spaniards checked in suppression of Netherlands Protestants.	1573	Curate Thomas Granger's slander case against John Rosell senior.
1575	Elizabeth declines offer of sovereignty of the Netherlands.	1575	Queen Elizabeth visits Kenilworth castle. Francis Willoughby knighted.
1576	First playhouse in England opens at Shoreditch. Spanish 'fury' in Antwerp.		
1577	Francis Drake begins voyage round the world.	1577	Sir John Zouch acquires Radcliffe rectory lands.
1579	Founding of the Dutch Republic.	1579	John Rosell senior and curate John Alred quarrel.
1580	Introduction of Jesuit missionaries into England.	1580	Building of Wollaton Hall begun. First mention of Radcliffe's church clock.
1581	First English colony in North America at Roanoke, later Virginia Jesuit. Edmund Campion executed.	1581	Earl of Rutland buys Newark Castle. John Rosell senior entails his estates.
1582	Edinburgh University founded.	1582	Death of John Rosell senior.
1583	Throgmorton plot for Spanish invasion of England.		
1584	Assassination of William of Orange.		
1585	Elizabeth aids the Dutch against Spain.	1585	Act for paving of Newark.
1586	Babington plot to murder Elizabeth. Sir Philip Sidney dies of wounds in Netherlands.	1586	General distress in Nottinghamshire due to bad harvests.
1587	Mary Stuart executed at Fotheringhay.	1587	Lady Anne Stanhope of Shelford dies.
1588	Spanish Armada defeated.	1588	Marriage of William Cecil, grandson of Lord Burghley and Elizabeth Manners at Newark Castle.
1589	Invention of first flushing water closet. England aids Protestant Henry of Navarre (Henry IV of France).	1589	Rev. William Lee of Calverton invents stocking frame.
1590	Edmund Spenser's 'The Fairie Queen'.		
		1591	Rectory lands of Radcliffe transferred to Sir Thomas Stanhope.
1592	Plague in London kills 15,000.	1592	Isabel Dewsbury's breach of promise (RoT).
1593	Christopher Marlowe murdered. Henry IV of France becomes a Catholic.	1593	George Cotes curate then vicar (RoT). Dispute over Stanhope's weir comes before Star Chamber.

Year	National and International events	Year	The Midlands - including Radcliffe-on-Trent
1594	First of five consecutive bad harvests.		
1595	Londoners riot for bread. Irish rebellion.	1595	Mustering of Nottinghamshire troops.
1596	Tomatoes introduced into England.	1596	Death of Sir Thomas Stanhope.
1597	Bacon's essays published.	1597	Hardwick Hall completed. Special collections for poor in RoT and other Nottinghamshire villages.
1598	Parish registers to be kept in books, and copies sent annually to the bishop. Edict of Nantes grants toleration to Protestants in France.		
1599	Oliver Cromwell born.	1599	Fight between Sir Charles Cavendish and John Stanhope and followers in Sherwood Forest.
1600	Gowrie conspiracy in Scotland.	1600	Rosells sell some lands to Pierreponts.
1601	Poor Law codifies previous acts. Essex's rebellion.	1601	First workhouse in Nottingham.
1602	Jesuits ordered to leave England.	1602	Stanhopes acquire 'Beaumont's' manor in RoT.
1603	Accession of James I of England and VI of Scotland.	1603	King passes through Newark Plague at Newark.
		1604	83 die of plague in 3 months at Colston Bassett.
1605	Gunpowder plot.	1605	Francis Willoughby builds a pit-head railway at Wollaton.
1606	Execution of Gunpowder plotters and Jesuit Henry Garnett.	1606	Death of John Rosell junior. Puritans under William Brewster secede from church at Scrooby.
1607	Foundation of Jamestown, Virginia under Captain John Smith.	1607	Thomas Jordan acquitted of murder. Midlands revolt. Commission on Enclosure on six Midlands counties
1608	First municipal library at Norwich.	1608	Scrooby congregation flees to the Netherlands. George Cotes before archdeaconry court.
1609	Tea first shipped to Europe.	1609	Plague at East Markham -115 die. At Upton - 83 die. George Cotes before magistrates.
1610	Arabella Stuart imprisoned in the Tower of London.		
1611	Authorised version of the Bible. Colonisation of Ulster.		
1612	Death of Henry Prince of Wales.	1612	King visits Newark. Two new church bells (RoT).
1613	East India Company sets up its first trading post.		
1614	Napier's tables of logarithms published.		
1615	Coal being substituted for expensive firewood. Arabella Stuart dies.	1615	First brick house built in Nottingham. Death of Sir Henry Pierrepont.
1616	William Shakespeare dies aged 52. George Villiers, later Duke of Buckingham, becomes King's favourite.	1616	King visits Nottinghamshire. Death of George Rosell?
1617	One-way streets introduced into London.	1617	Jeffrey Limner leaves money to Radcliffe poor. Widow Margaret Rosell marries Francis Hacker of East Bridgford.
1618	Sir Walter Raleigh executed. Start of Thirty Years' War in Europe.	1618	Death of Mary Rosell.
1619	First black slaves arrive in Virginia.		
1620	Voyage of 'Mayflower' including five from the Scrooby congregation.	1620	Donation of a prize cup for horse races held at Coddington Moor near Newark.
1622	Spanish marriage negotiations begun by Prince Charles (abandoned in 1623).	1622	Gervase Rosell marries Elizabeth Hacker. Richard Rumney replaces George Cotes as vicar (RoT).
1624	Failure of expedition to help Frederick of the Palatinate to recover lands from the Hapsburgs.	1624	Serious fire in Sherwood Forest - 4 miles by one-and-a-half miles. Daniel Willcockes becomes vicar (RoT).
1625	Accession of King Charles I. He marries Henrietta Maria of France. Plague kills 41,000 in London.	1625	11 out of 45 county gentry refuse to contribute to King's 'forced loan'. Two new church bells (RoT).
		1626	Death of Anne Ballard. Newark acquires a mayor.
1627	War with France.	1627	Birth of Thomas Rosell.
1628	Petition of Right. Assassination of Buckingham.	1628	Robert Pierrepont created Earl of Kingston-upon-Hull; Lord Stanhope of Shelford created Earl of Chesterfield.
1629	Parliament dissolved for 11 years.		
1630	Charles Stuart born. Peace with Spain.	1630	Plague so bad in Nottinghamshire that the musters did not take place (also 1631).
1631	Resentment against Court of High Commission's harsh sentences in ecclesiastical matters.		
1632	Taj Mahal begun.	1632	First surviving parish register for Radcliffe. Paul Sherwood appointed vicar of Radcliffe.
1633	Trial of Lancashire witches. William Laud becomes Archbishop of Canterbury.	1633	Case of Anne Byrde's disputed will.
1635	King Charles demands ship money.	1635	Impact of Laudian policy felt in Radcliffe.
1636	Harvard College founded.	1636	A middle arch of Trent Bridge collapses. Plague in East and West Bridgford, Cotgrave and Bingham.
1637	John Hampden refuses to pay ship money.	1637	Plague in Cotgrave - 93 die.
1638	Solemn League and Covenant signed in Scotland.	1638	William Creswell becomes vicar of Radcliffe.
1639	First Bishops' war.		

Year	National and international events
1640	First stage coach routes opened. Long Parliament meets
1641	Rebellion in Ireland. Execution of Strafford.
1642	King's attempt to arrest five Members of Parliament. Civil Wars begin. Battle of Edgehill.
1643	Royalist victory at Roundway Down. Parliamentary victory at first battle of Newbury. Louis XIV becomes king of France.
1644	Queen flees to France. Parliamentary victory at Marston Moor. Date of birth and parents' names to be given when recording baptisms.
1645	William Laud, Archbishop of Canterbury, executed for treason. Cromwell defeats King at battle of Naseby. Wallpaper used for the first time.
1646	End of first Civil War.
1647	Scots hand Charles I over to Parliament. Army enters London. Charles flees to Isle of Wight.
1648	Second Civil War. Cromwell defeats Scots at Preston. Pride's Purge leaves a 'rump' parliament.
1649	Charles I executed. Commonwealth created. Cromwell subdues Ireland.
1650	First coffee house opens in Oxford. Charles II lands in Scotland. Cromwell defeats Scots at Dunbar.
1651	Charles II crowned King of Scotland at Scone. Charles defeated at Worcester and escapes to France.
1652	First tea reaches England. First Anglo-Dutch war.
1653	Cromwell expels Parliament. Barebones parliament lasts 5 months. Cromwell becomes Lord Protector.
1655	Division of country under major-generals. English occupy Jamaica.
1656	Spain declares war on England.
1657	Humble Petition and Advice increases Cromwell's powers.
1658	Oliver Cromwell dies and is succeeded by his son Richard.
1659	Richard Cromwell forced to resign. First cheque drawn on a British bank.
1660	Charles II returns and is proclaimed king.
1661	Cavalier parliament meets.
1662	Anglicanism imposed. Settlement of the Poor Act. First Hearth Tax. Royal Society founded. Charles marries Catherine of Braganza.
1663	Yorkshire plot or Northern plot.
1664	Conventicle Act against nonconformists.
1665	Five Mile Act. Second Anglo-Dutch war. Great Plague begins. 68,000 die in London.
1666	Great Fire of London. Isaac Newton establishes laws of gravity.
1667	Peace with Dutch. Burial in Wool Act. John Milton's 'Paradise Lost'.
1670	Secret Treaty of Dover between Charles and Louis XIV.
1671	Thomas Blood tries to steal Crown Jewels.
1672	Declaration of Indulgence. Stop of the Exchequer. War with the Dutch.

Year	The Midlands - including Radcliffe-on-Trent
1641	Gervase Rosell marries Jane Ayscough.
1642	Protestation return. King raises standard at Nottingham. First Newark siege. Quarter Sessions abandoned.
1643	John Hutchinson appointed Parliamentary Governor of Nottingham Castle. Church courts abandoned. Earl of Kingston killed. Vicar of St Mary's, Nottingham, and rector of West Bridgford imprisoned.
1644	Tower of St Nicholas' Nottingham used by snipers and subsequently demolished. Second siege of Newark relieved by Prince Rupert marching via Rempstone and Bingham.
1645	West Bridgford and Wilford plundered by Royalists. Shelford House stormed; Col Philip Stanhope and 200 men killed. Wiverton taken Plague in RoT. Henry Pierrepont created Marquess of Dorchester.
1646	Charles I surrenders to Scots at Southwell. Newark Castle surrenders and is dismantled. Quaker George Fox preaches in Mansfield.
1648	Battle of Willoughby Field. Michael Stanhope killed. Quaker George Fox imprisoned after disturbance at St Mary's, Nottingham.
1650	Hutchinson in charge of Nottinghamshire militia. Wm Creswell, vicar of RoT, to have income augmented.
1651	Nottingham Castle demolished. General Ireton of Attenborough (Cromwell's son-in-law) dies of plague.
1652	John, first Lord Byron, dies in exile. Start of William Creswell's struggle to receive promised income. Resumption of Quarter Sessions records.
1655	Rising of 300 Nottinghamshire Royalists quickly dispersed. Major-Gen Whalley in charge of county.
1656	Bridewell at Southwell erected. Presbyterian church established in Nottingham and district.
1657	Death of Roger Campion, Radcliffe's parish clerk for 80 years.
1658	Thomas Smith buys Nottingham house from which he later begins first bank outside London.
1659	Failed Royalist rising; 60 to 120 men collected near Samson Wood in Sherwood Forest.
1660	Death of Gervase Rosell - probably end of December.
1661	Death of George Rosell.
1662	Thirty-eight puritan ministers ejected in county. Thomas Rosell marries Elizabeth Wright. Death of William Creswell? Church courts reconvene.
1663	John Hutchinson arrested over Yorkshire or Northern plot.
1664	John Hutchinson dies in Sandown Castle after 11 months imprisonment. Gervase Rosell born.
1665	Plague in Newark: one-third of population dies. Plague in Eyam.
1666	Francis Hacker of East Bridgford executed as 'regicide'.
1667	Plague in Nottinghamshire. Joseph Hawkins curate of Radcliffe.
1668	Edge and Pierrepont families acquire Radcliffe rectory lands.
1669	Over 2,000 non-conformists registered in Nottingham under the Conventicle Act.
1671	Peter Titley becomes curate of Radcliffe.
1672	Francis Willoughby, the naturalist, dies aged 37. Edward Cludd of Norwood Park who saved Southwell Minster from destruction, dies.

Year National and international events

1673 Test Act.
1674 Peace with the Dutch.
1675 Greenwich Observatory established. Christopher Wren begins St Paul's cathedral.
1676 Influenza epidemic.
1677 William of Orange marries Mary, niece of Charles II.
1678 Popish plot invented by Titus Oates. John Bunyan's 'Pilgrim's Progress'.
1679 Habeus Corpus Act. Exclusion crisis.
1681 Dissolution in Oxford of Charles II's last parliament.
1682 Halley's comet seen. First museum in Britain, the Ashmolean at Oxford, opened.
1683 Rye House plot to kill the king.
1684 Thames and the sea for two miles out freeze over.
1685 Accession of James II. Duke of Monmouth defeated at Sedgemoor and executed. Louis XIV revokes Edict of Nantes.
1686 James puts Catholics in church and army.
1687 James II grants freedom of worship.
1688 'Glorious Revolution'; William of Orange lands in England James II flees to France.
1689 Accession of William and Mary. Toleration Act. Bill of Rights.
1690 William III defeats James II at the Battle of the Boyne.
1692 War against France. First land tax at 4s in the pound. Massacre of Glencoe.
1693 William III initiates national debt.
1694 Bank of England chartered.
1696 Plot to murder the king. Window Tax.
1697 Treaty of Ryswick between England, France and Holland.
1698 London Stock Exchange founded.
1700 Princess Anne's last surviving child dies.
1701 Act of Settlement on heirs of Sophia of Hanover. Jethro Tull invents seed-planting drill. War of Spanish succession.
1702 Accession of Queen Anne. London's first daily newspaper published.
1703 England devastated by hurricane-force winds. Samuel Pepys dies aged 70.
1704 Marlborough's victory at Blenheim.
1705 Newcomen invents improved steam engine.
1706 Battle of Ramillies. First Turnpike Trust created.
1707 Act of Union of England and Scotland.
1708 Battle of Oudenarde.
1709 Battle of Malplaquet. Abraham Derby introduces new iron-smelting process at Coalbrookdale.
1710 Copyright Law introduced.
1711 Duke of Marlborough dismissed. Addison and Steele begin 'The Spectator'.
1712 Last execution for witchcraft in England.
1713 Peace treaties of Utrecht end wars.
1714 Death of Queen Anne. Prince George of Hanover succeeds as King George I.
1715 First Jacobite rebellion.

Year The Midlands - including Radcliffe-on-Trent

1674 Duke of Newcastle begins to re-build Nottingham Castle.
1675 Thomas Rosell's tithe dispute.
1676 Rector's book at Clayworth. Religious census.
1677 Publication of Robert Thoroton's 'Antiquities of Nottinghamshire'.
1678 Robert Thoroton dies aged 56.
1682 Nottingham given a new charter.
1683 Flooding in Trent Valley. Trent Bridge almost destroyed. Josiah Redford becomes curate of RoT.
1684 Ralph Edge of Strelley dies, having been town clerk of Nottingham for 20 years and mayor three times.
1685 Death of Thomas Rosell.
1686 Newark has new charter. Peter Laycock curate of RoT.
1687 Belton House completed. Gervase Rosell dies; birth of his son Gervase.
1688 Earl of Devonshire occupies Nottingham for William of Orange. Princess Anne flees to Nottingham.
1689 Rosell children's appeal to the Master of the Rolls.
1692 First fire engines in Nottingham by public subscription.
1694 John Holles, Earl of Clare, made Duke of Newcastle - said to be the wealthiest man in England.
1695 William III visits Nottingham.
1696 Celia Fiennes visits Nottingham.
1698 Joseph Hawkins curate of Radcliffe.
1700 Quaker Meeting House at Blyth.
1701 Anne Rosell's draft act of Parliament.
1702 Presbyterian meeting house at Mansfield.
1704 Count Tallard imprisoned in Newdigate House.
1706 Blue Coat School, Nottingham, established for 60 boys and 20 girls.
1709 Collins almshouses founded in Nottingham.
1710 First printing press in Nottingham. Map drawn of Rosell lands.
1711 Sir Thomas Willoughby created Baron Middleton. Southwell Minster damaged by fire and collections made throughout the county. Rosells' lands advertised for sale.
1712 John Haggar becomes curate of Radcliffe.
1713 Ancient wall dividing English and French boroughs cleared away from Nottingham market place.
1714 400 stocking frames in Nottinghamshire.
1715 Evelyn Pierrepont created Duke of Kingston-upon-Hull. 'Nottingham Post' started by Mr Collier.

MEASUREMENTS

Square measures of land

square mile	640 acres		2.59 square kilometres
acre (a)	4 roods	4,840 square yards	0.405 hectares
rood (r)	40 perches		
perch (p)	30.25 square yards		

Acre - originally as much land as a yoke of oxen could plough in a day, so the measurement varied from place to place governed by the lie of the land and the nature of the soil. Statute of 1533 defined an acre as an area equivalent to 40 poles long by 4 poles wide i.e. 4,840 square yards. 40 poles = 1 furlong and 32 furrows made by a plough in average ground would measure 4 roods across, or 22 yards as a rod, pole or perch is equivalent to 5 1/2 yards. One rood is a quarter of an acre.

Carucate - measure of land varying with soil etc – as much as could be ploughed by one plough and eight oxen in a year; a ploughland. Generally taken to be about 120 acres. A basic fiscal unit in the Midland, comparable to the Hide in other parts of the country.

Oxgang:- **broad** - a yardland (see below); **narrow** - originally the area of land cultivable by one ox, half a yardland, or one-eighth of a ploughland. Later a conventional unit varying widely from parish to parish (and even within the same parish) from perhaps ten to twenty five acres.

Yardland or **virgate** - measure of land, originally as much as would serve to occupy a yoke of oxen. Later a unit varying widely in area, but always containing two oxgangs and forming a quarter of a carucate, hide or ploughland.

Measures of length

mile	8 furlongs	1,760 yards	1.61 kilometres
furlong	220 yards		
chain (ch)	22 yards		
yard (yd)	3 feet		0.914 metres
foot (')	12 inches		30.5 centimetres
inch (")			2.54 centimetres

Measures of weight

ton	20 hundredweight		1,016 kilograms
hundredweight (cwt)		112 pounds	
pound (lb)	16 ounces		0.453 kilograms
ounce (oz)			28.35 grams

Measurement of volume

gallon	4 quarts	4.545 litres
quart	2 pints	
pint		0.568 litres

Money

No attempt has been made to modernise monetary values in the text. The following explains currency terms prior to 1971 when the coinage was decimalised:

4	farthings	=	1	penny	(1d)	
2	halfpence	=	1	penny	(1d)	
12	pence	=	1	shilling	(1s)	(= modern 5p)
24	pence	=	1	florin		
		=	2	shillings	(2s)	(= modern 10p)
30	pence	=		half a crown	(2s.6d)	(= modern 12 1/2p)
120	pence	=	10	shillings	(10s)	(= modern 50p)
20	shillings	=	1	pound	(£1)	(= modern £1)
1	angel	=		6s.8d when originally minted in 1464/5		
1	groat	=	4	pence		
1	mark	=		13s.4d		
1	noble	=		6s.8d		

GLOSSARY

acre measure of area. (See p. 257.)
advowson right of presentation to an ecclesiastical benefice.
alb white tunic or vestment (with sleeves) reaching to the feet.
amerced to be fined in a manorial court.
ark hutch; wooden chest of boarded construction (often hanging) for dry stores.
assize statutory regulations or settling of price of bread and ale with reference to that of grain.
assizes courts presided over by judges on circuit for civil and criminal cases.
attainted convicted.
aumbry early form of doored cupboard at times with pierced doors for ventilation for storage of prepared food.
bald white streak on face of horses or cattle.
baulks ploughed ridges.
beastgate the right of pasture on the common for one animal.
bedhilling counterpane or quilt.
bedstock rectangular wooden frame that supported the mattress or, in the case of a pair, the head and foot of a bed.
bill weapon; type of pike.
board cloth tablecloth.
bordar villager holding less land than a villein.
bovate legal Latin equivalent to oxgang.
bowstaves or **bowstaffs** sticks to be made into a bow.
brandiron trivet or stand for a kettle.
buckler shield.
buffet stool stool of joined or framed construction used at the dining table.
camlet see chamlet.
carucate measure of area. (See p. 257.)
cessment rate, tax or assessment.
chafing dish small enclosed brazier containing hot coals, usually charcoal, for heating food and drink.
chamlet camlet; light material; in the 16th and 17th centuries the hair of the Angora goat.
champion open field, not in severalty, or enclosed and held by one person.
chevage payment by villein (non-free tenant) to lord for permission to live away from manor; payment to lord by outsiders for permission to live in manor.
close enclosed field; a hedged, fenced or walled piece of land.
coffer chest for storing documents and valuables.
commonable animals that may be pastured on common land; of land held in common.
coolen cooler; an oval tub, particularly used in brewing and dairying.
copyhold Usually a customary tenure, where the tenant was protected by title written in the manor court rolls of which he retained a copy; originally carried an obligation to perform services, but these were later commuted to cash payments called quit rents.
corden or **cordwain** leather.
cordwainer shoemaker or repairer.
corporax communion cloth.
coulter see culture.
croft piece of land, often enclosed, usually arable and near the house.
cuillyon quilted? (old French: cuilliz = gathered, collected).
culture or coulter - iron blade fixed in front of the share in a plough to make a vertical cut in the soil; this was then sliced horizontally and turned over by the blade of the ploughshare.
demesne part of manor reserved for lord's use, but sometimes rented out.
denvil *not known.*
doubler dish or charger of various size, usually of pewter.
enclosure conversion into severalty of open-fields, common meadow, common pasture or waste.
engross wholesale purchase of corn or standing crop in order to retail or hoard it, awaiting higher prices.
engrossing accumulation in the hands of one man and his family of agricultural holdings adequate to the maintenance of more than one family, and formerly serving for such maintenance.
essoin excuse for non-attendance at the manor court.
farrow harrow?
fee area of jurisdiction of a lord of the manor and subject to feudal obligations; an estate of inheritance; an interest in the land which is capable of being inherited.
fleakes or **fleakes herds** woven hurdles.
framed type of furniture construction with joined legs, stretchers & top rails.
frames wooden shafts.
freehold tenure not subject to customs of the manor but governed by common law.
froggs (frogs) implement in the hearth (*uncertain*).
gallowbalk or **gallowtrees** iron bar across inside of chimney on which cooking vessels hung over the fire on chains and hooks.
garth croft (Yorkshire).
gears animal harness.
glebe land assigned to the incumbent of a parish as part of his benefice.
hack agricultural implement of the mattock, hoe or pick axe type.
hades strip left unploughed as a boundary, access pathway or

greensward where the plough turns on the headland.
halberd combination of spear and battle-axe mounted on a handle, five to seven feet long.
haqueton stuffed jacket worn under mail; jacket plated with mail.
harden fabric made from coarse flax or hemp.
harness set of armour.
headborough petty constable.
headland space left at the head of the strips of arable land in the common field for the plough to turn on.
hecks racks to hold fodder; cheese rack; fence, rail, gate, lower half of door with parallel bars.
hempen fabric made from hemp.
henge house substantial outbuilding with hinged doors.
hogs lambs before their first shearing; male swine which have been castrated when under a year old.
houserow house by house; according to the order or succession of houses.
hovel rick frame, shed, open-fronted store place, outhouse, framework for cornstack - affording protection from the weather for farm produce or implements.
hursts eminence, hillock, knoll, bank, especially sandbank; wooded eminence.
impropriate place tithes or ecclesiastical property in lay hands.
incontinency wanting in self restraint chiefly in sexual matters.
jack padded jacket; leather bottle; labour-saving device.
kit wooden vessel of hooped staves with or without lid for dairying, washing clothes etc.
kimnel tub for kneading dough/dairying.
kirtle woman's skirt or outer gown.
knight's fee fee (q.v.) originally held by military service.
Lammas 1st August; observed as harvest festival in early English church.
lands selions i.e. strips of arable land in an open field, not of uniform size.
latten mixed metal of yellow colour identical with or resembling brass.
leads vats, sometimes lined with lead, used for brewing; cistern.
leet manorial court; a minor crown court where petty offences were tried.
ley land ploughed for several years, put under grass for a period, then ploughed again, and so on.
livery cupboard see aumbry.
manor unit of land over which, in feudal times, its lord had the right to hold a manorial court.
maslin mixed corn, usually wheat and rye, sometimes grown as a mixed crop.
meers green boundaries; walkways.
mercer one who deals in textile fabrics; also, occasionally, in small-ware, groceries.
messuage farm house with land annexed to it and its appurtenances i.e. outbuildings, gardens etc.
midling cloth of medium quality.
mortuary payment to priest from deceased, originally of the second best beast.
motte mound of earth, sometimes surmounted by a castle.
muniments documents (such as title deed, charter etc) preserved as evidence in defence of rights.
murage toll or tax levied for the building or repairing of the walls of a town.
neatherd cowherd.
nuncupative will not written down in the presence of the testator but prepared after his or her death on the word of witnesses.
oblations presentation of something to God for the use of the church, its ministers, relief of the poor or other pious uses. especially in connexion with the Eucharist.
oxlands oxgangs?
pales poles, stakes or fencing made of stakes.
palet bundle of straw; piece of armour for the head.
pancheon large cask for holding liquid.
pannage the right to feed swine on acorns and beechmast in a forest or wood.
pansion panshion - large earthenware bowl, used in making bread.
piccage a toll paid for breaking the ground in setting up booths, stalls, tents etc at a fair.
pillowberes pillowcases.
pinder constable with special duty of impounding stray animals.
pinfold in the Midland counties, a pound for stray animals.
pingle scrap of land (in the open fields); any small enclosure.
platter flat dish or plate of pewter, wood or earthenware.
plaunchers wooden boards or stone slabs for kneading dough or used in preparing meats, dairy or other farm produce.
plough timber shafts.
pluralism the holding of more than one church living.
pole measure equalling 1 rod or perch. (See p. 257.)
pontage toll paid for maintenance of bridge.
pooge *not known.*
porringer small dish for porridge, soup or broth.
pottinger apothecary.
press cupboard, usually a large one with shelves.
procuration payment for necessary entertainment of bishop, arch-

deacon or other visitor by incumbent, parish or religious house.

pullen poultry; domestic fowls.

purveyance the royal right of buying provisions etc for the household at prices below market rates.

pyx vessel in which the host or consecrated bread of the sacrament is preserved.

quartern a quarter peck measure.

quern a hand mill or two circular stones, one rotated on top of the other for grinding corn.

ratchet set of saw-like teeth on edge of a bar or rim of a wheel into which a cog or the like may catch.

reckons (reckan) hook which held a pot over fire.

recusancy refusal, especially by Roman Catholics, to attend services of the Church of England.

rood cross over entry of chancel. A quarter of an acre of land.

roundel iron ring holding candles.

sallet type of helmet, like a souwester in shape.

scutage tax levied on knight's fees paid in lieu of military service.

settle bench with high back and arms at each end.

severalty enclosed area of land held by one person as opposed to scattered strips in the open field.

shoat young weaned animal.

simony act or practice of buying or selling ecclesiastical preferments, benefits or emoluments.

sizar an undergraduate at the University of Cambridge or Trinity College, Dublin, receiving a college allowance to enable him to study.

skillet bronze three or four footed cooking vessel with long handle.

socage tenure of land by certain fixed services other than knight service, but not servile.

soe large tub with two ears used for carrying water or brewing.

sorrelled chestnut coloured.

sparkyall perhaps a 'sparky' - velvet cloth spotted with gold or some similar material; or a 'sparkle' - a small ruby or diamond.

specialty legal term meaning deed under seal, sealed contract; bonds on which money is lent out.

splent splint - armour or plate worn on the arms or legs for defence.

stallage toll for liberty of erecting a stall in a fair or market.

stint regulation of the number of cattle allowed to graze on a common.

strapper dry cow.

strike a dry measure, usually half a bushel; also the cylindrical wooden measuring vessel containing this quantity.

stoops posts.

subsidy a tax levied by the crown.

syke area of common meadow, often damp; a ditch or dyke.

synodal payment to a synod, or assembly of clergy of a particular church.

tags (teggs) - sheep in their first winter.

tang large girth used to fasten the load or panniers on a pack-saddle.

tat a piece of closely woven sacking made from coarse hemp, used to screen doorways, hold fleeces, cover ricks etc.

teams coupling harness.

teathers tethers.

theave female sheep of first or second year, that has not yet born a lamb (Midlands and some southern counties); in some parts a ewe between the first and second shearing.

thirdborough tithing man or deputy constable.

tithe ancient obligation of all parishioners to maintain their parish priest from the fruits of the earth in his parish. Great tithe (usually of corn, hay, wood or wool) was payable to a rector; small tithe (all else, including the annual increase of farm stock, fruit, eggs) to the vicar.

toft (toftstead) house, or the site of a former house; a plot big enough to grow vegetables for domestic use.

trenchers wooden table ware.

trental 30 massses.

trestles folding supports.

trundle a low bed, usually on wheels, oftenkept out of use beneath a standing bed.

trussle a travelling bed whose frame and hangings could be taken apart and packed into bed trusses or bundles

turkey woollen material worked on a loom in imitation of Turkey carpet work.

tynen (tynan) - to provoke, enrage. Tyne - a cow's collar.

unshod wheels bare as opposed to iron-bound wheels.

wapentake a subdivision of certain English shires, corresponding to the hundred of other counties.

wether castrated ram sheep.

wimble braces; boring tool; a device for twisting straw or hay bonds.

wong furlong in the open fields, an enclosed meadow; low lying land, often marshy

yardland measure of area. (See p. 257.)

REFERENCES

Unless otherwise stated, wills can be found under the name and date of testator as indicated in the text, either in the Nottinghamshire Archives Office or the Borthwick Institute, York. Individual references to parish registers or marriage licences are not normally given as they can also be deduced from the text.

Abbreviations

BM	British Museum
Borthwick	Borthwick Institute, University of York
Cal Inquis	Calendar of Inquisitions Post Mortem
CCR	Calendar of Close Rolls
CFR	Calendar of Fine Rolls
CPR	Calendar of Patent Rolls
DNB	Dictionary of National Biography
HMC	Historical Manuscripts Commission
NAO	Nottinghamshire Archives Office
PRO	Public Record Office
Thoroton	R. Thoroton (and J. Throsby), *The Antiquities of Nottinghamshire* (1790-1797 republished 1972)
Thor Soc Rec Ser	Thoroton Society Record Series
TTS	Transactions of the Thoroton Society
VCH	Victoria County History

The Historical Background (pages 9-25)

1. S. Revill, An Excavation at Gibbet Hill, Shelford, *TTS* 75, pp. 59-67; A.G. MacCormick et al, Three Dug-Out Canoes and a Wheel from Holme Pierrepont, *TTS* 72, pp. 14-33; Malcolm Todd et al, The Roman Settlement at Margidunum Excavations 1966-8, *TTS* 73, pp. 7-104; J.E.B. Gover et al, *The Place-Names of Nottinghamshire* (1940), pp. 240-1; M.W. Bishop, *The Anglo-Saxon Cemetery at Windmill Hill, Cotgrave*, Notts Co Council (1986); A.C. Wood, *A History of Nottinghamshire* (1947), pp. 9, 34-39; D. Roffe, Nottinghamshire and the Five Boroughs, *History in the Making*, (1987), pp.7-11; Brewhouse Yard Museum collection; A. Oswald, Some Unrecorded Earthworks in Nottinghamshire, *TTS*, 43, p.12.
2. John Morris, ed, *Domesday Book, Nottinghamshire* (1977), 10.55, 11.33; G. Black, and D. Roffe, *The Nottinghamshire Domesday, a reader's guide*, (1986); Philip Morgan, *Domesday Book and the Local Historian*, (1988); David Kaye, *A History of Nottinghamshire* (1987), pp. 35-37.
3. H.O. Houldsworth, Notes on an Excavation at Radcliffe-on-Trent, *TTS*, 55, p. 23.
4. Itinerary of Edward I Pt. II 1291-1307, *PRO Lists and Indexes*, 132, p. 207; Thoroton, I, pp. 182-5.
5. Thoroton, Ibid; *Cal Inquis 1219-1307*, Misc. C. p. 258 ref 848; Thor Soc Rec Ser, IV 1914, pp. 132 -3 and *Cal Inquis* Henry III, vol I, p. 277; *CPR* 1281-92, p. 87 and Thor Soc Rec Ser, IV 1914, p. 18.
6. *Feudal Aids*, IV, pp. 92, 134; Thoroton, I, pp. 182-5; *CCR*, IV, p. 193.
7. *Catalogue of Ancient Deeds*, VI, p.19; *Cal Inquis* Edward I, I, p. 262; NAO Torre ms microfilm Z392; Thoroton, I, pp.182-5.
8. Thoroton, Ibid.
9. Thor Soc Rec Ser, IV, 1914, pp. 116-117; *Catalogue of Ancient Deeds*, VI, Edward IV, c 5661, p. 251.
10. Thor Soc Rec Ser, IV, 1914, pp. 5,13, 57, 90, 93, 142, 151, 154,190, 194, 283; *CPR* 1247-58, p. 185.
11. Thor Soc Rec Ser, VI, 1939, pp. 20-1.
12. PRO SC11/536.
13. *CCR* 1323-27, p. 143; *CCR* 1327-30, p. 115; *CCR* 1330-33, pp. 59, 552; *CCR* 1333-37, p. 8: *Cal of Chancery Warrants*, I, 1244-1326, pp. 529-30; *CPR* 1338-40, p. 222; *CPR* 1364-67, p. 388; *CPR* 1401-05, p. 164.
14. *Book of Fees*, II, p. 988; *CPR* 1343-45, p. 427; Ibid 1467-77, p. 462; *Feudal Aids* 1248-1431, pp. 101, 120-1.
15. Thor Soc Rec Ser, IV, 1914, pp. 170-1; *Cal of Inquis* Edward III, vol. X, p. 82.
16. *CPR* 1348-50, p. 175; *CPR* 1350-54, p. 83.
17. PRO E179/159/5 (transcribed by Carl Harrison); Robin E. Glasscock (ed), *The Lay Subsidy of 1334*, Records of Social and Economic History, New Series 2, (1975).

18. *CPR* 1247-58, pp. 185, 662; *Catalogue of Ancient Deeds* , VI, pp. 388, 389.
19. W.G. Hoskins, *The Making of the English Landscape* (1977), pp. 48-9; Thor Soc Rec Ser, VI, 1939, pp. 20-1.
20. *CPR* 1334-38, p. 481; *CFR* 1347-56, p. 273; *CCR* 1337-9, p. 424; *CCR* 1339-41, p. 20; *CCR* 1343-46, p. 138.
21. *CPR* 1377-81, pp. 464-5; Thoroton, II, p.127; P.M. Losco-Bradley and C.R. Salisbury, A Medieval Fish Weir at Colwick, Nottinghamshire, *TTS* 83, pp. 15-22; Thor Soc Rec Ser, IV, 1914, p . 50; *CPR* 1313-1317, p. 431.
22. Thoroton, I, p.186.
23. Ibid pp. 183-5; T. Foulds, Thurgarton Priory and its Benefactors, with an edition of the Cartulary, Univ. of Nottingham, Ph.D. thesis (1984), pp. 51, 197, 233, 1050; *CPR* 1557-58, p. 31; *CPR* 1572-5, p. 370; *CPR* 1575-78, pp. 287, 323; PRO E 315/399.
24. T. Foulds, op. cit. pp. 197, 1001, 200, 201; Thoroton, I, pp.183-185; NAO Torre ms, microfilm Z392; J.T. Godfrey, *Notes on the Churches of Nottinghamshire, Bingham Hundred* (1907), pp. 372, 379.
25. Godfrey op. cit. pp. 367, 372; *Feudal Aids*, 1284-1431 p. 145.
26. *CPR* 1313-17, p. 633; *CCR* 1323-27, p. 143; *CPR* 1321-24, p. 410; NAO Torre ms, microfilm Z392; Godfrey op. cit. p. 372.
27. *CPR* 1377-81, p. 297; Godfrey, op. cit. p. 368.
28. Thoroton, I, p 186; Godfrey, op. cit. pp. 372-3.

Five Good and True Men (page 26)

29. PRO E101/412/19 I-E p. 21; PRO E404/79; Cornelius Brown, *Annals of Newark-on-Trent* (1879), p. 34 citing ms 4 Lel, Col p 210 in the Cottonian Library; M.W. Bishop, *The Battle of East Stoke 1487* (1987); additional information from Dr Ian Arthurson.

The Early Tudor Squires (pages 27-34)

30. Thoroton, I, p. 184; T. Cox, *Magna Britannia* (1727), p. 52; J.T. Godfrey, *Notes on the Churches of Nottinghamshire, Bingham Hundred* (1907), p.3; *Records of the Borough of Nottingham*, III (1883), pp. 310, 463; T. Bailey, *Annals of Nottinghamshire*, I, p. 374; BM Add Ch 67092; Borthwick wills vol. 9, f. 287.
31. Thor Soc Rec Ser, III, 1905, p. 9.
32. Thor Soc Rec Ser, II, 1904, p. 49 et seq; BM Eg 3543 f. 9.
33. Thoroton, I, p. 183; NAO DDM 87/38; *Cal Inquis* Henry VII, III, pp. 528, 531; PRO E150/73029.
34. *Cal Inquis* Hen VII, III, p. 531; C. Deering, *History of Nottinghamshire* (1751), p. 311.
35. The information concerning Jane (or Elizabeth) Eland comes from a pedigree in the Peverel manuscripts of the Revel/Eland families drawn up in Elizabethan times - U of NMD Mi Mp 102/1/18, 19. The Babington marriage appears in Thoroton, I, p. 184. Borthwick wills vol. 9, f. 287; Thor Soc Rec Ser, III, 1905, pp. 142, 190, 193.
36. PRO DL30/ 2017 Bundle 131; U of NMD Mi Mp.
37. PRO E101/882 M6/2, E179/159/142-173.
38. Thoroton, I, p.182; Borthwick wills vol. 13, f. 589, vol. 16, f. 61.
39. J. & J.A. Venn, *Alumni Cantabrigienses*, Part 1 (1922-7) - the date given for Harold Rosell is incorrect; *Miscellaneous Writings and Letters of Thomas Cranmer*, Parker Society (1846), pp. 256, 262.
40. Borthwick ADM 1539/1; *Letters and Papers of Henry VIII*, pp. 482, 457; T. Blagg, The Manors of Cotgrave, *TTS* 13, pp. 69-79; PRO Ward 7 40/150, E150/730/29.
41. NAO DD27/1; Thoroton, I, p.182; Burke's *Peerage*; S. Glover, *Derbyshire*, II (1831-33), p. 308; Yorks Arch Soc, Burghwallis MD 218; A. Mawer, and F.M. Stenton, (eds), *The Place Names of Nottinghamshire* (1940), pp. 240-1. They associate the name of Hall Farm with Woodhall. The farmhouse was built in the former open fields after their enclosure in the 18th century, and was the working part of Radcliffe Hall, the 'gentrified' house now on the site.
42. Thor Soc Rec Ser, II, 1904, p. 55; Thor Soc Rec Ser, III, 1905, p. 142.
43. Bromley House Library, Boun ms Cc 260; PRO Ward 7 20/69; Thoroton, pp. 182, 262; T. Cox, *Compleat History of Nottinghamshire* (1730), p.52.
44. Thor Soc Rec Ser, III, 1905, p.142; PRO Sc11/540 73/21.
45. T. Bailey's *Annals of Nottinghamshire* (1853), I, p. 446; NAO DDSK 16/14, 16/27.
46. Borthwick Act Books 1553-1571, vol. 2, p. 8; North Country Wills, vol. I, p. 231.

The Muster (page 35)

47. PRO E101/882 M6(2). *DNB*.

Religious Changes 1485 to 1558 (pages 36-45)

48. Cornelius Brown, *Annals of Newark-on-Trent* (1879), p. 34; NAO Torre ms, microfilm Z392.
49. Borthwick, Dean and Chapter wills in Archbishops' registers, vol. 27, f. 148.
50. Ibid vol. 27, f.153.
51. See note on p. 261 on general location of wills; see also Appendix p. 243.
52. J.T. Godfrey, *Notes on the Churches of Nottinghamshire, Bingham Hundred* (1907), p.368.
53. W. Page (ed), *VCH Nottinghamshire*, vol. 2 (reprinted 1970), p.125; PRO SC6 Hen VIII/7384.
54. Borthwick, ADM 1549/1.
55. *Miscellaneous Writings and Letters of Thomas Cranmer*, Parker Society (1846), p. 321; Thoroton, III, p. 176; *VCH Nottinghamshire*, op. cit. p. 119.
56. PRO C142 279/163; Thor Soc Rec Ser, 16, 1912, pp. 123-30; A.H. Thompson (ed), Chantry Certificate Rolls, *TTS* 18, p. 128; *CPR* 1549-51, p. 180; PRO SC11/540 73/21; *CPR* 1549-51, p. 180; A. Cameron, The Dissolution of the Monasteries in Nottinghamshire, *TTS* 79, p. 56.
57. PRO E117/7/80; *CPR* 1550-53, p. 393.
58. Thoroton, I, p. 186.
59. Borthwick, Dean and Chapter wills in Archbishops' Registers, vol. 29, f. 91.
60. A.G. Dickens, *Lollards and Protestants in the Diocese of York* (1959), p. 199.
61. *CPR* 1555-57, pp. 544 and 546; John Stow, *Survey of London*, (1965), p. 397; *CPR* 1557-58, p. 318.
62. Borthwick, ADM 1549/1; PRO E326/12921; *CPR* 1557-58, p. 420.

The Thrave Family (pages 46-48)

63. PRO Sc11/540 73/21, E179/159/153 and 165, C1 1330.
64. Thor Soc Rec Ser 25, 1966, p. 138.
65. PRO C78 11 28.
66. U of NMD Mi Mp 29, 35 etc; PRO Sc2/196/82, 86 etc.
67. NAO DDTS 14/26/1 pp. 141, 171, 174, 178.
68. U of NMD Mi Mp 34; NAO DDTS 14/26/2 p. 18.
69. PRO Sc2/196/89, E179 160/237. (Contemporary copy of William Thrave's will is in the Borthwick Institute, York.)

Elizabethan Landlords (pages 49-57)

70. Thoroton, I, p.185; PRO C 142 299/163; PRO Ward 7 40/150.
71. Borthwick ADM 1564/6; J.T. Godfrey, *Notes on the Churches of Nottinghamshire, Bingham Hundred* (1907), p.3; NAO M773.
72. Thoroton, I, p.188; PRO E150/730/29; PRO C142/196/38.
73. PRO C3 155/59.
74. PRO C3 7/93.
75. PRO C3 97/21, Ward 7 20/227.
76. PRO C66 1236 m 4.
77. Nottinghamshire Local Studies Library Doubleday catalogue citing Torre ms for Aslockton and Assoc. Arch. Socs ii, 1853, p. 341; PRO C 66 1335 m 27; NAO DDTS 14/26/6.
78. PRO C142 299/163.
79. PRO Ward 7 20/266.
80. Thor Soc Rec Ser III, 1905, p.155; BM Eg 3543 ff. 9 & 150; PRO Ward 7 56/278.
81. *CPR* 1558, p.318; PRO Ward 7 40/150, Ward 7 56/278.
82. U of NMD MaB 236/51; *CPR* 1572-1575, p. 457; Thoroton, I, p.186 [Pat 44 Eliz is transcribed in U of NMD MaB 236/46]; NAO QDS 1/22.
83. U of NMD MaB 236/50; NAO QDS 3/7.
84. PRO C142 196/38, C142 299/163, Ward 7 20/266.
85. U of NMD Ma 2P 115.
86. NAO DDTS 14/26/10; U of NMD Mi Mp; BM Eg 3453 f. 150.

The River and Sir Thomas Stanhope's weir (pages 58-60)

87. *Geographical Journal*, cxxi (1955) pl. 3; Thor Soc Rec Ser 25, 1966, p. 98; Thoroton, II, p. 127; PRO Sc11/540 73/21; BM Eg 3543 f. 12.
88. PRO STAC 5 F2/27; Stanley Revill, A 16th Century Map of the River Trent near

Shelford, *TTS* 1971, pp. 85-87.
89. PRO C260/206, MPF 10; U of NMD MaB 236/50.
90. BM Harley 6996/5 and 7; *HMC Salisbury*, 4, pp. 312, 318; *HMC Rutland*, 1, p. 315.
91. PRO C260/206, STAC 5 F2/27.
92. U of NMD MaB 236/17, MaB 236/51, MS 4309.

Religion in the Reign of Elizabeth I (1558-1603) (pages 61-66)

93. See note on p. 261 on general location of wills; see also Appendix p. 243.
94. NAO DDTS 14/26/1 pp. 79, 105, 141, 171, 174, 199; U of NMD A 1.
95. Borthwick, ADM 1564/6.
96. NAO DDTS 14/26/1 pp. 141,171.
97. Borthwick, CPG 1654.
98. NAO DDTS 14/26/1 pp. 79, 105, DDTS 14/26/2 pp. 18, 22, 40.
99. Ibid pp. 61 and 71.
100. NAO DDTS 14/26/22 pp. 36, 48.
101. Borthwick, ADM 1579/15, 1585/22; NAO DDTS 14/26/22 pp. 217, 219, 221; Ronald Marchant, *The Puritans and the Church Courts in the Diocese of York 1560-1642*, (1960), p. 294.
102. NAO DDTS 14/26/22 pp. 21, 25, 43.
103. NAO DDTS 14/26/2 pp. 130, 140; DDTS 14/26/25 p. 61.
104. U of NMD PB 292 ff. 7, 5; *CPR* 1575-78, p. 323; Thoroton, I, p.186.
105. NAO DDTS 14/26/3 pp. 166, 23; DDTS 14/26/4 pp. 37, 54, 90, 95, 104, 108-9, 149, 247, 260, 262; DDTS 14/26/5 pp. 5, 40, 44, 155, 157; U of NMD LB 217/5/16/1-4, 218/2/41/1-4.
106. W.P.M. Kennedy, *Elizabethan Episcopal Administration*, vol. III, (1924), pp. 317 -325.
107. U of NMD PB 292 Nottingham and Bingham May 1596, f. 32.
108. U of NMD PB 292 Mixed Deaneries, ff. 35, 42, 53.
109. U of NMD PN 354, A24 etc; NAO DDTS 14/26/6 pp. 222; DDTS 14/26/7 pp. 106, 107, 116, 117, 118, 125, 130; DDTS 14/26/10 pp. 88, 121, 131.
110. NAO DDTS 14/26/8 p. 60; 14/26/6 p. 253; 14/26/8 pp. 17, 135; U of NMD PB 293/5 f. 37.
111. NAO PR 25,546.

Isabel Dewsbury's Breach of Promise (pages 67-69)

112. A. Mawer and F.M. Stenton (eds), *The Place Names of Nottinghamshire* (1940), p. 241; U of NMD LB 218/2/41/1-4; NAO DDTS 14/26/4.

Constraints and Obligations in Tudor Times (pages 70-78)

113. Thor Soc Rec Ser 25, 1966, pp. 34-5, 111, 151.
114. PRO MPF 10.
115. Thor Soc Rec Ser 25, 1966, pp. 70, 137, 138.
116. J.T. Godfrey, *The court of the honour of Peverel in the counties of Nottingham and Derby* (1882); Peter B. Park, *My Ancestors were Manorial Tenants* (1994); N.W. Alcock, *Old Title Deeds*, (1986); PRO DL 30/2014 and 2017.
117. U of NMD Mi Mp 36, 142/1c
118. U of NMD Mi Mp 89.
119. U of NMD Mi Mp 5; PRO Sc11/ 540 73/21; U of NMD Mi Mp 10, 20.
120. U of NMD Mi Mp 38, 40; PRO Sc2/196/80.
121. U of NMD Mi Mp 34, 89.
122. U of NMD Mi Mp 10 1b; PRO Sc2/196/82, 89; U of NMD Mi Mp 39.
123. U of NMD Mi Mp 17.
124. PRO Sc2/196/76,78, 89.
125. T. Blagg, The Manors of Cotgrave, *TTS* 13, p. 78.
126. Ronald Marchant, *The Puritans and the Church Courts in the Diocese of York 1560-1642* (1960), pp. 132, 133, 308; NAO DDTS 14/26/1, 2, 3, 4, 5, 6, 7, 22, 25 passim; U of NMD PB 292, 293/5, LB 217/5/16, 218/2/41, PN 354. (Individual items can be identified from the text and references for pages 61-66. Transcripts in possession of Radcliffe Local History Group.); Beryl Cobbing and Stephen Wallwork, unpublished research; David Marcombe, *English Small Town Life - Retford 1520-1642* (1993), p. 281.
127. W.E. Tate, *The Parish Chest* (1969), p. 191.
128. NAO DDTS 14/26/7 p. 130.
129. W.E. Tate op. cit. pp. 30, 191; Jasper Ridley, *The Tudor Age* (1988), pp. 343-4; U of NMD PB 292 Mixed Deaneries, ff. 35, 42, 53.
130. *Statutes of the Realm* (1819), IV, Part II, pp. 896-7, 899.

131. H.E.S. Fisher and A.R.J. Jurica, *Documents in English Economic History* (1977), p. 247.

Thomas Parker - a bailiff at odds with his landlords (pages 79-81)

132. U of NMD Mi Mp 17-45 passim; PRO E 179 160/237, 244, 247, 253; PRO Req 2 259/89; Brian Smith, *History of Malvern* (1964), pp. 164-5.

The Tudor Village - a social survey (pages 82-97)

133. PRO E179/159/142,153,165,173.
134. PRO E179/160/207,237,244,247,253.
135. U of NMD Mi Mp 17; PRO C142 196/38; BM Eg 3443 f.150.
136. PRO Sc11/540 73/21; C142 196/38.
137. P.B. Park, *My Ancestors were Manorial Tenants* (1990), p. 7; D.M. Palliser, *The Age of Elizabeth 1547-1603* (2nd ed. 1992), p. 77; A.J. Camp, *Wills and their Whereabouts* (1974), pp. ix-xix.
138. PRO Sc11/540 73/21; Park op. cit. p. 9.
139. PRO Sc11/540 73/21; R. Milward, *A Glossary of Household, Farming and Trade Terms from Probate Inventories* (3rd ed. 1991).
140. BM Eg 3543.

Farming in Tudor Times (pages 98-104)

141. Lucy Toulmin Smith (ed), *The Itinerary of John Leyland* (1907) I, pt. I, p 97.
142. PRO Sc11/540 73/21; U of NMD pre-enclosure map Ma 2p 116 (photocopy); A.H. Thompson (ed), Chantry Certificate Rolls, *TTS* 18, p. 88.
143. Thomas Tusser, *Five Hundred Points of Good Husbandry* (1984), p. 42; W.G. Hoskins, *Essays in Leicestershire History* (1950), p. 248; BM Eg 3543 f.9.
144. Joan Thirsk (ed), *The Agrarian History of England and Wales* vol. IV (1967), p. 192.
145. PRO C260/206.
146. Thoroton, I, pp. xvi and 286; Thor Soc Rec Ser, II, (1904), p. 49 et seq.

The Jordans - recusancy and 'murder' (pages 105-107)

147. Sir Clements Markham, *Markham Memorials* (1913); *HMC Salisbury*, 5, p. 227.
148. G.R. Elton, *The Tudor Constitution* (1965), pp. 412-3; NAO QSM 1/1 pp. 37, 66; DDTS 14/26/10 pp. 35, 65; U of NMD A24 2 July 1603, 6 April 1605, PB 292 Mixed Deaneries, f. 4, PB 293/6 f. 42.
149. PRO C 260/181/9; A24 19 Dec 1607, 5 March 1607/8.
150. NAO DDTS 14/26/12 p. 149, 14/26/13 p. 92, 14/26/14 pp. 92, 96, 105; U of NMD PB 295/5; H. Hampton Copnall, *Nottinghamshire County Records* (1915), pp. 131-2; W.F.Webster (ed), *Protestation Returns 1641/2*, Notts/Derbys (1980), pp. 23, 72; J.C. Hotten (ed), *Original Lists of Persons of Quality...* (1976), p. 219.

Two Pre-Civil War Squires (pages 108-113)

151. PRO C2 Jas I/S2/5; Derbyshire Record Office D518M/F4; Keith Train, *Nottinghamshire Families* (1969), pp. 20, 31; U of NMD Clifton mss Cl C 282-297.
152. *Harleian Society* 1986, NS vol. 5, p. 79; T.M. Blagg and F.A. Wadsworth (eds), *Nottinghamshire Marriage Licences* (1930) vol. I; Marriage Licences, London, *Harleian Society* 1887, p. 269.
153. Borthwick, Admonition Bond for Anthony Rosell July 1616; NAO PR 547 Holme Pierrepont Churchwardens' Accounts, pp. 52-3.
154. PRO C142 352/147, Ward 7 53/120; PRO E179/160/207-275.
155. NAO QSM 1/3 p. 1.
156. *Harleian Society* 1986, NS vol. 5, p. 79; A. Gibbons, *Lincoln Marriage Licences 1598-1628* (1888); NAO DD WN 2.
157. *Harleian Society* 1986, NS vol. 5, p. 79.
158. J.P. Briscoe (ed), *Old Nottinghamshire* (first series,1881), p. 131; H.L. Hubbard, Colonel Francis Hacker, *TTS* 1941, pp. 5-17.
159. PRO E179/160/ 275, 292, 284, 291, 299.
160. NAO QSM 1/73 p. 123; U of NMD marriage bond (Rosell/Hacker).
161. International Genealogical Index (microfiche); *Journal of the Derbyshire Archaeological and Natural History Society* 14, 1892, p. 96; J.P. Briscoe (ed) op. cit. p.131; *TTS* 1941, op. cit. pp. 5-17.
162. *HMC Welbeck*, II, p. 125.

163. U of NMD Cl C291.
164. NAO QSM 1/73 p. 215; NAO QSM 1/77 pp. 57, 82.
165. NAO DD WN 2.

The Will of Jeffrey Limner (pages 114-115)

166. U of NMD PB 295/5; Borthwick, Admonition Bond 8 Aug 1617.
167. Ibid 25 April 1616.
168. (Contemporary copies of the two Limner wills are in the Borthwick Institute, York.) Further information about the later history of the Jeffrey Dole can be found in P. Priestland (ed) *Radcliffe-on-Trent 1710-1837* (rev. ed. 1990), pp. 103-4, and *Radcliffe-on-Trent 1837-1920* (1989), pp. 189-293.

Church and Parish in the Early Stuart Period (pages 116-124)

(U of NMD Archdeaconry material referred to in the text can be found amongst the relevant set of documents for the Bingham Deanery, usually in chronological order. Current conservation will allow more precise referencing to some documents. Other documents, formerly consulted, are at present considered too fragile for examination.)

169. R.A. Marchant, *The Puritans and the Church Courts in the Diocese of York 1560-1642* (1960), p. 29.
170. Evelyn Waugh, *Edmund Campion* (reprinted 1987), p. 114; Edward Fitzpatrick, *A Study of the Village of Adbolton* (1989), pp. 54-5; NAO QSM 1/1 p. 174; U of NMD PB 293/6, 295/2, 295/5.
171. NAO DDTS 14/26/4 p. 262, 14/26/5 p.5; 14/26/5 p. 220.
172. U of NMD PN 352, A 24.
173. NAO DDTS 14/26/11 pp. 73, 78, 88.
174. U of NMD PN 364, A18, PB 293/8 ff. 21, 49; NAO DDTS 14/26/11 pp. 185, 206, 211, 225, 226, 231, 234; QSM 1/2 p. 82.
175. NAO QSM 1/2 pp. 119, 121.
176. T.M. Blagg and F.A. Wadsworth (eds), *Nottinghamshire Marriage Licences* (1930) vol. 1; U of NMD, marriage bond (Cotes/Goodwin).
177. U of NMD A 20, A 23/2, A 27/1, A 27/3, PN 355, PB 295/1; NAO DDTS 14/26/17 p. 43.
178. U of NMD A 22/1, A 23/1, A 24, A 34, PB 295/2.
179. U of NMD A 25, A 26/2.
180. U of NMD A26/2; J.T. Godfrey, *Notes on the Churches of Nottinghamshire, Hundred of Bingham* (1907), p 376.
181. U of NMD A 24, PB 293/8 f. 49, PB 295/2, PB 297, PB 314, A27/1.
182. Godfrey op. cit. p. 373; U of NMD CL 169/5 - 10.
183. J. Foster, *Alumni Oxonienses* 1500-1714 (1891); NAO Torre ms, microfilm Z392; U of NMD A29; NAO DDTS 14/26/18 pp. 116, 136, 203, 206.
184. J. and J.A. Venn, *Alumni Cantabrigienses* Part I (1922-27); NAO Torre ms, microfilm Z392.
185. Godfrey op. cit. p. 376; U of NMD PB 315, A 33, A35, A37, A39, PN 360.
186. U of NMD A35, PB 314, LB 224/4/1 3; Blagg and Wadsworth op. cit.
187. Uof NMD A39, CL 169/16.
188. U of NMD CL 169/17; *Alumni Cantabrigienses* op. cit.; Godfrey op. cit. p. 373.
189. U of NMD PN 360, PB 314.
190. U of NMD PB 315.
191. Uof NMD A43 at back of book, PB 315; NAO QSM 1/10 p. 121.

The Brass to Anne Ballard (pages 125-126)

192. J.T. Godfrey, *Notes on the Churches of Nottinghamshire, Hundred of Bingham* (1907), pp. 376-9; John Nichols, *History and Antiquities of the County of Leicester* (1795-1815), vol. III pt. 1, p. 507; Leicestershire County Records Office, William Ballard's will & Wymeswold parish register; Thoroton, I, p. 186; BM Eg 3543 f. 150; PRO C142 352/147, C142 299/103; NAO EA 292 microfilm of bishops' transcripts.

Anne Byrde's Disputed Will (pages 127-128)

193. T.M. Blagg and F.A. Wadsworth (eds), *Marriage Licences* (1930) vol. 1; NAO QSM 1/2, 1/4.
194. U of NMD A 27/1, A27/3; NAO DDTS 14/26/17 p. 43; Blagg and Wadsworth op. cit.
195. U of NMD Arch mss A23/1 and 2, A35.
197. U of NMD Arch mss LB 225/5/7, 226/1/7/1-2, 226/2/11-13, 226/3/8/1-2; International Genealogical Index (microfiche).

The Gentry from Civil War to Restoration (pages 129-133)

198. H.L. Hubbard, Colonel Francis Hacker, *TTS* (1941), pp. 5-17.
199. Cornelius Brown, *History of Newark-on-Trent* (1907), p. 59.
200. *Nottingham Evening Post*, July 30 1932; *Nottingham Guardian*, July 30 1932; A.C. Wood. *Nottinghamshire in the Civil War* (1937), pp. 101-4. (Information and advice on the 1932 finds from Mr Tom Carter of Jersey, and the curators of Brewhouse Yard Museum, Nottingham, the Victoria and Albert Museum, London, and the Royal Armouries, London is gratefully acknowledged.) Keith Train, *Nottinghamshire Families* (1969), p. 11. (Information on the find of Cavalier hats from Mr David Astill.)
201. BM Eg 3536 fol 66-76; Keith Train op. cit. p. 20; Robin Brackenbury, *Brothers at War* (1992); BM Eg 3536 ff.10-11.
202. Keith Train op. cit. p. 31; Thoroton, I, p. 148; PRO SP 23/77.
203. *TTS* 1903, p. 52, note by Rev J. Standish.
204. U of NMD Ma B 114/23-52.
205. Notts Local Studies Library Doubleday Catalogue, citing *Miscellanea Genealogie* 3rd series vol. 1, pp. 248, 196.
206. Keith Train op. cit. pp. 33-4.

The Protestation (page 134)

207. W.F. Webster, *Protestation Returns 1641/2* Notts/Derbys (1980), pp. 43-44; W.B. Stephens, *Sources for English Local History* (1983), p. 66.

The Breakdown of Religious Authority (pages 135-142)

208. L. Brettle, *A History of Queen Elizabeth's Grammar School for Boys, Mansfield* (1961), p. 33; J. and J.A. Venn, *Alumni Cantabrigienses* Part I (1922-27); *Admissions to College of St John the Evangelist* (1883); Borthwick, Act Books 1572-1619 vol. 3, p. 249.
209. U of NMD A 45, PB 315.
210. U of NMD A 45, A 46, A 47, LB 228/1/50-54, PB 315.
211. U of NMD A 47, A 48; NAO QSM 1/77 pp. 51, 93, 108.
212. W.F. Webster, *Protestation Returns 1641/2* Notts/Derbys (1980), pp.43-44.
213. H. Field, *The Date-Book of Nottinghamshire...* (1884), p.147; A.C. Wood, *Nottinghamshire in the Civil War* (1937), p. 120; QSM 1/12 p. 102.
214. PRO SP 23/77; Lambeth Palace Library, Comm. XIIa/13 ff. 248-50.
215. PRO SP 23/71 p. 349, SP 23/77 pp. 408-422, SP 22/2B p. 721.
216. A.C. Wood op. cit. pp. 140-1, citing Calendar of the Committee for Compounding I, pp. 543-4, 557, 595.
217. PRO SP 23/77 pp. 408-422.
218. NAO (microfiche) Cotgrave parish registers; Jocelyne Wood (ed), *Cotgrave, aspects of life in the 17th and 18th centuries* (1987), p. 13.
219. NAO (microfiche) Holme Pierrepont parish registers; Bernard Elliott, *The History of Humphrey Perkins School* (1965), pp. 22-44.

The Gambles and Their Daughters (pages 143-144)

220. NAO DDMM 71-74; 76-84; H. Hampton Copnall, *Nottinghamshire County Records* (1915), p. 19.

Laurence Henson - ship's carpenter (page 145)

221. PRO Will of Lawrence Henson pr 20 April, 1658; U of NMD LB 229/1/37; *Society for Nautical Research Occasional Publications No 5*, Lists of Men-of-War 1650-1700 (1939), p. 57; *Calendar of State Papers Domestic* 1657-8, pp. 245-6; John Charnock, *Biographia Navalis*, vol. I, (1794), p.158.

The Gentry, the Militia and the Colonel (page 146-7)

222. James Sutherland (ed), *Memoirs of the Life of Colonel Hutchinson by Lucy Hutchinson*, (1973), pp. 243–5; NAO DDP 37/3 pp. 47-53, 78-80, 228 and passim; Anthony Fletcher, *Reform in the Provinces - the Government of Stuart England*' (1986), pp. 282-348.

The Rosells in Retreat (pages 148 to 166)

223. PRO ASSI 80/11; NAO DD 625/1,4,5; NAO DDP 37/3 p. 32; T. Bailey's *Annals of Nottinghamshire* (1853), II, p. 976.
224. U of NMD M 4200, Ma B 114/23-52, 69, 75.
225. U of NMD A 49.
226. U of NMD LB 230/2, 230/3, 230/4 passim.
227. PRO C54 4171 (19-20), C7 481/48: NAO M 3835 and 6.
228. Borthwick, inventory of Thomas Rosell 9.12.1685; PRO E179/254/34: W.F. Webster (ed) *Nottinghamshire Hearth Tax 1664-1674*, Thor Soc Rec Ser 37, 1988, pp. 67, 69, 93, 94.
229. D.A. Wigley, Some Notes on the Wigley Family of Derbyshire, *Derbyshire Miscellany*, III, p.584.
230. NAO M24,193.
231. PRO C54 4640 (30 et seq); BM Eg 3642 f. 12.
232. BM Eg 3518 ff. 212-221.
233. Borthwick, Admonition Bond, 9 Sept 1686; BM Eg 3518 ff. 212-221.
234. BM Eg 3518 ff. 212-221.
235. Ibid; BM Eg 3642 f. 14.
236. BM Eg 3642 f. 15; Guildhall Library Ms. 11,598/1 and unfoliated; NAO DD WN 2; BM Eg 3517 f. 148, Eg Ch 7251.
237. PRO C8 639/61; BM Eg 3642 ff. 16, 17; *Calendar of State Papers, America and West Indies* 1706-8, p. 398; NAO DD WN 2.
238. BM Eg 3642 ff. 15-16, 20; U of NMD Ma 2P 115.
239. U of NMD Ma B 236/30.
240. U of NMD Ma B 236/17.
241. Burke's *Peerage* for 1850; Anthony Powell, The Hawksmores and Kindred Families of Nottinghamshire, Derbyshire and Lincolnshire in the 18th century, p. 411 et seq, *Genealogist Magazine* vol. 12, no. 12, December 1957; BM Eg 3642 f. 20.
242. *Derbyshire Miscellany*, III, op. cit. p. 643.
243. BM Eg 3564 f. 9; U of NMD MS 4312-15.
244. BM Eg 3642 ff.17, 18; U of NMD Ma 2P 115.
245. Thor Soc Rec Ser XVIII, 1958, p. 43; *DNB*.
246. BM 3642 ff. 18-19, 161-190; Bernard Elliot, *History of Humphrey Perkins School* (1965). Document plate II, said to be deposited in Leicester Record Office, but could not be found March 1993; NAO DDM 60/1; NAO DDM 89/12; W.E. Buckland, *History of Woodborough* (1897); P. Priestland (ed) *Radcliffe-on-Trent 1710-1837* (rev. ed. 1990), pp. 30-5; *Radcliffe-on-Trent 1837-1920* (1989), pp. 147-8.
247. *Radcliffe-on-Trent 1710-1837* op. cit. p. 18.
248. Derbyshire Record Office, Hurt A 74-5, A 88; U of NMD Ma 4496.

A Major Tithes Dispute (pages 167-168)

249. U of NMD Arch mss A 53, A 55, LB 230/4/53; Borthwick, CP H 3192.
250. U of NMD Arch mss LB 230/3/6, 230/3/32/2, 230/2/51, 230/3/48, 230/2/35, 230/2/37, 230/3/53/1, 230/3/53/2, 230/2/52, 230/2/53, 230/3/50/1, 230/3/50/3, 230/2/37, A53 on Walker's last case 20 March 1680, A55.

Religion Under the Later Stuarts (pages 169-176)

251. U of NMD Ma B 236/51, 52, Arch mss CL 170; P. Priestland, (ed) *Radcliffe-on-Trent 1710-1837* (rev. ed. 1990), pp. 37, 41-2.
252. U of NMD PB 304, CL 170, LB 229/2/15.
253. U of NMD A49, PB 304.
254. U of NMD A50, A51/1, LB 229/1/3, LB 215/1/63 (This document is out of order), CL 170; H. Hampton Copnall, *Nottinghamshire County Records* (1915), p. 139.
255. J. and J.A. Venn, *Alumni Cantabrigienses* Part 1 (1922-27).
256. E.L. Guilford, Nottinghamshire in 1676,*TTS* 1924, p. 110.
257. U of NMD A50, A51, PN 362, PB 305.
258. U of NMD A 51, A50, PB 305, A53, A54, LB 231/1/7, LB 231/1/13, LB 231/2/5/1.
259. U of NMD CL 170, IM 207/2, IM 208; BM Eg 3642 ff. 23-25, 64-67; U of NMD MS 4205, 4206, 4230, 4231, 4234.
260. U of NMD A56, A57, A58, C159/88, C160/60, C160/74, C160/179, PB319.
261. U of NMD CL 170, A 55, 60, 62, 63, 64, 65, PN 363, 364; U of NMD MS 4309-4318.
262. NAO DRI/3/2/1; *Radcliffe-on-Trent 1710-1837* op. cit. pp. 37, 41, 51-2.
263. U of NMD MS 4311, 4314, 4317, 4320; BM Eg 3564 f. 9; U of NMD LB 219/1/3/2.
264. U of NMD MS 4313; Ma B 236/51 and 52.

Constraints and Obligations in the Stuart Period (pages 177-194)

265. U of NMD Mi Mp 56-91; seal from *Derbyshire Archeological Journal* 1892, vol. 14, p. 40.
266. U of NMD Mi Mp 101b.
267. U of NMD Mi Mp 101b, 92, 97.
268. U of NMD Mi Mp 101b, 93, 94.
269. U of NMD Mi Mp 101a, b.
270. U of NMD M 4311, 4309; sketch of seal by W.L. Ashmore in Thomas Blagg, The Manors of Cotgrave, *TTS* 1909, pp. 69-79.
271. BM Eg 3623 - court days arranged chronologically and bound in one volume.
272. U of NMD MaB 114/28b, 61, 23b, 61, 66, 82.
273. (Individual cases are referenced in the relevant church section. See note on sources p. 266 under 'Church and Parish in the Early Stuart Period'). U of NMD A 18-43 passim, CL 169/5-10, 169/16, 169/17, LB 224/4/13, PB 293, 295, 297, 314, 315, PN 352, 355, 360, 364; NAO DDTS 14/26/4, 5, 11, 17, 18 passim. (Transcripts in possession of Radcliffe Local History Group.)
274. (Individual cases are referenced in the relevant church section. See note on sources p. 266 under 'Church and Parish in the Early Stuart Period'). U of NMD A 50-65 passim, C 159/88, 160/60, 160/74, 160/179, CL 170, LB 215/1/63, 219/1/3. 231/1/7, 231/1/13, 231/2/5, PB 304, 305, 319, PN 362-4. (Transcripts in possession of Radcliffe Local History Group); P. Priestland, *Radcliffe-on-Trent 1710-1837* (rev. ed. 1990), p. 44.
275. NAO QSM 1/3 p 28, 1/5 p. 61, 1/10 p 198,1/12 p 154; H. Hampton Copnall, *Nottinghamshire County Records* (1915), p. 19.
276. NAO QSM 1/9 pp. 180, 208, 444.
277. Ibid 1/5 p. 133, 1/6 p. 149, 1/8 pp. 215, 219.
278. Ibid 1/2 pp. 100, 106, 1/3 p. 142, 1/7 pp. 3, 6, 1/8 pp. 82, 86.
279. Ibid 1/2 pp. 119, 121, 1/3 p. 1, 1/6 p. 51, 1/9 p. 66, 1/10 p. 147, 1/2 p. 82.
280. Ibid 1/2 pp. 37, 54, 120, 1/4 pp. 120, 148, 1/9 p. 347.
281. Ibid 1/6 pp. 229, 250, 1/8 p. 250, 1/7 p. 189.
282. Ibid 1/6 pp. 24, 50, 127, 1/9 pp. 12, 61, 63, 448, 1/11 pp. 238, 240, 1/10 p. 102.
283. PRO SP16 329.
284. NAO QSM 1/4 p. 128, 1/2 p. 120, 1/6 p. 68.
285. Ibid 1/7 p. 73, 1/11 p. 222.
286. Ibid 1/3 p. 36, 1/8 pp. 123, 152, 1/9 p. 73, 1/11 p. 201, 1/12 pp. 57, 82, 126.
287. Ibid 1/3 p. 65, 1/5 pp. 194, 216, 1/10 p. 61, 1/12 pp. 51, 83, 108.
288. NAO DDTS 14/26/14 pp. 11, 15, 18.
289. NAO QSM 1/13 23 April 1655, 1/21 16 Jan 1708; *Collection of State Papers of John Thurloe Esq.* (1742), vol. IV pp. 411, 686.
290. NAO QSM 1/12 pp.169, 203, 223, 1/13 9 July 1655.
291. C.G.A. Clay, *Economic Expansion and Social Change: England 1500-1700* (1984), vol. II, pp. 243-4. vol. I, p. 230.
292. NAO QSM 1/14, 3 Oct 1687, 9 Jul 1688, 1/1515 Jul 1696, 13 Jan 1697.
293. *Radcliffe-on-Trent 1710-183* 7 op. cit. pp. 125, 118.
294. NAO QSM 1/15 7 Oct 1689; U of NMD Arch mss PN 363, PN 364, A 62, A 65; NAO QSM 1/20 28 Apr 1701, 1/21 21 Apr 1707, 1/22 9 Apr 1711.
295. NAO QSM 1/16 8 Apr 1678, 1/16 passim,1/16 3 Oct 1689, 1/15 16 April 1694, 1/17 14 July 1700, 1/22 14 Jan 1712.

The Pilkingtons and their Sons (pages 195-196)

296. J. T. Godfrey, The Pilkingtons of Nottinghamshire,*Notts & Derbyshire Notes and Queries*, June 1895; NAO QSM 1/16/17; BM Eg Mss 3517, ff. 166-169.

The Stuart Village - a social survey (pages 197-224)

297. Christopher Hill, *Reformation to Industrial Revolution* (1983) pp. 44-5; J.V. Beckett, *The East Midlands from AD 1000* (1988), pp. 103-4, 354; Uof N PB 295/5; A.C. Wood, An Archiepiscopal Visitation of 1603, *TTS* 46, pp. 3-14; E.L. Guilford, Nottinghamshire in 1676,*TTS* 28, pp. 106-113; W.F. Webster (ed), *Protestation Returns 1641/2* Notts/Derbys (1980) pp.43-4; W.F. Webster, (ed),*Nottinghamshire Hearth Tax 1664:1674* in Thor Soc Rec Ser 1988, 37, pp. xix, 69, 93.
298. PRO C142/381/152; BM Eg 3543; U of NMD MaB 236/50.
299. PRO E179/160/275 (1606), 282 (1621), 284 (1622), 291 (1625), 299 (1628), 294 (1629), 302 & 308 (1641); NAO QSM 1/9 pp. 12, 63, 1/7 p. 189.
300. W.F. Webster, (ed) *Nottinghamshire Hearth Tax 1664: 1674* , op. cit.
301. M.W. Barley, *The English Farmhouse and Cottage* (1961), p. 204; Elizabeth R. Perkins

(ed), *Village Life from Wills and Inventories Clayworth Parish 1670-1710* (1979), p. 8.

302. NAO QSM and PRs passim; BM Eg 3564 f. 9; U of NMD M4240; P. Priestland (ed) *Radcliffe-on-Trent 1710-1837*, (rev. ed. 1990), p. 135.

303. NAO QSM 1/1 p. 9, 1/9 p. 73,1/3 p. 82, 1/12 p. 83, 1/6 p. 68, 1/11 p. 238, 1/2 p. 37; U of NMD Mi Mp 101b p. 38; NAO QSM 1/10 p. 38; 1/9 p. 347; QSM 1/12 p. 80.

304. W.F. Webster (ed), *Nottinghamshire Hearth Tax 1664:1674* op.cit; J.P. Briscoe (ed) *Old Nottinghamshire* (second series 1884) Churchwarden Accounts of Holme Pierrepont by W.H. Stevenson, p. 100; U of NMD M4240; *Radcliffe-on-Trent 1710-1837* op cit, p. 130; U of NMD M4314; BM Eg 3564 f. 9; U of NMD M4314.

305. M.W. Barley, *The English Farmhouse and Cottage* (1961); U of NMD MaB 236/50; *St Mary's Parochial Magazine*, Sep. 1877, Notes from an Inhabitant; NAO QSM 1/3 p. 36; 1/9 p. 73; U of NMD M4309.

306. U of NMD Ma 2P 115.

307. Information from John J. McKay ARICS and Christine McKay MA is gratefully acknowledged.

A Seventeenth Century House - 37 Water Lane (pages 225-227)

308. Advice from Graham Beaumont about interpreting the building is gratefully acknowledged; P. Priestland (ed), *Radcliffe-on-Trent 1710-1837* (rev. ed. 1990), p. 116.

Some 17th Century Householders and their Inventories (pages 228-232)

309. BM Eg 3564 f. 9; W.F. Webster (ed), *Nottinghamshire Hearth Tax 1664: 1674* in Thor Soc. Rec Ser 1988, pp. xix, 69, 93; BM Eg 3642 f. 85, 3564 f. 9; U of NMD M4309; P. Priestland (ed), *Radcliffe-on-Trent 1710 to 1837* (rev. ed. 1990), p. 90.

Farming in Stuart Times (pages 233-240)

310. Joan Thirsk (ed) *The Agrarian History of England 1500-1640* (1984), vol. IV, passim. Keith Wrightson, *English Society 1580-1680* (1982) pp. 143-7; PRO E179/160/284, 292, 291; *VCH Nottinghamshire*, II, pp. 289-90.

311. Bm Eg 3543 f. 150; U of NMD MaB 236/50.

312. Bm Eg 3642 f. 85

313. NAO QSM 1/6 p. 229,1/8 p. 250.

314. BM Eg 3564 f. 9.

315. U of NMD MaB114/66; BM Eg 3543 f. 12; U of NMD M4309.

Literacy in Tudor and Stuart Times (page 241-242)

316. *Miscellaneous Writings and Letters of Thomas Cranmer*, Parker Society (1846), pp. 256, 262; W.F. Webster, *Protestation Returns 1641/2 Notts/Derbys* (1980), pp. 43-44; D. Cressy, *Literacy and Social Order: Reading and Writing in Tudor and Stuart England* (1980), p. 73; Signatures and marks from NAO PRNW:- 1&2 = will of Joane Needham 19 Feb 1658, 3 = inventory of John Taylor Feb 1664, 4 = inventory of John Yardley 4 Jul 1664, 5 = will of John Walker 16 Dec 1670, 6 = will of Simon Chadburn 2 Feb 1681, 7 = Ibid, 8 = will of Nathanial Markham, 13 Apr 1681, 9 = inventory of William Cooke 10 Nov 1682, 10 = bond to administer goods of Margaret Butler 26 Sept 1691, 11 = will of William Parr 4 Mar 1693, 12 = will of Richard Foster 3 Feb 1696, 13 = will of John Pare 1697, 14 = will of Richard Musson 29 Sept 1712 (similar mark in parish register).

FROM THE PARISH REGISTERS

1639 *Robert Leeson of Gedlinge drowned in Trent by a fall from a horse was buried June 7*

Elizabeth the wife of Thomas Bell a Londoner drowned in Trent by the same accident was buried June 7

1657 *Buried Edward Swinscoe aged 16 Yeares being Killed with ye strike of a horse October 15*

1684 *Thomas Beet a servant drowned in the Trent was buried July 3rd*

1698 *John Osbrook (who was drown'd in ye Trent) was buryed June 20*

1703 *John Pare the son of Bryan Pare & Mary his wife was buried May the 12th who was killed accedently by his fellow servant*

Available in the same series:

Radcliffe-on-Trent 1710-1837
(ed. Pamela Priestland)

Radcliffe-on-Trent 1837-1920
A study of a village during an era of change
(ed. Pamela Priestland)